Transnationalism in Ancient
and Medieval Societies

ALSO BY
MICHAEL C. HOWARD

_____

Transnationalism and Society:
An Introduction (McFarland, 2011)

Transnationalism in Ancient and Medieval Societies

The Role of Cross-Border Trade and Travel

MICHAEL C. HOWARD

McFarland & Company, Inc., Publishers
Jefferson, North Carolina, and London

LIBRARY OF CONGRESS CATALOGUING-IN-PUBLICATION DATA

Howard, Michael C.
Transnationalism in ancient and medieval societies :
the role of cross-border trade and travel /
Michael C. Howard.
p.   cm.
Includes bibliographical references and index.

ISBN 978-0-7864-6803-4
softcover : acid free paper ∞

1. Commerce — History — To 500.   2. Commerce — History —
Medieval, 500–1500.   3. International trade — History — To 1500.
4. Transnationalism — Economic aspects.   I. Title.
HF357.H69 2012   382 — dc23   2012000137

BRITISH LIBRARY CATALOGUING DATA ARE AVAILABLE

On the cover: Marco Polo travelling, miniature from the book *The Travels
of Marco Polo* (*Il milione*), circa 1324; background © 2012 Shutterstock

Manufactured in the United States of America

*McFarland & Company, Inc., Publishers
Box 611, Jefferson, North Carolina 28640
www.mcfarlandpub.com*

Table of Contents

Preface

I began work on this book at the same time that I started writing my earlier book, *Transnationalism and Society: An Introduction,* which was published in 2011 by McFarland. While that book focuses on transnationalism in the modern world, the present work shifts attention to the pre-modern world. I wanted to highlight that transnationalism is not unique to modern times, and to come to a better understanding of how and why people were able to maintain transnational relations in the past, given the many obstacles that they faced, such as limited capabilities to travel and communicate, relatively poor geographical knowledge, and a fragmented and shifting political landscape in which security often posed a problem. There is also a personal motivation behind the study. As a transnational scholar who has studied and taught in the United States, Australia, Fiji, and Canada — moving about within countries associated with the former British Empire — I recognize that I am part of a long tradition, and I felt the need to better understand and appreciate those who came before me.

While many studies look at the migration of people in ancient and medieval times, less attention has been paid to those who moved back and forth with some regularity or were at least able to maintain some sort of regular transnational contact. What we see in the study that follows is that there were significant numbers of such people and that they played important political, economic, and cultural roles. In regard to the latter point, we see that transnationalism was especially evident among elites, who had both the desire and the means to move back and forth across borders. To add flesh to such transnationalism I have discussed the lives of some of the better-known transnational elites such as the Hellenic scholar Herodotus, the Venetian merchant Marco Polo, and the Norwegian king Harald Hardradi, as well as some who are less famous like the ancient Roman civil servant Lollianus Mavortius and the Medieval Jewish merchant Abraham bin Yiju.

The nature of ancient and medieval historical records tends to emphasize the lives of these elites, but transnational non-elites also crop up throughout the study. Unfortunately we tend to get only glimpses of the lives of these people — perhaps the crews of the merchant ships that sailed between distant ports, or the teams driving camels along the Silk Road — and of the ports and oases where they lived and visited. Such people normally could not write and received little attention from those who could. Although they may not have contributed much directly to the major developments emerging from transnationalism, without them the trips across the seas and across the deserts of Central Asia and North Africa would not have been possible.

I have focused on transnationalism within the part of the world that was relatively integrated in ancient and medieval times, stretching from Western Europe to Eastern Asia. I also discuss transnationalism in central Mexico, primarily in relation to the Aztec Empire. Obviously there were also transnational relations between the various tribes, chieftanships, kingdoms, and empires elsewhere in the world. I hope that time and new discoveries will someday allow me fruitful study of these areas as well.

Introduction

"Stonehenge boy 'was from Med,'" announced a BBC News headline.[1] The British Geological Survey had reported that analysis of the teeth of the "Boy with the Amber Necklace," the name given to the remains of a teenager buried near Stonehenge around 1550 B.C., indicated that he came from the Mediterranean. Previous analysis of another skeleton known as the "Amesbury Archer" dating from 2450 to 2300 B.C., had indicated this person had come from the Alps.

Jane Evans of the British Geological Survey commented that the finds highlight "the diversity of people who came to Stonehenge from across Europe."[2] A *National Geographic* article wrote of the find, "Bronze Age teen was on epic 'grand tour'.... As a major attraction for more than 3,500 years, Stonehenge has inspired many an ancient road trip."[3] Said one of the archaeologists involved in the study: "We think that the wealthiest people may have made these long-distance journeys in order to source rare and exotic materials, like amber. By doing these journeys, they probably also acquired great kudos." The article notes that "crossing the English Channel — most likely by paddleboat — was probably one of the more challenging parts of his journey."[4]

The above story highlights the extent to which even in ancient times people traveled across great distances on a fairly regular basis. In addition it draws attention to the existence of transnational relations in the ancient world, since such grand tours or pilgrimages take place within a context in which people maintain a meaningful presence in or are part of a social system within one nation while also maintaining significant relations with others in different nations.[5] The story also points to two important motivating factors in regard to ancient transnationalism: trade and religion.

The present book is about transnationalism in ancient and medieval times. While it is easy to think of transnationalism in the age of inexpensive air travel and the internet, the ability of ancient peoples to travel and communicate across great distances and the extent to which they did so is often underestimated. While transnationalism today is of a scale that was inconceivable in the past, it is important to recognize that transnational connections existed even in ancient times and that they were quite significant.

One of the book's aims is to provide a balance to what can easily become an inaccurate view of transnationalism that suffers from what Bentley refers to as "modernocentrism."[6] He defines modernocentrism as "an enchantment with the modern world that has blinded scholars and the general public alike to continuities between premodern and modern times" and argues that scholars have tended to "discount the importance of long distance trade, travel, communication, and cross-cultural interaction in pre-modern times."[7] All too often such interaction is treated as intermittent, and not significant. By way of example, Bentley[8] cites Samuel P. Huntington's *The Clash of Civilizations and the Remaking of the World Order,* where it is stated, "During most of human existence contacts between civilizations were intermittent or nonexistent,"[9] and "For more than three thousand years after civilization first emerged, the contacts among them were, with some exceptions, either nonexistent or limited or intermittent and intense."[10] Yet a substantial body of empirical research indicates that this simply is not true.

One thing that is quite different between transnationalism in the past and at present is the number and range of people involved in transnational relations. In the past the difficulties and expense of travel and communication made it impossible for most people to maintain transnational links. Even those who migrated often made a one-way trip and once in their new home had little if any contact with their previous homeland. Nevertheless, there were people who traveled back and forth across borders, either on occasion or on a regular basis, who developed and maintained transnational lives. These individuals or groups had a major impact on societies far beyond their numbers in many ways and especially in regard to the cultures of societies and the ways that they evolved.

Chapter 1 begins with a look at some of the main points about transnational relations and their context in ancient and medieval times, including the enabling factors relating to transportation and communication. Chapters 2 and 3 offer an overview of the main empires since they play such a significant role in shaping transnational relations. The discussion in the chapters on empires is intended to provide an overview of the context such empires provided for transnational relations as well as to highlight the nature of transnational relations within these empires and beyond their borders.

In Chapter 4 we examine a number of the political entities that existed along the major maritime and overland trade routes. These trade routes served to link the major markets of the world and also facilitated the flow of ideas and people who were not directly involved in commercial activities. While attention is often focused on the markets connected by these routes such as imperial Rome in the west and the Han and Tang empires in the east, the polities along these routes not only functioned as conduits for the flow of people, goods, and ideas but were themselves consumers and suppliers of both goods and ideas.

The discussion then turns, in Chapter 5, to the main trade goods that traveled along these trade routes since the search for and provision of such goods was the main rationale for the existence of long-distance trade. In Chapter 6 we turn to the long-distance traders themselves. In particular we look at the main groups that were found among such traders. What is of relevance here is the fact that long-distance trade in the past tended to be a specialized activity carried out by particular ethno-national groups. Moreover, such long-distance traders comprised a major portion of the people engaged in transnational activities in the past.

Chapter 7 focuses on the specialized communities that arose along the trade routes, catering to the activities of the long-distance traders. Such communities, although often relatively small in size, were of considerable importance to transnationalism in the past and were the most transnational communities in the ancient and medieval worlds. As we shall see in Chapter 8, cities were also significant to transnationalism in the past just as they are at present. The major capitals of the ancient and medieval empires in particular served as destinations for goods and peoples and as centers from which people and ideas spread along the major trade routes. In addition to capitals such as Chang'an in China, Pataliputra in

India, and Rome in Italy, many of the cities in the ancient and medieval worlds grew up along long-distance trade routes, serving initially simply as transit points and then emerging as important markets, destinations, and centers of production in their own right.

The final two chapters focus on two of the other major groups that maintained transnational lifestyles in the past: soldiers (Chapter 9) and monks (using the term monk broadly to refer to all types of religious specialists) and scholars (Chapter 10). The category of soldiers includes both professional soldiers and mercenaries. Professional soldiers lived transnational lives primarily as members of imperial armies as they were posted in different parts of the empires that they served and sometimes even beyond their borders. Mercenaries, by virtue of their profession, tended to live transnational lives as they moved from one employer to the next, crossing borders in the process. Transnationalism was of relevance to monks and scholars in ancient and medieval times in two ways. First, even those who did not travel across borders were influenced by religious and secular ideas from elsewhere, especially from centers of study ranging from major monasteries and religious centers such as the Buddhist university at Nalanda in northern India to the secular Hellenic Mouseion at Alexandria. Second, there were secular and religious scholars as well as pilgrims who traveled across borders in search of enlightenment or employment and who helped to maintain the transnational flow of ideas.

1

Basic Features of Transnationalism in the Ancient and Medieval World

Societal Types

Transnationalism in ancient and medieval times took place between similar types of societies or polities as well as those that were quite different. In regard to differences, societies can be broadly divided into those commonly viewed as civilized and those that the civilized considered barbaric. These two categories are certainly contentious, but they were important distinctions in the past and reflect real differences in terms of social organization and adaptive strategies. Essentially, civilized peoples lived in sedentarized societies that boasted cities and an attendant complex physical and administrative infrastructure as well as a culture that was literate. Uncivilized societies, essentially, tended to feature kin-based forms of social organization, often were not sedentarized and lacked large permanent settlements, and usually lacked a system of writing. There was often a geographical dimension as well, with civilized peoples living in lowlands, where they had tended fields, roads, and cities, and barbarians living in highlands, jungles, deserts, or other wild places where there was relatively little evidence of human endeavor. Common distinctions were between the urbanized and sedentarized societies of the Mediterranean, Tigris and Euphrates river region, the Ganges and Indus river regions of South Asia, and the Yellow (Huang He) and Yangtze rivers in East Asia on the one hand, and the pastoral nomadic and tribal societies of Central Asia and Northern Europe on the other hand.

It is important to note that relations between civilized peoples and so-called barbarians were dynamic to some extent. Although tension, the potential for conflict, and even outright hostility or conflict were often present in such relations, there were also often instances of exchange. From the perspective of the civilized such exchanges were commonly aimed at securing peace and sought-after goods as well as promoting what were perceived to be beneficial changes in the nature of the barbarians. Thus, Central Asian nomads commonly traded goods with the Han, and the Han viewed the provision of luxury items such as silk cloth to the barbarians not simply as a means of obtaining desired items in exchange but also as part of a process of civilizing the nomads to make them less dangerous over the long run.

Contexts

The development of transnational relations in ancient and medieval times was more difficult than today not only because of the less developed state of transportation and communication, but also because of the political nature of the world. It was not simply technologically more difficult to travel; it was also more difficult to arrange for travel between the different sorts of political entities that existed, and more dangerous. An ability to move and communicate over distances is essential to transnationalism. By modern standards both were rudimentary in the ancient and medieval worlds, but they were sufficient for people, goods, and ideas to travel back and forth across large stretches of land and sea and to create and maintain transnational relations linking large parts of the globe. Prior to modern times, transportation relied largely on camels, horses, and ships with sails or oars. There were innovations in the case of sailing technology, but these were more incremental than revolutionary. Once basic forms of travel by ship or camel came into being, innovations in technology and improvements in knowledge helped a little, but these did not revolutionize travel; they only made it a little easier and faster.

The political context was often the most important one influencing the existence of transnational links in the past. This is particularly apparent in the case of long-distance land travel. Thus, as we will see, the trade routes associated with the Silk Road came into being within the context of the emergence of favorable political developments related to the emergence of the Roman and Han empires as well as political entities in between, and travel along these routes ebbed and flowed over the next thousand years or so in accordance with the degree of political stability along the route. The maritime sea route between China and Europe was more adaptable, but it too was subject to political considerations, as when China periodically sought to place greater restrictions on maritime travel or local conditions favored the use of one port over another along the way.

Our look at the ancient world begins with the Sumerians in the so-called Cradle of Civilization over 6,000 years ago and lasts until around A.D. 500. It focuses on relations within a portion of the world that stretched from the eastern Mediterranean to East Asia. Transnational relations reached their peak in the ancient world during the time of the Roman Empire in the west and the Han Empire (206 B.C. to A.D. 220) in the east when both overland and maritime trade between these empires flourished. The medieval world existed essentially between the ancient and modern periods, roughly from about A.D. 500 to 1500, although the years from 1350 to 1500 can also be viewed as a transitional period in some parts of the world, a period often referred to as early modern. In Europe the medieval period is popularly associated with feudalism, small states, technological backwardness, and relative isolation from the rest of the world. The medieval period began similarly in Asia, but gradually large empires emerged under the Mongols — who conquered China, Central Asia, and a large part of the Middle East — and various Muslim rulers who consolidated power over an extensive area of the Middle East. The medieval period also saw the rise of large empires in Mexico and Peru. While there were transnational relations in Europe, and to some extent in the New World, transnationalism was most in evidence during the medieval period in Asia, where the Silk Road continued to operate on and off and where maritime trade linking the Middle East, India, Southeast Asia, and East Asia flourished.

Two things are crucial to understanding the development and nature of transnationalism in the ancient world. First, long-distance trade was an important part of life in the ancient world. Second, while some ancient technologies were invented independently, for the most part they spread from centers of invention. Both of these activities, trade and technological diffusion, require human agents, and while diffusion may take place as a result of migration, long-distance trade involves a group of people moving back and forth over at least a portion of the trade route. The history of long-distance trade is at the heart of understanding transnationalism in the past. Mair refers to an "overemphasis on the utter distinctiveness of modern peoples" and a reluctance to admit that ancient people engaged in extensive long-distance trade.[1] As we will see, contact through long-distance trade has in fact been significant for thousands of years.

Trade routes move not only goods but also people and ideas. In addition to the traders, there are a host of support personnel, ranging from sailors to soldiers. In the stories of Jason it is important not to forget his Argonauts or in the tales of Sinbad his crew. Long-distance trade takes place within a context in which the traders seek security through diplomacy and, sometimes, armed protection. This context encourages the exchange of diplomats and the movement of security personnel over distances. In some instances, long-distance trade led to the creation of merchant colonies in important trading centers. The search for certain commodities, such as copper, also led to the creation of mining colonies. Ideas as well as goods travel along trade routes, including technical knowledge and more abstract notions. These ideas were transmitted by those engaged in long-distance trade and sometimes by religious specialists who began moving along these trade routes from very early times.

Traders in the ancient and medieval worlds also moved among a variety of political entities. The nation often coincided with a tribe or chiefdom and these in turn might be joined to form larger political entities such as confederacies or empires. Kingdom is a term that is used loosely and may refer to a relatively small territory occupied by a single cultural group or a fairly large territory incorporating numerous cultural groups. Thus, kingdoms might include different ethno-national groups. Since the term kingdom usually refers to more integrated political entities than confederacies or empires, transnationalism is of most relevance in reference to relations beyond the borders of kingdoms rather than within.

In addition to trade, the formation of empires through conquest was another important means of linking peoples in ancient times. The larger empires of the ancient world almost always were multi-national affairs that incorporated a number of distinct peoples within a single administrative system. Moreover, although the extent of administrative integration of empires, as we will see, varied considerably, empires did create a degree of security that generally was lacking beyond their borders. Such empires facilitated trade within their borders as well as creating structures within which administrative and military personnel moved back and forth between the lands linked by imperial domination. In addition to ports and oases, imperial capitals also often had multi-ethnic populations that included not only people from around the empire but those from beyond its borders who came in search of wealth from commerce, employment as artisans or in some other profession, or employment in a diplomatic capacity.

Although transnational relations between kingdoms and empires in the ancient and modern worlds were often difficult for logistical as well as political reasons, traders and others overcame these difficulties for a variety of reasons — including the hope for wealth, the search for enlightenment, and a sense of adventure. The nature of relations between kingdoms and empires could serve to help or hinder transnationalism. Attempts to foster better relations, often out of a desire to promote trade, included formal treaties as well as more indirect means such as establishing links through marriage and shared religious beliefs. The wealth generated by trade, of course, could also undermine relations when rulers sought to seize control of trade routes or the sources of trade goods.

Security was an important issue for maintaining transnational trade and other transnational relations. Maritime trade routes attracted pirates; overland routes, bandits. Sometimes the traders had to provide their own security in the form of hired guards. Governments concerned with promoting trade sometimes sought to protect trade routes with their own fleets and armies. As we will see, the breakdown or lack of security along a trade route could result in trade's dwindling and lead to diminished transnational relations or to alternative routes being used. This was an especially important issue in regard to the important trade between the Mediterranean and Middle East and East Asia and the overland route commonly referred to as the Silk Road in particular. This trade route (actually a variety of routes) was subject to fluctuations in security that at times made it virtually cease to function. The maritime trade route across the northern Indian Ocean, along the coast of India, across the Bay of Bengal to the Isthmus of Kra and later through the Strait of Melaka, and then on to southern China proved more enduring.

Until the opening of the New World to regular contact with the rest of the world in the 1500s, the inter-connected world within which transnationalism existed was to be found almost exclusively in Asia, Europe, and North Africa. International trade prior to 1500 primarily moved back and forth between the Mediterranean, the Middle East, Central Asia, South Asia, Southeast Asia, and China. While goods might move the entire distance from China to Mediterranean Europe, traders and other people usually did not travel so far. Romans moved mainly within the bounds of their own empire with a small number venturing as far to the east as southern India and Sri Lanka. Tamil traders sailed to Egypt's Red Sea ports to the west, but only rarely ventured further into the Roman Empire itself. To the east they sailed to Island Southeast Asia, but they seldom traveled as far as China. Malay traders from Southeast Asia occasionally sailed to China on the one hand and to India on the other hand, but they usually did not sail beyond southern India. As for the Chinese, they would at times travel overland to the Middle East or by sea to southern India, but travel further west was extremely rare.

Abu-Lughod divides the world system in the 1200s into eight interlinked subsystems that, in turn, can be grouped into three larger circuits: the Western European, the Middle Eastern, and the Far Eastern.[2] People tended to remain within these subsystems and to come into contact with the neighboring subsystem where they overlapped at what Abu-Lughod calls "beachheads." These beachheads were critical points for the exchange of goods and ideas between subsystems and boasted multiethnic commercial centers with transnational populations. Thus, Genoa and Venice emerged as important commercial hubs where the European subsystem that included France and England overlapped with the Mediterranean subsystem. Likewise, Melaka emerged as a major trading center where the South Asian and East Asian subsystems overlapped in Southeast Asia.

In addition to long-distance trade, the spread of religions was an important aspect of transnationalism in the ancient period, even more so in the medieval. Empires in the ancient world spread various religions within their domains. Zoroastrianism became effectively the state religion of the Achaemenid (Persian) Empire under King Artaxerxes I (r. 465–424); after his conversion to Buddhism, Asoka the Great (r. 273–232 B.C.) promoted this religion within the empire that he created, which encompassed much of modern India; and, after initially being suppressed, Christianity came to flourish within the Roman Empire, especially after the conversion of the Emperor Constantine I. Moreover, once such religions had become established in their respective empires, there was considerable missionary activity beyond imperial boundaries as well, usually along trade routes. Christianity survived the fall of Rome to be spread throughout Europe by missionaries in the medieval period. The medieval period also saw the rise of a new transnational religion, Islam, which was spread both by missionaries and by military conquest.

Motivations and Personnel

Given the difficulties of creating and maintaining transnational relations in the past, one may wonder why anyone bothered. The profit motive of long-distance traders is the most obvious and easiest to understand. Put quite simply the difficulties of long-distance trade in the past enhanced potential profits for those who succeeded. But profit is only part of the equation. What creates the market in the first place? Here things start to get more complicated. The grain trade between the Black Sea and ancient Athens or Egypt and Rome is not too difficult to understand, but most of long-distance trade in the ancient and medieval worlds was not in bulk commodities. It was in luxury items such as silks, spices, and incense. Here cultural and psychological factors often relating to social stratification come into play. The palaces and tombs of the elites of the past were piled high with expensive, exotic imports obtained through trade, tribute, or plunder. Understanding the motivation behind this is beyond the scope of the present study, but it is important to recognize the role that this desire for exotic goods played in promoting long-distance trade and transnationalism in the past.

The market for imports of bulk commodities and luxuries gave rise to the emergence of long-distance trade specialists. Obtaining such goods was not easy and it required both specialized knowledge and considerable organization. As will be discussed at length later in the book, this is a situation that gave rise to the emergence of specialized groups of people who engaged in long-distance trade. Sometimes these were ethnic groups, sometimes communities or towns. It is important not to forget that in addition to these traders the work of long-distance trade also required a supporting cast of specialists to sail the ships and drive the camels to their destinations.

There was more to transnationalism than trade in the past, however. Even in the economic realm, employment was another motivating factor. As we will see, people with specialized skills or knowledge not related to trade also moved across borders in search of better prospects. The imperial capital of the past served as a magnet for people with a variety of skills from within their empires and beyond. The desire to be trained in skilled professions was another motivating factor in cross-border movement.

The need and desire of rulers or governments to maintain relations or to undertake negotiations with other polities also led to the creation of transnational relations. Permanent embassies were a rarity in the ancient and medieval world, although some did exist. More common were periodic embassies sent for a particular purposes. Also rather than a corps of professional diplomats, past rulers tended simply to select particular individuals because they had skills necessary for the undertaking or simply because of their relative status. Such embassies did not always lead to the creation of transnational links between polities, but they did require the services of at least some people skilled in cross-cultural affairs, especially where there was a need for translation.

Religion provides a third important motivating factor for the creation of transnational relations. Transnational religious relations involved efforts at proselytization across borders as well as the movement of pilgrims and others seeking to contact co-religionists beyond their own borders. The numbers involved in such activities by modern standards were not huge, but such persons often played a significant role in the development of particular religious traditions.

Long-distance commercial relations often were relevant to transnational political and religious activities in the sense that ambassadors and the religiously motivated commonly traveled along established trade routes and often sought passage with commercial ships or caravans. It should be noted, however, that there were voyages and caravans organized specifically for political or religious purposes such as ambassadorial fleets sent by Japan to China and caravans organized for the Muslim pilgrimage to Mecca. Moreover, merchants often sought to join these for reasons of security or convenience.

Transportation and Communication

In an age of ever larger and faster aircraft that make it economically feasible for migrant workers to travel halfway around the world in a matter of hours to take on even relatively unskilled jobs, it is easy to forget that mass air travel is quite recent and that air travel itself dates back only about a century. Other relatively rapid means of travel such as cars, buses, and trains are only a little older. Humankind's oldest means of transportation is walking and our oldest means of communication is speech, but from a very early time humans have sought ways to augment or supplement these modes of transportation and communication and thereby enhance our ability to maintain links over distances.

DOMESTICATED ANIMALS USED FOR TRANSPORTATION

People ride on or carry goods on a variety of animals. These include horses, donkeys (or asses), mules (a mule is the offspring of a male donkey and a female horse), elephants, camels, llamas, water buffalo, oxen, bullocks, and yaks. Two of these animals have played an especially prominent role in overland long-distance travel: the horse and camel. Humans domesticated horses around 3500 B.C. on the steppes of Central Asia in what is now northern Kazakhstan. Their use spread relatively fast. They appear to have been widely domesticated in Central Asia and the Middle East by 3000 B.C., and the use of domesticated horses had spread throughout Europe and Asia by 2000 B.C. There are two varieties of camel: the one-humped dromedary or Arabian camel and the two-humped Bactrian camel. They are native to the dry desert regions of Asia and were domesticated by humans prior to 2000 B.C.[3]

Both horses and camels came to play an important role in transporting humans and goods over great distances in the dry areas of Central Asia, the Middle East, and North Africa. While horses were used mainly to carry people, camels assumed the major role in carrying goods overland in the dry regions of Asia and North Africa. These animals were closely associated with the development of pastoral nomadism and caravan routes across the deserts of Asia and North Africa. William Bernstein remarks, "Not until ... around 1500 B.C. would humans begin to exploit the camel's ability to carry hundreds of pounds of cargo across otherwise impenetrable territory," and, "Without the domestication of the camel, the trans–Asian silk and trans–Arabian incense routes would have been impossible."[4] In Europe, where there were no camels, horses along with oxen were used to pull carts, but this was a slow and inefficient means of transportation because of the scarcity of adequate roads.

In his book *Caravan,* Carleton Coon mentions four different kinds of caravan: "the military, religious, small commercial, and large commercial."[5] As an example of the first of these he draws on an account of a military expedition by the ruler of Tripoli to Cyrenaica in 1817. The expedition employed both camels and horses: "Aside from the Bedawin, who presumably had their own beasts, every five or six soldiers pooled their wealth to buy a camel. This animal carried barley for their horses, barley meal for their own consumption, palm-leaf mats on which the soldiers could sleep, a waterskin, and a wooden pail."[6] Religious caravans were formed to provide protection for pilgrims. As will be discussed in the final chapter, the travel writer Ibn Battuta joined one such caravan traveling from Mecca to Baghdad in 1326. Supplying such large caravans, which in this case included over 1,000 people and a larger number of animals, with water was a major concern. Ibn Battuta mentions that the caravan ran out of water near the end of its journey, but fortunately encountered merchants who provided them with dates, fruits, and other foods to sustain them for the remainder of the trip. Security was another concern. The caravan that Sir Richard Burton traveled with when he made a pilgrimage to the Arabian Peninsula in the late 19th century included a detachment of 500 Albanian cavalry to provide protection.[7] The commander of Burton's caravan also had to police the pilgrims themselves, for maintaining order in a caravan that included a mixture of people speaking Persian, Pashto, various Indian languages, and Arabic was no easy matter.

By far the most common form of caravan is the commercial caravan. Small caravans might be composed of a single merchant and his servants and goods, while larger ones included groups of merchants who had banded together primarily to provide security. In addition to the core members of such caravans, they would often be joined by others (e.g., merchants who were not part of the core group and pilgrims) seeking protection. Coon describes the use of camels by such caravans: "Camels ... are used to carry water, food, and merchandise; they are not ridden unless absolutely necessary. The number of animals to be taken depends on the distance to be covered and the frequency of water holes."[8] Captain J. Riley describes one large commercial caravan traveling from Timbuktu to the Mediterranean coast around 1812–15 consisting of 800 men and 3,000 camels and another traveling between Tripoli and Fez with 1,500 men and 4,000 camels.[9] The merchants of Tripoli and Fez would travel in such a large caravan to Timbuktu once a year and return with not only gold and ivory, but also up to 2,000 slaves.

The personnel making up a caravan also includes camel drivers and locally hired guides, with drivers doing the physical labor (such as cooking and breaking camp). In addition, the merchants often hire a professional "shaikh of caravans" or caravan leader. Thus, in the case of long-distance caravans it is not just the merchants who form the transnational group but also a group of transport and travel specialists.

SAILING CAPABILITIES

The importance of sailing craft to human history is underestimated frequently. People are often amazed to learn that humans settled in New Guinea and Australia over 30,000 years ago. How did the earliest migrants got there? Archaeological research in Indonesia indicates that *Homo erectus* used some type of watercraft to cross at least 25 km of open sea as early as 900,000 years ago.[10] The craft used for the earliest voyages were "floats, not boats."[11] Casson designates true boats as "something that would carry a man upon the water and at the same time keep him dry ... very likely the dugout, although experiments with bound reeds or with skins stretched over light frames must have been made quite early."[12] Sites found on Buka Island in the northern Solomon Islands indicate that 29,000 years ago people were able to cross over 100 km of sea using some type of sailing craft. Simple bamboo rafts and dugout canoes made from logs are still widely used around the Pacific and were probably the earliest means of sailing in this region. On the other side of the world, 10,000 years ago hunters were visiting the island of Malta on boats from the mainland, and they settled there between 7,000 and 8,000 years ago.[13]

It is not until perhaps 5,000 to 6,000 years ago that we see the advent of people sailing back and forth across the sea along coasts to engage in regular long-distance trade. This coincides with the invention of more sophisticated sailing vessels — the invention of the sail being especially important for long distance voyaging. Casson makes the point that "until the coming of the railroad, the water was the only feasible medium for heavy transport and the most convenient for long distance travel."[14] The Egyptians are often credited with inventing the first large boats made of planks in the Middle East some time prior to 3000 B.C., but relatively sophisticated boats were also being made in Mesopotamia then as well. About this time, the Malayo-Polynesian speaking peoples of Island Southeast Asia created a new type of canoe based on the dugout: the outrigger.

The importance of boats for the development of human civilization and of early transnationalism is considerable. Writing about the significance of boats in this regard Wachsmann remarks: "It was only with watercraft that ancient peoples could discover, explore, colonize, and supply the once uninhabited islands of the eastern Mediterranean, and it was mainly with watercraft that ancient peoples of the bordering African, Asian, and European coasts acquired raw materials — especially metals and timber — that allowed the rise of Bronze Age civilizations in the Levant."[15] A scribe writing around 2650 B.C. listing the accomplishments of the Pharaoh Snefru provides one of the earliest written records of such trade when he mentions "bringing of forty ships filled with cedar logs" to Egypt from the port of Byblos (north of modern Beirut).[16] As for the craft themselves, particular types of boat were developed in different regions of the ancient world, such as the dhow of the Indian Ocean and the outrigger of the Pacific Ocean. As Doran writes, "A boat type is a coherent, recognizable entity, a cultural pattern, a significant portion of a great tradition. Once developed, a type spreads gradually over a wide, contiguous area. Boat types are conservative features in which major changes are quite infrequent; they seem to endure for millennia in essentially unchanged form."[17] In the case of the ships that sailed out of Byblos, they were of a type that Wachsmann refers to as "Syro-Canaanite."[18]

The early history of sailing in the Mediterranean appears to be linked to trade in obsidian, the black volcanic stone that early humans valued for its sharp edges when chipped. Archaeologists have found evidence of obsidian being traded throughout the Mediterranean, including islands such as Malta, Crete, and Cyprus, prior to 6000 B.C.[19] Johnstone argues that reed-bundle boats were most likely used for this trade, and there is considerable evidence for the early and widespread use of such boats in ancient times by people living around the eastern Mediterranean, in Mesopotamia, and around the Arabian Sea (including along the Indus River).[20] With the advent of the Early Bronze Age more sophisticated and larger boats could be built of wood, using metal tools. Between 3000 and 2000 B.C. ships were being built in the Mediterranean to transport valuable cargoes such as copper and other ores and cedar logs as well as a host of other items ranging from cattle to cloth to fish. Such innovations led to considerable increases in commerce that in turn generated an even greater volume of commerce. Johnstone comments that as "boats became ships ... the first great island state came into existence" on Crete.[21] The type of ship that evolved in the Mediterranean had doubled rounded ends, a keel, and a single mast with a rectangular sail. Casson remarks, "Since the ancient mariner was as resistant to change as his later brethren, it remained the commonest type in the Mediterranean throughout ancient times."[22] Marine archaeologists have excavated a Phoenician merchant ship that sank off the southern coast of Turkey some time around 1200 B.C.[23] The ship was about 11 meters long and carried a cargo comprised mainly of metal and metal objects, including scrap bronze tools from Cyprus to be recycled and copper and tin ingots to be used for making new bronze.

The Greeks also became involved in ancient maritime trade and it is the Greeks who provide us with what Casson refers to as the "world's first recorded voyage of overseas exploration"—the voyage of Jason and the Argonauts.[24] The story is a quasi-mythical account of the voyage of Jason of Iolcus on Greece's northeast coast on a 50-oared galley named the *Argo* ("swift") in search of the Golden Fleece some time around 1000 B.C. The voyage took Jason and his crew to a land called Colchis located on the eastern side of the Black Sea in modern Georgia to claim the fleece. Despite the difficulties that Jason and the Argonauts encounter in the story, Casson argues that "the Black Sea [at that time] would be as familiar to Greek skippers as their own Aegean," but that as the "*Argo* coasted along the north shore of Asia Minor" it "met the usual problem that confronted a strange ship in those days: attacks by natives whenever it tried to put in for the night or for provisions."[25] So, although Greek sailors might have known the region to some extent, it was far from being part of an established trade route with safe harbors. Casson also suggests that the search for the Golden Fleece was perhaps in reality a search for gold: "Later ages knew that the peoples who lived at the farther end of the Black Sea where Jason's Aea was located had a way of washing gold from a river by tying fleeces in the stream so that particles of dust would adhere to them."[26]

While Greek ships used sails as a source of motive power, oars also played an important role. There were small merchant vessels with 30 oars on a single level that were known as triconters, while somewhat larger ones with 50 oars were called penteconters. Around 700 B.C. the Corinthians launched the first trireme, so named because of its three levels of oars. This particular one had a crew of 200 men. By the 400s B.C. the Greeks were making triremes of over 150 tons that were capable of carrying cargoes of as much as 500 tons. Adkins and Adkins report, "The largest recorded ship was built in the 3rd century B.C. for Hieron II, king of Syracuse.... It was a massive grain carrier with three decks and three masts and an estimated carrying capacity of 1,700–1,900 tons."[27] Ships that were designated for transport of goods rather than for warfare were called *holkades*. The word *holkas* means to tow and refers to their being towed in and out of harbors.[28] These ships lacked the ram of warships and instead had a rounded front. They were broad and deep and designed for stability and large cargo capacity. They were not built for speed. They also featured decks and usually some sort of quarters on the deck. In addition to cargo they also could carry passengers. Undoubtedly the most famous passenger on these ancient ships was the man Casson has dubbed "the first travel writer": Herodotus.[29] Born in Halicarnassus, a Greek city-state in Asia Minor under Persian suzerainty, into a wealthy family, he traveled extensively throughout the Persian and Greek world, finally settling in Thurii, a Greek colony in Sicily, where he died in 425 B.C. As Casson writes, "Like most travelers in ancient times, Herodotus went by ship whenever he could."[30]

One of the most prominent features of the Roman Empire is that it ruled the lands surrounding the Mediterranean. It also controlled the English Channel and parts of the Black Sea. Hence sea power and maritime commerce were important features of the empire. Roman ship designs followed existing traditions dating back to ancient Crete, but ships became larger. Merchant ships powered by sail and rowers carried unprecedented weights of cargo: "The freighters that carried official government cargoes were commonly 340 tons' burden, and those of Rome's crack grain fleet ... ran to 1,200 tons; seventeen centuries were to pass before merchant fleets of such tonnage again sailed the seas."[31] Significantly, as Casson notes, "The sailors and marines who manned the fleets were not Romans. They were Greeks, Phoenicians, Syrians, Egyptians, Slavs — members of those races who for centuries had gone down to the seas or rivers in ships."[32] Most of the officers were Greeks. Entering the maritime service around the ages of 18 to 23, they signed up for at least 26 years, at the end of which time they would be discharged and rewarded with Roman citizenship.

In the case of people around the Arabian Sea they too appear to have begun by using reed-bundle boats for long-distance trading voyages. Documents from ancient Ur refer to wood for building ships being brought as tribute. The wood was supplied via Dilmun (Bahrain) from the Indus region. Thus, in this part of the world as well, wooden ships were being built between 3000 and 2000 B.C. for long-distance trade. The Harappans of the Indus who shipped wood and other goods to Ur also built ships with keels, masts, and sails.

The early history of boat building in East Asia appears to indicate that there were distinct traditions to the north and south of the Yangtze River. Archaeological sites along and to the south of the Yangtze River and on the island of Formosa have turned up dugout boats used as coffins. This territory is associated with non–Han peoples linked to the cultural traditions of Southeast Asia. North of the Yangtze River the early boat traditions appear to include various types of bundled reed, inflated skin, and skin covered craft. However, there is evidence of the spread of boat-building traditions from south of the Yangtze River northward along the coasts and islands of northeastern Asia. Thus, Japan shares a boat-building tradition with the people to the south of the Yangtze River and the sampan ("three plans") developed from a style of dugout that is also found on Formosa.[33] Worchester says that the earliest clear representations of a sampan appear on pictographs dating from A.D. 25 to 225.[34] The other style of boat commonly identified with this part of the world, the junk, seems to have developed from bamboo rafts with sails, with wooden planks replacing bamboo poles.[35]

The junk's evolution into the most seaworthy ship of the pre-modern world entailed adoption of a number of innovations in the form of its sails, rudders, and other aspects of its design. Early Chinese documents describe junks undertaking voyages of up to twelve months by the 100s B.C. It is uncertain precisely how far they sailed, but at least as far as India and possibly to the Red Sea (though certainly not on a regular basis). Either destination served to link the Chinese with European and Middle Eastern commercial networks. Closer to home, Chinese junks joined the flow of ships and goods that were already present along the coasts and between the islands of Southeast Asia.

Chinese ships were not the only ones to sail the waters between South Asia and East Asia. In fact for most of ancient and medieval history they were in the minority. Most of the maritime trade that passed through these waters was carried on ships from southern India and Sri Lanka and from the Malay trading peoples of Southeast Asia. Chinese sources describe two types of ships used by the Malay peoples around the A.D. 200s.[36] One is described as being "12 xin [8 Chinese feet] long and 6 feet broad, with their bows and sterns like fishes.... The large ones carry a hundred men, each man carrying a long or short oar, or a boatpole."[37] The other type appears to have been the primary type used for long-distance trade: "The large ones [ships] are over 200 feet long, and are twenty to thirty feet high [above the water].... They can hold 600 to 700 men, and a cargo of over 10,000 ho [a Chinese corn measure; about ten pecks]. The men from beyond our frontiers use four sails for their ships."[38] To the north these Malay sailors are mentioned as visiting China as early as the 200s B.C. They also sailed into the Indian Ocean and reached the coasts of East Africa, where they exerted a significant cultural influence on the local population: "They were settled along the East African coast by the first century C.E. By the time of the Roman empire, there were permanent communities of Malayo-Polynesian speaking peoples on the coast of Malagasy."[39]

It is uncertain when the first outrigger canoe was built, but it was intimately associated with the spread of Malayo-Polynesian speaking peoples throughout Island Southeast Asia out into the Pacific as far as the islands of Hawaii, New Zealand, and Rapa Nui starting around 2,000 years ago and across the Indian Ocean to the coast of East Africa and the island of Madagascar almost 1,000 years ago.[40] Again, much of this sailing initially was uni-directional, but there was both regional and a limited amount of long-distance trade carried out by these sailors. Long-distance sailing and trading was commonly carried out using relatively large double-hulled canoes rather than the smaller outriggers. Smith writes that double-hulled canoes mainly made the long-distance voyages (large outriggers also made the voyages) and such canoes could cover 145 miles in a day.[41] The ancient Tahitians had several types of double canoe, including ones for albacore fishing, for traveling (it featured a thatched cabin), for carrying sacred objects, and for voyaging to distant islands (it had two masts and a plank-built hull).[42]

One of the largest double-hulled canoes ever built was the Fijian *wangga ndrua* (also sometimes called *wangga tambu,* sacred canoe). These were built "only by chiefs able to command the services of highly skilled hereditary canoe builders."[43] Hornell describes seeing what appeared to be the last of these when he visited Fiji in 1925.[44] It had been built in 1913 and was said to be a small one. The hulls were 40 and 44 feet long with a platform placed across them on top of which was a small thatched hut. Williams says that the largest *ndrua* that he knew of was 118 feet long, but that it "perished inland" (indicating that it could not be launched), while the longest functioning one at that time was a little over 99 feet long.[45] Such canoes were reported by European observers in the 19th century to have been used in warfare and to have carried from 200 to 250 men. But they were also used for peaceful voyaging. Their top speed is reported to have been between 10 and 15 knots. One European who had an opportunity to sail on one wrote: "Up went the huge sail, down went the steer oars, splashing into the sea, and away we shot like a racehorse.... We reached Lifuka [in Tonga] safely in about 3 hours, having run a distance of about 38 miles."[46]

It was not just to the neighboring islands of Tonga that the Fijians sailed. Commodore Wilkes,[47] who visited Fiji in 1840, also reported them as sailing to Rotuma and Samoa, and there is also a reference to Fijians sailing west to Vanuatu.[48] Most important for our consideration is a discussion by Hornell comparing Fijian and Tongan sailing abilities. He comments that while the presence of "Tongan settlements and culture in far distant islands of Melanesia" is an indication of their ability to sail such distances, their double canoe (the *tongiaki*) was "clumsy and ill-designed," and the Tongan presence on such distant shores was the result of their becoming involuntary castaways rather than by plan.[49] In contrast, he comments, "We heard nothing of such involuntary settlements on the part of the Fijians;

owing to the superior sailing qualities of their canoes, they were normally able to continue a given course, even against a head wind."[50]

In 1947 Norwegian explorer Thor Heyerdahl drew attention to the importance of large rafts to trans–Pacific voyaging when he and his crew drifted 4,300 miles for 101 days across the Pacific from Peru to the Tuamotu Islands in French Polynesia on a raft made of balsa logs.[51] Heyerdahl's belief that people from South America settled the Pacific Islands was proven to be wrong, but the expedition did serve to keep alive interest in trans–Pacific voyaging. More recently, Edwin Doran has drawn attention to the use of similar types of large sailing raft in southern China and Southeast Asia and Ecuador and Peru and argues that there was some kind of contact between the two regions in the distant past using such rafts.[52] In his study of the diffusion of the sweet potato from Ecuador to Polynesia, possibly on large sailing rafts, Scaglion dates its appearance in Polynesia around A.D. 1000.[53] While there is a great deal of circumstantial evidence pointing to contact between South America and the Pacific Islands there is no indication that this contact was on a regular basis or that there were established trading relations.[54]

Large sea-going rafts with sails were used, however, for travel on a regular basis along the coast of South America and north to Panama by the time of the Inca Empire in the 1400s A.D.. William Dampier describes large trading rafts carrying cargoes of 60 to 70 tons between Lima, Peru, north as far as Panama.[55] Edwards, basing his conclusions on early Spanish reports, describes these rafts as being able to carry such large loads as up to 50 men on these voyages and says that they appear to have been primarily associated with the coastal people of Ecuador, especially those living around the Gulf of Guayaquil.[56] As Scaglion notes, prominent among these peoples were the Cañari, whose name for the sweet potato *cumal* became *kumara* in Polynesia.[57]

The lateen-sailed dhow became the dominant style of vessel sailing along the coasts on the Indian Ocean in the medieval period.[58] The dhow evolved from earlier vessels that had been used for maritime trade between the Indus civilizations and the Middle East. Dhows weigh between 300 and 500 tons and have crews of between 12 and 30. In the popular imagination dhows are often associated with the voyages of the fictional character Sinbad the Sailor. The Sinbad stories were first compiled in Sassanid Persia and concern a Persian sailor from Basra who lived at the time of the Abbasid Caliphate, during the reign of Haroun al-Rashid, Caliph of Baghdad (r. A.D. 763–809). In these tales Sinbad voyages as far as Sri Lanka, where he visits the city of the king of Serendib where there are gemstones and pearls. The tales of Sinbad resemble many of those collected by the Persian sea captain Burzug Ibn Shahriyar from fellow sailors and published as *The Book of the Marvels of India*.[59] Basra was an important port and trade flowing along the Persian Gulf in the past was sometimes referred to as following the Route of Sinbad. Even today Sinbad's name is often associated with travel in the region.

Bernstein notes that nautical historians have wondered why the dhow continued to be used in the Indian Ocean even after superior ship designs were available from Europe and China.[60] To this question he provides three answers: the weight of tradition among shipbuilders, the lack of locally available iron for construction of these other type of ships, and "although the sewn craft may have been less seaworthy, they were more 'beachworthy,' that is, more pliable, and thus better able to survive the frequent encounters with the reefs, rocks, and shallows of the coasting trade than were the more rigid planked and ribbed Chinese and European ships."[61]

In East Asia, Chinese long-distance sailing increased under the Song Dynasty (A.D.

960–1279). The Song made considerable use of ships in their consolidation of power in the 900s, building ships that could carry up to 1,000 troops.[62] By the A.D. 1000s, the Chinese had developed a magnetic compass to aid in navigation and enhance their long-distance sailing capabilities.[63] In A.D. 1127, when the Song rulers lost control of the northern part of the empire and were forced south of the Yangtze River, the Song rulers initiated a spate of shipbuilding, harbor construction, and other improvements to maritime infrastructure to increase both maritime trade and naval military capabilities. Emperor Gaozong (r. 1127–62) of the Song Dynasty, a champion of maritime commerce, is quoted as saying, "Profits from maritime commerce are very great. If properly managed, they can amount to millions [of strings of coins]. Is this not better than taxing people?"[64] In 1132 the Southern Song established China's first permanent fleet. Louise Levathes notes that "by the thirteenth century the Chinese had the best boats in the Indian ocean and had captured the bulk of the sea trade from the Indians," and she provides the following description of their merchant junks: "The average oceangoing merchant junk was about 100 feet long and 25 feet wide at the beam, and carried 120 tons of cargo and a crew of 60. The largest ships carried three hundred tons and five to six hundred people."[65] These ships were capable of covering 300 miles in a day.

Chinese voyaging reached its peak during the reign of the Ming Dynasty Emperor Yung-lo (also spelled Yogle, r. 1402–24) with the voyages of seven great fleets under the command of Zheng He between 1405 and 1433.[66] The ships that were built for these fleets included 300- to 400-foot-long ships with up to nine masts featuring dozens of luxurious cabins for high-ranking officials. They were the largest ships the Chinese had ever built, and although they were built along traditional ship building lines, creating ships of this size required some innovations: "The strength of the treasure ships was created by another Chinese innovation, watertight bulwark compartments modeled after the multi-chambered structure of a bamboo stalk."[67] Around 300 vessels of varying size with around 30,000 crewmembers made up the fleets.

Each expedition lasted for about two years. They sailed south to Champa, stopping at the Cham port of Qui Nhon, and then on to the north coast of Java, the east coast of Sumatra, through the Strait of Melaka to Melaka (formerly spelled Malacca), and then on to Calicut in southern India with a stop at Sri Lanka (formerly spelled Ceylon) on the way.[68] Zheng He established an entrepôt at Melaka consisting of a stockade where goods that had been collected from throughout the region were stored for the homeward journey.[69] The last fleet left Nanjing in 1431 and arrived in Calicut at the end of 1432. The fleet then divided into smaller detachments. One of these sailed to Hormuz, Aden, and other ports on the Arabian Peninsula and then on the east coast of Africa as far as Malindi (in Kenya). The Chinese were especially keen to trade silks and porcelains for various types of incense and herbal medicines on this voyage. The fleet returned to China in mid–1433, bringing with it "the ambassadors of Sumatra, Ceylon, Calicut and Cochin, Hormuz, Dhufar, Aden, and the other Arab states" along with horses, elephants, and a giraffe.[70]

Yung-lo had died in 1424 and the new emperor, Yung-lo's eldest son, Hongxi (r. 1424–1425), cancelled further maritime expeditions as well as the overland trade to Tibet. This took place in the context of overseas military setbacks. In particular, China's naval power further declined when a fleet of junks sent to provide reinforcements to its army in Dai Viet was defeated with a loss of 300 ships. Hongxi died shortly after becoming emperor, and while the new emperor, Hongxi's son Xuande (r. 1426–36), allowed one more fleet to sail, he effectively maintained his father's policies of isolationism. Mills in his introduction to Ma Huan's account of his travels notes, "During 1431 regulations were made for the employment of naval men to transport grain on the canal, thus reducing them from fighting men to stevedores."[71] After the last treasure fleet returned, shipbuilding and voyaging declined during the remainder of the 1400s. Gradually the Chinese ceased their maritime activities: "By 1500 it was a capital offense to build boats of more than two masts, and in 1525 an imperial edict authorized coastal authorities to destroy all oceangoing ships and to arrest the merchants who sailed them. By 1551 ... it was a crime to go to sea in a multimasted ship."[72]

Perhaps no other European peoples are so closely associated with ships as the Vikings. The Vikings raided, traded, and colonized over extensive areas of Europe from the A.D. 790s to the 1060s. To the east they sailed in their longships down the Volga River and to the Black Sea and Caspian Sea, while to the west they sailed to and founded settlements in Iceland, Greenland, and Newfoundland. The use of sails on vessels in Scandinavia does not seem to appear until the early Viking period. It was the combination of sail and oars to propel these long, narrow, and relatively light ships with shallow drafts that gave the Vikings the ability to conduct their raids and terrorize so much of Europe. The longship was designed for speed and agility and was used for raiding, exploration, and long-distance trading. Small longships, known as *snekke,* had a length of about 17 meters and width of 2.5 meters, and a draught of 0.5 meters. They carried a crew of 24 oarsmen and one cox. These were the most common type of longship. Larger longships, known as *roskilde,* have been found measuring from 30 to 36 meters; these had crews of 70 to 80 men. The other main type of ship used by the Vikings was the *knarr,* which had a broader hull and a deeper draft. It was used mainly to carry cargo, but not for long-distance trade.

LANGUAGE

Transnationalism implies an ability to communicate across borders. This usually takes the form of communicating with those who share a common language. The language shared by those who are in communication may not necessarily be the language most commonly spoken in the two countries. Thus, an ethnic Vietnamese person living in Vancouver, Canada, may communicate with an ethnic Vietnamese person living in Sydney, Australia, in Vietnamese even though both also speak English and English is the dominant language in the two countries. Alternatively, two people living in different countries may employ a common language to communicate that is not the mother tongue of either one. An ethnic Vietnamese person living in Vancouver whose first language is Vietnamese may communicate with an ethnic Russian person living in Sydney whose first language is Russian or with a Cantonese speaking ethnic Chinese person in Hong Kong using English as a common language. In the latter case English serves as a vehicular or bridge language. When widely used such a vehicular language is often referred to as a lingua franca, a language that is used for communication between people who do not share a mother tongue. Today English is the world's leading lingua franca and is widely used in diplomacy, business, scholarly writing, science, technology, tourism, and aviation.

Whereas there are several thousand different languages spoken in the modern world, the linguistic picture was even more complex in the medieval and ancient worlds. Most people in the past could not communicate with those living across borders, and even more than at present, such transnational communication was the preserve of a relatively small proportion of the world's population. As today, in the past transnational communication sometimes took the form of a shared language such as between ethnic Greek traders from Rome visiting fellow ethnic Greek traders in Egypt. Otherwise, those engaging in transnational communication might employ a vehicular language or lingua franca. Such languages often were associated with the ethnicity of long-distance traders, the spread of religions, or the spread of imperial power.

Aramaic was an important early lingua franca in the Middle East.[73] It is a Semitic language that was spoken by the people of Aram in what is today central Syria as early as 1100 B.C. Tiglath-Pileser III conquered the Aramaean city-states and incorporated them into the Neo-Assyrian Empire in the mid–700s B.C., and the language became the lingua franca of the empire. It came to be used as the language of trade and diplomacy both within the empire and in neighboring territories. Darius I in turn made it the official language of the Achaemenid Empire around 500 B.C. Following Alexander's conquest of the Achaemenid Empire, the Hellenic rulers of the Seleucid Empire and Egypt established Greek as the language of administration. However, local versions of Aramaic continued to be used widely throughout the Middle East, such as in Judea, as well as by traders throughout the region and by subsequent Persian empires.

Sanskrit was another important lingua franca in the ancient world that was used widely in South Asia and in the context of the Hindu and Buddhist religions in neighboring areas as well. It was the liturgical language (i.e., holy language) of Hinduism and Buddhism and was used in Hindu epics such as the *Ramayana* and *Mahabharata*. It was also used for writing poems, dramas, and scientific and technical works. The spread of South Asian cultural influence to Southeast Asia, Central Asia, and East Asia meant that Sanskrit was also used in these area, especially within a religious context and by political elites.

Among European languages, Greek and Latin served as important lingua francas in the ancient world. The use of Latin spread with the Roman Empire, with local dialects serving as the bases for the development of the Romance languages such as French and Spanish later. Following the fall of the Roman Empire, Latin continued to be used in medieval Europe as the language of diplomacy, Christianity, scholarship, and science in a form known as Medieval Latin (as distinct from Classical Latin of the Roman Empire). Interestingly, under the influence of the Holy Roman Empire, its use also spread into Slavic and Germanic speaking areas that had never been part of the original Roman Empire.

Classical Chinese served as a lingua franca throughout East Asia in the ancient world. It was the written language of the Han and some of the earlier dynasties and many important books were written using Classical Chinese, such as the *Analicts of Confucius* and the *Tao Te Ching*. After the fall of the Han Dynasty in A.D. 220 numerous local dialects of Chinese emerged, and Classical Chinese evolved into a form known as Literary Chinese that is akin to Medieval Latin. Both forms of Chinese were widely used throughout East Asia and neighboring parts of Southeast Asia and Central Asia in diplomacy as well as in other contexts.

The spread of Islam from the A.D. 700s onward in the medieval period resulted in the rise of Arabic as an important lingua franca not only in Muslim territories in the Middle East, North Africa, South Asia, and Island Southeast Asia, but also in non–Muslim areas where Muslim traders were active, such as in some of the coastal trading ports of China.

WRITING

Being able to communicate with others at a distance is also important for the creation of transnational links. Prior to the invention of writing the means of long-distance communication were few and often not very reliable. Passing on messages by word-of-mouth is undoubtedly the oldest way of communicating over distance. Other ancient means included using sounds (such as those of drums) and smoke, but the content of such messages was limited as were the distances over which they could be sent. Writing represented a major step forward in long-distance communication. Important as it is, however, writing also requires that those in communication are literate in the writing system being employed, and until the advent of modern mass education literacy was not widespread.

Early sophisticated systems of writing were developed independently by ancient civilizations in Mesopotamia, China, Egypt, and Mesoamerica. The origins and evolution of systems of writing were as much connected with the need to keep records and communicate among people within a society as with communication across borders. As such the evolution of systems of writing has been intimately connected with political, commercial, and religious links between people.

Cuneiform uses wedge-shaped characters as a system of writing.[74] It evolved from pictographs in Sumer by around 2900 B.C. The early Sumerians employed about 1,000 distinct characters that were written with a blunt reed on clay tablets, which were hardened in the sun once completed. It was a logographic and syllabic system of writing rather than an alphabet. Of these early tablets Durant remarks, "For centuries writing was a tool of commerce, a matter of contracts and bills, of shipments and receipts; and secondarily, perhaps, it was an instrument of religious record, an attempt to preserve magic formulas, ceremonial procedures, sacred legends, prayers and hymns from alteration or decay."[75] By 2000 B.C. the Sumerians were writing historical chronicles. Their writings also include the Sumerian version of the epic *Gilgamesh*. Numerous other peoples in the Middle East adopted Sumerian cuneiform and adopted it to fit their own languages. The Hittites adopted it around 1800 B.C. and they gradually simplified their system to include only about 400 characters. Surviving Hittite tablets include a wide range of laws and regulations, prices for commodities, and comparative vocabularies with Hittite, Sumerian, and Babylonian equivalents. Although cuneiform continued to be used to a limited extent in the Middle East to at least A.D. 75, in evolutionary terms it was a dead end.

Egyptian hieroglyphics are an ancestor of most modern systems of writing.[76] Hieroglyphics contain logographic and alphabetic characteristics. There are proto-hieroglyphics written on clay tablets dating from around 3300 B.C. The Egyptian writing system evolved to include priestly (hieratic) and popular (demotic) scripts. The famous Rosetta Stone that allowed Europeans to begin deciphering Egyptian hieroglyphics in the early 19th century contains inscriptions in both hieratic and demotic hieroglyphics and Greek. In addition to religious, political, and historical subjects, hieratic hieroglyphics have also been found that tell stories. Included are tales of those who traveled beyond Egypt's borders. Adolf Erman has translated two of these.[77] One is the tale of a ship-wrecked sailor who "set out for the mines of the Sovereign" on board "a ship of 180 feet in length and 60 feet in breadth" with a crew of 120. The ship was wrecked in a storm and only the teller of the tale survived. The second is the tale of Sinuhe, who travels in exile around the Middle East from Egypt after the death of Amenemhet I (i.e., some time around 1900 B.C.) but decides to return to Egypt due to homesickness. Egyptians continued to use this system of writing, which in the Greco-Roman period included over 5,000 hieroglyphs, into the Roman period with the last known hieroglyphic writing dated A.D. 396.

The transition to the use of a true alphabet took a step further with the development of the Proto-Sinaitic consonantal alphabet some time around 1900 B.C. It was first employed by Semitic-speaking peoples who lived in northern Egypt. These people were influenced by Egyptian culture and adopted about 30 Egyptian hieroglyphics to write their language. It was still partly pictographic. Thus, a somewhat abstract drawing of an ox head represented the word for ox (*'aleph*). By around 1400 B.C. the Proto-Sinaitic alphabet was being used in Canaan, where linguists refer to its local form as the Proto-Canaanite alphabet. This alphabet in turn evolved into the Phoenician alphabet around 1050 B.C. In the early Phoenician alphabet the ox head comes to look something like an A on its side (this later is altered by the Greeks to become the letter A). As Phoenician merchants spread out across the Mediterranean world so did their alphabet and it came to be adopted by peoples throughout the region. The Phoenician alphabet in the form of Punic continued to be used until around A.D. 200.

Aramaic speakers settled in what today are Syria and neighboring areas of Iraq and Turkey around 1200 B.C. and adopted the Phoenician alphabet, which by 1000 B.C. began to assume some of its own characteristics (some letters remained the same such one for *'aleph*), with the style of the letters more square than Phoenician letters. Aramaic came to be widely spoken along the eastern coast of the Mediterranean and spread throughout the Middle East as a lingua franca, which it remained until it was largely replaced by Arabic after A.D. 637. It became the official language of Assyria in the 740s B.C. and was the official language of subsequent Persian empires. It was the native language of the Jews (including Jesus) and the early Christians. The Jewish migrants took the language with them to North Africa and Europe and Christian missionaries spread its use to Persia, India, and China. Most alphabets that subsequently developed around the world use scripts that can be traced back to the Aramaic and Phoenician alphabets. About 400,000 people in the Middle East speak Modern Aramaic today.

The important Brahmi alphabet of India is among the alphabets that evolved from the Aramaic alphabet around 500 B.C. The earliest surviving inscriptions using Brahmi are from the time of the Emperor Asoka (r. 273–232 B.C.). It formed the basis for a number of distinct alphabets that evolved in India, Nepal, Tibet, and Southeast Asia. It was first introduced to Southeast Asia during the time of Asoka, who sought to spread Buddhism to adjacent areas of southern Burma, and also formed the basis of the early Cham alphabet, which is the earliest known alphabet to have developed within Southeast Asia. The Cham alphabet developed from the Brahmi-based alphabets (including the Vatteluttu, Pallava, or Grantha scripts) of the Tamil people of southern India around A.D. 200 as a result of commercial and cultural ties between the Cham kingdom of Champa and southern India at that time. It was closely related to the Cham's adoption of the Hindu religion. Guillon reports that there are "some 210 stone inscriptions which survive from ancient Champa ... composed in Sanskrit, old Cham or in both languages."[78] All of the inscriptions relate to religion and aristocratic history. Thus, one famous stele from My Son that is dated A.D. 658 provides genealogical information relating to an alliance between Champa and the neighboring kingdom of Chen La (in Cambodia). The style of writing relies heavily on "Indian literary and religious clichés."[79]

The neighboring Khmer people of Cambodia, whose early culture and civilization was strongly influenced by the Cham, developed an alphabet based on Tamil script. Like the Cham inscriptions, those of the early Khmer are written in both Khmer and Sanskrit. In his survey of these early scripts, Vickery found "the majority, 134, of the published texts [about 190 in total] are in Khmer, of which 52 are preceded by, or contain, a Sanskrit section with significant information."[80] The Khmer alphabet in turn provided the basis for the Lao and Thai alphabets. The oldest Khmer inscription is from Angkor Borei dated A.D. 611. Tamil script was also used on Java to create Kawi script, the earliest form of writing for the Javanese language. Such early writing in Southeast Asia was not intended for a general audience, but could only be read by religious functionaries and educated aristocrats. It reflected important cultural ties with southern India, but the content of the writing focused on local matters of a political and religious nature.

The Mesoamerican writing systems combine pictures carrying meanings with a syllabary in which each picture represented a syllable.[81] The least known but earliest system of writing appears to be that of the Olmecs of Mexico's Gulf Coast region, whose Classic Period dates from 1200 to 900 B.C. The Zapotecs of Oaxaca developed a post–Olmec system of writing, as did the peoples of the Isthmus of Tehuantepec (the script is referred to as Epi-Olmec), the pre–Classic people associated with Izapan culture in the highlands of Guatemala who probably spoke a Mixe-Zoque language, and the Maya. The Epi-Olmec script may be a predecessor to Maya script and the Izapan script is similar to Maya writing as well. The Maya writing system, which was the most fully developed one in Mesoamerica, is composed of 700–800 symbols with about 100 of these forming the core. The peoples of central Mexico lacked a fully developed writing system, although the Aztecs employed a writing system that combined pictures with a limited range of pictographic symbols.

Another crucial component to allow writing to be used for long-distance communication is that the message needs to be written on something that is easily transportable. Early examples of such objects include clay tablets and pieces of bone, bamboo, and wood. Thin sheets of more pliable substances on which to write represent an advance over these more rigid objects and there are three major types of such sheets: papyrus, parchment, and paper.

The ancient Egyptians made papyrus from the pith of the papyrus grass (*Cyperus papyrus*), which was plentiful in the Nile Delta, by around 3500 B.C. Papyrus was made into sheets of varying length with longer ones often rolled into scrolls. The Phoenicians began shipping papyrus from Egypt to Greece around 1100 B.C. It continued to be shipped to Greece from Alexandria after Egypt's conquest by Alexander and later it was shipped to Rome as well. However, papyrus survives best in dry climates like that of Egypt. In Greece and Italy it was subject to mold and deteriorated more quickly than in Egypt.

Writing on animal skins also has a long history in the Middle East and Europe.[82] Parchment is made from calfskin, sheepskin, or goatskin. Rather than being tanned as with leather, the skin is stretched, scraped, and dried. Unlike papyrus, which cannot be folded without cracking, parchment can be folded, and the ancients made documents or books known as codices by folding long strips of parchment accordion-fashion. It is uncertain when parchment was first made from animal skins, but the Egyptians were using it by the time of the Fourth Dynasty (2613–2467 B.C.) and the Assyrians and Babylonians by the 500s B.C. The Roman Pliny the Elder says that a disruption in the supply of papyrus from Alexandria led to the introduction of parchment making in the Anatolian Greek city-state of Pergamom during the reign of either Eumenes I (r. 263–241 B.C.) or Eumenes II (r. 197–158 B.C.). Parchment became the dominant form of paper in Europe over the next few centuries and remained so throughout most of the medieval period until it was gradually replaced by paper.

Paper is usually made from cellulose material. Its origins can be traced to the making of beaten bark-cloth from the paper mulberry tree (*Broussonetia paperrifera*) over 6,000 years ago by ancient Southeast Asian peoples in what is now southeastern China.[83] The paper mulberry tree is indigenous to this area and served as a major source for bark-cloth making along with various other types of breadfruit tree (*Artocarpus*) and banyan or wild fig tree (*Ficus*) in Southeast Asia and the Pacific. Such bark-cloth was used mainly for clothing and sometimes for wrapping or decorative displays. According to what is likely an apocryphal story that has entered into official Chinese historiography, a court official named Cau Lun invented paper in A.D. 105 by combining paper mulberry and other bast fibers, along with scraps of fishnets, old rags, and hemp waste. Someone named Cau Lun may indeed have made paper in this manner, but he certainly did not invent it. Needham and Tsien mention that the Chinese were using paper for wrapping and padding by the 100s B.C., apparently as a substitute for more expensive silk cloth.[84] Archaeologists working near Dunhuang in northwestern China (Gansu Province), which was an important trading center between China and Central Asia and also an early center of Buddhist scholarship, have discovered paper with writing on it dating from about 8 B.C., but using paper as a medium on which to write was not widespread in China until the A.D. 200s.[85] Writing on paper in early China was closely related to Buddhism and many of the early documents are religious manuscripts, especially sutras (canonical scriptures). In general it came to be used to record scriptures and also by more secular scholars as well as by government officials and merchants.

The technology of making paper from paper mulberry pulp diffused to Korea during the period of the Three Kingdoms (100s B.C. to 600s A.D.).[86] Archaeologists have found a piece of paper in a tomb dating from A.D. 313 or earlier, indicating that paper was at least in use and probably being made in Korea by this time. The kingdoms of Goguryeo and Baecze produced lengthy histories written on paper during this century and the kingdom of Silla in the 500s. Silla conquered its two rivals and created a unified kingdom in 668. Archaeologists found the oldest Buddhist sutra that has yet to be discovered in a stupa that was sealed in 751, but it is obvious that Buddhist scriptures were being produced in Korea even earlier. A Korean Buddhist monk from Goguryeo named Damjing introduced papermaking to Japan in 610.[87] Korean paper was considered to be of exceptionally fine quality and it became an item demanded as tribute by China. Korean paper was also exported to China during the Koryo Dynasty (936–1392). Production of books on history, Buddhist scripture, and medicine and the printing of paper money during this dynastic period along with its export increased the demand for paper and led the government to encourage the growth of paper mulberry trees.

Papermaking diffused to the Middle East in the A.D. 700s as a result of Muslim conquests extending into Central Asia that brought them into contact with Chinese culture. Paper mulberry pulp was no longer available and came to be replaced with hemp and linen. Papermakers in Baghdad devised a means of making thicker sheets of paper and constructed the first paper mills in 794. This helped to reduce the cost of paper and make it more readily available. Papermaking spread from Baghdad throughout the Muslim world as far as Spain and India. Important papermaking centers were established in Damascus, Cairo, and in Xativa in Muslim Spain (where a paper mill was established in 1120). Paper mills were constructed in Fabrino, Italy, in the 1200s using technology imported from Muslim Spain. Over the next few centuries, paper mills appeared elsewhere in Europe, such as one in Dartford in England in 1588.

Writing in ancient Mesoamerica is commonly associated with glyphs on large stone stele, but the ancient Mesoamericans also produced codices. These codices date from between 1200 and 1520 and their readership included priests and secular elites. Their contents included histories and genealogies, descriptions of feasts and festivals, information of medicines and curing, and prophecies. There are two main groups of codices: those of the Maya, and those from central Mexico. Maya codices include the *Dresden Codex,* the *Madrid Codex,* the *Paris Codex,* and the *Groller Codex* (which may be a forgery). They are made from the inner bark of the fig tree, treated with a lime or lime-like coating and then written on with ink or paint. A number of scholars have examined bark-cloth making in Mesoamerica as an indication of maritime contact between Malayo-Polynesian speaking peoples and Mesoamerica.[88] In contrast the codices from central Mexico are made of animal hide parchment rather than bark paper. Professional codex painters (*tlacuilo*) made the codices of central Mexico and it is likely that there were such professionals in the Maya area as well. There are eight Mixtec codices including the *Codex Vindobonensis, Codex Nuttall,* and *Codex Bodley.* The *Codex Borgia* is a 39-page ritual and divinatory codex made of animal skin parchment that was probably written in Puebla. The *Codex Fejervary-Mayer* is a 23-page calendar codex believed to have originated in Veracruz made of deerskin parchment.

Papyrus, parchment and pre-industrial papermaking were time-consuming and relatively expensive processes that ensured that materials written on them were not widely circulated. The paper mills of the Muslim world made paper more readily available, but still out of reach to the bulk of humanity. At the beginning of the modern era paper was still an expensive commodity. This situation changed dramatically when mechanized production of paper was introduced in the 1800s. This new technology led to a revolution in communication allowing for the inexpensive production of paper for letters, newspapers, and books.

2

Ancient Empires

Since empires played such an important role in transnationalism in the ancient and medieval world and reference will be made to them throughout the book, in the next two chapters we will provide brief overviews of some of the most relevant empires, with particular attention to transnational aspects. The present chapter will look at empires in the ancient world and the following chapter at medieval empires. As was noted in the last chapter, generally an empire is a multi-national political entity. Moreover, they are commonly characterized by the rulers or ruling group being of a different ethnic or national background than many of the people incorporated into the empire.

Whereas nation building — whereby efforts are made to create a population that is relatively culturally homogeneous — is a common feature of many modern states, the attitudes of the rulers of older empires varied. Some, such as the Romans and Han, tried to promote a degree of shared values and institutions and identification with the imperial realm. Others were not overly concerned with creating such homogeneity beyond having a population that respected the general laws of governance and paid their taxes and tribute. Even where nation building took place on the imperial scale, local identities and loyalties tended to remain important, sometimes taking the form of independence movements whenever central power weakened. For such reasons it is often appropriate to think in terms of transnationalism when looking at relations between the component populations of many of these empires in addition to transnational relations beyond imperial borders.

In terms of transnationalism the status of vassal in relation to imperial rulers is an interesting one. It is commonly defined as "one holding lands from a superior on conditions of homage and allegiance."[1] However, the term is often used broadly to include those paying tribute to a sovereign who in practice has relatively little power to enforce his will, leaving the vassals largely autonomous. Such a status is commonly found along the frontiers of empires where imperial power is relatively weak. It allows the imperial power to create at least nominal influence over such a vassal and thereby promote commercial and cultural relations while also creating a degree of security along the frontier. From such a vassal's perspective such a link can be useful. It can in fact diminish the threat of imperial annexation while allowing beneficial commercial and cultural exchange and can also sometimes help to protect the vassal from threats by others. My own perspective is no doubt influenced by my study of the history of the Tai peoples of Southeast Asia. Living to the south of periodically expansive Han and Mongol empires, for over 2,000 years Tai rulers often paid tribute to the Han and Mongol rulers as a means of appeasing them in a way that served in some ways to bolster their own status and allowed them to retain a large degree of autonomy. This strategy worked for the Tai feudal rulers of Sipsongpanna in southern Yunnan from the time of the Mongol invasions in the 1200s until Mao's communists finally overran them in the late 1940s. In modern times the Tai rulers of what is now highland northwestern Vietnam found themselves wedged between the powerful lowland kingdoms of Dai Viet (modern Vietnam) and Siam (modern Thailand) as well as the Han Empire to the north, and the Tai paid tribute to the rulers of all three. Their relative autonomy provided a useful buffer between Dai Viet and Siam, which were often in direct conflict further south in Cambodia. It was only when the French arrived in the 1880s and laid claim to the Tai territory on the basis of the tribute paid to the Vietnamese that the structure collapsed. In the course of our discussions about empires it is often useful to examine such vassals since they occupy a status between that of an imperial province and an independent state.

My own research experience in Southeast Asia also made me more aware of another important aspect of vassalage in regard to tribute paying and its potential transnational aspects in that someone takes the tribute to the suzerain on a regular basis. This can create cross-cultural relations that may be of a transnational nature. In regard to cross-cultural relations, in the case of the Palaung villagers in Burma's Shan States who paid tribute in the form of opium to the ruling Shan feudal lords (*saopha*) in the past, it was the village headman who collected tribute due to the *saopha* and had to see to it that the tribute was delivered to the *saopha's* representatives.[2] As a result, while most Palaung remained in their villages and spoke only their own language, the headman and others who were responsible for delivering the tribute usually were bilingual, speaking their own Palaung language as well as the Tai language of the feudal lords, and tended to be more knowledgeable of the culture of the ruling Shan. Such people linked the two societies and served as conveyors of information about the respective societies. In this way, tribute paying helped to create a group of local elites and their assistants who lived transnational lives. Similar processes took place often in the past in the case of vassal states within empires and even those who paid tribute to distant rulers as an aspect of their foreign relations. The histories of the empires discussed in this and the next chapter contain numerous references to the payment of tribute by vassals and others. Unfortunately, the records are often quite sketchy and rarely provide details of the process of tribute paying, but what information does exist indicates that the pattern was not very different from that of the Palaung and Shan. It would seem that there were significant numbers of people, ranging from village headmen to princes, engaged in transnational tribute paying activities within and across the borders of ancient and medieval empires.

The Middle East

We begin this chapter with an examination of the ancient empires of the Middle East since this is where the world's first multi-national empires were created. In ancient times peoples speaking three major groups of languages inhabited the region. These are the Semitic languages and two groups of Indo-European languages: Indo-Iranian and Anatolian. Peoples speaking each of these groups of languages formed tribal groups and various other types of political entities including empires in the region in antiquity. It should be noted that there were peoples in the region who spoke other languages such as the Hattians of Anatolia (see below), the Hurrians of northern Mesopotamia, and the Elamites of southwestern Iran to add to the ethnic mixture of the region.

The Semitic languages appear to have first emerged in the Levant (the Eastern Mediterranean littoral) about 5,750 years ago.[3] Speakers of these languages spread from there to the east into Mesopotamia and south into the Arabian Peninsula. Semitic languages include Akkadian, Eblaite, various Canaanite languages such as Hebrew and Phoenician, Aramaic languages such as Nabataean, Syraic, and Chaldean, and Arabic languages.

Indo-European speakers initially lived in the Eurasian steppe of Central Asia, with peoples speaking Indo-Iranian languages found in the region between the Ural River and the Tian Shan mountain range.[4] Peoples speaking these languages included the Scythians, Sogdians, and Persians. The Scythians were nomads who lived in the steppes of Central Asia adjacent to the Caspian Sea. We will discuss the Sogdians later in relation to their involvement in long-distance trade across Central Asia. The Persians lived in what is now Iran and it is these peoples with whom we are primarily concerned in the present chapter. The Persians emerged as a distinct peoples as they moved from the steppes to the southeast in what is today Iran about 4,000 years ago.[5]

Ancestors of Anatolian speaking peoples emerged as a distinct group in the Eurasian steppe about 5,500 years ago and subsequently migrated to Anatolia (aka Asia Minor) in what is now Turkey about 4,000 years ago.[6] The indigenous Hattians and Assyrian traders were already living in Anatolia when the Hittites arrived. The Hittites absorbed many elements of the Hattian culture (and some from the Assyrians) as they organized themselves into city-states. By around 1600 B.C. these had coalesced into a single kingdom.[7] The Hittites were able to conquer territories to their south at various times, such as under Suppiluliuma I (r. *c.* 1344–1322 B.C.) when they conquered most of the Levant, but they did not hold territories outside of Anatolia for long periods, and they are of interest in relation to transnationalism largely because of there being so many mines in Anatolia that produced metals needed through the Middle East.

Another import feature of the imperial landscape in the Middle East is the relationship between settled peoples and pastoral nomads. In ancient and medieval times as today, the deserts and mountains of the Middle East were inhabited by groups of sheep-herding pastoral nomads. Economic relations between these nomads and settled populations include the nomads trading sheep and camel wool and other products of these animals for a variety of agricultural products and various other goods available from settled populations. Animal fibers obtained from the nomads were woven into cloth and rugs by settled peoples and some of these products became long-distance trade commodities. Water scarcity in particular at times leads to conflict between nomads and settled peoples and there are also instances of nomads raiding settled populations. The nomads themselves sometimes move into more fertile areas and settle to become farmers or town-dwellers — a process known as sedentarization.

In terms of who constituted the transnational populations of these empires, the range of people living such lives was relatively limited. Conquest and imperial policies often resulted in peoples being displaced or purposely relocated, but they rarely established transnational links once they had moved and instead usually simply became a local ethnic group that could trace its ancestry to some other place. Skilled artisans sometimes moved freely around empires, but often artisans either worked near home or were forcibly moved as war captives or slaves. Soldiers, of course, commonly moved around empires and across their borders, but often they were involved in short forays to conquer and to re-assert central authority and once the fighting and plundering was over they went home. Sometimes permanent garrisons were established around the empires or in distant imperial outposts and these could lead to the creation of transnational links. Most of the ancient empires in the

Middle East were fairly decentralized affairs in which administration tended to be localized. Only in the case of those few empires with a greater degree of centralized administration do we find the emergence of transnational imperial bureaucrats. The most common type of transnational was a person engaged in long-distance trade and this was an occupation that tended to be identified with particular ethnic groups or with people from particular towns or cities.

MESOPOTAMIAN EMPIRES

The earliest empires in the Middle East appeared in Mesopotamia, a region surrounding the Tigris and Euphrates river system and including the territory occupied by modern Iraq and adjacent parts of neighboring states. The Sumerians, a Semitic-speaking people who lived in southern Mesopotamia in a region bordering the Persian Gulf, created the first of these empires. In fact many of humankind's firsts are associated with the Sumerians. Sumerians created the first cities to be supported by populations practicing intensive year-round agriculture as early as 5300 B.C. By the Uruk period (4100–2900 B.C.) Sumer consisted of about a dozen city-states. At the beginning of this period, by 4000 B.C., the Sumerians had created an extensive system of canals to control the flow of water in order to reduce the threat of flooding and irrigate their crops as well as to facilitate transportation. As was noted in the first chapter, the Sumerians developed the first system of writing. This in turn allowed them to create the first business contracts and the first code of laws. While coinage had yet to be invented, gold and silver were used as standards for exchange and the Sumerians created what seems to be the first credit system.

The political power of Sumerian city-states rarely extended beyond control exerted by one city-state over some of its neighboring Sumerian city-states. However, a few of the city-state rulers were able to establish control over neighboring peoples for brief periods. Lugal-Anne-Mundu, ruler of Adab in the 2400s B.C., was the most famous of the kings to extend his power beyond the lands of his fellow Sumerians and, because of this, he is sometimes credited with establishing the first empire in history.[8] Among the non–Sumerians apparently under his rule were the neighboring Elamites of southwestern Iran; the people of Marhasi (aka Warahse), located to the east of Elam on the Iranian plateau; the people of Subartu (probably referring to what was later called Assyria)[9]; the Guti, a nomadic tribe living in the Zagros Mountains; the Amorites, a Semitic-speaking nomadic tribe living in the mountainous Jebel Bishri region of Syria[10]; and the people of the "Cedar Mountain land" (Lebanon). The reasons for his desire to control some of these regions, such as Marhasi, undoubtedly had to do with their association with valuable resources. While Lugal-Anne-Mundu may have actually ruled over at least some of these peoples, it would appear that most of them had the status of vassals who merely paid him tribute. Lugal-Anne-Mundu's empire quickly collapsed after he died and the various non–Sumerian groups reasserted their independence.

Sumerian transnational relations involved more than the occasional ability to exact tribute from other people. Long-distance trade on a regular basis was of far more significance. While there has been considerable debate on the contribution of long-distance trade to the emergence of Sumerian civilization, there is no doubt as to the substantial volume of such trade.[11] It is safe to say that both long-distance trade and increased agricultural surpluses helped to generate a society with a greater division of labor and more stratification along with promoting the rise of cities with populations exceeding 10,000 inhabitants.

Long-distance trade pre-dates the rise of Sumer in southern Mesopotamia. Obsidian was already being imported from the north in the Neolithic era (to be discussed in detail in another chapter). But as Sumerian civilization grew, so too did the demand for trade goods and increasingly the Sumerians had agricultural and other products to trade for these imports. The Uruk period saw a considerable volume of trade goods flowing along Sumer's rivers and canals, overland from various parts of the Middle East, and by sea through the Persian Gulf to Dilmun (Bahrain) and beyond on the Indus River in what is today Pakistan. Archaeologists have discovered an Uruk-era warehouse at Warka that is "literally brimming with objects made of imported woods, precious and semiprecious stones, and metals."[12] Enki was the Sumerian god of crafts and the text *Enki and the World Order* includes a prayer for timber and other articles to be brought to Sumer and for ships from Meluhha (Harappa in modern Pakistan) to bring gold, silver, and lapis lazuli.[13]

The list of imported items found in archaeological sites and mentioned in cuneiform texts is quite extensive and goes far beyond a few luxury items. Imports included pine timber used for roofing material; pure and alloyed metals in the form of ore, ingots, and finished products including gold, silver, copper, and lead; wool and woolen textiles; precious stones for decorative purposes and jewelry including lapis lazuli, carnelian, agate, chalcedony, amazonite, amethyst, aragonite, and jasper; semiprecious stones also for decorative purposes and jewelry as well as for use as building material including chlorite, obsidian, rock crystal, quartz, alabaster, gypsum, marble, diorite, and serpentine; common stones like basalt and flint as well as obsidian for making utilitarian implements; limestone for building foundations; and wine.[14] While a few of these goods came from within Mesopotamia, many of them came from beyond — from as far away as Lebanon, Anatolia, Afghanistan, and southern Pakistan — largely by water either along the Euphrates River or by sea via the Persian Gulf.

Although large quantities of trade goods flowed in and out of the city-states of Sumer, the Sumerians themselves do not seem to have been directly involved in the actual conduct of long-distance trade. Their role was primarily that of consumers of imported goods and suppliers of agricultural produce, leather, and a few other goods in exchange for these goods. The trade itself was carried out mainly by non–Sumerians and "many foreigners came to southern Mesopotamia for trading purposes."[15]

The Persian Gulf trade originated primarily from three locales, referred to by the Sumerians as Dilmun, Magan, and Meluhha. The location of Dilmun is uncertain, but it was probably located somewhere in the vicinity of Bahrain and Qatar and served as a transshipment center for trade goods from around the Persian Gulf and beyond. Magan refers to modern Oman and it was a source of copper and ornamental stone. Meluhha appears to refer to Harappa, located in the vicinity of the Indus River.[16] Meluhha provided Sumer with timber such as ebony that was used for shipbuilding, sesame oil, lapis lazuli from Badakshan in Afghanistan as well as other gems and minerals (some of these made into beads), cotton textiles, and possibly chickens.[17] In return Harappa received such goods as agricultural products, woolen textiles, and silver from Sumer. The actual trade route from Meluhha/Harappa probably began at the Harappan port of Lothal (near Ahmedabad in modern Gujarat) from where ships sailed to Magan/Oman, then on to Dilmun, and from Dilmun to Sumer.[18] It is unclear whether Harrapans actually sailed all of the way to Sumer, but it is a distinct possibility.

The navigability of the Euphrates allowed goods to be brought down the river from the Mediterranean littoral in what is today Lebanon and Syria as well as from the highlands of Anatolia. Such long-distance trade played an important role in the emergence of a number of small polities in what is now northern Syria.[19] Most of the peoples in this region spoke a variety of West Semitic languages and dialects.[20] Michalowski refers to ancient northern Syria as a region comprised of a series of city-states that were "largely independent of their cultural and linguistic cousins in Sumer and Akkad."[21]

The city-states of this region included the port of Ugarit, Ebla located inland to the northeast, Mari to the west along the Euphrates, and Nagar and Shekhna to the northeast. The Hurrian towns of Karkemish and Urkesh were located further to the north in the foothills of the Taurus Mountains of Anatolia. These towns in northern Syria are of particular interest in regard to transnationalism, located as they were in a frontier region of the Mesopotamian empires that was occupied by peoples who were ethnically distinct from those living within the imperial heartland but who, nevertheless, had important ties with the empires. These towns prospered providing the Sumerian and later other Mesopotamian markets with goods such as timber, building stone, various metals, and wine from northern Syria, Lebanon, and Anatolia.[22] These products and the wealth generated by their trade prompted the Sumerian Lugal-Anne-Mundu of Adab to invade the area in the 2400s B.C., but for the most part peaceful commerce and not conquest was the basis of contact between Sumer and the urban centers of northeastern Syria.[23] In addition to growing rich from their commerce with the Sumerians, the people of this region were influenced by Sumerian culture, adopting its system of writing and some of its gods, including Enki.

The Semitic-speaking Akkadians initially lived in the northern Arabian steppe and desert of the Levant and came into contact with Mesopotamia primarily by providing the settled peoples there with exotic goods through trade.[24] They migrated to the east and settled to the north of the Sumerians in central Mesopotamia where they became sedentarized and began to develop a civilization similar to that of the Sumerians. The cultures of the two peoples came into contact and during the 2000s B.C. became closely interrelated with bilingualism becoming common.[25]

While it is common to date the founding of the Akkadian empire as 2334 B.C., it did not become a large multi-national empire until the reign of Sargon (aka Sargon of Akkad, Sargon the Great; r .c. 2270–2215 B.C.).[26] Sargon conquered the Sumerian city-states as well as the Elamite city of Susa (modern Shush) and Marhasi (aka Warahse). While the territory ruled by Sargon was only a little greater than that ruled by Lugal-Anne-Mundu the nature of the empires was quite different. Not only did the rulers of these various cities and territories become Sargon's vassals and pay him tribute, he created an empire with greater centralized authority over his multi-national subjects that lasted beyond the end of his reign until 2154 B.C.[27] For this reason Sargon is often credited with creating the world's first multi-national, centrally ruled empire. The Akkadian Empire reached its greatest extent under its third ruler, Sargon's grandson Naram-Sin (r. c. 2190–2154 or 2254–2218 B.C.), the self-proclaimed King of the Four Quarters. Much of the coast of the Persian Gulf including Magan was added to the Akkadian Empire by Naram-Sin. He also defeated some of the nomadic tribes of the Zagros Mountains, although this period also witnessed the start of raids by the Guti who after Naram-Sin's death successfully invaded the Mesopotamian lowlands and brought the Akkadian Empire to an end.

There were a number of steps taken by Sargon and those who came after him to weld together their empire. While the rulers of local city-states often were left in place, their status became more that of a provincial governor than a tribute-paying semi-independent vassal. There were also instances where more direct rule was established with members of the royal family being appointed to governorships. The Akkadian rulers also undertook a program of road building to connect major parts of the empire. Sargon made Akkadian the official language of his empire, helping to establish it as the lingua franca in the region, a position that it maintained until the 700s B.C. when Aramaic assumed this role under the Neo-Assyrian Empire.

The long-distance overland, riverine, and maritime trade patterns of the Sumerians continued with the Akkadian Empire. While this tended to remain in the hands of foreigners who brought goods to the Akkadian markets voluntarily, the Akkadians sometimes sought to exert more direct control over this trade by establishing outposts along trade routes and in some instances by incorporating the trade centers into their empire. Thus, while Sargon is said to have "made ships from Meluhha, Magan and Dilmun come to the quay of Akkad,"[28] as mentioned above, Naram-Sin appears to have actually conquered Magan. The nature of the Akkadian presence in northern Syria is subject to some dispute among modern scholars. It is clear that Sargon and Naram-Sin did attack some of the towns in this region, such as Ebla,[29] but they do not seem to have established much of a permanent presence in the area. Michalowski diminishes the importance of raids by Sargon in Syria, noting that although Naram-Sin established a garrison at Nagar this was not indicative of widespread rule.[30] Urkesh, to the north of Nagar, for example, remained independent and Naram-Sin sought to strengthen ties with the city not through conquest but by marrying his daughter to a member of the ruling family of Urkesh.[31]

The collapse of the Akkadian Empire, possibly in part due to a drought in the region,[32] was accompanied by an invasion of lowland Mesopotamia by the Guti and a period of anarchy during which cities declined and long-distance trade collapsed. The drought also led nomadic groups such as the Amorites to come into conflict with settled peoples over water and during this period the Amorites gradually migrated towards Mesopotamia and eventually settled there. A Sumerian named Ur-Nammu (2112–2095 B.C.)[33] pushed the Guti out of the Mesopotamian lowlands and established an independent Sumerian kingdom associated with what is commonly referred to as the Ur-III dynasty that survived his death in battle with the Guti. The Sumerians managed briefly to establish control over the central area of Mesopotamia and to exert influence into northern Syria. Ur-Nammu began restoring roads and long-distance trade revived. Traders from Ebla and Mari in north Syria as well as Elamites once again began to visit Sumerian towns like Isin, where they traded goods from the north for local leather products.[34] This revival of long-distance trade in turn resulted in trading centers such as Ebla seeing their fortunes improve once again. The Ur-III dynasty did not last very long and some time around 2002 or 2004 B.C.[35] the Elamites and people of Susa sacked Ur and captured its king.

With the Guti out of the way and the Sumerians defeated, for a time there was again no dominant power in Mesopotamia. Rather there were a variety of kingdoms and city-states that were often associated with particular ethnic groups, although some were multi-ethnic. The Sumerians were divided into a number of small city-states such as Eshnuna, Isin, Larsa, and Kazallu. Sheep-herding nomadic Amorites had moved from the Khabur River area of Syria into northern Sumeria and the central Akkadian territories, where they lived around the sedentarized Akkadians and Sumerians and gradually came to settle with some moving into towns. The sedentarized Amorites adopted many aspects of Akkadian culture, including use of their written language, along with some elements of Sumerian culture. These sedentarized Amorites included some merchants who dealt in grain and other commodities. Babylon was one of the towns where the Amorites settled. Babylon at the time was a small town that after the fall of the Ur-III dynasty was ruled by the city-state of Kazallu.

A local Amorite leader named Sumu-Adama (aka Su-abu) declared Babylon's independence from Kazallu and established Babylon as an independent city-state in 1894 B.C.

To the north of Babylon the Akkadians of the city-state of Assur (aka Ashur) located along the upper Tigris River also established an independent city-state. This group of Akkadians is commonly referred to as Assyrians in reference to their city of Assur. The Assyrians are of particular interest in regard to transnationalism because of their involvement with long-distance trade at this time. In fact, the early history of the Assyrians prior to the establishment of their empire sets them apart from other early empire-builders in that their early fortunes were built largely on long-distance commerce rather than on agricultural or pastoral activities. Leeman argues that Assur came to depend on long-distance trade in part because "the possibilities for a flourishing agriculture were smaller than in Southern Mesopotamia,"[37] and he includes Assur in a list of "typical trading centres" along with Tilmun, Mari, and Ebla.[38]

The trade mostly involved trading textiles from Babylon for gold, silver, lead, and tin from mines in Anatolia, but other goods were also traded. Although the city's rulers as well as its temples were involved in long-distance trade, that trade was conducted mainly by family firms in which typically the head of the family lived in Assur, an eldest son or other family member was based in the Assyrian merchants' quarter (*kārum*) in the Hittite city of Nesa (aka Kanesh; modern Kültepe), and other family members traveled around Anatolia as agents of the firm (called *tamkārum*).[39] The Assyrian *kārum* in Anatolia, which were established between 1920 and 1740 B.C., will be discussed at greater length in a later chapter. Veenhof estimates that there were "as much as 2,000 inhabitants of the City of Assur" involved in long-distance trade in the mid–1800s B.C. with about one-third of this number living in or regularly traveling to Anatolia, adding, "This involvement of so many people must have had a serious impact on Assyrian society."[40]

An Amorite ruler named Shamshi-Adad conquered Assyria in 1813 B.C. His father ruled over a kingdom neighboring Mari and when Shamshi-Adad's brother inherited the throne, Shamshi-Adad conquered Mari after its king was assassinated. Shamshi-Adad then conquered the city of Shekhna to the north and eventually conquered Assur and deposed its ruler. Shamshi-Adad ruled Assur from his newly established capital of Shubat-Enlil (modern Tell Leilan) in the Khabur valley.[41] Importantly in regard to transnationalism, he allowed the Assyrians to continue their trade with Anatolia and to maintain their trading colonies there. He appointed one son, Ishme-Dagan, to rule over the city of Ekallatum, located to the south of Shekhna on the Tigris River, and another son, Yashmah-Adad, to rule over Mari. After Shanshi-Adad's death Ishme-Dagan also became ruler of Assur. A descendant of Mari's former ruler named Zimrilim overthrew Ishme-Dagan and Mari freed itself of Amorite rule.[42]

Having taken power from one Amorite ruler Zimrilim then allied himself with another Amorite, Hammurabi, the king of Babylon. Under Hammurabi (r. *c.* 1792–1750 B.C.) Babylon was emerging as an important regional power. Hammurabi defeated the Sumerian city-states to the south, but then faced stiffer resistance from Ishme-Dagan who established alliances with the Hurrians and others against Babylon — in the case of the Hurrians he had his son Mut-Ashkur marry the daughter of the Hurrian king. Hammarabi eventually defeated Ishme-Dagan in 1756 B.C. and made Assur a vassal state. Hammurabi was now master of a multi-ethnic empire composed of both directly ruled territories and more loosely controlled vassal states. Written Akkadian served as the administrative language of the empire with Sumerian being used in some religious contexts. The Amorite Assyrian kings (Mut-Ashkur had succeeded his father as king of Assyria) were able to retain a degree of autonomy under the Babylonians, but Assyrian trade with Anatolia effectively ceased as the direction of

Anatolian long-distance trade now shifted from Assur to Babylon, which had become both the political and economic center of Mesopotamia.

Hammurabi's empire did not survive long after his death. A number of its component parts sought to reassert their independence under his successor Samsu-iluna. In the case of Assur, a local Akkadian named Ashur-dugul seized the throne and a period of conflict with Babylon ensued that culminated in both the Babylonians and Amorites being driven out by an Akkadian named Adasi around 1720 B.C. Although the Amorites continued to rule over Babylon until 1595 B.C., the political power of Babylon was greatly diminished and once again Mesopotamia was divided into a number of relatively small political entities. Despite these political setbacks, the city of Babylon remained the region's most important economic center and hub of transnational commerce, in part because of its location as a bridge between the Tigris and Euphrates rivers.[43]

The Assyrian ruler Tiglath-Pileser I was able to create a large multi-ethnic regional empire for a brief time in the 1100s B.C. He became ruler of Assyria in 1115 B.C. and soon began attacks on the Hittites, first driving them out of the Hurrian territory of Subartu and then moving into the highlands of Anatolia. From there he took his armies into northern Syria and then on to the Phoenician towns of Gebal (modern Byblos, Lebanon) and Sidon and island of Arvad (modern Arad, Syria) along the Mediterranean coast. He sailed on a ship in the sea at Arvad, making him possibly the first Mesopotamian ruler to do so. The Phoenician cities paid him tribute and his incursion into this area also brought him into contact with Egypt since these Phoenician cities fell within their sphere of influence. Once again, this was a loosely tied empire composed mainly of relatively autonomous tribute-paying polities, and after Tiglath-Pileser died in 1076 B.C. his empire quickly began to crumble, with the Assyrians losing control of the areas outside of the Mesopotamian heartland in particular.

The political landscape of Mesopotamia and the Middle East in general change dramatically between the late 900s and 500s B.C. with the establishment first of what is commonly called the Neo-Assyrian and the Neo-Babylonian empires. This period saw the creation of more permanent and integrated empires that included territories beyond Mesopotamia. Although Assyria had lost control of most of its foreign territories after Tiglath-Pileser's death, the more inward looking kingdom itself fared relatively well. The capable administration of Ashur-dan II (r. *c.* 935–912) in particular saw effective provincial government and economic prosperity based on large agricultural surpluses, which helped to lay the basis for Assyria's re-emergence as a regional imperial power.

The Neo-Assyrian Empire is commonly seen as beginning with the reign of Assyria's next king, Adad-nirari II (r. 911–891 B.C.), who brought a number of neighboring territories under Assyrian control.[44] Initial expansion of the Neo-Assyrian Empire roughly followed the path of Tiglath-Pileser into Anatolia and Syria and once again exacted tribute from the Phoenicians. The Assyrians also moved westward into the Zagros Mountains and the lands of the Guti and Lullubi. Ashur-nasirpal II (r. 883–859 B.C.) moved the empire's capital to another Assyrian city, Nimrud (aka Kalhu, Kalkhu, or Kalakh) in 879 B.C. Despite being the capital of a large empire, Nimrud's population never exceeded 30,000 at a time when Babylon, which was economically the most important city in the region, had around 300,000 inhabitants.[45] The last years of the reign of Ashur-nasirpal's son Shalmaneser III (r. 858–823 B.C.) was marked by a revolt led by his eldest son, Ashur-nadinaplu, that greatly weakened the empire and allowed many of its subject peoples to reassert their independence for a time. Adad-nirari III, who assumed the throne in 810 B.C., was able to re-establish Assyrian power and even expand it by invading the Levant and large parts of Iran as far as the Caspian Sea. But after he died in 782 B.C. the Neo-Assyrian Empire was again weakened with the plague being added to its political misfortunes.

An Assyrian general and governor of Nimrud named Pulu seized power in 745 B.C. and murdered the members of the royal family. Taking the name Tiglath-Pileser III (r. 745–727 B.C.), he not only expanded the Neo-Assyrian Empire once again but he also radically reformed how it was administered. Archrival Babylon was made to pay tribute and eventually was conquered and for a time brought under more direct Assyian rule, but the Assyrians continually had difficulty in retaining control over the great city. Tiglath-Pileser III also re-established Assyrian control over the Levant. What set Tiglath-Pileser III apart from earlier Assyrian rulers was the extent to which he transformed it from what in effect was a collection of vassal states into a highly centralized and integrated empire.[46] Tiglath-Pileser III created a standing army to provide greater control over his empire and divided it into provinces that were administered by governors. The duties of these governors included enforcing imperial laws, collecting taxes, supplying labor for public works, and providing soldiers when needed. In an early form of empire-wide nation building, Tiglath-Pilser III established a policy of "deporting conquered populations to alien habitats, where, mingling with the natives, they might lose their unity and identity."[47] This practice failed in some ways and most of those who were forcibly moved retained their ethnic identities rather than viewing themselves as members of a larger Assyrian imperial nation, but it did result in some changes in the ethnic configuration of the region and in the blending of two of its larger ethnic groups, the Akkadians and Amorites.

Also of interest in relation to transnationalism was how the Assyrians themselves changed from being primarily traders to being mainly warriors. As Leeman remarks, as Assyria became "a state of conquerors and rulers over a large empire" it no longer "qualified as a trading country."[48] As imperialists the Assyrians were more interested in building a strong military and gaining wealth from plunder and tribute than in engaging in commerce. While the Assyrian's administrative reforms may have facilitated commerce, the Assyrians employed the infrastructure primarily to increase the flow of loot. As Durant comments, "The collection of wealth was facilitated by creation of what was without doubt the most extensive administrative organization yet seen in the Mediterranean or Near Eastern world."[49] Not only did non–Assyrians conduct commerce along the major trade routes outside of the imperial borders, even within the empire non–Assyrians conducted most of the long-distance trade. Thus, although the Syrian and Phoenician city-states were ruled by the Assyrians and remained important trading centers, Syrian traders were going to Assyria rather than Assyrian traders travelling west.

The Assyrians moved their capital once again in 706 B.C., when Sargon II decided to establish a new capital at Ninevah (aka Dur-Sharrukin, modern Khorsabad, near Mosul). Ninevah was already an old city at this time and had gained prominence as a center for worshippers of the cult of the goddess Ishtar over 1,000 years previously. Ninevah was located in a more favorable location to take advantage of northern trade routes and did manage to grow into a larger city than Nimrud (reaching a population of about 120,000). However, while Ninevah was a wealthy city, thanks in large part to the loot the Assyrians were able to extract from their subjects, and royal patronage resulted in massive construction programs, the city did not eclipse Babylon as the region's major transnational commercial hub.[50] Durant characterizes Nineveh and other Assyrian cities as being "not so much centers of commerce as they were centers for the collection of loot from their empire."[51]

The Neo-Assyrian Empire's climax of wealth and power was reached under the rule of Ashur-banipal (r. 668–631/627 B.C.), when "all the western Orient came to pay tribute to the Universal King."[52] Sending his armies to expand the empire even further while at the same time having to contend with ongoing revolts by the Babylonians and others within its borders took its toll, and like so many other empires in history, shortly after reaching its peak the Neo-Assyrian Empire collapsed. When Ashur-banipal's son Ashur-etililani assumed the throne after his father's death he was involved in a power struggle in which a general named Sinshumulishir briefly grabbed the throne. Another of Ashur-banipal's sons named Sinsharishkun came to power a short time later only to face a rebellion by the Babylonians to the south led by Nabopolassar (a Chaldean from southern Iraq) in 626 B.C., as well as incursions along his northern borders by a variety of Iranian-speaking nomadic groups including the Scythians, Cimmerians,[53] Medes, and Persians. The nomad hordes raided as far the southern Levant, destroying such towns as Ashkelon (in modern Israel). Nabopolassar's Babylonians attacked the Assyrian heartland itself in 616 B.C. and in alliance with the Iranian nomads besieged and then sacked Assur, Nimrud, and Ninevah.[54] The surviving Assyrians resurrected a small kingdom out of the ruins left behind with a new capital at Harran that survived until 609 B.C., when the Babylonians finally destroyed it as well.

Nabopolassar (r. 626–605 B.C.) is credited with establishing the Neo-Babylonian Empire, which is commonly dated from the onset of his rebellion in 626 B.C. to the Babylonian defeat by the Persians at the Battle of Opis in 539 B.C.—a total of 87 years with the first ten of these taken up fighting the Assyrians. Nabopolassar's nomad allies did not remain in the area and after the fall of Ninevah he assumed control over Assyria and some adjacent territories in Anatolia and Syria. However, the Egyptians had moved into the Levant and parts of Anatolia after the collapse of Assyrian power there and it took Nabopolassar most of the remaining years of his reign to establish control over this area.

Nabopolassar's son, who took the name Nebuchadnezzar II (r. 604–562 B.C.) on assuming the throne after his father's death, was active in promoting an Akkadian-Sumerian revival in the core areas of his empire in Mesopotamia. His program of re-building cities was the physical manifestation of this. Babylon in particular benefitted and grew into an even greater economic and cultural urban center. Cultural aspects of the revival included the restoration of Akkadian as the imperial language (although Aramaic remained firmly established as the common lingua franca). The growth of the Mesopotamian core surrounding Babylon coincided with its armies' exerting greater control over surrounding areas such as the Levant and southern Anatolia and thereby providing the core with both loot and labor. In regard to the latter, after crushing a revolt by the Jews in 572 B.C., Nebuchadnezzar II deported large numbers of them to Babylon.

The Jews who were deported to Babylon found themselves part of a multi-ethnic society, but one in which there was a strong tendency for those of foreign origin living in and around Babylon to adopt Akkadian-Sumerian culture. As Durant notes, the Jews "flourished on Mesopotamia's rich soil" and "enjoyed considerable freedom of custom and worship," but in the process "an ever-rising proportion of them accepted the gods of Babylon, and the epicurean ways of the old metropolis.... When the second generation of exiles grew up, Jerusalem was almost forgotten."[55] In the case of the Jews, of course, the memory of Jerusalem and their distinct identity did not entirely die out. Subsequently many of them returned to their ancestral land.

The Neo-Babylonian Empire began to fall apart soon after Nebuchadnezzar II's death during the reign of Nebonidus (r. 556–539 B.C.), who "preferred archaeology to government, and devoted himself to excavating the antiquities of Sumeria while his own realm was going to ruin."[56] When the Persian king Cyrus II invaded Mesopotamia in 539 B.C., many of the Neo-Babylonian Empire's subjects welcomed the invading Persians, resistance quickly collapsed, and the Persian army was able to enter Babylon without a fight. The Persian invasion marked a shift in regional power away from Mesopotamia east to Persia as Babylonia and Assyria were incorporated into the Persian-dominated Achaemenid Empire.

THE ACHAEMENID EMPIRE

The territory to the east of Babylon encompassing the modern state of Iran was occupied by diverse groups that included sheep-herding nomads and sedentarized people living in villages, towns, and small cities. The Elamites with their capital of Susa lived in the southwestern part of Iran, while Iranian-speaking tribes had settled over much of the remaining area between the 1100s and 800s B.C. The latter included the Medes (aka Medians), the Parthians in the east,[57] and the Parsu in the northwest (along the southeastern shore of Lake Urmiah). A Mede named Deioces formed the first Mede state some time around 700 B.C. with his capital located at Ecbatana (modern Hamadan in Iran).[58] Both the Medes and Elamites became vassals of the Assyrians, although Assyrian control over these eastern territories was far from firm. Not only was there local opposition to Assyrian rule, but the region was also subject to invasion by the Scythians. The nomadic Scythians not only invaded parts of Assyrian territory as mentioned above, but they also invaded Iranian territory. In so doing they pushed the Parsu southward where they settled in the vicinity of the Elamites under a leader named Achaemenes. Teispes succeeded him and then overran the Elamite capital of Anshan and subsequently established Parsu control over the surrounding area (corresponding roughly to the modern province of Fars). Teispes became king of Anshan, and thus ruler of both the Parsu and Elamites. The Parsu king of Anshan, Cyrus I, was defeated by the Assyrian king Ashur-banipal in 639 B.C. and forced to send his son to the Assyrian court to pay tribute.

The Scythians defeated the Medes in 653 B.C. and killed their king, Phraortes. Their leader Madius (r. 653–625 B.C.) then made himself king of the Medes. Scythian rule of the Medians ended when Phraortes's son Cyaxares killed the Scythian rulers at a banquet. After becoming king of the Medes, Cyaxares (1. 624–585 B.C.) allied himself with Nabopolassar in his war against the Assyrians. Cyaxares is also credited with reorganizing the Mede army and establishing control not only over much of Iran (including over the Parsu of Anshan), but also to the northwest over parts of northern Mesopotamia, Anatolia, and Armenia; he further extended his rule into the Central Asian territory of the Bactrians.[59] The Bactrians warrant mention since although they were largely nomadic peoples (their name being associated with the Bactrian camel) some of them were sedentarized and they occupied an important position in Central Asian long-distance trade.

Cyaxares went to war with Alyattes II, the king of Lydia, whose territory included most of Anatolia. After five years of fighting their forces met at the Battle of Halys in 585 B.C., which is also known as the Battle of the Eclipse since the fighting abruptly ended with the onset of a solar eclipse that both sides judged to be an omen to end the war.[60] In regard to transnationalism it is the aftermath that is important. In addition to establishing the Halys River as the border between the two kingdoms the kings also agreed to a marriage between their children, Cyaxares's son Astyages marrying Alyattes's daughter Aryrnis. This was not the first time that Cyaxares had sought to cement an alliance through the marriage of family members. He had also arranged for the marriage of his daughter or granddaughter Amytis to Nabopolassar of Babylon's son Nebuchadnezzar. She went to live with her husband in Babylon and is reputed to have been responsible for his decision to build the famous Hanging Gardens of Babylon where plants from her home were planted to ease her sense of homesickness.

When Cyaxares's son Astyages became king of the Mede Empire shortly after the Battle of Hayls he was allied to the rulers of both Lydia and Babylon through marriage. Astyages followed his father's practice and arranged for his daughter Mandane to marry Cambyses I, the Parsu king of Anshan. In this case, rather than forming an alliance, Cambyses was a vassal of the Mede king. The reign on Astyages was also noteworthy for the growth of the Zoroastrian religion within the Mede Empire. That religion was to become closely identified with long-distance trade across Asia in later years.

Cambyses had a son named Cyrus, who became Cyrus II as king. Cyrus II was more ambitious than his father and rebelled against his grandfather Astyages. A significant number of Medes sided with Cyrus II in the war and Cyrus was able to defeat his grandfather and make himself ruler of the Mede Empire.[61] While Cyrus is commonly perceived as a Persian it is worth remembering that he was of joint Parsu and Mede ancestry. As Cyrus the Great (r. 559–530 B.C.), Cyrus II is also associated with a line of Parsu rulers back to his paternal ancestor Achaemenes, whose name was used for the ruling dynasty and the multi-ethnic empire that Cyrus II established, the Achaemenid Empire, which was to last for over 200 years until it was conquered by Alexander the Great in 330 B.C. Cyrus the Great laid the foundation for the creation of the largest empire in the world to date and, more importantly in terms of transnationalism, one that not only included all of the Middle East, but extended far beyond. At its greatest extent the empire included portions of Afghanistan and Pakistan (e.g., the Punjab) to the east; adjacent areas of Central Asia to the north; Iraq, Turkey, Bulgaria, parts of Greece, Armenia, and the Caucusus to the west; Syria, Lebanon, Jordan, Israel, northern Saudi Arabia, much of Egypt, and as far as Libya to the southwest. About 40 million people of numerous distinct nationalities lived within its borders.

One other legacy of Cyrus the Great was his allowing the Jews of Babylon to return to their homeland in Yehud province in 538 B.C. and rebuild their temple. As was mentioned earlier, many of the Jews who had been brought to Babylon had become assimilated, but a number still retained enough of a distinct identity that they decided to move to Yehud even though by then none of them had been born there or knew it firsthand.

The Achaemenid ruler Darius I (r. 521–486 B.C.), also known as Darius the Great, is of particular interest because of his administrative reforms and economic policies. Rawlinson says of Darius: "He found the Empire a crude and heterogeneous mass of ill-assorted elements, hanging loosely together by the single tie of subjection to a common head; he left it a compact and regularly organized body, united on a single well-ordered system."[62] Durant comments, "The Persian Empire was the most successful experiment in imperial government that the Mediterranean world would know before the coming of Rome."[63]

All of the Achaemenid capitals were located in the imperial homeland in what is today Fars Province. Cyrus the Great had established his capital at Pasargadae. Construction of the new capital began in 546 B.C., but it had not been completed by the time Cyrus died. His son, Cambyses II, moved the capital to the former Elamite capital of Susa and made Pasargadae the provincial capital of Persis (i.e., Fars). Although Darius oversaw a program of construction at Susa, he moved his capital to another new site in Fars, known as Parsa, the City of Persians (aka Persepolis, north of the modern city of Shiraz), which he began building in 515 B.C. Among the monuments of the city was the Gate of All Nations, a grand hall that was named in reference to the subject peoples of the empire.

Darius divided the empire into twenty provinces under the supervision of a civil governor known as a satrap. During the course of the empire's history the number of satraps varied from 20 to 29. The satraps were appointed by the king and exercised supreme civil authority in their territories, including the collection of fixed amounts of tribute that were to be paid to the crown. The tribute included both money (gold and silver coins were minted) and commodities. The commodities were those that each province was known for. Egypt supplied grain; Media and Cappadocia, sheep, mules, and horses; Armenia, colts; Cilicia, white horses; and Babylonia, corn and boy eunuchs. Each province also had its own military commander, who was intended by the king in part to serve as a check on any thoughts that the satrap might have about revolting. Both satraps and military commanders often were chosen "from among the king's blood relations" or they were attached to the crown by marrying them to one of the royal princesses.[64] The king also appointed an independent financial controller in each province and would also send royal inspectors to the provinces. These inspectors were commonly sons or brothers of the king. They were accompanied by an armed force and had the power to correct anything that they found amiss in the province. Beyond these high offices there was a vast bureaucracy and a large army.

Durant comments, "Industry was poorly developed in Persia; she was content to let the nations of the Near East practice the handicrafts while she bought their products with their imperial tribute."[65] One of the important developments during the reign of Darius I was the promotion of commerce within the empire and trade with territories beyond its borders. Within the empire there was a great deal of infrastructure built to facilitate communication. One such project was the Royal Road, running 2,699 kilometers (1,677 miles) from Susa to Sardis, which boasted inns and royal stations that provided fresh horses for mail carriers: "though the ordinary traveler required ninety days to go from Susa to Sardis the royal mail moved over the distance as quickly as an automobile party does now [in the 1930s] — that is, in a little less than a week."[66] Rawlinson remarks, "The conveyance [of the post couriers] was so rapid that some even compared it to the flight of birds."[67] Herodotus wrote of these postal carriers: "Neither snow, nor rain, nor heat, nor darkness of night prevents these couriers from completing their designated stages with utmost speed."[68] In addition to being relatively rapid, movement over these roads was also, as noted by Herodotus, "safe" — such security being enhanced by the construction of guardhouses so that "the whole route was kept secure from the brigands who infested the Empire."[69] Roads were even built across parts of Afghanistan to improve communication with India. Bridges were built over important river crossings, including the Hellespont, "over which hundreds of skeptical elephants could pass in safety."[70] Darius I also built a canal to connect the Red Sea and Mediterranean.

Rawlinson notes that these improvements in communication reflected Darius's idea that it was "of the utmost importance that the orders of the Court should be speedily transmitted to the provincial governors, and that their reports and those of the royal secretaries should be received without needless delay."[71] As Durant points out, however, while these roads, bridges, and canals "were built primarily for military and governmental purposes, to facilitate central control and administration ... they served also to stimulate commerce and the exchange of customs, ideas, and the indispensable superstitions of mankind."[72]

While Achaemenid rulers such as Darius I encouraged trade, commercial activities themselves were left largely in the hands of non–Persians. According to Herodotus, the Persians expressed extreme contempt for trade and "only the very lowest and poorest were actual artisans and traders. Shops were banished from the more public parts of towns; and thus such commercial transactions as took place were veiled in what was regarded as a decent obscurity" in large part because it was felt that "shopping and bargaining involved the necessity of falsehood."[73] Citing Quintus Curtius, Rawlinson remarks that not only did Persian women disdain commerce, but they even looked down upon weaving: "The labors of the loom, which no Grecian princess regarded as unbecoming her rank, were despised by all Persian women except the lowest."[74] Babylonians, Phoenicians, and Jews were the main peoples who brought goods to the empire and who engaged in commerce within its borders.

The materials used to construct Darius's palace at Susa give an idea of the nature of commerce and production within the empire. The timber included cedar from Lebanon and a type of wood called *yaka* that was said to have come from Carmania (mountainous Kerman Province in southeastern Iran) and Gandhara (the Kabul region in Afghanistan). The gold came from Sardis (the ancient kingdom of Lydia, the modern Turkish province of Manisa) and Bactria (in northern Afghanistan and southwestern Uzbekistan); the lapis-lazuli and carnelian, from Sogdiana (to the north of Bactria including the provinces of Samarkand and Bukhara in Uzbekistan, and Sughud province in Tajikistan); the turquoise, from Chorasmia (part of the satrap of Parthia, in modern Uzbekistan); the silver and ebony, from Egypt; the ivory, from Ethiopia, Sindh (Pakistan) and Arachosia (modern Arghandab district in Afghanistan and neighboring areas of southeastern Afghanistan and northern Pakistan). Ornamentation was brought from Ionia (an area settled by Greeks in western Anatolia, modern Turkey). The stonecutters were Ionians and Sardians, the goldsmiths were Medes and Egyptians, and the wood-workers were Sardians and Egyptians, while Babylonians baked the bricks, and Medes and Egyptians adorned the walls.

The territory of the Sogdians, who are mentioned above, was incorporated into the Achaemenid Empire on its frontier. Beyond it lay the land of the nomadic Scythians, and Sogdians served as a buffer between these nomads and the sedentarized world of the Achaemenid-ruled empire.[75]

The Achaemenid Empire is also associated with the growth of the Zoroastrian religion. Although its origin is linked to the prophet Zarathustra (aka Zoroastres, Zoroaster), who lived long before the founding of the Achaemenid Empire, the religion nevertheless came to be closely linked with the empire and the Persian people.[76] Artaxerxes I (r. 465–424 B.C.), who moved the empire's capital temporarily to Babylon, is credited with establishing Zoroastrianism as the de facto state religion. Artaxerxes II Mnemon (r. 404–358), who was the longest ruling king of the dynasty and whose reign is associated with a period of relative peace and prosperity — he also moved the capital back to Parsu (Persepolis) — oversaw the building of Zoroastrian temples in the major cities of the empire, and Zoroastrianism was spread throughout Asia Minor and the Levant, to Armenia. The religion was later to be promoted by the Sassanid rules of Persia (who assumed power in A.D. 228) and its followers travelled and settled along the Silk Road as far as China prior to the 500s. The religion went into sharp decline with the Muslim conquest of Persia in the mid–600s A.D. and the number of its adherents was greatly reduced. The Muslim conquest created a Zoroastrian diaspora with many of its followers migrating to western India, where they came to be known as Parsis.

Darius III Codomannus (r. 336–330 B.C.) was the last Achaemenid king. He had the unfortunate luck to have to face the Macedonian Alexander, and his defeat by Alexander brought an end to over 200 years of Achaemenid rule and the expansion of a new nationality, the Greeks, across the region.

ALEXANDER AND THE SELEUCID EMPIRE

Scholars and the popular media in the West have paid considerable attention to Alexander III of Macedon (l. 356–323 B.C.), who is commonly referred to as Alexander the Great, and his dramatic conquests. In addition to conquering the Achaemenid Empire, he invaded neighboring areas in the vicinity of the Indus River before returning to Babylon, where he died. From a transnational perspective the most important aspect of Alexander's conquests was the insertion of Hellenic influence in the Middle East and adjacent parts of Central Asia and South Asia beyond its former toehold in Anatolia. This spread of Hellenic influence was manifest in the fact that even after Alexander's death and the division of his empire by the so-called Partition of Babylon and the subsequent Partition of Triparadisus (320 B.C.) Macedonions continued to rule territories he had conquered. Outside of Greece, Hellenic rulers retained a presence in the Kingdom of Pergamon (aka Pergamun) in Turkey, the Ptolemaic Kingdom in Egypt, and the Seleucid Empire, which occupied much of the territory that had been part of the Achaemenid Empire.

The Seleucid Empire (312–63 B.C.) was comprised essentially of the Middle Eastern and South Asian portions of Alexander's empire, stretching from eastern Turkey to the Indus River. Founded by Seleucus I Nicator, its Macedonian ruling class spoke Greek and maintained Greek culture. Seleucus came into conflict with Chandragupta Maurya, founder of the Mauryan Empire in India (to be discussed below), in 305 B.C. Peace was established between the two kingdoms through a treaty, followed by Seleucus giving Chandragupta Maurya the hand of his daughter (or perhaps another Macedonian princess) in marriage and in return receiving a gift of 500 war-elephants. There was also an exchange of ambassadors.

Perhaps of most interest in regard to the Seleucid Empire in terms of transnationalism are the efforts by its rulers to promote Hellenic culture. These included not only efforts to assimilate local populations, but also colonization by migrants from overpopulated areas of Greece, especially to southeastern Turkey and Syria. Such Greek influence was mainly evident in larger towns and cities, including newly founded colonies (known as *katoikiai*) and cities such as Seleukeia-Tigris (aka Seleucia Tigris) and Antioch.[77] Antioch was one of four cities founded by Seleucus I Nicator. Greek architect Xenarius was responsible for the city plan, which was similar to that of Alexandria in Egypt. Its initial population of around 50,000 Greek citizens, their families, slaves, and various migrants from the nearby region included Macedonians, Athenians, and other Greeks as well as Jews and other non–Greeks.[78] In part because of its commercial importance, over the next couple of centuries Antioch became the third largest city in the Mediterranean world after Rome and Alexandria with a population of around 500,000.

The nature of long-distance trade in the Middle East appears to have changed little under the Seleucid rulers, but there were some changes. For one thing, Seleukeia-Tigris (located south of modern Baghdad), which was founded by Seleucus I Nicator in 323 B.C. and served as the Seleucid capital, became a major regional trading center:

> "The principal land route from India and the one from Baktria [Bactria] and Central Asia (later to become the Silk Road) came together at Artakoana in Aria (near Herat), skirted the Dasht-i-Kavir desert on the north, crossed the Zagros by way of Ekbatana [Ecbatana] and arrived at Seleukeia-Tigris. A secondary land route from India, but more difficult, reached Susa after traversing Arachosia, Drangiane, Karmania [Carmania] and Persis, and continued on to Seleukeia-Tigris.... From Seleukeia-Tigris the goods collected from Arabia and India travelled west to Antioch and thence to Laodikeia and Seleukeia-Pieria for Mediterranean destinations or traversed Asia Minor to arrive at the Aegean ports, principally Ephesus and Smyrna."[79]

The rise of Seleukeia-Tigris as a commercial hub came at the expense of Babylon, which saw its economic fortunes decline under Hellenic rule.

Greeks become more involved in overland long-distance trade in the Middle East under the Seleucids, but most of the long-distance traders were still non–Greeks. Thus, maritime trade in the Persian Gulf and overland trade from the Arabian Peninsula remained in the hands of Arabs and other local groups. Part of the process of Hellenization also involved the more widespread use of silver coinage as a medium of exchange with one of the major mints being established at Seleukeia.

THE PARTHIAN EMPIRE

The Seleucid Empire was replaced by the Roman Empire in the west and the Arsacid or Parthian Empire elsewhere. We have already mentioned the Parthians as an Iranian nomadic group that had settled in Iran. Their territory lay in what later was known as Khorasan (aka Khurasan) located in northeastern Iran and adjacent portions of Afghanistan. The Medes ruled them and the Parthians acknowledged Cyrus II as their ruler. Their territory became part of an Achaemenid satrapy. The governor of the satrapy Phrataphernes surrendered to Alexander the Great in 330 B.C. and was rewarded by being reappointed as governor under Macedonian overlordship. The territory remained a satrapy under the Seleucids until the Seleucid Empire began to crumble. The governor of Parthia, Andragoras, proclaimed his independence around 247 B.C.[80]

Somewhat earlier, around 238 B.C., a group of nomads known as the Parni, who were living in the northern part of Parthia and appear to have been a Scythian tribe originally from the Caspian Sea area,[81] led by two brothers named Arsaces and Tiridates, had also declared their independence from the Seleucids and eventually they were able to assume control over all of Parthia.[82] Arsaces and then his brother ruled Parthia as an independent kingdom and Arsaces was subsequently considered to be the founder of the Arsacid Dynasty. Under Arsaces II the kingdom lost its independence and became a vassal state of the Seleucid ruler Antiochus III (aka Antiochus the Great) in 209 B.C. This status continued until Phraates I (r. 176–171 B.C.) regained their independence.

One of Phraates's sons, Mithrades (r. 171–138 B.C.), assumed the throne upon his father's death. Bivar refers to Mithrades as "the real founder of Parthia as a major power."[83] Mithrades invaded Babylonia in 141 B.C. and subsequently captured the Seleucid ruler Demetrius II Nicator in 139 B.C. and overran Mesopotamia and Media. The Arsacids' empire eventually came to include most of the Middle East, extending as far west as Armenia and east as far as Pakistan. The empire lasted until the defeat of Artabanus IV by the Persian Ardashir I in A.D. 224.

During their long history the Arsacid rulers were to have a number of capitals, sometimes more than one at a time, and some of these were outside of their original homeland. Arsaces I made Nisa (near modern Ashgabat, Turkmenistan) his capital. Bivar argues that the Arsacids probably moved their government westward from Nisa because of the vulnerability of that locale "to nomad raids by the fiercer tribes from beyond the Oxus."[84] Around 200 B.C. the Arsacids made Hecatompylos (modern Sahr-e Qumis, Iran) their capital. It was located along the Royal Road, which was also to become an important link in the Silk Road, and eventually grew into a fair sized city. As the empire expanded the Arsacids established new capitals away from the Parthian homeland, including Ctesiphon, located next to the Tigris River near the former Seleucid capital of Seleukeia-Tigris. This shift of capitals followed the Royal Road from one of its minor links to a more central location as was befitting such a powerful empire.[85] Moreover, just as the founding of Seleukeia-Tigris as the Seleucid capital had seen trade networks shift from Babylon to Seleukeia-Tigris, Ctesiphon replaced Seleukeia-Tigris as the main regional commercial center.[86]

Strabo refers to Ctesiphon as "a large village" but then goes on to say, "Because of the Parthian power ... Ctesiphon is a city rather than a village."[87] In fact, under the Arsacids Ctesiphon became one of the largest cities in the world, just behind Rome and Alexandria in population.[88] Strabo describes Ctesiphon as the Arsacids' winter capital: "The Parthian kings are accustomed to spend the winter there because of the salubrity of the air, but they summer at Ecbatana and in Hyrcania because of the prevalence of their ancient renown."[89] Hyrcania being their old city in the north of Parthia and Ecbatana an old city in the west of Iran associated with the Medes and Persians, the Arsacids thus established a transnational existence, moving between capitals in different parts of their empire. Ecbatana came to serve as their primary summer capital and also was the home of the Parthian mint. Strabo indicates that by establishing their winter capital at Ctesiphon the Parthians were able to maintain a degree of separation between their own Scythian people and the Greeks of Seleukeia-Tigris — "thus sparing the Seleuceians, in order that the Seleuceians might not be oppressed by having the Scythian folk or soldiery quartered amongst them."[90] He goes on the describe Ctesiphon: "Its size is such that it lodges a great number of people, and it has been equipped with buildings by the Parthians themselves; and it has been provided by the Parthians with wares for sale and with the arts that are pleasing to the Parthians."[91]

The Parthian or Arsacid Empire was more decentralized than many other ancient empires and local elites retained a considerable degree of independence as illustrated by the fact that many of the different territories could mint their own coins. At one point there were 18 vassal kings under Arsacid rule.

Imperial revenue was obtained largely in the form of tribute and tolls and, rather than being traders themselves, the Parthians sought to profit from the trade of others. It is worth noting that the overland caravan trade from the east to Roman territory continued even during times of war between the Roman Empire and Parthians. Young writes about the problems posed for the caravan trade by warfare.[92] The Parthian conquest of Mesene in A.D. 150–1 appears to have disrupted the Palmeyrene caravan trade (Palmyra dominated such trade in this region) and it only recommenced in A.D. 156 with difficulty. Having just re-started, when Rome under Lucius Verus and Parthia under Vologases IV (r. c. 147–191) went to war in 162 the caravan trade once again was disrupted and only began again after the death of Vologases IV. The conclusion that Young draws from this is that "the caravan traffic was not a great priority in setting ether Roman or Parthian foreign policy."[93]

The port of Siraf (in Bushehr Province, Iran) located on the shores on the Persian Gulf was a hub of the Parthian Empire's maritime commerce, which became especially important as overland caravan trade was disrupted during the latter days of the empire. Archaeologists working there have discovered ivory objects from Africa, stones from northwestern India, and lapis lazuli from Afghanistan. The port became involved in trade with China in A.D. 185. It remained a major port for the next few centuries and then gradually declined as trade routes shifted to the Red Sea and bypassed the Persian Gulf.

The Parthians were relatively eclectic in regard to culture and adopted elements from the various cultures within their empire, including Hellenic and Persian elements of art and architecture. They "maintained a policy of tolerance towards all religions" and their subjects included followers not only of local older religions such as Zoroastrianism, but also the newer religions such as Christianity and Buddhism.[94] This is in contrast to the Sassanid Dynasty that came after them and persecuted other religions after making Zoroastrianism their official religion. In the case of Buddhism, not only did it gain followers within the empire, but as will be discussed in a later chapter Parthian Buddhists were also prominently involved in the transmission of Buddhism to China. Especially important in this regard was a Parthian prince named An Shigao (aka An Shih-kao), An being a title for a person from Anxi, Parthia), who renounced his chance at the Parthian throne to travel to China as a Buddhist missionary — becoming the first Buddhist missionary to be named in Chinese historical sources.[95] An Shigao arrived in the Han capital of Luoyang in A.D. 148 and established a center for translating Theravada and Mahayana texts. After An Shigao died in 168 another Parthian Buddhist monk, An Xuan, arrived in 181 to take over the job of translation.

In the west, Parthia and Rome often found themselves in conflict and the border between the Roman and Parthian empires shifted frequently. Small states along this border area found themselves caught in a tug-of-war for influence between the two superpowers. The Romans managed to capture Ctesiphon three times (in A.D. 116, 164, and 197), but were unable to hold the city. Roman attacks on Parthian territories and a smallpox epidemic in A.D. 165 served to weaken the Arsacid Empire, but in the end it fell not to the Romans but to one of its own vassals, Ardeshir I.[96] Ardeshir was from the city of Istakhr (aka Estakhr) in Fars and ruled there as a vassal of the Parthians. He revolted against the Parthians and defeated them in a battle near Bandar Abbas in which the Parthian ruler Artabanus IV was killed. Ardeshir is considered the founder of the Sassanid Dynasty that came to replace the Arsacids as the rulers of most of the Middle East until it fell in A.D. 651. He made Istakhr his capital, but later Ctesiphon became the Sassanid capital.

South Asia

The earliest states in South Asia developed along the Indus River in the west and the Ganges River in the east. The earliest to emerge were city-states along the Indus, associated with Harappan Civilization. Later the kingdom of Magadha emerged in the vicinity of the Ganges River in the 600s B.C. in what is today Bihar State in India. Magadha's Nanda Dynasty conquered much of the lowland areas of what is today northern India as well as neighboring portions of Bangladesh and Pakistan in the 400s B.C. and created the Nanda Empire.[97] The first Magadha capital was located at Rajgir (aka Rajagriha, in modern Bihar State) and the capital was later moved to Pataliputra (also in Bihar). While the various polities under Nanda rule were able to retain a degree of autonomy, the Nandas appointed many of the high level officials in these territories and imposed a system of tax collection. Magadhi Prakit was the language of Magadha and the surrounding areas and became the imperial language.

Jainism initially was the dominant religion of Magadha, but Buddhism later came to be of considerable importance as well. One of the early prophets of Jainism, Parshvanath (aka Parshva), was born of noble parents in Varanasi, adjacent to the Ganges River.[98] Siddartha Gautama Buddha was born also of noble parents a little later and further to the north in Lambini. His family belonged to the Shakya people in what is now southern Nepal.[99] King Ajatashatru of Magadha convened the First Buddhist Council in a cave near Rajir and King Kalasoka of Magadha convened the Second Buddhist Council at Vaishali, where Gautama Buddha had delivered his last sermon. Both religions, but especially Buddhism, spread with the rising political fortunes of Magadha.

The Mauryan Empire

The Mauryan Empire (321–185 B.C.) that followed the Nanda Empire is of particular interest in relation to transnationalism in that under its rulers there were important political, commercial, and religious relations established with states and empires outside of the empire's South Asian heartland.

Alexander the Great's invasion of the area adjacent to the Indus River in the west appears to have played a crucial role in the fall of the Nanda Dynasty. The city of Taxila (aka Takshasila, in Punjab Province, Pakistan) was strategically located along several important trade routes: one linking the Nanda Empire with Gandhara to the west, another running northwest to Bactria, and a third passing through Kashmir, over the Khunjerab Pass, and then to Central Asia (and what later would become the Silk Road). Darius the Great had made it part of the Achaemenid Empire, but by Alexander the Great's time it was free of Persian rule. Its ruler Ambhi allied himself with Alexander and hosted Alexander and his army in Taxila. It was a wealthy and cosmopolitan city that was known as an educational center. A prominent teacher at Taxila named Chanakya (aka Kautila) was quite upset by Alexander's invasion and lobbied various kings to fight against the Macedonians and their allies, including Dhana Nanda, ruler of the Nanda Empire. Unsuccessful in these efforts, he elicited the support of one of his pupils, Chandragupta Maurya. There is considerable scholarly debate about Chandragupta's origins. Durant refers to him as "a young Kshatriya noble exiled from Magdha by the ruling Nanda family, to which he was related."[100] Whatever his origins, Chandragupta — with Chanakya acting as his mentor (Durant refers to him as "his subtle Machiavellian adviser"[101]) — organized a small military force that was able to defeat the Macedonian satrap Alexander had left behind and was declared king of Taxila around 303 B.C. He then attacked the Nandas and finally defeated them after laying siege to their capital of Pataliputra around 321 B.C.

Chandragupta Maurya, with Chanakya serving as his prime minister, made Pataliputra his capital and set about to expand his empire beyond the borders of the old Nanda Empire. In particular, he took control of areas in the west that had been destabilized by Alexander's withdrawal from the area around the Indus. Chandragupta's son Bindusara (r. 298–274 B.C) inherited the throne upon his father's death. Bindusara expanded the empire southward as far as the Tamil territories in the far south, which remained independent. He also failed to conquer the kingdom of Kalinga (roughly corresponding to modern Orissa). Bidusara's son Asoka was made viceroy of the territory occupied by the Avanti kingdom (roughly corresponding to modern Madhya Pradesh) and took up residence in its capital city, Ujjain, while another son, Susima, was made viceroy of Taxila. It was Asoka (r. 274–232 B.C) who assumed the throne upon his father's death. He conquered Kalinga and under him the Mauryan Empire reached its greatest extent, including a great deal of modern India (with the exception of most of northeastern India and Tamilakan, or Tamil Land, in southern India) as well as large parts of modern Pakistan and Afghanistan.

In terms of transnationalism what is of interest is the manner in which the Mauryan Empire united what had formerly been numerous distinct kingdoms and territories within a single administrative structure on the one hand and relations beyond its borders on the other hand. Stability and security were provided by a large military force, estimated by the Greek ambassador Megasthnes to have included 600,000 infantry, 30,000 cavalry, and 9,000 elephants.[102] Chandragupta and Chanakya created a centralized administrative system that included departments with well-defined duties. The latter included departments responsible for frontiers, passports, navigation, communication, and commerce.[103] There was also a single currency. It is easy, however, to over-emphasize the degree of control exercised by the Mauryan central government. Some regions remained nominal vassals and, as events were to prove, local loyalties remained strong in many of the newly conquered territories.

Asoka in particular sponsored the construction and maintenance of an extensive system of roads and canals, along which shade and fruit trees were planted and rest houses constructed. Rest houses on the major trade routes were built "at distances of one *yojana* (from five to nine miles, the original word denoting the distance at which cart-ox could safely be driven ... on long treks)."[104] Hospitals and veterinary clinics were also built throughout the empire, including along the trade routes. Kosambi remarks, "These new constructions, which must have been an absolute godsend for the traders; especially because of the doctors and veterinaries available at many of the stations, were located not only in Asoka's domains but also beyond his frontiers."[105] Among those traveling over these roads were not only traders, the emperor himself undertook to make a tour of inspection throughout his domains once in every five years — no small undertaking given the distances involved and the slow speed of travel. Water transportation was also well looked after. The department responsible for navigation "regulated water transport, and protected travelers on rivers and seas; it maintained bridges and harbors."[106]

In regard to harbors, the port of Tamralipti (aka Tamralipta, Tamalika, Tamalitte, Tamoluk, modern Tamluk in West Bengal) was of particular importance.[107] It was the main international port of the Mauryan Empire. Located on the Bay of Bengal at the mouth of the Ganges River, it also served as the capital of the kingdom of Vanga, which was incorporated into the Mauryan Empire. Overland trade routes carried goods to and from the port and ultimately linked it later to the Silk Road. It was an important center for maritime trade and travel between India and Sri Lanka and the Tamil territories of southern India to the south and Burma, Sumatra, Java, Champa, and elsewhere in Southeast Asia to the east. Most of the Buddhist pilgrims and missionaries (to be discussed in the final chapter) passed through Tamralipti. Tamralipti continued to serve as a major port during the Gupta period and there are references to it dating until the A.D. 700s.

In regard to religion, whereas Chandragupta Maurya had been a Jain, Asoka converted to Buddhism and actively promoted the religion. He convened the important Third Buddhist Council around 250 B.C. that was chaired by his brother Moggaliputta Tissa, who had been ordained as a monk.[108] Asoka also issued a series of edicts known as the Edicts of Asoka.[109] The edicts were written on stones and on stelae known as the Pillars of Asoka that were erected throughout the empire and served as physical manifestations of Asoka's efforts to promote Buddhism throughout his realm. Reflecting the multi-lingual nature of the empire, while the edicts were inscribed in Brahmi script using the Magadhi Prakit language in the eastern part of the empire, in the west they were written using the Kharosthi script of the Gandhara culture and a version of the Sanskrit language. There is also an edict written in Greek and another in both Greek and Aramaic. As will be discussed at greater length later, Asoka not only promoted Buddhism within his empire, but also beyond its borders by sending missionaries to many parts of the world. It is also interesting to note that Asoka's old university town of Taxila became an important center of Buddhist learning during his reign.

Despite the spread of Buddhism under the Mauryas, Jainism also remained an important religion, especially in the eastern part of the empire. Asoka's wives were predominantly Buddhist, but his first wife, Padmavati, was a Jain. Their son Kunala was blinded to keep him from becoming emperor and the throne went to Asoka's grandson Desharatha instead, but Asoka declared that Kunala's son Samprati was to become ruler after Desharatha.[110] As emperor, Samprati (aka Samrat Samprati, r. *c.* 224–215 B.C.) promoted Jainism within the empire, and this practice continued under the next emperor, Salisuka (r. 215–202 B.C.).[111]

In regard to foreign relations, those between the Mauryan Empire and the Hellenic polities to the west have received the most attention, although it is important to keep in mind that they also maintained significant commercial and cultural (largely religious) relations with the Tamil polities to the south and a variety of Southeast Asian polities to the east. After peace was concluded between Chandragupta Maurya and the Hellenic king Seleucus I Nicator in 303 B.C. a long period of sustained contact began between the Mauryan Empire and the Hellenic west. In regard to the peace agreement, in his description of the territory along the Indus, Strabo mentions: "Of these places, in part, some that lie along the Indus are held by Indians, although they formerly belonged to the Persians. Alexander took these away from the Arians and established settlements of his own, but Seleucus Nicator gave them to Sandrocottus [Chandragupta], upon terms of intermarriage and of receiving in exchange five hundred elephants."[112] This would seem to indicate some type of marriage arrangement to help cement the alliance.

Seleucus I Nicator also sent a man named Megasthnes (l. *c.* 350–290 B.C.), who was mentioned above, as his ambassador to the Mauryan court around this time. Megasthnes provided an account of his travels to India in his book *Indika*.[113] Megasthnes was an Ionian from Asia Minor who at the time of his appointment was living in the satrapy of Arachosia (located to the south of Bactria in modern Afghanistan). A former officer of Alexander's named Sibyrtius, who was from Crete, was the satrap at the time (previously he had been satrap of Carmania, modern Kerman in Iran). Megasthnes entered the Mauryan Empire along the border with the region referred to by the Greeks as Pentapotamia (the modern Punjab region) and proceeded from there by the royal road to Pataliputra.

Bindusara continued to maintain relations with the Hellenic world. The Seleucids sent Deimachus as ambassador to Bindusara's court. Bindusara is also known to have asked the Seleucid king Antiochus I Soter to send a Greek philosopher to his court.[114] No philosopher appear to have been sent, but their request highlights the cordial relations between the two courts. During Asoka's reign in addition to the Seleucids, Pliny the Elder mentions that Ptolemy II Philadelphia (r. 283–246 B.C.) of Egypt sent Dionysius as his ambassador to the Mauryan court.[115] The Edicts of Asoka in turn mention that he sent ambassadors to a number of Hellenic kings, including the Seleucid king Antiochus II Theos (r. 286–246 B.C.), Ptolemy II Philadelphia of Egypt, Antigonus II Gonatus of Macedon (*c.* 319–239 B.C.), Magas of Cyrene (Libya, r. 276–250 B.C.), and Alexander II of Epirus (located in neighboring parts of modern Greece and Albania, r. 272–*c.* 242 B.C.).

As a result of the relatively friendly relations that existed with the Hellenic world, trade grew between the Mauryan Empire and the Hellenic polities to the west. The Kyber Pass emerged as an important point connecting commerce and communication between the two worlds. Sea-borne trade also extended east along the coast of the Bay of Bengal and down the Isthmus of Kra. Textiles and spices formed an important part of the export trade at this time. Trade within and beyond the empire was conducted largely by private joint-family commercial enterprises (such as those called *sreni* that resembled modern corporations) rather than state-sponsored ones.

Desharatha was only about twenty years old when he assumed the throne upon Asoka's death in 232 B.C., and initially he ruled with the assistance of a group of ministers. The Satavahanas led by Simuka were vassals of the Mauryans in central India, and they successfully declared their independence of the Mauryas around 230 B.C. They established their own empire, known as the Satavahana Empire or Andhra Empire, which covered much of the Deccan Plateau of central India and adjacent coastal areas of what are today Andhra Pradesh and Maharashtra with their capital located at Dharanikota and Amaravati (in modern Andhra Pradesh) and Prathisthan (aka Paithan, in modern Maharashtra). They remained an important regional power into the A.D. 100s.

The Mauryan Empire shrank even further during the reign of Satadhaven Maurya (r. 195–187 B.C.) with the rise of a resurgent Kalinga under the leadership of Kharavela (aka Kharabeja), who established a short-lived empire (193–170 B.C.) of his own at the expense of the Mauryans that included parts of central and eastern India. Kalinga is of interest in terms of transnationalism also because of its extensive maritime commercial relations during this period with the Tamils to the south as well as with various parts of Southeast Asia.

When Brihadratha Maurya became emperor around 187 B.C. he was ruler of an already diminished and weakened empire.[116] Brihadratha's rule was cut short when he was assassinated around 185 B.C. by the commander-in-chief of his armed forces, Pusyamitra Sunga. Pusyamitra Sunga (r. 185–151 B.C.) founded the Sunga Dynasty (185 B.C.-78 B.C.). He was unable to hold on to all of the remaining Mauryan territories in the face of attacks from the Satavahanas and Kharavela from the south and the Greco-Bactrians from the west. Pusyamitra Sunga appears to have persecuted Buddhists and to have been responsible for the destruction of a number of Buddhist temples.[117] His persecution of the Indo-Greek inhabitants in the western part of his empire, who were mainly Buddhists, seems to have been a contributing factor to the decision of Demetrius I of Bactria to invade the western part of the former Mauryan Empire around 180 B.C. Indo-Greeks had been treated well by the Mauryans and relations between Hellenic rulers to the west of the empire and the Mauryans had remained cordial under the Mauryan rulers who followed Asoka. It is unclear how far Demetrius's army reached, but he succeeded in bringing territories in northern Pakistan (including Taxila), Afghanistan, and eastern Iran that had been under Mauryan rule into his domain. A later Greco-Bactrian ruler, Menander I Soter (r. *c.* 155–130 B.C.), appears also to have invaded the Sunga Empire and possibly to have reached as far as Pataliputra.

South Asia was now once again politically divided into rival empires. The Sungas held on to power in the northeast until they were overthrown by one of their ministers named Vasudeva Kanva in 75 B.C. The political and ethnic configuration of South Asia was changed even further with the onset of a series of invasions by various nomadic tribes of Scythians as well as the Kushans. Scythian tribes appear to have begun moving into Bactria, Sogdiana and other surrounding areas in the 100s B.C. A Scythian named Maues (aka Moga) invaded Gandhara around 85 B.C. and briefly established a kingdom that was heavily influenced by Hellenic culture and Buddhism.[118] The Scythians moved further south and occupied an area known as the Western Satraps comprising what are today parts of southern Pakistan and the Indian states of Gujarat, Maharashtra, Rajasthan, and Madhya Pradesh sometime around A.D. 20–35. In doing so they absorbed the Indo-Greek polities in this region. The Scythians and their Western Satraps occupied important portions of overland trade routes, including the city of Taxila, as well as the port city of Barygaza (modern Bharuch in Gujarat). Barygaza had served as an important seaport for maritime trade to the west since at least the 500s B.C. and continued to serve in this capacity under the Western Satraps. Rudrasimha III of Gujarat was the last Western Satrap. Chandra Gupta II defeated him in A.D. 395.

We will soon discuss the Kushans at greater length because of their importance to long-distance trade across Central Asia and their relations with the Roman and Han empires.

What is of relevance here is their conquest and incorporation of large parts of northwestern South Asia into their empire. By the reign of the Kushan ruler Kanishka I (r. *c.* A.D. 127–140) their empire stretched eastward in northern India to include the former Mauryan capital of Pataliputra.

THE GUPTA EMPIRE

The Gupta Empire (A.D. 319–550) succeeded in reuniting the northern portion of India and some adjacent areas. The Gupta Dynasty traces its origins to Sri Gupta (r. *c.* A.D. 240–280) who ruled over a kingdom located in the north-central part of Bangladesh.[119] The empire was expanded during the roughly 100 years of the successive reigns of Chandra Gupta I (r. A.D. 319–335), Samudra Gupta (r. A.D. 335–375), and Chandra Gupta II (r. A.D. 375–415), with Chandra Gupta II's reign being regarded as the empire's high point. While military might was a major force behind the expansion of Gupta power, the creation of strategic alliances through diplomacy and marriage was also important. The Guptas ruled over much of northern India with the core of the empire being divided into provinces with a centralized, hierarchical administration. The rulers of some adjacent polities like the Western Satraps and Kushan kingdoms accepted them as suzerain and paid tribute. In addition to government offices, there were also important guilds of bankers, traders, and craftsmen that Mookerji describes as functioning like modern chambers of commerce.[120] The emperors were Hindus, but other religions were tolerated.[121] In the case of Buddhism this was of transnational relevance in that Buddhist scholars and pilgrims from China, Sri Lanka, and other countries visited the empire. The king of Sri Lanka was even allowed to build a monastery at Bodh Gaya (where Gautama Buddha attained enlightenment) for Buddhist pilgrims.

The Golden Age of the Gupta Empire survived Chandra Gupta II's death, but by the 470s they were facing threats in the west from invading Hephthalite (White Hun) tribes, another group of Central Asian nomads. They had overrun Gandhara by around 475 and then attacked the central Indian empires. Narasimha Gupta Baladita, allied with Yasodharman the Aulikara ruler of the Malwa Plateau, finally pushed them back,[122] but the Guptas were in a much weakened state. Vishnu Gupta (r. 540–550) was the last of the Gupta rulers.[123]

The Roman Empire

The city of Rome's transformation from city-state to imperial capital began with a series of wars leading to its conquest of Italy from the late 300s to the early 200s B.C. It emerged as a major regional power after a series of three wars with Carthage, known as the Punic Wars, between 264 and 146 B.C. It reached its greatest extent under the emperor Trajan (r. A.D. 98–117), who captured the Parthian capital of Ctesiphon and became the only Roman emperor to stand on the shores of the Indian Ocean in A.D. 114. After his death a number of the territories that he had conquered regained their independence as his successor Hadrian (r. 117–138) sought to consolidate the empire and withdrew Roman troops from Mesopotamia, Parthia, and Armenia (making the latter a client kingdom), and "accepted the Euphrates as the eastern boundary of the empire."[124] The Roman Empire was essentially a Western European and Mediterranean empire with its territories encompassing most of Western Europe south and west of Germany, southern Eastern Europe adjacent to the Black Sea, Egypt and North Africa along the Mediterranean coast, Anatolia, and the Levant. Like Alexander the Great's short-lived Macedonian empire the Roman Empire included both parts of Europe and Asia, but unlike Alexander's the Roman Empire had a significant presence in both continents, as it was the first large multi-national empire in Europe. The population of the empire at the time of Octavian/Augustus (i.e., around 25 B.C.) was about 45 million. By the time of Hadrian its population was about 65 million.

When most people think of the Roman Empire what usually comes to mind first are its emperors and legions, followed by its architecture and roads (the empire boasted over 80,000 km of paved roads),[125] but it is important not to forget the crucial role that government officials and merchants also played in the life of the empire. High-ranking officials came primarily from the two principal levels of the Roman aristocracy: the patricians (*patricii*) and the equestrians or equestrian order (*equites* or *ordo equester*). The equestrians are often referred to as knights in English sources. The patrician class was comprised largely of a hereditary network of elite families. Over time the equestrian order in turn came to be divided into two groups — senators and their offspring and non-senatorial equestrians — with the senatorial class serving as the elite of the equestrians.[126] Senators were not allowed to engage in commerce, while the non-senatorial equestrians were allowed to do so and came to dominate certain sectors of the imperial economy such as manufacturing, mining, shipping, and tax collecting (through companies that collected taxes). Further down the social structure men of lower and middle-class backgrounds could move into the higher ranks of the imperial government by distinguishing themselves in military service. While in the early days of the Republic members of these higher classes were mostly Romans or other ethnic Italians, as the empire grew their ranks came to include an ever larger number of people from elsewhere in the empire and from other ethnic groups.

The small empire created by Rome's conquest of the Italian peninsula between 458 and 282 B.C. gave it control over a variety of polities (tribes, city-states, and the like) from diverse ethno-linguistic groups. Treaties (*foedus*) between Rome and these polities gave them the status of *foederatus* — a status that was to assume considerable importance centuries later in relation to the fall of the Western Roman Empire.[127] As a *foederatus* a city-state was able to retain a degree of independence, but it was subject to Roman decrees and laws and was expected to pay tribute and to provide soldiers to assist Rome when needed. As Durant remarks, "The resources and main power of the 'allies' were drained by wars whose chief effect was to enrich a few families in Rome."[128] To maintain support among *foederati* "a few rich men in the cities had been granted Roman citizenship,"[129] but most of the subject peoples were denied such rights and frequently found themselves the target of discriminatory decrees. Discontent among the so-called allies (*socii*) finally boiled over with the outbreak of the War of the Allies (aka the Social War) in 91 B.C. that led to a new citizenship law (the *Lex Julia*) that granted citizenship to all those who were citizens of allied states and who complied with the provisions of the law.[130] In this way the concept of nation in relation to the Roman state came to be expanded from the inhabitants of Rome and a few other individuals to include most people living in the Italian peninsula.

The transition of the Roman Empire from a republican to an imperial form of government under Gaius Julius Caesar (l. 100–44 B.C.) and Octavian/Augustus witnessed a number of changes that are of relevance to transnationalism. One of these had to do with determination of citizenship. The Roman Empire at the time included territories inhabited by a number of distinct nationalities that were afforded a variety of legal statuses including free citizens, soldiers, free foreigners, and slaves.[131] Those who were afforded citizenship expanded along with Rome's political fortunes to include an increasingly varied number of peoples, often over the opposition of existing citizens. Julius Caesar granted the freemen of Italy citizenship rights equal to those of Rome itself. He granted similar rights to the colonists that he sent out to found or populate numerous cities around the empire. His death stopped him from extending the franchise even further to include all adult males in the empire.[132] Octavian carried on Caesar's drive to expand citizenship and granted full citizenship rights to the freemen of Cisalpine Gaul. One implication of such an extension of citizenship was that such people became eligible to serve as senators and to hold other imperial offices.

Caesar's dream was not to become a reality until A.D. 212 when Emperor Caracalla extended citizenship to all free adult males in the empire.[133] Even before then, however, there were other ways by which people could become citizens. Soldiers, for example, received Latin rights on enrollment and were given citizenship when discharged.[134] In addition, manumitted slaves were granted citizenship if they were freed by a Roman citizen.[135] As a result of these various means of becoming a Roman citizen over time the percentage of non–Roman and then even non–Italian people holding Roman citizenship increased, until by the A.D. 200s ethnic Italians were a minority of Roman citizens.

Octavian also restructured the status of provinces, distinguishing between those whose governors were appointed by the senate and those whose governors were appointed by the emperor.[136] By the time Vaspasian became emperor in A.D. 70 there were 11 senatorial and 25 imperial provinces. Diocletian (r. A.D. 284–305) created a new imperial structure known as the tetrarchy in the A.D. 290s in which provincial boundaries were redrawn to make smaller units (in the process creating almost a hundred provinces), and these in turn were grouped together into a dozen dioceses (*dioecesis*) of varying size. Thus, the diocese of Oriens (Diocese of the East) was created in A.D. 313 and included 16 provinces in the Levant and southern Anatolia. Antioch was its capital. The head of most dioceses was referred to as a vicarious, but the head of Oriens, which was the largest diocese in the empire, was given the title of Count of the East (*Comes Orientis*). Diocletian's reforms served to weaken the power of provinces as well as to enlarge the imperial bureaucracy. Another administrative level above that of the diocese was the Praetorian Prefecture, which was created during the reign of Constantine I (r. 306–337), and became a permanent feature of the empire after Constantine's death in 337 when the empire was partitioned between his three sons.[137] The initial prefectures were Gaul, Italy, Illyricum, Africa, and the East. The prefecture of the East, for example, included the dioceses of Thrace, Asia, Pontus, and Oriens.

Under Julius Caesar the Senate had grown to have over 1,000 members, in part through influence and bribery. Augustus got it back down to its previous level of about 600.[138] The patricians and equestrians comprised an elite class of several thousand people who monopolized political, military and economic power in an empire of about 60 million inhabitants. By the A.D. 200s power within this elite had shifted from ethnic Italian patricians to equestrians with distinguished military careers who often had risen through the ranks. In addition, many of these officers as well as high-ranking civilians came from provinces outside of Italy.

The highest officials such as governors (*proconsul* or *prepraeter*) and managers of finance and taxes (*quaestor* or *procurator*) throughout the empire usually came from the elite class. Often they were from the senatorial equestrian rank. However, there were many exceptions. The governor of Egypt, for example, was usually a non-senatorial equestrian. Noting that even "a freedman [i.e., former slave] could be appointed deputy-prefect of Egypt," Talbert emphasizes that there was considerable flexibility in the level of those appointed to imperial administrative posts in the provinces even at the higher levels.[139] As Talbert points out, "The relatively small corps of senators and equites who occupied the higher posts were normally not natives of the provinces in which they served."[140] He adds though that there were "sufficient exceptions ... to assure us that this was not an inflexible rule."[141]

In terms of transnationalism what is of most interest in regard to imperial positions is the way in which individuals moved from province to province in the course of their careers. In the case of young men from elite Roman or Italian families it was common for them to begin with an administrative post close to home, then to spend ten years or so in the army, followed by a high level civilian administrative or military position in one of the provinces, and then, if all went well, to return to a higher level position back in Rome. While members of elite families in the provinces might be satisfied remaining at home, those with ambition often would follow a similar career path through the army, posts in various parts of the empire, and then on to Rome.

Lollianus Mavortius provides a good example of a successful Roman career.[142] He served as the governor of the province of Campania in Italy from 328 to 335 and then was appointed the first Count of the East in 330, a post that he held until 336. From 334 to 337 he also served as proconsul of the province of Africa (modern Libya). Having done his time in the provinces, he became a prefect in Rome in 342. After Constantius II became the sole ruler of the empire in 350 after ruling over Egypt and the Asian provinces as co-emperor with Constans since 340, Mavortius's fortunes improved once again. He was appointed consul in 355 and then Praetorian Prefect of Italy in 356 by the emperor.

The governor was the most powerful person in a province.[143] He was appointed for a term of only one year, which could be extended, whereas procurators and those holding posts of similar rank usually held them for several years.[144] The governor had an immediate staff that included a variety of lictors, messengers, slaves, and soldiers. In addition to the procurator provinciae there was also an assortment of civil and military legati, military tribunes, and commanders of auxiliary units. There was a governor's advisory council with members selected by the governor. Talbot refers to this as a "relatively small central bureaucratic superstructure" commonly numbering only about 300 officials that "depended upon an infrastructure of effective local administration in the towns and villages of provinces," which exercised varying degrees of autonomy.[145] It is important to note that this imperial bureaucracy was open to prominent locals and that wealthy provincials could even attain equestrian status. Talbert cites the example of the Euryclids family of Sparta that gained citizenship under Octavian and had a member with equestrian procuratorial status by the time of Claudius.[146]

Before leaving the subject of civil servants, mention should be made of the *frumentarii*.[147] Their official job was the collection of wheat in the provinces, often in order to provision legions. They were headquartered in Rome at the Castra Peregrina and travelled extensively in the provinces in the course of their work. Since they travelled so much and their job brought them into contact with local people in the provinces in the course of their duties, Hadrian put them to use as couriers and spies, and it was in this latter capacity that they came to be known throughout the empire. While they were useful to the emperors, their role as spies made them increasingly unpopular with the population at large. Diocletian did away with the *frumentarii* in the course of his reforms and replaced them with a new body called the *agentes in rebus*.[148] These were intended primarily as an imperial courier service, but they also carried out a variety of other tasks such as collecting customs fees, supervising public works, and serving as ambassadors on occasion.[149] Like the *frumentarii* the *agentes in rebus* were also used to collect intelligence, but they did so openly rather than covertly as spies.[150]

Turning to trade, as Paterson remarks, "That Roman imperial expansion, even from its earliest days, should be linked to a major increase in commerce should not be doubted. It deserves greater emphasis than it is usually given in modern accounts."[151] As for Rome's armies, he adds: "Traders accompanied armies. Indeed, they were frequently in advance of armies," and he mentions that prior to invading Britain, Caesar summoned a group of merchants for their local knowledge, "because no one, except traders, goes there without good reason."[152]

Durant provides an impressive list of the goods imported by the city of Rome and their sources including foodstuffs, dyes, wild animals, cloth, eunuchs, and slaves. Precious stones and metals came in raw form or worked into statuary and jewelry. Durant writes that "from Belgium flocks of geese were driven all the way to Italy to supply goose livers for aristocratic bellies."[153]

Importing such goods, especially from outside of the empire, came at a cost in silver and various manufactured goods. The outflow of silver was especially a problem and silver mines within the empire gradually gave out. However, while Rome's economy began to run into trouble after A.D. 10 due to its balance-of-payments problems, the empire itself continued to provide a framework within which international trade prospered for those living in many of its provinces: "Italian merchants, in this first century A.D., almost disappeared from Eastern ports, while Syrian and Greek traders established themselves at Delos and Puteoli and multiplied in Spain and Gaul. In the leisurely oscillation of history the East was preparing once more to dominate the West."[154]

There were a number of categories of people engaged in commerce in ancient Rome. There were the large-scale wholesalers known as *negotiatores* who financed trade. A similar role was played by the *navicularii* who financed the shipping of goods by sea. At the ports themselves there were wholesalers known as *magnarii* who sold goods that had recently arrived from abroad. These individuals might also be masters of ships, but often the two were different. Those who were more directly involved in moving and selling goods were called *mercatores*. Wealthy merchants often distanced themselves from the conduct of long-distance trade, preferring to leave the work to slaves and freedmen who acted on their behalf.[155] Writing about the merchants of Roman Egypt, Young cites the example of Marcus Julius Alexander, who was from a rich Jewish family in Alexandria, and who kept agents in the Red Sea ports.[156] Annius Plocamus, whose family was from Puteoli in Italy, was another merchant operating in Egypt, and there is an account of one of his freedmen being blown off course while sailing around Arabia.

Egypt served not just as the granary of Rome, but also as a source of many other goods. Imperial administration in Egypt was largely in the hands of local ethnic Greeks, and Greek was the language of administration and commerce. Goods from India and beyond were brought to the empire by sea via Egypt's Red Sea ports such as Myos Hormos and Berenike. After being unloaded these goods were transported overland to Coptos on the Nile River where duty was paid before they could go on to Alexandria. The fees collected here were used to pay for upkeep of the roads and the military stations along the roads between the coast and the Nile. The goods were then loaded on boats and shipped down the Nile to Alexandria from where they were then shipped to Rome or other destinations in the empire. Young provides a translation of a document from the time of Caesar Domitianus Augustus that lists the duties payable at Coptos.[157] This list of duties gives an idea of the sort of people who were traveling along the route as well as a sense of the expenses incurred by travelers and merchants seeking to transport goods. At Coptos duties of 5 to 10 drachmas were charged for a helmsman of a Red Sea, a ship's lookout, a guard, a sailor, and a shipbuilder's servant. An artisan paid 8 drachmas. Women arriving by ship and women of soldiers paid 20 drachmas, while prostitutes paid 108 drachmas. The duty for a camel was 1 oboli and 2 oboli were charged for an ass. A man going up the Nile paid 1 drachma and a woman going up the Nile paid 4 drachmas. A covered wagon carrying goods was charged 4 drachmas. Coptos itself had a large community of merchants, had a silver market (that was probably related to the need to export silver to India), and was a center for textile production. The imported merchandise could not be sold at Coptos, but had to be shipped on to Alexandria, where a 25 percent duty was payable.

Some of the wealthier merchants of Alexandria who were involved in the maritime trade to the south maintained agents at Coptos and at the Red Sea ports. Young describes the activities of some of these merchants. He mentions a group of five partners with Greek names who arranged for a loan to finance a trip to the "spice-bearing lands."[158] A somewhat different arrangement is described in a text discussing shipments of goods from Muziris in southern India to Alexandria: "The loan was contracted at Muziris in India with a financier who was wealthy enough to provide this kind of loan, as well as maintain agents in Egypt. The person was possibly a member of the Roman 'merchant colony' in Muziris."[159] The merchant paid the ship owner, ship's master, and cameleers to transport the goods. Unlike those merchants who worked through agents, Young describes the author of the important guide to the region, *Periplus Maris Erythraei,* as being "a Greek-speaking resident of Egypt, an experienced merchant who had been involved in the trade and possessed great first-hand experience of the voyages to India and Africa."[160]

Ethnic Greeks played an especially important role in the life of the Roman Empire. Prior to the spread of Roman rule, ethnic Greeks were already scattered well beyond Greece itself around the shores of the Mediterranean and Black Sea. They served prominently not only in Rome's navy and maritime trade, but also in its civil service and cultural life. Cleopatra (Cleopatra VII Philapator, 69–30 B.C.) was perhaps the most famous of these Hellenes. Her father, Ptolemy XII, was one of the Hellenistic rulers of Egypt who had been put in place as a result of Alexander the Great's conquests. While Cleopatra's main language remained Greek, she is noted as being the first member of her noble family to have learned Egyptian. Her reign marked the transition from Hellenistic to Roman rule in Egypt and she herself had relationships with and produced children by the prominent Roman Mark Anthony and Julius Caesar. Cleopatra lived in Rome with Julius Caesar for a few years (47–44 B.C.). While with Mark Anthony she became co-ruler of Egypt and Cyprus while her children were made rulers of various territories around the Mediterranean, including Armenia, Media, Parthia, Cyrenaica, Libya, Phoenicia, Syria, and Cilicia. After defeating Anthony at the Battle of Actium in 31 B.C., Octavian conquered Egypt and Cleopatra killed herself. Her son by Caesar was executed and her other children were taken to Rome.

The process of assimilation, in this case Romanization, among peoples within the Roman Empire is an important aspect of transnationalism. The relative success of this process in some parts of Western Europe is attested to by the existence today of Romance languages such as Romanian, French, Spanish, and Portuguese along with systems of law and other cultural institutions in these countries with roots in the Roman imperial system. As Talbert remarks, Romanization "went beyond simple intrusions like the building of arteries of communication or the introduction of the Roman currency and encouraged the persistence or development of certain kinds of institutions, fostering and molding the relationship between Rome and the individual community, between disparate elements within the provincial communities."[161] While the process was strongest and most long-lasting in the Romanized parts of Western Europe, it was evident in other parts of the empire as well where local elites were "encouraged to undertake the burdens of civic government in return for the prospect of prestige and social advancement."[162] Local loyalties among such elites did not necessarily disappear, but at the same time they often had a strong attachment to many aspects of Roman civilization. Roman cultural influences went beyond the imperial frontiers to tribes and client kings.

The process of Romanization is also of relevance in regard to various tribal groups such as the Franks, Vandals, and Visigoths that came to settle within Roman territory and were given the status of *foederati* starting in the A.D. 300s. The Romans saw them as useful allies to help fill the ranks of its army and populate border areas. Taking the Franks as an example, when the Romans first encountered them they were a confederation of tribes living along the Rhine River in the vicinity of what is now the Netherlands.[163] One of the main groups of Franks that lived near the sea was initially known as the Sicambri and later they were commonly referred to as the Salians (aka Salii), while another group of Franks was referred to as the Ripuarians.[164]

The Salians crossed the Rhine southward around A.D. 260 during a time of considerable upheaval, partially as a result of pressure from the Saxons. They became allies of Carausius, an ethnic Menapian who had been appointed commander of the Roman fleet in the English Channel, but he rebelled against Rome and established his own kingdom encompassing Britain and northern Gaul in A.D. 286.[165] Constantius I Chlorus defeated the Salians who were allied with Carausius in 293, but did not put down the revolt for another two years, and spent a few more years fighting the Franks along the Rhine.[166] In the meantime, in 297 in an effort to repopulate the area with allied tribes he allowed the Salians to settle in the Rhine River delta region of the Batavi, which they soon came to dominate, in return for their allegiance.[167] After being attacked by other German tribes the Salians moved further south within Roman territory and occupied Toxandria (located between the Meuse and Scheldt rivers). Both the Salians and the Ripuarians then began to enter Roman territory along the Mainz River, but in 278 a campaign launched by the emperor Marcus Aurelius Probus (r. 276–282) against the Franks and other German tribes drove them back. Then in 307 the Emperor Constantine I (r. 306–337) launched a new campaign against the German tribes along the Rhine and in 310 this came to include attacks against the Franks, after which he carried off a large number of them as war captives.

Conflict between the Romans and Franks resumed after Constantine's death, leading the Emperor Constans to lead a successful campaign against them in 341–2. After this the Franks were drawn increasingly into intra–Roman conflicts rather than fighting against the Romans. As Perry comments, "During the frequent struggles for the Purple which took place at this period, the aid of the Franks was sought for by the different pretenders, and rewarded in case of success by large grants of land within the limits of the empire."[168] The conflict between Constantius II and Magnentius that broke out in 350 highlights the role of the Franks. The growing unpopularity of Constans, especially within the army, prompted a revolt in the western empire in 350 led by Flavius Magnus Magnentius, commander of the Iovia and Herculia (aka Jovians and Herculians) Imperial Guard, whose supporters killed Constans. Magnentius was born in Gaul and his father may have been a Briton and mother a Frank.[169] Magnentius's ethnic background and his religious and cultural tolerance gained him widespread support among tribal groups in the western part of the empire, especially among the Franks and Saxons. In relation to his background, Potter remarks that Magnentius was "the first man to claim the throne whose recent ancestors could legitimately be said to have been born beyond the frontiers (as he may have been himself). In a sense his success is a sign of the expanding definition of Romanness. His ability to win acceptance from senior officials of impeccably Roman origins shows how membership in the governing class depended upon service rather than birth."[170]

Constantius II (Constans's brother and ruler in the eastern empire) opposed Magnentius and their armies met at the Battle of Mursa Major in 351, said to have been one of the bloodiest in the history of the Roman Empire.[171] With most of his army dead Magnentius was forced to retreat to northern Italy and then to Gaul the following year. There Constantius II defeated him once again at the Battle of Mons Seleucus in 353, after which he committed suicide.[172]

A Frank named Claudius Silvanus had played an important role in securing Constantius II's victory at Mursa Major. Silvanus was the son of a Salian Frank leader named Bonitus who had supported Constantine I, who appointed him to the position of *magister militium* (master of soldiers, a regional military commander under the emperor) in 324. Potter describes Silvanus as "the son of a Frankish chieftain who had thrived in Roman service during the reign of Constantine."[173] Silvanus held the rank of tribune and initially had supported Magnentius, but he defected to Constantius II at the Battle of Mursa Major, an act that played a crucial role in Magnentius's defeat. Silvanus was rewarded for his betrayal by being appointed *magister militium* of Gaul by Constantius II. Potter argues, "The appointment may have helped ease the transition to Constantius' rule among restive survivors of the defeated faction."[174] In any event, Silvanus soon found himself embroiled in factional infighting among Frankish military officers in Gaul that played upon fears of persecution of Franks within the imperial government and culminated in Silvanus revolting against Constantius II in 355. The revolt lasted only a few weeks and ended with Silvanus's assassination by an agent sent by Constantius II.[175]

Around the time of Silvanus's revolt independent Salian Franks in the north asserted control over Batavia and Toxandria.[176] Flavius Claudius Julianus Augustus (aka Julian the Apostate), who had been appointed Caesar of the west by Constantius II in 355, defeated them in 358. As Perry comments, Julian "was better pleased to have them as soldiers than as enemies" and rather than "reducing them to despair ... they were permitted to retain the newly acquired lands, on condition of acknowledging themselves subjects of the empire."[177] The Salian Franks were thus allowed to remain in Toxandria as *foederati* who provided a buffer between the Romans and Germanic tribes to the north as well as supplying troops to the Romans. Thus, status and greater integration into the Roman world resulted in the Salian Franks' adopting more aspects of Roman culture, including more widespread use of Latin.

As *foederati* along the Roman frontier the Salian Franks "were often engaged in endeavoring to drive back the ever-increasing multitude of fresh barbarians, who hurried across the Rhine to share in the bettered fortunes of their kinsmen."[178] The situation was especially difficult in the winter of 406–7 when the Vandals and Alans crossed the Rhine in large numbers and overran many Roman and Frank areas. The Salian Franks and Visigoths joined forces with the Romans commanded by the general Flavius Aëtius against Atilla and the Huns who had invaded Gaul and defeated Atilla at the Battle of the Catalaunian Fields in 451. As Roman power collapsed in Gaul the Salian Franks under Clovis, who became king of the Salians in 481 at the age of 15, were able to assert control over Gaul and established a kingdom with its capital at Paris and a mixed Germanic-Roman culture. Their ties to Roman culture were strengthened in 496 when Clovis was baptized as a Christian.

East Asia

As was the case in ancient Mesopotamia and South Asia, the rise of early sedentary civilizations in East Asia also centers around two rivers: the Huang He or Yellow River and the Chang Jiang or Yangtze River. The Yellow River is commonly referred to as the Cradle of Chinese (i.e., Han) Civilization and the Yangtze River can be seen as the Cradle of Tai Culture. Agriculture and the first states in East Asia developed along these rivers. In regard to the development of civilization within this region, it is important to note that rather than a single point of origin from which civilization diffused, the early history of East Asia is one of interaction between a number of regions with a variety of cultural characteristics.[179] Surrounding these sedentary riverine peoples were various Neolithic peoples who to the north and west formed nomadic tribal societies (to be discussed below); along and beyond the coasts to the east and southeast developed maritime tribal societies, such as those of the Austronesians of Formosa; and elsewhere developed various forms of small-scale agricultural tribal societies, such as the rice farming tribes of Japan (referred to by the Han as Wa) that emerged during the Yayoi Period around 400/300 B.C.

While the peoples of the Yellow and Yangtze rivers share some cultural characteristics related to a very ancient common heritage, such as shamanism and related dragon symbolism, by and large by 8000 B.C. or so they had developed distinctive cultures.[180] To start with, the people along the Yangtze River were physically different from the people living to the north (i.e., the Han or Huaxia), who were related to the nomadic peoples of Siberia and the steppes of Central Asia. Their languages were also different with the people of the Yellow River region speaking what evolved into Sino-Tibetan languages and the people of the Yangtze River speaking what evolved into Austric languages (composed of Daic, Austronesian, and Hmong-Mien languages). Reflecting the different environments within which the two peoples lived, as they domesticated plants and animals they raised different crops and some different animals. In particular, the people in the north grew millet and other crops suitable to a dry environment while those in the south grew rice and other crops suitable to a wetter environment.[181] Both peoples domesticated pigs, but water buffalo were found only in the south. There were also important differences in their material cultures. The people in the south produced distinctive cord-marked pottery and made bark-cloth.[182] The coastal peoples of the south associated with Dapenkeng Culture (aka Tapenkeng, 5000–2500 B.C.) also developed a distinctive maritime culture that evolved into that of the Austronesian peoples, who migrated by sea to settle Formosa and the islands to the south using outrigger canoes — a type of boat not found in the north. Later, the southern peoples also developed silk weaving, using silk worms that were fed on the leaves of the paper mulberry tree (the bark of which was used for making bark-cloth).[183] They also developed a bronze tradition distinctive from that of the north that included large drums. These drums became important items of exchange throughout the southern region as well as the islands to the south as far as New Guinea, leading Hirth to refer to the non–Han peoples of the southern region as "bronze drum nations."[184] Writing about the ancient bronzes of Sichuan, Xu makes the point that while the bronze making technology might have diffused from northern China to Sichuan, the shape of the items and their use was quite different.[185]

The emergence of states along the Yellow and Yangtze rivers formerly was associated with the so-called Three Sovereigns and Five Emperors Period (roughly 3500–2000 B.C.), but that is more accurately described as the "Ten Thousand States" period in which there were a large number of small, independent stratified states rather than just a few large ones — the 10,000 coming from a reference to the Xia ruler Yu summoning people from 10,000 states to his wife's state of Tushan (Jiangsu).[186] Accordingly, while they were no doubt large and important early states, the kingdoms of the Shang (aka Yin), Xia, and Early Zhou "were among the 10,000 states that were distributed throughout North China's Yellow River valley during the 2,000 years leading up to the establishment of imperial China."[187] As for the Xia kingdom (*c.* 2070–1600 B.C.), as indicated above, its founder Yu (aka Yu the Great) ruled its nine provinces (*zhou*) from his capital at Yang City (modern Dengfeng, Henan Province, site of the Shaolin Monastery) and as noted above was married to a woman from a neighboring state that was apparently part of his kingdom.

The core of the Shang or Yin kingdom lay along the Yellow River in Henan and Shanxi provinces. The kingdom reached its greatest extent during the reign of Wu Ding (*c.* 1250–1189 B.C.) who conquered some neighboring territories, made others his vassals, and also created alliances (some through marriage). His capital of Yin (near modern Anyang) grew into the most important city in northern China during his reign. Commenting on its archaeological remains, Bagley remarks, "No earlier site approaches Anyang in the scale of human sacrifice; no tomb is so rich as that of Wu Ding's consort Fu Hao; and the oracle bones are the first clear evidence for writing in China."[188] Beyond the riches discovered in the royal tombs, what is of particular interest transnationally is the presence of imported goods, especially jade, which was imported in raw form from the far west and in worked form from the south.[189] The Shang rulers also received items such as turtle shells and cattle scapulas for use in religious activities as tribute from vassals and allies.[190] The archaeological discoveries in particular indicate that, while the Shang may not have ruled over a very large area, they were active participants in an extensive trade network stretching out in all directions from their capital.[191]

Shang power and influence declined after Wu Ding's death in 1189 B.C., leading Keightley to remark that the area within which a Shang ruler and his entourage "could move with safety, and which, through his allies and dependents, he could make some claims to control, was not particularly large."[192] In particular, a number of former allies came to be referred to with the suffix-*fang,* indicating an ememy.[193] The Zhou were increasingly independent vassals of the Shang who were engaged in extending their own power, culminating in King Wu of Zhou overthrowing the Shang at the Battle of Muye in 1045 B.C. Wu died a short time after his victory and a civil war broke out. After the rebellion was crushed the victors found themselves in charge of a "dramatically enlarged state" incorporating a number of eastern territories in particular, which they sought to rule through a "program of rapid colonization, with members of the royal family sent out to defend strategic points all along the two main geographic axes of north China, the Yellow River and the Taihung Mountains."[194] The states formed in this manner included Jin, Ying, Wey, Lu, Qi, and Yan. As Shaughnessy notes, "Situated as they were at strategic points along the principal routes of transportation in North China ... all of these colonies were destined to thrive," and "after the fall of Western Zhou, they grew into the major independent states of the Spring and Autumn and Warring States Period."[195]

Although the Zhou became the dominant power in northern China after the fall of the Shang, the Zhou Empire was a loosely structured one with limited centralized power.

Moreover, while the ruler of the various states within the empire might have had a shared culture (many of them being related), Zhou influence beyond this small group of elites appears to have been minimal. Looking at the archaeological record, Rawson comments, "Outside of the principal centers, Zhou culture was absent, it would seem."[196] The Zhou attempted to extend their power south outside of the Han heartland towards the Yangtze River, but failed to do so. The Zhou king Zhao attacked the southern kingdom of Chu in 957 B.C. in a campaign that ended with the king and most of his army dead. As Shaughnessy notes, "the Zhou state never really recovered from this loss."[197] Rule by the so-called Western Zhou came to an end during the reign of King You (r. 781–771 B.C.), when the ruler of the southern vassal state of Shen and a group of allies that included the Quangrong nomads (Tibeto-Burma speaking Western Qiang) overran the Western Zhou capital of Haojing. The Eastern Zhou period that follows the Western Zhou period is commonly divided into the Spring and Autumn Period and the Warring States Period (it begins around 475 B.C.). During this time the states that were nominally under Zhou rule were effectively independent.

A number of states had developed along the Yangtze River from Sichuan in the west to the area around Hangzhou Bay (modern Shanghai and northern Zhejiang Province) in the east by the 1200–1000s B.C. These included, from west to east, Shu, Ba, Chu, Yue, and Wu. Shu and Ba were located in modern Sichuan and were important for their close association with the invention of silk weaving and for the abundant wet rice cultivation. The Mi clan established the kingdom of Chu some time around 1200 B.C.[198] Over the next few centuries Chu grew to become a multicultural empire that "absorbed over sixty states and a number of tribal peoples."[199] Chu exerted influence to the south beyond the realm of its vassal states and appears to be associated with the founding of early kingdoms as far to the south as northern Vietnam. Thus, Chamberlain notes that the Hung kings who established the early Tai kingdom of Van Lang in northern Vietnam around 696 B.C. are referred to by the Chinese using the same character to designate the Mi clan of Chu.[200] Chu also controlled the eastern coastal area south of the Yangtze at times, but this was largely the domain of various peoples commonly referred to by the Han as the 100 Yue, some of whom were ancestral to the speakers of modern Southwestern Tai languages. Aurousseau mentions several Yue clans, including the Min in Fujian Province, Nan in Guangdong Province, and Lo in Guangxi and the Red River Delta region.[201] Madrolle says that members of the Lo clan from Fujian moved south and settled in the Red River delta area in the 500s B.C.[202]

While conflict was common between the Zhou Empire and the states to the south and the nomadic tribes to the west, it is important to recognize that peaceful transnational relations also existed. Thus, while long-distance trade was not particularly well developed during the Zhou periods, jade certainly continued to be imported by the Zhou from the west along with other items such as bronze bells that were imported from the south.[203] Xu refers to the Upper Han River region, located to the south of the Zhou capital of Haojing (in modern Shaanxi Province), "as a crossroads where traffic from many regions met."[204]

Qin and Chu emerged as the two main powers during the Warring States Period. For a time Chu was by far the more powerful of the two. Expanding north towards the Yellow River and east to the sea, Chu came "within a political hair of dominating all of China."[205] This northern expansion brought numerous Sinitic speaking Han peoples into its empire, while their conquest of Yue in 334 led to the ruling Lo clan of Yue fleeing south to northern Vietnam. Meanwhile to the west of Chu, the Qin rulers in Shaanxi, where Xianyang became their capital in 350 B.C., were expanding their territory. Most significant in this regard was the Qin conquest of Ba and Shu in 316 B.C. Just as Egypt was the granary of the Roman

Empire, the rice of Ba and Shu served to feed the Qin's expansion. The Qin general Bai Qi captured the Chu capital of Ying in 278 B.C. and forced the Chu to move their capital east to Souchun (in modern Anhui Province). The Qin conquest of Shu in 316 B.C. also had an impact on regions further to the south ruled by Tai affiliated with the Shu kingdom. Shu had conquered Yunnan and subjugated its Tibeto-Burman speaking inhabitants shortly before the Qin invasion. The Shu army in Yunnan was cut off with the fall of Shu and established the independent kingdom of Tien (aka Dian) around 310 B.C.[206] Tai associated with Shu also established several independent kingdoms in the highland valleys further to the east, including the kingdom of Nam Cuong with its capital at Nam Binh in modern Cao Bang Province, northern Vietnam.[207] The son of the founder of the kingdom of Nam Cuong, Tuc Phan (aka Shu Pan), consolidated control over the neighboring highland areas of northern Vietnam and southern Guangxi, then conquered the Chu-related kingdom of Van Lang to the south and established an enlarged kingdom known as Ou Lo (aka Au Lac) around 258 B.C., moving his capital to a site along the Red River known today as Co Loa (located across the river from Ha Noi).

The Qin finally defeated Chu in 223 B.C. and emerged as the rulers of a large part of China that for the first time included both the northern Han area and the Yangtze River region. The Qin ruler Shi Huang is thus commonly seen as establishing the first empire that incorporates the core of modern China in 221 B.C. After he died in 210 B.C., his eldest son was murdered to keep him from assuming the throne and his younger son Qin Er Shi was made emperor at the age of 21— effectively under the control of the eunuch Zhao Gao. Qin rule quickly began to crumble in the face of a series of revolts starting in 209. Xiang Xu, the commander of the rebel Chu army, defeated the Qin army at the Battle of Julu in 207 B.C. Xiang Xu divided the Qin Empire into what are commonly referred to as the Eighteen Kingdoms. A struggle then ensued between Xiang Xu of Chu and Liu Bang, who gave himself the title of King of Han. This conflict known as the Chu-Han Contention, engulfed most of China in war between 206 and 202 B.C. After Liu Bang defeated Xiang Xu at the Battle of Gaixia he proclaimed himself to be the Emperor of China.

The kingdom of Nam Yue (aka Nam Viet) was a legacy of the Qin Empire.[208] Shi Huang invaded Yue around 218 B.C. The motivation for this invasion is interesting in regard to transnationalism: "The 'first emperor,' Qin Shi Huang, is said to have sent five armies totaling half a million men against the Yue people of the south, solely because of the economic lure of tropical items to be obtained in the markets there: rhinoceros horns, ivory, kingfisher feathers, and pearls."[209] The first Qin army was defeated, its commander killed. Shi Huang then sent another army commanded by Ren Xiao and Zhao Tuo (aka Chao To, Trieu Da) to renew the attack in 214. They succeeded and were placed in charge of commanderies to administer the region. When Ren Xiao died a short time later, Zhao Tuo assumed command of the entire region. Zhao Tuo then established his own kingdom of Nam Yue in 204 after the Qin Empire collapsed. Prior to founding Nam Yue, Zhao Tuo had succeeded in defeating the kingdom of Ou Lo in 208 B.C.; after Zhao Tuo captured its capital, Ou Lo's ruler and his army retreated south where they were finally defeated near Cao Xa in Nghe An Province.[210] Zhao Tuo (r. 204–137 B.C.) established his capital at Panyu (modern Guangzhou) and divided his empire into seven provinces. These were administered by a combination of his fellow Han and local Tai feudal lords, who appear to have undergone a degree of Hanization in the process. The adoption of Han culture was related to a policy of Harmonizing and Gathering the Hundred Yue Tribes through which Zhao Tuo and subsequent rulers of Nam Yue created a syncretic culture that was a blend of Han and Tai cultures.

Nam Yue's three southernmost provinces of Giao-chi, Cuu-chân, and Nhât-nam roughly corresponded to the old Tai kingdom of Ou Lo plus some territory further to the south in what is now central Vietnam. The region of what is now the lowlands of modern Nghe An and Thanh Hoa provinces prior to Zhao Tuo's conquest had been a frontier zone between the Tai to the north and Cham to the south. The Cham will be discussed at greater length in a later chapter, but what is of relevance here is that the conquest of this area by Zhao Tuo brought the Cham into contact with Han culture.

THE HAN EMPIRE

Liu Bang was given the name Gao Zu after his death in 195 B.C. and came to be known as the founder of the Han Dynasty. The Han Empire lasted from 202 B.C. until A.D. 220, with a break from A.D. 9 to 25. The period from 202 B.C. to A.D. 9 is commonly referred to as the Western Han since the capital was at Chang'an (aka Xian, in modern Shaangxi Province), whereas the period from A.D. 25 until A.D. 220 is commonly called the Eastern Han since the capital was moved to Luoyang (in modern Henan Province). At its greatest extent the Han Empire occupied some 6 million square kilometers (about 1 million more than the Roman Empire at its height) and had a population of almost 60 million.

The political structure of Liu Bang's empire included commanderies (*jùnxiàn*) as well as vassal kingdoms that were commonly ruled by members of his family. The various states within the empire were relatively independent politically and economically. Under Emperor Wen's (r. 180–157 B.C.) rule the empire was relatively prosperous and the component parts became more independent. The kingdom of Wu (occupying the area around modern Shanghai) with an abundance of natural resources such as copper and salt grew particularly wealthy. Shortly after the Emperor Jing assumed the throne in 157 B.C. a dispute broke out between the emperor and his distant cousin Liu Pi of Wu. Their disagreement culminated in what is commonly called the Rebellion of the Seven Kingdoms in 154 B.C. (they being Wu, Chu, Jiaoxi, Zhao, Jiadong, Zaichuan, and Jinan), led by Liu Pi. The rebels were defeated and the empire evolved towards a more centralized form of administration in which the core area was expanded beyond the northern Yellow River region to include areas further to the south along the Yangtze River in particular. This expansion had a cultural dimension in the form of Hanization of the peoples brought under imperial rule.

The reign of the Emperor Wu Di (r. 141–87 B.C.) is of particular interest in regard to transnationalism because of the continued process of internal integration within the core area of the empire, expansion of the borders of the empire, and the unprecedented extension of long-distance trade. In regard to territorial expansion, for which Wu Di's reign is best known, the Han Empire's borders were extended into the Korean peninsula in the northeast, westward into Central Asia as far as modern Kyrgyzstan, and south to the lowlands of modern northern Vietnam. It is important to recognize, however, that Han control over many of these newly incorporated areas was spotty and that Hanization was quite limited in these areas. Moreover, the expansion of the empire placed considerable strain on the empire's finances. The assumption of state control of a number of industries was one means employed to help pay for imperial expansion.

Relations with nomadic tribes living to the north and west of the Han Empire were of particular significance politically and militarily. The two most important of these tribes, the Xiongnu and Yuezhi, will be discussed in greater detail later. Relations with the Xiongnu were fraught with problems for the Han and Liu Bang himself had considerable difficulty in pushing them back and stabilizing his northern border. In contrast, Liu Bang's relations with the Yuezhi were relatively amicable and, as we shall see, the Yuezhi played a crucial role in developing long-distance trade across Central Asia. Wu Di was more successful in dealing with the Xiongnu militarily, and his initiative to seek an alliance with the Yuezhi, who had been forced to migrate westward by the Xiongnu since Liu Bang's time, helped to develop Central Asian long-distance trade even further.

Considering the Xiongnu a significant military threat, in 138 B.C. Wu Di sent a military officer named Zhang Qian (aka Chang Ch'ien), who knew about these nomadic tribes, with a party of 39 men as an emissary to the Yuezhi in the hopes of forming an alliance against the Xiongnu. Zhang Qian is credited with being the first official diplomat to bring back reliable information about these nomadic tribes to the imperial court, and by doing so he helped to lay the basis for an expansion of westward trade. A later Chinese historian described the emperor's reaction to Zhang Qian's report of the existence of prosperous settlements to the west as a motivation for promotion of long-distance trade: "The Son of Heaven on hearing all this reasoned thus: Ferghana (Dayuan) and the possessions of Bactria (Daxia) and Parthia (Anxi) are large countries, full of rare things, with a population living in fixed abodes and given to occupations somewhat identical with those of the Chinese people, but with weak armies, and placing great value on the rich produce of China."[211] Trade routes gradually expanded westward from the Han capital of Chang'an through Xinjiang and Central Asia and on to Parthia. The Han emperors sent missions to Parthia and the Parthians responded by sending envoys themselves around 100 B.C. An early Chinese historical account of the missions has this to say: "When the Han envoy first visited the kingdom of Anxi (Parthia), the king of Anxi dispatched a party of 20,000 horsemen to meet them on the eastern border of the kingdom.... When the Han envoys set out to return to China, the king of Anxi dispatched envoys of his own to accompany them.... The emperor was delighted at this."[212]

While Han relations with the West along the Silk Road have received by far the most attention by modern scholars, it is important also to mention relations to the south and the development of the maritime sea route. Nam Yue's ruler Zhao Tuo recognized Han suzerainty in 196 B.C., but this came to little and he reasserted his independence in 183 B.C. It is around this time that Zhou Tuo began referring to himself as emperor and the neighboring states of Min Yue (in Fujian) and Yelang (in modern Guizhou) became his vassals. He once again agreed to become a vassal of the Han in 179 B.C., but he and subsequent rulers of Nam Yue retained considerable autonomy and the Han do not appear to have exerted much formal authority over Nam Yue. When the Nam Yue ruler Zhou Xing suggested taking the step of integrating the kingdom into the Han Empire during the reign of the Han emperor Wu Di, he was murdered and Zhao Jiande was placed on the throne. This prompted Wu Di to attack Nam Yue. The Han defeated Nam Yue and incorporated it into the Han Empire in 111 B.C.

The Han conquest of Nam Yue had important implications for the development of long-distance maritime trade. There is considerable archaeological evidence of maritime trade between the Dongson culture of the Tai of northern Vietnam and the islands of Indonesia prior to the region coming under control of Nam Yue, and some evidence that this trade continued under the Zhao Dynasty of Nam Yue. Wu Di's conquest of Nam Yue gave him access to maritime commerce through Panyu on the Pearl River (Zhu Jiang) Delta, which was transformed from Nam Yue's capital to a Han provincial capital, and particularly via the Red River (Song Hong) Delta to the south.[213]

The Han Empire entered a period of relative stability and prosperity under the emperors who immediately followed Wu Di. The reign of Emperor Zhao (r. 87–74 B.C.) was note-worthy for economic reforms aimed at overcoming the financial problems that were a legacy of Wu Di's reign. Emperor Yuan (r. 48–33 B.C.) was especially successful in neutralizing the threat from the Xiongnu, whose ruler Chanyu Huhanye visited Chang'an twice. How-ever, by the time of these later rulers the empire was beset by corruption, financial mis-management, and increasingly higher taxes on the population. There were also serious problems within the core of the government as the increasingly powerful Wang clan conspired to control the Liu emperors. Wang Mang served as regent for the young Emperor Ping, had him poisoned in A.D. 6, and then arranged to have 1-year-old Liu Yang made emperor. Wang Mang's actions prompted other members of the Liu clan to revolt. After the first of these revolts was crushed Wang Mang declared himself emperor of the new Xin Dynasty in A.D. 8. Wang Mang's rule was beset with problems, including the loss of control over the far west of his empire, and he was finally killed by a mob in A.D. 23. After a further period of instability Liu Xiu (aka Emperor Guangwu, r. A.D. 25–57) restored the Han Dynasty under Liu clan rule. Since Emperor Guangwu established his capital at Luoyang rather than Chang'an, as noted above, the restored Han Dynasty is referred to as the Eastern Han.

The early years of the Emperor Guangwu's reign were far from peaceful and it took him the first ten years of it to consolidate his rule. Opposition was of two sorts. On the one hand there were others who wished to rule the empire. On the other hand, and of more relevance to transnationalism, there were those towards the frontier who wished to regain their independence. Among the most famous of the latter were the Trung Sisters who led a revolt in A.D. 40 in northern Vietnam aimed at establishing their independence from Han rule. That revolt was finally crushed in A.D. 43.

As the political situation stabilized during the Eastern Han period there were significant increases in political, economic, and cultural relations to the west.[214] Their improved fortunes were in part due to infighting among the nomadic tribes living to their west. Particularly important was the defeat of the Xiongnu confederacy by rival tribes (the Hsien-pi and Wu-huan). Some of these nomads accepted Chinese suzerainty, while other moved further west. The reign of Emperor Ming Di (r. A.D. 58–75) was an especially fruitful one for western relations. Contacts with the Kushan Empire (founded by the Yuezhi and to be discussed later) led to the introduction of Buddhism to China. The Kushan Empire had inherited local Greco-Buddhist culture and was tolerant of Buddhism and other religions. The Kushan Empire also provided a relatively secure environment for long-distance trade and served to link sea-routes in the Indian Ocean with the land routes of the Silk Road through the Indus River Valley.

The second restored Han ruler, Emperor Ming (r. 28–75), sent General Ban Chao westward in A.D. 73 to attack nomadic tribes that were considered a threat to security. Ban Chao was sent west again by emperors Zhang Di (r. 76–88) and He Di (r. 89–105) to secure Han control over the Tarim Basin (known as the Western Regions) and the Silk Road trade route. He allied himself with Kushan military forces to fight against the Sogdians in A.D. 84. After the victory the Kushan ruler sent emissaries to the Han court to request a princess in marriage. The request was denied and the Kushans retaliated by attacking Ban Chao's army in A.D. 86. Ban Chao defeated the larger Kushan force and the Kushans began paying tribute to He Di. Ban Chao was given the position of Protector of the Western Regions in A.D. 91 and took up residence at the important Silk Road town of Quici (modern Kucha in the west of Xinjiang Province).[215] He remained in this position until he retired and returned to Luoyang in A.D. 102, where he died.

Although Han power in Central Asia waned after Ban Chao's death, relations were maintained with the Kushan Empire. The Kushan rulers sent additional presents to the Han court during the reign of Emperor Huan Di (r. 146–168) that were followed by increased exchanges between the two empires. Especially important in this regard were increased activities by Kushan Buddhist missionaries such as Lokaksema, who came to China around A.D. 170 and was known for his translations of Mahayana Buddhist scripture into Chinese.

The *Hou Hanshu* or *Book of the Later Han* provides interesting accounts of relations between the Han court and the Parthians and Romans during the time of the later Han Dynasty.[216] Section 10 on "The Kingdom of Anxi [Parthia]" mentions that in A.D. 87 the Parthians sent an envoy to offer lions and a Persian gazelle to the emperor and in A.D. 101 they sent lions and ostriches. It says that in A.D. 97 General Ban Chao sent Gan Ying to visit the Roman Empire. When he reached Characene (a region that includes modern Basra) and Susiana (now Khuzestan Province, Iran) at the head of the Persian Gulf, local sailors dissuaded him from going any further: "The ocean is huge. Those making the round trip can do it in three months if the winds are favorable. However, if you encounter winds that delay you it can take two years. That is why all the men who go by sea take stores for three years. The vast ocean urges men to think of their country, and get homesick, and some of them die." Upon hearing this Gan Ying gave up.

Chapter 11 gives a description of the Roman Empire, noting, "The people of this country are all tall and honest. They resemble the people of the Middle Kingdom and that is why this kingdom is called Da Qin (Great China)." The products of the Roman Empire are listed in Chapter 12:

> The country has plenty of gold, silver, and precious jewels, luminous jade ["night-shining," may denote another stone], bright moon pearls, fighting cocks, rhinoceroses, coral, yellow amber, opaque glass, whitish chalcedony, red cinnabar, green gemstones [possibly peridot, all of which was mined on the island of Zebirget in the Red Sea], drawn gold-threaded and multi-colored embroideries, woven gold-threaded net [or perhaps rugs or tapestries with gold thread], delicate polychrome silks painted with gold, and asbestos cloth. They also have a fine cloth which some people say is made from the down of "water sheep," but which is made, in fact, from the cocoons of wild silkworms. They blend all sorts of fragrances, and by boiling the juice, make storax [used as incense].

The mention of silk as a product of the Roman Empire may come as a surprise, but highlights the fact that the knowledge of silk making was widespread in the ancient world, including in the Middle East and eastern Mediterranean.[217] The reference to "water sheep" relates to another type of cloth woven from byssus fiber.[218] Byssus fiber is made from secretions of the byssus gland in the foot of the *Pinna squamosa* mollusk. Weaving with this fiber was known in the ancient world from India to the Mediterranean, including Greece and Sicily. During the reign of the Roman Emperor Tertullian (r. A.D. 150–222) the center of byssus weaving was in Tarenton, Italy.

Chapter 12 has this to say about Roman trade: "They [the Romans] trade with Anxi [Parthia] and Tianzu [northwestern India] by sea. The profit margin is ten to one.... The king of this country [the Roman Emperor] always wanted to send envoys to the Han, but Anxi [Parthia], wishing to control the trade in multi-colored Chinese silks, blocked the route to prevent [the Romans] from getting through [to China]." It goes on to note, however, that in A.D. 166 the Emperor Marcus Aurelius "sent envoys from beyond the frontiers through Rinan [a prefecture in the southern part of Chinese-ruled northern Vietnam], to offer elephant tusks, rhinoceros horn, and turtle shell. This was the very first time there was [direct] communication [between the two countries]. The tribute brought was neither precious nor rare, raising suspicion that the accounts [of the envoys] might be exaggerated."

In addition to long-distance trade along the Silk Road, the Han were also developing long-distance maritime trade to the coasts and islands of Southeast Asia and as far as the east coast of India. This route involved travel from the southern province of Giao-chi (aka *Jiao Zhi*), which occupied portions of northern Vietnam, along the coast of Vietnam (inhabited by Cham at the time) to the emerging commercial center of Oc Eo in southern Vietnam and then across the Isthmus of Kra in southern Thailand, along the coast of the Bay of Bengal (which was inhabited by Mon), and on to Bengal. Malays and other non–Han conducted the trade and operated the ships (to be discussed below), but the Han did send some envoys along this route, including one delegation that visited India between A.D. 2 and 5.[219] Wang characterizes this maritime trade as being of relatively minor importance in the context of the Han Empire's economy as a whole and certainly of less importance than the overland Silk Road trade, but as being of considerable significance to those in Southeast Asia who were engaged in trade with the Han Empire.[220]

Han power declined after the reign of Emperor Zhang Di (r. A.D. 76–88) as palace intrigues and other internal squabbles sapped the government's strength. Centralized power was reduced until Cao Pi, the ruler of Wei, finally overthrew the last Han emperor in A.D. 220. One development related to this declining central power was the complete loss of the southernmost parts of the former Nam Yue in what is now central Vietnam. Not that the Han had ever been able to establish firm rule in this frontier area: "This was the extreme border of areas nominally subject to Chinese domination — a dangerous and impenetrable area" where people "remained insurgent and continually rose up invading centers where Chinese officials dwelt, staged raids, and plundered and killed, and then retreated before reinforcements, fleeing into their impenetrable forests."[221] Han reports indicated that after a group of Cham carried out a particularly audacious raid in A.D. 100 in which they "burned" the local Han officials, the Han seem to have had few relations with the people in the far south of this region.[222] Then in A.D. 192 the son of a sub-district head named K'iu Lien (aka Ou Lien) rebelled and proclaimed himself king of a territory encompassing most of the coastal region of central Vietnam — an act that is commonly associated with the founding of Champa.[223] These developments are of interest on several counts. One is that they show just how limited Han rule was in such frontier regions. However, the fact that K'iu Lien's father was a low ranking official in the Han imperial bureaucracy and that K'iu Lien and his father appear to have been Cham would seem to indicate that there were at least some local Cham who were partially Sinicized. We will return to K'iu Lien and the Cham in a later chapter and here merely note that over the next few decades the Cham expanded and consolidated their control over the coast of central Vietnam and remained independent.

Following the fall of the Han dynasty in A.D. 220 what remained of their empire broke up into the three kingdoms of Wei, Shu, and Wu. The Sima clan of Wei managed to consolidate power in the central region of China in 280 by defeating Wu and established the Jin Dynasty (aka Western Jin Dynasty). Their rule was not stable, however, and a civil war that is usually referred to as the War of the Eight Princes broke out in 291. It lasted until A.D. 306 and devastated the core Han region. The period that follows lasting until A.D. 439 is commonly called the Sixteen Kingdoms Period.[224]

What is of particular interest in regard to transnationalism of the civil war and period of political decentralization that followed is the incursion of nomads into the Han heartland and their subsequent Hanization. The chaos of the civil war provided an opportunity for various groups of nomads to invade and to conquer portions of the Han core area. The Han referred to the five main nomadic groups collectively as the Wu Hu, which included the Di, Jie, Qiang, Xianbei, and Xiongnu. During the Sixteen Kingdoms period, while Han ruled four of these kingdoms, nomads ruled most of the others and effectively controlled most of the traditional Han heartland. The Xianbei and Xiongnu were the most important of these nomadic tribes. We will discuss the Xianbei here and the Xiongnu shortly.

The Xianbei were a confederation of nomadic tribes that had established a state in what is now Mongolia during the time of the Han Empire. They invaded the Jin kingdom and seized control of the Northern Wei kingdom, which became the dominant kingdom in the north. Most of the population of the kingdom was Han and ethnic Han were placed in most administrative posts with the highest levels of power reserved for the Xianbei. Much later, during the reign of Xiaowen (r. 471–499), the kingdom underwent a period of Hanization. Xiaowen's father was Xianbei and mother Han. He changed his clan name to a Han one, Yuan, and towards the end of his reign, in 493, he instituted a Hanification campaign. This included moving the capital to Luoyang and having large numbers of Xianbei settle there, where they became Hanified. He also promoted adoption of the Buddhist religion. The Hanified Xianbei continued to rule over Northern Wei until the 500s.

As for the Jin, they lost control of Chang'an in 316 and the Jin and other nobles and wealthy Han families fled south to the territory of the Kingdom of Wu on the Yangtze River, where the remnants of the Jin made Jiankang (southern capital, modern Nanjing) in the Yangtze River delta their new capital and established what is known as the Eastern Jin kingdom (317–420). Under the Eastern Jin, Jiankang grew into a large, cosmopolitan city that served as a center of Han culture. Within the kingdom, Jin rule led to considerable Hanization of the population. This in part was related to the conscription of local non–Han people into the army.

Since the Eastern Jin kingdom was cut off from overland trade they pursued the development of maritime trade with Champa, Funan, and as far as India. This built on previous maritime relations between Wu and the south. Funan was in the Mekong River Delta region and in the vicinity of the important trading center of Oc Eo. Funan had sent a mission to the previous kingdom of Wu between A.D. 226 and 231 and Wu had responded by sending a mission to Funan in 231. There were other diplomatic exchanges, but these became increasingly rare after A.D. 252 as Wu went into decline.[225] A revitalized Eastern Jin kingdom now revived this trade on an even larger scale than previously, encouraging ships from the south to bring goods to the north.

The end of the Han Empire contributed to a decline in long-distance trade along the Silk Road. Developments further west were equally important to this development. At the other end of the Silk Road the Roman Empire was also entering a period of decline. It is common to date the beginning of the collapse of the Roman Empire from the chaos that ensued following the assassination of the emperors Commodus and Pertinax in A.D. 193. The economic decline within the Roman Empire led to a deterioration of international commerce as well. Long-distance trade along the Silk Road was already into decline by A.D. 200 and by the 300s it had virtually stopped in part because of the activities of nomadic groups. In addition to the nomadic groups that invaded the former Jin Empire in the east, further to the west another confederacy of nomads known as the Huns arose in the 300s, further disrupting international overland commerce along the Silk Road.[226] The Silk Road at the Chinese end was effectively closed to major caravan traffic in A.D. 439. Under pressure from the Huns, who had reached the Volga River and Black Sea around 370, the Goths moved into Roman territory in 376 and in 410 the Visigoths under Alaric sacked Rome.[227] With the relatively stability that had been created by the Han and Roman empires at an end, the transnational social relations that this period had helped to create largely disappeared for a time.

THE XIONGNU

The Xiongnu played an especially important role in shaping the Han Empire's foreign relations. The Xiongnu (aka Hu or Hsiung-nu) were Altaic-speaking nomadic peoples who lived in what is now Mongolia. Their ruler was known as *chanyu* or *shanyu*. The Qin emperor Shi Huang invaded Xiongnu territory in 215 B.C. to secure a large piece of land on which to resettle demobilized troops and refugees — while also initiating construction of the Great Wall in an effort to keep the nomads out of his empire. The leader of the Xiongnu, Chanyu Touman, was forced to flee northward and in 209 B.C. his son Modu (aka Maodun, Mao-tun; 1. c. 234–174 B.C.) killed him and became *chanyu*. Di Cosmo comments, "The account of the killing of Touman by his son suggests a struggle between an old aristocracy, evidently unable to meet the challenge presented by the Chinese invasion, and the junior leaders," adding that the Chinese "displacement of the Xiongnu must have caused widespread relocation and migration [of the nomads], upsetting the established territorial makeup and balance of power among the peoples" in this area to the north of China.[228] Such unsettled conditions allowed Modu and the Xiongnu to gain the ascendency over other nomadic groups. Moreover, Modu's seizure of power came just after the Qin emperor had died in 210 B.C., which resulted in a civil war breaking out within the Qin Empire, leaving the Chinese unable to follow up on their initial incursions. Eventually Chanyu Modu succeeded in uniting the nomadic tribes of Mongolia and the Tarim Basin and making the city-states of the Tarim Basin recognize his suzerainty. The Xiongnu Empire had no settled capital, but an annual gathering at Longcheng (in Mongolia) served to function administratively as a capital.

Shortly after establishing the Han Dynasty, Emperor Gao Zu (aka Liu Bang) was faced with an attack by Modu and the Xiongnu who laid siege to the city of Taiyuan, the capital of the province of Bing (modern Shanxi), in 200 B.C.[229] The Han army broke the siege, but as the emperor and his army pursued the Xiongnu army northward, Modu was able to defeat the Han at the Battle of Baideng (in the far north of Shanxi). The peace negotiations that followed included recognition of the Great Wall as the boundary between the two states, an agreement by the Han to pay periodic tribute to the Xiongnu, and an agreement that the Han emperor would send Modu a princess to marry. This last part of the agreement became a common feature of Chinese relations with its nomadic neighbors known as *heqin* (peace marriage) and was part of an overall policy aimed at civilizing the nomads by introducing them to Chinese culture.[230]

The Han sent Modu a total of three of these so-called princesses to marry and continued to arrange such marriages to the reigning Xiongnu *chanyu* on a fairly regular basis, and the *heqin* practice remained a part of Chinese foreign policy towards nomadic peoples and other so-called barbarians into the A.D. 800s under the Tang Dynasty. The brides were usually not actual princesses, although the Han emperor Jing (r. 188–141 B.C.) did send one of his own daughters, the Princess Nangong, to marry Chanyu Gunchen in 152 B.C., shortly after putting down the Rebellion of the Seven Kingdoms in 154 B.C. Wang Zhaojun was undoubtedly the most famous of these brides.[231] She is one of the Four Beauties of ancient China and her beauty is reputed to have caused birds to fall from the sky. The stories about her say that the Xiongnu *chanyu* Huhanye, who had come to the Han court of Emperor Cheng in Chang'an to pay homage, requested a princess as a bride, but instead he was given five women from the emperor's harem. Wang Zhaojun was one of these. Huhanye died a couple of years later and Zhaojun asked Emperor Cheng to allow her to return to China. The emperor refused her request and she had to marry the new *chanyu*. As the story of Wang Zhaojun indicates, *heqin* brides usually went on a one-way trip.

The Han emperor Wu Di was able to reduce the power of the Xiongnu, and under Chanyu Huhanye and Emperor Cheng, relations between the two imperial powers changed from one of relative equality to the Xiongnu becoming vassals of the Han, though what the Chinese referred to as outer vassals. When the Han lost control during the Xin period and China underwent a period of instability the Xiongnu once again asserted their independence and ended their vassalage. As was discussed above, Xiongnu power and autonomy were once again reduced in the Eastern Han period. The Xiongnu suffered a defeat by the Han in A.D. 89 and subsequently divided into northern and southern branches when the Han chancellor Cao Cao (1. A.D. 155–220) resettled a large number of them in the Ordos Desert region and Bing Province (modern Inner Mongolia and Shanxi provinces) in the early 200s. While many of the southern Xiongnu maintained their nomadic lifestyle, their elites in particular became increasingly Sinicized.

During the Sixteen Kingdoms Period, Xiongnu nobles established three of these kingdoms: the Northern Han (Beihan) from 304–319, established by Luu Yuan with its capital at Taiyuan (in modern Shanxi Province); the Former Zhao (Qianzhao or Han Zhao) from 319 to 329, established by Liu Yao with its capital at Chang'an; and the Xia (aka Daxia) Kingdom from 407 to 425, established by Helian Bobo with its capital at Tongwa, which was built in 413 (in modern Shaanxi Province). The kingdoms of the Xiongnu during the Sixteen Kingdoms Period were multi-ethnic in nature and included a mixture of nomadic and sedentary peoples, and the rulers and other elites in particular had developed a syncretic Xingnu-Chinese culture. To start with, many members of the leadership lived mixed nomadic and sedentary, even sometimes urban lives. Some of them such as Liu Yuan and Liu Yao adopted Han surnames. In the case of Liu Yuan he had been educated as a young man in the Jin capital of Luoyang and had a reputation of being well versed in classical Chinese scholarship. Han attitudes towards the Xingnu and other nomads who had adopted Han culture were ambivalent. They actively sought to have the nomads adopt Han ways, but nomads who did so often still found themselves discriminated against and treated as inferiors.

3

Medieval Empires

While the medieval period is characterized by political fragmentation in some parts of the world, especially in Europe, it also witnessed creation of empires of an unprecedented scale under the Mongols and Arabs. The religiously inspired imperial conquests of the Arabs and their fellow Muslims are particularly noteworthy in the way that they sought to bind people together. The empire-wide nation building initiatives of the Romans and Han were associated with the spread of what emperors perceived as superior cultures. Empire building under the Arabs focused instead on the perceived superiority of a single religion.

The Byzantine Empire

Greek colonists founded the city of Byzantium in 657 B.C., and in A.D. 330 the Roman emperor Constantine I made it the capital of the Eastern Roman Empire under the name Nova Roma (although the city came to be known as Constantinople). In 335 Constantine divided the empire between his sons, but after a period of instability following his death the empire was re-united in 353 under Constantius, who had been ruler of the eastern part of the empire.

Economic and political power within the empire gradually shifted from Rome to Constantinople and the city grew into one of the largest and richest cities in the world — and it remained so for around 1,000 years. Its population in 337 was around 50,000. By A.D. 500 it had a population of over 1 million. It was essentially a Greek city with a small Roman elite at the top, while most of its inhabitants were Greeks (who called themselves Romans as citizens of the Roman Empire). Latin was the language of the state, but Greek was the main language outside of government circles, and by the 600s the use of Greek had largely replaced the use of Latin within the government as well. The Roman Empire had a population of around 70 million in the A.D. 300s, but only about 6 million of these were Italians. The remainder included some 20 million Gauls with most of the rest comprised of Greek-speaking easterners. The end of the western line of Roman emperors came in A.D. 476, during the reign of Zeno the Isaurian (r. 474–91). The Isaurians were a tribal group from southwestern Turkey, and Zeno, whose original name was Tarasicodissa, served as a general in the imperial army before becoming emperor. He consolidated the Eastern Roman Empire, but effectively relinquished control over the Western Roman Empire to Odoacer (1. 435–93), the son of a Scirii (a tribe from eastern Germany) chief who was a vassal of Attila the Hun, who came to rule in Rome.

The Byzantine or Eastern Roman Empire initially included modern Greece, Albania, the former Yugoslavia, Bulgaria, and eastern Hungary in Europe. In the Middle East it included modern Turkey, Cyprus, Syria, Jordan, Lebanon, Israel, northwestern Saudi Arabia, Egypt, and northern Libya. It reached its greatest extent in the 500s under the Emperor Justinian I, when it extended control in the west over Italy, Tunisia, northern Algeria, and southern Spain, as well as over a portion of the Crimean Peninsula. After being defeated by the Turks at the Battle of Manzikert in 1071 it was relegated to a relatively small area that included about half of modern Turkey, Cyprus, Greece, Bulgaria, Albania, the former Yugoslavia, and a portion of the Crimean Peninsula. Constantinople fell to the Republic of Venice and crusaders in 1204 and a portion of its territory was ruled as the Latin Kingdom of Constantinople from 1204 to 1261. In 1261 the Emperor Michael Palaiologos (r. 1259–82) re-established Byzantine rule over Constantinople. Constantinople finally fell to the Muslim forces in 1453.

In regards to transnationalism we are concerned primarily with the movement of ruling elites, mercenaries, traders, and scholars within and to the empire. The emperors themselves came from various parts of the empire. The emperor Justinian I (r. 527–65) was born in the province of Dardania in present-day Macedonia and was of mixed Thracian or Illyrian and Roman background. He was brought to Constantinople while he was a boy. The Emperor Heraculius (r. 610–41) was born to Armenian parents from Cappadocia. His father, Heraculius the Elder, was a general who served in Africa, where the young Heraculius grew up. Leo III the Isaurian (r. 717–41) was born in Syria. After entering imperial service he undertook diplomatic missions to Georgia and the Caucusus before becoming emperor. Basil I the Macedonian (r. 867–86) was born to Armenian parents from what is now eastern Turkey near the Greek and Bulgarian borders. He initially spoke Armenian. Bulghars captured his family and he was carried off to live among the Bulghars as a child. He escaped in 836 and entered the service of a relative of the emperor as a groom. He was taken in by a wealthy woman while on a visit to Patras (in Greece) and later became a bodyguard of the emperor.

Antioch and Alexandria continued to serve as important commercial hubs as they had under the old Roman Empire. Faced with the hostility of Persia, Justinian I sought to develop alternative trade routes to the one that ran from Syria through Persian territory to Central Asia. He established cordial relations with the Himyarite Kingdom (modern Yemen) of southwestern Arabia and with the rulers of Ethiopia in order to promote trade through the Red Sea and on to India. For a short time Byzantine merchants sailed this route to India, but the high tolls charged by the Persians who controlled the Indian ports defeated this effort. Justinian I then turned his attention to a northern route. He developed ports on the Black Sea and goods were shipped across the sea to the Christian kingdom of Lazica-Egrisi (the ancient kingdom of Colchis in western Georgia, which had been the destination of Jason and his Argonauts in earlier times). From there caravans transported goods to Samarkand and Bukhara in modern Uzbekistan (ancient Sogdiana) "where Chinese and Western merchants could meet and haggle without Persian scrutiny."[1] This was part of the ancient Silk Road and it was over this road in 552 that a group of Nestorian monks brought silkworms and mulberry trees from Central Asia in an effort to end Byzantium's reliance on China as a source of silk.[2] Their initiative paid off and before long major silk industries had emerged in Greece and Syria as well as in Constantinople itself. Trade was largely in the hands of non–Greeks — "Armenians, Syrians, Egyptians, Amalfians, Pisans, Venetians,

Genoese, Jews, Russians [Rus, Scandinavians], and Catalans."[3] Such merchants maintained their own factories or agencies in or near Constantinople.

The Byzantine Empire is widely credited with keeping Greek cultural traditions alive. As in ancient times many prominent scholars moved about the Empire. It was also the home to a number of important universities including ones in Constantinople, Antioch, Alexandria, and Athens. Curriculum focused on literature and rhetoric, philosophy, and medicine. The School of Constantinople was created in 425 during the reign of Theodosius II. Initially it had 1 philosophy teacher, 2 teachers of law, and 28 who taught Latin and Greek. The school at Alexandria was a major center of medical scholarship. The Greek Oribasius (1. *c.* 320–400) studied at Alexandria under Zeno of Cyprus prior to becoming the personal physcian of Emperor Julian the Apostate. Aëtius Amidenus (he was from Amida in Mesopotamia) was another famous physician who studied at Alexandria in the late 400s or early 500s prior to moving to Constantinople to practice medicine at the court. Not all prominent scholars were linked to these universities. The historian Procopius (1. c. 500–c. 565) — compiler of the most prominent histories of Justinian I's reign — was born in Caesarea (in modern Israel) and may have been educated in Greek at the School in Gaza and perhaps later in Beirut or Constantinople in law and rhetoric before becoming legal adviser to Justinian I's leading general, Belisarius.

South Asia

After the fall of the Gupta Dynasty in A.D. 550 South Asia was divided into numerous small polities for the next two centuries. A general named Gopala (r. 750–770) was elected to head the kingdom of Gaur in 750 and under his rule the kingdom expanded its control over most of Bengal. Gopala is commonly considered the founder of the Pala Empire and its ruling dynasty, although it was his son Dharmapala (r. 770–810) who enlarged the kingdom into a multi-ethnic empire extending across most of northern South Asia as far as Kamboja/Gandhara (Afghanistan). The city of Gaur served as the imperial capital. His was a fairly decentralized empire, however, with imperial power only being firmly established within the vicinity of Bengal and neighboring Bihar. Beyond that the territories under his suzerainty were mostly vassals and some little more than allies.

The Palas were Buddhists and Dharmapala was an avid patron of Buddhism. The large Buddhist structures built during his reign include the Somapura Mahavihara (at Pahapur, Bihar). This was one of five mahaviharas in Bihar and Bengal (the others being Vikamashila, Nalanda, Odantapura, and Jaggadala) that served as centers of Buddhist learning under state patronage of the Palas. They formed a network and as Dutt notes, "it was common for great scholars to move easily from position to position among them."[4] More importantly in terms of transnationalism, Buddhist monks from these centers also moved back and forth between them and Buddhist centers in other countries as well, especially in Southeast Asia. Moreover, while the actual process is not known, the Somapura Mahavihara also served as a model for the construction of a number of Buddhist (and Hindu) temples in Burma, Java, and Cambodia.[5] Its influence can be seen in two temples built at Prambanan in Central Java during the reign of the Hindu king Rakai Pikatan, the Buddhist temple Candi Sewu (built between 835 and 860) and the Hindu temple dedicated to Siva of Cadi Loro Jonggrang that was completed in 856 and built to celebrate the victory of Rakai Pikatan over his rival Sailendra who was a Buddhist (Rakai Pikatan's queen, however, was a Buddhist).

Dharmapala's son Devapala (r. 810–850) extended the Pala Empire even further, claiming suzerainty over parts of Assam along the Brahmaputra River, parts of Orissa and the Deccan Plateau to the south, and further west into Afghanistan (Kamboja). Subsequent Pala rulers lost control of many of these vassal states in part as a result of the increasing power of the Chalukyas of Karnataka and the Cholas of southern India. Under their king Rashtrakutas after 973 the Chalukyas had revived their fortunes and taken control of most of the Deccan Plateau and some areas beyond. After conquering Orissa, Rajendra Chola I (r. 1012–1044) attacked the Palas around 1021–24 and appears to have made them and neighboring Kalinga vassals.[6] Mahapala I (r. 995–1043) was able to regain control over most of Bengal and subsequent Palas were briefly able to seize control of neighboring territories (i.e., briefly gained control of the kingdom of Kamarupa in the Brahmaputra River valley), but their power did not extend very far and the dynasty came to an end in 1140.

The Caliphates

The spread of Islam had important implications for transnationalism in the medieval world. It served not only to create a new religion with universalist claims with followers spread across a great expanse of the globe, but it also served as a vehicle to promote the creation of large multi-national political units and long-distance trade.

Political expansion of the Arabs under the aegis of Islam gained momentum during the rule of Umar (Omar) the Great (r. 634–44), who was born in Mecca and became the second caliph after Abu Bakr. He expanded the territory under Arab-Islamic rule beyond Arabia by conquering the southern parts of the Byzantine Empire including Palestine, Syria, and Egypt, and Armenia as well as the western parts of the Sassanid Empire including Mesopotamia and parts of Persia. The expansion of Arab political power and the Islamic religion beyond the Arabian peninsula created an Arab feudal elite that ruled over a variety of non–Arab lands as well as serving to spread the use of Arabic as the transnational language of the Islamic world.

Caliph Muawiyah (r. 661–80) established the Umayyad Caliphate (661–750). Muawiyah became caliph after a period of considerable conflict between rival factions in the empire and moved its capital from Kufa in Arabia to Damascus in Syria. The Umayyads expanded their territory in all directions. To the west they captured Carthage in 698 and then invaded Spain in 711. To the east one of their generals sailed to Sindh (aka Sind) in 710 and conquered Sindh and Punjab (modern Pakistan). At its greatest extent around 750 the Umayyad Caliphate encompassed about 7 million square kilometers (inhabited by over 60 million people) and included most of the Middle East with the exception of western Turkey (which remained under Byzantine control), North Africa from Egypt to Morocco, most of Spain and Portugal, parts of southwestern Central Asia that included Bukhara and Samarkand, and most of modern Pakistan and Afghanistan.

Expansion came to an end under the reign of Hishm (r. 723–43), which was marked by a defeat of the caliphate's armies by the Byzantines in Anatolia and the Franks in Europe and by internal revolts such as those by the Berbers in North Africa and by the Sogdians in Uzbekistan. The decline of the empire accelerated under Marwan II (r. 744–50), culminating in its being overthrown by the Abbasid family in 750. The Abbasids killed most of the members of the Umayyad family, except for 'Abd al-Rahman, who fled to Spain where he established the Emirate of Córdoba. Previté-Orton argues that the fall of the Umayyad

Caliphate was linked to the rapid expansion of Islam beyond Arabia and the incorporation of so many non–Arabs including many who were better educated than their Arab masters into the empire as well as to rivalry between Syria and Mesopotamia.[7]

The Abbasid Caliphate (750–1258) achieved the high point of Islamic imperial expansion during the medieval period, covering some 10 million square kilometers. The Abbasids established control over virtually all the Islamic world for a time and ruled over about 50 million subjects. Their capital was moved from Harran to Baghdad in 762. This move exemplified a shift in political and cultural influence from Arabs to Persians and other non–Arabs. This shift did not go unchallenged and from the outset there was a lack of support for the Abbasids not only from surviving Umayyad elements in the Emirate of Córdoba, but also from other Arabs.

The Abbasid Caliphate evolved into a relatively decentralized empire. This decentralization took two forms. One was the emergence of a powerful bureaucracy dominated by Persians and military dominated by Turks that was distinct from the older Arab aristocracy. The other was creation of positions such as those of vizier and emir that allowed for the establishment of local bases of power to challenge central authority. The creation of the caliphate and its imperial institutions resulted in the creation of an extensive transnational society that was a mixture of Arabic, Persian, and Turkic cultures. At the same time, the decentralized nature of the caliphate provided scope for the retention of more localized social and cultural traditions.

The role of the caliph in Baghdad became increasingly ceremonial as a result, while greater power lay in the hands of the bureaucracy and local rulers. By the time of Al-Radi (r. 934–41) the caliph in Baghdad had ceased to exert any effective power. Considerable local autonomy was evident as early as 819 as the Persian Samanid Dynasty (819–999) emerged as a local and relatively independent power in parts of Persia, Afghanistan, Tajikistan, Uzbekistan, and Turkmenistan. The Arab Hamdanid Dynasty (890–1004) likewise established itself as the local power in northern Mesopotamia and Syria in the late 800s. The Turco-Persian Ghaznavid Dynasty (963–1187) established effective political control over Persia, Mesopotamia, and adjoining areas. In addition, the Abbasids had virtually lost control of the empire's bureaucracy to the Persian Buwayhid Dynasty (945–1055) by the early 900s. The Seljuk Turks established a dynasty (1037–1157) that took over control of most of Turkey, Syria, Palestine, and parts of Mesopotamia and Persia. The Fatimid Caliphate (909–1171), with its capital at Cairo, ruled over most of the western empire, until they were supplanted by the Ayyubid Dynasty (1171–1250) founded by Saladin in 1171 that ruled over Egypt, Syria, Yemen, parts of Arabia, and northern Mesopotamia. In the far west, the Emirate of Córdoba (929–1031) of the Arab Umayyads ruled over most of the Iberian Peninsula.

The Seljuk Turks seized parts of Turkey from the Byzantine Empire and established the Sultanate of Rûm (1077–1307; Rûm being derived from the Arabic word for Rome). The Seljuks promoted maritime and caravan trade with Persia and Central Asia and maintained important commercial relations with the Genoese in the Mediterranean. In 1243 the Seljuks were made vassals of the Mongols and the sultanate went into decline.

As for the military, like so many imperial rulers the Abbasids soon came to depend on foreign troops to maintain their empire. In this case, however, the army during the reign of Al-Ma'mun (r. 813–33) came to be comprised mainly of Turkish slaves, called Mamluks, along with smaller numbers of Slavs and Berbers. The Mamluks were slaves who had been captured mainly among non–Muslim peoples from the Caucasus region and from Turkish groups living north of the Black Sea. They were purchased for military service while young and raised in a compound in Cairo where they underwent religious and military training. They spoke Turkish and retained their ethnic identity as Turks. They lived in garrisons scattered throughout the caliphate in the service not only of the ruler in Baghdad but also of local emirs. They were able to attain high ranks within the army. Their military power was translated into political power with the assumption of Mamluk rule in Egypt in 1250 and subsequent establishment of the Mamluk Sultanate (1250–1517).

Even nominal Abbasid rule came to an end in 1258, when the Mongol leader Hulagu Khan (r. 1217–65) sacked Baghdad. With the fall of Baghdad power and influence in the Islamic world shifted to the Mamluks in Cairo, while the core of the old Abbasid empire came under Mongol rule in the form of the Ilkhanate (1256–1335). The Mongol rulers for a time were Buddhists who created a relatively benign environment for Christian and Jewish minorities, but after Ghazan (r. 1295–1334), who had at various times in his life been a Buddhist and Christian, converted to Islam (to gain military support in his struggle for political supremacy), the situation deteriorated for such religious minorities. The territory of the Ilkhanate was unified once again under the empire of Timur (aka Timurlane, l. 1336–1405), a Muslim Turkic tribesman from Central Asia. Timur was the founder of the Timuric Dynasty (1370–1526) that ruled over much of Central Asia, Persia, Afghanistan, Mesopotamia, Pakistan, and the Caucasus region, and extended its rule and Islam into India (Timur sacked Delhi in 1398).

The Mamluks succeeded in halting the Mongol advance towards the Mediterranean and extended their own control beyond Egypt as far north along the eastern Mediterranean as Antioch. To their north in Anatolia, the region had seen the emergence of a number of small states known as the Ghazi Emirates after the Mongol invasion, including that of the Osmanoglu, whose ruler Osman I (r. 1281–1326) laid the foundations for the Ottoman Empire (1299–1923). The Ottomans extended their power into the Balkans in the late 1300s. Ottoman power was temporarily eclipsed when Timur attacked them in 1402 and took their sultan prisoner. After a period of instability Ottoman power was re-asserted by Mehmed II (r. 1444–46, 1451–81), who is best known for seizing Constantinople in 1453. Mehmed II made Constantinople his capital and proclaimed himself Kayser-i-Rûm (Roman Emperor).

Despite the numerous political divisions and frequent conflicts, the Islamic world of the Middle East during the medieval period is noteworthy not only for its transnational rulers, bureaucrats, and soldiers, but also for its transnational scholars and traders. Sharing a common religion and language (Arabic) that transcended political boundaries allowed traders and scholars to move with relative ease over a large part of the world.

In addition to sharing a common religion and language, the traders of the Islamic world operated under similar political systems that shared a general view of the benefits of trade. From the outset, as noted by Durant, "the Arabs did not share the European aristocrat's scorn of the merchant" and "soon they joined Christians, Jews, and Persians in the business of getting goods from producer to consumer with the least possible profit to either."[8] In order to promote trade, "the state left industry and commerce free, and aided it with a relatively stable currency."[9] Long-distance trade included both transport overland by camels and across the sea on ships.

Maritime commerce included trade routes along the east coast of Africa, from the coasts of India to the Middle East, and from the Middle East through the Strait of Melaka to China. The Persians already had a long history of trade with China, and soon after the

Muslims had defeated the Sassanids in 636, Arab and Muslim Persian merchant ships were sailing to China, where Muslim merchants established communities in most of the coastal ports. Bernstein cites *An Account of China and India* (apparently written by Arab merchants in the mid–800s) that describes the trip from Baghdad to Guangzhou.[10] The ships were loaded at the ports of Basra and Siraf in the Persian Gulf, sailed down to Oman and then had one month to sail across to the Malabar Coast (where a local tax had to be paid). The trip across the Bay of Bengal to the Isthmus of Kra took another month, with a stop along the way at the Andaman Islands to renew provisions. Goods would then either be off loaded and carried across the isthmus to be re-loaded for the onward voyage or carried through the Strait of Melaka. The trip from the Isthmus of Kra to the ports of Champa took about three weeks. It then took another month to sail to Guangzhou.

Taking into account the weather and bureaucratic delays, a round trip took about a year. In fact, not many sailors or merchants undertook the entire trip and usually it was divided into more manageable segments — commonly three. "A [non–Muslim] Gujarati merchant, for example, would typically load his ship with the fine cotton cloths and indigo of his native land, sail the summer monsoon to Malacca [Melaka], exchange there his goods for silk, spices, and porcelain, and return home on the winter monsoon. Or he might choose to sail west in the winter and return in the summer from Aden with horses and incense, or to Malindi on the East African coast and return with gold and slaves."[11]

The eastern portion of this trade was severely disrupted as the Tang Empire went into terminal decline during the 800s (see the next section), especially after a rebel named Huang Chao killed thousands of the foreigners living in Guangzhou.[12] It revived again in the 1100s during the time of the Southern Song Dynasty and continued into the early 1400s, when the political situation in East Asia once again undermined such international commerce.

The Tang and Song Empires

A large portion of East Asia was once again unified within a single imperial order after the Northern Zhou rulers were overthrown by Yang Jian in 581. He established the Sui Dynasty (518–619), which can be compared to the earlier Qin Dynasty for its oppressive rule, its undertaking large building projects, the brevity of its duration, and is serving as a precursor to a more stable empire, in this case the Tang. The Xin rulers reunified the northern Han core area under Han rule and conquered the south as well. Chang'an became the capital once again under the Sui. They also completed the Grand Canal, which reached Hangzhou in the south in 609, and rebuilt large portions of the Great Wall. Such projects put considerable strain on the empire in the form of the use of large amounts of forced labor and heavy taxation of the populace, which contributed to their rapid fall from power.

The Tang Dynasty (618–907) at its height is widely regarded by historians as representing the Golden Age of medieval China.[13] The dynasty began when Li Yuan seized power from the declining Sui Dynasty in 618 and proclaimed himself emperor (aka Emperor Gao Zu, r. 618–626). The initial years of the Tang Dynasty under the Li emperors were devoted to consolidating power. The second Tang emperor, Taizong (r. 626–649), in particular is credited with bringing about a number of administrative reforms that helped to stabilize the empire. It is the time from his reign until the outbreak of the An Shi Rebellion in 755 that constituted the Golden Age — a period of a little over 100 years.

The early Tang emperors expanded the territory under their control, especially to the west, and also actively sought recognition of suzerainty from neighboring rulers. The Tang Empire reached its greatest extent during the reign of the third Tang ruler, Li Zhi (aka Emperor Gao Zong, r. 650–683), when the area under Tang rule and suzerainty was about 11 million square kilometers. They also oversaw the re-distribution of the ethnic Han population towards the south, a policy that had important implications in regard to the assimilation of many southern non–Han peoples.[14] In the 600s and first half of the 700s the Tang ruled over more than 50 million people. Most of them were ethnic Han and at the outset about three quarters of these people lived north of the Yangtze River. Migration of Han people south of the Yangtze River resulted in about half of the empire's population coming to live south of the Yangtze River. This included a movement of Han people into what is now the Red River Delta area of northern Vietnam. This movement had begun during the Sui Dynasty in part as a result of construction of the Grand Canal that ran from Beijing to in the north to Hangzhou in the south. It was the southern leg of the canal that promoted the movement of people south from the Yellow River to Jiangsu and Zhejiang provinces.

The canal also served to facilitate the flow of goods (especially grain) and gave rise to the growth of urban centers along its route. In particular, during the Tang period the city of Yangzhou, which lay along the canal, became the economic hub of the empire. Yangzhou became a center of trade and industrial production and was headquarters of the government's salt monopoly. Flooding and warfare along the Yellow River and Grand Canal in the mid–700s led to a deterioration of economic conditions in northern China and to a shift in economic activity from Yangzhou to Kaifeng.

Buddhism was a major religious influence during the Golden Era of the Tang Dynasty, but during the later years of the dynasty it came to be persecuted. As will be discussed in the final chapter a number of Buddhist monks visited China from India and other countries and Chinese monks also visited India and neighboring countries.

The Tang capital of Chang'an (modern Xian) was the largest city in the world. While the majority of its inhabitants were Han, it was a multi-ethnic and cosmopolitan city populated not only by many of the ethnic groups ruled over by the imperial Han, but also by a sizeable number of foreigners. The foreign population in Chang'an reflected the fact that the city was not merely the Tang capital, but also the terminus at the Chinese end of the Silk Road. The Silk Road had been in operation during the Han Dynasty, but, as was mentioned in the last chapter, it had fallen into decline as political conditions within and outside of China deteriorated. Trade along the Silk Road resumed intermittently under the Tang after General Hou Junji's (d. 643) successful campaign against the king of Gaochang (an important oasis city in what is now western Xinjiang near the modern city of Turpan) and the Western Tujue (a Turkic people who lived in what is now Kyrgyzstan) in 640. The Tang sought to protect the route by establishing what were known as the Four Garrisons of Anxi in the newly established Protectorate General to Pacify the West in 648. The four garrisons included Kucha (the capital of the prefecture), Khotan, Kashgar, and Karashahr (which was replaced by Suyab in 679, with Suyab in turn being replaced by Turgesh in 719). These garrisons were, in effect, Han outposts, although even the troops stationed there at times were non–Han.

The Tang lost control of the prefecture in 651 to a Turkic prince named Ashina Helu (d. 658) who rebelled against the Tang. The garrisons were recaptured in 657 and Ashina Helu was captured and allowed to live in exile near Chang'an. The Tibetans began threatening the prefecture in 662. Between 670 and 692 control of the area changed hands between the Tang and Tibetans several times. After 692 the Tang were able to retain control of the four garrisons, except for in 709, when control was lost again for a time to the Turgesh. Tang control over the Silk Road increased with the capture of the portion of the route that passed through the Gilgit Valley (in what is now northern Pakistan) in 722. The Tang lost the valley to the Tibetans in 737, but recaptured it with troops under the command of a general from the Goguryeo, an ethnic group from what is now northern Korea. That general, Gao Xianzhi (d. 756), came to be known as the "Alexander the Great of the East." His push to the west came to an end at the Battle of Talas in 751, where the army of the Abbasid Caliphate defeated him.

The weakening of the Tang Dynasty as a result of the An Shi Rebellion (755–63) led to a gradual loss of Tang control over the Silk Road. Between 764 and 787 the Tang lost control of the Hexi Corridor prefectures (Liangzhou, Ganzhou, Suzhou, Guazhou, Yizou, and Shazhou) to the Tibetans for varying periods and the Protectorate General to Pacify the West finally fell to Tibet in 791, effectively cutting China off from trade with the Middle East for the next 60 years. Political instability in Tibet that began 848 allowed the Tang to re-assert control over the western territories that it had lost earlier,[15] but trade over the Silk Road did not resume its earlier importance.

Mention of the Goguryeo general Gao Xianzhi points to the importance of foreigners within China's military under the Tang. Foreign troops and military leaders also played a prominent role in the An Shi Rebellion that broke out in late 755. The rebellion was led by An Lushan, a Sogdian-Turkic general who served as commander of three northern garrisons: Pinlu, Fanyang (near present Beijing), and Hedong (in what is now Shanxi Province). He declared himself emperor after capturing the city of Luoyang (in western Henan Province). After the rebels captured Chang'an, the fleeing Tang emperor was replaced with a new one, Suzong, who promptly appointed two new generals. These generals raised troops from the Turkic Tujue and Huihe (ancestors of the Uyghurs) tribes and with them recaptured Chang'an and Luoyang. Internal dissent among the rebels (including the murder of An Lushan by his son An Qingxu and the son's subsequent murder by one of his generals) led to the collapse of the rebel forces in 763. The devastation caused by the war was considerable. An estimated 36 million people died during this period from violence and starvation (roughly two thirds of the population). The Tang Dynasty survived but in a weakened form that allowed considerable autonomy for the provinces. Not only had the Tang Dynasty become dependent on non–Han soldiers, but its perceived weakness led the nomads living around its borders to increase their attacks along the frontiers.

Despite the political decline of the Tang Empire following the An Shi Rebellion and the devastation caused by it, the post-rebellion period proved to be one of relative economic prosperity. This resulted from economic reforms in the 780s that saw the general withdrawal of the central government from economic management, with the salt monopoly being an exception. The reign of Emperor Xian Zong (r. 806–20) in particular was a period of economic recovery and relative stability. One legacy of Xian Zong's reign was his creation of a large standing army led by court eunuchs. This army proved effective in suppressing a number of rebellions, but after Xian Zong's time imperial power once again began to wane and the power of the eunuchs increased.

Foreign trade during the latter years of the Tang Dynasty focused primarily on maritime trade. Chinese maritime trade, as has already been discussed, dates back to the Han Dynasty, but had gone into decline after the fall of the Han. The early Tang emperors promoted maritime trade. Unlike in the past, it was a two-way affair with considerable numbers of Chinese ships sailing south from its coastal ports and numerous foreign ships coming to the southern coasts of the Tang Empire. The most important of these ports was Guangzhou (Canton). The Buddhist monk Jian Zhen described the port as being crowded with large ships from Borneo, Java, and Persia carrying spices and pearls as well as "jade piled up mountain high."[16] The foreign merchants and sailors coming to Guangzhou and other ports included Chams and Malays from Southeast Asia, Sinhalese from South Asia, and Persians and Arabs from the Middle East. One of Muhammad's uncles and fellow Quraysh tribesman Sa'd ibn Abi Waqqas (1. c. 584–664) led a delegation to the Tang court sent by Caliph Uthman ibn Affan during Li Yuan's reign (r. 618–26). After receiving the delegation the emperor ordered that a mosque be erected in Guangzhou, the Huaisheng Mosque, to serve the port city's Arab and Persian merchant community.[17]

There was also important maritime trade between the Tang Empire and Korea and Japan further north across the Yellow Sea and East China Sea.[18] Conflict between the Korean kingdom of Silla and Japan resulted in Japanese ships, which sailed from the port of Nagasaki, heading for the coast in the vicinity of Shanghai and sometimes even further south to ports in Zhejiang, Fujian, as well as to Guangzhou.[19] Reischauer mentions a Japanese embassy to the Tang court arranging to sail back to Japan on nine ships manned by Korean sailors from the cities of Lianshui (Jiangsu Province) and Chuzhou (Anhui Province), located along the Huai River to the north of Shanghai, pointing not merely to the presence of Korean settlements but to the active engagement of these ethnic Koreans in international maritime commerce.[20]

The Chinese themselves sailed mainly to nearby destinations in Southeast Asia, but they were known sometimes to venture much further to the Persian Gulf, Red Sea, and even to have visited Somalia and Ethiopia in East Africa.[21] Such voyages, however, do not appear to have resulted in the establishment of any permanent Chinese settlements in these areas.

As with the Silk Road trade, the 750s also witnessed a severe disruption of Tang maritime trade. However, sea trading eventually recovered during the later Tang Dynasty. In addition to the disruptions caused in the north by the An Shi rebels, a group of Arab and Persian pirates burned and looted Guangzhou in 758.[22] Tang officials responded by closing the port for foreign commerce for the next 50 years and re-directing maritime traffic to Tong Binh instead.[23]

Tong Binh (modern Ha Noi) was the capital of the Tang province that includes the lowlands of northern Vietnam. As has already been mentioned, Han rule over this area already dated back centuries. The Han had referred to the area as Jiao Zhi (Giao-chi) and the region subsequently had remained under the control of the Wu and Eastern Jin kingdoms. Long Bien, on the north side of the Red River, was made the province's capital in 264. In 679 the Tang changed the name of the province to the Protectorate General to Pacify the South (*An Nam do ho phu* in Sino-Vietnamese, or An Nam — i.e., Pacified South — for short) and moved the capital across the river to a new site called Tong Binh. Under the Tang Dynasty Tong Binh's population reached about 50,000 plus a military garrison in the Dai La citadel. The closing of Guangzhou to foreign maritime commerce helped to boost Tong Binh during the latter half of the 700s. Tang rule dramatically changed the ethnic nature and composition of the population of lowland northern Vietnam as large numbers of Han migrated to the area, the Mon-Khmer speaking ancestors of the modern Kinh (Viet) people came to settle in the lowlands from the southwest, and the resident Tai-Kadai speaking peoples were assimilated to a greater extent than previously. It is from a blend of these three elements that the Kinh ethnic majority in modern Vietnam developed.

Guangzhou was re-opened to foreign trade in the early 800s and once again the port thrived and boasted an important foreign mercantile community. The Arab trader Suleiman al-Tajir visited Guangzhou in the 840s. Durant refers to the account that an anonymous author wrote in 851 of Suleiman's journey as "the oldest Arabic account of China."[24] This account describes the local mosque, the treatment of foreigners, and the goods available in the city, including fine porcelain.[25] By this time, ceramics had emerged as another of China's major exports along with silk, and large quantities of Chinese ceramics were being shipped throughout Southeast Asia and beyond. Initially Arab traders carried the ceramics to the Middle East and East Africa, but in 785 the Chinese began sailing to these areas themselves in an effort to cut out the Arab middlemen.[26] In 863 the Chinese administrator and writer Duan Chengshi (from Shandong, d. 863) published an account of Chinese trade along the coast of Somalia.[27] The demand for Chinese ceramics and other trade goods in Fustat (present day Cairo) resulted in many Chinese merchants traveling to Egypt.[28]

In the face of a weakened Tang Dynasty, attacks on its territories as well as piracy and banditry increased after the mid–800s. One example of this was the invasion by the Nan Chao kingdom of An Nam (northern Vietnam) in 862–863. The Tang regained control of the province, but An Nam was able to throw off Chinese rule after the fall of the Tang Dynasty. Even more telling was the Huang Chao Rebellion (874–84). The rebels sacked Chang'an and Luoyang, and in 879 they sacked Guangzhou and killed not only thousands of its Chinese inhabitants, but also many of its resident Muslims, Christians, and Jews as well. The rebels were eventually defeated in 884, but this time the dynasty did not recover and the empire drifted into terminal decline. By the time the rebellion was over the emperor Li Xuan's (aka Xixong, r. 873–888) empire was only about 3.7 million square kilometers — about one-third of the territory under Tang domination at the empire's height. A salt smuggler named Zhu Wen (l. 852–912) who had joined the Huang rebels and then betrayed them, resulting in his being rewarded by the Tang court, deposed and then ordered the murder of the last Tang emperor, Aidi (r. 892–907), and proclaimed himself emperor. The region then entered what the Chinese refer to as the Five Dynasties and Ten Kingdoms Period (907–60) during which time there was not only political decentralization but also a decline in long-distance foreign trade.

With the end of the Tang Dynasty the Han lost control of all of the western regions of their empire and large parts of the north and south as well. The emperor Taizu (r. 960–1127) unified some of the territories of the former Han Empire and established what came to be known as the Northern Song Dynasty (960–1127). His capital was at Bianjing (Kaifeng). The Northern Song also re-established relations with a number of states in Southeast Asia, South Asia, and the Middle East and sought to revive maritime trade. They were unable to regain control over the western territories or the far south. To their immediate west the nomadic and semi-sedentarized Khitan people of Mongolia established the Khitan Empire (915–1125), which is sometimes called the Liao Dynasty to give it a Chinese appearance even though the Khitan rulers were strongly opposed to Han acculturation. West of the Khitan Empire the Tibeto-Burman speaking Tangut people established the Tangut Empire (1038–1209) in what are now the provinces of Gansu, Shaanxi, and Ningxia (this empire is sometimes referred to as the Western Xia).

The Northern Song Empire soon found itself beset by political factionalism. In such a weakened state they were attacked from the north by the Jurchen peoples of Manchuria, which was part of the Mongol region and had remained outside of Han political control (they were the ancestors of the Manchus). The Jurchen sacked the Song capital in 1127 and captured the emperor. The Jurchen assumed control over the Han heartland along the Yellow River. Chinese historians commonly refer to the Jurchen Empire as the Jin Dynasty (1115–1234). The Jurchen established their capital at Yanjing (modern Beijing). The Song remained in control of the southern part of their empire, which included about 60 percent of the Han population and the most fertile lands, but by the Treaty of Shaoxing in 1141 they ceded claims to all land north of the Huai River to the Jurchen. Further conflicts followed, but finally the Treaty of Longxing in 1164 led to a degree of stability and several decades of peace. The ascendancy of the Jurchen in northern China resulted in 3 million Jurchen people and other northern peoples migrating into the Han lands. The Jurchen rulers opposed Hanization and Han were not allowed to marry Jurchens until 1191.

The Southern Song capital was at Lin'an (present day Hangzhao), located to the west of Shanghai in the Yangtze River Delta. Lin'an had been the capital of the Wu Yue Kingdom (907–978), which was known for its promotion of the arts and Buddhism and had maintained relations with Japan, Korea, and the Khitan Empire. Under the Southern Song, Lin'an became the center of Han culture as well as the political and economic center of their empire and an important hub of domestic and foreign commerce. Large numbers of refugees resulted in the population swelling to over 1 million. Crowded conditions resulted in frequent outbreaks of fires.

As was discussed earlier in the chapter in the section on sailing, maritime commerce flourished under the Southern Song Dynasty (1127–1279), especially during the reign of Emperor Gao Zong of Song (aka Zhao Gou, r. 1127–62). Ship building during the Southern Song period was centered in Fujian Province, while Chinese and foreign ships called at a variety of ports along the coast, including Guangzhou. The famous Arab geographer Muhammad al-Idris (1. 1100–65/66) wrote in 1154 about large Chinese merchant ships carrying silk, porcelain, and other goods to trading centers in South Asia and the Middle East.[29] Numerous Muslim merchants also visited the Southern Song ports where once again there were thriving merchant settlements. Increasing attacks by the Mongol on the Southern Song in the 1200s resulted in the period of prosperity and foreign trade once again coming to an end.

The Mongol Empires

Although the term Mongol was initially used by the Tang to refer to a few small tribes living in the vicinity of the Ono River in what is now part of Mongolia, by the 1200s it came to be used to refer to a large confederation of nomadic tribes speaking both Mongolic and Turkic languages that had been united by Temüjin (1. *c.* 1162–1227), who assumed the name Genghis Khan in 1206 after he had succeeded in uniting these nomadic tribes.[30] After uniting these tribes he attacked the Tangut Empire (Western Xia), which he defeated in 1209. The Mongols then attacked the Jurchens and captured their capital at Yanjing (Beijing) in 1215, forcing them to move their capital to Kaifeng and to surrender control of much of the northern part of their empire to the Mongols.

Seeking to establish trade relations with the Khwarazm Empire that ruled over much of Central Asia, in 1218 Genghis Khan sent a trade mission to it, but the governor of the town of Otrar (an important trade center along the Silk Road in what is now Kazakhstan) executed the members of the caravan and seized its goods. In retaliation in 1220 the Mongols invaded the empire, captured its capital at Urgench (in modern Turkmenistan) as well as

Bukhara and Samarkand, and assumed control over its territories. Genghis Khan himself then led a portion of his army into Afghanistan and northern India and then sent another part of his forces west where they conquered Armenia, Azerbaijan, and Georgia (in the process destroying the Genoese trading entrepôt of Caffa) and defeated the Rus of Kiev and Bulghars of the Volga. The Mongols later conquered the Bulghars and Rus between 1237 and 1240. While Genghis Khan had been away in the west the Tanguts formed an alliance with the Jurchens in the hopes of defeating the Mongols. Upon his return, in 1227 Genghis Khan defeated the Tanguts and had their imperial family executed.

Genghis Khan died a short time after the defeat of the Tanguts and Ögedei (l. c. 1186–1241), Genghis Khan's third son, became Great Khan in 1229. In terms of conquests carried out during his reign, in the east the Mongols completed their conquest of the Jurchen Empire in 1234 (thereby solidifying Mongol control over northern China), began attacks on the Han of the Song Dynasty, and made the Koreans vassals. In the west they conquered much of the remaining Russian steppes as well as large parts of modern Hungary and Poland. They had launched an attack on Western Europe and were advancing on Vienna when Ögedei died and the attack was called off. A particularly important development in regard to transnationalism during Ögedei's reign, besides spreading a number of Mongols around their newly conquered territories, was that the relative political stability created in the wake of the Mongol conquest of Central Asia and portions of the Middle East allowed the re-establishment of the Silk Road.

After Ögedei died the unity of the Mongol Empire began to unravel in the face of political rivalries that emerged. Kublai Khan (l. 1215–94, r. 1260–94)[31] emerged as the Great Khan after a period of instability and civil war, but he was unable to re-unify the empire. Before turning to a discussion of Kublai Khan's reign let's briefly examine the other Mongol territories. We have already mentioned the Ilkhanate that emerged in the Middle East and assumed control over a large part of the old Abbasid caliphate.

To the north of the Ilkhanate was the territory of the Golden Horde, also known as the Kipchak Khanate (1240s-1502), that encompassed a large portion of the western part of modern Russia and neighboring areas that included parts of Eastern Europe.[32] Under Batu (r. 1242–55) it assumed a relatively independent existence. The Kipchak Khanate ruled over a diverse group of peoples. The population of the Golden Horde itself included Turkic peoples and Mongols, with Turkic peoples being in the majority. The Mongols formed a ruling elite that gradually lost its distinct ethnic identity and became Turkified and increasingly sedentarized. The peoples produced from this blending later were referred to as Tartars. This transformation included adopting the Muslim religion of the Turkic peoples. Subject peoples of the Golden Horde included Russians, Armenians, Georgians, Circassians, Greeks and Goths from Crimea, Bulghars, and Serbians. The Khanate's capital was located at Sarai Batu, along the lower Volga River in present-day Russia. The city became one of the largest in the world in the mid–1200s, with a population of around 600,000. The court attracted Russian princes and other notables from within the khanate and it also served as an important commercial hub along the Volga River. The capital later moved to Sarai-al-Jadid, or New Sarai, in the mid–1300s. Trade was conducted across the Black Sea with Genoese and across the Mediterranean with Mamluk Egypt (with whom an alliance was maintained against the Ilkhanate).

The Chagatai Khanate (1225–1687) was located to the east of the Kipchak Khanate in Central Asia. Genghis Khan's second son, Chagatai Khan (r. 1225–42), ruled the khanate during the reign of Ögedei. Officials who answered to the Great Khan administered the khanate for a time, but it became independent during the reign of Alghu (r. 1260–66). As in the Kipchak Khanate, the Mongols formed a political elite within the Chagatai Khanate. In this case they ruled over an almost entirely Muslim Turkic population. While some of the Mongol rulers in this khanate became Turkicized and converted to Islam, others resisted. This resistance took the form of a revolt by Mongol nomads living within the khanate in the mid–1300s, dividing the khanate with the rebels forming the Moghul Khanate.

As we can see from the above discussion, by the time Kublai Khan assumed power in 1260, his effective power did not extend beyond the borders of present-day western China. Kublai Khan's brother Mongke had become Great Khan in 1251, and he appointed Kublai governor over the southern part of the Mongol Empire in what is today central China, where he ruled over a largely Han population. Mongke subsequently sent Kublai to conquer the Kingdom of Nan Chao (centered in modern Yunnan) in 1253. Kublai was engaged in an attack on Sichuan when his brother died. His younger brother Ariq Boke was proclaimed Great Khan, a move that Kublai opposed. Kublai won his war against Ariq Boke, but had difficulty in asserting his authority over the khanates to the west. A revolt by some of the Han who had served as officials under Kublai while he was at war with his brother was crushed and served to create a distrust of Han officialdom on Kublai's part. Kublai Khan was able to push into Song territory following the six-year Battle of Xiangyang (Hubei Province, 1267–73). The defeat of the Song forces here allowed the Mongols to move along the Han River and enter the Yangtze. The Song royal family surrendered to the Mongols in 1276 and the remaining Song supporters were finally defeated at the naval Battle of Yamen in 1279.

A Mongol now was ruler over all of the territory comprising modern China. Even before this, in 1271 Kublai Khan had named his empire China Dai Yuan and sought to portray himself as Emperor of China and founder of the Yuan Dynasty (1271–1368). This move reflected Kublai Khan's years of living among the Han and his desire to gain the support of these subject peoples. Some Mongols opposed these initiatives, but Kublai Khan was able to establish firm control over the territories within the heart of his empire. Kublai sought unsuccessfully to extend his empire further to the south and east and met with defeat when he invaded Japan, Dai Viet (modern Vietnam), and Java.

The effects of his policies on transnationalism are of primary concern here, but Kublai Khan himself presents an interesting study in transnationalism. A Mongol by birth, he spent most of his adult life living in parts of what is today China and came to rule over a large multi-ethnic empire. After the old Mongolian capital of Karakorum was destroyed in the process of the civil war with Kublai's brother he established a new capital at Dadu (Beijing). Kublai Khan adopted many aspects of Han culture, but these remained mixed with his Mongol heritage and with other influences. His relationship with Tibetan Buddhism is especially noteworthy. Genghis Khan had established diplomatic relations with Tibet in 1207 and the Tibetan rulers sent tribute to him. They ceased to pay tribute after his death and this prompted Ögedei to send Prince Godan to invade in 1240. Tibet was incorporated into the empire in 1247, but the leader of the Sakya Buddhist sect Sakya Pandita was granted religious authority over the region. Kublai Khan established a relationship with Tibet whereby Tibet recognized him as its secular ruler, while the head of the Sakya sect had authority in religious affairs. Kublai Khan converted to Buddhism and maintained a close relationship with Drogön Chögyal Phagpa (l. 1235–80), the fifth leader of the Sakya sect, who not only served as the priest-king of Tibet but also functioned as Kublai Khan's spiritual adviser. Kublai Khan gave him the title Imperial Preceptor in 1260 and he played an important role in introducing Buddhism to Mongolia. At Kublai Khan's request, in 1268 he also designed a new writing system, called Phagpa script and based on Tibetan script, which was considered to be more suitable for the multi-ethnic empire than the system of characters used by the Han. It became the official writing system of the empire in 1271.

Drogön Chögyal Phagpa was not the only non–Mongol and non–Han to hold an important position within Kublai Khan's empire. In fact, Kublai Khan proved to be extremely open to allowing non–Han from within and outside of his empire to conduct business and hold office within his domain. In part because of his distrust of the Han, he appointed not only many Mongols to high-level administrative posts, but also many people from Central Asia as well as Muslims and even a few European Christians. Such appointments were a reflection of Kublai Khan's views of the relative reliability of his subjects and sojourners within his empire, which were ranked hierarchically into four categories. Mongols were at the top, followed by a variety of Central Asian (including the Uyghurs) and Western peoples. Next came the Khitans, Jurchens, and Koreans. The Han and other former subjects of the Southern Song Dynasty were placed at the bottom.

Despite ongoing problems in his relations with other Mongol rulers, sometimes Kublai Khan was able to establish alliances with his fellow Mongols. He was especially successful in forging an alliance with his nephew Ilkhan Abagha, ruler of the Ilkhanate. This was motivated in part out of a desire to oppose the Mamluks, but also from a desire to promote long-distance trade. As a result, the Silk Road once again began to function relatively well. He also promoted maritime trade, and the volume of shipping along the maritime route between China, Southeast Asia, South Asia, and the Middle East grew. Foreigners were welcome to visit and carry out business and religious affairs within the empire. Kublai Khan's international interests were reflected in his court, where large numbers of foreign ambassadors, merchants (including Marco Polo), and religious figures were constantly in attendance. A relatively large number of foreign businessmen resided in and visited the empire, including Chams from Southeast Asia, Persian Muslims from the Middle East, and even a few European Christians.

After Kublai Khan's death, one of his grandsons, Temur, became the Great Khan (r. 1294–1307). Temur essentially consolidated Kublai's empire. He made peace with the western khanates and with neighboring countries such as Dai Viet (northern Vietnam), Champa (central Vietnam), Ava (Burma), and Sukhothai (Thailand). In general he maintained cordial relations with states willing to accept largely symbolic submission as vassals. In 1297 he sent troops to Ava to help the local Bama rulers fend off an attack by the neighboring Tai (Shan). He received numerous foreign emissaries. Ghazan Khan of the Ilkhanate sent an ambassador with gifts to cement good relations between the two Mongol rulers after first breaking relations following his conversion to Islam. Temur was not as hostile to the Han as his grandfather and appointed more Han to offices, but he continued to appoint Mongols along with Muslims and Christians as well. His more favorable disposition towards the Han is reflected in his promotion of Confucianism.

Subsequent Yuan rulers in general became more Han and less Mongol in their cultural outlook, although this was not always the case. Ayurbarwada Buyantu Khan (r. 1314–20) was the first Yuan emperor to actively promote Han culture. In contrast, Yesun Temur Khan (r. 1323–28) temporarily reversed this tendency. He actively sought to eliminate Han influence in the government and appointed mainly Mongols and Muslims to positions. The running of the government, in fact, was largely in the hands of Dawlat Shah, a Muslim.

The Italian Franciscan monk Odoric of Pordenone (1. c. 1286–1331) visited China during the reign of Ayurbarwada Buyantu Khan as a missionary. Odoric traveled from

Venice to Constantinople by sea and then passed through the Middle East to Hormuz, often stopping in towns were the Franciscans maintained houses. He then sailed to Thana (near modern Bombay) and traveled along the coast of India. Next he sailed to Sumatra, Java, Borneo, and Champa, and finally landed at Guangzhou. During his travels in China he established houses of the Franciscan Order in the port of Amoy (Xiamen, Fujian Province) and visited the Yuan capital. There he remained for three years, attached to one of the Christian churches there that had been established by John of Monte Corvino (1. 1246–1328). John of Monte Corvino had been sent by Pope Nicholas IV as a missionary to Asia in 1275 and was responsible for establishing missions in Persia, India, and China. He served as archbishop in Beijing until his death. Odoric returned overland through Mongolia, Tibet, and Persia. A friar named William of Solagna wrote down an account of Odoric's travels in Padua in 1330.[33]

Yesun Temur's son Ragibagh Khan (1. *c.* 1320–28) briefly became emperor after his father's death, but a revolt by those opposed to the power that had been wielded by Dawlat Shah and his associates resulted in the execution of Dawlat Shah and also, apparently, young Ragibagh. Tugh Temur (1. 1304–32), who assumed the name Jayaatu Khan upon becoming emperor (r. 1328–32), reverted to the promotion of Han culture and especially Confucianism. This included taking steps to encourage Mongols and Muslims to adopt Han culture. His reign was also noteworthy for his efforts to improve relations with the western khanates that included sending diplomatic missions to the Ilkhanate and the Kipchak Khanate. Their rulers responded by sending their own missions with tribute indicating their recognition of Tugh Temur as suzerain.

The Yuan Empire faced severe droughts and floods along the Yellow River and resultant famines during the 1340s. The government's inability to deal with these problems effectively and increasing taxation created growing opposition among the subject Han that culminated in the outbreak of the Red Turban Rebellion in and around Guangzhou in 1351. Supporters of the rebellion were drawn initially primarily from Han followers of the millenarian White Lotus Buddhist sect (which often functioned as a secret society) and Persian Manichaeism (which was especially popular in the coastal areas of southern China). Zhu Yuanzhang, a Buddhist monk associated with the White Lotus sect, became leader of the rebellion.[34] He was able to gain widespread support among the Han by portraying the revolt in ethnic terms — i.e., overthrowing the Mongols and restoring the Han to power. Factional fighting among the Mongols meant that they were unable to respond effectively to the rebellion.

After capturing a large part of the former Southern Song territory from the Yuan the rebels made Nanjing their capital in 1355. By 1387 Zhu Yuanzhang had gained control over most of the Yuan Empire with the exception of Mongolia. He proclaimed himself emperor with the title Hongwu in 1368 and established the Ming Dynasty (1368–1644). The Mongol emperor fled to Shangdu in Mongolia and the Red Turbans entered Dadu. Basalawarmi (d. 1382), the Yuan Viceroy of Yunnan and Guizhou, resisted the Ming until he was defeated in 1382. The defeat added this region to the new Han Empire and launched the career of Zheng He, who was to become a famous Ming admiral. Zheng He was born in Yunnan in 1371 and at the age of 11 he was captured, castrated, and brought to the Ming court to serve as a eunuch. The Yuan Dynasty did not end with the ascendancy of the Ming, but continued to rule in Mongolia as the Northern Yuan Dynasty.

The new Ming Emperor Hongwu (r. 1368–98) reversed Yuan policies favoring openness and international commerce and sought to create a closed, self-sufficient society.[35] He focused on promoting agriculture and was opposed to commerce and urban life. After a period of instability following Hongwu's death, Zhu Di assumed the throne with the title Yung-lo (Yongle)

Emperor (r 1402–24). Yung-lo moved the Ming capital from Nanjing to Beijing and reversed many of Hongwu's isolationist policies. The Mings' interests in the outside world waned later in the 1400s, but maritime trade revived a little in the 1500s with the arrival of Europeans.

The Aztec Empire

Transnational relations also existed within North and South America in ancient and medieval times, primarily in the form of trade within regions, but also trade with adjacent regions. Such trade was especially well established in relation to the Aztec Empire of Mesoamerica. Mesoamerica, a region encompassing modern Mexico and the countries of Central America, included a number of kingdoms between the A.D. 500s and 1500s. The most important of these were associated with Teotihuacán and the Aztecs of central Mexico and the Maya of southern Mexico and Central America. Here we will focus on the Aztec Empire and its relations with neighboring peoples.

The geography of Mesoamerica has played an important role in the political and economic history of the region. The highlands of central Mexico consist of a series of rather arid valleys that supported relatively dense populations on the basis of intensive agriculture. The highland valleys of southern Mexico and Guatemala are less arid, but still required intensive agriculture to support their populations. The lowlands of the gulf coast of Mesoamerica receive relatively high amounts of rainfall, but suffer from poor soils and also required careful and intensive use of resources.

All of the kingdoms of Mesoamerica during this period engaged in trade not only with neighboring peoples but also with more distant lands. While the trade closer to home often involved relatively low-value foods and other items, long-distance trade focused on high-value items of interest primarily to elites (this long-distance trade will be discussed at greater length in a later chapter). Such items included exotic bird feathers, stones for jewelry and other decorative purposes, and fine ceramics.

The Nahuatl-speaking Mexica founded the Aztec Empire. The Nahuatl-speaking peoples were hunters and gatherers who migrated to central Mexico from northern Mexico in the A.D. 500s where they came into contact with the existing sedentary population. The Valley of Mexico was home to a number of small states. A Nahuatl group known as the Tepanecs, who lived in Azcapotzalco (in the northwest of modern Mexico City), became dominant in the valley of Mexico in the 1100s. Another group of Nahuatl, known as Mexica, migrated to the region and settled at Chapultapec (in central Mexico City) around 1248. They then moved to Tizapan in 1299. They were ejected from Tizapan and moved to an island in Lake Texcoco where they founded Tenochtitlan in 1325.

When the Mexica leader Tenoch died in 1375 the Mexica elders sent a delegation to the more powerful Culhua of Culhuacan and requested that the Culhua provide them with a new leader. Acamapichtle, whose father was a Mexica leader and mother the daughter of a Culhua noble, who was living with his mother at Texcoco at the time, was chosen. Acamapichtle became governor (*cihuacoatl*) of the Mexica in 1376 and took as his first wife a daughter of the ruler of Culhuacan. Tenochtitlan became a vassal of the Tepanecs of Azcapotzalco, paying it annual tribute and fighting against neighboring states on its behalf. Acamapichtle was crowned ruler (*huey tlatoani*) of Tenochtitlan in 1382 and the city grew increasingly prosperous and powerful for the remainder of his reign.

Prior to his Acamapichtle's death in 1395 the Mexica elders named his son Huitzilihuitl by the daughter of the ruler of Tetepango as his successor. Huitzilihuitl married a daughter of the ruler of Azcapotzalco and managed to negotiate a reduction in tribute payments. He also married a daughter of the ruler of Cuernavaca. The weaving industry grew in Tenochtitlan during his reign and wearing cotton rather than maguey fiber clothing became more widespread. Woven cotton cloth became an important export to neighboring states including Azcapotzalco and Cuernavaca. Tenochtitlan continued to assist Azcapotzalco in waging war on some of its neighbors and profited from the loot obtained by these wars.

Acamapichtle's son Itzcoatl by a slave of noble birth became Tenochtitlan's fourth ruler in 1427 (r. 1427–40). Itzcoatl allied himself with the ruler of Texcoco and put an end to Azcapotzalco's suzerainty. Forming a triple alliance between the Mexica of Tenochtitlan, the Acolhuas of Texcoco, and the Tepanecs of Tlacopan, Itzcoatl initiated a series of conquests that laid the basis for the formation of the Aztec Empire. Not only did this Triple Alliance of Nahuatl-speaking peoples subsequently dominate the Valley of Mexico, but under Moctezuma I (r. 1440–69) and Axayactl (r. 1469–81) the Aztecs built an empire that included territory in the adjacent lowlands of the Pacific and Gulf of Mexico. Thus it became a multi-ethnic empire that included non–Nahuatl peoples. The Aztec Empire reached its greatest extent during the reign of Moctezuma II (r. 1502–19) when the territory of the Zapotecs of Oaxaca was also conquered and the empire came to stretch as far south as the Isthmus of Tehuantepec and Soconusco on the Pacific coast of Chiapas. Prescott remarks that early Spanish chroniclers of the Aztecs such as Sahagun began to use the term emperor to refer to the later Aztec rulers instead of king, which they employed in reference to the earlier rulers, "intimating, perhaps, his superiority over the confederated monarchies of Tlacopan and Tezcuco."[36]

Beneath the Aztec emperor were about thirty Aztec nobles, some of them descended from the founders of the ruling dynasty,[37] ... as well as a number of vassals — "powerful chieftans, who lived like independent princes on their domains."[38] The nobles and vassal chieftans were required either to spend part of the year in the capital themselves or required by the emperor to send "hostages in their absence."[39] The duties of these nobles and vassals varied and included providing troops when needed, helping to repair buildings, and presently tribute that ranged from "fruits and flowers" to agricultural produce that was stored in "spacious granaries and warehouses in the capital.[40] In addition to military garrisons that were established around the empire, the imperial government outside of the capital included a variety of office holders. There were judges appointed by the emperor in each of the main towns. These judges had "final jurisdiction in both civil and criminal cases" and, once appointed, kept their positions for life.[41] There were also tax collectors, "who were recognized by their official badges, and dreaded from the merciless rigor of their exactions."[42] The chief tax collector was stationed in Tenochtitlan "with a map of the whole empire, with a minute specification of the imposts assessed on every part of it."[43]

Like other empires, the Aztecs sought to link their conquered territories through a series of roads. The Aztec roads included a royal highway (*ohquetzalli*) that linked the cities of the Valley of Mexico with some of the more distant cities. According to Torquemada, such roads allowed the ruler to eat fresh fish from the Gulf of Mexico daily.[44] The road network eventually stretched as far as Soconusco (in modern Chiapas). Lacking animals for transportation, travel was on foot. Subject peoples were required to maintain the roads, which included establishing inns with food and toilets every 10 to 15 km. The rulers communicated over these roads by a system of couriers (*paynani*) and sought to ensure that travel was safe. The couriers worked in relays so that individual couriers did not travel far from their homes.

4

Polities Along the Major Trade Routes

This chapter focuses on the polities along the overland Silk Road through Central Asia and along the maritime trade route that stretched from China to the Middle East. Long-distance trade was of considerable importance to the economies of all of these polities and also contributed to the cosmopolitan nature of their societies. The oases and ports of these kingdoms and empires served as conduits for the flow of both goods and ideas. While most of the inhabitants of these polities, including many of their rulers, did not travel beyond their borders and foreigners tended to be concentrated in a few locales, the lives of virtually all of their inhabitants were greatly influenced at least indirectly by the flow of trade goods and the wealth that such trade generated as well as by the ideas that travelled along the trade routes.

The Yuezhi-Kushan

Central Asia provided a crucial link in long-distance overland trade between Europe and China from the time of the Roman Empire and well into the medieval period and is therefore of considerable interest in regard to transnationalism. Throughout the ancient and medieval periods the region was the home of various groups of nomads who sometimes united to form confederacies and even occasionally kingdoms and empires.[1] In ancient times the Yuezhi are of particular interest among the nomadic groups in relation to long-distance trade.

The Yuezhi (aka Yue Shi, Niuzhi) were an Indo-European speaking nomadic people who lived initially in the Tarim Basin (modern Xinjiang and western Gansu). As Liu notes, "While the Xiongnu were famous in history because of their conflicts with Chinese empires, the Yuezhi were better known to the Chinese for their role in long-distance trade."[2] In particular, as early as the 600s B.C. the Chinese knew them for their role in supplying jade from Xinjiang.[3] During the reign of the first Han emperor, Liu Bang (aka Gao, Gao Zu; r. 202–195 B.C.), the Yuezhi came to be known to the Chinese as suppliers of horses. Sima Qian mentions a Yuezhi chief named Lou who supplied the Han horses in return for silk and cattle. The silk was resold to other nomads at considerable profit, making Lou quite wealthy, and he was granted an audience with the emperor. Based on Sima Qian's history, Liu argues, "we may consider the Yuezhi to have been the very people who initiated the Silk Road trade. Around the third century B.C.E. their role in distributing silk to tribes on the steppe stimulated the silk-for-horse transactions, and also spread the fame of Chinese silk products as yarn, floss, and textiles."[4]

The increasingly powerful and belligerent Xiongnu under Chanyu Modu attacked the Yuezhi in 176 B.C. and drove them out of western Gansu. Chanyu Jizhu (aka Laoshang, r. 174–158 B.C.) attacked them again in 162 B.C.[5] The attacks by the Xiongnu prompted the majority of the Yuezhi to migrate westward to the vicinity of the Ili River (in the border region between modern Xinjiang and Kazakhstan) and a smaller group to move south to settle among the highland Qiang peoples in Nan-shan (modern northwestern Sichuan).[6] Xiongnu attacks finally prompted the Yuezhi to move to the south, where they settled in the vicinity of the Oxus River in a region known as Transoxiana to the north of the kingdom of Bactria.[7] The migration of the Yuezhi across Central Asia had a number of consequences. For one, in the course of their movement they absorbed other nomadic groups. As Enoki, Koshelenko, and Haidary note, "The Yüeh-chih proper, having drawn into their orbit a number of other nomadic peoples, passed through Ferghana (Ta-yüan) [located in modern Uzbekistan, Kyrgyzstan, and Tajikistan; Alexander the Great established a Greek colony here and at the time that the Yuezhi arrived the valley was occupied by Greco-Bactrians] and reached the borders of Bactria."[8] Not all the nomadic groups that they encountered were absorbed and their westward movement also "set off a whole series of displacements of nomadic peoples in Central Asia" that had repercussions as far as the Roman Empire in Europe.[9]

The Yuezhi came into conflict with the sedentary people of the Greco-Bactrian kingdom and they or a related group of nomads are believed to have burnt the city of Alexandria on the Oxus (aka Ay Khanum), an important commercial center located in the north of modern Afghanistan, around 145 B.C.[10] There were also conflicts between the Parthians and Yuezhi, including a battle in 124 B.C. in which the Parthian king Artabanus I died. His successor, Mithridates II, managed to stop further incursions into Parthian territory and so the Yuezhi turned their attention towards the weaker Bactrians. By the time that the Han ambassador Zhang Qian (aka Chang Ch'ien) visited them between 130 and 125 B.C. the Yuezhi were in firm control of Sogdiana and northern Bactria, and the southern Bactrian towns were under their suzerainty.[11] Sima Qian provides the following account by Zhang Qian of the situation in Daxia (Bactria): "Its people cultivate the land, and have cities and houses. Their customs are like those of Dayuan [aka Ta-yüan, Ferghana]. It has no great ruler but only a number of petty chiefs ruling the various cities. The people are poor in the use of arms and afraid of battle, but they are clever at commerce. After the Great Yuezhi moved west and attacked and conquered Daxia, the entire country came under their sway.... The capital is Lanshi [Bactra, modern Balkh] where all sorts of goods are bought and sold."[12] The Hellenic king Hermaeus Soter (r. *c.* 90–70 B.C.) ruled over a region known as the Parapamisade (Hindu-Kush in eastern Afghanistan) around 70 B.C., when this region came under Yuezhi control.

As the Yuezhi established control over Bactria, which came to be known as Tokharistan, two important developments occurred. One is that the Yuezhi underwent a degree of acculturation to their new environment and especially Hellenization. Evidence of Hellenization can be seen in their use of a form of the Greek alphabet and their production of coins resembling those of the Greco-Bactrians (many of their early coins bore the likeness of Hermaeus Soter and later ones still resembled earlier Greco-Bactrian coins).[13] The other development is that the Yuezhi and Han resumed commercial relations. This had especially important implications for long-distance trade over the Silk Road. The initiative for this came from the Han emperor Wu Di (r. 141–87 B.C.) in the aftermath of Zhang Qian's visit to the region and led to the development of fairly regular long-distance trade between China and the Parthian Empire passing through Yuezhi territory, along with visits of subsequent Chinese embassies to the Yuezhi. Another caravan route through Kushan territory linked Parthia and China to India. This route passed through Tirmidh, Balkh, Bamiyan, and Taxila and also served as a conduit for Buddhist beliefs into Central Asia.

Rather than a unified kingdom the Yuezhi formed a confederation in Bactria that was divided into five polities referred to as *xihou* (aka *his-hou*).[14] The ruler of one of these *xihou* named Kujula Kadphises (r. *c.* A.D. 30–80) united them around A.D. 30 and laid the foundation for the creation of the Kushan Empire. The Kushan ruler Vima Kadphises (r. *c.* A.D. 95–127) expanded the empire's territory to the southeast as far as northwestern Pakistan. The Kushan Empire reached its greatest extent during the reign of Kanishka I (r. *c.* 127–140) who conquered large portions of the lowlands of northern India including the city of Patiliputra and possibly including Champa (the modern state of Chhattisgarh). The empire had multiple capitals: their principal one at Purushapura (modern Peshawar, Pakistan), another at Mathura (in modern Uttar Pradesh and an important holy city to Hindus who believe it to have been the birthplace of Krishna), and a summer capital at Kapisa (modern Bagram, Afghanistan). In regard to the latter, Alexander the Great had built a Greek-style city there, known as Alexandria on the Caucasus, on the site of an earlier settlement. Seleucus, the Mauryans, and the Greco-Bactrians successively ruled the city. It became the capital of a Greco-Indian kingdom after the Yuezhi had taken control of Bactrian territory to the north until this territory also fell to the Yuezhi. In addition to its political importance Kapisa was also a center for long-distance trade.

The Kushan Empire split into western and eastern parts after the death of Vasudeva I (r. c. A.D. 190–230). The Sassanids attacked the Western Kushan Empire around this time. They deposed the Western Kushan rulers in 248 and replaced them with vassals known as the Kushanshas. The Eastern Kushan Empire, with its capital at Peshawar, had lost control of its eastern territories by A.D. 270 and was finally conquered by Samudra Gupta in the mid–300s.

Liu refers to the "cosmopolitanism of the Kushan empire."[15] This related in part to their assimilation of cultural elements from those they conquered and came into contact with as well as to their involvement in long-distance trade between the Han Empire to the east and the Roman Empire to the west. Such trade made them wealthy and contributed to the development of their cosmopolitan culture. In addition to their participation in long-distance trade from the east and west, there were exchanges of ambassadors not only between the Kushans and the Han, but also with the Roman Empire. The items found as a result of excavations of the Kushan palace at Bagram in the 1930s serve to highlight not only the wealth of the rulers but also their acquisition of valuable goods from a wide range of sources including the Roman Empire, the Han Empire, and South Asia.[16] Their cosmopolitanism can also be seen in their religious beliefs that drew on Buddhism, Zoroastrianism, and Hinduism, as well as ideas from the Greeks. Liu relates this in part to the desire of the Kushan rulers to establish their legitimacy in the eyes of their sedentary conquered subjects: "The Kushan rulers patronized religious cults to claim their legitimacy of ruling the conquered sedentary societies — Central Asian territory influenced by Persian religions, Hellenistic Bactria, and Bramanical and Buddhist South Asia."[17] Their syncretic religious beliefs were built on a tolerance of different religions. Thus, Buddhists commonly view Kanishka I as a second Asoka, not because he converted to Buddhism, but for his lavish patronage of the religion and its associated Gandharan art style based upon tolerance.

Tamil Kingdoms

The Tamils lived to the south of the Mauryan Empire. Ancient Tamil history focuses on three different clans or Tamil peoples: the Cheras, Cholas, and Pandyas.[18] Our interest here is on their international trade relations, and especially their involvement in international maritime trade. The southern part of India served not only as a source for a variety of local goods such as spices and gems that were shipped to both the east and west, but also as a transshipment point for goods from the east destined for markets to the west and for western goods going east.

Such long-distance commerce dates back to at least the time of Ptolemy II (r. 282–246 B.C.), who encouraged contact and trade with Arabia and India and established posts in India. This trade with southern India expanded with the discovery by Greek navigators of how to best use the monsoon winds to sail across the Indian Ocean and improvements in knowledge of the geography of the Indian coast. Such discoveries are commonly linked to the Greek merchant-navigator Hippalus some time in the 1st century B.C. One of the important aspects of this knowledge was that it allowed merchants to make the return voyage fairly efficiently without having to remain in India too long. Trading ships were able to leave the Red Sea ports of Egypt in July, arrive in India in September or early October, and then commence the return voyage in November.[19]

This maritime trade grew considerably under the Roman Empire. Beyond simple economic considerations, "the inspiration for Indo-Roman trade can be traced to Alexander, whose achievements loomed large in the Roman mind."[20] It is important to keep in mind, however, that the so-called Romans (the Tamils called people from the Roman Empire Yavanas) trading with and living in India were not ethnically Roman but were primarily ethnic Greeks.[21] Although spanning a period from the 1st century B.C. until the A.D. 200s, the peak period of trade between the Tamil kingdoms and the Roman Empire was from the time of the reign of Octavian/Augustus (r. 27 B.C.–A.D. 14) to the reign of Nero (r. A.D. 54–68).[22] It went into decline from then until the end of Caracalla's disastrous reign in A.D. 217 — launching a war against Parthia, he was assassinated by one of his imperial guards while urinating along the roadside near Harran — when it effectively came to an end. Strabo, writing during the peak period of such trade, says 120 ships sailed for the ports of northwestern and southern India from the Red Sea port of Myos Hormos.[23]

Turning to the three principal Tamil clans, the Cheras were a hill people from the interior region of Western Ghats of southwestern India. They also occupied and exerted control over the adjacent lowland coastal plain known as the Malabar Coast (modern Kerala). Their capital was located at Vanchi, which appears to be modern Karur in central Tamil Naidu. They were engaged in international trade from ancient times, providing spices (such as pepper), ivory, timber, pearls, and gems to Arabia, Mesopotamia, Egypt, Phoenicia, Greece, and Rome. Their principal port was Muziris, which appears to have been located at Pattanam (near Paravur) on the Malabar Coast. Muziris was already a bustling international port by 500 B.C. and it may have been functioning as a port as early as 1500 B.C. During Roman times the main exports passing through the port for the Egyptian Red Sea ports were pepper and malabathron (the Greek name for Indian bay-leaf, *Cinnamomum tamala*), as well as nard, Chinese silks, and gemstones. The Romans paid for these goods with gold and silver coins as well as by exporting wine, Egyptian papyrus, lead (often alloyed with copper or tin) and copper largely for coinage, and glass.[24]

There appears to have been a permanent Roman merchant colony located at Muziris.

Young mentions a map depicting the Roman world in the first century A.D. that "shows a building marked as *Templum Augusti* (Temple of Augustus) at Muziris. Such a structure would have been built only by subjects of the Roman Empire, and presumably ones who were living in Muziris or who spent a significant portion of their time there."[25] He adds, "It would seem that the pepper and malabathron trade from southern India was lucrative enough to encourage Roman merchants to settle in the area."[26] Romans were not the only foreigners living at Muziris. Tomber characterizes the Muziris community as being "heterogeneous" and including "non-local Indian traders from the north-west" as well as Romans.[27] It should also be noted that these foreigners included sailors as well as merchants. As for the Roman traders themselves, Tomber describes them as private individuals rather than agents of the state, but notes, "The enormous cost and complexity of the undertaking would not have precluded private enterprise, but did preclude small merchants acting on their own; instead extremely wealthy merchants or a consortia of merchants would have been required to finance such ventures.... The Muziris papyrus implies a hierarchy in which a wealthy financier recruited merchants to undertake the trips."[28]

The Pandyas lived to the south of the Cheras. They are mentioned in ancient texts as early as 500 B.C. The kingdom was invaded by the Kalabhras, but was revived in the A.D. 500s under Kadungon. They are known to have conducted considerable trade with Ptolemic Egypt and then with the Roman Empire via the Egyptian Red Sea ports. They also began trading with China in the A.D. 200s. Early Chinese sources describe them as good traders who provided sea pearls. A Roman merchant colony was established at the mouth of the Vaigai (Vaitai) River in the vicinity of modern Ramanathapuram. A Pandyan king sent an ambassador to visit the emperor Octavian/Augustus around A.D. 13. Another Pandyan ambassador was sent to visit the emperor Julian the Apostate in A.D. 361.

The Cholas established a kingdom around 300 B.C. in the Kaveri River valley of eastern Tamil Naidu. They ruled over the Coromandel Coast of southeastern India. Karikala Chola, who ruled around A.D. 120, was one of their most famous kings. The important port of Arikamedu (aka Poduke) was located in their territory.[29] The main period for trade between Arikamedu and the Red Sea ports appears to have been from the first century B.C. and the 100s A.D., but trade continued well into the 300s. There has been some debate among scholars as to the nature of the foreign community at Arikamedu, but it appears as if there was a distinct Roman emporium located in the northern part of the town.[30] Arikamedu was also an important center for working with beads, metals, glass, gemstones, ivory, and shells. The port was also engaged in considerable trade to the east as evidenced by the presence of a good deal of pottery from southern India in archaeological sites in Champa (central Vietnam), northwestern Java, Sambiran on Bali, and Beikthano (southern Burma). Goods from Southeast Asia and China also passed through Arikamedu on their way to the Roman Empire.

The Roman presence in the Tamil region went beyond traders living in a few coastal enclaves. There were also Romans living inland such as those at Kaveripattinam (in northwestern Tamil Naidu)[31] and Roman mercenaries served in Tamil armies. Nagaswamy provides translations of early Tamil texts describing the Romans and Tamil trade with them.[32] One of the texts relating to the Pandyas mentions the ships of Yavanas (Romans) coming to the ports of the Malabar Coast laden with gold and returning with pepper. The gold was not only in the form of coinage. One passage describes the Pandya Nan Maran drinking delicious Roman wine, imported in jars, daily from a gold cup. There is also a passage mentioning Roman-made lamps being used by the Pandyan ruler. Romans serving as bodyguards for the Pandyan king are described as having sturdy bodies and in one passage as having a terrifying look and another as a fearful appearance. The final reference mentions the capture of Romans by Nedum Cheral Adan. He seized their vessel that was carrying diamonds. He then had their hands tied and molten ghee poured over their heads. Nagaswamy speculates the reason for inflicting such a treatment is probably that they transgressed the law of the land in some way, possibly not paying duty on the diamonds, and were therefore punished.[33] The Romans are described as using a barbaric language and as being quarrelsome.

The Tamil epic *Silappadhikaram* also contains accounts of the Yavanas. It says that they had a colony called Yavanar Irukkai (called Kaberis by Ptolemy) near the mouth of the Kaveri River and close to the important Chola city of Thanjavur. The account describes the colony as being quite noticeable and the Yavanas as possessing powerful and destructive weapons. Another Tamil text, the *Manimekhalai,* refers to Roman artisans. It says that the palace of the Chola ruler Mavan Killi, who had conquered the Chera capital of Vanchi (Karur), employed Roman sculptors in his palace. Roman artisans are also described as constructing chariots for the king. Men and women of high society are said to have had a preference for decorative Roman-made crystal boxes to store their jewelry, gems, and gold. One Tamil text also mentions a wealthy Roman colony called Yavancceri (or Yavanappadi) located at Rajagiri (Cochin, Kerala).

In addition to foreigners coming to visit and reside in the Tamil kingdoms, there is also some evidence of Tamils travelling abroad as well in ancient times, although for the most part "the Tamils of the south did not sail across to the west."[34] As has already been mentioned, the Pandyas sent ambassadors to Rome on at least a couple of occasions. Warmington comments, "After the discovery of the monsoons the presence of Indians in Alexandria was more or less continuous."[35] However, they rarely appear to have travelled on to Rome and accounts of Indians in Rome mention them as embassies and slaves. Moreover, such Indians also included people from northwestern India as well as Tamils. As for Tamils in Alexandria and elsewhere in Egypt, although the growth of commerce with the Roman Empire led some Indian merchants to go to Egypt, the number was fairly small. Warmington lists several reasons for this, including "the partial exclusion from the Red Sea of Indians by Arabians" and "the imposition by the Romans of differential customs-dues at Egyptian ports against Indian and Arabian vessels."[36] Despite such constraints, in addition to the mention of Indians being present in India in published sources there is archaeological evidence of their presence. Tomber mentions, "Graffiti in Indian languages strongly imply that Indians were living at Red Sea sites."[37] Such graffiti includes three Tamil-Brahmi personal names at two sites dating from around the 1st century A.D. Archaeologists have also found characteristic Indian domestic pottery at three sites that "may also relate to Indian communities, rather than representing trade in ceramics or their contents," and they have found remnants of some Indian textiles that may have been personal possessions.[38] The distribution of the pottery at one site suggests that the people associated with the items lived or worked in a distinct area.[39]

The Chera Kingdom went into decline in the A.D. 200s and, though it survived during the medieval period, it did not play a major role in transnational relations during this time. The Pandya Kingdom underwent a revival in the A.D. 500s and the Pandya king Arikerari Parankusa Maravarman (r. *c.* 730–65) gained control over the Malabar Coast at the expense of the Cheras. Later in the century, however, the Pallavas (assisted by the Cheras) defeated the Pandyas. The Pandya Kingdom re-emerged as an important state between 1150 and 1350. During this period they controlled portions of Sri Lanka for a time and also were actively engaged in trade with the Middle East as well as with Srivijaya and other Southeast Asian kingdoms. The Delhi Sultanate invaded Pandya territory in 1311, and continued Muslim attacks eventually led to the defeat of the Pandyas and the founding of the Madurai Sultanate (1333–78). This sultanate's first ruler was Jalaluddin Ahsan Khan (r. 1333–9) and one of his daughters was married to Ibn Battuta. The Madurai Sultanate became part of the Vijayanagara Empire in 1378.

The medieval Chola Empire, with a territory that included the Coromandel Coast, was established by Vijayalaya Chola in 848 and lasted until 1279. Rajaraja Chola I (r. 985–1014) expanded the Chola Empire over southern India, the Maldives, and parts of Sri Lanka. His son Rajendra Chola I (r. 1012–44) sent military expeditions that managed to establish suzerainty over territory along the east coast of India as far as the Ganges region. The Cholas were driven out of Sri Lanka in 1069–70 and by the early 1100s they had lost control of most of their empire outside of the Tamil heartland. The empire subsequently went into decline. After 1279 the center of political and economic power in the Tamil world shifted to the resurgent Pandya Kingdom.

The Vijayanagara Empire (1336–1646) was an inland empire based on the Deccan Plateau that came to exert control over most of southern India, including the Tamil kingdoms and their important coastal trading ports. Its capital of Vijayanagar is located near the modern city of Hampi (Karnataka State).

In addition to imperial conquest, transnationalism manifested itself among these medieval Tamil kingdoms primarily through international trade. As in ancient times the Tamil ports were important entrepôts along the maritime trade route that stretched from the Middle East to southern China. Regional goods such as spices (e.g., pepper and ginger), gems, and textiles were exported from these ports, while goods from China, Southeast Asia, and the Middle East were imported and transshipped. The maritime trade also generated an important shipbuilding industry. Foreign traders and seamen from a variety of countries resided in and passed through these ports and they also served as bases for Tamil merchants who engaged in international trade.[40] The west coast port of Calicut was the major center catering to the trade with the Middle East. Persians, Arabs, and other Middle Eastern merchants took up residence in Calicut during the medieval period. The Cholas in particular conducted trade with China and the Abbasid Caliphate of Baghdad, as well as with the Malay Kingdom of Srivijaya, the Javanese Sailendra Kingdom, and the Cham kingdom of Champa.

Tamil maritime trade was conducted primarily by merchant guilds. In addition to the merchants themselves the guilds also had military personnel to provide protection. They also undertook religious and charitable activities on behalf of their members, including the construction of temple compounds. One of the most important of these guilds was named Nanadesa Tisaiyayirattu Ainnutruvar or Disai Ayirattu Ainnurruvar, meaning the five hundred from four countries and a thousand directions. Its members were itinerant merchants who ranged over an extensive area. Its headquarters were at Aihole, in what is now Karnataka State, and they had a second base at Pudukottai, in what is now Tamil Naidu. This guild was closely associated with the Chola kingdom and followed close on the heels of its conquests in India and beyond. The Chola rulers developed a navy that engaged in military attacks as far as island Southeast Asia. Srivijaya had control of the most lucrative part of the trade between China and the Middle East with the Cholas overseeing the trade that passed through southern India. Envy of Srivijaya's relative prosperity seems to have motivated the Cholas to send their fleet eastward in 1025 to sack the capital of Srivijaya at Palembang (southern Sumatra) as well as to raid other Malay coastal towns.

Prior to the attacks of 1025 the merchant guilds already had a significant presence in and proximity to Srivijaya. Initially Takola (aka Takkolam, after the Tamil word for *piper cuveba* or tailed pepper, a type of pepper that was exported from Sumatra and Java) was the most important port catering to maritime trade along the Isthmus of Kra (later the port was named Takua Pa, in Phang Na Province, Thailand; *takua* is Thai for lead and refers to the region's later development as a tin mining center).[41] In addition to Persians and Arabs, there was a large Tamil population here and the Tamil merchants built a Saivite Hindu temple here in the 700s. Later a Tamil merchant guild named Kodumbalur Maninramam built a water tank for the temple. Takola's status as a trading center began to deteriorate as it became embroiled in regional political conflicts in the 1060s, when troops of the Bama (Burmese) king Anawratha (r. 1044–77) captured the port and forced its ruler to flee. The exiled ruler of Takola sought aid from the Cholas who then attacked and drove out the Bama in 1067. So much conflict led foreign merchants to seek a more secure base in the region and they moved their operations south to Kedah (known by its Tamil name Kadaram and called Kalah by Arab merchants), which Rajendra Chola I's forces had also attacked but was now deemed to be a more secure base.

The Bama were soon indirectly drawn into conflict with the Cholas again when the Buddhist Sinhalese king Vijayabahu (r. 1055–1110) of Sri Lanka requested assistance from fellow Buddhist Bama king Anawratha of Bagan in his fight against the Hindu Cholas in 1071. Anawratha responded by sending products from Bagan that were used to pay the Sinhalese soldiers, who succeeded in driving the Cholas out of Sri Lanka: "The *Culavamsa*, the Sri Lankan Buddhist chronicle, records that in 1070, after Vijayabahu I gained control, many costly treasures were sent to the Pagan [Bagan] king; then in 1075 Buddhist priests from Burma [Bagan] were sent to Sri Lanka to purify the order."[42]

We have already seen how Tamil merchants built Hindu temples where they were active. For instance, in addition to the temple at Takola, Hall mentions an inscription from Bagan dating from the 1200s describing a donation made by a merchant connected with one of the Tamil merchant guilds to build a new shrine in the compound of the local merchants' temple.[43] Such temple construction was not a one-way affair, and Hall also notes, "In the early eleventh century [a] monk's abode was endowed by the Srivijayan monarchs at Nagapattinam, the centre of the Saivite Hindu Cola [Chola] realm."[44] Maritime activities of the Chola not only served to promote transnational interaction among Hindus. One of the consequences of the Hindu Chola attack on the Buddhist Sinhalese was the forging of close relations between the Buddhist kingdoms of Bagan in Burma and the Sinhalese in Sri Lanka. This relationship "worked both ways, the Theravada communities in each helping those of the other."[45]

Malay Kingdoms

Southeast Asia formed the next link in the maritime trade route heading east from southern India. While all of the medieval kingdoms of Southeast Asia engaged in international trade to some extent and many of them had at least some ties with this maritime trade route, two kingdoms in particular were associated with it: Champa and Srivijaya. Malay peoples founded both kingdoms. The Malays originally lived along the coasts of the island of Borneo and from there migrated by sea north to southern and central Vietnam and west to the Malay Peninsula and the eastern side of the island of Sumatra.

SRIVIJAYA

The Kingdom of Srivijaya was a Malay kingdom located along the east coast of the island of Sumatra and at times exerting control over adjacent areas of western Java and the Malay Peninsula. An account of a visit by a Chinese Buddhist monk named Yijing (aka I-Ching), who will be discussed at greater length in the final chapter and who spent six months there in 670–671, is the earliest written reference to the kingdom.[46] Srivijaya's first capital was in the vicinity of Palembang in southeastern Sumatra.

Between the early A.D. 100s and the 300s maritime trade between southern India and Oc Eo in southern Vietnam passed to the north of the Strait of Melaka across the Isthmus of Kra, but gradually the route shifted south through the Strait of Melaka and around the tip of the Malay Peninsula. A number of Malay ports at the mouths of rivers along the Isthmus of Kra and the Strait of Melaka and further south on the east coast of the island of Sumatra grew to channel local goods (e.g., camphor and pepper) to this trade through the Strait of Melaka. The port of Palembang on the Musi River in southeastern Sumatra emerged as the most important of these ports and came to rule over an empire known as Srivijaya. Palembang defeated its rival Jambi around the 670s or early 680s. Palembang, with a large harbor, at this time was a "prosperous entrepôt where ships going to and coming from China and India gathered while waiting for the winds to change. The ruler was a great patron of Buddhism, and a large international community of monks resided nearby; Chinese monks came here to study with Indian teachers. In a more prosaic vein, ships with fighting men were being sent to intimidate potential rivals along the Straits of Melaka and of Sunda."[47]

Who exactly was involved in this trade between India and China through Indonesian waters has been the subject of considerable scholarly debate. The evidence would seem to indicate that those involved in this portion of the trade from the 300s to the 900s were largely Malays and other Indonesians.[48] The Chinese referred to these people as *K'un-lun*. Wang indicates that in the 600s these *K'un-lun* were sailing to Guangzhou every year and that one group of these traders was involved in the killing of a corrupt Chinese port official.[49]

By the late 600s and early 700s Palembang had become an important political, economic, and religious center for the region around the Strait of Melaka. The rulers of Srivijaya also developed close relations with the neighboring Sailendra rulers of central Java with whom they intermarried. Thus, prior to his becoming ruler the Sailendra Samaratungga married Dewi Tara, the daughter of the ruler of Srivijaya Dharmastu (r. *c.* 782). This relationship took an interesting turn when the Sailendras lost power to Hindu rivals around 852 and fled to Srivijaya as refugees. The Srivijayan rulers sought to develop ties with their more distant trading partners as well. Thus, they began sending emissaries to the Tang court in the early 700s.

In addition to promoting the spread of Buddhism locally, the Srivijayan rulers also promoted ties with fellow Buddhists in India, Sri Lanka, and China. Dharmastu, for example, is associated with the erection of three Buddhist sanctuaries in the vicinity of Ligor (modern Nakhon Si Thammarat in Thailand). Following the arrival of the Sailendra refugees in Srivijaya the ruler of Srivijaya financed the building of a Buddhist monastery at the Buddhist center of Nalanda (in modern Bihar), which was located within the Pala Empire, around 860. Casparis and Mabbett make the interesting point that whereas the Srivijanyans built few large Buddhist monuments in Sumatra, possibly because of the lack of a large population from which to recruit laborers, they did sponsor the building of "great monuments in countries as far away as India and China."[50] The latter refers to a temple that they had built in Guangzhou and is an indication of the significant presence of Malays in this

Chinese port. Wolters comments on the ways in which Buddhism and maritime trade complemented one another in reference to the role of Buddhist pilgrims in collecting commercial intelligence.[51] More generally, Buddhism helped to provide a cultural dimension to the links maintained by Srivijaya with its important trading partners.

Srivijaya's paramountcy in the Strait of Melaka area was challenged in the early 1000s. An expedition from Srivijaya attacked central Java in 1016 and the Javanese counter-attacked. Then in 1025 the Cholas sacked the Srivijayan capital and raided some of towns linked to Srivijaya on the Malay Peninsula. Economic changes were also beginning to undermine Srivijaya. Chinese merchants had begun to appear on their own ships in the 900s. By the 1100s the growing presence of Chinese ships in the waters had reduced the importance of local Malay ships for international commerce. Hall argues, "The effect of increased Chinese shipping was to disperse authority in the Malay world."[52] Malay ports in the region became increasingly independent, the Srivijiayan "system of paramountcy" began to unravel, and "the position of Palembang receded to the level of other ports with access to the Straits of Melaka."[53] Political authority shifted north to Palembang's rival Jambi (aka Malayu). In the late 1200s Srivijaya began to lose control of territory to the Javanese Tumpael-Singhasari Kingdom, which made Jambi a vassal state. Writing of the situation in the early 1400s, the modern editor of Ma Huan's account of Chinese expeditions to the region remarks, "Palembang had some economic importance in maritime commerce, though Djambi [Jambi] had replaced it as the capital of the state."[54]

From a transnational perspective, it would appear that one of the important developments during this period was the growth in the number of Chinese residing in and passing through the region. Ma Huan mentions that by the time of his visits in the early 1400s there were a large number of "men from Kuang tung [province] and from Chang [chou] and Ch'üan [chou], who fled away and now live in this country."[55] Later Ma Huan adds, "Some time ago, during the Hung-wu period [1368–98], some men from Kuang tung [province], Ch'en Tsu'i and others fled to the place with their whole households; [Ch'en Tsu'i] set himself up as a chief; he was very wealthy and tyrannical, and whenever a ship belonging to strangers passed by, he immediately robbed them of their valuables."[56] In effect, after 1377 Palembang became "a nest of Chinese pirates."[57] In response to this threat to commercial shipping, in 1407 Zheng He and his fleet intervened: "Ch'en Tsu-i and others were captured alive by the grand eunuch Cheng Ho [Zheng He] and taken back to the court; [and] they were put to death."[58] "Shih Chin-ch'ing who was also a man from Kuang tung" was also taken to China where he was made governor of Palembang.[59] After Shih Chin-ch'ing's death the emperor appointed his son governor. As Gordon notes, "There was a general idea at court that some of the Chinese in Southeast Asia were still connected to China, called the Central Country."[60]

Zheng He's activities also served to strengthen the position of Melaka as a new regional trading center as the Chinese offered protection for the local Malay ruler Paramesvara from threats by the Tai of Ayutthaya. As Taylor observes, "Paramesvara of Melaka took full advantage of this opportunity to place himself under Chinese protection. He welcomed the Chinese fleets, sent envoys to China, and in 1411 personally went to the Chinese capital to demonstrate his loyalty."[61]

Champa

Malayic speaking ancestors of the Cham migrated from Borneo to the coast of Vietnam as early as 600 B.C. First settling along the coast of what is now central and southern Vietnam, they also later moved inland along the Mekong River in eastern Cambodia and as far as Champasak Province in southern Laos. Some of these Malayo-Polynesian speaking people also settled in the adjacent highlands of central Vietnam. Archaeological evidence, especially bronze drums, indicates that there was some contact between the ancestral Cham and the Tai associated with Dongson Culture to the north, but the cultural orientation of the Cham was primarily seaward with the coastal regions of what are today the countries of Indonesia, Malaysia, and the Philippines. Stone jewelry made by Sa Huynh (a culture associated with the Malayo-Polynesian peoples of central Vietnam) craftsmen has been found in archaeological sites in coastal areas of Thailand, the Philippines, and Formosa, indicating the existence of maritime trade at this time. Evidence of the maritime activities of the Cham can also be seen in the close linguistic relationship between the Cham language and that of the Acehnese language in northern Sumatra.

As the Malayic speaking peoples who settled along the coast of the Mekong River Delta were drawn into long-distance maritime trade linking South Asia and China, Oc Eo emerged as an especially important trading center for the transshipment of goods as well as for providing goods from its hinterland for trade and as provisions for sailors. As was mentioned previously, Oc Eo and the associated region known as Funan sent emissaries to the kingdom of Wu in relation to trade in the early A.D. 200s. As was also noted, some of the Cham living further to the north had come under Chinese rule until K'iu Lien (aka Ou Lien) successfully rebelled in A.D. 192. Despite contact with the Chinese through commerce and conquest, Han culture exerted little if any lasting influence on the Cham. Instead the dominant external cultural influence came from distant South Asia in the form of the adoption of Hindu and Buddhist religious beliefs, a system of writing derived from South Asia, and notions of statecraft.

The Chinese referred to K'iu Lien's kingdom, located in the vicinity of modern Hue, as Lin Yi and to the Cham it was known as Shri Mara.[44] Eventually the Cham established a larger kingdom commonly known as Champa (not to be confused with the Indian kingdom of the same name) that at its height stretched from just north of Saigon (Baigaur in Cham) in the south to Ngang Pass in Vietnam's Quang Binh Province in the north. Thus, it occupied most of the coastal region of what is today central and southern Vietnam. Champa reached its greatest extent from the A.D. 700s to the mid–900s. Despite periodic wars with its neighbors and gradual loss of territory to Dai Viet starting in 1069, it remained an important kingdom into the late 1400s — Dai Viet annexed a large part of Champa in 1471 — and was not completely conquered until 1832. Thus, the kingdom of Champa had an incredibly long history, stretching from the latter part of the ancient period, throughout the medieval period, and into early modern times.

International trade was extremely important for Champa and was largely responsible for the kingdom's considerable wealth. Some sense of the kingdom's wealth and its economic resilience as a result of international commerce comes from accounts of the large amounts of loot taken away in the course of the periodic sackings of its capitals and the fact that the Cham were able to recover time and time again. The Southern Song emperor sent a large army to attack Champa in 446. The Southern Song army succeeded in defeating Champa's army and it sacked Champa's capital of Simhapura. This was the first of several sackings of a Cham capital by invading armies and the Chinese account notes that they found so much treasure and such a huge quantity "of extraordinary and rare objects that they were no longer called precious."[63] Maspero comments, "The huge loot taken from Champa by Tan Ho-chen [the Chinese general who sacked Simhapura] had left a deep impression on the Chinese. For them this kingdom had become a fabulous country in which gold and precious and curious objects were so abundant that one would not know what to do with them."[64] In the early 600s an army of the Sui emperor Yang Di (r. 604–618) defeated the Cham and sacked their capital, once again carrying off fabulous treasures, including a group of musicians from the neighboring kingdom of Funan. The Chinese were not accustomed to tropical diseases, however, and losses due to malaria and other tropical diseases soon forced the Sui army to retreat. Despite the loot from the Cham capital, Yang Di's ill-fated military ventures combined with large-scale construction projects left his empire bankrupt and prompted the population to revolt, leading to the fall of the Sui Dynasty.

The early history of Champa's maritime trade is poorly understood. Using Chinese sources relating to the Cham ruler Fan Yi (r. ?–336; Fan is a title), who sent the first Champa embassy to the Western Jin Empire in 284, Maspero mentions an important aid of Fan Yi named Wen.[65] Wen was Chinese and had been captured and sold into slavery as a boy. He ran away and "sought refuge with a Cham merchant whose trading activities obliged him to make long journeys."[66] In the service of this merchant, Wen "visited many countries, stayed in China under the Min emperor around the year 315, and finally returned to settle in Champa, where he went into the service of Fan Yi."[67] Wen managed to become king after Fan Yi's death as Fan Wen (r. 336–49).

Prior to the founding of Champa, Oc Eo on the southern coast of the Mekong Delta region had served as the major regional port. With the rise of Champa maritime trade shifted northward and international shipping began to frequent the ports of Champa especially the southern port of Panduranga (Phan Rang). It is interesting to note that Panduranga maintained a fair degree of autonomy within Champa and served as the kingdom's most important center of international commerce: "Here at the extreme southern edge of the Cham realm the 'ferocious' threatening foreigners could be isolated."[68] However, trade goods also were shipped from the more northerly port of Bini (modern Qui Nhon), near the Cham capital of Cha Ban (1000–1471), and while most foreigners do appear to have carried out their activities in Panduranga foreigners were to be found elsewhere in the kingdom as well.

Although maritime shipping from the Malay ports to southern China sometimes bypassed the Cham ports, incentives to stop on their way to and from southern China included not only using the ports to take on provisions, but more importantly the desire to trade for local goods. Such goods included valuable agar wood (often called aloe wood in the European literature; it will be discussed in detail later) as well as sandalwood, camphorwood, gold, cinnamon, cardamom, beeswax, lacquer, elephant ivory, rhinoceros horn, tortoiseshell, pearls, peacock and kingfisher feathers, and areca nuts.[69] Another important item that is often not included in lists of Champa's trade goods is ceramics. Glazed celadon and stoneware mainly from Bini (Qui Nhon) in Champa's Vijaya Province (modern Binh Dinh Province) was produced and exported in relatively large quantities until the late 1400s. Ceramics from Vijaya Province have been found in archaeological sites along the coasts and in shipwrecks in the Philippines, Indonesia, Thailand, Malaysia, as far north as Japan and west as far as the Sinai Peninsula.

Trade with China was especially important. The Cham ruler Jaya Simhavarman V (r. 1400–41) sent a delegation to the Ming emperor to ask for assistance against Dai Viet. The Ming did intervene and assumed control over Dai Viet, until Le Loi forced them out in 1428 and re-established Dai Viet's independence. Jaya Simhavarman V was able to regain control of the provinces that he had lost to Dai Viet and began sending costly annual tribute to the Chinese emperor. Maspero notes that the tribute was also paid because "the Cham had commercial interests in China's markets."[70]

Foreigners trading with Champa included mainly Chinese, Malays, and Javanese. The close relationship that developed between Champa and the Javanese kingdoms in the 700s included not only intermarriage between nobles and an intermingling of religious ideas and architectural styles, but also trade partnerships. The increasing importance of Muslim traders was evident in Champa by the 900s. Muslim traders included Chinese Muslims from the ports of southern China as well as Persians and Arabs. Two Muslim gravestones dating from the early 1000s have been found in Champa. Muslim involvement in Champa's international trade had grown considerably by the 1400s, and, as evidenced by the marriage of Champa's Princess Davavati's sister to a Muslim Arab in the early 1400s, this presence was not confined to traders found in Champa's ports. The king of Champa did not convert to Islam until the 1600s, but prior to this at least a small number of Cham had converted. During the early modern period there were also a few Europeans coming to Champa to trade. Nicolo de Conti visited Champa in 1435: "Having left the Giave [Java] isles and taken with him things that could be traded, he headed west toward a maritime city called Champa, rich in aloe wood [agar wood], camphor, and gold."[71]

As noted above, in addition to commercial relations there were also diplomatic, religious, and marriage relations between the people of Champa and other kingdoms. Champa and China frequently exchanged ambassadors and Champa periodically sent tribute to the Chinese emperor. Ambassadors were also exchanged periodically between Champa and Dai Viet. The Cham ruler Jaya Sinhavarman III (r. ?-1307), for instance, sent an ambassador to Dai Viet to mark the accession of a new Tran Dynasty (1225–1400) ruler there, Tran Anh-ton, in 1293. The new emperor of Dai Viet's father had abdicated and entered a Buddhist monastery, where he assumed the name Thuong Wang. Desiring to visit holy places in neighboring countries, when another embassy from Champa arrived in Dai Viet in 1301, Thuong Wang accompanied it on its return trip to Champa. Thuong Wang lived in Jaya Sinhavarman III's court for nine months and, as Maspero records, the Cham ruler "was so kind to him that before his departure he promised him the hand of one of his daughters."[72] Jaya Sinhavarman III had already married a daughter of the ruler of the Javanese kingdom of Majaphahit and now sought to marry a noblewoman from Dai Viet as well. Members of the Dai Viet court were strongly opposed to the marriage, but negotiations proceeded despite these protests. The marriage between Jaya Sinhavarman III and princess Huyen Tran finally took place in 1306 and in exchange for the royal bride Champa ceded a significant portion of its northern territory (including the northern province of Indrapura). Jaya Sinhavarman III died a short time after his marriage and, following rather delicate negotiations, the princess was allowed to return to Dai Viet rather than following Cham custom and being burned on the pyre of her deceased husband to accompany him to the next life.[73]

As indicated above, the rulers of Champa also maintained relations with Hindu and later Muslim nobles on the island of Java. There was some intermarriage between noble families. There is also mention of a man named Po Klun Pilih Rajadvara who served four of the rulers of Champa in the late 800s and early 900s and twice was sent to Java "to obtain a knowledge of magic."[74] Jaya Simhavarman III's older sister married a Muslim Arab and converted to Islam, while the younger sister, Daravati, went to Java to marry the ruler of the kingdom of Majaphahit. The king of Majaphahit was a Buddhist, but when the son of Daravati's older sister, Raden Rahmat, visited Java he was allowed to settle near Surabaya and to propagate the Muslim religion. Oral history in Java credits this Cham prince with introducing Islam to Java and the story also points to the growing influence of Islam in Champa itself.

There are a number of accounts from Champa of people moving about internationally for religious purposes. One of the earliest of these concerns Ti Chen, the son of Fan Hou Ta (aka Bhadravarman I, r. 380–413), who had established a new capital at Simhapura ("Lion City") east of modern Danang and is also credited with initiating construction of the first structure at the nearby temple complex of My Son. Following his father's death Ti Chen (aka Gangaraja) assumed the throne, which he then abdicated in order to undertake a pilgrimage to the Ganges River in India — a trip from which he did not return. Maspero remarks, "During this period when the unknown seas were populated with terrors, navigators who undertook such journeys were scarce and rarer still were kings who did so. Of all those who reigned in eastern Indochina whose names we possess, he is the only one to have undertaken such a journey."[75] There appears to have been some movement of religious personages from India to Champa as well. Thus, an account mentions that the Dai Viet army that sacked the capital of Champa in 982 brought back with them not only treasure but also "a hundred women of the king's entourage" and "an Indian monk."[76]

The attacks on Champa by Dai Viet over the centuries not only resulted in the absorption of a portion of the Cham population into that of Dai Viet, but also created a flow of refugees. The first mention of such refugees concerns a group of Cham in the northern part of Champa who fled northward into Chinese territory where they settled on Hainan Island as a result of attacks by Dai Viet in 986. Their descendants on Hainan Island are known as Utsuls and their language is referred to as Tsat. Champa suffered a major defeat at the hands of Dai Viet in 1044 that resulted in the death of the Cham ruler, the sacking of its capital (once again), and the forcible resettlement on some 5,000 Cham in southern Dai Viet (in modern Nghe An Province). Subsequent attacks on Champa from the 1400s until the final fall of Champa resulted in large numbers of Cham migrating west to Cambodia, Thailand, and Malaysia. While there are some contemporary transnational relations between Cham who scattered as a result of these later dispersals, the Utsuls lost contact with their fellow Cham and have not re-established relations.

5

Long-distance Trade Goods

A look at the main trade goods is central to our discussion of transnationalism in the ancient and medieval worlds, since it was the search for and movement of such goods that provided the basis for most transnational relations during both periods. We have mentioned a number of different goods that were traded over long distances in the previous three chapters. In the present chapter we will examine the most important of these goods in more detail. It is interesting to note that many of the same goods were traded in both periods. Differences in part reflect the marginality of Europe to international trade following the decline and fall of the Roman Empire. Few goods were shipped to Europe and Europe exported little to the rest of the world after the fall of Rome. The major markets were to be found in China and the Middle East, and international commerce reflected the needs and tastes of peoples in these regions.

Obsidian

Obsidian is a volcanic glass that is usually black. It breaks to produce razor-sharp edges and prior to the advent of metal blades was greatly valued throughout the world as a source of cutting implements. It is found worldwide, but readily only in certain areas of volcanic activity. Its desirability to all Neolithic peoples, many of whom lived at some distance from sources of obsidian, led to the emergence of trade in the volcanic glass as early as 14,000 B.C. Archaeologists Renfrew, Dixon, and Cann also have pointed to another characteristic of obsidian that is of considerable value in the study of ancient trade: it has characteristics that allow its point of origin to be determined.[1]

Renfrew and his colleagues focused on the Middle East where in ancient times the main sources of obsidian were located in Anatolia (modern Turkey). Especially important sources were in Cappadocia in central Anatolia and further east in and around Bingöl. As early as 14,000 to 12,000 B.C. obsidian from these sources was being transported to distant lands in Mesopotamia via what archaeologists call the Hilly Flanks route and the Levant via what they refer to as the Levantine Corridor. This trade grew more extensive as the weather warmed between 12,000 and 9500 B.C. and obsidian from these northern sources was traded along the Euphrates River and throughout the Levant. The amount of obsidian finding its way along these routes grew considerably with the founding of early farming communities between 9500 and 8500 B.C. By this later date it is even found as far as southern

Cyprus. Even after metal made its appearance, obsidian continued to be traded and used in the Middle East. Thus, archaeological excavations at a site dated 4500 to 3500 B.C. at Gilat, Israel, have turned up obsidian from three locales in Anatolia.[2]

Obsidian was also traded from very early dates along the volcanic rim of the western Pacific. The oldest archaeological evidence of obsidian trade in this region comes from the Bismarck Archipelago northeast of New Guinea. The islands of the archipelago were settled by sea around 35,000 to 30,000 years ago. Archaeological research on Manus Island in the Admiralty Islands in the northwest of the Bismarck Archipelago indicates that obsidian from Lou Island was being taken to Manus 12,000 years ago. Peoples speaking Proto-Oceanic variants of Malayo-Polynesian languages arrived in the area around 3000 B.C. on outrigger canoes and developed what is known as the Lapita Culture some time later.[3] Bellwood has characterized these people as "highly mobile groups of sea-borne colonists and explorers who expanded very rapidly throughout Melanesia."[4] The culture's classic period in the Bismarck Archipelago dates from 1350 to 750 B.C. Evidence of Lapita Culture ranges to the west from Aitape in the central northern coast of New Guinea and eastward out into the Pacific to the Solomon Islands, Vanuatu, and New Caledonia. Lapita people were the first settlers of Fiji, Tonga, and Samoa between 1300 and 800 B.C. Lapita Culture is associated in particular with distinctive pottery. In addition to pottery, the items found in Lapita sites include obsidian blades. Lapita people not only settled distant islands but also developed long-distance trade and transport of goods by canoe. Thus, obsidian from Talasea on New Britain in the Bismarck Archipelago was carried on outriggers as far as the Reef Islands of the Santa Cruz Group (2,000 km) and New Caledonia (2,600 km).[5] While colonizers may simply have carried some of the obsidian found in Lapita sites with them,[6] in other instances the distribution was the result of trade.

Green has characterized the Lapita people as mobile traders in an area already settled by peoples speaking Papuan and Trans–New Guinea languages.[7] Some idea of the possible nature of how they organized trade comes from ethnographic accounts of trade relations along the coasts and offshore islands of New Guinea. The pattern of settlement of the Malayo-Polynesian speaking descendants of the Lapita people is to first found communities on the small offshore islands that are found all along the coast, and in some locales then to establish villages facing the sea on the coasts. In some cases settlements are established next to important resources such as clay deposits for making pottery. Such pottery-producing villages still exist in Papua at Batu Pulau (in Jayapura Bay), Abar (in Lake Sentani), Tarfia (west of Demta), Serui Laut (on Yapen Island), and Mansinam (near Manokwari).[8] Pottery from these villages is traded to other offshore island and coastal communities as well as to some located in the hinterland of the mainland that are part of a series of trade networks that also involve trade in goods besides pottery (such as woven bast-fiber cloth that was produced in a few specialized villages). There were three main trading areas along the north coast of Papua: one involving the communities in and surrounding Cenderawsih Bay; another, communities along the coast and on adjacent islands from the mouth of the Mamberamo River to the vicinity of Demta; and a third around the Jayapura area. Locally produced goods rarely traveled between these areas or beyond. Such wider regional trade only began about 2,000 years ago when Bronze Age traders from further west began to visit in search of trade goods. If obsidian was traded so extensively to the east by Lapita traders this was possibly because of its not being available within the local trading networks, thereby requiring that it be carried across their boundaries.

Trading obsidian was also important in the New World, where metal implements were largely unknown until the arrival of Europeans. Obsidian was traded extensively throughout North America and South America. The ancient Mesoamericans used obsidian to make both utilitarian cutting implements and implements for ritual bloodletting and sacrifices. In the case of ancient Mexico and Guatemala, obsidian was obtained primarily from a limited number of highland locales. Thus, almost all of the obsidian found in ancient Maya sites comes from four sources in the Guatemala highlands (Tajumulco, El Chayal, Ixtepeque, and San Martin Jilotepeque). Hammond, for example, found that obsidian from two highland sites occurred in 23 Classic Maya sites.[9]

Teotihuacán in central Mexico engaged in extensive long-distance obsidian trade and while there are a number of sources in the highlands of central Mexico, the milky green-gold colored obsidian from Pachuca was especially valued. Long-distance trade was of considerable importance to the lowland Maya who sought to obtain a variety of goods that were not locally available (including obsidian) from the highlands of Guatemala. Rathje argues that such long-distance trade played a crucial role in the development of states among the lowland Maya.[10] Making blades from raw obsidian by the ancient lowland Maya was centralized in such locales as Tikal, Uaxactun, and Palenque, and from there it was redistributed or traded to other places. Pires-Ferreira makes a similar case regarding the emergence of early states in the highlands of central Mexico, where specialist obsidian blade monopolies developed within the context of regional redistributive economies.[11] Again, ethnographic accounts help to give us an idea of how the trade was organized among the Maya.

The Kekchi Maya (aka Q'eqchi') are indigenous to the Alta Verapaz region of the highlands of Guatemala and also live in the adjacent lowlands of the Peten and in southern Belize. They migrated to Belize in the 1800s. Young Kekchi men, called *Cobaneros* after the town of Coban in Alta Verapaz, travel—walking along the jungle trails on foot with their goods on their backs—to the Kekchi and Mopan Maya villages of southern Belize as traders.[12] They pass through the villages selling a variety of handicrafts (including items made of volcanic stones) and commercial goods not locally available or that are more expensive in local markets. These traders often establish social relationships with families in these lowland villages to facilitate their travels and in some instances these young men eventually marry local women and settle in the lowlands as farmers.

Beads

In his foreword to Dubin's *The History of Beads from 30,000 B.C. to the Present* Liu makes the point that "beads are probably the first durable ornaments humans possessed."[13] The earliest beads in fact predate 30,000 B.C. and were found in the Neanderthal site of La Quina, France, dating from around 38,000 B.C., making them the oldest form of human figurative art known.[14] Of particular interest here, however, is not just bead making but the trading of beads. While many early beads were made of relatively common locally available materials such as clay, bone, and shells, between 8,000 and 6,500 B.C. bead-making industries developed in Asia using stones (e.g., agate, carnelian, jasper, fossilized coral, lapis lazuli, and sometimes obsidian) that were available only in certain locales. By 6,500 B.C. beads were being traded throughout the Middle East: "Made of scarce, durable, and easily recognizable raw materials to which commercial value could be easily assigned, and produced in small, standardized, and readily portable sizes, beads became a major commodity for traders."[15]

The early trade was a two-step process by which the raw materials would be shipped to centers of production and then on to markets. The Sumerians had a fondness for beads made of lapis lazuli. The lapis lazuli used to make the beads came from the Badakshan region of Afghanistan, 2,000 km away from Sumer and outside of its political control. Tosi and Piperno describe this trade, as it existed around 2600 to 2400 B.C.[16] The raw material was shipped to towns such as Shahr-i Sokhta on the Iranian Plateau. Here the limestone surrounding the lapis lazuli was removed and then small blocks of lapis lazuli were sent on to the urban centers of Sumer where the beads were made and then traded throughout the region. Ur was an especially important center of bead making.

In addition to lapis lazuli, Afghanistan was (and remains) an important source of agate and turquoise, from which beads were also made. The royal tombs of Ur also contain beads made of carnelian, gold, and silver. The gold and silver was imported from a variety of sources, while the carnelian came by sea from the trading centers of the Indus River Valley. Beads made of glass have been found in sites associated with the Akkad Dynasty in Mesopotamia (2340 to 2180 B.C.)[17] and from the Caucasus region (dating about 2400 B.C.).[18] Glass beads were an important trade item for the Phoenicians, who were highly skilled glass-makers.

The ancient Greeks also made glass beads and Rhodes was an important production site around 300 B.C.[19] The most common type of glass bead produced in Rhodes was a small, monochrome oblate-shaped bead that was made from tubes with constrictions that formed bulges that were cut apart to form the beads.[20] This same style of bead was later to be made in Egypt, in Alexandria[21] in Roman times and later in Fustat.[22] Beads from these two sources were traded extensively throughout Europe, the Middle East, and Africa.

Dubin comments, "The manufacturing and trading of glass beads on a truly global scale commenced with the Romans."[23] She adds, "Everywhere the Romans went they brought glass beads to trade."[24] Francis points out, however, that most of these beads were not made by ethnic Romans, but by other peoples living within the Roman Empire.[25] Thus, Egypt (the towns of Alexandria and Fustat in particular), which had already become an important center of glass bead manufacturing around 300 B.C. during the Greek period, remained a center of production under the Romans (and under Muslim rule as well). As Francis notes, while some styles of glass bead were produced by the Egyptians for relatively short periods, others "were essentially unchanged for some 1,500 years."[26] Glass beads manufactured in the Roman Empire found their way as far north as Scandinavia, southward in Africa to Mali and Ethiopia, and eastward throughout the Middle East, to India, Sri Lanka, the Isthmus of Kra (Khlong Thom), southern Vietnam (Oc Eo), and as far as China and Korea.

The ancient bead industry in South Asia and Southeast Asia is identified primarily with beads made from carnelian and agate. As in the Middle East, the source of bead material (and the material for making the bits used to drill the holes in the beads) and the place of manufacture were different, giving rise to trade over varying distances. The earliest evidence of making carnelian beads comes from Mergarth, Pakistan, dating from around 4000 B.C.[27] During the period of Harappan Civilization (2600–1300 B.C.) bead centers were found in several locales, such as the urban centers of Harappa and Mohenjo-Daro as well as closer to the sources of raw materials such as at Lothal near the Gulf of Cambay and the Narmada River (which was a source of stones for bead-making).[28] Some of these Harappan beads were exported to Mesopotamia. By 200 B.C., Ujjain (located inland north of the Narmada River and Vinhya Range) had become an important center of bead making and gemstone working.[29] Beads were exported from here through the port of Barygaza at the mouth of the Narmada River to the Roman Empire. The wealth from these trades helped to turn Ujjain into the second largest city in India (and the ninth largest in the world) with a population of around 100,000.[30]

Beads were made in southern India as well (especially at the port cities of Arikamedu, located near Pondicherry, and Muziris, located at the mouth of the Ponnani River on the southwestern coast). Some of these were made of gemstones (such as almandine and hessonite garnet, amethyst, and beryl) and will be discussed in the section on gemstones, but the artisans of Arikamedu also made carnelian, black onyx, and banded agate beads. The sources of such stones in this case included rivers such as the Godavari and Krishna,[31] which flow into the Bay of Bengal in central India, far to the north of Arikamedu. Diamonds were also imported from the Golconda region of central India for use as drill bits in bead making. Tamils dominated the bead and gem industries and trade in southern India. The port of Muziris served as the main center for the export of beads to the Roman Empire and beads from Arikamedu were shipped to Muziris for re-export to the Roman Empire and eastward to Southeast Asia.

The maritime trade route from Arikamedu to the east during the Roman Period went across the Bay of Bengal to the Mon kingdoms of southern Burma, down the coast to the Isthmus of Kra, then across the Gulf of Thailand to Oc Eo, and from there north to Chinese territory and southeast to the islands of Indonesia. In addition to beads that were made in Arikamedu being exported along this route, local bead industries modeled on Arikamedu's developed at various locales such as at Khlong Thom (aka Khuan Luk Pat)[32] and Oc Eo.[33] As in India, the raw materials for making beads at these locales also had to be imported from elsewhere. In the case of Oc Eo the materials probably came from inland sources in the Central Highlands of Vietnam. Francis also argues that the bead makers themselves moved along this maritime route: "Before or at the abandonment of Arikamedu the bead makers went to Mantai [in northwestern Sri Lanka] (ca. 1st to 10th Century), Khuan Luk Pat ([southern] Thailand; ca. 2nd to 6/7th Century) and Oc Eo ([southern] Vietnam; ca. 2nd to 6th Century)."[34]

After the fall of Rome the European Mediterranean declined in importance as a market for beads, but bead making continued to be centered in Egypt, Syria, and the Levant from the 600s to the 1500s. The only difference was that this region became part of the Islamic world rather than the Roman world. Moreover, as Dubin notes, "Although Islamic craftsmen developed their own glassmaking aesthetics, fine Islamic glass beads were primarily derived from Roman Period beads made after the division of the empire in the late fourth century A.D."[35] Cities associated with glass bead making in the Middle East during this time (and earlier) include Alexandria, Fustat (modern Cairo), and Thebes in Egypt; Hebron, Jerusalem, Acre, Tyre, Damascus, Tripoli (Lebanon), Antioch, Armanaz, and Aleppo along or near the shores of the eastern Mediterranean; and Samara in Mesopotamia. Around 1400 Samarkand also emerged as a center of making glass beads. Muslim traders carried these beads throughout the Middle East, across the Indian Ocean, and throughout Africa.

In northern India, during the medieval period, bead making was no longer centered in Ujjain but moved to other locations nearer to the Gulf of Cambay, and the city of Cambay served as a center for their export to the Middle East and East Africa. In southern India, according to Francis, "When Mantai [in Sri Lanka] was abandoned the bead makers returned to India, probably somewhere near Nagapattinam, eventually to settle at Papanaidupet (Chittor District, Andhra Pradesh)," and within Southeast Asia "the bead makers at Khuan Luk Pat [Khlong Thom] apparently went to Kuala Selinsing (Malaysia; 6th to 10th Century) and then Sungai Mas (Malaysia; 9th to 13th Century). Those of Oc-Eo seem to have gone to Sathing Pra (Thailand; 7th to 10th Century) and then to Takua Pa (Thailand; 9th to 10th Century)."[36] More or less the same style of beads were made in the medieval period as in ancient South Asia and Southeast Asia; they were simply sometimes made in different places.

Textiles

The components of textile production include weaving technologies, weaving skills, thread materials and thread-making capabilities, and dyes and dyeing skills. These have never been distributed universally and the desire for clothing made of woven material has generated important trade relations from very ancient times up to the present. Flax (*Linum usitatissimum*) was the earliest plant to be domesticated in order to produce thread for weaving cloth (linen in this case). Textiles were being woven from flax thread by 6000 B.C.[37] Weaving with flax appears to have diffused from northern Iraq to southern Iraq, and on to Anatolia and Syria. Flax weaving then diffused from this region between 5000 and 3000 B.C. south to Egypt and west to Europe as far as Germany. The other important ancient fiber used in weaving was sheep's wool. Domesticated wooly sheep were known in the Middle East as early as 5000 B.C., but were not plentiful until around 3000 B.C.[38] The weaving techniques employed were relatively simple and the cloth generally was not dyed. While weaving was known in many parts of the Middle East by 3000 B.C., people living in many areas did not weave and there were definite centers of weaving and textile trading.

As Bernstein has remarked, "For most of recorded history, the primary manufactured trade commodity was cloth."[39] During the 2000s B.C. regional trade in textiles developed with the Sumerians of Ur being prominent exporters and traders of textiles. Wool thread and woolen textiles were among the main items exported from Ur.[40] Thus, the Sumerians shipped woolen textiles south to Magan (Oman) to exchange for copper. Between 1920 and 1740 B.C. the Assyrians of Assur in northern Mesopotamia were sending textiles north to their trading colonies (*karum*) on the Anatolian Plateau to exchange for lead and tin. Textiles were traded to the Iranian Plateau and beyond in exchange for lapis lazuli and other stones.[41] Possehl also points to important differences in trading cultures within the region, making a distinction between the market-based trade of the Mesopotamians (who comprised the main traders) and the prestige-conscious exchange of those with whom they traded on the Iranian Plateau.[42] Textiles were also exchanged for particular types of pottery.[43]

Two other fibers began to assume increasing importance in the ancient international textile trade: silk and cotton. Despite the often-repeated claim, the Han Chinese did not invent silk thread and silk weaving. In eastern Asia at least that honor goes to the ancestors of the Tai who lived along and to the south of the Yangtze River in ancient times in areas where the paper mulberry tree grew.[44] It is upon the leaves of the tree that silk worms (*Bombyx mori*) are mainly fed in eastern Asia. The Tai spread silk making across Mainland Southeast Asia, but it was the Chinese who conquered the early Tai silk-making kingdoms along the Yangtze River in the 300s B.C. and who came to dominate the commercial production of silk thread and cloth in eastern Asia and the subsequent export of silk cloth westward over the Silk Road.

There are, in fact, over 500 species of silkworm and many can be fed something besides the leaves of the paper mulberry. Weaving using thread from other varieties of silkworm was also found in various parts of South Asia and the Middle East in ancient times. Such silk is often described as wild or natural to distinguish it from silk made from the thread of the *Bombyx mori*. Thus, archaeologists have found such natural silk in graves dated 1500 to 1200 B.C. in Uzbekistan.[45] So-called wild silk was also well known and widely used for weaving cloth in ancient India. The reason for this distinction is that the thread of the *Bombyx mori* is far superior to thread from other varieties of silkworm[46] and this difference resulted in the thread and cloth made from it being exported westward from China. As an indication of how old this trade is, Barber cites chemical tests on antique silk textiles in Europe indicating that the thread was made of silk from China, including cloth from a tomb from Hohmichele, Germany, dating from the mid–500s B.C. and another from Altrier, Luxemburg, dating from the late 400s B.C.[47]

Cotton comes mainly from plants belonging to the genus *Gossypium*. There are 42 species of the genus, but only four are cultivated: *G. arboreum*, *G. herbaceum*, *G. hirsutum*, and *G. barbadense* (also known as Pima cotton and Sea Island cotton). The first two of these are indigenous to Asia and the latter two to the New World. One of the characteristics of these plants is that they grow well only in relatively dry climates, and they do not grow in the colder northern climates of Europe or Asia or very well in wet, humid tropical climates. The oldest evidence of cloth made from cotton in Asia comes from the Indus River Valley civilizations and dates from the 2000s B.C.,[48] although it is likely that the plant was being grown earlier. Interestingly, cloth made of mixed cotton and local wild silk threads has been found in southern India dating from around 1500 B.C.,[49] indicating that cotton thread was being made in this area at this time or that it was being imported from the north. The Assyrians imported cotton from India during the time of Sennacherib around 700 B.C.[50] By the 1st century A.D. traders from the Roman Empire were importing Indian cotton from the north Indian ports of Barbarikon and Barygaza via the Red Sea.[51] Indian varieties of cotton plants were introduced to Southeast Asia around this time, and although they did not grow well in the tropical climate that is characteristic of most of Southeast Asia, they grew well enough to meet local needs.

One important development in the medieval world in regard to textiles was the diffusion of cotton cultivation, the *G. herbaceum* variety in particular. Although India remained a major source of cotton, *G. herbaceum* cotton also was grown in other parts of Asia during the medieval period. Cotton began to be grown in the Middle East during the time of the Sassanid Empire (A.D. 226–651). The Moors introduced its cultivation to Spain in the 800s, but cotton was never widely grown in Europe. Although Egypt today is known as a major grower of cotton, it was not grown on a large scale there until after 1821. The trade in cotton cloth also increased as Muslim maritime traders shipped large amounts of Indian cotton eastward to Southeast Asia and west where it was traded throughout the Middle East and North Africa.

Copper and Bronze

Although copper is often singled out as the first metal to be adopted for human use, as Sherratt reminds us, "from the beginning" metallurgy was "a multimetallic tradition, embracing not only copper but also gold, silver, and lead."[52] Nevertheless, it is copper that dominated early metalworking during the so-called Copper Age.

There is no consensus on when copper was first used, but it is significant that all of the earliest sites where there is evidence of working with copper are also located near where it was mined and smelted. This gave rise to early specialized communities and social groups that engaged in the array of activities involved in obtaining, processing, and producing objects from metal. The oldest copper artifacts have been found in burial sites associated with the Mehrgarh Culture in Balochistan, Pakistan, that date from the Mehrgarh I Period (7700–5500 B.C.).[53] These burials also include lapis lazuli that was imported from Badakshan in Afghanistan, indicating some kind of link between these two early mining areas. During the later Mehrgarh period (5500–2600 B.C.) there is evidence of a considerable copper industry that includes copper tools. To the west, in Iran, Caldwell and his team of archae-ologists discovered copper artifacts and evidence of copper mining and smelting dated around 5000 B.C. at Tal-i Iblis (aka Tal-i Eblis) in the Kerman Range of western Iran—along with the oldest known oven for making bread.[54] Caldwell does not believe that those working with copper at this site were fulltime specialists. Other early mining and smelting sites in Iran include Sialk (near modern Kashan), Ahangaran (near modern Ghaen), and Veshnaveh (near modern Qom).[55] Over the next thousand or so years copper mining and making copper objects spread throughout the Middle East as far as Egypt to the southwest, to Anatolia in the west,[56] and north to Turkmenistan and the southern Ural Mountains.[57] Copper beads have been found in Sitagroi (Macedonia) dated around 4800 B.C.[58] and copper axes have been found in Switzerland dated around 3300 B.C.

As indicated in an Egyptian document on mining and metallurgy produced during the reign of Ramesses III (r. 1186–1155 B.C.), ancient Egypt obtained copper from a variety of sources.[59] Some were fairly close at hand, such as a copper mine at Bir Umm Fawakhir, located near Wadi Hammamat about halfway from the Nile (north of Luxor) and the Red Sea, which was located within Egyptian territory.[60] The Sinai Peninsula was a more distant important source of copper that initially lay outside of Egyptian territory. Prior to 3500 B.C. various tribal peoples—including the Horites, Rephaim, Edomites, Amalekites, and Medianites (nomads who came from the Arabian Peninsula)—settled in the vicinity of Jeb Katherina to mine turquoise and copper. A profitable trade in both turquoise and copper had developed with Egypt by 3500 B.C. By 2600 B.C. the Egyptians had established direct control over the area and established labor camps at the mines. These laborers were respon-sible for creating the Proto-Sinaitic alphabet. The copper and turquoise was transported from the mines to the port of Markha (near Abu Zneima), from where it was transported by ship across the Red Sea to Egypt. The goddess Hathor (goddess of love, music, and beauty) came to be associated with turquoise and Egyptian women often wore turquoise amulets. A large temple dedicated to Hathor was erected near the mines and many of the workers worshipped her. Timna (near Eilat in southern Israel) became another important source of copper. Timna is located in an area associated with the Edomites, but Medianites are also mentioned in association with the mines. The document from the time of Ramesses III mentioned above describes an expedition by ship and donkey to Timna to obtain copper. The Egyptian presence there was significant as indicated by the presence of another temple dedicated to Hathor that was built during the reign of Seti (aka Sethos) II (r. 1203–1197 B.C.).

The Egyptians also obtained copper from more distant locales. One of these was the important copper mining district of Fenan in Jordan,[61] where mining began some time between 3000 and 2000 B.C. The island of Cyprus was perhaps the most distant source of copper for ancient Egypt. Cyprus became a major source of copper in the ancient world—the name for the metal in many European languages is derived from *aes cyprium* in Latin, which means Cypriot copper.[62] Pharaoh Tutmose III (r. 1479–1425 B.C.) is reported to have received 108 ingots of copper from Cyprus as tribute.

In addition to evidence of the diffusion of copper-related technology throughout the Middle East and Europe, numerous copper objects have turned up in Copper Age archaeological sites in the Middle East, South Asia, and Europe that indicate the existence of trade in copper objects within regions. Production became increasingly refined as people learned to form the metal into thin sheets and these in turn into elaborate objects. Copper production became a highly skilled craft with a limited number of production centers. Thus, in the case of Europe, Sherratt argues, "sheet-working techniques were initially confined to specialized east Mediterranean workshops at centers like Troy or Mycenae, and only slowly spread to their European hinterlands," and such metalworking "was confined to a narrow set of social contexts and closely linked cultural traditions within it, initially in urban and para-urban settings."[63] The implication is that although traders could move the metal objects from their places of origin, to spread the technology required moving craftsmen or sending people to centers of production as apprentices.

The Bronze Age in the Middle East dates from 3300 B.C. to 1200 B.C. Bronze is an alloy that is 85–95 percent copper, with tin or arsenic making up most of the remaining 5–15 percent, and other metals sometimes present in small amounts. Arsenic ores are far more common than tin ores in the Middle East, and the first bronze was made using arsenic — which, of course, is also a poison. The Maykop Culture (c. 3500–2500 B.C.) of the vicinity of the Kuban River valley in the northern Caucasus produced the oldest bronze from an alloy of copper and arsenic, but bronze made with arsenic does not cast as well as that made with tin and gradually tin came to replace arsenic. The change was gradual, however, and bronze continued to be made with arsenic in Egypt, Crete, and the western Mediterranean long after its use had ceased elsewhere in the Middle East.

Bronze made with tin appears to have been first made in western Iran and by 3000 B.C. large numbers of bronze objects were to be found in the cities of Mesopotamia. Whereas copper mining was already well established around the Middle East, tin was rare. Tin mining was first developed in the Taurus Mountains of southeastern Turkey, an area that also contains deposits of gold, silver, and lead. Archaeologists have discovered more than 40 ancient mining sites in this region. One of these is the Göltepe (aka Kestel) mining complex. Yener reports that metal exploitation in this area began prior to the metal ages in the 7000s B.C.[64] The village associated with the Göltepe mine was occupied from around 3290 to 1840 B.C. The area does not have copper deposits and the tin was clearly exported from here on donkey caravans to centers of metal working and trading. Sargon of Akkad (r. 2334–2279 B.C.) invaded Anatolia around 2350 B.C. in large part to secure the sources of tin and other metals and the trade routes associated with them. Tin was carried from the mining region to Assur and then on to Assyrian merchant colonies (*kärum*) at Kültepe (c. 1974–1836 B.C.) and Acemhüyük (c. 2000–1800 B.C.), where it was sold to local smiths.

The dates for the Bronze Age in the Indus River Valley are similar to those in the Middle East — c. 3300 B.C. to 1500 B.C. It is associated with Harappan civilization and bronze artifacts from this period have been found over a wide area as far east as West Bengal and as far south as Karnataka.[65]

The Sintashta-Arcaim Culture developed as an important Bronze Age culture in the southern Ural Mountains between c. 2000 and 1600 B.C.[66] This Eurasian Bronze Age culture appears to have played a pivotal role in the diffusion of bronze technology across Central Asia to East Asia with the nomadic peoples of the steppes playing an intermediate role.[67]

The Chinese quest for jade in the western lands of these nomads and their adoption of the regions bronze technology helped to lay the basis for the creation of the overland trading network that came to be known as the Silk Road.

It is interesting to note that copper does not play a significant role in the early development of East Asian and Southeast Asian civilizations. Small quantities of copper artifacts have been found scattered about the region dating back as far as 4000 B.C., but copper in this part of the world only seems to have become significant with the onset of the bronze age in its role as the primary ingredient for making bronze.

The earliest bronze objects from China are associated with Qijia and Majiayao cultures (*c.* 3100–1700 B.C.) in Gansu Province along the upper Yellow River and have been dated around 2000 B.C.[68] This was a frontier region between the Han Chinese heartland to the east and the deserts and steppes to the north and west. The Hexi Corridor within the province later formed an important part of the Silk Road by which trade goods moved to and from China. A center of bronze production developed further to the east at Erilitou, in Henan. During the Neolithic Period, Gansu was at the western extremity of what is known as Yangshao Culture (5000–3000 B.C.) and Erilitou at the eastern end, with the Wei and Yellow rivers flowing through the territory. During the Erilitou Period (*c.* 1900–1350 B.C.), the number and size of settlements along the Yellow River increased significantly and Erilitou itself emerged as China's first major urban center. There is no evidence of bronze production or craft specialization at smaller sites associated with Erilitou culture, but at Erilitou itself there were craft specialists and bronze casting was carried out in specialized workshops. It is also interesting to note that it was not only bronze making technology that diffused to China at this time. Wheat (*Triticum aestivum*), which is native to southwestern Asia, also arrived around 1500 B.C.

Political power in this region came to be identified with what is called Erligang Culture of the Early Shang period from the 1400s to 1300s B.C. Important sites associated with this culture are located at Zhangzhou (east of Erilitou) and Yanshi (near Leoyang and west of Erilitou), both of which are also located in Henan Province. Erligang expanded rapidly and exerted influence over an extensive area in northeastern China, but its power declined in less than 200 years. Bronze production increased during the Erligang period and knowledge of the technology spread to neighboring polities and peoples, although the means of this diffusion is unknown. The expansion of Erligang political and cultural influence to the south appears to have been closely linked to the search for supplies of copper and other metals that were to be found most plentifully beyond the Han region south of the Yangtze River. Bagley has described Panlongchen, which was located in eastern Hubei on a tributary of the Yangtze River, 450 km to the south of Erligang, as a "site of Erligang civilization" where the "indigenous population was ruled by an intrusive Erligang elite."[69] The reason for this intrusion so far from home appears to have been the desire to provide security for the trade routes that brought copper from even further south — the closest being about 100 km to the south of Panlongchen. Panlongchen itself developed into a center of bronze making, indicating that artisans from the bronze making centers of Erligang Culture to the north probably settled in the city along with Erligang elites and soldiers.

Erligang Culture appears to be responsible for the introduction of bronze technology to the peoples living along and to the south of the Yangtze River, and Erligang bronzes appear in numerous sites in this region. As was noted above, this contact initially was related to the copper trade. The underground and open-pit copper mines at Tonglong (near Ruichang City, Jiangxi Province), dating from around 1300 B.C., are the oldest mines discovered so far in China. The mines are associated with the local Wucheng Culture. Bagley refers to Wucheng having "received the Erligang stimulus" and having "a ruling class wealthy enough to a supply large-scale bronze industry with raw materials and to support specialized workers employing a complex foundry technology."[70] He adds, "We might speculate that the Wucheng culture owed its wealth to the copper trade."[71]

As was discussed in an earlier chapter, the lands along the Yangtze River were inhabited in particular by the ancestors of the Tai peoples, who were associated with the formation of a series of early kingdoms located along the Yangtze and to the south that include what are now Sichuan, Jiangxi, Hunan, Anhui, Jiangsu, Zhejiang, Fujian, and Guangdong provinces. Von Falkenhausen comments, "Local bronze-casting industries, established already during the Erligang period, appear to have expanded in tandem with the increased intensity of mining. The ore was smelted close to the mines and the raw material was cast into ingots of portable size, which could be traded.... Such activities must have played an important role in the economy of the area and should not be underestimated as possible factors in the rise of the Wu and Yue kingdoms."[72] Fertile lands for growing rice provided the initial impetus for economic growth and political development in this region and prior to the Bronze Age they were already engaged in some long-distance trade.

The Baodun Culture of Sichuan flourished in the fertile rice-growing areas of Sichuan from around 2500 to 1200 B.C. Burial sites in the vicinity of Sanxingdui that date from the end of this period have revealed considerable wealth in jade and bronze. Ba and Shu, located in Sichuan, are the oldest of the Yangtze kingdoms and emerged some time around this time. The kingdom of Chu emerges somewhat later and it too possessed fertile rice-producing lands and is associated with wealth in bronze, jade, and silk. The eastern Yangtze kingdom of Wu possessed important copper mines in the hills of southern Anhui and Jiangsu provinces and the kingdom was associated in particular with large-scale mining, smelting, and bronze casting as well as with playing an important role in the development of porcelain. Wu also seems to be linked with Japan, where the ancient Wo people claim to have come from Wu. Tai polities in the Yue region also had an important bronze making tradition.

All of these local kingdoms along the Yangtze River and to the south developed distinctive bronze traditions in terms of techniques, the types of object they made, and the motifs found on them. The bronze of Wu and Yue was particularly noteworthy for its use of more tin in the alloy than elsewhere. Von Falkenhausen remarks, "Over time, local casters' technical versatility improved to a point at which extremely fine casting was possible."[73] The bronze casters of the courts of Wu and Yue were famous for the weapons that they made, including bronze blades with gold inlay. Bronze items were traded over a wide area and often were given as gifts to nobles of other states. Commenting on Chu bronzes found in the tombs of Wu nobles, von Falkenhausen speculates, "They may have reached Wu as war booty, through trade, or as tokens of political or marriage alliance."[74] The extent to which bronze objects were traded or given as gifts can clearly be seen from a tomb found at Moutuo (Maoxian, Sichuan), dating 500 B.C., the contents of which "strike one as being the most heterogeneous of those known from the entire East Asian bronze Age."[75] The tomb contains local bronzes as well as bronzes from the Western Zhou, Chu, the Huai River basin, Yunnan, and the Central Eurasian steppes.

As was mentioned in an earlier chapter, some of the most distinctive bronze objects made by these southern peoples were drums. These spectacular drums received attention in early Chinese writings on the southern barbarians as well as from European scholars.[76] Bronze objects from the Yangtze region were traded south along the coasts and rivers to

Neolithic peoples in the vicinity of modern Guangzhou and Hong Kong and as far south as northern Vietnam. Higham writes, "The period which saw the arrival of exotic bronzes from the *zhongyuan* and the middle reaches of the Yangtze saw, in the context of the Late Neolithic, the beginnings of a local tradition in casting which involved the production in bronze of a limited range of artifacts long since rendered in stone or bone."[77] This development appears to have taken place around 1300 to 1000 B.C.[78] More sophisticated bronze items, including the large drums, are associated with what is commonly referred to as the Dongson Culture (*c.* 600 to 200 B.C.) of northern Vietnam. This period coincides with the establishment of political rule over the area by Tai nobles associated with the northern kingdoms of Chu and Yue. Similar developments occurred in Yunnan, where the leader of a Tai army from Shu established the kingdom of Tien (Dian) around 310 B.C. after being cut off from his homeland when the Qin conquered it in 316 B.C.

Tai bronze making spread with the Tai throughout Mainland Southeast Asia. The bronze drums that they made also came to be highly regarded by non–Tai peoples in the region and a trade in these drums developed. Cooler describes the last bronze drum-making center at Nwe Daung in Kayah State, Burma, where Shan (the local Tai people) metalworkers were still making bronze drums in the late 1800s.[79] These drums were "sold to various sub-groups of the Karen as well as to tribal groups in Thailand and Laos such as the Lamet, and Tsa Khmu."[80] Older bronze drums are also found among highland peoples in Vietnam. One of Cooler's informants estimated that 100 drums were produced yearly and that they were taken away on foot by various tribes.[81] Shan craftsmen, who were forced to settle in Nwe Daung by a local Karen chief, made the drums — "every house had its individual compound and the bronze casters used their compounds for transacting business."[82] Cooler refers to "master bronze casters" who passed on their knowledge to members of the families and who were required to recite prayers and whose work was surrounded by behavioral proscriptions and rituals.[83] Not only did these highland tribes use the bronze drums, but they also played a symbolic role in establishing relations between these groups and lowland rulers. Even today one of the events of the Royal Ploughing Ceremony that is associated with the monarch of Thailand involves a parade that includes Karen playing bronze drums.

While archaeological evidence points to the existence of long-distance trade in bronze items involving these southern states and territories further to the south in ancient times, the nature of this trade is difficult to determine. Nineteenth century accounts of the trade in bronze drums at Nwe Daung provide an idea as to how the trade probably took place in ancient times as well. It should be noted that Nwe Daung was not just a center of bronze drum production, but an important center for the production of several types of items including other objects made of bronze as well as a special type of shoulder-bag. The shoulder-bags and other bronze objects were traded all over northern Burma whereas the bronze drums were traded over a more extensive area.[84] Nwe Daung also served as a trading center to which people came from northern Burma, northern Thailand, and Laos over established trade routes to obtain the drums and other items rather than as a distribution center from which people in Nwe Daung carried the trade items elsewhere: "The drums were cast and awaiting purchase when a customer arrived."[85] In addition to the initial purchase the drums were also sold second-hand, taken as war booty, and exchanged as gifts. Evidence of the latter practice is still to be seen in Thailand where drums are on display in various palaces and temples where vassals of rulers and those wishing to make merit have given them as gifts.

Large numbers of Dongson era bronze drums have also been found in burial sites in

Dak Lak Province in the Central Highlands of Vietnam. How they got there remains some-thing of a mystery, but they point to the links that existed between the Tai people of northern Vietnam and the peoples to the south such as the Cham.

Another mystery that has intrigued scholars for quite some time is just how these drums made it as far as the Bomberai Peninsula in western Papua. Swadling has linked the presence of Dongson bronze artifacts in eastern Indonesia to the trade in Bird of Paradise (Cenderawasih) feathers.[86] The bird is found in significant numbers in certain part of the north coast of Papua (such as Yapen Island and the Cyclops Mountains near Lake Sentani), and Swadling argues that these are the bird feathers represented prominently on many of the human figures appearing on Dongson bronze drums in Vietnam. After the fall of the Ou Lo kingdom in northern Vietnam to the Qin general Zhao Tuo in 208 B.C. and the regions coming under the rule of Nam Yue, the nature and routes of trade changed to focus on the islands further west and trading for sandalwood.

As with the bronze drums made at Nwe Daung, it is unlikely that Tai traders from northern Vietnam sailed south into Indonesia. Rather, it is more likely that Malay-speaking traders from the south came to northern Vietnam during the Dongson period just as the Malay maritime traders from Oc Eo and Champa are known to have sailed to the region at a later date. In the case of Papua, the feathers and drums (along with other goods) that were traded probably passed through several hands before arriving at their destinations. Towards the north the Malay traders of Oc Eo and other locales of southern Vietnam may have played a role in moving goods. Within Indonesia itself there were numerous long-established trade networks. At the Papuan end there was also a well-established trade route from the islands of Ternate and Tidore to Biak Island in Cenderawasih Bay.[87] The Biak Islanders acted as intermediaries for the long-distance traders. The traders of Biak established trade relationships (known as *manibob* or trade friends) with those living around the bay and exchanged imported goods for local ones. The Biak Islanders sometimes established permanent or temporary communities around the bay to serve as bases for trade.

Gemstones

The gemstone trade began in the ancient Middle East in relation to the emergence of civilizations in Egypt and Mesopotamia. Gemstones were greatly sought after in the ancient world and not simply to be used for decorative purposes. They were often assigned sacred qualities and believed to have mystical powers. Moorey mentions a document from ancient Assur in Mesopotamia that lists 54 stones as being suitable for magical amulets.[88] Ancient Egypt was fortunate in that there were a number of local sources of gems, whereas Mesopotamia had to import its gems. Besides Egypt, gemstones were obtained primarily from sources scattered throughout the northern arch of mountains from Anatolia to Afghan-istan and northern Pakistan. As today, most gemstones were collected from river sands and gravel or rock fissures located on or near the earth's surface. The Egyptians appear to have been the first to mine gemstones from quarries. Relatively little has changed in this regard. As Schumann has remarked, "With the exception of diamonds, mining methods in most countries are very primitive. In some districts, they have not changed in the last 2000 years."[89]

The most famous passage relating to gemstones in the ancient world appears in Exodus (28: 17–22) in the Old Testament of the Bible, written around 1300 B.C.: "And you shall make a breast-piece of judgment, in skilled work; ... you shall make it: of gold, blue and purple and scarlet stuff, and fine twined linen.... And you shall set in it four rows of stones. A row of sardius, topaz, and carbuncle shall be the first row; and the second row an emerald, a sapphire, and a diamond; and the third row a jacinth, an agate, and an amethyst; and the fourth row a beryl, an onyx, and a jasper.... There shall be twelve stones with their names according to the sons of Israel; they shall be like signets, each engraved with its name, for the twelve tribes."[90] Few who have read this passage have given much thought to how the ancient Israelites obtained these stones, most of which were not locally available in their homeland. There are also interesting questions as to the actual identity of several of the stones mentioned in the passage since the ancients often simply named gemstones according to their color.[91]

Let's look at each of the stones mentioned in turn. Sardius (*odem* in Hebrew) may refer to sard, a type of agate with parallel layers. If so, it is likely to have come from Egypt. However, the biblical term also may refer to carnelian, which also was mined in Egypt. The term topaz in antiquity did not refer to the same gemstone that is associated with that name today, but was used to refer to all gemstones of related yellow, brown, and green colors. In this case it probably referred to the peridot, which was mined on an island in the Red Sea that today is called Zabargad, but in ancient times was called Topazios. The island was the sole source of peridot in the region in ancient times and the Egyptians had begun mining the stone there by 1500 B.C. Carbuncle (*nophek*, glowing coal, in Hebrew) was a term used in ancient times for a variety of red stones and in this case it probably refers to almandine garnets. Although almandine garnets have been found in the vicinity of Mt. Carmel in Israel, it is more likely that the garnets of the Bible came from the vicinity of Mt. Sinai in the Sinai Peninsula, where the Egyptians had been mining them since 2000 B.C. The Egyptians believed that garnets were an antidote for snakebites and food poisoning and they were widely believed in the Middle East to give the wearer guidance at night. Noah was believed to have hung a large garnet from the ark to provide illumination.

Turning to the second row, emeralds in the ancient world were associated primarily with what is popularly referred to as Cleopatra's mine, located in the desert hills of the Sikait-Zabara region to the east of Luxor. The mine itself predates Cleopatra (Cleopatra VII, 1. 69–30 B.C.) by at least a couple of thousand years. According to Ward, "India traded for Egyptian emeralds from 2000 or 3000 B.C. until Cleopatra's mines were exhausted in the 13th century"[92]—the mines, in fact, not being completely abandoned until the A.D. 1700s.[93] But were these stones actually emeralds? As Ward points out, "The Greek word *smárdados,* which we translate as *emerald,* was an ancient catchall term for green color in a variety of materials — quartz, glass, ceramics, feldspar, and peridot — all later misidentified and mistranslated as emerald."[94] Several of the so-called emeralds in existing ancient Egyptian jewelry when tested have turned out to be green beryl crystals, a less valuable relative of the emerald with trace elements of iron. However, the emerald of the biblical passage (*bareketh* in Hebrew) may have been chalcedony. Chalcedony was also mined in Egypt and was far more common than emeralds (or green beryl).

The sapphire mentioned in the Old Testament passage probably was lapis lazuli: "our word for sapphire is from the Latin form of the Greek word for blue. Similar Hebrew and Persian words also associate blue with sapphires."[95] Mineable deposits of lapis lazuli are rare and the only source in the ancient world was in the Kokcha River valley in Badakshan Province of northwestern Afghanistan. Lapis lazuli from this source was being mined at Sar-e-Sang as early as 4000 B.C. It was being traded to Egypt and Mesopotamia as early as 3300

B.C. and by 2000 B.C. it was traded to the Indus River Valley as well.[96] Diamonds were being mined at Golconda in central India as early as 800 B.C.,[97] although some accounts date the discovery to the 300s B.C., and India was the only source of diamonds in the ancient world. In fact, except for small numbers coming from southeastern Borneo, India was the world's only source until diamonds were discovered in Brazil in 1725. The earliest date for diamond mining at Golconda is well after the Old Testament reference, so India could not have been the source. Small quantities of diamonds have been found from time to time in various locales in the Middle East and it is possible that the diamonds referred to here were from some unknown source in the region.

The identity of the stone called jacinth (*lesham* in Hebrew) that was to be placed in the third row has given rise to considerable debate among biblical scholars. Various scholars have identified it as amber, a brown variety of sapphire, and agate. In mineralogical terms, jacinth refers to either red zircon or hessonite garnet. The hessonite garnet (*esson* in Greek, also called cinnamon garnet) is a possible candidate. Hessonite is a brown-orange variety of grossalar garnet with well-known deposits located in northern Pakistan and Afghanistan as well as in Sri Lanka. The ancient Greeks and Romans commonly used it in jewelry. It was also widely used in India and features prominently in Vedic astrology. Agate (*shebo* in Hebrew) was commonly worn by the ancient Israelites and was mined in Egypt and traded throughout the Middle East.

Amethyst (*ahlamah* in Hebrew) is a Greek word meaning not drunken and the stone was worn as an amulet against drunkenness. Amethyst played an important role in ancient Egyptian commerce. Wealth generated from the trade in amethyst not only helped to spur conspicuous consumption in Egypt but also helped to fund ventures into neighboring areas. It was mined as early as the First Dynasty (2920–2770 B.C.). The Wadi el-Hudi region, 35 km southeast of Aswan, was the primary amethyst mining location from the 11th Dynasty (2125–1985 B.C.) to the end of the Middle Kingdom.[98] During the Middle Kingdom (c. 2055–1650 B.C.) there were also important mines at the Gebel el-Asr quarries, 65 km northwest of Abu Simbel. Amethyst fell out of favor during the New Kingdom (c. 1570–1070 B.C.), but it was popular again in the Roman Period. The Romans mined it at Wadi el-Hudi and elsewhere in Egypt. In addition to Egypt, other sources of amethyst in ancient times were located in Syria, Arabia, Anatolia, and Iran.[99]

Beryl today refers to a variety of gemstones of the beryl group that are not emerald-green or aquamarine blue. The beryl referred to here may have been a golden beryl or heliodor (they are lemon yellow or golden colored). There are no major deposits in the Middle East (the closest ones being in Sri Lanka), but they were mined in small quantities in Egypt.[100] Onyx was called *shoham* in Hebrew. There are two candidates for the identity of this stone: malachite and turquoise. The Egyptians mined malachite and used it for jewelry, amulets, and (in powder form) as eye shadow. The Egyptians mined turquoise from deposits in the Sinai Peninsula that were worked as early as 4000 B.C. Jasper is a multicolored stone (its Greek name means spotted stone) of the chalcedony quartz group that is sometimes treated as chalcedony. It is called *yashpheh* in Hebrew. India was an important source in ancient times, but it was also found in various locales in the Middle East. Schumann notes, "In antiquity, it was used for cylinder seals and as amulets against sight disturbances and drought."[101]

Gemstone mining and the gemstone trade grew considerably under the Roman Empire from the 100s B.C. to the 300s A.D. Ward refers to the famous Roman writer Pliny as "the world's first gemologist."[102] The range and quantities of gemstones available within western

Europe is relatively limited — i.e., jet from Britain, amber from the Baltic, possibly emeralds from Austria,[103] and amethyst and citrine from the Ural Mountains — and the Romans turned to the Middle East and India to obtain most of the gems that they desired. The Romans continued to exploit existing mines in Egypt and elsewhere in the Middle East that were now within the borders of their empire and to import lapis lazuli from Afghanistan. Most importantly for our purposes, however, was the growth in the shipment of gemstones from India to Rome via the ports of the Red Sea. Gems had been finding their way to the Middle East for a couple of thousand years already, but the trade grew considerably during the Roman period. Ships engaged in trade between the Roman Empire and India either went north to the ports of Barbarikon (Barbarike) and Barygaza or south to the Tamil ports of Muziris, Nelkynda, and Arikamedu. A few Roman traders also appear to have made it to Sri Lanka, which the Romans called Tabrobane. In addition to such goods as silk from China and cotton and pepper from India, the traders picked up gemstones to take back to the Roman Empire. Turquoise and lapis lazuli were shipped from Barbarikon and agate (onyx) from Barygaza. The port of Arikmedu was an especially important center of the gem and bead industry.[104] The stones worked by local artisans here included diamonds, sapphires, rubies, spinels, beryls, amethyst, citrine, prase (a green colored jasper), rock crystal, agate, black onyx, and almandine and hessonite garnets. As was noted above, the diamonds came from Golconda in central India. There were important beryl mines in Coimbatore, Tamil Naidu, where a large number of Roman coins have been discovered.[105] Sapphires, rubies, spinels, and other gemstones came from the Ratnapura District of southwestern Sri Lanka.

Jade was the dominant gem in East Asia and Mesoamerica in ancient times. In fact, the term jade refers to two stones, jadeite and nephrite. Nephrite is far more common and in ancient China the term jade generally refers to nephrite; jadeite from Burma became available to the Chinese only in modern times.[106] Ancient Chinese interest in trade beyond their western borders and the early development of the Silk Road was intimately related to their desire to obtain jade (nephrite). The main source of nephrite in ancient times in Asia was in the Kunlun Mountains and along the Karakash (Black Jade) River and Yurunkash (White Jade) River (*kosh* means nephrite in Uyghur) near the oasis of Khotan (called Hotan today and located in the southwestern corner of Xinjiang).[107] Caravans brought nephrite down from the mountains to Khotan, which also became an important center of silk weaving.

Jadeite and nephrite were highly valued by all of the ancient civilizations of Mesoamerica, starting with the Olmecs. Archaeologists have discovered a site for working jade in the Rio Balsas region dating from around 1000 B.C.[108] Jade artifacts have been found in archaeological sites throughout central and southern Mexico and in Central America as far south as Costa Rica. Those found in Costa Rica date from as early as 500 B.C.[109] Yet there are only two known sites for mining jade in Mesoamerica: the Rio Balsas region in Mexico's Guerrero State and in Guatemala's Motagua River Valley.[110] Coe uses the designation "the jade route" in reference to the route the stone was traded from its source in Guerrero State to the Olmec lands on the Gulf.[111] Jade was carried over other important trade routes throughout ancient Mesoamerica.

Incense

Incense refers to a wide range of aromatic materials that release fragrant smoke when burned. Incense comes from a variety of sources. These include woods and barks (agar wood, cedar, sandalwood, cypress, juniper, and cassia), resins and gums (frankincense, myrrh, benzoin, copal, labdanum, galbanum, elemi, camphor, sandarac, gugul, opoponax or sweet myrrh, and Tolu balsam), leaves (balsam, bay, patchouli, and sage), roots and rhizomes (calamus, couch grass, galangal, orris, spikenard, and vetiver), seeds and fruits (coriander, harmalla, juniper, nutmeg, star anise, and vanilla), flowers and buds (clove, lavender, and saffron), essential oils (jasmine, rose, and ylang-ylang), and animal-derived sources (ambergris, musk, and gastropod operculum). Various types of incense have been widely used since ancient times in religious ceremonies as well as in medicinal curing and simply for their aesthetic value. Incense was used in ancient Egypt, Mesopotamia, India, China, Greece, and Rome. Its spread to East and Southeast Asia was associated with Buddhism. The ancient Chinese employed various types of incense in medicine and the promotion of wellbeing as well as for veneration and religious ceremonies. The Japanese and Chinese considered agar wood and sandalwood to be the two most important incenses. Sandalwood is considered important incense for meditation.

While local materials were sometimes used, there is also a long history of trade for incense. The ancient Egyptians imported gums and resins of aromatic trees from Oman, Yemen, and Somalia as early as 3000 B.C. The Incense Route or the Incense Road was a series of trading routes by land and sea stretching from the Mediterranean across Egypt and the Levant to southern Arabia and the Horn of Africa. It was also connected to the important sea trade route from the west coast of India. Frankincense and myrrh were the two main types of incense that gave the route its name. Frankincense is an aromatic resin obtained from trees of the genus *Boswellia* such as the *Boswellia sacra*. The best frankincense comes from Oman, but it is also produced in Yemen and the north coast of Somalia. Myrrh is an aromatic resin that is obtained mainly from the *Commiphora myrrh* tree. Its main source was Oman.

In Greco-Roman times frankincense and myrrh were obtained mainly from the Sabaean kingdom of Hadramawt with its capital at Shabwa (in modern Yemen).[112] From them it was traded to the Gebbanitae, whose capital was Thomna (aka Qataban), for shipment overland or to ports such as Kane and Mosca Limen for shipment by sea via the Red Sea to Egypt.[113] There were two caravan routes carrying the incense northward from Thomna. One of these turned northeastward to Gerrha on the Persian Gulf (near modern Al-Hasa in Saudi Arabia and Dilmun, modern Bahrain). The trip from Thomna to Gerrha normally took 40 days. Chaldeans (aka Kaldu) were the original inhabitants of the area around Gerrha. The Chaldeans became involved in the affairs of the Mesopotamian kingdoms to their north and ruled Babylon for a time. Gerrha itself was an independent kingdom from about 650 B.C. to A.D. 300. Gerrha served as a port for goods coming from India, and overland trade routes left Gerrha heading north to Mesopotamia and northwest towards Petra and Damascus. Gerrha controlled the shipment of incense to Babylon and also shipped some to the Levant via Petra.

The other caravan route carrying incense to the Levant, also part of the route known as the Incense Road, traveled in the northwesterly direction through Mecca, Medina, Petra, and on to other locales in the Levant. Caravans traveling from Thomna to Gaza normally made 65 stops for the camels. The Nabataeans controlled the northwestern end of the incense trade route through the city of Petra. Petra served as a crossroads for caravans bringing goods from India and Arabia to Egypt, Damascus, and ports along the Mediterranean. Young translates a reference to the Nabataeans written in 31 B.C. by Diodorus Siculus: "Although there are not a few of the Arab tribes using the desert as pasture, these [the

Nabataeans] greatly exceed the others in wealth, being not much more then ten thousand in number. For not a few of them are accustomed to bring down to the sea frankincense, myrrh and the most valuable of the aromatics which they receive from those who carry them from Arabia called Eudaimon."[114] In addition to conducting trade in incense close to home the Nabataeans also ventured to more distant points along the trade routes. At a distance of 320 km to the south of Petra the Nabataeans occupied the city of Meda'in Salen (in modern Saudi Arabia). It served as an important stopping point for the incense caravans and itself grew into a large and wealthy city — as attested by over 100 large tombs of Nabataean military officers and government officials dating from A.D. 1 to A.D. 75. Young argues that Meda'in Salen's main function was to protect the incense trade.[115] As for the caravan trade itself, "The Nabataeans would thus seem to have been involved in the commerce chiefly as transporters.... Their role seems to have been that of taking over the incense from the Minaean and Gerrhaean caravans when they arrived in Nabataean territory, and then conveying them to the sea at Gaza and Alexandria, or for consumption in the cities of Roman Syria itself."[116] While most Nabataean traders appear to have operated within their own borders or in cities close at hand there is "some evidence of a Nabataean presence in southern Arabia, so it seems that at least some Nabataean merchants traded this far afield."[117]

Sandalwood and agar wood are two of the most important types of incense in South, Southeast, and East Asia. Agar wood, or agar (from the Malay *gaharu*) incense, is made from the resinous heartwood of the *Aquilaria* tree. This is a large and rare evergreen tree that is native to Southeast Asia. Not all of the trees can be used to produce incense. They produce an aromatic resin in response to an infection by a parasitic fungus and it is this rich, dark resin that produces the aroma. Other names for the incense are *jinko* (*jin-koh*) (Japanese), *chen-xiang* (Chinese), *mai ketsana* (Lao), eaglewood or aquilawood (Lignum aquila Latin) aloeswood, and *oud* (Arabic). The complex and pleasing aroma of agar wood is quite distinct and it became one of the most valuable commodities traded in the ancient world. Even today the highest grades are worth more by weight than gold. Like diamonds, agar wood is carefully graded and priced according to grade.

Agar wood was an important commodity carried by sea from Southeast Asia north to China and Japan and west to the Persian Gulf and as far as Egypt. The ancient Egyptians used it for embalming the dead. Elsewhere it was (and is) used mainly as incense, although the wood is also sometimes carved, especially to make religious images such as Buddhas. The Central Highlands of Vietnam were an especially important source of the wood in the past and early Chinese accounts often mention it as coming from this area (then referred to as Rinan). Mountain people in the Central Highlands collected it and traded it to the Cham from the coast and it then entered the international maritime trade. Some indication of how the trade operated comes from Vietnamese accounts from the 1500s. In the late 1500s, the Nguyen lords who ruled over much of the lowlands of central and southern Vietnam promoted the export of agar wood, especially to China and Japan. There were three grades, with that called *Khi Nam* (Calambac) being the highest grade. The Nguyen lords established a monopoly over the sale of Calambac grade agar wood and this became a major source of revenue for them. A pound of Calambac was sold in the central Vietnamese port of Hoi An for 15 tael (one tael being a little over one ounce of silver). When sold in Nagasaki, Japan, the price was 600 tael.

Sandalwood is a fragrant wood of trees belonging to the genus *Santalum*. The trees are native to India, Australia, Indonesia, and numerous Pacific Islands. It is called *candanam* in Sanskrit, *chandan* in Hindi, *cendana* in Malay, and *sandanon* in Greek. It was used in

India as perfume, medicine, incense, and the material for religious statues as early as the 400s B.C. and probably much earlier. Its use in Southeast Asia, China, Korea, and Japan spread with the adoption of Hindu and Buddhist beliefs and practices.

An interesting account of the maritime trade between India and China that passed through the port of Oc Eo prior to A.D. 350 relates to the introduction of local incense as a trade item.[118] In addition to Indians, Chinese, and Persians, there were also Malays who not only helped to carry goods from each end of the trade route but also introduced regional goods to the international markets. The Indians, Chinese, and Persians initially were not particularly interested in goods from Southeast Asia: "The traders at Fu-nan [Oc Eo] went to China in order to exchange Mediterranean, Indian, Middle Eastern, and African goods (items such as frankincense and myrrh, other plant resins, and other substances used to manufacture perfumes and incense) for China's silk."[119] However, the sailors and traders from the region "responded with entrepreneurial skill and began to introduce their own products, beginning with those that might be construed as substitutes for products destined for the China market. Sumatran pine resins were substituted for frankincense, and benzoin (a resin from a plant related to the laurel family, also known as Benjamin gum) was substitute for bdellium myrrh."[120] Other Southeast Asian goods were soon introduced to the trade as well: "One of the most important was camphor, a resin that crystallized in wood and that was valued as a medicine, as incense, and as an ingredient in varnish. Throughout the ages the most highly prized camphor has been that of Barus, a port on Sumatra's northwestern coast. Aromatic woods such as gharuwood [agar wood] and sandalwood (a specialty of Timor) became important commodities, and the fine spices of Maluku [such as cloves and nutmeg] also began to appear in international markets at this time."[121]

Various types of incense also remained important trade items in the medieval world. After international maritime trade through Southeast Asia bypassed Oc Eo and focused on Champa's ports further to the north along the coast of central Vietnam, trade in aromatic commodities continued. Chinese sources often mention Champa sending incense to China. For example, included among the gifts sent by the queen of Champa to the Chinese emperor in A.D. 962 along with elephants, rhinoceroses, silk and cotton cloth was "a thousand pounds of incense."[122] When Nicolo de Conti (1. 1395–1469) visited Champa in 1435 he reported that the Cham were major traders in agar wood ("aloes"), camphor, and gold.[123] Ma Huan, whom we have cited before, sailed with the fourth of the Ming Dynasty's treasure fleets commanded by Zheng He in 1413 in the capacity of a translator of foreign documents.[124] He was a Muslim from the vicinity of Hangzhou. His memoir provides a description not only of the voyage of the fleet, but also of the places and peoples that it visited, one of these being Champa. His description of Champa includes reference to agar wood incense ("ch'ieh-lan"), which he describes as being "produced only on one large mountain in the country, and comes from no other place in the world; it is very expensive, being exchanged for [its weight in silver]."[125] While Champa was not the only source of agar wood at this time, it was the source for most of the agar wood incense that found its way into international commerce.

Tropical Spices

Most spices are found only in the tropics. *The Oxford Universal Dictionary* defines spice as "strongly flavored or aromatic substances of vegetable origin, obtained from tropical plants, commonly used as condiments, etc."[126] In addition to flavoring they also play an important role as preservatives for food and often as medicines as well. Important tropical spices that have a long history of being traded internationally include pepper, cinnamon and cassia, cardamom, cloves, mace, nutmeg, mustard, saffron, turmeric, and ginger.

Since the tropics are the source of most of the world's spices those living outside of the tropics must import them. The Middle East, Europe, and East Asia were important markets for tropical spices from ancient times and most spices came from southern India's Malabar Coast and Southeast Asia.

The spice trade may have begun with pepper. Peppercorns of South Indian origin were placed by Ramesses II's nostrils when he was buried in 1213 B.C., and they were also imported by the ancient Greeks, but it was not until Roman times that large amounts of pepper were exported from the Tamil area of southern India to Rome. Bernstein comments on its popularity: "Filling the holds of many a Greek ship, pepper arrived in bulk to flavor the otherwise bland wheat- and barley-based Mediterranean cuisine of rich and poor Romans. It proved so popular that when the Goth Alaric held Rome to ransom in A.D. 408, he demanded three thousand pounds of the black spice."[127] He also mentions that a popular cookbook from ancient Rome "called for pepper in 349 of its 468 recipes."[128]

The spice trade grew in importance in the medieval period. The Middle East was the largest market for imported tropical spices, but China and Europe also emerged as major consumers. In regard to Europe, "After undergoing an agricultural and commercial revolution and crusading in the eastern Mediterranean for some two hundred years, the Western Europeans had begun to consume meat in quantity, and had developed a taste for and subsequently a need for Asian spices to flavor dried or salted meat and preserved vegetables and fruits."[129]

Spices from the Malabar Coast of southern India and Southeast Asia continued to be shipped by sea westward to the Middle East and Europe and northward to East Asia. As in Roman times, today pepper is the most important spice traded globally (about 20 percent of all spices) and it was the main spice traded in the medieval world as well. There are three principal types of pepper (genus *Piper*)—*Piper nigrum* (black pepper), *Piper cubeba*, and *Piper longum*—with *Piper nigrum* being the main commercial variety.[130] Black pepper is native to southern India and Southeast Asia and the Malabar Coast was the main source of pepper in antiquity (the word pepper comes form Sanskrit *pippali* via the Latin *piper*). The Malabar Coast remained the major source of pepper in the medieval world, but it also was exported from parts of Southeast Asia as well.

The main sources of black pepper in Southeast Asia were Sumatra and west Java.[131] The pepper trade in Southeast Asia was linked primarily to the growing demand for pepper in China. While pepper was used in China by the A.D. 200s (it was called *hujiao*, "foreign pepper"), it was not widely used in ancient times. Pepper had become popular in food in China by the 1100s and Marco Polo indicated that in the 1200s large amounts were being imported. The Srivijayan Empire, which came into being around A.D. 670 along the eastern coast of Sumatra, initially was the main Chinese source of pepper. In the 1000s as Arab and Indian Muslim traders became more involved in the spice trade the Acehnese port of Samudra in northern Sumatra became an important entrepôt for the sale of Sumatran pepper. While Sumatra continued to export pepper,[132] the center of the pepper trade in Indonesia shifted to Java at this time as a result of actions by the east Javanese king Airlangga (r. 1019–1049) aimed at promoting trade.

Airlangga initiated a project to dam parts of the Brantas River in northeastern Java in part to provide "a better harbor for international shipping at the royal port of Hujung Galah [in the vicinity of the modern city of Surabaya]. The new port facilities serviced a growing international trade. It was not long before east Java had gained a dominant position in the international spice market, a market that grew to include most of the eastern hemisphere."[133] Airlangga and subsequent Javanese kings gave charters to merchants at the ports. Revenue from such trade helped the rulers to provide greater security for merchants, an important factor in the decisions concerning where to operate: "during this era the Chinese were aware that they could get a superior variety of pepper (pepper at a better price) in the Sunda Strait region, but did not bother to go there since it had a reputation for brigandage."[134] In 1282 Samudra applied to the new Mongol rulers in China to once again become a preferred port for trading pepper and other goods. This inspired the Javanese under Kertanagara to invade the region and establish control over the Strait of Melaka by 1286. This in turn led to a confrontation between Kertanagara and the Mongols and a disruption of trade. Raden Vijaya established the new Majapahit kingdom in the 1290s after Kertanagara died, and he re-established commercial relations with China. Majapahit then continued to be a major supplier of pepper as well as cloves, nutmeg, and mace to the Middle Eastern and European markets.

Hall provides the following description of the spice merchants coming to Majapahit:

> The international traveler who came to Majapahit in the latter part of the fourteenth century, at the peak of its glory, would approach on a merchant ship, riding the west wind, and first enter the core region of the realm at the port of Surabaya, a town of about a thousand families (including some that were Chinese).... After going some thirty to fifty kilometers [up the Brantas River on a small boat], one would come to Canggu, a ferry crossing and a marketplace. From Canggu it was a half-day's walk further up the river to the 'twin cities,' Majapahit and Bubat.[135]

The history of the trade involving cinnamon has generated more controversy than any other spice. This is related to questions about the identity of plants mentioned in early sources (i.e., whether the references are to cinnamon or some other plant) and debate about the source of the cinnamon that was traded. True cinnamon (*Cinnamomum verum* or *Cinnamon zeylanicum*) is native to Sri Lanka and Madagascar. Related species from Southeast Asia are actually cassia, but they are commonly referred to as cinnamon. These include *Cinnamomum aromaticum*, *Cinnamomum loureiroi*, and *Cinnamomum burmannii*. These are variously also sometimes called Chinese cinnamon, Vietnamese cinnamon, Saigon cinnamon, and Indonesian cinnamon. True cinnamon has less of a strong flavor than cassia and somewhat different physical and chemical properties.

There are references to what many modern authors believed to be cinnamon being used in Egypt and elsewhere in the ancient Middle East prior to Roman times, but as Crone points out, what is described in the ancient texts is not cinnamon but "a xerophilous shrub" that was found around the Red Sea area and thus did not need to be shipped very far.[136] By Roman times, however, what can be identified as cinnamon was being imported from a distant source, the identity of which is again subject to debate. Since it is widely believed that *Cinnamon zeylanicum* is only found in Sri Lanka this trade has caused considerable scholarly argument about how the cinnamon got from Sri Lanka to East Africa and then to Arabia. The debate becomes especially interesting when one considers that *Cinnamon zeylanicum* "does not appear to have been cultivated commercially in Ceylon until the Portuguese and Dutch conquests."[137]

The identity of the source from where the Romans obtained their cinnamon (*Cinnamon zeyanicum*), in fact, appears to be East Africa via southern Arabia. Pliny recorded in the

Periplus, which was written in A.D. 70, that cinnamon was transported to Arabia by "raft" (actually outrigger) from the East African port of Mosyllum.[138] He describes the port in Chapter 10 of the *Periplus* as follows:

> Beyond Mundu, sailing toward the east, after another 1000 or even 1500 stades, we reach Mosyllum, on a beach, with a bad anchorage. There are imported here the same things already mentioned, also silver plate, a very little iron, and glass. There are shipped from the place a great quantity of cinnamon, (so that this market-town requires ships of larger size), and fragrant gums, spices, a little tortoise shell, and mocrotu, (poorer, than that of Mundus), frankincense, ivory, and myrrh in small quantities.[139]

Those engaged in the cinnamon trade nearest the source were Malayo-Polynesian speaking peoples who had sailed from Southeast Asia across the Indian Ocean via Sri Lanka and southern India to settle along the coast of East Africa and especially on the island of Madagascar. They brought with them from Southeast Asia plants like bananas, coconuts, and cocoyam (along with the technology of bark-cloth making), but not, it would appear, cinnamon — unless they brought it with them from Sri Lanka, which does not seem likely. The name cinnamon is derived from a Malayo-Polynesian word via Phoenician and Hebrew,[140] from which the Greeks adopted the name *kinnamomon.* Shaffer mentions an Arabic text from the 1200s that refers to a "Malay settlement in the vicinity of Aden sometime around the Roman conquest of Egypt in 31 B.C.E. Vast fleets of Malay outrigger canoes came and went from this place, it tells us, but eventually the settlers 'grew weak, lost their seafaring skills, and were overrun by neighboring peoples'.... According to the text, this happened after Egypt's decline ... and scholars have tentatively dated the settlement to the first century C.E."[141] It is still not widely known that *Cinnamon zeylanicum* grows wild in the east and northwest coasts of Madagascar.[142] Madagascar was the main place of Malayo-Polynesian settlement in East Africa and it is most likely that this was the source of the cinnamon that they transported on outriggers to Mosyllum and southern Arabia.

Madagascar virtually disappears as a source of cinnamon in the medieval period following the Muslim conquests of the Middle East. Moreover, it would seem that during the medieval period cinnamon comes to be associated with cassia and no longer with *Cinnamon zeylanicum. C. zeylanicum* does not seem to re-emerge as an item of international trade until the modern era and the advent of European colonialism.

Even though cassia was commonly referred to as being Chinese in the medieval period — in the Middle East it was called Chinese wood — it seems to have come mainly from sources in Southeast Asia and southeastern China. The Chinese themselves appear to have begun using cassia/cinnamon only at the outset of the medieval period. It enters the Chinese medical literature only in the A.D. 400s or 500s, and did not play a significant role in Chinese commerce or culinary habits at this time. Champa was an important source of cassia/cinnamon. It was collected by highland peoples and traded to the lowland Cham and then exported through their ports. It is interesting to note that the port of Quang Ngai, located in what was once part of Champa, was still exporting cassia/cinnamon in the early 20th century during the French colonial period. Cassia/cinnamon seems mainly to have been shipped to the west from Champa to India and then on to the Red Sea or the Persian Gulf from where it spread across the Middle East and Europe.

The ginger family (*Zingiberaceae*) of plants has produced a number of important spices. Cardamom is one of these. It comes in two principal varieties: *elettaria* (green cardamom) and *amomum* (black cardamom). Both varieties are grown in South Asia and Southeast Asia. There are also three native varieties found in Kerala, and Mysore, and a variety known as *amomum tsao-ko* cardamom that is cultivated in Yunnan and northwestern Vietnam. Cardamom is popular in Indian and Middle Eastern cuisines and green cardamom is used in traditional medicine in India, Vietnam, China, Japan, and Korea. Like cinnamon, cardamom was also obtained by the Cham from interior regions and exported from the ports of Champa.

Turmeric (*Curcuma longa*) also belongs to the ginger family. It is native to South Asia and Southeast Asia and requires temperatures above 20 degrees Celsius and a great deal of rainfall to grow well. A related species, *C. xanthorrhiza*, grows in Java. Turmeric is widely used in South Asia and Southeast Asia in foods, as a medicine, as a dye, and as a cosmetic and sunscreen. It was traded to the Middle East and Europe from India (the center of the turmeric trade in India today is in the town of Sangli in Maharashtra). It was known as Indian saffron in medieval Europe, where it was used as a less expensive substitute for saffron.

Cloves, nutmeg, and mace were three of the most important spices in the medieval world and no spices have influenced world history as much as these three.[143] Cloves come from the clove tree (*Syzygium aromaticum*) that originally grew only in northern Maluku in eastern Indonesia on the small islands of Ternate, Tidore, Bacan, Makian, and Moti. Nutmeg and mace come from the *Myristica fragrans* tree that originally grew only on the Banda Islands of Maluku. The trade in cloves is especially ancient. Cloves were being traded to the Middle East via India as early as 1721 B.C.[144] Onyx beads and silver from India have been found on these islands dating from around 200 B.C. Cloves were traded to China during the Han Dynasty, when high-ranking court officials used them to improve the smell of their breath when addressing the emperor. Cloves have been documented in Mediterranean Europe by 100 B.C. The nutmeg trade developed later, apparently spurred by increased Chinese interest in such spices. When the Chinese elites who had fled south of the Yangtze River in the 400s had their access to overland goods from the west cut off in A.D. 439 they turned to maritime trade routes and came to rely more on Southeast Asian goods. By the 500s to 600s these included nutmeg and mace. Nutmeg began to be traded to the west around that time as well and by the 700s it had become popular in European cuisine.

The sources of these three spices were unknown to the Muslim, European, and Chinese spice traders. The early European and Muslim traders thought that they came from India since they were obtained from the ports of western India. The Chinese believed that they came from Java and told this to Marco Polo. Later Muslim traders believed this to be the case as well. This was because these traders obtained the spices from northern Java as was described in the passages above concerning Majapahit. Marco Polo wrote that Java (i.e., the Kingdom of Majapahit) "is of surpassing wealth, producing ... all ... kinds of spices, ... frequented by a vast amount of shipping, and by merchants who buy and sell costly goods from which they reap great profit."[145] Java lay to the south of the main trade route that ran from Champa, around the Malay Peninsula, through the Strait of Melaka, and then across the Indian Ocean, but by serving as a source of cloves, nutmeg, mace, and pepper it was able to attract a clientele of international traders. In fact, while they preferred to come to Java to trade for pepper for reasons of security, they came for cloves, nutmeg, and mace because Java had a monopoly and no other source was available to foreign merchants.

Bugis traders brought the three spices to Java from the islands of Maluku and they and the Javanese initially at least do not appear to have been keen on letting foreign merchants know where they came from. The homeland of the Bugis was the southwestern part of the island of Sulawesi. From there they ranged throughout island Southeast Asia and even to northern Australia in search of trade goods. Their homeland as well as the clove islands of

Maluku became dependencies of Kertanagara's Javanese kingdom during the latter part of the 1200s and Javanese influence in the area continued during the Majapahit period. As Majapahit's influence over regional maritime trade declined in the 1400s the pattern of the spice trade remained more or less the same. The main difference now was that the traders increasingly were Muslim, either Muslims from India or the Middle East or local converts (conversion of Ternate and Tidore took place around 1470). Most of the spices continued to be transported mainly by Bugis — although some foreigners now also were involved directly in the trade — to ports on Java's north coast, but there was also a northern trade route from Ternate and Tidore across the Sulu Sea and to the Champa port of Panduranga.

Before leaving the medieval spice trade, we should note the role of the Venetians and Genoese. We will discuss them again later, but they should be mentioned here since their wealth was built on the spice trade: "The most visible legacy of the wealth and splendor generated by the medieval spice trade still dazzles the eye today in Venice, whose grand palazzi and magnificent public architecture were built largely on profits from pepper, cinnamon, nutmeg, mace, and cloves."[146] The Muslim conquest of the Middle East cut off European traders from the Indian Ocean, leaving that part of the spice trade entirely in the hands of Muslim traders. Even if they had to buy their spices in Alexandria, "a hundred pounds of nutmeg, purchased in medieval Alexandria for ten ducats, might easily go for thirty or fifty ducats on the wharves of Venice. Even after payments for shipping, insurance, and customs duties at both ends, profits well in excess of 100 percent were routine."[147] Some idea of the wealth generated can be surmised from Lane's estimate that Venetian ships yearly carried an average of 3.5 million pounds of spices across the Mediterranean a year in the 1400s.[148]

Tea

Another commodity that rose to importance in international commerce during the medieval period is tea. While tea continues to be a very important crop in the international economy, its production and export today is associated to a large extent with countries other than those that were its main suppliers in medieval times. India and Sri Lanka (Ceylon) did not produce tea commercially until the British arrived and even China initially only got involved in the trade as an intermediary to trade tea from southern Yunnan to Tibet for horses.

While teas are made from many substances, the tea that we are concerned with here is that made from the *Camellia sinensis* plant.[149] The plant is native to the mountainous region of southern Yunnan and adjacent parts of northern Laos, northern Burma, and northeastern India. The oldest tree known is located in Fengqing County, Lincang Prefecture, Yunnan Province. The Tibeto-Burman speaking Wa people are the ancient inhabitants of this area, which lies to the west of the Mekong (aka Lancang) River, and tea as a beverage was initially associated with the Tibeto-Burman and Tai-speaking peoples of this region of southern Yunnan. As was mentioned previously, the Tai kingdom of Shu sent an army to conquer the area and when Shu fell to the Chinese the local Tai ruler in Yunnan established his own kingdom, the Kingdom of Tien (called Dian by the Chinese), around 310 B.C. The capital (near the present city of Kunming) was located to the north of the tea-growing region. The Han made Tien a tributary state in 109 B.C., but do not appear at that time to have had much interest in tea. The area regained its autonomy after the fall of the Han

Dynasty, but broke up into a number of small independent states. The area was eventually reunited into the Kingdom of Nan Chao (aka Nan Zhao, or Six Chao), which was founded in A.D. 732. Nan Chao fell to the Mongols in 1253. The heart of the tea-growing area was located in a region that came to be called Sipsongpanna (Twelve Panna, Xishuangbanna to the Chinese) in 1570, a region inhabited by Tibeto-Burman and Tai, speaking peoples. The Tai-speaking Lue (called Dai by the Chinese) settled mainly in the valleys, especially around Jinghong and Menghai, and formed the ruling class of Sipsongpanna. Their kingdom was incorporated into Nan Chao until 1253. After the fall of Nan Chao the area eventually became a dependency of the Chinese for a time. The Lue region of Menghai (Muang Hai to the Lue), which has an altitude of 1,400 meters, was an especially important tea-producing region. Today this region is know for the production of a variety of tea known as *puer* (pu-erh) tea that is usually sold made into flat round disks or balls.

Ukers recounts the early history of tea in relation to the Chinese.[150] Chinese legend associates tea with the legendary emperor Shen Nung, known as the Divine Healer, who lived around 2737 B.C. His medical book says, "Bitter *t'u* [tea] is called *ch'a hsuan,* and *yu.* It grows in winter in the valleys by the streams, and on the hills of Ichow [in Sichuan]."[151] However, the book was written during the Second Han dynasty (25–220 A.D.) and the tea reference was only added in the A.D. 600s. There are several other references to *t'u* (tea) during the later Han period, all treating it as a medicinal plant and referring to its being brought to Sichuan to be planted: Wang Piu in *Contract with a Servant* mentions buying *t'u* from a mountain in Sichuan called Wutu; the Buddhist monk Gan Lu (Wu-Li-chien) went to India to study Buddhism and is said to have brought *t'u* plants with him on his return to plant on Ming Mountain in Sichuan; and the physician Hua T'o in *Shin Lun* wrote, "To drink *k'u t'u* [bitter tea] constantly makes one better."[152] The earliest definite mention of tea cultivation in China is by Kuo P'o in *Erh Ya* (a dictionary), written around A.D. 350. It advises that "*kia,* or *k'u t'u,* a beverage, is made from the leaves by boiling" and mentions that the young tea leaves are called *t'u* and later ones *ming.*[153] There are several references to tea during the time of the Northern Wei Dynasty (A.D. 386–534): Chang I in *Kuang Ya* (a dictionary) mentions tea leaves being picked and made into cakes in Hubei and Sichuan (this appears to be the earliest reference to tea being processed into cakes); Shan Ch'len-Chih's *Wu Hsing Chi* (written in the A.D. 400s) mentions that tea reserved for the emperor was grown on a mountain in Zhejiang Province; and the *Family History of Chiang* (also written in the 400s) mentions tea becoming a trade good. A Qin Dynasty (A.D. 557–89) poet, Chang Meng-yan, mentions "fragrant *t'u*" being grown in terraces in Sichuan Province.[154]

Tea began to be consumed as a refreshing beverage and not just as a medicinal drink in China during the reign of Wen (r. 581–604), founder of the Sui Dynasty. Tea began to be called *ch'a* around 725, during the Tang Dynasty (618–907). Lu Yu wrote the famous *Ch'a Ching* (Book of Tea) in 780 at the request of tea merchants. It was now considered a commercial crop and the government imposed a tax on it in 780 (opposition to the tax resulted in its being withdrawn for a time but it was re-imposed in 793). The *Man Shu,* which was written in A.D. 860, describes tea trees growing in southern Yunnan (Sipsongpanna).

The tea trade in Asia during the time of the Tang Dynasty was associated with the Tea and Horse Road (*Chamadao*).[155] Horse caravans carried sugar and salt from Sichuan to Yunnan to exchange for tea and carried tea, sugar, and salt to the Tibetan plateau to trade for horses (especially war horses). Travel over this route dates back to at least 1000 B.C., but it only emerged as the famous Tea and Horse Road during the Tang Dynasty. Tea became popular in Tibet during the reign of King Chiusongzan (aka Khri 'Dus-sron) (r. 676–704). The Tibetans conquered parts of northwestern Yunnan at this time in the vicinity of Lijang and Dali and established military posts. The trade route followed the military route. Shaxi (Jianchuan County, Dali Prefecture, Yunnan) was one of these important trading posts from the time of the Tang Dynasty (618–907) to the Ming and Qing dynasties. The route went from Sipsongpanna to Dali and then on to Lijiang, Zhongdian, Deqin and Hangkang along the Hengduan Mountains, and then it turned west to Lhasa (and on to northeastern India) and east to Ya'an in Sichuan.

Trade over this route increased considerably during the Song Dynasty (960–1279) as tea became an important daily drink in Tibet and the Song sought to acquire Tibetan war horses that were used in their struggles against Central Asian nomads. The Song court established the Tea and Horse Office in 1074 that established markets for trading in tea and horses. Jia Daquan mentions 20,000 warhorses being acquired a year during the Northern Song period (960–1127) and about 15 million kg of tea was exported to Tibet from Sichuan (half of the total output of Sichuan).[156] Similar offices were maintained during the Yuan Dynasty (1271–1368) and Ming Dynasty (1369–1644).

India has its own mythical origin of tea that is as untrue as China's. India's mythical origin comes from the Ramayana (written around 750–500 B.C.). The belief is based on the part of the story where Hanuman is sent to the Himalayas to bring the *sanjeevani* plant to revive Lakshmana who was seriously wounded by Indrajit (Ravnana's son). In fact the *sanjeevani* plant was not tea but *Selaginella bryopteris,* a plant that is used for medicine in relation to strokes, urinary problems, and menstrual irregularities, and is also said to be able to revive a dead person. As for the origin of tea in India, it appears to have been harvested as a wild plant by Tai peoples such as the Ahom and Khamti and Tibeto-Burman peoples like the Singpho in Assam and neighboring areas of northeastern India from at least the 1100s. It may have been introduced into the area by the Tai speaking groups when they invaded Assam at this time. Commercial production did not begin until the arrival of the British East India Company in the 1700s.

6

Long-distance Traders

Discussing the dangers of travel and market difficulties faced by early long-distance traders, Bernstein asked the question, "Why would anyone risk life, limb, and property on journeys that might carry him from hearth and home for years on end, yielding only meager profits?"[1] The answer to this, he says, is simple: "the grim trading life was preferable to the even grimmer existence of the more than 90 percent of the population who engaged in subsistence-level farming." Even small profits from trade were sufficient "to support an upper-middle-class existence" and made the trader "a rich man" when compared to most other people.[2] Moreover, it is important to understand that trading in ancient and medieval times was rarely an individual undertaking. For the most part long-distance trading was the business of extended families or clans whose members quite often were part of entire societies or ethnic groups that specialized in trade. Thus, long-distance traders in the past commonly were members of transnational societies that focused on commerce across borders. Moreover, in the past such traders comprised the majority of those who lived a transnational existence. In the sections that follow we will look at some of the most prominent groups of long-distance traders in ancient and medieval times.

Phoenicians

The Phoenicians, who dominated trade throughout the Mediterranean region for almost 1,000 years from around 1200 B.C. to the fall of Carthage to the Romans in 146 B.C., can be described as the world's first global capitalists. Not only did the Phoenicians conduct trade throughout the Mediterranean, but important overland trade routes in the Middle East also converged on the Phoenician coast, allowing the Phoenicians to exert considerable influence over the trade between Mesopotamia in the east and Egypt and Arabia to the south.

The Phoenicians were a maritime trading people with society organized around city-states. Their initial homeland was along the coast of present day Lebanon and included cities such as Tyre, Tripoli, Beirut, and Sidon. From here they spread throughout the Mediterranean and established over fifty settlements. These included numerous settlements on Cyprus, Hippo (in Algeria), Ikosium (modern Algiers), Genoa, Panormos (modern Palermo), Oeo (modern Tripoli), Acra, Tingis (modern Tangier), Abyla (modern Ceuta), Akra (modern Alicante), Gadir (modern Cadiz), Qart Hadsat (New Carthage, modern

Cartagena), Olissipona (modern Lisbon), Qart Hadasht (Carthage), and Calpe (modern Gibraltar). A study by the Genographic Project indicates that 6 percent or one in 17 men in the Mediterranean region today may have Phoenician ancestry.[3] The Phoenicians also sailed beyond the Mediterranean to Britain, the Canary Islands, and down the west coast of Africa as far as the Gulf of Guinea, and, according to Herodotus, they may have circumnavigated Africa around 600 B.C.[4] Migrants from Tyre founded Carthage in 814 B.C. Carthage was the capital of an important empire and was one of the greatest trading centers in the ancient world for centuries prior to the rise of the Roman Empire. As Carthage rose, however, Phoenician fortunes in their homeland declined with Tyre becoming a tribute state of the Assyrians in 666 B.C.

Trade in the Phoenician homeland of Lebanon has very ancient roots. About 5,000 years ago the Egyptians began importing timber, metals (especially silver from the Taurus Mountains), and other goods from this region. Such goods also began to find their way to Mesopotamia. Among those who came to settle in this region were the nomadic Amorites with cultural affinities to Sumer and the Canaanites, whose cultural orientation was more towards Egypt and the Mediterranean. Amorites founded the city of Byblos from which cedar logs were shipped to Egypt around 2600 B.C. The rulers and merchants of Byblos had close relations with Egypt and its rulers assumed Egyptian titles. Following the defeat of the foreign rulers of Egypt known as the Hyksos by Ahmosis I in 1570 B.C., Egyptian dominance over the region was re-established during the 18th Dynasty (1570–1314 B.C.). Cedar logs no longer were the main Egyptian imports from Lebanon at this time but rather purple cloth, wine, and oil. Egyptian paintings show purple-clad merchants from the ports of Lebanon as well as Syrian traders in white. Culican says that "colonies of Canaanite and Syrian traders were certainly settled in Egypt from the reign of Amenophis II (1440–1415 B.C.)" and "during his reign the worship of Canaanite deities grew in Egypt."[5] Design elements from this region are also featured conspicuously in the tomb of Tutankhamen.[6]

The Phoenicians emerge in this area some time around 1200 B.C., perhaps out of a mixture of marauding sea peoples who had come from the north and the coastal Canaanites. Tyre was their first major trading center, followed by Sidon, and it was the city-state of Tyre that initiated Phoenician colonization of other lands around the Mediterranean. Phoenician trade was founded on the manufacture and dyeing of textiles. Particularly important was a purple dye that is commonly referred to as Tyrian purple in reference to the Phoenician city of Tyre. The dye is made from a mollusk, the banded dye murex *Hexaplex trunculus*.[7] The oldest piles of such shells used for dyeing have been found in and around Crete dating from 1800 and 1600 B.C., but it was the Phoenician cities to the east that became most associated with the production of the dye and its trade. The earliest trace of the dye itself comes from an amphora discovered at a Phoenician site in Sarepta, Lebanon, dating from 1300–1200 B.C.[8] As noted by Barber:

> The purple industry continued to flourish on the coast of the Levant throughout the 1st millennium, making its purveyors rich and famous throughout the Biblical and Classical worlds on account of Tyrian purple and Phoenician red. But each animal [mollusk] yields only a single drop of the dye, and even that only when freshly caught. In their quest for new sources of the mollusks, among other commodities, the Phoenicians eventually set up colonies all around the Mediterranean and out on the Atlantic shores of Spain and Africa, leaving a trail of shell heaps behind them.[9]

It was not just the dyes that the Phoenicians were famous for in antiquity. They were also a major source of woven textiles made from wool, linen, cotton, and silk. The raw materials were imported from a variety of sources. So-called white wool came from Damascus.

Lamb's, ram's, and goat's wool came from Arabia. Linen came from Egypt, which was a linen manufacturing center in its own right. Persian merchants brought raw silk from further east to Tyre and Berytus. Phoenician cloth was highly regarded for its brilliant colors and for the delicacy of its embroidery.

The Phoenicians were also major manufacturers of glass, which was widely exported. Sidon was the center of the glass industry, but glass was also produced in Tyre and Sarepta. They produced three kinds of glass: transparent colorless glass, translucent colored glass, and opaque glass. They also produced a wide variety of objects from metal, including items made of copper that was imported from Cyprus. Relatively low quality ceramics were manufactured, in large part for export to peoples who did not produce their own pottery. Among the raw materials that the Phoenicians shipped were Lebanon cedars to Egypt, where wood was in short supply.

Greeks

As Durant has remarked of ancient Greece, "Commerce was the life of Hellenistic economy. It made the great fortunes, built the great cities, and employed a growing proportion of the expanding population."[10] A distinct merchant class emerged in many of the ancient Greek city-states and coinage and banking systems were developed to encourage commerce. Athens was the most important Greek trading state, with international trade goods passing through its port of Piraeus, which was the busiest port in ancient Greece. Most other Greek cities were involved in international commerce to varying degrees as well. The powerful Athenian fleet was able to eliminate the threat of piracy in the Aegean Sea between 480 and 430 B.C. and this created a tremendous boost in international commerce for a time. Thucydides boasted, "The magnitude of our city draws the produce of the world into our harbor, so that to the Athenian the fruits of other countries are as familiar a luxury as those of his own."[11] Immediately to the east of Greece, Rhodes flourished as an important trading center starting in the 300s B.C. It was eclipsed by Delos, which became a free port in 166 B.C.

The ancient Greeks moved beyond their own shores and established numerous settlements and colonies on nearby islands such as Crete, Rhodes, and Cyprus, along the coasts of Turkey, throughout the eastern Mediterranean from Syria to Egypt, north along the coast of the Black Sea, and west on Sicily and along the coasts of Italy, Gaul, Spain, and northern Africa. The sites selected for establishing colonies usually related to their association with particular resources. As Durant notes, "The colonies served not only as markets, but as shipping agents to send Athenian goods into the interior."[12] While most of the settlers or colonists tended to stay put once they had settled down, there were some who adopted more of a transnational lifestyle. As in Greece itself, merchants played an important role in the life of overseas Greek communities. The merchants of the Greek city of Acragas on the island of Sicily in the 500s B.C., for example, "became the American millionaires of their time, upon whom the lesser plutocrats of older Greece looked with secret envy and compensatory scorn."[13] In Egypt the Greeks were allowed to establish a trading post along the Nile at Naucratis around 650 B.C. since the pharaohs found them a good source of mercenaries and revenue from customs taxes. The city grew into an important center for manufacturing pottery as well as a trade emporium where Greek olive oil and wine was traded for Egyptian wheat, linen, and wool, and ivory, frankincense, and gold from elsewhere in Africa.

Describing trade and travel in Ancient Greece (500 to 300 B.C.) Casson writes, "And so Greek traders were to be found shuttling back and forth the length and breadth of the Mediterranean. You saw them in south Russian ports dickering for grain to feed Athens, on the docks of the Piraeus picking up olive oil to ship to Greek colonists along the Black Sea, putting into Beirut for ship timber cut from the cedars of Lebanon, negotiating at Miletus on the Asia Minor coast for fine woolen fabrics that brought two to three times the purchase price in shops at Athens or Syracuse."[14] The exports of ancient Athens were varied and included olive oil, grape wine, wool, marble and other minerals, pottery, armaments, and books and works of art. Grain was the most important import,[15] but a wide range of goods was imported. Merchants brought to the port of Piraeus every conceivable commodity — from food stuffs ("fish from the Black Sea, nuts from Paphlagonia [in northern Turkey along the Black Sea]") to household items ("beds from Chios and Miletus, boots and bronzes from Eturia") to human beings ("slaves from Lydia, Syria, and Scythia").[16] Tsetskhladze remarks that "the export of grain from the Bosporan kingdom [on the Black Sea] to Athens was on a massive scale,"[17] but also points out that most of the grain exported from this region was grown by Greek settlers rather than by the indigenous population and that the trade itself was largely in the hands of Greeks.[18] Dio Chrysostom (aka Dion of Prusa, 1. *c.* A.D. 40–120) wrote regarding the Scythians of Olbia that they "had neither the ambition nor the knowledge to equip a trading-centre of their own after the Greek manner," while characterizing the Greek traders who came to the wilds of Olbia themselves as being "really barbarous."[19]

Particular goods were often sold in markets that were located in specified parts of the city where the merchants selling them lived (e.g., honey sellers and cheese sellers). Large cities such as Athens had specialized wholesale market halls (*deigmata*) that were run by the state to allow foreign merchants to display and sell their wares to local merchants.[20]

While during certain times of the year large numbers of people might travel to take part in religious or other festivals, "Traders, journeying regularly year in and year out, no doubt made up the biggest number [of travelers] both on land and water."[21] As Casson points out in his account of the Greek travel writer Herodotus, his "fellow-travelers were more often than not traders and commercial agents, and he surely whiled away many a long day on deck or donkey back talking business with them."[22] The Greeks recognized various types of merchant: *kapeloi* (retail merchants who sold such things as cattle and leather), *palinkapeloi* (entrepreneurs and middlemen), and *emporoi* (long-distance traders). Merchants who traveled by sea chartered ships themselves or booked passage on ships. Ship owners were referred to as *naukleroi*. Those who went by land traveled with teams of donkeys or mules to carry goods (up to about 100 kilograms per animal) and sometimes to ride (if they could afford such a luxury). Roads able to handle wheeled vehicles were rare and so wheeled carts were not common means of transport for long-distance traders. As for accommodation, "Traders counted on being lodged with business associates or to stay in privately run inns or rented accommodation if they stayed for longer periods."[23] Such forms of accommodation were readily available in the major ports. As the hub of the Greek trading world, Athens boasted the largest population of *emporoi*, and merchants in general made up a sizeable proportion of its population. In his study of the population of ancient Athens, Gomme mentions that in addition to slaves, there were 43,000 citizens and 28,500 *metics* (*metoikoi* meaning sharing the home; i.e., resident aliens).[24] This last category was mainly comprised of non–Athenian merchants, while the number of citizens also included many merchants.

Ancient Greek and Phoenician traders overlapped in time and space and while there was no doubt competition at times, "Greeks and Phoenicians seem to have explored the markets together,"[25] especially in the western Mediterranean. Thus, Greek merchants appear to have operated out of Carthage from the early days of that city and Greek and Phoenician trade goods turn up together in many sites around the Mediterranean.

Sogdians

The Sogdians were an Iranian people whose original homeland was between the Amu Darya (aka Oxus) and Syr Darya rivers in what is today Uzbekistan and Tajikistsan. The Aral Sea lies to the north and the high mountains of the Pamirs to the south. The region itself is comprised largely of the Kyzyl-Kum Desert. Within this area the Sogdians occupied fertile valleys that were surrounded by desert. Lacking a powerful state of their own, nevertheless, they dominated long-distance trade throughout Central Asia from A.D. 500 to 1000.

In ancient times Sogdian territory formed a buffer between the Persian Empire to the south and the Scythians to the north and east. Alexander the Great captured their main citadel in 327 B.C., established Macedonian garrisons in their territory, and united it to form a satrapy. It was part of the Seleucid Empire until the local Seleucid ruler Diodotus I Soter rebelled and established an independent kingdom in 248 B.C. The rise of the Parthian Empire cut Sogdiana off from the rest of the Hellenistic world. The Sogdians subsequently organized themselves into city-states — the territory is commonly referred to as Sogdiana — that paid tribute to whoever was the dominant regional power. Scythian and Yuezhi nomads overran the Sogdiana some time around 150 B.C. and the confederacy of Scythian tribes became the dominant regional power for the next several centuries. The Hephthalites (aka White Huns) displaced the Scythians and conquered Sogdiana in the early A.D. 420s.

Local Sogdian rulers wielded little more power than other members of the nobility. In addition to nobles Sogdian society included merchants, priests, common peasants and workers, and slaves.[26] Before the conquest of the area by Arab-led armies in the early 700s, Zoroastrianism was the most common religion among the Sogdians, but there were also many Buddhists, Nestorian Christians, and Manichaeans. After the Arab conquest Islam became the dominant religion. They wrote their language using Aramaic script and as their influence spread along the Silk Road so too did use of their language and of the Aramaic alphabet (which served as the basis for Uyghur and Mongol alphabets).

The Sogdians occupied a link along the Silk Road and long-distance trade was an important part of their economy, culture, and social organization from a very early time. As Boulnois comments, "Under one master and then another, these Sogdians had continued to develop their civilization, and to carry out their commercial activities."[27] Some of the Sogdian towns specialized in the production of particular goods. Local products that were exported included silk, wool garments, carpets, glass, worked gold and silver, chain mail, wine, fruits, and musk deer hides. They also traded horses and slaves and dealt in trade goods from other areas including amber, furs, and honey from the northwest. There were military slaves called *chakar,* who were trained as guards for the homes of merchants since the merchants were often away from home on long trips. Wealthier merchants sometimes possessed a large enough number of such slaves that they formed what can be viewed as private armies.

Many Sogdians died in the course of the Arab conquest and local society was severely disrupted. A period of Persianization followed along with the disappearance of the Sogdian language. The nobles who survived adopted many elements of Islamic culture, and "the mercantile population of Central Asia, accustomed to accept foreign rule so long as the rulers could protect the trade routes and their businesses, accepted Islam much more readily than the communities of Iran."[28] The merchants did not merely accept Islam: "Merchants, of course, saw advantages in joining the Arabs with their far-flung caliphate.... Sogdian merchants even gave loans to the government for its expeditions, expecting rich returns from the acquisition of booty by conquests."[29]

While they are best known for their involvement in trade across Central Asia to China, the Sogdians also actively traded to the west with the Parthians and later with Byzantium.[30] In regard to trade to the west, the Sogdians were "at the forefront of the silk trade with their western neighbors, Persia and Byzantium."[31] Menander the Guardsman provides a contemporary account of an unsuccessful attempt by the Sogdians to establish direct trade links with Byzantium following the defeat of the Hephthalites in 565.[32] The Sogdians asked the Western Turkish ruler Dizabul (aka Istemi), who had formed an alliance with the Persian king Khosroes to defeat the Hephthalites, for permission to approach the Persian king to seek permission to trade across Persia with Byzantium. He refused their request, burning the silk that they had brought after buying it from them. Dizabul sent a second embassy at the request of the Sogdians and this time Khosroes had the embassy's members poisoned. A Sogdian named Maniah then suggested that Dizabul send an embassy directly to Byzantium via the Caucasus. Dizabul agreed and the embassy arrived in Byzantium around 568–9 carrying silk as a gift to Justinian II. While the Sogdians were only interested in trade, the Turks in the embassy proposed an alliance against the Persians. Justinian agreed to form such an alliance and sent an embassy to the Turks. The creation of this alliance (which lasted until the death of Dizabul) allowed the Sogdians to establish direct trade with Byzantium.

The Sogdians' ability to work with the nomads who lived around them was crucial to the development of their trading activities beyond their own homeland. As indicated by the above passages in reference to the Western Turks, while the Turks taxed the Sogdians and other vassals, they also encouraged commercial activities and provided safety for those travelling within their territory.[33] Frye comments, "The Sogdian merchants were adept at dealing with nomads, and much of their success came from cooperation with the political powers who ruled the steppes and even their own oases. The nomads, inclined to extortion from, or protection of settled communities, found it to their advantage to use Sogdian merchants as their intermediaries in international trade."[34] He adds, "Chinese merchants were not trusted because of the political ambitions of their rulers."[35]

It is uncertain when the Sogdians first became involved in trade with China, but there is documentary evidence that the Sogdians became actively engaged in trade between China and the Parthian Empire following the Han emissary Zhang Qian's mission to the Yuezhi in 138 B.C.[36] De la Vassière cites Chinese sources that mention what appear to be Sogdians visiting the Han court in 29 B.C. and 11 B.C.[37] Somewhat later there are references to Sogdians living along the Silk Road, especially in the Gansu area. There is mention of resident Sogdian merchants serving as a delegation to an invading army in Gansu in A.D. 227. Aurel Stein discovered letters dated A.D. 313 sent by Sogdian traders in the ruins of a watchtower.[38] One of these letters was sent from Gansu with Samarkand as its intended destination. It describes the turmoil in China after the emperor fled Luoyang and warns the intended recipient that there was no profit to be made in Luoyang and that the Indian and Sogdian merchants had fled the ruined city. A large group of Sogdian traders continued to reside in Gansu, however. These traders were captured by the Wei in A.D. 439 and held for ransom.

Despite political instability in East Asia and adjacent parts of Central Asia the Sogdians continued to expand their trade networks and settle across the Tarim Basin and Gansu corridor and into Chinese territory in the 400s and 500s. De la Vassière cites funerary epitaphs describing the settlement of Sogdian families in Gansu during this period.[39] One describes how a *sabao* (chief caravaneer) came from Anxi (western Sogdiana) and settled in Jiuquan in western Gansu during the Wei period. One of his descendants named An Tugen "rose from the position of merchant to Grand Minister of the Northern Qi in the middle of the sixth century."[40]

Greater stability in East Asia under the Sui (589–620) and Tang (618–907) dynasties provided opportunities for the Sogdians to extend their trade networks and to settle even more widely within and around Chinese territory.[41] The *Sui shi* (History of the Sui Dynasty) describes the Sogdians as "skilled merchants" and notes that "many foreigners travelled to their land to trade."[42] During this period the Sogdians achieved the status as the preeminent traders along the Silk Road, serving as "middleman in the transfer of goods, techniques and religious beliefs across continental Asia."[43] Chinese officials encouraged Sogdian merchants to settle in northern towns in particular in order to supply Chinese army garrisons in this area. Under the Tang in particular it was relatively easy for Sogdians to settle in Chinese territory and the Tang saw them as having essentially the same "responsibilities and benefits" of other tax-payers.[44]

The Sogdians began moving into Chinese territory and settling there in unprecedented numbers. During this time, as Hansen notes, "Sogdians formed the most visible and the most influential of the non–Chinese groups resident in China."[45] Various sources "describe whole communities of Sogdians moving to China with the support of merchants."[46] Sogdians came to settle extensively throughout Chinese territory. Rong Xinjang, for example, mentions a family of 3,000 Sogdians moving from the Chinese capital of Chang'an to the provincial town of Xiangyang in Hubei around 420.[47] Some of the Sogdians came as merchants while others came, at least ostensibly, as envoys. Many of these so–called envoys settled, bought land, and married Chinese women. A Chinese document written in 787 refers to envoys living in Chiang'an for over 40 years: "They had all married, purchased land and housing made other investments on which they earned interest, and ... they had no intention of ever returning to their homelands."[48] There were an estimated 4,000 such envoys living in the city at the time. Rong Xinjang comments that a large number of Sogdians had already left the city by this time because of the An Shi Rebellion of 755–63, and so more are likely to have lived there earlier.[49]

Inititally the Sogdians tended to form distinct communities. In Chang'an and Luoyang, for example, they lived mainly in the market areas, where they also established Zoroastrian temples. In regard to such temples, as soon as a community reached about 100 households its members would build a Zoroastrian temple. The Sogdians used the title *sabao*, which initially had referred to the chief of a caravan, for the head of their communities. They exercised both political and religious authority. De la Vassière remarks, "Most of the main towns of Northern China had in the sixth and seventh centuries their Sogdian community headed by a Sabao, who received a mandarinal rank in the official hierarchy, at least from the Northern Qi to the Tang."[50]

Over time the Sogdians living in China, especially those away from the frontier areas, became increasingly integrated into Chinese society. De la Vassière cites the funerary beds that they used as symbolic of this integration: "These nouveaux riches had some wealthy funerary beds carved for them, where they displayed both their Sogdian culture and their integration into Chinese society.... These funerary beds were an old Chinese tradition well suited for Zoroastrian purposes because it isolated the body from earth and water."[51] During the 600s many Sogdian communities within Chinese territory were integrated into the general administrative structure and the distinctive Sogdian hierarchy, including the title of *sabao,* disappeared. Even though the communities had lost their distinctiveness, this did not mean that individual Sogdians were being suppressed. Rather they were becoming socially more integrated into Chinese society. Moreover, they were able to retain many aspects of their culture, and Persian culture, with which the Sogdians were associated, exerted considerable influence on the Chinese during this period. From a transnational perspective it is also important to recognize that Sogdians were increasingly to be found in a wide variety of occupations within China (e.g., serving as monks, soldiers, and government officials). Many Sogdians continued to be active as merchants who were linked to long-distance trade.

The Sogdian presence in China began to decline following the An Shi Rebellion led by An Lushan. We discussed An Lushan earlier in relation to the Tang Dynasty. An Lushan's father was a Sogdian and his mother a Turk. He grew up in northeastern China, where in his youth he worked as a translator in the markets. He joined the Chinese army and climbed through the ranks to become the military governor along the northeastern frontier. His rebellion, which began in 755 and was finally defeated in 763, had ethnic overtones. The rebels at times referred to it as a Sogdian revolt and beyond the military An Lushan had the support of many Sogdian traders (although there were also quite a few who sided with the Tang). Many contemporary Han sources also referred to it as a Sogdian rebellion.[52] Although Sogdians continued to take an active part in long-distance trade between China and the west after the revolt, Sogdians within China began to conceal their ethnic identity. De la Vassière gives the example of "An Chongzhang, the Minister of War. In 756 he asked for the authorization to change his family name, 'being ashamed to bear the same name' as An Lushan. He became Li Baoyu and the exchange was retroactive: his ancestors' family name changed also."[53]

Trans-Saharan Caravan Traders

Camels are sometimes referred to as the ships of the desert and indeed they served much the same purpose as ships for overland long-distance trade in Central Asia and North Africa. In the medieval Islamic world there were two main areas where such caravans were employed: in Central Asia to connect the Middle East with China and in North Africa to connect the sultanates along the southern shores of the Mediterranean with the interior of Africa. The North African caravan routes included one that ran from Fez in the west to Cairo in the east. This route lay within the territories of the Islamic sultanates. Of more interest here are the north-south caravan routes that crossed the Sahara desert and served to extend Islam and related economic and political influences southward across the deserts and into sub–Saharan Africa.

The peoples who are of particular relevance here are speakers of the Berber and Chadic language families of the Afro-Asiatic phylum of languages (that also includes Semitic and Egyptian language families). The Berber (Tamazight) languages are mainly spoken in

Morocco and Algeria, with smaller groups also found in Tunisia, Libya, Egypt, Western Sahara, and Mali. Berber-speaking peoples in Northern Africa were well known to the ancient Phoenicians, Greeks, and Romans, and one Berber, Septimus Severus (r. 193–211), became a Roman emperor. St. Augustine of Hippo (l. 354–430), the famous Christian theologian, was also a Berber. Arabs invaded the Berber area along and near the Mediterranean in the mid–600s and the Berbers in this area were converted to Islam and influenced by Arab culture.

Our interest is primarily in those Berbers living away from the Mediterranean coast in and around the Sahara Desert, and especially those who are known as Tuareg (they refer to themselves as Kel Tamasheq or Kel Tamajaq). The Tuareg initially lived in the vicinity of the Tafilalt oasis in Morocco, which is located ten days' journey by camel south of Fez. The Tuareg adopted camel herding from the Arabs and came to play a major role in the camel caravan trade in the Western Sahara. Many of them migrated southward into the desert as the caravan trade developed. In the desert the Tuareg lived as tribal nomads largely beyond the borders of existing kingdoms.

People speaking Chadic languages live further south in what are today Chad, Central African Republic, Cameroon, Niger, and northern Nigeria. Hausa is the most widely spoken Chadic language today and serves as a lingua franca throughout much of the interior of West Africa. The Hausa originally lived in Nubia. They began migrating westward between A.D. 500 and 700 and settled in what is now northern Nigeria. Eventually there were seven Hausa city-states known as the Hausa Bakwaia. One of the earliest of these was Kano (originally known as Dalla Hill), which began as a center of iron working. The *Chronicle of Kano* mentions Bagauda (r. 998–1063) as the first ruler of Kano. Other city-states that were founded between 1000 and 1200 included Gobir, Rano, Biram, Katsina, Zazzau, and Daura. The Hausa rulers converted to Islam in the 1000s, but Islam was slow to spread more widely among the populace. By the 1200s these city-states, which remained independent of one another, were functioning as important trading centers at the southern end of the trans–Saharan caravan routes exporting such goods as gold and kola nuts northward. Katsina became the largest of the Hausa city-states and commercially the most important one. It was at the terminal point of one of the trans–Saharan caravan routes that ran northward to the Tuareg oasis town of Ghadames (in western Libya). The Romans had established a garrison at Ghadames (they called it Cydamus). Byzantine missionaries converted the population to Christianity in the 500s. It was taken over by the Muslim Arabs in the 600s and they converted the population to Islam.

The western north-south caravan routes in North Africa start in cities such as Marrakech and Fez in the west and Tunis and Tripoli in the east and then head south into the Sahara. They pass through important oases such as those of Ghadames in Libya and In-Salah and the Tuat region of central Algeria and on to trading centers such as Timbuktu. These caravan routes served as routes for the spread of Islam across the Sahara and into adjacent areas of sub–Saharan Africa. In the case of Tuat, Jews settled around the oases of the Tuat region in the A.D. 100s. The area was conquered and occupied by Berbers in the 600s and the Jews either fled or were absorbed into the Berber population. Arabs then took over the oases in the 900s and converted the local people to Islam and rulers thereafter were either Berbers or Arabs.

The caravan routes from Tunis and Tripoli ran southward across what is now Niger to the Hausa city-states and the Kanem Empire west of Lake Chad in what is now northern Nigeria. These caravans were mainly interested in obtaining such goods as ivory, slaves, and kola nuts, which they exchanged for salt, beads, metal goods, and cloth. Caravans from Tunis went southward to Ghadames and then on to Ghat (in southwestern Libya near the border with Algeria), which served as a major point along the trans–Saharan caravans and was a stronghold of the Tuareg. From there they went on to Agadez (in what is now central Niger). Agadez was founded in the 1300s and became the most important Tuareg city. There was also a more easterly route from Tripoli south to Bilma (in what is now northeastern Niger). Bilma was known not only as an oasis, but also as a center of date and salt production. Salt from Bilma was carried not only along the north-south route but also west to Ghat. After leaving Bilma caravans travel south for 15 days without sighting any vegetation or water.

The Kanem Empire (700–1376) was located to the east of the Hausa city-states and to the west of Lake Chad in what is now Niger and northern Nigeria.[54] It emerged as a result of the migration of the Nilo-Saharan speaking Zaghawa nomads into the area that was already occupied by the sedentary So peoples around A.D. 700. Berber and Arab traders initially brought Islam to the region, and in either 1075 or 1085 a Muslim from the nomadic Sayfawa confederacy named Hummay seized the throne and made Islam the official state religion. During the reign of Dunama Dabbalemi (r. 1221–1259) the kingdom's expansion peaked. He also established relations with the sultans of North Africa and arranged for a hostel in Cairo for pilgrims from his kingdom. The center of political power moved west to Bornu around 1376.

Caravan routes further to the west mainly crossed the Sahara to obtain gold, which came primarily from the Bambuk goldfield near the headwaters of the Senegal River (between the Bakoy and Faleme rivers in the southwestern corner of Mali), which seems to be the oldest major source of gold in West Africa. Roman Carthage issued gold coins that appear to have come from here in A.D. 296 and gold may have been exported from Bambuk even earlier. The gold trade grew as Berbers began crossing the Sahara on camels in the A.D. 400s to obtain gold from the Soninke peoples (who today live mainly in Mali and adjacent states) in response to increased demand for gold from the Mediterranean region. Islamic scholars came to refer to the sub–Saharan lands as the Land of Gold. By the 700s the trade had grown to involve large caravans crossing the desert. The wealth generated from the trade among the Soninke helped them to establish the Ghana or Wagadou Empire around 750 (c. 750–1076), which occupied southeastern Mauritania, western Mali, and eastern Senegal.

The Berbers mainly sold the gold to Arab merchants in town of Sijilmasa, which is located in what is now southeastern Morocco at the Tafilalt oasis (near the modern town of Rissani). This interaction led to the spread of Islam among the Berbers and subsequently among other peoples along the caravan routes and at the southern end of the routes. From Sijilmasa one of the main routes went south to Tuat and then to the important Berber oasis of Tidikelt in southern Algeria. A caravan route from Tunis also joined this route here on its way to the southern goldfields. The route then headed south to the town of Timbuktu on the Bend of the Niger River.

One of the most important goods heading south over this route was salt. The main source of salt for this trade were the Taodeni (aka Taoudenni) salt mines, located about 600 km north of Timbuktu in northwestern Mali near the border with Algeria. The mines were described in the late 19th century as being run by Arabs and worked by several thousand African slaves.[55] At that time there were two large salt caravans per year traveling between Timbuktu and the mines. The trip took three weeks each way and involved thousands of camels. In the late 1930s, Miner estimates that 7,000 camels were involved in each caravan.[56]

Timbuktu, located in central Mali near the Niger River, began as a seasonal camp for the nomadic Tuareg and developed into a regional commercial center in the 900s. It was incorporated into the Mandinkas' Manding or Mali Empire (1230s-1600s), which was centered in southwestern Mali in the vicinity of the Bure goldfield. The Mandinka rulers were responsible for spreading Islam to Timbuktu. According to Miner, "Important Islamic influences reached Timbuctoo in 1336 when the Songhoi [Songhay] came under Mandingo control. Returning from a pilgrimage to Mecca, the Emperor of Mali, Mansa Mousa, stopped at Timbuctoo and had the Great Mosque erected."[57] Mansa Mousa also sought to promote Islamic scholarship and ordered a number of local scholars to go to Fez to study. After they returned the city began to develop a reputation as a center of Islamic learning in its own right and Muslim scholars from North Africa and Spain visited the city.

At the southern end of this route the gold trade initially was centered in the town of Audaghost (located north of the Bambuk goldfield in what is now southern Mauritania), which was established by Berbers in the 400s as a gold-trading center located outside of Soninke territory. The Soninke conquered Audaghost in 1050 out of a desire to gain greater control over gold trading. In the late 1100s, however, the gold trade began to bypass Audaghost as the Bambuk goldfield declined in importance and the center of gold production moved east to the Bure goldfield in southwestern Mali near the head of the Niger River and within the territory of the Mali Empire. The king (*mansa*) of the Mali Empire claimed exclusive ownership of all gold nuggets found within his realm, and they were exchanged with the royal treasury for an equivalent weight in gold dust.

Oualata (aka Walata, located in southeastern Mauritania) replaced Audaghost as the main trading center for a time. Soninke people were the initial inhabitants, but by the time that Ibn Batutta visited in 1352 Berbers were the main inhabitants. The route followed by Ibn Battuta was from Sijilmasa, 25 days to Taghaza (where salt was obtained from the nearby Taodeni salt mines), then on to another oasis (possibly Bir Ksaib), and another arduous 10 days to Oualata.[58] Ibn Batutta indicated that while salt might be exchanged for gold at Oualata, it was far more profitable to sell it in the kingdom's capital of Niani (located in modern Guinea). In the latter half of the 1300s Timbuktu replaced Oualata as the main terminus of the trans–Saharan caravan trade in this region, and Oualata declined, becoming a small kingdom.[59]

The trans–Saharan caravan trade had a number of important implications for transnationalism in the medieval period and beyond. First of all there was the introduction of Islam and linking the peoples of the region to the larger Islamic world in cultural and economic terms. The Sahara and sub-Saharan areas involved in the caravan trade remained outside of the caliphates, but there was significant interaction as traders as well as religious scholars and pilgrims moved back and forth. Conversion to Islam and the wealth generated by the caravan trade was influential in the creation of numerous political entities south of the Sahara, including multi-ethnic empires, while Islam and the caravan trade ensured that people continued to move back and forth between these states and empires and that there were transnational residents involved in commerce and religious affairs living in them.

Vikings

The Vikings are normally thought of in terms of their raiding throughout Europe and their exploration of the North Atlantic. Often ignored are their transnational activities as long-distance traders and as mercenaries. Their employment as mercenaries serving in the Byzantine Empire's Varangian Guard is discussed in another chapter. Here we will focus on the Vikings as long-distance traders. As Simpson notes, these long-distance traders "always went by water, whether by sea or along river-systems."[60] Thus, Viking traders not only were active all along the coasts of Europe, but also along many of its major rivers. Muslim and Byzantine writers who have left us descriptions of these traders often refer to them as Varangians as well. Davidson says that the term "was probably derived from the Old Norse *vàr*, 'pledge,' used of a group of men binding themselves into a company and swearing to observe certain obligations and to support one another loyally, as well as sharing the profits."[61]

The term Viking loosely refers to Scandinavian peoples from Sweden, Norway, and Denmark who engaged in raiding, trade, conquest, and settlement throughout Europe and the North Atlantic. The Viking Age begins in 793, when Norwegians carried out a raid against the English monastery of Lindisfarne. The Viking Age roughly coincided with the Medieval Warm Period (*c.* 800–1250), when relatively mild temperatures prevailed in northern Europe, and came to an end around the time of the onset of the Little Ice Age (*c.* 1250–1850) in Northern Europe.

Raiding was conducted initially mainly by Norwegians and later the Danes became involved as well. They also established colonies in the Orkney, Shetland, and Faeroe Islands and later in Ireland, the Isle of Man, Scotland, and England. Simpson mentions, "They established fortified harbors (Dublin, Wexford, Waterford, Cork, Limerick), which were valuable bases for voyages to the west coast of France and Spain, and these became flourishing centres of trade."[62] In the 870s Norse settlements were established on Iceland. These settlers, like those on the Isle of Man, were largely farmers. Danes and Norwegians also settled in large numbers in England from the 870s to the 950s. The Danes established rule over much of England from 1017 to 1042. Norse settlement of Greenland began in 982 and later a small settlement was established in northern Newfoundland.

As the raiding commenced, Scandinavians from Gotland and elsewhere in Sweden "were amassing wealth as traders and importing European glass and woolen fabrics, possibly in exchange for iron ore."[63] Davidson refers to the island of Gotland as "a kind of Clapham Junction of the Viking Age, a centre from which routes led out in many directions."[64] Immediately to the east, Swedes and Gotland islanders in particular established colonies in the 700s in Latvia, Lithuania, Estonia, and Finland.

During the 800s enterprising Viking traders expanded their activities to the southeast along the Volga River where they came into contact with the Khaganates of the Volga Bulghars, whose capital of Bulghar was an important trading center, and of the Khazars, whose capital of Itil was located adjacent to the Caspian Sea. These two peoples controlled the trade along the Volga River and with the Caliphate of Baghdad. Muslim traders would sometimes travel north to trade with the Vikings, buying slaves and northern products in exchange for silver and sometimes goods such as silks and spices. While some Viking traders conducted their business in Bulghar or Itil, a few would sail across the Caspian Sea and carry their goods on camel to Baghdad. Davidson remarks, "The market at Bulghar drew Swedish merchants along the Volga route because they could met with eastern merchants there and get good process for slaves and furs."[65]

In 921 the Caliph of Baghdad sent the Arab geographer Ahmad ibn Fadlan as his ambassador to the Volga Bulghars. His mission was not a success, but he wrote an account of his travels that included an important description of the Vikings he encountered: "They arrive from their own lands [at certain seasons] and moor their ships along the Itil [Volga], which is a great river, and build large wooden houses on its banks. In one such house 10 or 20 people (more or less) will gather."[66] Each of the traders had his own quarters in one of these buildings, where he would reside with his concubines and slaves. Ibn Fadlan says the traders exchanged sable pelts for goods.

Commenting on the wealth of Gotland's traders, Davidson notes, "About half the vast number of silver coins from abroad discovered in Scandinavia have been found in Gotland, and a large proportion of these came from the Islamic East."[67] The desire for silver coins was an important motivating factor driving Viking traders to the Muslim world and most of the silver coins discovered in Viking sites come from this area rather than from Christian locales.[68] Scandinavia had no silver of its own and political instability in Europe following the fall of the Western Roman Empire had put an end to that source of silver. The Muslim world then became the primary source. From the late 700s until the late 800s most of the silver was mined near Tashkent. Then in the late 800s a new source of silver was discovered at Benjahir in Afghanistan. This was an incredibly rich mine that produced vast amounts of silver for the caliphs. Silver production declined in the mid–900s, creating a silver crisis in the Middle East and a sharp drop in the amount of silver available to Viking traders.

As the flow of silver along the Volga River dried up, Viking traders shifted to the Dnieper River, although Byzantium did not ever provide as much silver for the Vikings as had the Volga River route. This can be seen from the fact that in contrast to the 85,000 Arabic silver coins found in archaeological sites in Sweden only some 500 Byzantine silver coins have been found.[69] During the latter part of the 900s Scandinavian trade with Germany grew in importance as the Vikings sought German silver that was being mined in the Harz Mountains. About 70,000 German silver coins have been discovered in Scandinavia dating from the later 900s and 1000s.

The Vikings did not trade solely for silver. Some gold made it north, mostly in coin form, which was then made into "ornaments, gold leaf or thread."[70] Excavations of gravesites from the trading center of Kaupang (near Oslo), for example, have turned up "Frankish glass, Rhineland pottery, and many objects from the British Isles."[71] In addition to silver and gold coins, the other important trade good sought from Byzantium was silk. Byzantine silk was considered a particularly precious commodity.[72]

What did the Vikings trade? Slaves were an especially important item of trade. Simpson mentions walrus and seal rope that was very strong and walrus ivory that was used to make a variety of decorative objects such as crucifixes and sword-grips.[73] *Egil's Saga* describes a trading expedition by Thorolf Kveldulfsson of Halogaland (Norway) to England:

> Thorolf had a large ship, which was waiting to put to sea. It was elaborate in everything, beautifully painted down to the sea-line, the sails also carefully striped with blue and red, and all the tackling as elaborate as the ship. Thorolf had this ship made ready, and put aboard some of his house-carles as crew; he freighted it with dried fish and hides, and ermine and gray furs too in abundance, and other peltry such as he had gotten from the fell; it was a most valuable cargo. This ship he bade sail westwards for England to buy him clothes and other supplies that he needed; and they, first steering southwards along the coast, then stretching across the main, came to England. There they found a good market, laded the ship with wheat and honey and wine and clothes, and sailing back in autumn with a fair wind came to Hordaland.[74]

Traders came to Kaupang from the far north (including Greenland) bringing goods such as seal and walrus rope, walrus ivory, furs, steatite (soapstone), narwhale tusks, and bird feathers. From there merchants would then often sail to the important trading center of Hedeby at the base of the Jutland Peninsula. From there traders went east across the

Baltic Sea and on to Russia, west across the North Sea to northern France and England, or south by land into Germany.

Hedeby was established as a trading center around 808 and expanded until the mid–900s, when it went into decline until it was sacked and then abandoned in the mid–1000s. The town housed traders as well as craftsmen (including those who made amber and glass beads, others who carved stag and reindeer antlers and walrus tusks, and a variety of metal workers who made objects from bronze, tin, and lead, and some gold and silver as well). The inhabitants included various Scandinavians as well as Frisians and Saxons.[75] Slaves also passed through Hedeby mainly on their way to Muslim markets. This trade seems to have been the motive behind a visit to the town by Ibrahim ibn Ahmed at-Tarishi of Córdoba in the 950s — he had little good to say about the town or its inhabitants.

Birka, on the island of Björkö in Sweden, was another important trading center on the shores of the Baltic Sea. While some trade went west from Birka, most went east through Finnish territory along the Gulf of Finland to Starya Ladoga near the southern shore of Lake Ladoga. Traders then went south to Novgorod and then either continued south along the Dnieper River to Kiev, on to the Black Sea, and then to Byzantium, or east down the Volga River to Bulghar and on to Itil on the Caspian Sea, and across the sea to Baghdad. Birka was an especially important center for exporting furs to the south. Starya Ladoga was a mixed Finnish and Swedish community, while further south mixed Swedish and Slavic communities were established along the Dnieper. Novgorod was inhabited mainly by Slavs, but was ruled by Scandinavians.

As was mentioned above, during the 900s the focus of eastern Viking trade shifted from the Volga River to the Dnieper River. While the Baghdad Caliphate and other Muslim territories across the Caspian Sea had been the southern focus of the Volga River trade, trade down the Dnieper River aimed ultimately at crossing the Black Sea and trading with the Byzantine Empire. Swedish traders had first made contact with Constantinople in 838, but it was not until the next century that this route became important. The Persian Abu'l Qasim Ubaid'Allah ibn Khurdadhbih (l. *c.* 820–912), a geographer and Director of Posts and Intelligence of the province of Djibal (northwestern Iran), wrote *The Book of Roads and Kingdoms* around 870, in which he describes Rus traders (likely Swedes) traveling along the Dnieper "bringing beaver skins, and skins of black foxes, and swords, from the furthest parts of the Slav lands down to the Black Sea."[76]

The Byzantine emperor Constantine VII Porphyrogenitus (r. 912–59) provided an account written around 944 of the Viking traders in his book *De Administrando Imperio:* "In June the expedition sets out for Greece. For a few days the merchant fleet assembles at Vytechhev, a fortress of the Rus just below Kiev. When the fleet is complete they all set off downstream, so as to face the difficulties of the journey in company." They pass through seven gorges. "Then they succeed in reaching an island, named after St Georges, to which they bring their offerings because a gigantic oak-tree grows there." Then they sail on to the island of Berezanj at the mouth of the Dnieper and then on to the Black Sea and Byzantium.[77]

While there were Viking mercenaries who resided permanently or for very long periods in Byzantium, the merchants appear to have come to trade on an annual basis and then returned north once their business was complete. The activities of Viking traders who came to Byzantium from Kiev, Novgorod, and other towns were outlined in commercial treaties in 907 and 911.[78] The 907 treaty stipulates that upon arrival the Scandinavian traders were to dock their ships at a specific harbor. A government official then recorded their names and they were required to take up residence in the St. Mamas quarter that was located on the Bosporus and outside of the city walls. They could only enter the city through one gate and had to do so unarmed and accompanied by an official. They were exempted from taxes and those who arrived with merchandise were provided for by the state: "Whoever come as merchants shall receive supplies for six months, including bread, wine, meat and fruit. Baths shall be prepared for them in any volume they require. When the Rus return homeward, they shall require from your Emperor food, anchors, cordage and sails and whatever else is needed for the journey."[79] The 911 treaty also made provision for Scandinavians who wished to enter imperial military service to reside in the city and dealt with settling the estates of those who died while residing in the empire. It is apparent that a Scandinavian community had come into existence in Byzantium that included relatively permanent mercenaries and temporarily resident merchants. As will be discussed in a later chapter at least some of the mercenaries can be viewed as transnationals in that they retained ties to their northern homes, but it is unclear whether there were other transnational Scandinavians living in the city.

The Vikings established several fortified towns south of Novgorod along the Dnieper River. Kiev was the most important of these settlements and was established some time before 840. Swedes were the rulers in Novgorod, while Norwegians ruled Kiev. Scandinavians and their descendants formed a ruling class of warrior aristocrats, who collected tribute from the surrounding area. The remainder of the population was a mixture of Slav and Scandinavian. Simpson comments, "Relationships between the two races were certainly complex: on the one hand, the Scandinavians exacted tribute from the Slavs, and carried many of them off as slaves, but at the same time they themselves became increasingly Slavicised in customs and by intermarriage."[80] Davidson remarks, "The Vikings were practical colonists and explorers, they would travel light and adapt to existing conditions, while intermarriage with women of different races or the taking of concubines among their captives must have complicated household arrangements and possessions to an even greater degree."[81] In addition to the rulers and their allied warriors there were artisans and merchants who resided in the towns. The larger towns often had a separate quarter for the artisans. The Persian Muslim geographer Ahmad ibn Rustah describes these Scandinavians (probably referring specifically to those living at Novgorod) in the 900s: "They fight with the Slavs and use ships to attack them; they take them captive and carry them to the Khazars and Bulghar and there sell them as slaves.... They have no villages, no estates or fields. Their only occupation is trading in sable and squirrel and other kinds of skin, which they sell to those who will buy from them. In payment they take coins, which they keep in their belts."[82] While many of the Scandinavians who settled in these towns along the Dnieper River settled down and gradually lost their ties to their northern homelands, it would appear that there were both merchants and mercenaries who maintained more mobile, more transnational, lives as Varangian Guards.

Nestorian Christians

It is unfortunate that so little attention has been paid in modern times to this group of Christians since they played such an important role not only in the spread of Christianity across Asia but also in their activities as long-distance traders. As has already been mentioned, it was a group of Nestorian monks who brought silkworms and mulberry trees to the Byzantine

Empire from China in A.D. 552. The most famous Nestorian merchant monk was Cosmas Indicopleustes. He was a Greek from Alexandria who produced an account of his travels around the Red Sea and to South Asia known as the *Topographia Christiana* around 550.[83] In this work he describes trading activities as well as the Christians that he encountered. Thus, he describes Taprobane (the ancient name for Sri Lanka) as a "great emporium which was connected by seaways with trading marts over the world" and mentions "there is a church of the Christians, and clerks and faithful" on the island.[84] He says that the Nestorian church had a bishop in the important trading center of Kalliana. He describes Malé on the Maldives as also having a Nestorian church. He made several voyages to India and visited the Malabar Coast in 522 where he encountered Nestorians.

The Nestorians take their name from Nestorius (1. *c.* 386–451). He was born in the Roman province of Syria and received his clerical training in Antioch from Theodore of Mopsuestia (1. *c.* 350–428), a Universalist who believed that all people eventually would be saved. Nestorius served as Archbishop of Constantinople from 428 to 431. He was accused of heresy because of his preference of referring to the Virgin Mary as the Mother of Christ rather than the Mother of God and was removed as archbishop by the Council of Ephesus. He died in exile in the Egyptian desert. His followers, commonly referred to as Nestorians or Chaldean Christians, came to be associated with the Holy Apostolic Catholic Assyrian Church of the East, which is also called the Nestorian Church or the Church of the East.

When Byzantine Christians began persecuting Nestorius's followers the Sassanid Persians granted them protection in 462. Their church established its Patriarchate at Seleukeia-Ctesiphon (located along the Tigris River and known as Al-Mada'in in modern Iraq). Newman writes of this period, "In the day of their power, Edessa was their sacred city, and the city of Nisibis was their seat of learning and the centre of their grand missionary operations."[85] Edessa (modern Sanliurfa) and Nisibis (modern Nusaybin) are located in what is today southeastern Turkey. The area was incorporated into various ancient empires, including various Persian empires and the Roman Empire. The School of Nisibis was famous as a Christian center of scholarship. Nestorians gravitated to the school after their school in Edessa was closed in 489. The school remained an important center of learning until it went into decline after a new school was established in Baghdad in 832. It was around this time that the Nestorians moved their headquarters to Baghdad. Newman remarks, "Not less than one hundred and fifty authors [attached to the school] contributed to advance literature in the East. They were commentators of the whole or parts of the Bible; they were sacred and profane historians; they were lexicographers, grammarians, logicians, metaphysicians, geographers, astronomers, writers on natural philosophy; and more than a hundred were poets."[86] They wrote in Greek, the Syriac language, and Persian, and translated many works from other languages into these languages.

The Nestorians were active missionaries in many parts of the Middle East, across Central Asia and the Indian Ocean to the coastal areas of southern India, Sri Lanka, and China. As a marginal minority within Persia they turned to trade as a means of supporting themselves. From their base in Persia the Nestorians conducted missionary activities and long-distance trade widely across Asia.[87] The two often went hand-in-hand. The Nestorians prospered under the rule of Kavad (r. 488–531) and his son Khosru (r. 531–79). Thus, they accompanied the Persian army to Turkestan in 498 where they sought to convert the Hephthalite Huns, and after Khosru made Yemen a province of Persia in 575 they set about to gain converts there as well. The Persians had sent their first embassy to China in 455 and, although relations were limited until the 600s, the Nestorians took advantage of the opportunities presented by these relations. Soon there were Nestorians visiting China, and in 579 there is a reference to a Nestorian settling in China. They also followed commercial routes to the southeast and established a church in Kalyana (modern Karachi) in the 500s.

The founding of the Tang Dynasty in China and its re-opening of the Silk Road in 630 was a major impetus for the expansion of the Nestorians. The Nestorian missionary Alopen Abraham arrived in China in 635. In 638 the Tang Emperor Tai Taizong issued an Edict of Toleration for Christians. The same year Alopen built a church in the Tang capital of Chang'an and completed work on the first Christian book in Chinese, *The Sutra of Jesus the Messiah*.[88] Taizong's successor Gao Zong of Tang (r. 650–83) continued to tolerate the Nestoraians and awarded Alopen with the title Great Spiritual Lord, Protector of the Empire. Christians then fell out of favor for a time (roughly 683 to 744) and local Christians and missionaries were persecuted. The situation for Christians began to ease towards the end of the reign of Emperor Xuanzong (r. 712–56) and a new group of Nestorian missionaries arrived in China in 744.

Nestorian missionaries and traders were also active in the areas around China. Nestorianism gained a foothold among the Huihe (Uyghars) to the west of China and in 755 the Nestorian son of the Huihe ruler joined forces with the Tang to defeat the An Shi Rebels. A few years later, in 762, the Huihe adopted Manichaeism (a syncretic religion that included elements of Nestorianism) as their state religion. Nestorians remained active among the Huihe, however, and around 1180 a metropolitan was appointed for the important Uyghar town of Kashgar. Further to the west a number of inscriptions dating from 1249 to 1345 appear on Nestorian gravestones in Bishkek (modern Kyrgyztan). Nestorians were also active in Tibet and in 781 a Nestorian bishop was consecrated there. Nestorians went to Japan as well. It is unclear when the first Nestorians arrived in Japan, but they were certainly active in the 600s. Researchers have found a version of the Gospel of Saint Matthew in Chinese dating from the 800s in the Koryuji Buddhist Temple in Kyoto. The temple was built in 818 on top of the ruins of a Nestorian Christian church that had been destroyed by fire.

The Nestorian religion declined again in China with the collapse of the Tang Dynasty. An imperial edict in 845 led to renewed persecution of Christians in China and Nestorian monks visiting China in 981 found no evidence of any remaining Christians there. Around the same time, Nestorians in the Middle East were facing persecution during the reign of the Abbasid Caliph al-Mutawakkil (r. 821–61).

Nestorian fortunes were reversed in the 1200s, particularly during the time of Kublai Khan. A Nestorian metropolitan for Khanbalik (Beijing) was appointed in 1248 and Nestorians began to play a role in the religious, commercial, and political life of the empire. A Nestorian named Mar Sergius served as governor of Gansu Province from 1278 to 1281. Kublai Khan created a special department to deal with Christians in his empire in 1281 and appointed a Nestorian named Ai-hsueh as its first head. In addition to Khanbalik (Beijing), the Nestorians established churches along the Silk Road in His-ning (modern Xining, Qinghai Province) and Tun-huang (Dunhuang, Gansu Province), in the port cities of Chen-chiang (Shanghai), Ch'uan-chou (Quanzhou, Fujian Province), Hang-chou (Hangzhou, Zhejiang province), and Kuang-zhou (Guangzhou, Guangdong Province), as well as in Ch'eng-tu (Chengdu, Sichuan Province). Thus, they had churches in virtually all of the important centers of international trade linking China to the outside world.

The Nestorians survived the fall of the Yuan Dynasty in 1368 and Nicolo de Conti reported meeting with some of them when he visited China in 1440, but their numbers were in decline. The Italian Jesuit Matteo Ricci who lived in China most of the time from the 1580s until his death in 1610 reported finding only a small number of Nestorians.[89]

As was mentioned above, Nestorians were also active in India. Christianity has a long history in India centering along the Malabar Coast (modern Kerala). Thomas the Apostle landed there in A.D. 52 and established a Christian community. When Cosmas Indicopleustes visited the Malabar Coast in 522, he found them living in the important port of Kollam (modern Quilon). This Nestorian community is also mentioned in a letter by the Nestorian Patriarch Jesujabbus (d. 660) to Simon of the church's metropolitan see in Persia. The Nestorian church sent two bishops to India in 822 to look after the local Christian communities in the ports of Kollam and Cranganore (modern Kodungallur). Mar Sapor became the bishop at Kollam and later lived in Thevalakara (about 25 km from Kollam), where he was buried in a church that was built in the 300s. Later Nestorian churches were also established outside of Kerala, including in Bombay and Patna (Bihar State). The Nestorians established a metropolitan see in Patna in 1222. When the Franciscan Odoric of Pordenone visited India in 1324 he found that all of the Christians there were Nestorians. The Nestorian community in India was still active when the Portuguese arrived in 1498. A delegation of them had traveled to visit the Nestorian patriarch in Gagarta (near Mosul) in order to bring back bishops for India. The Portuguese were not particularly tolerant of the Nestorians, and forced those falling under their control to convert to Catholicism.

Radhanites and Other Jewish Traders

The term Radhanites was used during the medieval period to refer variously to specific groups of Jewish merchants as well as to Jewish merchants in a more general sense.[90] They played an important role in long-distance trade connecting Europe, the Middle East, Central Asia, East Asia, and North Africa, especially during the early medieval period (A.D. 600–1000) when communities of Jewish traders could be found scattered along the most important trade routes.

The Persian Abu'l Qasim Ubaid'Allah ibn Khurdadhbih, who was mentioned in the section on the Vikings, provides an account of the activities of the Radhanites during the latter half of the 800s. He says that the traders were sophisticated and multilingual and describes their trade routes between the Rhône Valley in France and China and the goods that they carried. They transported slaves as well as a wide range of valuable goods including spices, oils, incense, perfumes, jewelry, silk, furs, and steel weapons. The Radhanites were pioneers in developing long-distance trade directly from Western Europe to China rather than relying on intermediaries in Persia and Central Asia. They were able to conduct this trade on a fairly regular basis for several centuries. Their role as traders developed in part because of restrictions the Christian rulers in Western Europe and the Muslim rulers in the Middle East placed on their fellow Christians and Muslims conducting trade with one another. The Jewish Radhanites were considered neutral middlemen.

Although their position began to erode during the reign of Charlemagne, who banned Jews from engaging in money lending in 814, the early Carolingian rulers in France afforded Jewish merchants privileges from the 600s until the time of Charlemagne that encouraged their activities in long-distance trade. The merchants and their benefactors were able to amass considerable wealth from this trade, but this served to generate hostility on the part of local Christian authorities. To avoid carrying large quantities of cash, Jewish communities developed a system of using letters of credit. This form of credit was widely used by the Radhanites and other long-distance Jewish traders in the medieval period. In the face of political changes in China and Central Asia the Silk Road trade effectively collapsed in the 900s and with it the long-distance trade of the Radhanites between Western Europe and China ceased.

This was not the end of long-distance Jewish trading, however, for Jews continued to engage in long-distance trade between the Middle East and South Asia, primarily dealing in spices, but also carrying silk, ceramics, and other goods. A network of Jewish traders was formed between Cairo, Aden, and the ports of the Malabar Coast. One of these traders, Abraham bin Yiju, was active in the spice trade in the 1100s.[91] He came to the Malabar Coast port of Mangalore in 1138 to purchase cardamom. At the time there was a "heterogeneous community of Arabs, Gujaratis, Tamils, Jews, and others" numbering between 2,000 and 3,000 living around the harbor, with the merchants living in fortified houses that also served as warehouses.[92] Abraham bin Yiju was born in the port of Mahdia (in modern Tunisia) and his father was a rabbi. Abraham and his two brothers decided to become traders, but while his two brothers remained in Mahdia to engage in Mediterranean maritime trade, Abraham, like many other Tunisian Jewish traders, went to the more important commercial center of Cairo around 1120 carrying with him a letter of introduction from his father to the leading Jewish merchants of that city. After spending a few years in Cairo, Abraham sailed to Aden. There a man named Madmun ibn Bandar, who was the town's most important trader and head (*nagid*) of the Jewish trading community in Aden, employed him as an apprentice keeping accounts. Madmun maintained an extensive trading network with Jews and Muslims that reached from Spain to India. Madmun sent Abraham to Mangalore as a junior partner after he completed an apprenticeship of three years.

Abraham established his new home in Mangalore and began dealing in spices. Gordon makes the important point that, although Abraham bin Yiju was a Jew, he "neither lived nor worked in an isolated enclave of Jews. The Mangalore trading society included local Hindus, resident Gujaratis, and local Muslims, in addition to periodic arrivals of Middle East Muslims," and he "regularly formed partnerships with Gujaratis and local Hindus."[93]

After several years of successful trading Abraham was able to establish himself as an independent trader. A male slave assisted Abraham in his business and functioned as an agent and was entrusted to carry money and goods between Mangalore and Aden. As for his family life, Abraham married and had children by a slave he had purchased and then manumitted. Though such a marriage were a common enough practice, Abraham's fellow traders in Aden and Cairo did not approve of the marriage since the woman was not a Jew. It is not that there were no local Jewish women available. The Jewish community at the nearby port of Cochin, for example, at the time numbered several thousand.

The Jewish communities of North Africa suffered as a result of attacks by Christian crusaders. Roger II of Sicily kidnapped members of Abraham's family in 1148 and forcibly took them to Sicily. Abraham left his wife in Mangalore the following year and returned to Tunisia (with his son and daughter) in an effort to assist his family. One brother remained in Sicily where he lived in poverty and the other defrauded Abraham of money. Abraham then went to Aden, where his son died, and then settled in southern Yemen to work as a trader once again. He had left his daughter in Aden and after settling in Yemen arranged for her to marry the son of his brother in Sicily.

The Jewish traders of Egypt remained active until around 1300, when Muslim merchants largely pushed them out of the spice trade. The Jewish community in Aden also lost some of its influence in long-distance trade at this time, although the community itself remained an important one until the twentieth century when attacks on the community by Muslims culminating in a wave of attacks in 1967 led the remaining Jews to leave. A community of several thousand Jews continued in the spice trade in Cochin, India, until they migrated to Israel between 1970 and 2000.[94]

Marco Polo and the Venetians

A new group of long-distance trading centers emerged in Western Europe during the latter part of the medieval period. These were Italian city-states such as Venice, Genoa, Pisa, and Amalfi. Venice and Genoa became the dominant Italian trading city-states with commercial interests scattered across Western Europe and the Mediterranean. These northern Italian cities profited from overland trade moving across the Alps, which they then shipped across the Mediterranean. Genoa dominated maritime trade in the Tyrrhenian Sea and Venice the Adriatic. These city-states traded with both Christian and Islamic states: Venice with Egypt, Pisa with Tunisia, and Genoa with the Moors of North Africa and Spain. During the Crusades they sold goods to crusaders and provided them with transport while still trading with Muslims, including the selling of arms to the Saracens. Merchants from Amalfi, Pisa, Venice, and Genoa engaged in trade in the Byzantine Empire and established factories at Constantinople. Curtain makes the point about these city-states, "Venice, Genoa, and other Italian port cities organized trade diasporas that depended heavily on the use of force; commerce and coercion were closely linked, if not inseparable."[95]

In addition to merchants and powerful fleets, these city-states also possessed important financial institutions that supported overseas trade. As Durant remarks, "The Italians ... developed banking to unprecedented heights in the thirteenth century. Great banking families rose to supply sinews of far-reaching Italian trade: the Buonsignori and Gallerani in Siena, the Frescobaldi, Bardi, and Peruzzi in Florence, the Pisani and Tiepoli in Venice.... They extended their operations beyond the Alps, and lent great sums to the ever-greedy kings of England and France, to barons, bishops, abbots, and towns.... By the middle of the thirteenth century these 'Lombards,' as the North called all Italian bankers, were the most active and powerful financiers in the world."[96] The rise of both Italian merchants and bankers came largely at the expense of the Jews who had previously dominated these activities.

The present discussion will focus on Venice, which became the richest European city of the late medieval period and the main European financial center for centuries. The Republic of Venice emerged in the late A.D. 600s and lasted until 1797.[97] Initially it was under Byzantine rule, but after achieving de facto independence in 803 it became an increasingly important ally of the Byzantine Empire, an alliance in which economic fortunes of the two were closely interrelated. Venice was the dominant Italian power operating in Constantinople. Curtain notes, "From 1082 to 1204, the Byzantine Empire recognized the value of Venetian naval services (and the threat of Venetian naval power, if unfriendly) by exempting Venetians from the duties normally payable in Byzantine territory."[98]

By around 1100 the Venetians began to expand their operations beyond the confines of the Adriatic and Aegean seas into the eastern Mediterranean to the shores of the Levant and Egypt. This enhanced the wealth of Venice while also increasingly involving it in the affairs of the crusaders. In 1123 they were granted autonomy to operate within the crusader-established Kingdom of Jerusalem. Jealousy of their wealth and status resulted in attacks on the Venetians in Constantinople in 1182 with many being killed and others having their property seized and being forced to leave the city. Partially in revenge for the events of 1182, in 1204 the Venetians in league with crusaders of the Fourth Crusade sacked Constantinople.

Historians consider this to be one of the most profitable sackings of a city in history and the Venetians made off with most of the loot.

During the period of the Latin Kingdom of Constantinople from 1204 to 1261, Venice laid claim to parts of the Byzantine Empire and established colonies in the Black Sea and eastern Mediterranean. Venice already had well-established trade connections in the Black Sea through its association with the Byzantine Empire. This was viewed as important since it provided a link with the overland Silk Road routes that reached the shores of the Black Sea. Venetians were quite active at the important trading center of Tanaïs that was located adjacent to where the Don River empties into the Sea of Azov. After the sacking of Constantinople the Venetians established colonies in a number of towns around the Black Sea, including Theodosia (aka Caffa, Kaffa) and Sudak. Theodosia was an ancient town founded by Greeks in the 500s B.C. It had been destroyed by the Huns in the A.D. 300s, but had re-emerged as a trading center, for a time under the Kipchaks and later under Mongol rule. Venice built a fort and trading center there called Soldaia, which it controlled from 1204 to 1261 and again from 1296 to 1307. Genoa purchased it from the Golden Horde in 1261 and turned it into an important slave-trading center. Genoa regained control of it in 1307. Sudak was founded in A.D. 212. Greek merchants occupied it for a time and Khazars ruled it from the 800s to 1016. The Venetians asserted control over it after 1204 until it was ceded to Genoa in 1365. After the end of the Latin Kingdom of Constantinople the Genoese gained the upper hand in the Black Sea at the expense of Venice, until the Ottomans drove them out in 1475.

The Venetians also established colonies on the islands of Euboea and Crete after 1204.[99] The smaller islands that were Venetian colonies in the Aegean Sea were administered as the Duchy of the Archipelago from 1207 until 1579. Crete was administered as the Venetian colony of Candia from 1211 until it fell to the Ottomans in 1669. McKee argues that Candia was distinct from most other colonies of the medieval period for the unprecedented degree to which the colonial power was directly involved in its governance.[100] A paid civil service fully accountable to the Venetian Senate governed the colony. It was a multi-ethnic and multi-religious colony with the majority of its inhabitants being Byzantine Greek Cretans and there also being minorities made up of Venetian Catholics and Jews. Over time there was considerable mixing of the Greek and Venetian populations and their cultures, although the colonial administration and Venetian and Greek Cretan elites promoted notions of ethnic distinctions. The Jewish community of Candia was comprised mainly of Armenian Jews.[101] A number of Jews also migrated to Crete from Spain after the expulsion of Jews from Spain in 1492. Jews were the third largest ethnic community of the colony and numbered about 800 in the city of Candia in 1627 (about 7 percent of the population). The administration of Proveditor General, Sindace, and Inquisitor Giacomo Foscarini (1547–77) began a period of discrimination against both Jews and Greeks in which all non–Catholics were required to pay significantly higher taxes than Catholics.

Venetian merchants conducted considerable trade with Egypt. They were attracted to Egypt, primarily the port of Alexandria, by the trade in pepper and other spices.[102] Venetian trade with Alexandria increased sharply between 1173 and 1184, and after Venice lost access to the Black Sea to the Genoese in the late 1200s the spice trade through Alexandria became even more important to Venice and Venetian merchants established a permanent settlement there. This maritime trade route became even more important to Venice after the overland Silk Road route was disrupted once again in the 1400s.

Venetian traders, financiers, and seamen were also found in the centers of trade in northern Europe. Venetian ships sailed to Bruges in Flanders to provide spices and other goods to northern European markets. Agents of Venetian banking interests could be found in most of the major cities of northern Europe.

Let us now turn to the most famous Venetian transnational of the medieval period, Marco Polo. Marco Polo (1. 1254–1324/25) was a trader and explorer whose travels were published in the book *Il Milione* (*The Million*), better known as *The Travels of Marco Polo*.[103] Marco Polo's father Niccolo and his uncles Maffeo (Maffio) and Marco (Marco il Vecchio, Marco the Elder) were prosperous merchants who traded with Asia. Niccolo and Maffeo were living in Constantinople's Venetian Quarter in 1259 when they decided to move north to the Venetian colony of Soldaia (Caffa) on the Crimean Peninsula. It was a fortunate decision since when Michael VIII Palaiologos captured Constantinople in 1261 the Venetian captives in the city were blinded and many of those who sought to escape by fleeing to the Venetian colonies in the Aegean Sea perished when the crowded ships that they were fleeing on sank. Soldaia (Caffa) was within the territory of the Golden Horde. In search of better profits, the Polo brothers traveled to Sarai Batu, the capital of Berke Khan, the ruler of the Golden Horde. The Polos remained in Sarai Batu, which was in reality a large camp rather than a sedentary town, for about a year. Motivated in part by conflict between Berke Khan and his cousin Hulagu Khan, the Polo brothers then headed further east to the important trading center of Bukhara, where they remained for three years. In 1264 Niccolo and Maffeo accompanied an embassy sent by the Ilkhan Hulagu to his brother Kublai Khan. The embassy arrived at Kublai Khan's capital of Khanbaliq (aka Dadu, modern Beijing) in 1266.

According to Marco Polo, Kublai Khan favorably received the Polo brothers and then sent them back to Italy accompanied by a Mongol named Koeketei as the Khan's ambassador to the Catholic Pope. They also took with them a letter from Kublai Khan requesting that educated Europeans be sent to China to teach about the Christian religion and Western customs. To help them on their return trip the Khan gave them a tablet stating that the travelers should be given horses, lodging, and food throughout the Khan's domains. Koeketei did not complete the journey. The Polo brothers traveled to the Armenian port of Ayas (in what was then the Kingdom of Cilicia) and then sailed to Saint Jean d'Acre (aka Acre), the capital of the Kingdom of Jerusalem. Pope Clement IV had died in 1268 and, at the suggestion of the papal legate for the realm of Egypt, Theobald Visconti, who was living in Acre, they returned to Venice to wait until the nomination of a new Pope.

Gregory X became Pope in 1271 and sent a response back to Kublai Khan with Niccolo and Maffeo the same year. Niccolo's son Marco and two friars (who turned back and did not complete the journey) accompanied them. Marco got along well with Kublai Khan and was sent on a variety of missions around the Khan's empire. He also served as governor of Guangzhou for three years. Marco was sent on his last mission for Kublai Khan in 1291. This entailed accompanying a Mongol princess named Koekecin (aka Cocacin) who was betrothed to the Ilkhan Arghun. They sailed from Quanzhou to Sumatra, Sri Lanka, India, and Persia. The Polos arrived in the Ilkhanate in 1293 or 1294. Arghun had died by then and there was a new Ilkhan on the throne, Gaykhatu, with whom they left the princess. They traveled on to Trebizond (modern Trazon, on the Black Sea in Turkey) and from there sailed to Venice.

Gujaratis

The modern state of Gujarat in western India was part of the ancient Mohenjodaro-Harappan civilization and the center of that civilization's and subsequent civilizations' ties with international maritime trade. There were a number of important ancient ports located along its coast. This tradition of maritime commerce around the Gulf of Cambay continued into the medieval period.

There are conflicting views about the origins of the Gujaratis, and it is apparent that by the medieval period they were a mixture of various peoples, including migrants from north India.[104] The region's ports were important trading centers under the Maurya and Gupta empires. Following the collapse of the Gupta Empire in the A.D. 400s, the region became relatively autonomous from the Gupta Empire under the Gupta general Bhatarka. Dronasimha broke ties with the Guptas and founded the Maitraka Dynasty (c. 475–770). The Maitrakas appear originally to have been Persian Zoroastrians. An additional influx of Zoroastrian refugees from Persia settled in the area in 775, where they came to be known as Parsis. After the Muslim ruler of Sindh sacked the Maitraka capital of Vallabhi in 770, the Pratihara Dynasty ruled the region. Gujarat became part of the Delhi Sultanate in 1297–98, but it regained its independence under the local Muslim governor Zafar Khan Muzaffar after Timur sacked Delhi in the late 1300s. His son Ahmed Shah (r. 1411–1442) became sultan and established his capital at Ahmedabad. The sultanate remained independent until 1576, when it became part of the Mughal Empire. Bharuch initially was Gujarat's most important port during the medieval period, but later Cambay emerged as the main port. The Portuguese established enclaves along the coast of Gujarat, including Daman (1531) and Diu (1535).

Tomé Pires, writing in the early 1500s, described Gujarat, which he referred to as the kingdom of Cambay, as "not large but noble, and rich and civilized, with large, strong cities with good walls and towers."[105] He also notes that it was constantly at war with its neighbors and that it employed a significant number of foreign soldiers, including "*Maçaris,* Arabs, Turkomans, *Rumes,* Persians, that is from Guilan and from Khorasan, and Abyssinians" as well as "renegade Christians."[106]

It is trade, however, that receives most of his attention: "These [people] are [like] Italians in their knowledge of and dealings in merchandise. All the trade in Cambay is in the hands of the heathen. Their general designation is Gujaratees.... There is no doubt that these people have the cream of the trade. They are men who understand merchandise; they are so properly steeped in the sound and harmony of it, that the Gujaratees say that any offence connected with merchandise is pardonable. There are Gujaratees settled every-where."[107] He adds that, while there are also traders from Cairo, Aden, and Hormuz living in the ports of Cambay, "none of these count in comparison with the heathens, especially in knowledge."[108] Pires goes so far as to recommend that his fellow Portuguese who want to engage in business would do well "to go there and learn, because the business of trade is a science in itself which does not hinder any other noble exercise, but helps a great deal."[109] He lists its most important ports as Cambay, Surat, Rander, and Diu, with the interior capital of Ahmedabad (he calls it Chamapne) also serving as an important commercial hub.

"These merchants do not merely carry out their trade at home, but they and the other merchants who have settled in Cambay," according to Pires, "sail many ships to all parts, to Aden, Ormuz [Hormuz/Ormus], the kingdom of the Deccan, Goa, Bhatkal, all over Malabar, Ceylon, Bengal, Pegu, Siam, Pedir, Pase (*Paeçe*) and Malacca."[110] He adds, "Cambay chiefly stretches out two arms, with her right arm she reaches out towards Aden and with the other towards Malacca.[Melaka]"[111] These are the two most important destinations for the traders of Cambay. Pires rates Melaka as the most important of these arms: "Malacca cannot live without Cambay, nor Cambay without Malacca."[112] This link, however, was a recent one and Pires says that only a century earlier, "Before the channel to Malacca [Strait of Melaka] was discovered," the Gujaratis sailed through the Sunda Strait at the southern end of the island of Sumatra to Gresik on Java's north coast.[113]

Pires notes that there were 1,000 Gujarati merchants living in Melaka and 4,000–5,000 Gujarati seamen regularly sailing between the two locales.[114] He remarks, "The Gujaratees were better seamen and did more navigating than the other people of these parts, and so they have larger ships and more men to man them. They have great pilots and do a great deal of navigation."[115] Merchants from the Middle East and elsewhere in India who were either resident in Cambay or who had traveled from their more distant homes sometimes accompanied the Gujarati traders and sailors to Melaka. Occasionally they too would settle in Melaka. Pires lists the following goods as being exported from Cambay to Melaka: "cloths of many kinds and of a fair quality, rough clothing, seeds such as nigella, cumin, *ameos,* fenugreek, roots like rampion, which they call pachak, and earth like lac which they call catechu, liquid storax and other things of the kind."[116] From Melaka they brought back to Cambay "all the rich merchandise of the Moluccas, Banda and China, and they used to bring a great deal of gold."[117]

Ryukyuans

The Ryukyu Islands are a long chain of islands that lie between Formosa and Japan with Okinawa, the main island of the group, located near the center of the chain. A degree of political unity was established in the 1300s with the founding of the three kingdoms of Sanzan (aka Chuzan). The entire region was then unified into a single kingdom in 1422 with the Kingdom of Ryukyu lasting as a distinct entity until 1879. The capital of the Kingdom of Ryukyu was located at Shuri on the island of Okinawa. The three kingdoms of Sanzan established tributary relations with the Ming Dynasty court of China in 1372 and the Kingdom of Ryukyu maintained this relationship. The kingdom was invaded by Japanese in 1609 and forced to pay tribute to the Japanese shogun as well. It was annexed by Japan in 1879.

Their status as vassals of China encouraged Ryukyuans to engage in maritime trade not only close to home but also throughout East and Southeast Asia.[118] The port of Naha is located on the small island of Ukishima that is connected to the capital of Shuri by a causeway. While it is not known when the port became an active center of trade, archaeologists have discovered pottery from the Japanese archipelago and Korean peninsula dating from the A.D. 1000s in the vicinity that indicates the existence of trade with these areas by this time. Naha included a port area, a marketplace with a government office, and an embassy and residence for Chinese officials. Adjacent to Naha and Shuri was a walled community known as Kumemura, which was a center of classical Chinese learning and also a residential area for other Chinese attracted to the area for trade.

Ryukyuans engaged in international maritime trade prior to 1372, but their new status as vassals of the Ming Empire and the Ming Dynasty's policies towards trade created opportunities that enterprising Ryukyuans took advantage of to become involved in maritime trade to an unprecedented extent. Ryukyuan maritime trade flourished as a result of preferential treatment granted to the Ryukyu kingdom and the Ming policy of *hai jin* (sea bans) that limited trade with China to vassal states and those with formal permission. Thus, the king of Sanzan was granted formal permission for his ships to trade in Ming ports.

Ryukyuans, on their own ships or as crew on Chinese ships, came to sail not only to neighboring ports in Japan, Korea, and China, but also to venture to ports in Southeast Asia, including ports in Annam (northern Vietnam), Champa, Java, Sumatra, Melaka, Patani, and Ayutthaya. Japanese merchants operating in a private capacity or on behalf of local nobles often used Ryukyuans to gain access to China. This was accomplished sometimes by transporting envoys from the Ryukyus who were officially traveling to China to present tribute as a cover for their trading activities. When the Ming court restricted overseas trade by Chinese, many Chinese merchants and seamen left China and settled in neighboring countries, especially in Southeast Asia. These overseas Chinese merchants continued to trade with China, often employing Ryukyuan ships that were under the command of Chinese officers.

The Portuguese king sent the merchant and pharmacist Fernao Pires de Andrade to make contact with China in 1517. Pires de Andrade had heard of the Ryukyu Islands while in Melaka and during the course of his visit to Fujian he sent one of his captains, Jorge Mascarenhas, to explore the Ryukyu Islands.[119] Another Portuguese, Tomé Pires, makes numerous references to the Ryukyuans in his *Suma Oriental,* referring to the islands of Liu Kiu and the islanders as *Lequeos.* In his preface, Pires refers to the Ryukyu Islands as "the noble island of Liu Kiu (*Lequeos*)."[120] In his description of the kingdom, Pires says that the people "have small ships of their own type; they have three or four junks which are continuously buying in China, and they have no more. They trade in China and in Malacca, and some times in company with the Chinese, sometimes on their own."[121] He adds, "One, two or three [of their] junks come to Malacca every year, and they take a great deal of Bengal clothing."[122] In regard to trade with Bengal, Pires lists "large green porcelain wares from Liu Kiu (*Leqios*)" among the main trade goods taken to Bengal from Melaka.[123] In his description of "native administration" of the rulers of Melaka, Pires says that there were "four *Xabamdares,* which are municipal offices" that "receive the captains of the junks" of foreign traders.[124] One of these was responsible for traders from China, the Ryukyus, and Champa. In addition to Melaka, Pires mentions that the people of Liu Kiu sailed to the port of Gresik in Java.[125]

After the Portuguese seized Melaka in 1511 traders from China and the Ryukyu Islands shifted the bulk of their trade in Southeast Asia to Patani. Previously Patani had been a minor port, but by the 1530s it was a major entrepôt that even attracted a large number of Portuguese traders. Later in the century Ryukyuans came to engage in an increasing amount of trade directly with Ayutthaya, which became the destination for the vast majority of their ships. A much smaller number of Ryukyuan ships continued to sail to Patani, Melaka, and Java.

The Ryukyuans carried a wide range of trade goods. Local exports included sulfur and horses. From Japan they carried silver, swords and other weapons, lacquerware, and fans and folding screens. They carried Japanese goods and such Chinese goods as porcelain, silk and other textiles, various metal goods (including coins), and medicines to the ports of Southeast Asia. Pires listed the main goods that they carried to Melaka: "The chief is gold, copper, and arms of all kinds, coffers, boxes with gold leaf veneer, fans, wheat, and their things are well made. They bring a great deal of gold."[126] They brought back from Southeast Asia exotic animals, rhinoceros horn and other medicinal items, camphor, various types of incense, dyewoods, ambergris, and spices. They also brought back goods from India and the Middle East that they obtained in Melaka or Patani such as ivory and frankincense. Alcohol was another important trade item. Pires remarks, "Among the *Lequjos* Malacca wine is greatly esteemed. They load large quantities of one kind which is like brandy, with which the Malays make themselves [so drunk as to run] amuck."[127] Ayutthaya was another source of alcohol and it is credited as the place where Ryukyuans learned the art of distilling rice alcohol (rice *shochu* or Awamori) in the 1400s. From there the art diffused to Japan.

Ryukyuan maritime trade declined in the late 1500s in the face of greater competition from Europeans and a loss of preferential treatment by China. The Ryukyuan maritime trade with Southeast Asia suffered in particular with the bulk of trade coming to involve shipping goods between Japan and China.

Aztec Traders

Prescott describes the market of Tenochitlan when Cortez and his men arrived in the early 1500s:

> on drawing near the *tianquez,* or great market, the Spaniards were astonished at the throng of people pressing towards it, and, on entering the place, their surprise was still further heightened by the sight of the multitudes assembled there, and the dimensions of the enclosure, thrice as large as the celebrated square of Salamanca. Here were met together traders from all parts, with the products and manufactures peculiar to their countries; the goldsmiths of Azcapozalco, the potters and jewelers of Cholula, the painters of Tezcuco, the stone-cutters of Tenajocan, the hunters of Xilotepec, the fishermen of Cuitlahuac, the fruiters of the warm countries, the mat and chairmakers of Quauhtitlan, and the florists of Xochimilco.[128]

Prescott's famous history of the Spanish conquest of Mexico and overview of Mexican society at the time of the conquest based largely on early Spanish sources devotes several pages to Aztec traders and trade. He comments, "Trade was held in avowed estimation by the Aztecs" and "the occupation particularly respected was that of the merchant."[129] As an indication of their importance, Prescott notes, traders "were allowed to assume insignia and devices of their own," they formed a "council of finance," "they were much consulted by the monarch, who had some of them constantly near his person," and "they were allowed to have their own courts, in which civil and criminal cases, not excepting capital, were determined; so that they formed an independent community, as it were, of themselves."[130]

There were several categories of traders. The Aztecs called local and regional traders *tlanecuilo* or *tlanecuiloani,* while more important merchants belonging to guilds were called *pochteca.* The *pochteca* belonged to hereditary guilds.[131] The merchants of Tenochitlan lived in the merchant district of Tlatelolco. These merchants even had their own deity, Yacatecutli (Yahcatecutli), the patron god of itinerant merchants, to whom a large shrine was dedicated in Tlatelolco. A person known as the *pochtecatlailotlac* (first of the *pochteca*) governed the merchants of Tlatelolco and was accountable directly to the king. Under him were three to five market judges (*tianquizpan tlayacanqui*) who heard cases daily and a number of *tlanquzt-lacanqui* who looked after the day-to-day operation of the market and collected taxes.

A typical example of the Aztec *pochteca* is described by Prescott as "a sort of itinerant trader, who made his journeys to the remotest borders of Anahuac [the Aztec Empire], and to the countries beyond, carrying with him merchandise of rich stuffs, jewelry, slaves, and other valuable commodities."[132] Turning to long-distance trade, he says:

> With this rich freight, the merchant visited the different provinces, always bearing some present of value from his own sovereign to their chiefs, and usually receiving others in return, with a permission to trade.... He performed his journeys with a number of companions of his own rank, and a large body of inferior attendants who were employed to transport the goods.... The whole caravan

went armed, and so well provided against sudden hostilities, that they could make good their defense, if necessary, till reinforced from home.[133]

In this regard, quoting an account from Sahagun's *General History of the Things of New Spain*,[134] he says, "In one instance, a body of these militant traders stood a siege of four years in the town of Ayotlan [in Jalisco], which they finally took from the enemy.... Their own government, however, was always prompt to embark in a war on the ground, finding it a very convenient pretext for extending the Mexican empire."[135] Prescott mentions, "In the Mendoza Codex is a painting representing the execution of a cacique [ruler] and his family, with the destruction of his city, for maltreating the persons of some Aztec merchants."[136]

There is evidence of the existence of long-distance traders in central Mexico as early as the time of Teotihuacán. Hassig points to a mural at Teotihuacán that depicts Yacatecutli, the patron god of itinerant merchants.[137] Acosta Signes argues that such merchant guilds may have originated with the Olmecs of the Gulf Coast and then spread among the pre–Aztec Toltecs.[138] He lists merchant guilds from a number of locales in central Mexico as well as to the south in the Mixtec region and in Yucatan. In regard to central Mexico, during the Aztec period, in addition to Tlatelolco, Sahagun lists eleven other towns with merchants' guilds in the Valley of Mexico.

In his discussion of the *pochteca,* Hassig notes, "The merchants' trading areas were expanding with the empire. As the borders of the empire were pushed back, Aztec merchants traded within these areas."[139] What goods did these merchants trade in? Bird feathers were especially important items of trade. Around 1400 the *pochteca* of Tlatelolco dealt mainly in red arara and blue and scarlet parrot feathers. In the 1410s and 1420s they added trade in quetzal and troupial feathers as well as turquoise and various green stones and cotton cloth. By the mid–1400s the repertoire of traded goods had grown to include "gold lip and earplugs, necklaces with radiating pendants, fine turquoise, enormous green stones, long quetzal feathers, wild animal skins, long troupial feathers, and blue cotinga and red spoonbill feathers."[140] Later in the century they also traded for "costly red capes with the wind-jewel design. White duck-feather capes, capes with cupped-shaped designs in feathers, embroidered breechcloths, embroidered shirts and shifts, long capes and chocolate."[141] These were items for elite markets that were brought not only from the adjacent lowlands of the Pacific Coast and Gulf Coast but also from as far away as Guatemala to the south and New Mexico to the north. For the most part, the *pochteca* were seeking rare and exotic raw materials for local artisans to turn into products for the Aztec elite. To obtain these raw materials they traded manufactured goods from central Mexico that included "worked cotton capes, golden crowns, rosettes and necklaces, and rings, as well as crystal and obsidian earplugs, tin, obsidian razors, and needles and lake products."[142] Most of these goods were, in turn, intended for elite markets where they were trading.

As for trade beyond the borders of the empire, this posed some difficulties since hostile neighbors surrounded the Aztec Empire. Despite such obstacles Aztec traders brought increasing quantities of goods to the imperial center to feed the growing appetite of urban elites. In the south they did so in part through mercantile colonies that are commonly referred to as ports of trade.[143] These served primarily to give Aztec traders access to goods from the Maya area.

Trade heading south departed from Tochtepec (in the modern state of Puebla). This was a border town where the porters (*tlamemes*) were stationed who carried the trade goods. From here the traders either went to Cimatan and Xicalango on the Gulf Coast or to

Socunusco on the Pacific Coast. From Soconusco there was a maritime trade route along the coast to Suchitepéquez (in modern Guatemala), which was known for its cacao, as well as overland routes into the highlands of Chiapas and Guatemala. Tzutuhil and Cakchiquel Maya inhabited Soconusco as well as Aztec colonists who over time intermarried with the local Maya.

Aztec merchants going to the Gulf Coast first reached Cimatan (aka the Three Cimatans). It was located along the Grijalva River where the Dos Bocas River branches off towards the Gulf. Scholes and Roys comment, "The three Cimatans occupied an important strategic position commercially, for they were the first Tabasco towns encountered by the merchants from the Valley of Mexico. Sahagun tells us that before they arrived they sent word ahead and were met in the hostile territory through which they were passing by the friendly 'lords' of Anahuac Xicalango, as the Aztecs called the country between Coatzacoalcos and Laguna de Terminos, and conducted to their towns."[144] In addition to going to Cimatan or Xicalango, some merchants went to the Chontal towns of Mecoacan, Chilateupa, and Teutitlan Copilco "where they had their factories and warehouses" and "sold their goods to local traders."[145] The town of Cimitan "controlled the most important trade routes from the highlands of Chiapas as well as that from the Valley of Mexico."[146] It was a fortified town with large houses and temples.

Xicalango was located near the western end of the Laguna de Terminos. Its ruins today are referred to as Cerrillos. It lies immediately to the east of where two of the great rivers of the Gulf Coast, the Grijalva and Usumacinta, join and flow into the gulf near the modern city of Alvaro Obregon. Xicalango was "a Nahuatl-speaking town" that "commanded the trade route to Yucatan and through its subject town of Jonuta probably controlled much of the Usumacinta trade."[147] Moreover, "just as Cimatan was favorably situated to handle foreign trade from the south and west, Xicalango enjoyed a very similar advantage in regard to Yucatan, Acalan [Chontal territory in modern Campeche], and the Usumacinta valley."[148] As for the population of the town, while the important local merchants and members of the ruling class were Nahuatl-speaking, most people were probably Chontal.[149] Xicalango appears to have had commercial links with the Chontal town of Potonchan, which was located at the mouth of the Grijalva River. Cortés described Potonchan as well populated with a large army and as an important trading center with extensive cacao orchards.[150]

Once Aztec traders reached the lowlands of Tabasco they came into contact with Maya traders who made extensive use of canoes along the region's rivers and coasts. The importance of canoe travel in the Maya lowlands can be seen from the name that the Aztecs assigned to the Chontal kingdom that they called Acalan: "it is reasonably certain that Acalan is a corruption of a Nahuatl word *acaltlan,* 'place of canoes.'"[151] The Aztec merchants were not sailors and once in the lowlands they became dependent on the Chontal (aka Putun) for water transport. According to Thompson, at certain exchange points the Culhua-Mexica merchants "handed over to the Putun their cargoes to be carried thence by water."[152]

On his fourth voyage Columbus encountered a large trading canoe near the Bay Islands of Honduras. The canoe was as long as one of Columbus's ships, though narrower, and had 25 men along with women and children on board. Thompson argues that the canoe probably had sailed around the Peninsula of Yucatan from Xicalango [or perhaps Potonchan] and that the "merchants and crew were Putun (Chontal Maya), the Phoenicians of Middle America."[153] People from Xicalango and neighboring communities in Tabasco were able to describe to Cortés communities along the coast "as far as the residence of Pedrarias Dávila."[154] The latter is located in modern Panama and Thompson believes that on the basis of these interviews it would appear "that there was sea trade between the bottom of the Gulf of Mexico and at least present-day Costa Rica, if not with Panama."[155] The trade with Costa Rica and Panama was probably to obtain gold. The sea trade from the Bay of Honduras and around the Peninsula of Yucatan carried cacao, bird feathers, wax and honey, salt, textiles, and a variety of stone and metal implements.

Chetumal was the most important trading center along the sea route between Tabasco and the Gulf of Honduras. When first visited by the Spanish the town of Chetumal is said to have had 2,000 households. It was sufficiently powerful that it was able to fight off the initial Spanish attack and even sent a fleet a war canoes to the Gulf of Honduras to fight the Spanish. Its wealth was derived from its cacao orchards, its apiaries that produced honey, and its maritime trade.[156] Thompson notes that only Chetumal and Potonchan yielded significant amounts of gold to the Spanish conquerors in this region.[157] There is no evidence of any resident Aztec merchants at Chetumal, but Spanish accounts do mention merchants from Xicalango and Potonchan visiting the important shrine of Ix Chel (wife of the sun god and patroness of weaving, childbirth, medicine, and divination) on the island of Cozumel on their voyages between the Gulf of Honduras and Tabasco.[158] This would seem to indicate that at least some Aztec merchants passed through Chetumal.

The main trading center in the south was at Nito, which was located in the vicinity of the modern town of Livingston in Guatemala where the waters from Lake Izabal and the Polochic River empty into the Gulf of Honduras. In addition to being a port for sea-going canoes traveling around the Yucatan Peninsula and along the northern coast of Central America, Nito was strategically located close to several rivers that were important for inland trade (i.e., the Ulua, Motagua, Polochic, Cahabon, Chamelcon, and Sarstoon rivers) and was located near to important cacao growing areas. Thompson characterizes Nito and the coastal region from the Chamelecon River to the Rio Dulce as forming "a single economic, but probably not political, unit with a large population."[159] Cortés described there being four towns in the area with populations of 2,000 households or more.[160] Cortés mentions the area having broad roads, trading quarters, factories of Putun (Chontal) merchants, extensive cacao orchards, and maritime trade. It is unclear who exerted political authority over Nito. Chetumal exerted control over the maritime trade with Nito and may have maintained a factory there. There was a quarter of the town occupied by Chontal merchants from Acalan who were governed at the time that the Spanish arrived by a brother of the ruler of Acalan. Chol Maya were the primary inhabitants of the surrounding region and Chol traders were present in the town.

There is disagreement among scholars concerning the presence of Aztec traders in Nito and other communities in the vicinity. Roys is of the opinion that Nito may have been an Aztec trading post and that Aztec traders may have occupied other communities such as Naco.[161] Thompson, however, believes that "evidence for supposed Nahuatl-speaking villages in the area is tenuous."[162] He argues that the Spanish use of Nahuatl names in the area only means that the local names were given to them "in translations through Nahuatl-speaking auxiliaries."[163] He does admit though that there may have been a "Culhua-Mexica merchants' quarter in the town."[164] Whether or not Aztec merchants were present, it is clear that Nito served as an important entrepôt for the movement of trade goods, many of which ultimately found their way to the Valley of Mexico, and that it was an important base for transnational long-distance traders.

7

Merchant Communities

As in ancient times, during the medieval period distinct communities were formed along the major overland and maritime trade routes that served as commercial hubs for those engaged in long-distance trade. While not all people living in these communities themselves adopted a transnational lifestyle, the primary rationale for these communities was transnational in nature in that they were formed to facilitate the movement of goods and people over long distances and across borders. Those directly engaged in transnational activities in these communities included long-distance traders as well as crews and captains of ships and those who were employed in the movement of animals used for overland transportation. Within the communities there were also numerous artisans and others engaged in support activities ranging from ship-builders to prostitutes, who themselves sometimes moved from center to center.

The term port of trade is also used to denote these communities. Such a port is defined as a town or city "whose specific function was to serve as a meeting place of foreign traders."[1] While such locales were often coastal or riverine ports in the literal sense, port in this case is used more generally as a transshipment point for goods. It was common for them to have developed for ecological and political reasons. In regard to both they often were located in borders or frontiers. Geographically they were often located not only along coasts or rivers, but also between highlands and lowlands, deserts and more fertile areas. In regard to politics, "Ports of trade usually developed in politically weak spots, such as small kingdoms near the coast, or chieftans' confederacies."[2] Moreover, they tended to be located in places that were politically neutral and relatively safe from the vagaries of imperial conquest. If located within the boundaries of a large kingdom or empire, they usually were afforded special status where the normal laws did not apply. Such neutrality was in the interest of both the long-distance traders and the kingdoms or empires where the goods were ultimately destined. As Revere notes, "Continuity of the supply of goods was essential, since it could not be expected that traders — under the difficult conditions of archaic long distance trade — would come to an outlying place unless they knew for certain that a safe exchange of goods was possible."[3]

The Middle East

The Middle East was home to many of the earliest known merchant communities and there were many of these during ancient and medieval times. We briefly discussed the ancient

157

trading centers of northern Syria and Anatolia in Chapter 2 in relation to Mesopotamian markets.

Archaeologists have discovered evidence of what was perhaps the earliest community of expatriate long-distance traders at Hacinebi Tepe, in Anatolia at the point furthest to the north where the Euphrates River is navigable. A settled community came into existence here around 4100 B.C. Within this community, archaeologists discovered a distinct area with artifacts from the Sumerian city of Uruk dating around 3700 B.C.[4] The site appears to have been occupied by early traders from Uruk and was probably associated with copper mining in the vicinity. The Sumerians established small colonies of settlers beyond their heartland and Sumerian traders and settlers traveled east as far as central Iran, west to the coast of the Mediterranean Sea (e.g., Nagar, modern Tell Brak in Syria), and north to Turkey (e.g., Harran, aka Carrhae, in southeastern Turkey, which was a major commercial and religious center for the Sumerians where Abram stopped on his way to Canaan). Though their outposts had an influence on neighboring peoples, the Sumerians were unable to maintain effective political control over distant areas and, thus, did not incorporate them into an empire.

As was mentioned in an earlier chapter, Assyrian long-distance traders established merchant colonies (*kārum*) and stations (*warbartum*) in Anatolia between 1920 and 1740 B.C.[5] Kanesh (aka Kanis, modern Kültepe) was the most important of these *kārum* in Anatolia and served as a center for the other colonies and stations in the region. In addition to Kanesh other *kārum* in Anatolia included Purushattum, Wahsusana, Hahhum, Zalpa, Turunmit, and Hattus. The Assyrians were mainly interested in obtaining metals that were mined in the region, including copper, lead, tin, gold, and silver, although they also traded in wool. While the Assyrian colonies were part of local Anatolian communities — Kanesh was located in the city of Nesa — they were physically separate and were afforded a special legal status (including a differential tax status). As was noted previously, family firms (*tamkārum*) conducted most of the trade, with the head of the family living in Assur, an eldest son or other family member based in Kanesh serving as the head of operations in Anatolia, and other members of the family and employees conducting business around the region. In addition to those permanently residing in either Assur or Anatolia members of the firms also regularly carried goods back and forth between the two locales. The *kārum* was especially important as a center for assembling copper from the nearby mines. The ore was stored in local houses prior to shipping. Pálfi comments, "The great market and copper-distribution centre of Turhumit was very important for every significant family firm."[6]

In later antiquity the city of Palmyra served as the center of the caravan trade between the empires of Parthia and Rome. Gawlikowski says of Palmyra, "Ever since Rostovtzeff's famous book, Palmyra is commonly called a 'caravan city.' As a matter of fact, it is the only real caravan city among those considered as such by the great scholar."[7] Palmyra originally was an oasis called Tadmor that evolved into an important trading city in the first century A.D.[8] It was incorporated into the Roman Empire some time between A.D. 11 and 32.[9] As Young points out, Palmyra did not become an important trading center simply because of natural geographical features. Rather, "we see the merchants of this oasis city, in concert with the landowning aristocracy of the town, deliberately utilizing the city's qualities and contacts with the surrounding tribes to *develop* a trade route which enabled them to prosper" and therefore, "the commercial vocation of Palmyra was the result of an initiative of its citizens, not the chance location of its oasis."[10] While Palmyra boasted considerable local resources, it was the caravan trade that turned it into an opulent city with a substantial proportion of its population engaged in trade or involved in occupations that were supported by the wealth generated by trade: "Without this trade, Palmyra would have been a small, struggling community on the fringe of the desert. It can only have been the wealth generated by the caravan commerce that raised Palmyra to the splendor that is still visible today."[11]

There are numerous inscriptions from Palmyra in Greek and the local variant of Aramaic that commemorate the activities of those who commanded caravans and those who were their patrons. From these it is clear that Palmyrian society was organized around the caravan trade.[12] The leaders of caravans were called *synodiarch* or *archemporos*. The local patrons of the caravans provided money, animals, and often armed guards for the caravan. The patrons were not merchants, but were wealthy estate owners on whose properties the herds of animals for the caravans were raised. The merchants themselves formed yet another distinct group that was involved in the caravan trade. While such patrons no doubt existed, Young cautions that the inscriptions indicate that roles of those involved in the caravan trade were often not so clear cut and may often have overlapped. He concludes, "The caravan trade seems to have been a privately initiated, organized and funded affair, in which groups of merchants would attach themselves to a wealthy Palmayrene aristocrat who would provide them with the means to make the journey. These magnates would act, either personally or by a representative as the caravan leader for the journey."[13] In addition to private caravan guards who accompanied the caravans on their journeys, the city maintained its own militia whose primary duty was providing additional security for the caravans as its primary duty. This militia maintained permanent garrisons at various points not only along the land routes of the caravans, but also at strategic points along the Euphrates River (such as at Dura Europos) within territory under Roman control.[14]

The inscriptions indicate that most caravans headed east to cities in Mesopotamia (largely within the Parthian Empire) and then returned from there with goods from a variety of sources, but especially goods that had arrived by sea from northern India. These routes in particular went overland to the cities of Calinicum, Dura Europos (an important commercial hub of trade along the Euphrates that was founded in 303 B.C. by the Greek Seleucids), and Hit that were located along the Euphrates River. Goods were carried up the river from Spasinou Charax, the capital of Mesene at the head of the Persian Gulf that for a time appears to have been allied with Rome but after 151 was a vassal of Parthia. After A.D. 140 the city of Vologasias also became an important trading center for the Palmyrenes along the rivers. Palmyrene merchants are mentioned as living in the various centers of trade along these routes. Palmyrenes are also mentioned as owners of ships that sailed between Spasinou Charax and India. Ships sailed from Spasinou Charax to Tylos (Bahrain) and then on to the port of Barbarikon at the mouth of the Indus River and sometimes continued further south to the port of Barygaza at the top of the Gulf of Cambay. Silk was among the goods that they obtained from the Indian ports.

Merchant communities of varying size were to be found scattered throughout the trade routes of the Muslim world in the Middle East with particularly important ones associated with the maritime trade route heading east to South Asia. Alexandria and Cairo served as important bases for long-distance traders and as collection points for goods from the surrounding area as well as Venice and elsewhere in Europe that were then shipped along the maritime route to South Asia. Along the route the ports of Aden and Hormuz were the two most important.

Aden was a port of the Kingdom of Awsan between 600 and 400 B.C. Known as Eudaemon in Roman times, Aden served as a port for the transshipment of goods along the Red Sea for a time. After a long period of decline, it re-emerged as a commercial center in the

1100s. Aden established its independence from Egypt in 1229 under the Rasulid Dynasty and became one of the Middle East's leading trading centers. When Ma Huan visited Aden in the 1430s he described it as a rich and populous country. The Chinese fleet traded for gemstones, pearls, coral, and exotic animals.[15]

In the early 1500s Pires describes Aden as "the only populous town in this Arabia, and [it] is the key not only of Arabia but of all the strait, both for those entering and for those leaving."[16] He mentions that it boasts a strong fortress and a force of many people "who are paid to fight."[17] Turning to its trade: "This town has a great trade with the people of Cairo as well as with those of all India, and the people of India trade with it. There are many important merchants in the city with great riches, and many from other countries live there also. It is one of the four great trading cities in the world."[18] After a lengthy description of the goods that pass through the port from a wide variety of locales and are exported from its hinterland, Pires says, "People come to the port of Aden from all the above-mentioned places, and they [the merchants of Aden] go everywhere."[19] Pires also describes Muslim Arabs and Egyptians and Christian Jacobites and Melchites living in Jeddah, Tor, and Mecca who are engaged in trade with Aden. "These merchants carry goods from Venice that have been placed in warehouses in Alexandria to factories in Cairo, on to warehouses in Jedda," then to "the warehouses they have in Aden and from Aden [the goods are] distributed to Cambay, Goa, Malabar, Bengal, Pegu and Siam."[20]

Hormuz (aka Ormus or Ormuz) was a city-state and small kingdom located in the Strait of Hormuz. The port was located on Hormuz Island, adjacent to the modern town of Bandar-e Abbas in Iran. The kingdom was founded in the 900s and came under the suzerainty of Persia in 1267. It was one of the most important trading centers in the Middle East for a time, reaching its peak as a hub of maritime trade in the 1200s to 1300s, when it boasted a large merchant fleet and navy. It was captured by the Portuguese under Alfonso de Albuquerque in 1515 and remained under Portuguese control until 1622. Duarte Barbosa, writing in 1518, said that "the merchants of this isle and city are Persians and Arabs."[21] Pires describes the "kingdom, besides being rich and noble," as "the key to Persia," adding that he considered it to be one of the four great cities "on this side of Asia."[22] He says, "The city has people in it from many parts, big merchants," and "ships from outside are constantly coming there with merchandise and Ormuz trades with them all."[23] He mentions that it is not very involved in the shipment of Venetian goods to South Asia, but primarily ships goods from around the Middle East to Cambay and other points in India.

South Asia

We have already discussed such South Asian ports catering to long-distance trade in ancient times as Barygaza at the mouth of the Narmada River, Muziris on the Malabar Coast, and Arikmedu near modern Pondicherry. There were also a number of such ports in South Asia during the medieval period that not only exported regional goods, but also served as trans-shipment points for goods from East and Southeast Asia heading west and goods from the Middle East and Western Europe heading east. There were quite a number of medieval South Asian ports that took part in the international maritime trade and that had international merchant communities. The most important of these included Cambay, Calicut, and Cochin.

Cambay (modern Khambhat) was the principal one among several ports in what is now the modern Indian state of Gujarat. As an important international port it was visited by many medieval travel writers, including al-Mas'udi in 915, Marco Polo in 1293, and Nicolò de Conti around 1440. Pires describes the port of Cambay as having "the best merchandise" in the region.[24] Although local Gujaratis comprised the majority of merchants working out of Cambay, in Pires's time there were also Egyptians from Cairo and "many Khorasans and Guilans from Aden and Ormuz" living in and trading through Cambay.[25] These merchants brought goods from Europe and the Middle East to Cambay and returned home with goods from Cambay as well as spices and other trade goods brought from Melaka. The main local goods included cotton and silk cloth and carnelian.

To the south the Malabar Coast included several important trading ports during the medieval period, starting with Manjeshwaram in the north (located in the far north of modern Kerala State) to Quilon (modern Kollan in the south of Kerala State). Tamils inhabited the Malabar Coast and largely as a result of international trade and migration the Tamils there developed a distinct local culture and came to be known as Malayali, a culture that developed from Tamil mixture with migrants from the Middle East and elsewhere. While the majority of the people of the Malabar Coast are Hindus, especially around the trading ports the region includes a significant number of Christians, Muslims, and Jews.

The Jewish community was established as early as 700 B.C.[26] Jewish merchants originally settled at the trading port of Cranganore near Cochin, where the ruler of Cochin allowed them to establish their own principality called Anjuvannam. Muslims who sought to force the Jews out of the pepper trade attacked the Jewish community in 1524 and most of the Jews fled to Cochin. There they were offered protection by the local Hindu raja, who allowed them to establish their own community that came to be known as Jew Town. St. Thomas brought Christianity to the region in A.D. 52 and the community subsequently grew under the Nestorian Christians.[27] Pires reported, "There are fifteen thousand Christians in the province of Malabar.... Two thousand of these are men of repute, noblemen, merchants, estimable people, and the others are craftsmen, poor people.... These Christians live in the district from Chetwayi (*Chetua*) to Quilon (*Coulam*). Outside this area there are none of the early Christians."[28] Arab traders brought Islam to the Malabar Coast in the A.D. 600s, when they were allowed to settle and form a community.

Udaiyavar of Ernad (aka Swami Nambiyathiri Thirumulpad) founded Calicut (modern Kozhikod) in the 1200s and it subsequently grew into an important port. The Chinese referred to Calicut as Ku-Li. Zheng He's fleet visited the port and Ma Huan noted, "Foreign ships from every place come there; and the king of the country also sends a chief and a writer and others to watch the sales; thereupon they collect the duty and pay it in to the authorities."[29] Among the local products that he mentions are pepper, silk, precious stones, and pearls. He does not, however, describe foreign residents in the port. Pires provides a more detailed description: "

> The town is large and has many inhabitants, and a great deal of trading is done there by many merchants, natives of Malabar as well as Klings, Chettis and foreigners from all parts, both Moors [i.e. Muslims] and heathens. It is a very famous port and is the best thing in all Malabar. Many nations used to have factories here; each country used to bring its merchandise here, and a great business of barter and exchange took place. It is a great place; it is renowned in all this part of Asia as an important place.[30]

The foreigners living in and visiting Calicut around 1500 included Muslims from the Malabar Coast, Arabia, Persia, Turkey, Somalia, and the Maghreb. Indians involved in the Calicut trade included Bengalis, Deccans, Chettis from the Coromandel Coast, and Gujaratis. There was also an important shipbuilding industry at Calicut.

Prior to 1341 Cranganore (known as Muziris in ancient times and Kodungallur in modern times) was one of the most important ports of the Malabar Coast. It was the main port of the Cheras and was an especially important source of pepper. The Periyar River flooded in 1341 and this resulted in the destruction of Cranganore harbor and creation of a new harbor at Cochin (modern Kochi and known as Yavanas in ancient times), which then became the main port in the area. The Chinese referred to Cochin as Ko-Chih. Ma Huan describes the local traders as being composed mainly of "Che-ti" (the local trading caste) and the only significant export product being pepper.[31] Pires depicts Cochin as being "very small and very great. The kingdom is no more than the Island of Vypin (*Vaipim*) and that of Cochin, which together contain about six thousand Nayars."[32] To this he adds that the king "has a good city and a good port, and many ships, and does a great deal of trade."[33]

The Portuguese took considerable interest in the Malabar Coast. Vasco da Gama first visited the Malabar Coast in 1498, landing at Calicut, and Pedro Alvares Cabral visited Cochin in 1500. The local ruler sought Cabral's support in attacking Calicut and signed a treaty of friendship that allowed the Portuguese to establish a factory at Cochin. Faced with a strong show of force by the ruler of Calicut, Cabral called off his attack. Later Vasco da Gama attacked Calicut and destroyed the Muslim factories there. This attack led to an outbreak of war between Calicut and Cochin in 1503. To protect themselves and to help defend the local ruler from attacks by Calicut the Portuguese built fortifications (Fort Manuel) around their factory at Cochin. Portuguese influence in Cochin increased to the point that they became the de facto rulers of the port (until 1663) and it served as the capital of Portuguese India until 1510, when it was moved to Goa. In 1505 the Portuguese established a second base at further north at Kannur, which was another important port catering to the Middle Eastern trade. They also put pressure on the ruler of Calicut and in 1509 he allowed them to establish a third base at Chaliyar. In addition to the brief work of Saint Francis Xavier in the Malabar Coast in the 1540s in general the Portuguese promoted the Catholic mission there at the expense of the Nestorians and Jews.

Melaka

Melaka (aka Malacca) is undoubtedly the most famous of the ports along the maritime route from the Middle East to China and yet its history as a trading port is a brief one; its moment of glory comes only during the end of the medieval period in what is sometimes referred to as the early modern period. Melaka is also of interest since its rise spans the period in which Muslim traders consolidated their control over the maritime trade route at the expense of non–Muslims.

At the time of the founding of Melaka in 1402 the Malay Peninsula was effectively under control of the Tai kingdom of Ayutthaya (often referred to as Siam) with the Javanese kingdom of Majapahit laying claim to some of the southern parts of the peninsula. Pasai, on the northeast coast of Sumatra, was the most important trading port along the Strait of Melaka. It was also in Pasai that Islam first became firmly established along the Southeast Asian portion of the maritime trade route.

The early history of Melaka is associated with a man named Paramesvara (also spelled Parameswara, 1. 1344–1414). He was a prince from Palembang who left the city following its conquest by the forces of Majaphahit. He fled to Temasak (modern Singapore) around 1396 where the regent, who was a Malay from Patani appointed regent of Temasak by

Ayutthaya, offered him protection. Paramesvara subsequently killed the regent and set himself up as ruler. After fending off an attack by Majapahit, threats from Ayutthhaya forced him to flee along the northwest coast of the Malay Peninsula around 1402. Pires says that a group of people he calls *Celates* Bugis accompanied him to Melaka.[34] These people were not Bugis (a group of people from Sulawesi), but appear to be Malays from the Sumatra-Riau area.[35] Paramesvara and these Celates eventually settled at the mouth of the Bertam River, which was later re-named the Melaka River. Pires states that initially there were around 300 settlers.[36]

Within three years of its founding (i.e., about 1405) the settlement had grown considerably and had established relations with Ayutthaya. According to Pires: "People began to come from the Aru side and from other places, men such as the Celates robbers and also fishermen, in such numbers that three years after his coming Malacca was a place with two thousand inhabitants, and Siam was sending rice there."[37] Paramesvara seems not to have been satisfied with the status of his new settlement as a vassal of Ayutthaya and sent envoys to the Ming court in China seeking recognition as ruler of Melaka. It is unclear how successful he was in this, but according to some accounts he was given a seal recognizing his status as a vassal ruler, although this status was not recognized by Ayutthaya. The situation changed when Zheng He sailed to Melaka on his third voyage in 1409 and brought with him a seal elevating Melaka to a kingdom and recognizing Paramesvara as its ruler. Paramesvara married a daughter of the ruler of Pasai around this time and adopted the Persian title Iskandar Shah. To consolidate his position with the Chinese, Paramesvara visited the Ming court personally in 1411.

After Paramesvara died in 1414 his son visited the Ming court and was recognized as the new ruler. He took the title Raja Sri Rama Vikrama, but was known as Sultan Sri Iskandar Zulkarnian Shah or Megat Iskandar Shah to his Muslim subjects (r. 1414–24). He married a Tamil Muslim woman. There was a growing Tamil population in Melaka by this time, forming the basis of what eventually would become a mixed Tamil-Malay culture in the Malay Peninsula (sometimes referred to as Mamak). The population of Melaka at this time was about 6,000.[38]

Raja Sri Rama Vikrama sent a mission to Ayutthaya led by his brother-in-law requesting assistance: "The said king of Siam sent him people and foodstuffs and merchandise from his country, saying that he was delighted for it to be peopled like this, and that he would help him if he cultivated the land."[39] He also sent an ambassador to Majapahit requesting friendship now that his father was dead and asking for Majapahit to send ships to Melaka to trade. The ruler of Majapahit replied that he already was sending ships to Pasai, which was a vassal, and did not wish to upset the ruler of Pasai. The ruler of Melaka then sent an embassy to Pasai asking permission for Javanese ships to trade with Melaka. The ruler of Pasai sent ambassadors to Melaka saying that he would grant permission if the ruler of Melaka would convert to Islam. The ruler of Melaka did not take the request well, again according to Pires, and held the ambassadors prisoner for three years. In the intervening years, even though the ruler of Pasai had not agreed, a few Javanese ships began to visit Melaka, but there appears to have been little trade at this time. After the ambassadors were released relations improved between Melaka and Pasai:

"The kings made friends, and they traded from Pase [Pasai] in Malacca, and some rich Moorish [Muslim] merchants moved from Pase to Malacca, Parsees, as well as Bengalles and Arabian Moors, for at that time there were a large number of merchants belonging to these three nations, and they were very rich, with large businesses and fortunes, and they settled there from the said parts, carrying on their trade; and so having come they brought with them mullahs and priests learned in the sect of Mohammed — chiefly Arabs, who are esteemed in these parts for their knowledge of the said sect."[40]

Raja Sri Rama Vikarama finally converted to Islam at the age of 72 and married a daughter of the ruler of Pasai. After conversion he sought to convert his subjects as well.

Chinese relations were maintained during Raja Sri Rama Vikrama's reign. Not only did Zheng He's fleet continue to visit Melaka, but Rama Vikrama himself made a trip to the Ming court. This trip took three years and after this the ruler took a Chinese woman as one of his wives.[41] Zheng He made his last visit to Melaka in 1431 during the reign of Melaka's third ruler, Muhammed Shah (r. 1424–44). Raja Ibrahim became ruler in 1444 and adopted the Hindu title Sri Paramesvara Dewa Shah. Ayutthaya made an unsuccessful attack on Melaka in 1445, being defeated by a Melakan army led by Tun Perak. There appear to have been tensions between the Tamil Muslim and Hindu Malay communities in Melaka at this time. After less than two years as ruler Sri Paramesvara Dewa Shah was stabbed to death, and his half-brother by a Tamil Muslim mother, Raja Kasim, then assumed the throne and adopted the title Sultan Madzafar Shah.

During the reign of Sultan Madzafar Shah (r. 1446–59) Islam became more firmly entrenched as the dominant religion and the kingdom grew in importance as a trading port. Tun Perak defeated another invading army from Ayutthaya in 1456 and was rewarded by being made *bendahara* (prime minister).

The next ruler, Sultan Mansur Shah (r. 1459–77), sought to expand his territory and sent his prime minister Tun Perak to conquer neighboring territories in the Malay Peninsula and on the island of Sumatra. As a result of Melaka's military ventures, the rulers of these territories converted to Islam. Pires recounts, "He was a great man of justice; he devoted much care to improvements of Malacca; he bought and built junks and sent them out with merchants."[42] He also notes that as a result of his conquests and conversion to Islam of neighboring lands "his name became so famous that he had messages and presents from the kings of Aden and Ormuz and of Cambay and Bengal, and they sent many merchants from their regions to live in Malacca."[43] When Dai Viet conquered Vijaya, the capital of Champa, in 1471 a large number of Cham fled to Cambodia and Melaka, where they came to be influenced by the local Malay culture and Islamic religion.

During the reign of Alauddin Riayat Shah (r. 1477–88) Melaka continued to prosper as a trading center but internally there was ongoing tension between the Malays and the local Tamils. Sultan Alauddin married the daughter of the ruler of Kampar and sought to keep the rulers of other neighboring regions under his control close at hand: "This king Alaodín [Alauddin] always had the kings of Pahang, Kampar and Indragiri, and their relatives, with him in Malacca, at court as it were, and he instructed them in the things of Mohammed."[44] While preparing to leave for Mecca on a pilgrimage, Sultan Alauddin died under mysterious circumstances, possibly being poisoned by his brother. Raja Mahmud, Sultan Alauddin's son by his second wife, then became ruler as Mahmud Shah (r. 1488–1511). Mahmud was a young man and Tun Perak served as regent until he died in 1498.

The Portuguese Diogo Lopes de Sequeira arrived at Melaka with five ships in 1509. He survived an attempt by the Malays to kill him, but nineteen seamen on shore were made prisoners, including Rui de Ajaújo who became the first factor in Melaka in 1511. Pires says that when Sequira visited Melaka there were over 4,000 foreign merchants living in Melaka.[45] These included about 1,000 Gujarati merchants, a large number of Tamils (Pires calls them Kling), as well as numerous Parsis, Bengalis, and Arabs. At the time the Tamils were the dominant traders. In addition to Bengali merchants who visited Melaka, Pires had the following to say about the Bengali community in Melaka: "There are a large number of Bengalees, men and women, in Malacca. The men are fishers and tailors — most of them — and some of the women do very bad work [i.e., are prostitutes]."[46] The Portuguese under the command of Afonso de Albuquerque captured Melaka in 1511 and Mahmud Shah fled to Kampar, Sumatra, where he ruled until his death.

Pires commented on the linguistic diversity of the people living in Melaka: "Very often eighty-four languages have been found spoken."[47] About 40 of these were languages from nearby areas but this left many languages being spoken by people from far more distant lands as well. Pires provides an often quoted list of the people who traded with Melaka that highlights the multi-ethnic nature of maritime commerce in this part of the world at the time:

> Moores from Cairo, Mecca, Aden, Abyssinians, men of Kilwa [in Tanzania], Malindi [in Kenya], Ormuz, Parsees, *Rumes,* Turks, Turkoman, Christian Armenians, Gujaratees, men from Chaul [India, south of Bombay], Dabhol, Goa, of the kingdom of the Deccan, Malabars and Klings, merchants from Orissa, Ceylon, Bengal, Arakan, Pegu, Siamese, men of Kedah, Malays, men of Pahang, Patani, Cambodia, *Champa,* Cochin China, Chinese, *Lequeos,* men of Brunei, *Luçoes* [traders from Luzon, Philippines], men of Tamjompura, Laue, Banka, Linga..., Moluccas, Banda, Bima, Timor, Madura, Java, Sunda, Palembang, Jambi, Tongkal, Indragiri, Kappatta, Menangk-abau, Siak, *Arqua (Arcat?)*, Aru, Bata, country of the *Tomjano,* Pase, Pedir, Maldives."[48]

Many of the merchants from the Middle East first went to Gujarat and from there took ships for the onward journey to Melaka.[49] Indian merchants commonly sailed to Melaka on ships from coastal ports such as Cambay, but merchants from Chaul, Dabhol, and Goa first went to Bengal or Calicut and from there sailed to Melaka. While many of the Muslim traders left after the Portuguese conquest, others such as the Hindu Tamils remained and continued to trade under Portuguese rule, but Melaka's importance as a trading port declined as the Muslim traders took their business elsewhere.

Guangzhou

There were several ports in China where foreign merchants were allowed to settle and form communities during the medieval period. The two most important of these ports with foreign communities were Guangzhou (Canton) in Guandong Province and Quanzhou (aka Zaiton) in Fujian Province. We will discuss Guangzhou in the present section in detail. Hirth and Rockhill provide the following overview of Quanzhou's trade relations from the 800s to the 1000s:

> Somewhere about the ninth century, possibly even earlier, a portion of the southern sea-trade of China was diverted to Ts'üan-chóu, near Amoy, which had commercial relation with Japan and Korea for centuries past, and where Arabs [Muslims] found the products of those countries and of remote parts of China not easily reached from Canton, besides probably receiving more favorable treatment from the local customs. Two centuries later [i.e., the 1000s] this port became of nearly equal importance with Canton; the Arab [Muslim] settlement became much larger than at the latter place, and the fame of the city extended throughout the medieval world.[50]

The foreign trading communities in Guangzhou, Quanzhou, and other ports in the early medieval period included a significant number of Muslims. Islam was brought to Guangzhou some time between 618 and 626 and the relatively large foreign community at the time was comprised mainly of Persians and Arabs.[51] Although the reasons for the act is not clear, in 758 Guangzhou's Muslims are reported to have sacked and burned the city and to have then sailed away with their loot.[52] For a time thereafter, presumably, the foreign community in Guangzhou was smaller and comprised largely of other peoples. Among the other foreigners living there were people from various parts of Southeast Asia. These included a number of Cham. One of them, a Hindu, is described as follows:

> The most prominent among them [the Cham] was a man named P'u (Abu) who was by birth a noble of Chan-ch'öng [Champa]. Later he took up his permanent residence in China, to attend to his import and export trade. He lived in the city where his home was furnished in the most luxurious fashion, for in wealth he was the first of the time. His disposition was very superstitious, and he loved neatness. For his prayers he had a hall in which was a tablet which served as a god. Whenever there was a gathering (of his people) to feast (at his home), they did not use spoons or chopsticks: they had very large platters (lit. 'big troughs') of gold and silver in which was fresh water porpoise and millet (or rice) cooked together. They sprinkled rose (water) about, and put their right hands under their skirts, all picking up food with their left hands.[53]

Li Chan in his *T'ang-Kuo-shï-pu,* which recorded historical data between 713 and 825, provides the earliest written mention of foreign trading vessels visiting Guangzhou: "From it we learn that the ships engaged in this trade and which visited Canton were very large, so high out of the water that ladders several tens of feet in length had to be used to get aboard. The foreign (Fan) captains who commanded them were registered in the office of the Inspector of Maritime Trade (Shï-po-shï)."[54]

Accounts from the 800s by Persian merchants from Basra recorded by Abu Zayd Hasan ibn Yazid Sirafi are the earliest Muslim descriptions of trade with China.[55] These accounts mention frequent fires in the godowns of Guangzhou and report that ships engaged in the trade with China carried goods such as ivory, frankincense, copper, tortoise-shell, camphor, and rhinoceros horns from Basra, Oman, and other locales in the Middle East and sailed from the Persian Gulf port of Siraf (it was destroyed around 970). The Chinese authorities appointed a member of the local Muslim community to maintain order within the community. This included administering Muslim law.

Domestic political disturbances in China in the late 800s caused the foreign residents of Guangzhou to flee to Palembang and ports on the Malay Peninsula. For a time it seems that Chinese and other local ships carried goods from the ports in China to the Malay ports. Foreigners returned to Guangzhou in the late 900s with the establishment of order under the Song Dynasty and as a result of the dynasty's efforts to promote foreign trade.

The *P'ing-chóu-k'o-t'an* by Chu Yü provides an account of the foreign settlement in Guangzhou in the early 1100s:

> In the foreign quarter in Kuang-chóu reside all the people from beyond the seas. A foreign head-man is appointed over them and he had charge of all public matters connected with them. He makes it his special duty to urge upon the foreign traders to send in tribute (to the Chinese court). The foreign facial wears a hat, gown, shoes, and (carries) a tablet just like a Chinese. When a foreigner commits an offense anywhere, he is sent to Kuang-chóu, and if the charge is proved (before the Chinese authorities?), he is sent to the foreign quarter. (There he is) fastened to a ladder and whipped with a rattan from head to foot, three blows of a rattan being reckoned equal to one of the heavy bamboo. As foreigners do not wear drawers and like to squat on the ground, beating with the heavy bamboo on the buttocks proves most painful, whereas they do not fear beating on the back. Offenses entailing banishment or more severe punishments are carried out by the Department Magistrate of Kuang-chou.[56]

Chóu K'ü-feï, in his work *Ling-wai-tai-ta*, which was written in 1178, makes the point that at this time the activities of foreign traders was confined to the ports of Guangzhou and Quanzhou. He describes the government agency responsible for looking after the foreign traders and where they come from:

In its watchful kindness to the foreign Barbarians our Government has established at Ts'üan-chóu and at Kuangchóu Special Inspectorates of Shipping, and when ever any foreign traders have difficulties or wish to lay a complaint they must go to the Special Inspectorate. Every year in the 10th moon the Special Inspectorate establishes a large fair for the foreign traders and (when it is over) sends them (home). When they first arrive (in China) after the summer solstice (then it is that the) Inspectorate levies (duties) on their trade and gives them protection. Of all the wealthy foreign lands which have great store of precious and varied goods, none surpasses the realm of the Arabs (Ta-shï) [i.e., Muslims from the Middle East]. Next to them comes Java (Shö-p'o); the third is Palembang (San-fo-ts'i); many others come in next rank.[57]

By the time Pires arrived on his ill-fated mission to China in 1517 Ming Dynasty isolationism was in full swing. According to Pires, "The city of Canton (*Quantom*) is where the whole kingdom of China unloads all its merchandise, great quantities from inland as well as from the sea."[58] Relying on secondhand accounts of those who had been there prior to his visit, he says that they describe the city as being surrounded by a sturdy wall and a port with a large number of junks. At the time, he says, foreign traders were required to conduct their business outside of the city: "Thirty leagues on this side of Canton, towards Malacca, there are some islands near the mainland of Nan-t'ou (*Namtoo*), where are the ports already allotted to each nation, viz., *Pulo Tumon* and others. And as soon as the junks anchor there, the lord of Nan-t'ou sends word to Canton and merchants immediately come to value the merchandise and to take their duties."[59]

Western Europe

We have already discussed the commercial activities of Italian cities such as Amalfi and Venice. Further north, the Hanseatic League of the Baltic region formed "one of the oldest, most complete and complex merchant organizations in the Middle Ages."[60] When the League was formed the Baltic Sea and northern Europe in general was relatively warm, facilitating commerce. The League was comprised of a group of towns in north Germany whose traders were in competition with merchants from southern German and the Dutch towns further to the south. It was formed in the 1300s and continued to function until 1630. Members of the League established several trading posts, the most important of them being in Novgorod, Bergen, London, and Bruges. Bruges served as the main center for the redistribution of goods from Eastern Europe, the Mediterranean, and beyond to northern and northwestern Europe until Antwerp assumed this role in the 1500s. Each trading post had "its tribunal, its bank, and a legal personality.... Each year, the general assembly of merchants elected the elder, who had heavy responsibilities and no compensation.... Within the structure of the Hanseatic League existed associations of merchants that were at once professional, religious, choral, and recreational. The center of each association was a house with at least one big meeting room administered by the elders elected by the general assembly of the members."[61]

Mauro makes the important point that "in contrast to local merchants, whose interests were identified with those of the city, the members of these communities were foreigners who formed the 'nations,' autonomous groups with their own privileges and rivalries."[62] Concerning use of the term nation in this regard, he writes, "During the fifteenth century, the term 'nation' was used for the merchant association of a certain nationality.... A merchant nation was established with the tacit approval of the territorial prince and with the consent of the prince of the merchants' land.... During the first half of the 1500s the term mainly applied to Portuguese who controlled the spice trade."[63] Lyon was an important inland trading center in Western Europe. A list of merchant "nations" residing in Lyon in 1483 includes Savoyards, Germans, Milanese, Florentines, Genoese, and Venetians. In 1571 the list grew to include other Italians (still the majority), as well as a few Portuguese, English, Flemish, and Spanish. These merchant nations depended on favorable policies and attitudes on the part of those who governed these cities. Often this included the granting of a special legal status to foreign merchants that allowed them to carry out their activities largely outside of the rules and regulations that applied to local residents. Writing of Antwerp in the 1500s, Mauro says, "In Antwerp the foreign merchants were treated very favorably, and the port was an islet of economic liberty in Europe."[64]

8

Cities

In addition to the relatively specialized merchant communities discussed in the last chapter, cities also often played important roles in transnational life in the ancient and medieval worlds. Urban life dates to a time when agriculture had developed to a point that surpluses were available allowing for greater specialization of labor and concentrations of non-farming peoples. Trade was often significant in the development of early cities. In fact, as Tellier argues, "It is most likely that trade caused urbanization, at least as much as, and probably more than, agriculture."[1] The development of trade and, in turn, cities is also related to improvements in communication such as in water transport and writing. From our perspective what is significant about this argument is that it highlights the importance of transnational relations linked to long-distance trade for cities.

We have already discussed transnational aspects of some of the major ancient and medieval cities in earlier chapters. All of these cities served as important regional political, economic, and cultural centers as well as (to differing degrees) focal points of international commerce and bases for long-distance traders. Most people living in these early cities were not transnationals, but there were always at least some transnational traders, diplomats, scholars, priests, and soldiers living in them. Just as today, however, it is important to keep in mind that in the past too there were cities where transnational relations were not so important, cities that were oriented largely towards their immediate hinterland.

The Black Death, an outbreak of the bubonic plague that swept across the Old World in the mid–1300s, warrants mention here because of its close association with urban life, its impact on medieval cities, and its transnational character. This plague originated in China in the aftermath of the Mongol conquest and a resultant famine that broke out in 1331.[2] By the time the plague had run its course China's population had declined from about 120 million to around 60 million.[3] The plague travelled across Central Asia along the Silk Road with the long-distance traders and Mongol armies, reaching the city of Caffa on the Crimea Peninsula in 1347. (The Mongols who placed the city under siege catapulted infected corpses over the city walls.) Over the next couple of years the plague spread down the east coast of the Mediterranean through Constantinople, and on to Alexandria, Antioch, Damascus, and Jerusalem. Initially it was carried by trading ships, but as people fled the cities they carried the plague further afield. Hecker remarks, "India was depopulated, Tartary, Mesopotamia, Syria, Armenia were covered with dead bodies."[4] Ibn Battuta encountered the effects of the plague in his travels: "I went to Damascus.... The number of deaths among them had risen to two thousand four hundred a day.... Then I went to Cairo and was told that during the plague the number of deaths had risen to twenty-one thousand a day. I found that all the shaikhs I had known there were dead."[5] Genoese traders fleeing Caffa carried the plague to Sicily, from where it entered Western Europe. Cantor estimates that around 20 million people died of the plague in Western Europe, representing 30 to 50 percent of the population.[6] The Black Death was largely to blame for the population of the world declining by about one-quarter during the 1300s, with cities being particularly hard hit.

Mesopotamian Cities

Since urbanization began in the Mesopotamia around 3200 B.C., we will start our discussion in that part of the world. The earliest cities in Mesopotamia were tiny by modern standards with populations of 20,000 or less, but huge compared with other settlements at the time. They were centers of administration and trade and had a relatively complex mix of people: "They were inhabited by farmers ... and craftsmen, as well as traders, soldiers, priests, priestesses, civil servants, political leaders, slaves, servants, prostitutes, water carriers, women and children."[7]

The earliest cities were associated for the most part with the Sumerians. The Sumerians established around thirty small city-states in the vicinity of the Tigris and Euphrates rivers. Ur was the largest and most important of these cities. The original village of Ur was flooded and then re-established around 4300 B.C. and by 3200 B.C. it had developed into a city.[8] By 2800 B.C. the city had a population that archaeologists have estimated to have been between 12,000 and 24,000 with some 500,000 people living in the surrounding area.[9]

At the time Ur was located close to the Persian Gulf and it was connected to the Euphrates River by a canal. This allowed the city to develop as an important trading center and such trade in turn helped to generate the city's wealth — as exemplified in the items found in its royal tombs.[10] The city's artisans produced an array of goods for domestic consumption and export. Raw materials for these products were brought overland and down the rivers from the north and by sea from the south. As was mentioned in the discussion of trade goods, lapis lazuli from Afghanistan was imported to Ur as early as 2600 B.C. and carnelian was imported from the Indus Valley. Some of these stones were made into beads, which were subsequently exported from Ur to other parts of the Middle East. It was also noted that Ur was a center of wool textile production. These textiles were also exported, including some to Magan (Oman), where they were exchanged for copper.

Ur was the dominant Sumerian power until Sargon of Akkad defeated it and established the Akkadian Empire (c. 2270–2083 B.C.). Ur again rose in power during Sumer's third dynasty, which is also known as the Ur III Period. The founder of the new dynasty, Ur-Nammu, revitalized the kingdom and the city of Ur. He ushered in a period of major construction and economic development and trade. The Elamites put an end to Sumerian power around 1940 B.C. and for a time there was no major power ruling over Mesopotamia. Although no longer capital of an empire, Ur's favorable location in relation to trade by inland waterways and by sea meant that it continued functioning as a major port in the Persian Gulf and it remained an important urban center until around 550 B.C. It was abandoned around 500 B.C.

Babylon, located to the north of Ur along the Euphrates River, was a large regional city by the time of Sargon and was to remain an important city on and off for the next two thousand years.[11] Its rise and significance over such a long period of time was largely related to what Tellier refers to as the "triumph of the Euphrates-Mediterranean" trade axis.[12] As a result Babylon served as the world's most important trading center during much of this period. This role in turn saw the city emerge as the world's first "authentic 'heterogenetic' and cosmopolitan metropolis"... "the first 'London' or the first 'New York' the world has known."[13]

The rise of this trade axis began during the reign of Hammurabi (r. *c.* 1728–1686 B.C.), the sixth king of the dynasty, who captured all of the major kingdoms and cities of Mesopotamia (including Assur and Ur) and assumed control over their extensive trade networks. Under his rule the core trade routes shifted from Sumer to the south northward and towards the Mediterranean. Babylon grew in size and wealth as the commercial hub of the Middle East. Ships with crews of up to 90 men carried goods along the Euphrates River. An increasing number of skilled trades emerged and this period witnessed the organization of skilled workers into guilds (called tribes) with masters and apprentices.

Babylon fell to the Hittites around 1531 B.C. (dates recorded for this event vary from 1651 to 1499 B.C.) and the city came to be ruled from 1530 to 1155 B.C. by the Kassites, who renamed it Karanduniash. Later it came under Assyrian rule. Under the leadership of Nabopolassar the Chaldean, Babylon threw off Assyrian rule in 627 B.C. and became the capital of the Neo-Babylonian Chaldean Empire.

Nabopolassar's son Nebuchadnezzar II (r. *c.* 605–562 B.C.) initiated a spate of construction in Babylon and throughout his empire. Of particular relevance to the present discussion was that he facilitated trade by improving highways and canals. Quoting Nebuchadnezzar—"I have turned inaccessible tracks into serviceable roads"—Durant remarks that during his reign "countless caravans brought to the bazaars and shops of Babylon the products of half the world. From India they came via Kabul, Heart and Ecbatana; from Egypt via Pelusium [near modern Port Said, Egypt] and Palestine; from Asia Minor through Tyre, Sidon and Sardis to Carchemish [a Hittite city], and then down the Euphrates. As a result of all this trade Babylon became, under Nebuchadnezzar, a thriving and noisy market-place, from which the wealthy sought refuge in residential suburbs."[14] He adds that Babylon at this time "was essentially a commercial civilization. Most of the documents that have come down to us from it are of a business character."[15] Nebuchadnezzar is best known for his conquest of Judea and the subsequent forcible removal of the Jews to Babylon. The Jewish presence in Babylon serves to emphasize the multinational character of the city.

The Neo-Babylonian Empire fell to the Persian king Cyrus the Great in 539 B.C. Under the Persians Babylon was no longer the capital of an empire, but it remained an important center of government, commerce, and learning. Alexander the Great captured Babylon in 331 B.C. Alexander was well disposed towards the city—he died there in 323 B.C.—and under him it continued to flourish. After Alexander's death and the division of his empire, however, the fighting between his successors resulted in the city's drastic decline until in 275 B.C. its remaining inhabitants were moved to Seleukeia-Tigris, the new capital of the Seleucid Empire.

The Middle East boasted a number of large cities during the medieval period, many of them being placed along important trade routes, especially those associated with the Silk Road. The Silk Road route to Antioch passed through Samarkand and Tehran. Samarkand was built on the site of the Zeravchan oasis around 600 B.C. and served as the Sogdian capital. Muslims captured it in A.D. 712. The more southern route of the Silk Road heading to Petra and Alexandria passed through Shiraz. The city of Isfahan was also built on the site of an oasis (located on the banks of the Zayandeh River) and is mid-way between Tehran and Shiraz and served as a meeting point between north-south and east-west trade routes. Timur captured the city in 1387 and after its inhabitants revolted against the heavy taxes that he imposed he had his troops slaughter its estimated 70,000 inhabitants. Largely due to its important position in relation to trade routes it revived and the city flourished again. It became the Safavid capital of Persia during the reign of Shah Abbas the Great (r. 1587–1629). It was during this period that it became an important center of rug production.

The city of Nishapur (Neyshabur), in the northeast of modern Iran, had a population of around 125,000 in A.D. 1000 — placing it within the top ten cities in the world by population — and owed its prominence in large part to its proximity to nearby important turquoise mines and its strategic location along the Silk Road. According to tradition, the Sassanid king Shapur I (r. 241–72) established the city. It declined in importance for a time, but its fortunes rose once again in the 800s, when it became a center of the production of distinctive glazed ceramics that were exported widely, including to Europe. The founder of the Seljuk Dynasty, Toghrül (1. c. 990–1063), conquered the city in 1028–29 and made it his residence for a time. The city was within the borders of the Khwarezmian Empire (1077–1231), which was attacked by Genghis Khan in 1220. One of Genghis Khan's sons-in-law was killed in the attack on the city and at the request of his widow all of the city's inhabitants were put to death and their skulls placed in piles. Subsequent earthquakes destroyed the city's kilns.

Tabriz was the third largest city in the Middle East in 1500 with a population of around 250,000.[16] Its growth and prosperity was also linked to its political importance and its role in international trade. Although the city was established earlier,[17] it was destroyed by an earthquake and rebuilt under the direction of Zubaidah a wife of the Abbasid caliph Harun al-Rashid, in A.D. 791. She is commonly credited as the founder of the city. Tabriz became capital of the Ilkhanate during the reign of Arghun Khan (r. 1284–91), and Ghazan Khan (r. 1295–1304) undertook a program of construction that included new city walls, numerous public buildings, and caravansarais to serve traders coming overland along the Silk Road. The city also served as capital of the Kara Koyunlu (Black Sheep Turkomen) confederation (encompassing adjacent parts of Armenia, Azerbaijan, Turkey, Iran, and Iraq) from 1375 to 1468 and the Ak Koyunlu (White Sheep Turkomen) confederation from 1469 to 1501. Timur sacked the city in 1392, but this did no lasting damage. Shah Ismail I (r. 1502–24) made it the capital of the Safavid Persian Empire. It remained capital of the empire until 1548, when the capital was moved to Qazin. In addition to its political importance, throughout this long history the city served as an important commercial center especially for long-distance traders with goods flowing through the city from Central Asia, the Middle East, and South Asia. The local population is predominantly Azeri, but as the capital of various empires and an important commercial center the city has also been populated by a range of different ethnic groups from the surrounding area (e.g., Persians, Kurds, Armenians, and Assyrians).

Mediterranean Cities

Maritime commerce around the Mediterranean helped give rise to a number of cities on or near its coasts in ancient times. In the northeastern Mediterranean, the relatively poor lands of Greece and the neighboring island of Crete contributed to the development of a civilization oriented towards long-distance trade and colonization, and cities developed here under conditions that highlight the importance of trade to urbanization. Castleden compares the ancient Greek city-states with medieval Venice and modern Singapore "whose wealth depends on commercial enterprise, on human resources" rather than exploitation of local natural resources.[18]

Urban life in ancient Greece began on the Peloponnese peninsula with a citadel named Mycenae. Settled sometime around 2000 B.C., Mycenae was an important regional power from around 1400 B.C. until about 1200 B.C.[19] Mycenaean traders travelled extensively and Mycenaean goods found their way around the eastern Mediterranean and as far west as Italy. Thus, Castleden notes, "substantial amounts of Mycenaean pottery have been found in southern Italy and Sicily."[20] He adds, "The main reasons why the Mycenaeans reached out to other lands was the poverty of their own."[21] As for the organization of this trade, "Trade at places like Ugarit in the Levant was probably organized by freelance traders operating according to the local pattern of exchange. In Egypt, Mycenaean goods arrived in a completely different way, as part of a formal exchange of royal gifts, described by the Egyptians as tribute."[22] Relations with Egypt were not a one-way affair: An inscription from Kom el-Heitan in Egypt dating from around 1380 B.C., recording the itinerary of an Egyptian embassy to the Aegean Sea region, mentions Mycenae. Mycenaean trade grew over time: "By the end of the fourteenth century, political links with Egypt and the Levant had been developed, and by the thirteenth century the Mycenaeans had gained control of the eastern trade routes. This was marked by significant increase in the number of oriental objects and raw materials arriving in Greece."[23] The Mycenaeans also established colonies along the coast of western Anatolia. These included Ephesus, Iasos, and Miletus. They were coastal enclaves in a territory that was otherwise controlled by the Hittites. Mycenae was attacked either by the Dorians or by a group known as the Sea People around 1150–1200 B.C. and its inhabitants scattered.

Subsequent Greek city-states ranged in population from around 40,000 to 100,000 and many of them followed the Mycenaean pattern of seeking opportunities through long-distance trade and establishing colonies. Athens was the most important of these city-states. Founded around the same time as Mycenae, it had grown into a small city by 700 B.C. Athens emerged as a significant political and economic power in the 500s B.C. Peisistratus, who was in power roughly from 546 to 527/8 B.C., was especially influential in promoting the city-state's economic development and international activities. He encouraged silver mining at Laurium, created a new coinage, established the Panathenaic games, established colonies along the Dardanelles, and made a number of commercial treaties around the region. As Durant notes, until the time of Peisistratus, Athens "had been a second-rate city in the Greek world."[24] That changed under the rule of Peisistratus and his sons and Athens began its ascent to preeminence among Greek city-states in the following century. At its peak, the population of Athens between 500 and 450 B.C. was somewhere between 160,000 and 100,000, making it by far the largest Greek city in its day.

The Spartans destroyed the Athenian fleet in 405 B.C. and power shifted within the Hellenic world. The Roman general Sulla destroyed Athens in 86 B.C. It was rebuilt and once again emerged as an important cultural center in the Mediterranean under Roman rule. The Goths and Heruli destroyed much of the city again in A.D. 267, and although it was rebuilt it did not achieve the same cultural status as before.

The building of warships and merchant ships, paid for in part by the silver from Laurium, played an important role in the rise of Athens: "The Athenian fleet for two generations keeps the Aegean clear of pirates, and from 480 to 430 commerce thrives as it never will again until Pompey suppresses piracy in 67 B.C."[25] The Athenian navy provided safety for a commercial fleet that allowed the Athenian economy to grow. The growth of the commercial fleet and international trade in turn meant that more and more Athenians were directly involved in transnational activities and this had an important effect on life in general in Athens: "The merchants who accompany their goods to all quarters of the Mediterranean come back with changed perspective, and alert and open minds; they bring new ideas and ways, break down ancient taboos and sloth, and replace the familial conservatism of a rural aristocracy with the individualistic and progressive spirit of a mercantile civilization."[26] Such people were able to travel in greater safety than before and also more cheaply: "Passenger tariffs are low: for two drachmas ($2 [in 1939]) a family can secure passage from Piraeus [the port of Athens] to Egypt or the Black Sea."[27] Not only did the silver of Laurium help to pay for ships, but it also allowed Athens to establish a reliable coinage that was "accepted gladly throughout the Mediterranean world,"[28] unlike the debased coins of many other Greek city-states.

Like the Myceneans before them, the Athenians and a number of other Greek city-states established colonies outside of Greece. Such colonization was motivated by a variety of factors. The poor soils of Greece played a role, as did the development of international trade networks. There were also political factors as those at the losing end of political conflicts sometimes left their homes and went into exile. Colonies were established to the northeast in Anatolia and around the Black Sea. In Asia Minor the Greek colonial cities of Ephesus and Miletus emerged as important financial centers linked to long-distance trade. In fact, in the 500s B.C. Miletus was the wealthiest city in the Greek world, in addition to being an important center of literature, philosophy, and the arts. Moreover, it in turn established around eighty colonies of its own and merchants from Miletus were to be found around the Baltic Sea and throughout the eastern Mediterranean. Byzantium was founded in 660 B.C. as a colony of Megara. These colonies allowed the Greeks to assume control over the Grain Route from the Black Sea. Colonies were established to the south on the island of Cyprus and as far away as Egypt (another important source of grain), where Miletus established the colony of Naucratis around 650 B.C. To the west colonies were established in Italy, France, and Spain. Syracuse on the island of Sicily was an important Greek commercial center in the west. Phoenicians founded the colony of Massalia (Marseille) in 550 B.C. It served to give the Greeks access to trade routes carrying goods such as amber (brought from the Baltic Sea area) and pewter (which was carried across Gaul from England).

The Phoenicians were the other great transnationals of the ancient Mediterranean. Carthage was an especially important Phoenician city in North Africa.[29] According to Roman legend it was founded in 814 B.C. as a colony of the Phoenician city of Tyre. The population of Carthage before its destruction by the Romans in 146 B.C. was over 700,000 (it was later rebuilt by Rome and remained an important city until destroyed by Muslims in A.D. 698). The Phoenicians built two large artificial harbors for the city. One of these served the city's navy that at one time numbered 220 warships and the other was used for mercantile trade.

While Carthage's navy recruited mainly among the Punic (local ethnic Phoenician) citizenry, as will be discussed in a later chapter Carthage relied heavily on foreign mercenaries for its army. The core of its army was from territories directly under Carthage's control in North Africa and included Punics, ethnic Libyans, and Numidians. There were also mercenaries from different ethnic groups and geographic locations around the Mediterranean and beyond. Many of the mercenaries were from the Iberian Peninsula and the Balearic Islands.

Carthage's economy began as an extension of that of its parent city, Tyre, and its merchants initially followed Tyre's trade patterns. Over time, however, it developed a more extensive trade network. Carthaginian merchants traveled by land in caravans south across the Sahara and east as far as Persia and in ships by sea throughout the Mediterranean and out into the Atlantic down the coast of West Africa, west to the Canary Islands, and north to Britain (a source of tin). Carthage possessed a huge merchant fleet with vessels that were capable of carrying over 100 tons of goods. Carthaginian merchants are credited with inventing auctions as a means of selling goods and used this technique extensively in trade with people living to the south in Africa, where they sold manufactured goods and agricultural products and obtained gold as well as exotic goods such as ivory, ebony, and live animals and birds as well as feathers and hides.

Traders from the ancient harbor of Tartessos at the mouth of the Guadalquivir River in Andalusia, Spain, appear to have initiated trade with the Cassiterides (the Tin Islands), whose identity is debated by modern scholars, where tin was obtained for making bronze. The Phoenicians entered into partnership with them and built their own port of Gadir (modern Cádiz) nearby. Over time Carthage came to control much of tin and lead (as well as silver) trade in the western Mediterranean and emerged as an important producer of bronze goods as well. Trade in these metals and metal goods served as a major source of Carthage's wealth, but the range of its trade goods was extensive. Carthage produced the valuable Tyrian purple dye as well as less expensive red dye made from cochineal and exported a wide variety of types of locally produced cloth dyed with them. Other goods traded by its merchants included pottery, incense, perfumes, furniture, jewelry, and objects made of glass, wood, alabaster, ivory, lead, gold, and silver. Carthage also manufactured and exported wine (including a famous raisin wine) and traded in a variety of food items that included salted fish from the Atlantic, fish sauce, olives and olive oil, dates, and a variety of fruits, nuts, and grains. Carthage was famous for its horses and these too were exported.

Carthaginians established a number of permanent settlements along the coast of the Mediterranean such as the port of Gadir mentioned above as well as on islands in the Mediterranean like Malta and the Balearic Islands as an extension of their trade. Elsewhere they often established permanent trading facilities in other people's ports. Their overseas colonists not only engaged in trade but also often produced goods for trade. Thus, for centuries Carthage was the center of a large trading network that encompassed a great deal of Western Europe, Northern Africa, and the Western Middle East.

Alexander the Great founded Alexandria in 332 B.C. It served as a center of Hellenistic culture and commerce in Egypt and grew in economic and political prominence under Ptolemy I Stoler (1. *c.* 367–283 B.C.) who became satrap of Egypt after Alexander's death. Although the Phoenician city of Tyre continued to serve as an important trading center linking the Mediterranean world with the Middle East and regions further to the east, Alexandria came to eclipse Tyre and Carthage in commercial importance under Ptolemaic rule. It became the largest city in the world in the 200s B.C. and even after Rome conquered Egypt Alexandria remained the second largest city in the Roman Empire and one of the largest in the world.

Alexandria was essentially a Greek city in Egypt, but it developed a unique syncretic Greco-Egyptian and Greek culture. As Erskine points out the inhabitants of Alexandria included "an extraordinary mix of Greeks from many cities and backgrounds, all with different civic, social, and religious traditions behind them. There would be no one tradition to look back to, a tradition which would unite the people."[30] He contrasts Alexandria with

Greek colonies that were linked to a single Greek city-state. In addition to Greeks and Egyptians, Alexandria also had a large Jewish population, the largest in the world at the time. The growth of Rome coincided with increasing trade between Egypt and Rome through Alexandria and with increasing Roman influence on the city. The Romans asserted jurisdiction over the city in 80 B.C. Octavian conquered the city in 30 B.C. and it along with Egypt subsequently was incorporated into the Roman Empire. A great deal of the city was destroyed by Roman troops of Emperor Trajan in A.D. 115 in response to a Jewish revolt and was then rebuilt by Emperor Hadrian along Roman lines. The city was destroyed by a tsunami in A.D. 365 and again rebuilt.

Alexandria's population reached its peak under the Romans at around 800,000 and it was the second largest city in the Roman Empire.[31] Moreover, it was the Roman Empire's leading city of industry and commerce. Raw materials were brought to Alexandria where they were turned into manufactured goods. Thus, frankincense from Arabia was processed here and silk thread was woven into cloth. It was an important center of glass making and some of this glass was exported to the East.

Richard Alston remarks of Alexandria under Roman rule, "All the races of the world met and traded in Alexandria."[32] Those living there included Greeks, Egyptians, and Romans (Italians), as well as Jews, Phoenicians, Arabs, Persians, Syrians, Libyans, Nubians, Scythians, and even Indians. Durant mentions, "It was also a tourist center, equipped with hotels, guides, and interpreters for visitors coming to see the Pyramids and the majestic temples of Thebes."[33] The Jews comprised as much as 40 percent of the city's population.[34] Originally they had been confined to a distinct part of the city, but over time many lived outside of this area as well. The Romans allowed them to continue living under their own laws and to be governed by their elders as they had under the Ptolomies. The head of the Jewish community in Alexandria was called the *arabarch*. The Jews were engaged in industry and trade and made up a significant part of the merchant class.

Alexandria may have been the leading city of commerce and industry in the Roman Empire, but Rome was its largest city and its capital. As such it was the largest and wealthiest city in the ancient Mediterranean. The city of Rome was supposedly founded in 753 B.C., probably as a colony of the Latium city of Alba. Located about 30 km inland on the alluvial plain of the Tiber River, Rome became an important commercial city. Especially significant in this regard was its strategic location as a link in the long-distance salt trade from Salona (near Split in Croatia) to the western Mediterranean region.[35] Rome's port of Ostia also served as a transshipment point for grain coming from Egypt and the Black Sea. The maritime trade itself was largely monopolized by the Carthaginians and in 510 B.C. Rome signed a treaty with Carthage recognizing this monopoly in return for Carthage agreeing not to interfere with Roman activities of a more domestic nature. By the 300s B.C. Rome had grown into a rich commercial city with a population equal to or greater than that of Athens.

Rome's rise as a power beyond Italy came in the wake of the decline of Carthage and the Greek city-states. This transition was marked by a series of wars, starting with the First Punic War (264–41 B.C.), which resulted in Rome seizing control of Sicily, Corsica, Sardinia, and parts of Gaul. By 146 B.C. Rome had taken over Carthage and Greece and continued to expand its empire throughout the Mediterranean region until it reached its maximum extent during the reign of the emperor Hadrian (r. A.D. 117–38).

We have already discussed the Roman Empire in an earlier chapter. What is of concern here is the transnational character of the city of Rome. With a population of around 500,000 to 1 million at its height, imperial Rome was the largest city in the Mediterranean region at the time.[36] Beyond sheer size it was also the capital of a large multi-national empire. Despite its Eurocentrism, the saying "all roads lead to Rome" does point to how ancient Rome was at the center of an extensive road network linking it to its vast empire.[37] In fact there were 29 highways radiating from Rome.[38] As Matz notes, "Although the road system was built primarily for the use of the army, civilians also frequented it. Overland travel, however, was slow and often dangerous. Thieves and muggers, seemingly lurking behind every tree and boulder, awaited the weak and unwary. So river and ocean transit was the preferred method of getting from one place to another."[39]

In addition to the roads Rome was linked by sea to its empire through the ports of Ostia, Puteoli, and Portus. The Romans imported large quantities of bulk goods and luxuries through these ports, and a large number of people passed through them coming and going from the far reaches of the empire and also worked in them building and repairing ships and loading and unloading goods and passengers: "Of corn barges alone twenty-five were drawn up the Tiber every working day; if we add the transport of building stone, metals, oil, wine, and a thousand other articles, we picture a river teeming with commerce and noisy with loading and carrying machines, with dockmen, porters, stevedores, traders, brokers, and clerks."[40] The port of Ostia, located at the mouth of the Tiber River about 30 km to the northeast of Rome, had a permanent population of 50,000 to 75,000 people during the 1st to 3rd centuries, as well as a large transient population that included "travelers from Africa and the western Mediterranean and the merchantmen's crews, who often would lie over for a considerable time: the travellers waiting for passage to a specific place, the seamen waiting for favorable weather or permission from the bureaucracy to go home."[41] As would be expected, Ostia had a multi-ethnic population of people from around the empire who were engaged in trade and seafaring. The Ostia Synagogue, built during the reign of Claudius (A.D. 41–54) and one of the oldest Jewish synagogues in the world outside of Israel, is indicative of the port's multi-ethnic character.[42]

Prior to its imperial expansion Rome does not appear to have been inhabited by many non–Italians, but its involvement in long-distance trade did serve to create transnational interests among at least some of its residents. As Rome became the center of a large empire, the composition of the city became increasingly varied and a greater number of the people living there were engaged in activities of a transnational nature, whether in relation to administration of the empire, commercial activities beyond Italy, or artistic or educational activities linked to distant lands.

People living in Rome who were engaged in transnational activities or whose lives had transnational aspects can be placed in a number of categories including free citizens, soldiers, free foreigners, and slaves. The category of free citizens is somewhat ambiguous. As was discussed in an earlier chapter, the numbers of those who were afforded citizenship expanded along with Rome's political fortunes to include an increasingly varied group of peoples, often over the opposition of existing citizens. As was also discussed previously, the progressive extension of Roman citizenship to a greater range of people meant that the percentage of non–Roman and then even non–Italian people holding Roman citizenship increased, until by the A.D. 200s ethnic Italians were a minority of Roman citizens. The implication for the city of Rome was that a large number of people from a wide variety of national backgrounds around Europe and the Mediterranean had legal, political, and cultural ties to the city and this was increasingly reflected in the population living in the city as well.

Most of the people living in ancient Rome at any given time were free Roman citizens (although of diverse national origins) and most of these people were born in Rome and spent their lives there. There were, however, quite a few free Romans who worked in public or private capacities that linked them to the world beyond Rome and even Italy. Moreover, there were a substantial number of Romans, especially elites, who spent large parts of their lives working or traveling in other parts of the empire, including those whom Plutarch called "globe-trotters who spend the best part of their lives in inns and on boats."[43] While those Romans involved in imperial administration or long-distance trade may not have traveled as easily or as frequently as their modern counterparts, maritime travel in particular was relatively inexpensive and efficient. It took only a day to cross the Adriatic and "with favorable winds, six days carried one from Sicily to Alexandria or from Gades [Cadiz] to Ostia."[44]

Nor was travel around the empire restricted to those engaged in commercial or administrative affairs. Writing in the 1940s, Durant comments, "Despite all difficulties, there was probably more traveling in Nero's day than at any time before our birth…. Educated Romans flocked to Greece and Egypt and Greek Asia, scratching their names on historic monuments, sought healing waters of climates, ambled by art collections in the temples, studied under famous philosophers, rhetors, or physicians, and doubtless used their Pausanias as their Baedeker."[45] Pausanias was a 2nd century ethnic Greek geographer who wrote a description of Greece that is often credited as being the world's first travel guide.[46]

In addition to local-born and foreign-born free Roman citizens living in Rome the city was also home to a substantial number of foreigners who were not citizens, including slaves, non–Roman military personnel, free foreigners (*peregrinis*) from within the empire, and a mixture of people coming to Rome from outside of the empire as part of embassies and in other capacities. Noy estimates that free foreign-born immigrants constituted on average about 5 percent of Rome's population with the number of migrants coming from outside of Italy increasing from the 1st through the 3rd centuries.[47] After then, with the onset of the Crisis of the Third Century, Rome "lost some of its appeal to immigrants" as a result of its "economic, cultural and political decline" and this "reduced the numbers of immigrants across a whole spectrum from slaves to professors to merchants."[48]

In a survey of several hundred inscriptions from ancient Rome that provide evidence of a person's place of origin, Noy found that among Pagans many came from Asia and Bithynia in Asia Minor; Gaul and Hispania in western Europe; and Africa, Numidia, and Egypt in North Africa; while among Christians and Jews the largest number came from Syria and Palestine, with a significant number also coming from Galatia (modern Turkey).[49] Most of those who were from Asia Minor were ethnic Greeks, and ethnic Greeks from the eastern part of the empire in general were one of the largest citizen and non-citizen ethnic groups in the city. Jews comprised another group in Rome that rivaled ethnic Greeks in size. There were between 20,000 and 60,000 Jews in Rome in the early 1st century A.D., equal to between 2 percent and 6 percent of Rome's population.[50] Some were citizens, but not all. North Africans, especially people of Punic (i.e., Carthaginian) ancestry and Egyptians, comprised a third major group of foreigners in Rome. It was a prosperous region and an especially important source of grain. Many affluent families were able to send members to Rome and many merchants and others engaged in commerce from the area also at least visited Rome. Some of the rulers of the region, including members of the Ptolemaic family like Cleopatra VII, lived in Rome for periods of time. There were over 100 senators from North Africa: "In the third century perhaps one in eight of the Roman Senate was of African origin."[51] As would be expected a number of migrants and visitors came from Alexandria, including merchants, sailors, and doctors. There were also a number of priests of Egyptian cults (especially the cult of Isis, which became one of Rome's religions, *Isis et Serapis*) living in Rome.

Tiberius Sempronius Gracchus (aka Tiberius Graccus the Elder, l. *c.* 217–154 B.C.) and his family provide an example of a Roman elite family during the early days of the empire who spent a limited amount of time out in the empire in the course of their careers.[52] The elder Tiberius came from an influential Roman family. He was elected tribune of the people in 187 B.C. and then praetor in 179 B.C. In this capacity he went to Spain to put down a revolt by the local tribes. He married a woman named Cornelia, a daughter of Scipio Africanus Maior (l. 234–183 B.C.), who also had been a military commander in Spain and who had led Roman forces successfully against Carthage in 202 B.C. The couple had two sons, Tiberius and Caius. The younger Tiberius (l. 168/163–133 B.C.) served as an officer in the Third Punic War and then held the post of *quaestor* (an overseer of financial affairs) in Numantia in Spain. Back in Rome he was elected a tribune of the people in 133. His populism infuriated his fellow senators and he was killed and his body thrown in the Tiber. Tiberius's younger brother was then elected tribune in 124, only to die a few years later and to have his body also tossed into the Tiber. These were fairly cosmopolitan Romans who moved about the empire while retaining Rome as their home. In the case of Spain, although they resided there for a time, they sought to spread Roman power and civilization to the region rather than to integrate themselves into local society in any way. Beyond this, however, like many elite Romans at the time and afterwards, they were also familiar with and influenced by Greek culture, especially Greek philosophy, and fluent in the language. Thus, Tiberius Graccus the Elder addressed the people of Rhodes in Greek during a visit to the island some time around 168 B.C.

As the Roman Empire grew and citizenship came to encompass a wider range of peoples, a greater number of free Roman citizens moved back and forth between Rome and the provinces during the course of their lives. Moreover, family networks developed that included citizens living in Rome as well as other members in provincial towns and cities. While many of these family networks were among ethnic Italian Latin speakers who formed enclaves throughout the empire, networks sometimes were multi-ethnic and included both Latin-speaking ethnic Italians and people of other ethnic groups who also spoke other languages. It is interesting to look at the Roman emperors in this regard. In part because many of them served in the military before becoming emperor and continued to take an active part in military campaigns after assuming the emperorship, many of Rome's emperors spent parts of their lives away from Rome. Moreover, a number of them were born outside of Italy and had family members scattered around the empire.

The Emperor Claudius (r. A.D. 41–54) was the first non–Italian emperor. He was born in Lugdunum, Gallia Lugdunensis (modern Lyon in what is now France).[53] Founded in 43 B.C., Lugdunum was the most important city in the western Roman Empire. Claudius was a member of the same family as the previous emperors, but they had all been born in Italy. Trajan (r. A.D. 98–117) was the next foreign-born emperor. He was born in Italica (near modern Seville), Hispania Baetica, and was the adopted son of the previous emperor, Nerva (r. A.D. 96–98). Hadrian (r. 117–136) was also born in Italica. Trajan was a maternal cousin of Hadrian's father. The emperor Caracalla (r. 198–217) was also born in Lugdunum.

Outside of Europe the coastal cities of North Africa produced two emperors. These cities were of Carthaginian origin, but also had large ethnic Italian populations. Septimus Severus (r. 193–211) was born in Leptis Magna, Africa Province (modern Al Khums, Libya), in A.D. 145.[54] His father was of Carthaginian-Punic ancestry and his mother was from an influential Roman family. Raised in Leptis Magna, Septimus Severus spoke Punic as a young man, but was taught Latin and Greek. He left Leptis Magna around 162 to start a public career in Rome, where he was granted senatorial rank through his mother's family connections. He went back to Leptis Magna around 166 and then returned to Rome to take up the office of quaestor. When his father died he went back to Leptis Magna for a short time to deal with family matters and then was posted to Sardinia. In 173 he was appointed to a higher position back in Africa to serve under a relative who had been made proconsul of the province. During his tenure there he married a woman who was of Punic ancestry. He then moved back to Rome, where he became a people's tribune. His first wife died in 186 and he sought the advice of fortune-tellers concerning whom he should marry next. Based on this advice he married a Syrian woman from Emesa named Julia Domna who was from the Syrian royal family and at the time was serving as a priestess to the local sun god Elagabalus. They married in 187. Then in 191 the emperor Commodus appointed Septimus commander of the legions of the province of Pannonia (occupying the western half of modern Hungary and parts of neighboring countries). Septimus was with his troops at Carnuntum (in modern Austria) in 193 when the emperor Pertinax was murdered (he had been emperor for only 3 months) and his troops proclaimed him emperor. Before assuming the position, however, he had to defeat other claimants in battles in various parts of the empire. As emperor, Severus spent some time away from Rome leading military campaigns in the Middle East, Britain, and North Africa.

The emperor Marcus Opellius Macrinus (r. 217–8) was born in Iol Caesarea, Mauretania (modern Cherchell, Algeria), around A.D. 165. He is of interest not only because of his birth in North Africa, but also because he was of Moorish ancestry. He was well educated and trained as a lawyer. Macrinus rose through the ranks of the Roman bureaucracy under Septimus Severus and the emperor Caracalla made him prefect of the Praetorian Guard. While Caracalla and Macrinus were in the east campaigning against the Parthians, Caracalla was assassinated and Macrinus proclaimed himself emperor.

Marcus Aurelius Antoninus, who is commonly known as the emperor Elagabalus (r. 218–222), is an especially relevant emperor from a transnational perspective because of his substantial ties to the eastern part of the empire. He was born in Emesa, Syria (modern Homs, Syria). His father, Sextus Varius Marcellus, was a Syrian Roman. His mother, Julia Soaemias, was the daughter of a Syrian nobleman and a Syrian Roman woman who was a niece of Emperor Septimus Severus's wife, Julia Domna. Because of their relationship to Julia Domna, the family moved to Rome while the future emperor was still a small child. Imperial connections then resulted in his father being posted to Britain in 197, where he served as procurator. While his father was appointed to additional imperial posts in Rome, the boy moved back to Emesa with his mother where he took up the position of a high priest of the sun god Elagabalus. They were living there in 217, when the emperor Caracalla was murdered in Syria and Macrinus was proclaimed emperor. In large part through his mother's initiative, the following year Roman legions in Syria revolted against Macrinus and declared Marcus Aurelius Antoninus emperor. Before long he had the support of most of the eastern armies. He took the name Elagabalus after the sun god, and the cult of this god played an important role not only in his garnering support among the eastern troops, but also in his subsequent reign as emperor. His accession to the emperorship was accompanied by the notion that the empire would benefit by his bringing together the religious cult of the Syrian sun god and the cult of the Carthaginian goddess Tanit in Rome. Accordingly, stones that were central to the worship of these two cults were brought to Rome. His reign was a disaster, ending in he and his mother being murdered and their bodies being thrown into the Tiber, but the religious cults that he promoted did continue.[55]

Alexander Severus (r. 222–35), who had been born in Arca Caesarea, Iudaea (modern Arqa, Lebanon), succeeded his cousin Elagabalus. Alexander's parents were Syrians and he was related to Elagabulus through his mother. Although his reign ended with he and his mother also being assassinated, on the whole he was considered to be a competent ruler. Among other things, he had a reputation for religious tolerance and he allowed the Jews to erect a synagogue in Rome. The period following his death from 235 to 284 is commonly referred to as the Crisis of the Third Century. It was a period marked by almost constant civil war, foreign invasions, and economic collapse. It also began a period in which other parts of the empire produced more Roman emperors than previously.

Prior to its decline in the 3rd century, who else migrated to Rome? Noy makes the point that unlike modern cities and even many other cities in the Roman Empire, Rome was not a particularly attractive destination for poorer, unskilled people since they had to compete for employment with the abundant number of slaves in the city.[56] In addition to the slaves themselves, many of the city's free citizens were manumitted slaves and their descendants, who were also available in abundant number to make finding work for poor, uneducated migrants quite difficult. It would appear then that the city mainly attracted affluent or skilled migrants from other parts of the empire lured by the prospects of better education, employment opportunities, or career advancement.

We have seen how movement to Rome from the provinces figured in the careers of several of the emperors and members of their families. As was mentioned in an earlier chapter, this was a fairly common pattern, especially on the part of elite provincial families seeking to improve their fortunes by sending family members to Rome, or to see members of their families posted to Rome in the course of their career advancement. The famous 2nd century historian Lucius Cassius Dio Cocceianus (better known simply as Cassius Dio) provides a good example.[57] Although he was a Roman citizen and his father served as a Roman senator, the family was of Hellenic origin and lived in Nicaea in Bithynia Province (modern Iznik, Turkey), where Cassius Dio was born and raised. In later life Cassius Dio continued to write in Greek. During his career Cassius Dio moved between Nicaea, Rome, various parts of the empire, and finally back to Nicaea to retire. Thus, in addition to living in Rome where he held the post of senator and later consul, he served as governor of Smyrna (in modern Turkey) and as proconsul in the provinces of Africa and Pannonia.

As the most important market and economic center in the empire Rome also attracted a number of merchants and others from elsewhere in the empire who were engaged in various aspects of trading commodities and other goods. Such people included non–Italian Roman citizens and non-citizens from within the empire. Most of them only visited Rome or its ports to conduct business and then returned home, but some took up residence on a more permanent basis. Noy cites the example of a *curator* (i.e., manager or steward) of Carthaginian ships named L. Caelius Aprilis Valerianus who lived in Ostia with his family.[58] Individuals or groups engaged in trade with Rome sometimes sent agents there to assist with their activities at that end such as "P. Clodius Athenio, a *negotians salsarius* (dealer in garum) from Malaga" and "an officer of the Corporation of Traders of Malaga."[59] Foreign traders came to Rome from all over the empire, but certain regions or cities featured prominently, such as Spain, Alexandria and other North African ports, and Syria. The Syrians, for example, came from Palmyra and other eastern cities and were known especially for trading in luxury items and slaves.

Some of the foreign commodity traders and ship-owners engaged in maritime trade had centers known as *stationes* in Ostia and the city of Rome. The majority of these were associated with cities in the eastern Mediterranean (e.g., in the provinces of Cilicia, Asia, Syria, and Palestina) and the language used was Greek, although in Ostia there were also several from North African cities such as Alexandria and ports further to the west in Africa and Mauretania.[60] They appear to have been subject to their "home city councils" and also "had some involvement in the cult of the gods of the homeland."[61] There were also organizations associated with the trade in specific commodities from particular regions or cities such as the *negotiatores olearii ex Baetica* formed by olive oil traders from Baetica, the *corpus inportantium et negotiantium vinariorum* formed by wine importers also from Spain, and the *mercatores frumentarii et olearii Afrari* formed by grain and olive oil traders from Africa.

Rome also attracted a large number of people with skills such as doctors, teachers, artists, craftsmen, and entertainers. As with the merchants discussed above many of these skilled people came to Rome on a temporary basis, while others came to reside there permanently. Ethnic Greeks from the eastern part of the empire figure prominently among such migrants. People with certain skills were particularly encouraged to come to Rome by its citizens for cultural or practical reasons. In regard to the former, "The taste for Greek culture among Roman aristocrats in the second and first centuries B.C. created a demand for philosophers, poets and private tutors in great houses,"[62] and this continued to be the case in the imperial period. As Durant has commented, "When Rome became mistress of the Mediterranean, Greek artists poured into the new center of wealth and patronage."[63] The state also sometimes became involved. In regard to state involvement, "two groups of non-citizen foreigners were repeatedly encouraged to come to Rome by the state because they had skills which were not felt to be sufficiently available in the indigenous population: doctors and, to a lesser extent, teachers."[64] It would appear that most of the doctors in Rome were ethnic Greeks from the east or Egyptians. Ethnic Greeks from the east also figured prominently among certain skilled crafts; for example, marble traders and workers came from Bithynia and elsewhere in Asia Minor, and gold and silver smiths came from Corinth.

Rome, like most great cities, was also a magnet for those seeking fame or fortune in leisure activities. They included actors, musicians, dancers, charioteers, boxers, keepers of exotic animals, and prostitutes. Such people came to Rome from all over the empire. Whether or not they remained in Rome sometimes depended upon their success. In addition to the performers themselves were those who helped to organize the events, who staged the performances and recruited the people and animals. Chariot racing was an extremely popular sport in Rome. Matz describes "a crisp autumn afternoon in A.D. 146," when 250,000 fans turned out at the Circus Maximus "to watch the great driver of the Red team, Appuleius Diocles, compete in what may be the final race of his storied career."[65] Noy comments that for aspiring charioteers, "the city must have had an attraction like that of Series A for top-class European footballers now."[66] In the case of Gaius Appuleius Diocles, who came from Lusitania (modern Portugal) and started racing at the age of 18, he won 1,462 races during his 24 year career and received over 35 million sesterces in prize money by the time he retired. Peter Struck puts this in perspective: "Last fall, *Forbes* magazine was all atwitter as Tiger Woods closed in on becoming 'the first athlete to earn over $1 billion' in the course of his career... but *Forbes* missed the mark — taking the long view, Tiger was never all that well paid to begin with when compared with the charioteers of ancient Rome." Struck compares Woods' compensation to that of Gaius Appuleius Diocies: His total take-home amounted to five times the earnings of the highest paid provincial governors over a similar period — enough to provide grain for the entire city of Rome for one year, or to pay all the ordinary soldiers of the Roman Army at the height of its imperial reach for a fifth of a year. By today's standards that last figure, assuming the apt comparison is what it takes to pay the wages of the American armed forces for the same period, would cash out to about $15 billion."[67]

Entertainment in ancient Rome also included concerts, mimes, and plays. In the early days of imperial Rome 55 of the 76 festival days included performances of plays or mimes. The theater focused on old Roman and Greek tragedies, old Roman comedies, and mimes. There was little innovation in the theater except through mime. Like audiences of modern action movies, mime attracted multilingual crowds. Durant remarks, "There was a profit in foregoing language; the polyglot population of Rome of which a considerable part could understand only the simplest Latin, followed the action better when unburdened with words."[68] Pylades of Cilicia and Bathyllus of Alexandria (Bathyllus was a companion of Gaius Cilinius Maecenus, a close friend of Octavian-Augustus and a wealthy patron of the arts) introduced the pantomime to Rome in 21 B.C. This style was already popular in the eastern Mediterranean and it became the dominant stage form in Rome.

The rise of pantomime made dance fashionable as well. Previously dance had been looked down upon by the Roman elites. Many wealthy Roman households now employed dancing masters. Roman music came largely from Greece. Formal concerts were also held and there were musical competitions. *Symphoniae* were performed at the pantomimes with a chorus that sang and danced to the accompaniment of an orchestra. Performances might include as many as 6,000 singers and dancers. While Rome attracted performing artists from throughout the empire, professional performers also went on extended concert tours. The performing arts not only served as a means of culturally uniting the empire, but they played an additional political role as Roman emperors and consuls used the theater as a means of placating and distracting the populace of Rome and its empire. Theaters were constructed throughout the empire with an emphasis on making them as large as possible.

As for the military, there were foreigners in the military who were stationed in Rome on a long-term basis and those who spent only a short time there. Since few local Romans were recruited into the military, most soldiers stationed in Rome would have been foreigners. Noy makes the point that "living in barracks and sometimes performing repressive functions cannot have made for good relations between troops and the rest of the population, and most of them appear to have left Rome when they were discharged" (their normal term of service was 16 to 17 years.)[69] The number of soldiers stationed in Rome at any given time numbered from 10,000 to 30,000, with the largest number serving in the Praetorian Guard. The soldiers serving in the Praetorian Guard tended to come from "smaller cities and Romanized areas" initially in Italy, but by the time of Septimus Severus many were recruited from elsewhere in the empire.[70] Le Bohec estimates that 86.3 percent were from Italy, 9.5 percent were from elsewhere in Europe, and only 4.2 percent were from the east in the 1st-2nd centuries. In the 3rd century he estimates that 60.3 percent were from Europe outside of Italy (there were no Italians any longer) and 39.7 percent were from the east.[71] In regard to the impact of this change on Rome, Noy cites Cassius Dio, who complains that this change in recruitment patterns had resulted in "filling the city with a throng of motley soldiers most savage in appearance, most terrifying in speech, and most boorish in conversation."[72] In addition to the Praetorian Guard some of the emperors such as Claudius and Nero used German bodyguards. There were about 1,000 of them living in a distinct camp. The sailors in Rome's navy tended to be recruited from places other than those used by the army, such as Egypt, and some of these foreign sailors lived in barracks in Rome when not at sea, especially in the winter.[73]

People from outside of the Roman Empire tended to come to Rome in one of three ways, as members of embassies, as hostages, and as slaves or prisoners of war. Embassies generally came to Rome while the emperor was in residence or when the senate was in session and, while the intent was for an embassy to remain only a short time, in some cases unexpected circumstances difficulties in performing their intended tasks, "or personal complications, sometimes led to an extended visit."[74] Some embassies were housed at public expense in the Villa Publica, while others had to fend for themselves. The number of ambassadors in Rome at any given time varied from a dozen or so to hundreds. Most of these embassies came from nations or empires on the imperial frontier (such as Scythia and Parthia), while others came from further away (such as Tamil ambassadors). As for hostages, "There was a long tradition of taking hostages from enemy states to live at Rome. This gradually developed into members of the ruling families of client states being brought up at Rome and eventually sent back home as (it was hoped) pro–Roman rulers."[75]

Slaves were brought to Rome from different regions within and on the frontier of the empire at different times, in part reflecting the course of military conquest. Thus, in the early days of the empire many of the slaves came from Gaul, Hispania, other nearby areas in Western Europe and North Africa. Later a large proportion came from the eastern part of the empire such as Syria and its border regions.[76] Whatever their origin, slaves in Rome were mixed together in the market and subject to forces of assimilation once sold. Relatively few retained much in the way of identification with their places of origin.[77]

Most foreigners living in Rome did not form distinct ethno-national communities. There were no distinct residential areas for foreigners and interaction among co-nationals was largely related to shared kinship or commercial interests. Shrines or temples linked to foreign religious cults sometimes also served as a point of contact among co-nationals and as links to their ancestral home. Egyptian cults such as the one devoted to Isis had shrines and priests in Rome, but it is important to note that the worshippers were not exclusively Egyptian and included some upper class Romans.[78] Thus, such shrines were not exclusive ethno-national centers. There were also quite a few shrines devoted to deities from Syrian cities in Rome. While sometimes these attracted non–Syrians, for the most part worshippers had some connection with Syria.[79] Thus worshippers at the Palmyrene shrine included temporary visitors from Palmyra, recent immigrants from Palmyra, and residents of Palmyrene ancestry.[80]

Jewish synagogues were another group of ethnically exclusive religious shrines and temples that served as community centers. There were at one time at least 11 and possibly more synagogues in Rome, more than were found anywhere in the empire outside of Israel.[81] The Jews were a relatively old group in Rome. A large number of Jews had been brought to Rome as slaves who had been captured as prisoners of war and many were subsequently freed and became Roman citizens. Despite this long history of residence in Rome, unlike other groups of slaves the Jews retained a strong sense of identity and of being connected to Israel. As Rutgers notes, even though they were scattered throughout the empire, the Jews formed a distinct community based on shared religion and history.[82] The Roman state recognized this and treated them as a distinct group. Synagogues played an important role in maintaining this identity and ties with Israel for the Jews in Rome: "The Jewish synagogues in Rome were a form of organization without parallel among other foreign groups. By establishing communal institutions which took on a life of their own, the Jews had the means to pass on a separate identity from one generation to the next, irrespective of immigration."[83] Moreover, Jews in Rome did not merely send money back to the Temple in Israel, for despite considering Rome as their home, they "felt an overriding loyalty to Jerusalem."[84]

Economic and political power within the Roman Empire gradually shifted from Rome to Constantinople, which grew into one of the largest and richest cities in the world — and it remained so for around 1,000 years. It was founded by the Greeks in 657 B.C., and in A.D. 330 the Roman emperor Constantine the Great made it the capital of the Eastern Roman or Byzantine Empire. It was given the name of Nova Roma (New Rome), but quickly became known as Constantinople in honor of the emperor. Noy comments on the shifting fortunes of Rome and Constantinople in regard to immigration: "The foundation of Constantinople provided an alternative destination which must have been particularly attractive to people whose first language was Greek."[85]

Constantinople's population was around 50,000 in A.D. 337. By the time of Justinian I (aka Justinian the Great; 1. 483–565), 200 years later, its population was around 500,000.[86] In contrast, by A.D. 500 Rome's population had fallen to less than 100,000 and after the destruction caused by the Gothic War (535–54) there were only around 30,000 people still living in the ruins of the city.

Constantinople was essentially a Greek city with a small Roman elite at the top. Latin was the language of the state, but Greek was the main language outside of government circles, and by the 600s Greek had largely replaced Latin within the government as well. As for Constantinople, while most of its inhabitants were ethnic Greeks (who called themselves Romans as citizens of the Roman Empire), as the capital of the Eastern Roman or Byzantine Empire it was also an imperial city and home to a wide variety of peoples from throughout the empire and beyond: "Constantinople attracted people from a diversity of linguistic, cultural, and regional backgrounds. The city streets resounded with a cacophony of Latin, Greek, and Syriac, Aramaic and Armenian, Coptic and Ethiopic, Gothic and Hunnic, Persian and Arabic."[87]

In addition to those living in the city because of its political status as the imperial capital, there were also a large number of people whose lives were related to the city's extensive trade networks. Durant comments, "From the fifth century to the fifteenth Constantinople remained the greatest market and shipping center in the world."[88] The city's most important import was grain, most of which came from Egypt, and there were four to five kilometers of wharves for the grain ships.[89] Imperial policies served to promote commerce: "Commerce was encouraged by state maintenance or supervision of docks and ports, governmentally regulated insurance and loans on bottomry [a form of contract where the owner or master of a ship borrows money at fixed interest to allow him to conduct a voyage by pledging his ship as security for repayment], a vigorous war on piracy, and the most stable currency in Europe."[90]

The city was also an important religious center for Christians in Eastern Europe and the Middle East. Monks from Alexandria, for example, established monasteries and churches in the city. It also attracted a large number of Christian refugees fleeing persecution by non–Christians beyond the empire.

Constantinople grew and prospered at the outset of Justinian I's reign, but in 541 it suffered a setback in the form of the Plague of Justinian.[91] It seems that the plague was brought on the grain ships from Egypt and from Constantinople it spread to the other port cities of the Mediterranean. An estimated 40 percent of the city's population and perhaps a quarter of the population of the eastern Mediterranean as a whole died from the plague, and it played a major role in the decline of the empire until the 800s.[92] The empire and city recovered for a time, but suffered another setback in the 1200s in part because of the rivalry between the Christian church based in Rome and the eastern Christian church. Constantinople fell to the Republic of Venice and crusaders in 1204 and a portion of its territory was ruled as the Latin Kingdom of Constantinople from 1204 to 1261. In 1261 the Emperor Michael VIII Palaiologos (r. 1259–82) re-established Byzantine rule over Constantinople, but by this time the city and empire faced an even greater threat in the form of the rising forces of Islam.

Constantinople fell to Muslim forces commanded by Mehmed II (aka Mehmet II) in 1453 and again had its name changed, this time to Istanbul. The majority of the 30,000 inhabitants of the Byzantine city still living there when it fell were deported and Mehmed II then set about to repopulate the city by forcing Muslims, Christians, and Jews from around his empire to move to the city.[93] The census of 1477 gave the population of the city as consisting of 9,486 Muslim households, 3,743 Greek households, 1,647 Jewish households, 267 Christian households, and 31 Gypsy households. There was also a spate of construction including the Grand Bazaar in 1455, Topkapi Palace in 1459, and the Faith Mosque in 1463. There was a great deal more construction during the reign of Suleiman I (aka Suleiman the Magnificent, r. 1520–1566). At the time of Mehmed II's death in 1481 the population of the city had reached 80,000. By 1500 the city had a population of around 200,000. As capital of the Ottoman Empire the city again attracted a wide range of diverse peoples from around the empire as well as diplomats, merchants, and others from beyond its borders.

Political and economic conditions under the Muslim caliphates influenced the development of a number of cities around the Mediterranean as well as further to the east in the Middle East and South Asia. Beyond strictly political considerations the caliphates were important in regard to transnationalism not only by providing a context for long-distance trade, but also by encouraging the movement of scholars and people engaged in religious activities.

The spread of Islam into Egypt led to the rise of a new city there: Cairo.[94] A settlement named Babylon had been founded on the site of Cairo in Roman times around A.D. 30. The Romans also established a military camp (*fossatum* in Latin) on the other side of the Nile. The town of Babylon came to be inhabited primarily by Christians. When the Muslim Fatimids occupied the area in A.D. 641 they first set themselves up on the site of the old Roman military camp, naming their town al-Fustat (a derivative of the Latin name). The Fatimids founded a new city nearby called al-Mansuriyah in 969. The city's name was changed to al-Qahirah (The Victorious) in 972 — the name Cairo being a European version of the name. Serving first as the Fatimid capital, then as the capital of Saladin of the Ayyubid dynasty (Salah ad-Din Yusuf ibn Ayyub), and next becoming the Mamluk capital in 1260, by 1300 Cairo had grown to a population of around 400,000. The first century of Mamluk rule was especially prosperous for the city and there was a great deal of construction of public and religious buildings at this time. By the middle of the 1300s its population had increased further to around 500,000, making it "the greatest city of Africa, Europe and Asia Minor" at the time.[95] The city's growth owed a great deal to the trade in Asian spices that passed through Cairo.

Cairo suffered from the Black Death in 1348 and this and other epidemics saw the city decline in size and wealth during the latter part of the 1300s. The city's marginalization to the spice trade in the late 1400s added to its decline. The Ottomans defeated the Mamluks in 1517 and the status of the city was reduced from an imperial capital to that of a provincial capital, though still with a population of around 400,000.

When the Muslims conquered Spain between 711 and 714, Córdoba (aka Cordova) and Seville (aka Sevilla) were already important Christian cities located on the banks of the Guadalquivir River. The Phoenicians had founded Córdoba, which came under control of Carthage in 230 B.C. It was captured by the Romans in 152 B.C. and served as the capital of the Roman province of Hispania Baetica. In Roman times it had produced a number of notable persons including the philosopher Lucius Annaeus Seneca the Younger. The Vandals captured the city in A.D. 476. It was incorporated into the Byzantine Empire in 554 and then into the Visigoth kingdom in 572. Despite such political changes, it remained an important city in the Byzantine Empire and under the Visigoths. After the Muslims captured it in 711 the city became the capital of the Umayyad's Emirate of Córdoba in 756 under Abd al-Rahman I (r. 756–788). The city's prosperity was a result in part of its being located in a fertile area where cereals and olives were grown and exported.

The city prospered under Umayyad rule and by A.D. 1000 it had a population of around 450,000, making it the second largest city in Europe after Constantinople and the largest Muslim city in the world (Seville, the second largest city in Muslim Spain, had a population of around 150,000 in 1200). Córdoba's growth stalled at this point in part because of the outbreak of civil war in Muslim Spain in 1031, but it remained economically and culturally an important city until the mid–1100s.

Among the famous people of the medieval period to have been born in Córdoba were Abū 'l-Walīd Muhammad ibn Ahmad ibn Rushd (aka Averroes) and Moses Maimonides. Ibn Rushd (1. 1126–98) is associated with the Averroism school of philosophy and is widely viewed as the founder of secular thought in Western Europe. He held judicial appointments in Córdoba, Seville, and Marrakech (where he died). Moses Maimonides (aka Rabbi Moses ibn Maimon;1. 1135–1204) was a Jewish rabbi, philosopher, and physician and is widely considered to be one of the greatest Torah scholars. After conquering Córdoba in 1148 the Almohades forced local Jews to either convert, face execution, or go into exile. The decline of the city began at this time. The majority of Jews went into exile and the Maimonides family settled in Fez, Morocco. Moses Maimonides attended Al Karouine University there, traveled for a time, and then settled in Fustat, Egypt, where he became the physician of the Grand Vizier Alfadhil and Sultan Saladin (he also treated Richard I the Lionheart). The Christians led by the king of Castile captured Córdoba in 1236 and the city continued to decline in size and importance.

In contrast to the relative wealth and overall development of Muslim Spain in the 1000s to 1200s, Christian Europe was an underdeveloped backwater. This was reflected in the general lack of urbanization in the region. Moreover, Christian Europe's population peaked in the 1200s and, in part because of the Black Death, then declined through the 1300s and well into the 1400s. Paris and London at the time were small towns with popu-lations of less then 25,000, while the largest cities of Christian Europe were to be found in Italy, cities such as Amalfi, Naples, Milan, Venice, Florence, and Genoa. Amalfi was the first of these cities to develop primarily because of the pioneering efforts of its merchants to build trade links with Constantinople. They were the first group of western Europeans to establish a presence in Constantinople in the 900s and they are noteworthy for creating a maritime code of law — the *Tavola Amalfitana* — that was widely recognized around the Mediterranean over the next 500 years. Amalfi's dominance in Italian long-distance maritime trade came to an end when the Normans of Sicily conquered the city in 1091. Venice then emerged as the dominant commercial center in Italy, serving as an important link between Western Europe and the trade networks across the Mediterranean to the east. While small by world standards, by 1500 Venice had a population of around 100,000.

South Asian Cities

Cities first emerged in South Asia along the Indus River. These were associated with Harappan civilization and included the cities of Mohenjo-Daro and Harappa. They were founded around 2300 B.C. They and other Harappan cities were located along rivers and these rivers played an important role in their commercial activities, including their involvement in long-distance trade. They were relatively large cities for the time, with Mohenjo-Daro having a population of between 30,000 and 40,000 people by 2000 B.C. These cities disappeared around 1750 B.C. when Aryans invaded the area from the north. The Aryans were pastoralists and urban life in the region came to an end under their influence.

Urbanization was not to reappear in South Asia until the 500s B.C., when cities began to appear to the east along the Ganges River. Smith refers to this as the Early Historic period of South Asian urbanism, lasting until roughly the A.D. 300s — thus, encompassing the period of the Mauryan Empire — and reports over 60 sites from this period.[96] In addition to their association with the rise of empires, as Smith notes, "early Historic cities grew along with Buddhism."[97]

Pataliputra (modern Patna) was the most important of the South Asian cities of this period. Pataliputra was built originally as a small, fortified town on the banks of the Ganges River (where it is joined by the Gandhaka River) around 490 B.C. It grew in part as a center of trade along the two rivers and then became the capital of the Mauryan Empire. As the imperial capital the city received numerous ambassadors, including the ethnic Greek Megasthenes (1. c. 350–290 B.C.), who travelled to Pataliputra as ambassador of Seleucus I Nicator and wrote a description of the city.[98] Pataliputra also served as the capital of the Gupta (A.D. 320–550) and Pala (750–1175) empires. In addition to its political and economic preeminence the city was an important Buddhist center with several major monasteries located in and near the city that attracted scholars, artists, and others from throughout India. The city went into decline and was partially destroyed by Muslims in the late 1100s, but its fortunes were partially reversed when Sher Shah Suri (1486–1545) made Patiliputra his capital after conquering Bengal in 1539, changing its name to Patna.

Many of the South Asian cities entered a period of decline in the early A.D. 300s. As the cities began to grow once again during the Gupta era (A.D. 319–550), "they were less prosperous than before," and were built of "reused, broken bricks recycled from earlier structures."[99] This was a period of religious revival that saw many new religious structures being built within urban areas, but this building boom did not carry over into the secular structures of cities. In addition to serving as administrative centers for regional political powers, the cities of the Gupta and Pala periods were often centers of industrial production and trade. Some of these cities were known for particular goods. Cities like Ahmedabad, Multan, Boach, Masulipatam, and Thatta were known for textile production and Cambay for making stone beads.

In A.D. 1000 the city of Patan (in modern Gujarat State, India) with a population of around 100,000 was the second largest city in India. Vanraj Chavda founded the city in

A.D. 746. His father was assassinated before he was born and his mother fled to the jungle where he was born and given the name Vanraj (king of the jungle). He was educated by Jain priests and then established his kingdom with an army of Bhil tribesmen. He named his newly established capital Anahilavada (aka Anhilpur Patan) after his close friend Anahil, who had helped him establish his kingdom. Mulraj (r. 942–96) became the ruler of the kingdom in 942 and founder of the Solanki Dynasty. Patan grew to become a large and prosperous city under the Solankis and a noted center of religious learning. Although Patan benefitted greatly from the wealth produced for the kingdom by international trade, most of the actual international commerce was centered in coastal trading towns such as Cambay under the control of Patan's rulers. This wealth helped to support the construction of numerous public buildings as well as Jain and Hindu temples in the city. Patan is described in the Jain books known as the *Kumarpala Rasa,* which are accounts of the life of the Solanki ruler Kumarpal (r. 1143–72) who was responsible for building a number of the city's famous temples. According to these books Patan was 18 miles in circumference and contained 84 town squares, 52 bazaars, mints for making silver and gold coins, well laid gardens with fountains and trees, a grammar school that taught Sanskrit and Prakrit, numerous Jain and Hindu temples, and the Sahastralinga Talav (tank of 100 Shiva shrines). The city also developed its *patola* weaving industry during his reign. The Solankis lost power in the mid–1200s.

The spread of Islam into South Asia initially had a negative impact on cities when Mahmud of Ghazni began raiding the cities and temples in A.D. 1001, and it was only later, once Muslim rule had been established, that urban growth in those areas that had been subject to conquest resumed. In the case of Patan, the Muslim ruler Alauddin Khilji of the Khilij Dynasty (1290–1320) sent his army under the command of Ulugh Khan and Nusrat Khan to attack Gujarat in 1297. Ulugh Khan sacked Patan and destroyed much of the city including most of its temples. Gujarat regained its independence in the 1400s, but Ahmedabad became its capital.

Vijayanagar (City of Victory, aka Hampi; located in modern Karnataka, India) was the second largest city in the world in 1500 with a population of around 500,000. Durant remarks that it was "probably the richest city that India had yet known."[100] The city was founded in 1336, built on the site of a religious center, by Harihara Raya I (r. 1336–56) of the Sangama Dynasty (1336–1485), which was the first dynasty of the Vijayanagara Empire.[101]

Nicolo de Conti visited Vijayanagar in 1420 and estimated its circumference to be about 60 miles. Domingo Paes visited the city around 1520–22 as a member of a Portuguese delegation from Goa to the court of King Krishnadevaraja and described it as being "as large as Rome" and "the best-provided city in the world ... for in this one everything abounds."[102] Paes said that it had over 100,000 houses, implying a population of around 500,000 people. Most of the city's inhabitants were poor serfs and laborers, but in addition to the nobility there were also merchants. Paes described the city's marketplace as well:

Going forward, you have a broad and beautiful street, full of rows of fine houses and streets of the sort I have described, and it is to be understood that the houses belong to men rich enough to afford such. In this street live many merchants, and there you will find all sorts of rubies, and diamonds, and emeralds, and pearls, and seed-pearls, and cloths, and every other sort of thing there is on earth and that you may wish to buy. Then you have there every evening a fair where they sell many common horses and nags, and also many citrons, and limes, and oranges, and grapes, and every other kind of garden stuff, and wood; you have all in this street.[103]

Vijayanagar served as the capital of the empire that bears its name. The empire encompassed much of southern India and although the city itself was inland like Patan it too controlled important coastal trading ports that generated considerable wealth for the capital. As noted by Paes, "The said kingdom has many places on the coast of India; they are seaports with which we are at peace, and in some of them we have factories, namely, Amcola, Mirgeo, Honor, Batecalla, Mamgalor, Bracalor, and Bacanor."[104] Cotton was among the important agricultural products in the drier regions of the empire and its production supported a large weaving industry with a number of major weaving centers. The rainy hill region of Malad (in modern Karnataka) produced spices such as pepper, cardamom, turmeric, and ginger. Textiles, spices, and other goods such as gemstones and gold were transported to Vijayanagar for sale in its markets.[105] Foreign merchants sometimes visited Vijayanagar to purchase such goods, but for the most part they operated from out of the coastal trading entrepôts and it was from these ports that the empire's goods were exported to the Middle East, Europe, Southeast Asia, and China.

Although international commerce in the Vijayanagara Empire was limited mainly to a few coastal towns, this trade had an important impact of the lives of people throughout the empire. In addition to producing goods destined for the international market, the inhabitants of the empire also received benefits from the wealth such trade generated. For example, the wealth produced from this trade helped to support patronage of the arts and literature in the capital and throughout southern India. The rulers promoted the Hindu religion and the capital boasted a large number of religious buildings and numerous lavish religious festivals. The empire encompassed peoples from a variety of different cultures throughout southern India and its capital included people from the various groups under its control.

The empire came under attack from Muslim invaders in the latter part of the 1500s, and in 1565 Vijayanagar was captured and partially destroyed by Muslim forces. An Italian traveler named Cesare Frederici visited the city in 1567 and described it as only partially destroyed.[106] Tirumala Deva Raja (r. 1565–72) revived the empire and sought to re-establish Vijayanagar as its capital, but this attempt proved unsuccessful and the center of political power shifted to Andhra Pradesh. The city was abandoned and today is a UNESCO World Heritage Site located adjacent to the village of Hampi.

East Asian Cities

Urbanization began in East Asia later than in the Middle East and South Asia, around 1250 B.C., and initially occurred mainly in what is today northeast China along the Yellow River. While population growth and politics were certainly factors contributing to the growth of China's first cities, the economic considerations linked to early Chinese urbanization are poorly understood.

The earliest Chinese cities, such as Hao and Feng, which were capitals of the Western Zhou (1045–771 B.C.), were largely ceremonial in character and archaeologists have not found palaces or administrative buildings at either site. A number of larger cities developed in China during the Warring States Period (480–211 B.C.). Archaeologists have identified more than fifty urban sites from this period. Linzi of Qi and Ying of Chu were the largest and wealthiest cities of this time, with Linzi having a population of over 200,000 adult males.[107] The transnational character of these early Chinese cities is difficult to determine, but many of the later cities were linked to important long-distance trade routes.

Luoyang (aka Henan-fu), in present-day Henan, was founded around 1125 B.C. It was capital of the Zhou kingdom from 770 to 232 B.C., and the Han capital from A.D. 23 to

220. Von Falkenhausen says, "urban remains have yet to be found" at Luoyang from the period before it became the Zhou capital, indicating that it only became a city at that time.[108] During the period when it served as the Han capital, Luoyang's population grew to an estimated 500,000.[109] Significantly, during the Han period it was also an important commercial hub located at the Chinese end of the Silk Road.

Chang'an (modern Xi'an), which served as the Han capital during the earlier years of the dynasty and as the Tang (A.D. 618–907) capital, became China's and the world's largest city for a number of centuries. It was located along the Yellow River in what is now Shaanxi Province. Under the Tang Dynasty Chang'an's metropolitan area had a population of about 2 million people and it encompassed an area of over 80 sq km. While the majority of its inhabitants were Han, it was a multi-ethnic and cosmopolitan city with people dwelling there not only from many of the ethnic groups ruled over by the Han, but also a sizeable foreign population. Around 25,000 foreigners lived in the city.[110] Most of these foreigners were merchants or others associated with commerce, but there were also monks and others who were attracted by the city's wealth. Foreigners living in the city included Sogdians and others from Central Asia, Persia, India, Tibet, Korea, and Japan. Schafer mentions green-eyed, blond-haired Tocharian women from the Tarim Basin (modern Xinjiang) dancing, singing, and serving wine in taverns, and there were many "barbarians" who had come to the city from the newly conquered territories to the west.[111] Thus, unlike Rome where most foreigners were from territories within its empire, Chang'an also attracted a large number of foreigners from outside of its imperial borders. These foreigners brought with them their religions that included Buddhism and Islam as well as Nestorian Christianity, Judaism, Zoroastrianism, and Manichaeism. The influx of foreigners prompted the Tang in 628 to pass an edict requiring a foreigner who married a Chinese woman to remain in China and forbidding such foreigners from taking their brides home with them should they leave.[112]

Kaifeng (aka Bian, Bianjing, Dongdu, Eastern Capital) was the capital of the Northern Song Dynasty (960–1127). A city known as Daliang was built on the site near the Yellow River in 364 B.C. and it served as the capital of the Wei kingdom. The city was largely destroyed when the Qin conquered Wei and survived as only a small market town. It began to grow in size and importance again in the A.D. 600s after it was connected to the Grand Canal. A new city named Bian (aka Bianjing) was constructed on the site in 781 during the Tang Dynasty. Bian served as a capital city during the Later Jin (936–46), Later Han (947–50), Later Zhou (951–60), and Five Dynasties (906–59) periods.

Kaifeng emerged as a major city by world standards after it became the Northern Song capital. Kaifeng's population grew to over 400,000 in the late 900s and in the 1000s reached between 600,000 and 700,000. It was probably the largest city in the world from 1013 to 1127. Younguosi (Xiangguo) Pagoda was built in 1049. This served as the royal temple and was the largest Buddhist temple in China at the time (and remains the largest Buddhist temple in China today).

Although the city became the political, economic, and cultural center of China, its transnational character varied over time. The Silk Road was disrupted during the late 700s and after the fall of the Tang Dynasty. As was mentioned in an earlier chapter, the Song focused more on maritime commerce with transnational activities shifting mainly to a handful of ports. The city went into decline after it was captured by the Jurchen (a Tungusic people from Manchuria) who had founded the Jin Dynasty (1115–1234) in northern China. It subsequently fell to the Mongols in 1234.

The so-called Kaifeng Jews were one of the immigrant communities to have lived in

Kaifeng in medieval times.[113] Although of considerably less importance than during the Tang Dynasty some travel and trade continued along the Silk Road during the Song period, and the first group of Jews to settle in Kaifeng appears to have come from Persia along the Silk Road during Emperor Taizu's reign. The Song rulers gave them Chinese surnames (Zhao, Zhang, Shi, Jin, Ai, Gao and Li) and allowed them to take the imperial exams and hold government offices. They were also permitted to retain Jewish customs and in 1163 they built a synagogue in the city, which survived until it was destroyed in the 1860s. Kaifeng under the Song rulers also had a Zoroastrian community from Persia. As was noted previously, Zoroastrians had come from Persia along the Silk Road to settle in China from a very early date, but by the time of the Song they were a relatively small community.

The capital of the state of Yan, which was named Ji, was established on the site of modern Beijing during the Warring States Period, but it was only a minor town for the next several centuries. It was made the secondary capital of the Liao kingdom in 938. The Jurchen conquered the Liao kingdom in 1125 and they made Ji their capital in 1153, changing its name to Zhongdu (Central Capital). The Mongols destroyed the city in 1215. Then in 1272 Kublai Khan built his new capital of Khanbaliq (aka Daidu, Great Capital) on the site (the Han called it Dadu). Under Kublai Khan the city attracted a relatively large transnational population. Its transnational character declined after Zhu Yuanzhang captured the city from the Mongols in 1368. He renamed it Beiping (Northern Capital) and made it his co-capital along with Nanjing. The city became the primary capital of the Ming rulers in 1421 with the name of Jingshi (Nanjing became a secondary capital). The city underwent a period of considerable public construction and from around 1425 until the mid–1600s was the largest city in the world (it regained this status from the early 1700s to the early 1800s). Beijing had a population of around 672,000 in 1500. As with the Song, under the Ming transnational relations were limited mainly to a few ports while their capital city remained fairly isolated from the world beyond China's borders.

Elsewhere in China, as was discussed previously, Hangzhou and Guangzhou had grown and prospered from maritime trade during the time of the Southern Song Dynasty (1127–1279) and, although the Mongols moved the center of political power back to the north, both cities continued to flourish as centers of international maritime trade. While Guangzhou suffered following the outbreak of the Red Turban Rebellion in 1351 both cities again grew and prospered under Ming rule in the 1400s as China's foreign maritime flourished. While the population of Hangzhou was still smaller than during its peak under the Southern Song, by 1500 it had a population of around 250,000 and the population of Guangzhou had recovered to around 150,000. The transnational character of these two cities was about to change, however, as China progressively closed itself off to the outside world during the 1500s.

Cities also developed in East Asia outside of China, with the largest of them being found in Japan. Kyoto, the world's third largest city in 1000, had a population of around 200,000. From a transnational perspective it was even more isolated than Beijing—intentionally so. Kyoto's original name was Heian-kyo (tranquility and peace capital). The emperor Kammu established it as his capital in 794. Japan's fist capital had been at Heijo-kyo (modern Nara) from 710 to 784. Heijo-kyo was modeled after the Chinese capital of Chang'an and served as an important center of Buddhism. It was a relatively international city through which foreigners and foreign ideas entered Japan. It attained a population of 100,000 before the capital was moved. Emperor Kammu established his capital at Heian-kyo in large part to escape from what he perceived as the meddling influence of Buddhist monks and his new capital became much more of an inward looking city. The city's name was changed to Kyoto (capital city) in the 1000s and it remained Japan's imperial capital until 1868. The city suffered considerable destruction and loss of population during the Onin War (1467–77), and during the Edo Period (aka Tokugawa Period, 1603–1868) political power shifted to Edo (modern Tokyo).

Southeast Asian Cities

In ancient and medieval times the population density of Southeast Asia was considerably lower than that of neighboring South Asia and East Asia. As Reid remarks, "Most of the region was still covered with jungle as late as 1800, so that attacks by tigers were not uncommon even on the outskirts of substantial population centres."[114] Nevertheless, by around A.D. 1000 the region had produced a few large cities by world standards. This is part was a reflection of extent to which, largely because of geographical factors, the population of Southeast Asia was highly concentrated in a few areas that were particularly fertile or along some of the major rivers. This rise of such cities was also a reflection of political factors as well as economic factors related not just to agriculture but also to trade. In regard to cultural influences on these cities these included a mixture of local cultural influences from within the region as well as influences from both China and India. We will look at the four largest cities to arise in Southeast Asia during the medieval period: Thang Long, Bagan, Angkor Thom, and Ayutthaya.

Ly Thai To (r. 1009–1028), founder of the Ly Dynasty of Dai Viet, founded Thang Long (Ascending Dragon, modern Ha Noi) in 1010 as his capital on the site of the existing Dai La citadel. The new capital was located inland on the southern bank of the Red River not too far from the old Ou Lo capital of Co Loa, which was located to the north of the river and in the vicinity of the provincial capitals of the region under prior Chinese rule (i.e., Tong Binh and Long Do). Co Loa had also briefly served as Ngo Quyen's capital after he had thrown off Chinese rule and established an independent Dai Viet in 938. The Dinh Dynasty (968–980) had moved the capital further south to Hoa Lu (in Ninh Binh Province) and Ly Thai To decided to move it back to the more central location along the Red River.

Construction of the new Thang Long citadel was completed in 1011 and gradually a small city grew around it that was modeled on Chinese imperial cities. There was a small Forbidden City (Tu Cam Thanh) in the center where the king and his family lived. The Imperial Citadel (Hoang Thanh), where imperial administrative offices were located and members of the imperial court lived, surrounded the Forbidden City. The Imperial City (Kinh Thanh), where the general public lived, formed the outermost part of the city. A number of important historical sites in Hanoi date from this period, including the One Pillar Pagoda (Chua Mot Cot) that was built during the reign of Ly Thai Tong (r. 1028–1054) and the Temple of Literature (Van Mieu) that was established in 1070 during the reign of Ly Thanh Tong. Chinese influence was evident in the city's architecture and in the cultural life of the city with Mahayana Buddhism being the dominant religion. The 36 artisans guilds of Thanh Long established themselves in a part of the city in the 1200s with each one being associated with a particular street.

The Mongols sacked Thang Long in 1257 and briefly occupied the city in 1285. The period after the final Mongol defeat in 1287 witnessed increased conflict between Dai Viet and Champa with the Cham army occupying Thang Long for a short time in 1371. Dai

Viet was in a state of decline and Thang Long as well. The regent General Ho Quy Ly moved the capital south to Tay Do (Western Capital) in Thanh Hoa Province in 1397 and Thang Long's name was changed to Dong Do (Eastern Capital). The Chinese invaded and annexed Dai Viet in 1407 and the following year made Thang Long, which they renamed Dong Quan (Eastern Gateway), their administrative capital. Le Loi led a rebellion against the Chinese in Thanh Hoa in 1418 and in 1427 the rebels forced the Chinese to leave and regained control of Thang Long/Dong Quan.

Le Loi declared himself king of Dai Viet in 1428, assuming the name of Le Thai To (r. 1428–33), and made Thang Long/Dong Quan his capital, renaming it Dong Kinh (Eastern Capital, Tonkin in English). The early years of the Le Dynasty were a period of relative prosperity for Dai Viet, based in part on the conquest of a large part of Champa in 1471, in which agriculture flourished, roads and irrigation canals were built, and education was promoted. It was also during this time that Dong Kinh/Thang Long became a large city with a population of over 100,000 by the late 1400s.

As the capital of a relatively small kingdom, Thang Long did not receive a large number of foreign embassies. The primary ones mentioned, as would be expected, are from China. Nguyen, for example, cites a description of the Ly court written by a Southern Song envoy in 1174.[115] Thang Long also attracted at least a few foreign merchants. While recent archaeological excavations of the site of the early Thang Long citadel (at modern 18 Hoang Dieu Street) have turned up a large number of domestic items and items from China, porcelain and bronze coins from Japan and western parts of Asia have also been found, highlighting the continued association of the city to maritime trade. Hall points to the importance of international commerce to Dai Viet from the early days of the Dinh Dynasty in relation to the need for imported clothing (primarily from China) for members of the court and high ranking military officers: "To meet these clothing needs, as well as the other material requirements of the emergent Vietnamese court, foreign trade was a necessity. Envoys were sent to China with many gifts, presumably to proclaim Vietnam as an international marketplace as well as to secure political recognition."[116] International trade was also an important part of the economy of the Le Dynasty from the 1400s, which the rulers saw as an attractive alternative to "squeezing additional tax revenue from the land."[117]

While kingdoms and the imperial designs of the Han and others to the north were the source of some economic and political influences on the development of early kingdoms and towns of ancient and medieval Burma, Indian influence was of greater relevance. Maritime trade along the coast of the Bay of Bengal created commercial relations between the peoples of Burma and India (and Sri Lanka) and with these came religious and other cultural influences as seen in the widespread adoption of Buddhist beliefs and use of Indian derived alphabets in Burma.

There were several Mon city-states that emerged along the coastal areas of southern Burma and Thailand starting around A.D. 200. The kingdom of Dvaravati with its capital at Lavapura (aka Lavo, near modern Lopburi, Thailand) was the most prominent of these. Kasetsiri characterizes Dvaravati as "a group of cities ... loosely linked together by marriage and cultural ties."[118] Prominent Mon city-states in southern Burma included Sudhammavati (modern Thaton) and Hamsavati (modern Pegu or Bago), which was founded in 573 and served as the capital for a coalition of city-states known as Suvannabhumi. Dvaravati appears to have been a vassal of Funan for a time in its early years. These and other Mon towns were involved in maritime trade and also developed close religious ties with fellow Buddhists in India and Sri Lanka. A number of Buddhist centers were located in these Mon territories, with Nakhon Phanom being the most prominent. It is likely that the Emperor Asoka sent Buddhist missionaries to this area, establishing it as the first center of Buddhism in Southeast Asia. The Mon city-states also were responsible for spreading Buddhism into interior regions of Burma and Thailand and eastward to Funan and Champa.[119]

The Tibeto-Burman speaking Pyu settled in the central area of Burma by A.D. 100 and established the kingdom of Beikthano in the A.D. 400s. They were influenced by Indian culture largely via the Mon. Sriksetra (modern Thayekhittam near Prome) became its capital in the 500s, but they moved their capital to Halin after they were invaded by Nan Chao in the mid–700s and made a vassal of that kingdom.

Another Tibeto-Burman speaking group, the Bama, migrated from the north and had settled in central Burma by the A.D. 800s. Their initial capital was at Tampawadi (modern Pwasaw), but King Pyinbya (r. 846–878) moved his capital to Bagan (aka Pagan) in 874. Bagan was abandoned for a time, but King Anawratha (r. 1044–1077) re-occupied it as his capital in 1057. Anawratha's conquests of the surrounding area including the Mon states to the south transformed Bagan into the capital of a large kingdom, and befitting its new status its name was changed to Arimaddanapura (aka Arimaddana, City of the Enemy Crusher). During the roughly two centuries between the 1050s and its decline after 1287, when the Mongols briefly occupied the city, Bagan/Arimaddanapura grew into a large, cosmopolitan city occupying some 41 sq km and containing over 2,000 mostly Buddhist temples. The population of Bagan at this time is difficult to gauge. Much of the labor to build the temples was undertaken by people brought to Bagan temporarily from surrounding areas and the region around Bagan itself was not particularly fertile, meaning that the city's rulers had to rely on other parts of their kingdom for food, but it was clearly a large city by world standards.

Inscriptions on the Mya-zedi pillar written during the reign of King Alaung Si-thu (r. 1112–1167) in Pyu, Mon, Burmese, and Pali highlight the diverse cultural influences on Bagan.[120] Mon influence on Bagan is the most noticeable and the Bama adopted a version of Mon script for their writing. Anawratha took some 30,000 Mon and re-settled them around Bagan, where they formed several distinct communities.[121] These Mon included artisans, artists, musicians, Buddhist monks, and even hairdressers. Many of the temples at Bagan, especially those built during the early period, are Mon in style. However, there are also many temples that reflect stylistic influences from various parts of India and Sri Lanka. As Taylor points out, Anawratha's conquest of the Mon states brought him into contact with maritime trade and with the kingdoms, empires, and cultures of India and Sri Lanka in particular.[122] The culture, architecture, and art of the Pala Empire in India is particularly evident in Bagan. Fraser-Lu comments, "Pagan sculpture was greatly influenced by the canons of eighth-twelfth century East Indian Pala art, a style which, at its best, combined a bold plasticity of form and ornamental detail rendered with great delicacy and precision."[123] There was a degree of reciprocity in this relationship. King Kyan-zit-tha (r. 1084–1112), as a merit-making undertaking, supported repairs of the Mahabodhi temple at Bodh Gaya. Then a century later, around 1218, King Nan-taung-mya (r. 1210–1234) built a small replica of Bodh Gaya, called the Mahabodhi temple, at Bagan.

Anawratha initiated exchanges of monks and texts with Buddhist centers in India and Sri Lanka. This interchange continued under subsequent rulers as Bagan emerged as an international center of Buddhist learning that attracted Buddhists from South Asia as well as other parts of Southeast Asia. The local Buddhist scholar Aggavamsa completed a famous Pali grammar known as the *Saddaniti* in Bagan in 1154.[124] In fact, Bagan continued to serve as an important center of Buddhist learning even after its political and economic decline in the late 1200s. Perceiving that the Mon-derived style of Buddhism had become increasingly corrupt, King Narapati-si-thu (r. 1173–1210) began promoting the introduction of Sri Lankan Theravada Buddhism in 1192. As Hall notes in this regard, the rulers of Bagan began sending "selected monks to Sri Lanka, which was considered to be the centre of Buddhist piety in that era, to be purified (ordained). When they returned, these monks would in turn lead the reordination and purification of all Burmese monks."[125] Because of Bagan's status as a regional center of Buddhism, this promotion of Sri Lankan Theravada Buddhism in turn influenced Buddhism elsewhere in Southeast Asia, especially within the Khmer Empire and in the emerging Tai kingdoms to the east.

Bagan maintained only limited relations with China. There was some overland trade through the highland areas to the north to Yunnan, but this does not seem to have been well developed at this time. Kyan-zit-tha sent missions to the Southern Song court to promote overland trade with Yunnan.[126] As was mentioned earlier, the Southern Song court at this time was also seeking to promote overland trade with Southeast Asia. However, this was near the end of the Southern Song period and nomadic incursions soon made such trade even more difficult than usual. The Mongol invasions then effectively put a halt to significant overland long-distance trade between the Burmese lowlands and China.

The Mongol invasion of Bagan in 1287 resulted in the city being largely abandoned. Many of the city's inhabitants moved to Taungoo, which gradually emerged as the center of Bama political power and center of a small kingdom.

The ancestors of the Mon-Khmer speaking Khmer migrated down the lands adjacent to the Mekong River and settled in what is now southern Laos and northern Cambodia some time prior to A.D. 200, where they came into contact with the Malay kingdoms and cultures that straddled the coast of southern Vietnam and the lower parts of the Mekong. The Khmer established the kingdom of Chenla with a capital at Sresthapura (near modern Stung Treng) that initially was a vassal of Funnan during the reign of Funan's king Fan Shih-man (r. *c.* A.D. 105–225). The king of Chenla Bhavavarman I (r. *c.* 550–598) defeated Funan and extended Chenla's control over a good deal of Cambodia and adjacent parts of southern Laos and northeastern Thailand. Chenla went into decline in the early 700s in part as a result of internal divisions and also because of external attacks by the Sailendras of Java who also carried out attacks on Champa and Dai Viet between 767 and 787. A portion of Chenla known as Chenla of Water became a vassal of the Sailendras, who referred to it as Indrapura. The Sailendras appointed Jayavarman II to rule over the territory. He apparently made at least one trip to Java during his tenure. Some time after his return from Java he renounced the Sailendras' suzerainty and in 802 declared himself to be the Devaraja (God King) of his newly independent kingdom. The kingdom came to be known as Kambuja, which is the name of a mythical founding dynastic ancestor, Kambu, who is said to have been an Indian who arrived by ship and married the daughter of the local serpent king. Jayavarman II's initial capital was at Indrapura on the Mekong, but he moved the capital eastward to Hariharalaya near Tonle Sap.

King Yasovarman II (r. 889–900) built a new capital named Yasodharapura not too far from Hariharalaya. King Suryavarman I (r. 1002–1050) undertook a series of conquests that laid the basis for the creation of a multi-ethnic empire that eventually would include Cambodia, and a good deal of modern Thailand, as well as portions of southern Laos and Vietnam. After a period of instability during the latter part of the 1100s and a change of dynasties, dynastic and imperial control was re-established for a time by Suryavarman II (r.

1113–*c.* 1150), who is best known as the builder of the Angkor Vat complex. Champa sacked Yasodharapura in 1177 and killed the Khmer king. After another period of instability, Jayavarman VII (r. 1181–*c.*1218) drove the Cham out. The Khmer empire reached its greatest extent during his reign. He claimed to have ruled over 306,372 subjects living in 13,500 villages.[127] He also re-built Yasodharapura and gave it the new name of Angkor Thom and erected the Bayon temple complex in its center. Modern estimates place the population of Angkor Thom as high as 150,000, but this may be on the high side.[128]

The rulers of Kambuja followed both Hinduism and Buddhism, often in a mixed form. The imagery depicted at Angkor Vat, for example, is Hindu. Jayavarman VII promoted Mahayana Buddhism, but foreign monks promoting Theravada Buddhism are known to have visited Kambuja during this time, laying the groundwork for establishing this brand of Buddhism among the populace. His activities put considerable strain on the people and the resources available, and after his death the Kambuja began a period of decline, culminating in the Siamese sacking of the capital in 1352 (and again in 1430) and the Champa re-occupation the Mekong delta region in the 1420s. Like Bagan, Angkor Thom remained a Buddhist center of learning after the onset of its political and economic decline. In 1432–37 the Khmer capital was moved to Phnom, Penh, which was considered safer from Siamese attack.

A Chinese official named Zhou Daguan provides us a glimpse of life in Kambuja in the late 1200s in a written account of a visit to the kingdom in 1296. Zhou Daguan sailed from the port of Mingzhou (modern Ningbo) in 1296 as part of a delegation sent by the Yuan Emperor Temur Khan to the kingdoms of Champa and Angkor. His is the only eyewitness account that we have of the ancient Khmer kingdom from this period. In his introduction to Zhou Daguan's account Harris informs us that the author was born in the vicinity of the southern Chinese port city of Wenzhou, was a native speaker of the Wu dialect, and was probably "from a well-connected trading or official family. He may also have been something of a linguist, and taken along to help as an interpreter."[129] The delegation sailed across the South China Sea and the Gulf of Tonkin to Champa and then on to "Zhenpu" (possibly in the region of Vung Tau in southern Vietnam), on Kambuja's frontier. They then entered the mouth of the Mekong River and sailed up the river for another 15 days to Tonle Sap and then on to the Khmer capital of Yasodharapura, where Zhou Daguan remained for about a year, probably staying with "the family of a local Chinese."[130]

Our interest here is primarily with what Zhou Daguan tells us about Kambuja's relations with non–Khmer peoples. The Khmer maintained commercial relations with their non–Khmer neighbors to their north to obtain slaves and a variety of jungle products. Zhou's account makes it clear that slavery played an important role in Khmer society at time.[131] Slaves included prisoners of war as well as individuals obtained through trade. Zhou Daguan lists local products as including "kingfisher feathers, elephant tusk, rhinoceros horns, and beeswax" as well as "rosewood [laka wood, *dalbergia odorifera*], cardamom, gamboges, lac, and chalmoogra oil."[132] Most of these goods were in fact not local, in that they were not products of the lowland Khmer, but were obtained by the Khmer from other peoples living in the highlands to their north. "Cardamom for example was cultivated entirely by the savages in the mountains."[133]

The so-called savages also provided Kambuja with woven cloth. Zhou Daguan mentions that they not only grow cardamom, but also grow "kapok and weave cloth for a living."[134] Local textile production was relatively limited: "None of the locals produces silk. Nor do the women know how to stitch and darn with a needle and thread. The only thing they can do is weave cotton from kapok."[135] The resultant local market for textiles and clothing attracted both migrants and traders. The Tai people from the north were skilled in the textile arts, and Zhou noted, "In recent years people from Siam have come to live in Cambodia, and unlike the locals they engage in silk production. The mulberry trees they grow and the silkworms they raise all come from Siam.... Siamese women do know how to stitch and darn, so when the local people have torn or damaged clothing they ask them to do the mending."[136] Cloth was also imported: "Although cloth is woven domestically, it also comes from Siam and Champa. Cloth from the Western Seas is often regarded as the best because it is so well-made and refined."[137] The "Western Seas" locale is uncertain, but may refer to India.

Zhou Daguan also provided some information about the local Chinese community and Chinese trade with Kambuja. He provides a list of Chinese goods that were imported including gold, silver, fine silk, pewter ware from Zhengzhou (in Henan Province), lacquer ware from Wenzhou (in Zhejiang Province), celadon ware from Quanzhou (in Fujian Province) and Chuzhou (in Anhui Province), mercury, cinnabar, writing paper, sulphur, saltpeter, sandalwood, lovage, angelica, musk, hemp, yellow grasscloth, umbrellas, iron pots, copper dishes, glass balls, tung tree oil, fine-toothed combs, wooden combs, needles, and mats from Mingzhou (Hangzhou, in Zhejiang Province).[138] He says that the local traders were all women, "So when a Chinese goes to this country, the first thing he must do is take a woman, partly with a view to profiting from her trading abilities."[139] At this time there were an increasing number of Chinese coming to the capital to trade, including some living there on a permanent basis. In addition to traders, he mentions Chinese sailors who had run away from their ships as among the foreigners living in Cambodia.[140]

Kambuja lost control over the territories to the west to Tai peoples who had come to settle within its northwestern territories from further north in greater numbers. Tai Yuan had established *muang* (small polities) to the north of Khmer territory in what is now northern Thailand starting in the A.D. 600s and with the collapse of Khmer power to the south the Tai established a number of kingdoms in central Thailand in the 1200s. The most prominent of these, Sukhothai, was established in 1238. Its ruler, Ram Khamheng (aka Rama Khamhaeng, r. *c.* 1283–1317), expanded the kingdom to include parts of Laos, additional portions of central Thailand, and as far south as the Malay Peninsula into territory that had been under the dominion of Srivijaya. The Sukhothai kingdom absorbed aspects of Khmer and Mon culture and adopted Theravada Buddhism. The kingdom rapidly broke apart after Ram Khamheng's death.

The city-state of Lavo (modern Lopburi) was one of the territories included in Ram Khamheng's conquests. The Mon had built the earliest town in the vicinity of Lopburi in the 400s, which served as the eastern capital of Dvaravati and played an important role in the spread of Mon culture and Buddhism to the north. It was conquered by Kambuja a little after A.D. 1000 and became a center of Kambujan administration, although Kambujan control over the area was "intermittent."[141] Kasetsiri makes the point that while Lopburi had been an important seat of Buddhist learning under the Mon, under the Khmer it experienced a period of Hindu influence that produced "a kind of religious syncretism" that was to become a hallmark of subsequent Ayuttahayan, Siamese, and Thai culture.[142] Lopburi had regained its independence by the mid–1200s and emerged as a small local power.

A man named U Thong (b. 1314) founded the city of Ayutthaya in 1351 and proclaimed himself king Rama Thibodi (r. *c.* 1351–1369). The site was located on an island in a bend of the Chao Phrya River where it is joined by the Pa Sak River, some 100 km north of the sea, to the south of Lopburi, and to the east of Suphanburi. The new city of Ayutthaya was located within an existing state (*muang* in Thai) named Ayodhya that at the time was a vassal of Lopburi.[143] U Thong's life has been subject to various historical interpretations and many aspects of it remain unclear. According to a Dutch account written in 1640 by Jeremias van Vliet, U Thong was the son of a provincial ruler from China named T'Jaeu ou-e who was sent into exile.[144] He and his followers sailed to Pattani and then traveled north to the Chao Phrya Basin area where he established himself as a trader based at Phetburi (which was a vassal of Suphanburi).[145] He appears to have been very successful. His exporting of goods to the Chinese court in particular gained him the award of a royal title that resulted in his changing his name to Thaeu Outhongh (aka Thao U Thong) and he was given a Chinese princess in marriage. While living in Thailand he became a Buddhist and married a princess from Suphanburi, then another one from the ruling family of Ayodhya, and he also seems to have had family ties through these marriages to the rulers of Lopburi.

U Thong was one of many Chinese merchants living in Thailand in the early 1300s. The region was linked to long-distance maritime trade from an early period. Archaeological evidence from the coastal area of the Chao Phrya Basin indicates that it was linked to the early maritime trade that flowed from the Bay of Bengal, across the Isthmus of Kra, and then on to Oc Eo. Goods found from Mon-era sites there include beads and coins from the Roman Empire as well as a lamp from Alexandria dating from the A.D. 200s.[146] Ayutthaya was founded during a period of relatively free trade with China under Kublai Khan's Yuan Dynasty (1271–1368), prior to its becoming more restrictive under the Ming Dynasty (1368–1644).[147] On the Thai side trade was also relatively free for merchants from China and elsewhere wishing to do business there. Only later did the Ayutthaya court seek to establish greater centralized control. Within this environment of free trade private Chinese merchants settled at coastal towns along the Malay Peninsula, the Isthmus of Kra, and further north along the coast of the Chao Phrya Basin (e.g., Phetburi).[148] Chinese merchants and artisans also settled inland in the Chao Phrya Basin and beyond. These merchants engaged in both domestic and long-distance trade, with the exports to China including "hardwoods, aloes, incense, ivory, kingfishers' feathers, tin, cardamom, and chaulmoogra-seed, which was used as a treatment for leprosy."[149] In return they imported silk and satin textiles and porcelain. Chinese potters and merchants established the important kilns at Sawankhalok along the Yom River north of Sukhothai in the 1200s. The best-known product of these kilns was celadon-glazed pottery. Initially the Sawankhalok pottery was shipped to domestic markets. Its markets expanded within Thailand with the rise of Sukhothai. Chinese also settled to the southeast in Chanthaburi Province where they engaged in mining of sapphires (and some garnets and zircons). About 200 Song refugees from the Mongols also came to Thailand in 1282, where they settled in a Chinese community that had already been established along the Chao Phrya River just south of where U Thong would later establish Ayutthaya.[150]

Not only was U Thong part of a fairly large Chinese community in Thailand, he was also not alone as a Chinese immigrant in the degree of his acceptance by local Tai, in the extent of his assimilation of Tai culture, and in his ability to integrate himself into elite Tai society, although he certainly proved to be the most successful example of such early Sino-Tais. In U Thong's case his marriage into the royal family of Suphanburi may have resulted in his being made ruler of Phetburi, and his subsequent claim to a kingship was based on his marriage into the ruling family of Ayodhya that was without a male heir.[151] Using his connections with the two leading city-states in the area, Lopburi and Suphanburi, and his link to the royal family of Ayodhya, and taking advantage of a relative power vacuum as a result of the decline of Kambuja and Sukhotai, U Thong was able to create a kingdom that quickly became an important local power. At the outset he was able to unite the main city-states in the Chao Phrya Basin, and he sent the elder brother of one of his wives to rule in Suphanburi and his eldest son to rule Lopburi.[152] The kingdom that he founded was a multi-ethnic one with Khmer, Tai, Mon, and Chinese inhabitants.

The kingdom that U Thong established was a loosely structured affair comprised of a unified center surrounded by vassal states with varying degrees of autonomy. The core area lay within the Chao Phrya Basin. This was an area that had been part of the Kambujan Empire and that had developed a syncretic Khmer-Mon-Tai culture that was distinct from that of the Tai polities further to the north, where the rival kingdom of Lan Na was forged by Mangrai between 1259 and 1288. The Kingdom of Sukhothai, reduced in power after the death of Ram Khamheng, had a culture that was largely Tai and formed something of a buffer between Ayutthaya and Lan Na. Unification of the Kingdom of Ayutthaya began in earnest with the rule of King Trailok (aka Borommatrailokanat, r. 1448–88), Ayutthaya's eighth king. Trailok's ability to unify the kingdom was in large part related to his own transnationalism. He was the son of the Ayutthayan king Boromracha II (r. 1424–1448) and was born in Ayutthaya in 1431, but his mother was a princess from Sukhothai and it was she who raised him in Ayutthaya. After the King Maha Thammaracha IV of Sukhothai died, King Boromracha II was able to place his son Trailok on the throne in 1446. Thus, at the age of 15, Trailok, accompanied by his mother, moved to Phitsanulok, the capital of the Sukhothai kingdom, where the pair were relatively successful in overcoming local resistance to such an imposition by adopting many of the local customs. When Boromracha II died in 1448 Trailok was made king of Ayutthaya and he moved back there. Problems for King Trailok emerged in 1456 when the ruler of Lan Na in alliance with a rebel prince from Sukhothai invaded from the north. The ruler of Lan Na succeeded in capturing Sukhothai and removing its entire population to its capital of Chiang Mai in 1460. After Trailok's son was killed in battle against Lan Na in 1463, Trailok decided to move his capital north to Phitsanulok. Peace was finally established between the two kingdoms in 1474 and Trailok spent the remainder of his reign ruling from Phitsanulok and taking steps to create a more unified kingdom.

After moving the capital to Phitsanulok, Trailok made his son Intharacha regent of Ayutthaya. The city of Ayutthaya was given a reduced status as *muang luk luang* or the southern cardinal city of the kingdom. Despite its loss of political status Ayutthaya continued to develop as an important commercial center. Intharacha became King Boromracha III after Trailok's death and he moved the capital back to Ayutthaya, which once again became the political and commercial center of the kingdom.

Like the kingdom, the city of Ayutthaya had a multi-ethnic population comprised of the various ethnic groups found within the kingdom as well as an increasing array of people of different nationalities who had come to the city as a result of its growing importance as a center of international commerce. As the kingdom of Ayutthaya became an important political entity that encompassed most of modern Thailand, the capital city of Ayutthaya grew into a large, cosmopolitan city. By the early 1500s, Ayutthaya had developed what Wyatt refers to as a capital culture as expressed in "language, literatures, and the public rituals of sacral life" of the city that was contributing to the creation of a distinctive Siamese culture.[153] It was a culture that reflected the mixed Mon, Khmer, and Tai background of the region. It also was influenced by the city's role in international commerce through immigrants such as the Chinese and the interaction with others who passed through the city.

In regard to culture, at the outset even though U Thong was Chinese, the political culture that he promoted was largely one derived from the Khmer Hindu-Brahmanical tradition associated with the former Kambujan Empire. Accordingly the kings of Ayutthaya were viewed as reincarnations of the leading Hindu gods, with U Thong taking the name Rama Thibodi — Rama being a reincarnation of Vishnu. Wyatt comments that Ayutthaya's bureaucracy consisted initially of a "Khmerized urban elite" from nearby towns.[154] These people spoke Khmer, and a special court vocabulary evolved based on Khmer and Sanskrit. This political culture also created links to India itself. Thus, U Thong is reported to have sent a mission to India to request sending Brahmans to officiate at his coronation and eight were sent from Benares.[155]

Ayutthaya also served as an important center of Theravada Buddhist learning. Ayodhya had already replaced Lopburi in this regard, and as such attracted Buddhist scholars not only from around the kingdom, but also from neighboring countries and sometimes further afield. In addition, as Kasetsiri notes, because its location gave it "much readier access to the centres of Theravada Buddhism in Lower Burma and Ceylon and Nakhon Sithhamarat," Ayodhya had become "a natural stopping place for religious men travelling from the hinterland of the Menam [Chao Phrya] Basin to Lower Burma or Ceylon."[156] There are a number of reports of monks and other Buddhist pilgrims stopping at Ayodhya and Ayutthaya on their way back and forth between Sri Lanka (Ceylon) and various places in East Asia. Like Bagan, Ayutthaya established important links with Sri Lanka. Thus, when King Trailok was ordained as a monk (along with 2,348 other men) in Phitsanulok in 1465 he imported a monk from Sri Lanka to officiate.[157]

Ayutthaya does not appear to have received many foreign ambassadors prior to the arrival of Europeans in the 1500s. The states in the area had a history of exchanging embassies with the Chinese and this relationship continued to be of importance for Ayutthaya. The Yuan court is reported to have sent a mission to Sukhothai in 1292, in part it seems to check on the activities of the Song refugees mentioned above ten years earlier. Sukhothai reciprocated by sending a mission to the Yuan court with tribute.[158] Lopburi (Lo-hu to the Chinese) had been more pro-active in seeking to establish good relations with the Yuan court and had sent missions to the court in 1289, 1291, 1296, and 1299.[159] Such missions combined diplomacy with trade and were aimed at promoting good political relations as well as increased trade with the Yuan court. Recognition by the Yuan court also helped to bolster the legitimacy of the rulers back in Sukhothai and Lopburi. Kasetsiri say that there is no record of such missions during the first half of the 1300s and associates this with the fact that "the China trade was increasingly being carried on by private Chinese traders," which reduced the importance of the state.[160]

Ayutthaya renewed the practice of sending embassies to China and the Chinese also sent a number of embassies to Ayutthaya. The new Ming ruler in China sent an embassy to Ayutthaya to demand tribute in 1370, and the king of Ayutthaya, Boromracha, sent an embassy headed by a prince with gifts that included "six tame elephants and some six-legged tortoises."[161] U Thong's death in 1369 was followed by a period of several years in which various parties vied for the throne, during which time those involved in the struggle sent a number of embassies to China seeking China's support. These included embassies sent by male royals to the Ming emperor as well as by female royals to the empress.[162] Intharacha, who became king in 1409 and prior to that became king of Suphanburi in 1388, in particular, "was assiduous in cultivating good relations with the Chinese court" even before he became king. He sent a number of missions to China starting in 1374 and even appears to have led three of them himself in 1375, 1377, and 1384.[163] If he did so, Intharacha was the only king of Ayutthaya to have gone to China.[164]

Zheng He, commander of the Ming Treasure Fleet, visited Ayutthaya in 1408 while on his way to Calicut, the year before Intharacha became king.[165] The Ming emperor had received an embassy from Ayutthaya the year before, bringing gifts that included "elephants, parrots, and peacocks." Now he was sending the ambassador home with Zheng He along with counter-gifts of "money, Chinese court costumes, and fine writing materials."[166] Kasetsiri emphasizes the impact this visit had on Intharacha's rise to power (Zheng He granted a personal audience to Intharacha), while Levathes discusses it within the context of the Ming foreign policy of "fragmentation" of the barbarians in terms of promoting Ayutthaya against Kambuja.[167]

Noting that Ayutthaya sent by far more tribute goods to the Ming court than any other country, Kasetsiri points out that this not only meant that Ayutthaya received major trading privileges, but that the Chinese also sometimes asked Ayutthaya to serve as "middlemen in passing messages from the Chinese court to other states in South-East Asia."[168] Receiving favorable treatment in regard to trade by the Ming court was important since the court had created a much more restrictive trade environment than had been the case under the Yuan. The Ming emperor not only sought to tighten control over foreign trade but he also tried to put a stop to Chinese migration to other countries. This served to hamper the movement of independent merchants and of Chinese immigrants to Ayutthaya in general. The emperor raised this issue to Intharacha's ambassador in 1409. The emperor told the ambassador "he was concerned about his 'wandering' countrymen, in particular, a man named He Baiquan and his followers, and wanted them returned to China for punishment."[169]

The most significant aspect of Ayutthaya's transnationalism is undoubtedly its position as a center of international trade. This is highlighted in Wyatt's reference to the city as a "port-capital."[170] It is important to recognize that Ayutthaya's emergence as a major commercial center was gradual. When Ma Huan visited the area in the early 1400s, he reported that the rulers of Ayutthaya sent "sappan-wood, laka-wood, and other such valuable things" to China as tribute.[171] He also indicates, however, in regard to the conduct of trade locally that this was centered at Lopburi (he calls it Upper Water): "In this place there are five or six hundred families of foreigners; all kinds of foreign goods are for sale; red ya-ku [probably red garnets], [and] its brightness resembles that of a pomegranate seed. When the treasure ships of the Central Country [China] come to Hsien Lo [Siam], [our men] also take small boats and go to trade [at Upper Water]."[172] Ma Huan also mentions that Lopburi served as a point of origin for travel north to Yunnan, noting that from there you "can go through into Yünnan by a back entrance."[173] A century later when Pires wrote his account of Ayutthaya, however, the city had become a major regional trading center. This change in its status was related in large part to administrative reforms undertaken by King Trailok.

Management of the kingdom of Ayutthaya's international trade was increasingly concentrated in the port-capital of Ayutthaya.[174] Although the process began earlier, this centralization became more pronounced during and after King Trailok's reign. King Trailok's Law of the Civil Hierarchy placed foreign trade, immigration, and other aspects of foreign affairs under the jurisdiction of the *phra khlang* (minister of finance).[175] Direct responsibility for overseeing trade was given to two habormasters, the *chularatchamontri* (an Indian harbormaster) and *chodukratchasetthi* (a Chinese harbormaster), reflecting the two directions of Ayutthaya's trade and the dominant nationality conducting the trade in each direction.

Later these positions of habormaster became departments known as the *Krom Tah Kwah* (Port of the Right), which was oriented towards the Indian Ocean to the west, and the *Krom Tah Sai* (Port of the Left), which was oriented towards the South China Sea to the east.

The volume of international trade flowing in and out of Thailand increased markedly under the Kingdom of Ayutthaya and in turn this generated increasing revenue for the royal treasury. In the case of Sawankhalok ceramic production, for example, this began to increase a great deal during the latter part of the 1300s and in the 1400s it reached levels that made it a world-class industrial center of ceramic production. There were major improvements in kiln construction and ceramic techniques and in the 1400s over 200 kilns were in operation, many of them making specialized products. This growth was related to an expansion of the markets for Sawankhalok ware, which was exported in large quantities throughout Southeast Asia, to China and elsewhere in East Asia, and also to the west as far as Egypt. The industry continued to thrive into the 1500s, when it went into decline as a result of competition from Burmese celadon ware. In addition to exporting Sawankhalok ware, the port of Ayutthaya also served as a transshipment point for ceramics from Champa, Dai Viet, and China that were destined for the international market.[176]

Ayutthaya also exported rice, especially to the trading entrepôt of Melaka. In return Ayutthaya imported cloth and various luxury goods from India via Melaka. Tamil traders carried the cloth to Melaka from India and then it was shipped on to Ayutthaya. The imported cloth included "Kling" cloth from Masulipatam and Pulicat on the Coromandel Coast, muslin from the Coromandel Coast and Bengal, and a variety of types of cloth including "carpets and brocades" from Cambay.[177] The Ayutthayan elite had an especially strong desire for imported cloth. Reid cites an example of this attitude from the *Traibhumikatha*, which was written around 1345 (just prior to the founding of Ayutthaya): "When seeking to emphasize the magnificence of a royal gift, a Thai chronicle explained that it was woven entirely from imported silk 'without any admixture of Thai thread.'"[178] While Ayutthaya was happy to sell rice to Melaka, it did not like the extra cost of importing goods from India via Melaka. It seized the port of Tenasserim in the 1460s and Tavoy in 1488 "apparently to gain direct access to maritime trade in the Bay of Bengal."[179]

As an example of new markets, the *Rekidai Hoan*, a history of the Royal Household of the Ryukyu Islands, discusses the nature of trade relations between Ayutthaya and the Ryukyu Islands, which appear to have commenced in the 1380s.[180] In addition to importing products of the Kingdom of Ayutthaya such as sappanwood, the Ryukyu Islanders also imported a variety of products from India such as velvet carpets and cotton and silk cloth that had been transshipped through Ayutthaya.

Pires describes Ayutthaya in the early 1500s as "large and very plenteous, with many people and cities, with many lords and many foreign merchants, and most of these foreigners are Chinese, because Siam does a great deal of trade with China."[181] He adds in relation to those conducting trade in Ayutthaya, "There are very few Moors in Siam. The Siamese do not like them. There are, however, Arabs, Persians, Bengalees, many Kling [Tamils], Chinese and other nationalities. And all the Siamese trade is on the China side, and in Pase, Pedir and Bengal. The Moors are in the seaports."[182] The Chinese continued to dominate trade to the east, while westward trade was becoming more important and Muslim Arab-speakers dominated this trade, especially Persians. The presence of Persian merchants appears to date back at least to the early days of the Sukhothai kingdom. Kasetsiri points to the use of the Persian word for bazaar for a local market in Sukhothai in an inscription written in 1292.[183] The Persian presence in Ayutthaya was to become much more important in later years, culminating in a Persian becoming prime minister during the reign of King Narai (r. 1656–88).[184]

As was mentioned earlier there were Chinese living in the vicinity of Ayutthaya even before the city was founded. There appear to have been a large number of Chinese living in Ayutthaya. Kasessiri remarks, "In 1429, only seventy-eight years after Ayudhya's foundation, the local Chinese community was so influential that it joined with the king building Wat Ratburama, one of the most important temples in Ayudhya."[185] A chamber in the temple was opened in 1957 and a number of inscriptions were discovered written in Thai, Arabic, Chinese, and Khmer. The Chinese inscriptions include the names of a number of Chinese with different family names who supported construction of the temple and participated in religious activities associated with it.[186]

New World Cities: Teotihuacán

Pre-modern cities were not found exclusively in the Old World, although urban areas in the New World generally developed a little later and tended not to be as large. Teotihuacán, located to the north of modern Mexico City, was the largest city in the pre-Columbian Americas.[187] The history of the city is generally divided into four periods: Teotihuacán I (Late Formative), 300 B.C. to 100 B.C.; Teotihuacán II (Proto-Classic), 100 B.C. to A.D. 300; Teotihuacán III (Early Classic), A.D. 300 to A.D. 600; and Teotihuacán IV, after A.D. 600, when the city was abandoned. The largest structure in the city, the Pyramid of the Sun, was completed by A.D. 100. The city reached its zenith between A.D. 150 and 450. Its population grew from around 60,000 in A.D. 100 to around 125,000 (and possibly as high as 200,000) by A.D. 600, when the city contained 2,600 buildings (including 2,000 apartment compounds) and covered around 20 sq km,[188] making it one of the largest cities in the world at the time. In addition to areas that were under its direct control, the city exerted substantial political, economic, and cultural influence throughout Mesoamerica. The fall of Teotihuacán in the 600s created a diaspora as people left the area and scattered both to nearby locales such as Cholula (near present day Puebla) and further to the south.

Teotihuacán was a multiethnic city, drawing the bulk of its population from the diverse ethnic groups of the immediate surrounding area of central Mexico. Of particular relevance for the present discussion is the importance of craft production and trade. In his survey of the city, Millon found over 500 craft workshops and estimates that as much as 25 percent of the population was comprised of craft specialists.[189] The largest number of these worked obsidian (mainly to make cutting tools), while others made ornamental objects from other imported stones (including turquoise and cinnabar). Ceramic production was also important, including both fine and utilitarian wares. For example, mould-made ceramic incense burners were mass-produced for local use and for export. There were also specialists who made elaborate feathered costumes for elites. Such production required a large volume of imports not only from the surrounding area, but also from much further away as well. In addition to merchants who dealt in local goods, there were "also long-distance merchants who handled the transport and exchange of goods to far-off areas."[190] The Maya region far to the south, for example, was an important source of such things as cacao beans and quetzal feathers.

Millon's survey of Teotihuacán shows that there was at least one neighborhood set aside for foreigners.[191] This was an area towards the western edge of the city occupied by Zapotec peoples associated with Monte Albán in Oaxaca. The residents of this neighborhood appear to have included at least some individuals of relatively high status as indicated by the presence of tombs modeled after Monte Albán in Oaxaca. Ceramics found in this neighborhood include Monte Albán–style funerary urns as well as domestic pottery and household objects in Oaxaca styles. There is also archaeological evidence that people from Teotihuacán may have lived in Monte Albán as well. One tomb and a number of stone monuments depict people dressed in Teotihuacán fashion, including a group of men approaching a Zapotec ruler. On the eastern edge of the city there was another neighborhood that Millon refers to as the Merchants Barrio. Archaeologists found concentrations of fine pottery from the Gulf Coast here as well as a structure that appears to have been a merchant's warehouse. The Huastecs, who lived to the northeast of Teotihuacán in an area that includes the modern Mexican states of Hidalgo, San Luis Potosí, Veracruz, and Tamaulipas, were another distinct residential group in Teotihuacán. Their presence is marked by a round temple dedicated to the Quetzalcoatl-Ehecatl wind god cult located in the northwest of the city. There is also archaeological evidence that indicates that there was trade with the Maya to the south and perhaps at least temporary visits by Maya to the city. Pottery shards identified as Maya in origin were initially found during excavations of Teotihuacán in 1932.[192] Murals painted in a Maya fashion as well as Maya pottery were also discovered at Teotihuacán in 1978.[193] In addition, Lowland Maya polychrome pottery found in the Merchants Barrio of Teotihuacán suggests the visitation of Maya foreigners to Teotihuacán.[194] The culture of Teotihuacán also influenced the styles of dress, pottery, and architecture of such Maya cities as Tikal, Rio Azul, and Copan.

9

Soldiers

Soldiers are commonly identified with a particular country or nation and not thought of in terms of transnationalism. Yet, there are a number of contexts within which soldiers develop transnational lives. Taking service in the military of a country other than one's own while retaining some ties to one's country of origin is one way. Soldiers in the service of a country may also be posted to other countries for prolonged periods where they develop transnational relations. In the past this was often the case with the standing armies of imperial powers. Service as a mercenary is a third means by which a solder may develop a transnational life. Mercenaries are soldiers who usually are not from any of the national groups directly involved in a conflict whose participation is motivated by the promise of private gain. Whereas short-term service as a mercenary is not likely to result in a person developing a transnational lifestyle, it can happen in cases of longer service or service with a particular country at intervals over a long period.

Large empires of the past required large armies to maintain internal order as well as to defend themselves from external threats. While the leading ranks of these armies often came from the dominant ethnic group of the empire, it was common for imperial armies to contain people not only from other nationalities within the empire, but also people from nationalities living outside of the empire. The latter includes those who might join the imperial army on a regular basis as well as those taking temporary employment as a mercenary. Whatever their origin, such imperial soldiers often were posted in countries other than their original ones.

Mercenaries in the Ancient Mediterranean

Mercenaries have been used in warfare in the eastern Mediterranean since at least the 1200s B.C. While one of the hallmarks of the rise of the ancient Egyptian Empire was its creation of a professional army, the ancient Egyptians also appear to be the first to have employed mercenaries.[1] The Egyptian ruler Ramesses II (r. 1279–1213 B.C.), who is generally considered to have been the most powerful of ancient Egypt's pharaohs, employed thousands of mercenaries. Many of the Egyptian mercenaries came from Nubia, while others were recruited from Libya, Canaan, and Syria, as well as the Sherdens. These soldiers came from territories where Ramesses II was involved in military campaigns; in the case of the Sherdens (aka Shardana), they were a group of Sea People, probably from southwestern Turkey, who had been raiding Egypt's coasts.[2] Sherdens subsequently became prominent within Ramesses II's military including service as bodyguards for the pharaoh.[3] The Sherdens are known to have taken part in the Battle of Qadesh (aka Kadesh) against the Hittites in Syria in 1274, as did another group of mercenaries who are referred to as Ne'arin (aka Nearin) who may have been Canaanites.[4]

Southwestern Turkey's association with mercenaries re-emerges prominently in the 600s B.C. during the reigns of the Lydian king Gyges (r. 687–652 B.C.) and the Egyptian pharaoh Psammetich I (aka Psammeticus, Psammetichos, r. 664–610 B.C.). Gyges was the son of the commander of the royal guards and appears to have murdered the incumbent king in connivance with the king's wife and then assumed the throne himself, thereby ending the long-ruling Herakleid Dynasty and laying the foundation for the Mermnad Dynasty. He kept Sardis (in modern Manisa Province) as his capital.

In his rise to power Gyges appears to have relied heavily on the use of mercenaries, especially those known as Misthophoroi Uazali. They were mercenaries from the Lycian Coast region of southwestern Turkey, which was not part of the Lydian kingdom. Most of these mercenaries were Karians (aka Carians), but there were also Lycians, Pamphylians, and Pisidians among them. Caunos (aka Caunus) was the main Karian city. The early Karians had close ties with the Greek Islands (the island of Rhodes lies immediately to the south of Caunos) and Crete and they served as sailors and soldiers on the Minoan fleets. Uazali is a Lycian word for warrior. This region is also associated with the Sea Peoples. Among the Sea Peoples named by the Egyptians who had attacked them, the Shardana, Tereh, Lukka, Sheklesh, and Ekwesh appear to have come from the coastal region of Turkey and Syria. The Shardana may have come from the east in the vicinity of coastal Syria, whereas the Teresh and Lukka probably came from the Lycian Coast with Lukka referring to the Lycians. Lycian is a Luwian language related to Hittite and it is important to note that these people were not Greeks. As a result of their interaction with the nearby Greek colonies and city-states, however, over time they became increasingly Hellenized while retaining a distinct identity. Initially the Sea People are associated with piracy and maritime combat, but later the Karians and others from the Lycian Coast fought mainly as infantry (the Greek term *thureophoroi* came later to be associated with such soldiers). Many of those who went abroad to serve as mercenaries appear to have come from the interior highlands.

By the time of Gyges the Karians and their neighbors were commonly employed as mercenaries by many of the city-states and kingdoms around western Turkey. The Karians appear to have allied themselves with the Lydians. Alyattes II (r. 619–560 B.C.), who is considered to have created the Lydian Empire through his more extensive conquests than his predecessors, had two wives, one a Greek and the other a Karian. This latter marriage appears to have resulted in the Karians becoming subjects of Lydia. Alyattes had two children by his Karian wife and one of them, Croesus, became king after his father died. Writing about the Lydian Empire under Croesus, Herodotus says that the Lycians had remained independent, while the Karians and Pamphylians had become Lydian subjects.[5]

One of the most important issues concerning mercenaries is how to pay them. In this regard the rise of the use of mercenaries in the eastern Mediterranean region appears to be intimately interrelated with the development of coinage, with which Lydia is closely associated. One early means of paying mercenaries, prior to the invention of coinage, may have been with copper and bronze ingots that were used by both the ancient Greeks and Egyptians. The wealth of the Lydians was famous in the ancient world and this was associated in part with their access to electrum, a natural alloy of gold and silver (with trace elements of copper). There were two main sources of electrum in the ancient Mediterranean. One was a site mined by the Egyptians between the Nile and the Red Sea, but the metal was even more plentiful in western Turkey, where large deposits were found on Mount Tmolus (modern Bozday, 2,200 m) and in the silt of the Pactolus River that flowed down from the mountain. The Lydian capital of Sardis was built on a northern spur of the mountain and the river flowed through the city. The electrum and gold obtained from the mountain and the alluvial deposits of the river contributed greatly to the wealth of the Lydians and Alyattes II is credited with the invention of the first coins.[6] Electrum ingots were already in use in western Turkey and these probably were already serving as a means of paying mercenaries, but coins were far more efficient. Moreover, whereas the gold content of natural electrum around Sardis was between 70 percent and 90 percent, the coins produced by Alyattes II had a gold content of 45 percent to 55 percent. This percentage was accomplished by adding refined silver to the natural electrum and it allowed the Lydians to enhance their wealth even more.[7] The Lydian coins weighed 4.7 grams and were given the denomination of 1/3 stater. Three of these, or 1 stater, was roughly equivalent to a month's pay for a soldier, and the Lydian kings Alyattes II and Croesus used their electrum coins extensively to hire soldiers from around the Mediterranean world.

The ability of Croesus to hire soldiers is apparent from Xenophon's account of Cyaxares's report to Cyrus II on the state of the Lydian army on the eve of the Battle of Pteria in 547 B.C.:

> Croesus the Lydian is coming, we hear, with 10,000 horse and more than 40,000 archers and tar-geteers. Artamas the governor of Greater Phrygia is bringing, they say, 8000 horse, and lancers and targeteers also, 40,000 strong. Then there is Aribaius the king of Cappadocia with 6000 horse and 30,000 archers and targeteers. And Aragdus the Arabian with 10,000 horse, a hundred chariots, and innumerable slingers. As for the Hellenes who dwell in Asia, it is not clear as yet whether they will send a following or not. But the Phrygians from the Hellespont, we are told, are mustering in the Caystrian plain under Gabaidus, 6000 horse and 40,000 targeteers. Word has been sent to the Carians [Karians], Cilicians, and Paphlagonians, but it is said they will not rise; the Lord of Assyria and Babylon will himself, I believe, bring not less than 20,000 horse, and I make no doubt as many as 200 chariots, and thousands upon thousands of men on foot; such at least has been his custom whenever he invaded us before.[8]

While the numbers may not be accurate, the account gives an idea as to where Croesus was able to recruit soldiers. Moreover, Anthon describes it as an army "consisting entirely of mercenaries."[9] The imperial army of Cyrus II, which was larger than the mercenary army of Croesus, was equally international with Persians accounting for perhaps one-third of the number and the remainder being made up mainly of Arabians, Armenians, and Medians.

The battle ended indecisively and Croesus headed back to Sardis to assemble a larger force. In this case in addition to the various groups of mercenaries he had already assembled, he was reinforced a large contingent of troops from Egypt sent by the reigning pharaoh Amasis II (r. 570–526 B.C.). That pharaoh, as we will discuss below, himself relied heavily on the use of mercenaries from Greece and Turkey. The two armies met at the Battle of Thymbra and Croesus was defeated despite having the larger force. Cyrus then captured Sardis after a 14-day siege and Lydia became a satrapy in the Achaemenid Empire (known as Sparda).

While the presence of mercenaries in Croesus's army from nearby regions is no surprise, the presence of a large number of soldiers led by Aragdus the Arabian raises interesting questions of relevance to transnationalism. In particular, how were these soldiers recruited and how did they get to Turkey? Unfortunately the early sources shed little light on these important questions. However, as we will see when we discuss the presence of mercenaries in Egypt, transport by sea seems to have been a common means of moving mercenaries around in the ancient Mediterranean region, and the Lydians and their neighbors certainly had ready access to maritime transport.

The actual process of recruitment indicates that there had to have been persons who could function cross-culturally to make the arrangements. This was not much of a problem in the case of mercenaries within the Turkish region where people of different nationalities were accustomed to interacting with one another, but in the case of more distant lands where people spoke very different languages things were not so simple. Some indication of the problem comes from a passage by Assurbanipal concerning emissaries sent to him by Gyges to seek assistance after he was attacked by the Cimmerians:

> Gyges' rider set out [...]. He reached the border of my country. My men spotted him and asked him: "Who are you, stranger, you, whose country's rider never traveled the road to the frontier?" They brought him [...] to Nineveh, my royal city, into my presence. But of all the languages of east and west, over which the god Aššur has given me control, there was no interpreter of his tongue. His language was foreign, so that his words were not understood.[10]

In this case a solution was obviously found to the problem since "a treaty was concluded and after Gyges had paid tribute, the Assyrians and Lydians jointly fought against the Cimmerian mounted archers."[11] Unfortunately, the means by which such solutions were found in the ancient world are rarely recorded, although the Egyptian case to be discussed below does provide one example of how a problem was overcome.

Karians (this terms is used generally to include all of those mercenaries coming from the Lycian Coast) and ethnic Greek mercenaries from Turkey were employed extensively in Egypt by the pharaohs of the Saite Dynasty (664–525 B.C.). After Assurbanipal's army had re-established Assyrian suzerainty over Egypt in 667, he placed Necho I on the throne as his vassal. When Necho I died in 664 his son Psammetich I (aka Psammeticus, Psammetichos, r. 664–610 B.C.) became pharaoh and a short time later succeeded in ending Assyrian suzerainty.

Psammetich I's consolidation of his position as pharaoh faced local opposition. Diodorus Siculus sheds light on Psammetich I's background and how he came to use mercenaries to consolidate his power:

> Psammetichus of Sais, who was one of the twelve kings and in charge of the regions lying along the sea, furnished wares for all merchants and especially for the Phoenicians and the Greeks; and since in this manner he disposed of the products of his own district at a profit and exchanged them for those of other peoples, he was not only possessed of great wealth but also enjoyed friendly relations with peoples and rulers.... Psammetichus, calling mercenaries from Caria and Ionia [Karia and the nearby Ionian colony of Colophon], overcame the others in a pitched battle near the city called Momemphis, and of the kings who opposed him some were slain in the battle and some were driven out into Libya and were no longer able to dispute with him for the throne.[12]

Modern historians commonly refer to these mercenaries as Greeks, but it is important to recognize that although they spoke Greek, most of them were non–Greek Hellenized Karians.

As for payment, Diodorus reports: "among the mercenaries he distributed notable gifts over and above their promised pay, gave them the region called The Camps to dwell in, and apportioned to them much land in the region lying a little up the river from the Pelusiac mouth; they being subsequently removed thence by Amasis, who reigned many years later, and settled by him in Memphis."[13] Herodotus say that these mercenaries "were the first men of alien speech" to settle in Egypt,[14] adding that he placed young Egyptian boys among them to learn Greek and to serve as interpreters.

Diodorus makes the point that after assuming the throne with the help of the Hellenized and Hellenic mercenaries, Psammetich I continued to develop ties with the Hellenic world, and he was far more open to the outside world than his predecessors:

> [Psammetich] then formed alliances with both Athens and certain other Greek states. He also reg-
> ularly treated with kindness any foreigners who sojourned in Egypt of their own free will, and was
> so great an admirer of the Hellenes that he gave his sons a Greek education; and, speaking generally,
> he was the first Egyptian king to open to other nations the trading-places throughout the rest of
> Egypt and to offer a large measure of security to strangers from across the seas. For his predecessors
> in power had consistently closed Egypt to strangers, either killing or enslaving any who touched
> its shores.[15]

As for the mercenaries now living in Egypt, "And since Psammetichus had established his rule with the aid of the mercenaries, he henceforth entrusted these before others with the administration of his empire and regularly maintained large mercenary forces."[16] Such favoritism at times appears to have caused problems:

> Once in connection with a campaign in Syria, when he was giving the mercenaries a more honorable
> place in his order of battle by putting them on the right wing and showing the native troops less
> honor by assigning them the position on the left wing of the phalanx, the Egyptians, angered by
> this slight and being over two hundred thousand strong, revolted and set out for Ethiopia, having
> determined to win for themselves a country of their own.[17]

Use of Karian and Ionian mercenaries continued under subsequent Saite rulers, although by the reigns of these later pharaohs it may be best to view those who were resident in Egypt simply as ethnically distinct members of the imperial Egyptian army rather than as mercenaries. Psammetich I's son as Necho II (r. 610–594) used these mercenaries in his Syrian campaign of 608 B.C. Psamtik II (r. 595–589 B.C.) employed Karian mercenaries in his Ethiopian campaign in 591 B.C. These mercenaries "carved inscriptions on the legs of the colossi of Ramesses II at Abu Simbel in Nubia, which indicate the mercenaries' origins."[18] Apries (r. 589–570 B.C.) turned to Hellenic mercenaries to thwart Babylonian efforts to conquer Egypt and to defend Egyptian territory in Libya against Dorian Greek invaders. After the Dorians defeated Apries and his Hellenic mercenaries, indigenous Egyptian troops revolted and placed an Egyptian general on the throne as Amasis II (r. 570–526) after Apries was forced to flee the country.[19]

Karian and Ionian mercenaries played an important role in the fall of the Saite Dynasty to the Persians under Cambyses II in 525 B.C.[20] Prior to Cambyses II's invasion of Egypt, a close advisor to Amasis II named Phanes, who was an Ionian from Halicarnassus (modern Bodrum, located southwest of Karia), had a dispute with the pharaoh and sailed to Lycia, apparently with the intent of going over to the Persians. He was captured there by an agent of Amasis II's but managed to escape and then went to serve Cambyses II as an advisor for his invasion of Egypt. Shortly after Amasis II died and his son became pharaoh Psammetich III (aka Psamtik III), Cambyses II invaded and was able to defeat the Egyptian army at the Battle of Pelusium in 525 B.C., which set the stage for the Persian conquest of Egypt. The army of the Egyptians included Karian and Ionian mercenaries, whereas the Persian army included a number of Hellenic mercenaries who had gone over to their side. Psammetich

III had hoped to be able to stop the Persian invasion with the assistance of Hellenic mercenaries, but his efforts were undermined when significant numbers of these Hellenes not only failed to support him, they went over to the Persians. Especially important in this regard was the decision of Polycrates (r. *c.* 538–522) from the Ionian island of Samos, who commanded the largest fleet in the region (comprised of about 40 triremes), to support the Persians. To punish Phanes for his treachery, according to Herodotus, prior to the battle Psammetich III gathered Phanes's sons and drained their blood into bowls of wine, which he and his advisors then drank.

With the Persian conquest of Turkey and Egypt, the primary source and market for mercenaries in the eastern Mediterranean were now part of the Persian Empire. This did not put an end to the use of mercenaries in the region, far from it, but the main source of mercenaries shifted from the Hellenized coastal areas of Turkey to Greece itself. Not only did the city-states of ancient Greece have their own armies, but limited employment opportunities for soldiers also encouraged many of them to leave Greece in search of work to the extent that mercenaries from Greece were a common feature in the ancient eastern Mediterranean after 400 B.C.[21] Writing of Greece during this period, Durant comments, "While Plato talked of philosopher kings, soldier kings were growing up under his nose. Greek mercenaries sold themselves impartially to Greek or 'barbarian' generals, and fought as often against Greece as for her."[22] Seeking employment as a mercenary did not become widespread in Greece until after the Peloponnesian War (431–404 B.C.). As Hamilton notes, "Almost thirty years of constant warfare had produced a class of soldiers who were skilled at their craft but unable to find a livelihood through traditional means — farming, trade, or manufacture at home — and who turned to the profession of arms as an alternative."[23] The mercenaries came from a variety of places in the Greek world, especially from poorer rural areas, and gathered in the larger cities such as Athens and Corinth in search of employment.

Significantly, while the Achaemenid Empire was able to raise large imperial armies internally, it also continued to employ Hellenic mercenaries. As with other great empires, a large percentage of the male population in the Achaemenid Empire spent its time in military service. Rawlinson estimates that "at the very least, one-third, if not one-half, of the adult male population" of "Persia Proper" served in the military at any given time.[24] Added to this number were soldiers recruited from other parts of the empire. In general the army was comprised only of Persians and closely related peoples such as the Medes and Hyrcanians. "Order was maintained by large and numerous garrisons of foreign troops — Persians and Medes [and perhaps Hyrcanians] — quartered on the inhabitants, who had little sympathy with those among whom they lived, and would be sure to suppress sternly any outbreak."[25] The Persian army in Egypt, for example, was comprised of 120,000 Persians.[26] Foreign troops were employed only during major campaigns. Thus, when Darius gathered an army to invade Europe he assembled an army estimated to have numbered between 700,000 and 800,000 men "which was made up of contingents from all the nations under his rule."[27] Even in this case, however, as Briant points out, the core of the fighting army was composed of Persians and closely allied peoples, while non–Persian soldiers were often used for show to demonstrate the great power of the ruler. Moreover, he notes that many of these ethnic troops likely came from multi-ethnic garrisons and permanent military colonies that existed throughout the empire.[28]

Artaxerxes III Ochus (r. 358–338 B.C.) was forced to rely heavily on Greek mercenaries to put down a series of revolts and re-conquer Egypt shortly after assuming the throne. Greek mercenaries played an important role on both sides of many of these conflicts.

Nectanebo II (r. 360–342 B.C.) of Egypt sent a force of 4,000 Greek mercenaries under the command of Mentor of Rhodes (1. c. 385–340 B.C.) to aid Tennes, the ruler of the Phoenician city of Sidon, in a revolt against the Persians in 345 B.C. The revolt failed after Tennes secretly sold the city out to the Persians in return for a promise of his own safety. A massacre followed, with the survivors being taken off in captivity to be sold as slaves, and Tennes was executed.[29] The Persians later captured Mentor. He was pardoned and then employed by them as a mercenary. When the Persians invaded Egypt, their force of 330,000 included 14,000 Greeks — 6,000 of them coming from the Greek cities of Asia Minor, 3,000 sent by Argos, 1,000 from Thebes, and another 4,000 under Mentor's command.[30] Each of the three Persian armies involved in the invasion was placed under the command of both a Persian and a Greek general — the Greek generals being Lacrates of Thebes, Mentor of Rhodes, and Nicostratus of Argos. The opposing Egyptian army of 100,000 included 20,000 Greek mercenaries as well as 20,000 Libyans. Mentor and his men's familiarity with Egypt played an important role in the Persian defeat of the Egyptians at the Battle of Pelusium in 342 B.C. After the victory Mentor was made governor of a portion of the coastal area of Asia Minor as a reward and held the post until his death a few years later.

Darius III Codomannus (r. 336–330 B.C.) was the last Achaemenid king. He had the unfortunate luck to have to face the Macedonian Alexander the Great. Of particular interest here is the nature of his armies. During the initial battles of Granicus and Issus as Alexander began his attacks on the empire, Darius's forces relied heavily on Greek mercenaries. In the final battle of Gaugamela, near Arbela, soldiers from throughout the empire joined the Persians and Greek mercenaries. Besides the Persians and Greek mercenaries Darius's army included Medes, Babylonians, Susianians, Armenians, Cadusians from the Caspian Sea region, Bactrians, Sogdonians, Arachosians, Arians from Herat, Indians from Punjab, Sitaceni, Albanians, Sacesinae from Sacassene, Cappadocians, Coele-Syrians, Syrians of Mesopotamia, Tapri, Hyrcanians, Parthians, Daans, tribes of the Red Sea coast, Mardians, Karians, Massagetae, Kassites from the Zagros Mountains, Belitae, Gortae, Phrygians, Catatonians, and Saka (aka Sacae, a Scythian tribe) from Kashgar and Yarkand on the borders of the Gobi Desert.[31] This was undoubtedly the most international army that had ever been assembled up to that time.

Greeks also played an important role in seafaring in and around the Persian Empire. The Persians had no navy of their own and when ships were needed they conscripted those of seafaring peoples under their rule, especially Greeks and Egyptians. Thus, a fleet of 600 ships mainly belonging to Greeks from Asia Minor accompanied Darius's army that invaded Greece. Likewise, sea-going trade to and from the empire was carried out aboard ships of Phoenicians, Greeks, Babylonians and other non–Persians.

In an examination of various military campaigns by the Hellenic Seleucids in the Middle East, Aperghis estimates the size of the Seleucid field armies to have been between 70,000 and 80,000 men.[32] This included around 35,000 regulars and 15,000 mercenaries, composed of ethnic Greeks as well as others from Mesopotamia, Syria, and elsewhere, with the remainder being made up of local allies and levies. In regard to the latter, the Greek historian Polybius refers to the presence of 5,000 Medes, Kissians, Kadusians (a Mede tribe), and Karmanians, along with 2,000 Agrianian and Persian bowmen and slingers in one campaign.[33] In addition to the field armies there were garrisons scattered around the empire. These garrisons, like the field armies, were composed of a mixture of ethnic Greeks as well as "soldiers brought from other parts of the empire, a regular practice also of the Achaemenids."[34]

Further to the west, Carthage also made extensive use of mercenaries. In fact, most of its army with the exception of those of the highest ranks was comprised of mercenaries recruited mainly from neighboring parts of northern Africa, especially Libya, and the Balearic Islands. The defeat of Carthage by Rome in the First Punic War led to a revolt by its mercenary soldiers when Carthage was unable to pay them that is commonly known as the Mercenary War.[35] To give some idea of the numbers involved, around 20,000 mercenaries sailed from Sicily at the outset of the revolt and attacked Tunis. Later some 70,000 Libyan mercenaries were said to have been involved.

The Roman Empire's Army

During the early days of the Roman Republic its army was comprised entirely of well-off citizens who served without pay. By the 1st century B.C. the Republic's army had grown into a much more professional force of 60,000 to 70,000 men.[36] All male citizens between the age of 17 and 45 had the duty of serving in the military for at least 6 years and they remained liable to be called up at any time for an additional maximum period of 16 years. Those who decided to remain in service formed a core of professional soldiers. Prior to this time the cavalry, drawn from the equites, served from a minimum of 3 years to a maximum of 10 years. Later the ranks of the cavalry were filled by allies and from those living elsewhere in the empire. Since soldiers were no longer necessarily recruited from the well to do, it had become necessary to pay them and the rate at this time was about 160 *denarii* a year.[37] Julius Caesar increased this to 225 *denarii* around 49 B.C.[38]

In addition to the legions of Rome's own army there were also supporting units of auxiliaries recruited from newly conquered territories as well as allied tribes and states. "Recruitment ... served to draw off the young tribesmen and harness their vigor in the empire's defence."[39] Since such units tended to be stationed close to home they were not particularly transnational in character, but rather served as a form of imperial nation-building. People from their own nationality commonly commanded them, but there were instances where Roman officers were in command and in these instances transnational relations can be said to have been created between the Roman officers and their non–Roman troops. There were some instances during the Republican period when auxiliary units were stationed away from their homelands, "including bodies of Cretan archers and Numidian cavalry, [that] seem to have been kept in Roman service on a more permanent basis, and served throughout the Mediterranean."[40] Auxiliaries participated in the campaigns during the civil war (49–30 B.C.) and at times found themselves far from home:

> Caesar's wide-ranging campaigns carried Gallic, German and Spanish troops to the furthest corners of the empire; 10,000 Spanish and Gallic cavalry participated in Anthony's Armenian campaign. Octavian continued to recruit auxiliaries from the western provinces under his control. In the East Pompey, the Liberators and later Anthony were able to draw on the armies of client kings in Thrace, Asia Minor, Syria, Judaea and Egypt.[41]

The military affairs of allies and vassals of Republican and early Imperial Rome tended to be transnational in a variety of ways. Herod I of Judea (r. 37–4 B.C.) provides a good example.[42] As Judea became embroiled in the rivalry between Rome and the Parthian Empire, Herod sided with Rome, which provided him with troops under the command of Roman generals to oust the Parthian-backed Antigonus II Mattathias and install himself on the Judean throne in 37 B.C. Herod made trips to Rome and also became involved in the civil war. His lobbying efforts with Octavian resulted in the victor of the civil war confirming Herod as king of Judea in 30 B.C. As king, Herod made considerable use of ethnic Greeks for administrative purposes, with Nicolas of Damascus and his brother Ptolemy serving as his close advisors (Ptolemy was placed in charge of finance). Roman officers commanded his troops, which included a mixture of Thracian, German, and Galatian mercenaries, who were from territories either under Roman rule or vassal states. The Galatians, were a Celtic people from a region in central Turkey that had become a vassal state of Rome in 64 B.C., often hired themselves out as mercenaries around the Mediterranean. The Tracians lived in an area comprised of adjacent parts of European Turkey, northeastern Greece, and southeastern Bulgaria. They served as mercenaries for the Macedonians and had fought with Alexander the Great. They also served as mercenaries for the Romans, and Rome had become increasingly involved in Thrace's affairs, annexing part of their territory and making the rest of it a vassal state.

We have already discussed the troops that were stationed in the city of Rome. Outside of Rome the soldiers in the legions that were stationed around the empire at least potentially lived transnational lives. Their role was to serve as guardians primarily of the empire's cities and commercial arteries against bandits, rebels, and outside armies. Under Octavian/Augustus the placement of Rome's 25 to 28 legions primarily reflected the nature of imperial conquest, with legions being posted increasingly to frontier regions while the numbers found in the more secure parts of the empire were reduced. Thus, whereas there were 7 legions in Spain in 208 B.C., the number had been reduced to 3 by A.D. 14.[43] In A.D. 14 there were a total of 25 legions stationed in Spain, along the Rhine River, along the Danube River, and in Egypt, Tunisia, and Syria.[44] The largest number of legions was in Syria and the two German districts, each with 4 legions. Legions could be moved around when necessary, especially in relation to conflicts along the Rhine and the Danube and in the East. For example, Tiberius sent legion IX Hispania from the Danube to Africa for four years.[45] By A.D. 200 they were also to be found in Britain, across the Danube in Dacia (Romania and Moldavia), in eastern Cappadocia, Mesopotamia, Palestine, and Arabia.

Under Octavian/Augustus Rome's army became increasingly professional, being made up of career soldiers. After the civil war in A.D. 5 the period of military service was increased to 20 years plus 5 in reserve and in the salary paid to soldiers, which was raised to 3,000 *denarii* in the same year.[46] Another reform that took place at this time was that soldiers were forbidden to marry (existing marriages were dissolved upon enlistment). There was also a change in land allocations given as a reward to certain groups of soldiers on retirement. Caesar had given such troops land in southern Gaul and Italy. After the civil war this was no longer politically feasible and Augustus initiated a program of giving them land in the more distant colonies. As was noted previously, those who joined the army were granted Roman citizenship upon being discharged if they were not already citizens (eventually along with their family members).

As was noted above, units could be moved around the empire for short periods. However, all legions were associated with a particular province where they were normally stationed. As Campbell notes, "Initially there was a considerable degree of movement and transfer of troops, but eventually things settled down and greater continuity was established."[47] Thus, the Third Legion was stationed in the North African province of Africa (Carthage was its capital). The legion founded the city of Lambaesis (Lambese) in A.D. 123. It set up its permanent headquarters nearby and over time many of the soldiers married local women, settled down, and established homes in the town. Integration into local societies by the Roman legions stationed there was in part related to the non-combat activities of the soldiers. In addition to becoming involved in local security-related activities such as policing, "the army also formed a useful reserve of disciplined manpower" and soldiers were often drafted into construction and other sorts of work.[48] When they retired solders were provided with a cash settlement and some were given land near where they had served. Retired Roman soldiers in Britain during Claudius's reign, for example, were settled at Camulodunum (Colchester); those on the Rhine were settled at Cologne (founded in A.D. 50), and those serving in Syria were settled at Ptolemais (Akko).[49]

We have also already commented on the changing ethno-national identity of troops serving in the Roman army over time. During the civil war "all the protagonists from Caesar onwards succeeded in augmenting their forces by forming 'legions' from the non-citizen populations of their provinces and by training and arming them in the Roman manner."[50] Moreover, "Italians who had been prepared to serve in the civil wars for a fairly short term proved unwilling to spend a span of twenty-five years or more, much of their adult life, in a frontier province far from home. Greater emphasis was placed on seeking recruits in the provinces, where (it seems clear) men were eager and willing to serve, and saw in legionary service a route to social advancement."[51]

The number of Italians in Rome's army declined until "by the mid-second century A.D. (in the reign of the emperor Hadrian), there were hardly any Italians serving in the legions."[52] Initially "recruiting centered on the more Romanized provinces, such as Narbonese Gaul, Spain, and Asia Minor," but later "more men were recruited from the frontier zones, and also from Syria and Egypt."[53] Many of these soldiers either remained in their provinces of birth and became Roman citizens or permanently settled in other provinces. In this way the military served to spread Roman culture and encouraged some migration, but did not necessarily promote a transnational lifestyle for most soldiers.

While Rome's soldiers generally became increasingly sedentary, they did not always stay put. Those of higher rank were more mobile than the rank and file, but even lower ranking soldiers sometimes moved about the empire, especially during times of internal conflict such as in the case of one of Rome's more spectacular civil wars in A.D. 69. Lucius Vitellius had already held a number of administrative posts in Rome and served as proconsul of the province of Africa when he was appointed governor of Lower Germany in A.D. 68. When the troops in Upper Germany revolted against the emperor Galba in A.D. 69, associates of Vitellius in Lower Germany proclaimed him emperor and other legions in Gaul, Britain, and Raetia joined the revolt. By the middle of the year the troops backing Vitellius were victorious and he assumed the emperorship in Rome. His opponents characterized these troops who marched on Rome as foreigners and aliens. Vitellius had hardly set foot in Rome when word arrived that the legions in Egypt had proclaimed their support for Titus Flavius Vespasianus, the governor of Judea, as emperor. Soon legions from Syria and the Danube region joined Vespasian's side and those from the Danube marched on Rome and defeated those troops supporting Vitellius, who was captured, tortured, killed, and thrown into the Tiber River.

By A.D. 70 the nature of the Roman Empire's army had altered considerably as a result of changes in the nature of recruitment of the military. "Rome was a city they were pledged to defend, but which they would mostly never visit. Increasingly they began to identity their interests with those of the provinces in which they were stationed." Moreover, they felt little attachment to the Roman Senate or to the people of the city of Rome, "rather they were loyal to the emperor."[54] The nature of the auxiliaries also changed. After the turmoil of A.D. 69–70 and the revolt of troops in Gaul and along the Rhine, policy was changed from keeping auxiliary troops close to home to moving them away from their homes, and from keeping the units ethnically homogeneous to mixing them more. Also the practice of placing units under the command of local tribal leaders was ended.[55]

The reign of Emperor Septimus Severus (r. 193–211) was an especially important one for the Roman army, especially since he witnessed the start of a process of decentralization within the army.[56] He was born in 145 in Leptis Magna (near modern Tripoli) in North Africa, and prior to becoming emperor served in several different parts of the empire. As emperor, Severus enlarged the empire and also increased the overall size of the regular Roman army and the auxiliary as well as substantially raising a soldier's pay. While the enlarged empire provided more income to Rome, the enlarged and better paid military put a substantial strain on imperial finances that led to a drastic debasement of the Roman currency and also contributed to a loosening of centralized control.

The Romans employed mercenaries at various times. For example, when faced with a depleted army and invading barbarians in A.D. 167, Emperor Marcus Aurelius hired other barbarians, Germans and Scythians, to attack the invaders. Over the years the Romans relied increasingly on others to do their fighting. Rome no longer had the wealth to pay for a permanent professional army and increasingly came to rely on mercenaries largely recruited from the *foederati* discussed in an earlier chapter. As Durant comments, "The armies of Rome were no longer Roman armies; they were composed largely of provincials, largely barbarians; they fought not for their altars and their homes, but for their wages."[57] When Attila (aka Attila the Hun, r. 434–453) invaded the Western Roman Empire in 451 an army composed of Franks, Celts, Burgundians, and assorted *foederati* under the Roman general Flavius Aëtius defeated him. The situation eventually led in A.D. 476 to "the barbarian mercenaries who dominated the Roman army" deposing ruling emperor Romulus Augustulus and naming their leader, Odoacer, as ruler.[58]

Medieval Mercenaries in Europe

Mercenaries were widely employed in Western Europe and the Middle East after the fall of the Western Roman Empire. While we will focus on the use of mercenaries by the Byzantine Empire and in Christian Western Europe, from the example of Muslim Spain discussed below it is important to realize that the Muslim caliphates also employed mercenaries. Mercenaries in Medieval Western Europe sometimes lived transnational lives during their time as soldiers, but often they came to settle in the areas where they were employed, living out their lives more as migrants than as transnationals.

THE BYZANTINE ARMY

The Byzantine Empire that survived after the fall of the Western Roman Empire relied heavily on mercenaries who were often recruited from outside of the empire. Durant makes the point that "the imperial army [of Byzantium] was composed almost wholly of barbarian mercenaries from a hundred tribes and states" who "lived by plunder, and dreamed of riches and rape. Nothing united or inspired them except regular pay and able generals."[59] Davidson notes, "The tradition of reliance on barbarian troops from outside the Empire was as old as the city itself, for Constantinople showed great honor to the Coruti [a Germanic tribe] for the part which they played in the Battle of the Milvian Bridge in A.D. 312."[60] This was the battle at which Constantine I defeated his rival, Maxentius, at the Milvian Bridge over the Tiber River.

Among those serving in the Byzantine military were special units responsible for guarding the city and capital. Initially these units were comprised of local Greeks, but by the 800s foreign mercenaries were being recruited as well. Davidson mentions, "The presence of the Rus [Vikings from along the Dnieper River] in the imperial forces is recognized as early as 911.... Vikings might serve along with Germans, Hungarians, Goths, Lombards, Normans and Pechinegs [a Turkic people from Central Asia], and there were also two separate contingents of Turks from Central Asia known as the Pharangians, and a company of Khazars [another Turkish group from the region north and west of the Caspian Sea]."[61] The divisions within the guards served in part to keep people of markedly different backgrounds apart, especially separating Christian from non–Christian. The captain of the guard "was usually a member of some aristocratic Greek family, possibly a kinsman of the Emperor."[62]

The origins of the Varangian Guard, which served as an imperial guard, date to 988, when Vladimir of Kiev (l. 958–1015) dispatched 6,000 men to help Emperor Basil II (r. 976–1025) subdue a revolt in Anatolia. The troops were sent after Vladimir had converted to Christianity the year before and after Basil II had agreed to marry Vladimir's sister Anna. After the revolt was put down Basil II recruited Rus to serve as imperial guards. Scandinavians comprised the majority of the guard until it ceased to exist in 1204, following the sack of Constantinople. Scandinavian members of the guard were recruited from as far away as Iceland and the Orkney Islands and also included Danish nobles who left England after the Norman Conquest in 1066. The guards were well paid and played an active role in the ceremonial life of the court as well as being called upon occasionally to fight. Some of the commanders of the guard were ethnic Greeks while others were Scandinavians.

Among the commanders was Harald Hardradi (aka Harald Sigurdson or Harald the Ruthless), a prominent transnational figure of the medieval period. Harald was forced to leave Norway in 1030 at the age of 15 after his half-brother was killed. He went to Russia, where he spent about four years in the service of Prince Yaroslav the Wise (l. 978–1054) of Kiev. Harald commanded a company of soldiers that fought against the Poles. He left Kiev for Constantinople (called Miklagard by the Vikings) around 1034, apparently in search of glory to gain the respect of Yaroslav's family so that he could marry Yaroslav's daughter Ellisif. Harald arrived immediately prior to Michael IV's (r. 1034–41) assumption of the throne. Harald found service in the empire's navy under the command of the Greek general Georgios Maniaces and attained command of a company of Varangian Guards. Harald fought in campaigns in Sicily, Bulgaria, and other parts of the empire. After returning from the campaign in Bulgaria in 1041 Harald became part of the Palace Guard. Under the next emperor, Michael V (who ruled for 4 months in 1042), Harald was put in prison for a time. Michael V was overthrown and Harald appears to have been the one responsible for blinding the former emperor before he was sent to live out the remainder of his life in a monastery. After this event Harald left Constantinople (under circumstances that are debated by historians) and returned to Kiev with considerable wealth. He married Ellisif. He then returned to Norway to become co-ruler with his cousin Magnus. During his reign (r. 1046–66) Harald maintained relations with Byzantium, and Greek priests were sent to Norway. The English throne was in dispute after the death of King Edward in England in 1066. Harald Hardradi invaded from the north but was defeated and died at the Battle of Stamford Bridge.

WESTERN EUROPE

Crowley and Parker comment, "By the end of the medieval period, mercenaries were everywhere in Europe, from the famed Swiss pikemen to Italian *condottieri* like Sir John Hawkwood."[63] We will return to John Hawkwood shortly. In the decentralized political world of Western Europe after the end of the Western Roman Empire the kingdoms and city-states of the region often found themselves in need of soldiers, but frequently they were unwilling or not in a position to support a permanent army. The disadvantage of securing soldiers through feudal levies was that the men recruited served only for a limited period of time before returning home, making it difficult to fight a long campaign. The alternative was to hire mercenaries. Mercenaries cost more than feudal levies, but they could fight at any time throughout the year and this made them increasingly popular with medieval European rulers.[64] Moreover, the almost constant state of warfare in and around Europe and market demands ensured that mercenaries were available in plentiful supply. The Crusades (1095–1291) and the Hundred Years' War (1337–1453) in particular added to the supply of trained soldiers looking for work. Those employed as mercenaries came from a wide variety of national backgrounds, and while some mercenary groups were comprised exclusively of co-nationals, others were multi-national in composition. Moreover, it is interesting to note that not only did the Muslim rulers of Spain hire Christian mercenaries as mentioned above, but Christians in Italy hired Muslim mercenaries.

Although mercenaries no doubt were hired in Western Europe between A.D. 500 and 1000, it is not until the 1000s that written accounts of mercenaries begin to appear with some frequency. The reign of the Umayyad caliph of Córdoba Hisham II al-Hakam (r. 976–1008, 1010–1013) provides a good example of the use of foreign mercenaries by a caliphate. When caliph Hakam II died in 976, Al-Mansur ibn Abi Aamir (aka Almansor) secured the throne for the 12-year-old Hisham by arranging the murder of a rival claimant. Al-Mansur became the young king's vizier and effectively was the ruler of the kingdom. "To consolidate his position, Ibn Abi Amir reorganized the army mainly with Berber and Christian mercenaries, who, hostile to the Arabs, felt no obligations to the state, but rewarded with personal loyalty his [Ibn Abi Aamir's] liberality and tact."[65] Ibn Abi Aamir launched a series of annual attacks on the Christian kingdoms of northern Spain with his mercenary army. As a result of their successes he added the title Al-Mansur (i.e., the victorious) to his name. Ibn Abi Aamir died in 1002 while returning from a campaign against Castile. The kingdom fell on hard times after his death. The Berber mercenaries were given land to settle on, but poor land: "The Berbers, scorned and impoverished in the realm that their arms had won, and relegated to the arid plains of Estremadura or the cold mountains of Leon, periodically revolted against the ruling Arab aristocracy."[66]

The misrule of Ibn Abi Aamir's sons, who served as viziers after their father's death, culminated in a revolt in 1009 led by Muhammad II al-Mahdi, who proclaimed himself caliph and imprisoned Hisham II.[67] A short time thereafter, an army of Berbers led by Sulayman II ibn al-Hakam (aka Sulayman al-Musta'in) in alliance with Sancho Garcia of Castile captured Córdoba and forced Muhammad to flee to Toledo. After the Berbers and Castilians pillaged the city and killed half of its population the Berbers declared Sulayman caliph of Córdoba. Muhammad re-grouped in Toledo and the next year built a new army composed of Slavs and other mercenaries from around Europe. He also allied himself with Ramon Borrell of Barcelona, and their forces defeated Sulayman and re-captured Córdoba. The city was pillaged once again — this time by the Catalans — and Muhammad declared himself caliph again. Muhammad was assassinated by some of his mercenaries a couple of months later and Hisham II was restored to the throne. Meanwhile, Sulayman, who had retreated to Algeciras, re-grouped his Berber forces and in 1013 they captured Córdoba and deposed Hisham II for the final time. Sulayman was forced to make considerable concessions to the Berbers, Slavs, and others that allowed considerable autonomy for the regions beyond Córdoba. A Berber army led by Hammudid of Cauta captured Córdoba in 1016 and Sulayman was executed. After a time the Muslim part of Spain, known as Al-Andalus, was divided into a number of mostly Berber-ruled kingdoms, including those of the Almoravid (1040–1147) and Almohad (1121–1269) dynasties that also ruled over a portion of northwestern Africa.

In addition to the wars in Spain during the 1000s, mercenaries also played a significant role in Normandy's conquest of England. The death of Robert II the Pious in 1031 started off a prolonged war over succession to the throne of France that lasted until 1039. Henry I won but at the cost of the impoverishment of France that resulted in the loss of centralized power and the rise of fairly autonomous principalities. Flanders and Normandy were two of these. Normandy, which was ruled by the descendants of Viking conquerors and had a mixed population of Franks, Gauls, and Norse, emerged as particularly powerful among these principalities under the rule of the Duke of Normandy Robert I's bastard son William I (aka William the Conqueror), who assumed the throne in 1035. His power increased after he married the daughter of the Count of Flanders. The Normans had close relations with England and when King Edward III the Confessor of England died in 1066, William became involved in the struggle to rule England. While Harald Hardradi of Norway invaded England from the north, William invaded from the south with an army that included soldiers recruited from various parts of France.[68] An especially large contingent — as much as one-third of his army — was made up of Flemish mercenaries recruited from his wife's heavily populated homeland of Flanders.

William's conquest had major effects on English society, at least two of which were of direct relevance to mercenaries and transnationalism. One effect was that many of the Flemish mercenaries settled in England after the conquest, and Flemish mercenaries continued to be recruited by subsequent rulers of England over the next century.[69] A second, and generally less known, effect relates to the flight of Anglo-Saxon refugees from England in the wake of the conquest to Constantinople. According to William of Tyre's history, commonly known as the *Latin Chronicle,* written between 1170 and 1184, the largest group of Anglo-Saxon refugees sailed from England to Constantinople on a fleet of 235 ships in the 1070s.[70] The main reason for their choosing this destination appears to be their knowing that the Byzantine Empire was a good employer of mercenaries. As Ciggaar notes, "The Greeks were generous to them and offered them quarters in the capital, a town on the Sea of Marmara (Civetot), jobs and money."[71] In fact, the English replaced Scandinavians as the main members of the Varangian Guard.[72] The Anglo-Saxon refugees also settled along the coast of the Black Sea on the frontier of the Byzantine Empire, where they founded towns with English names.[73]

Back in England after William I's death, a group of Flemish mercenaries under the command of William of Ypres (1. *c.* 1090–1165) — an illegitimate son of one of the sons of Robert I, Count of Flanders, who claimed at various times himself to be the count of Flanders — fought for King Stephen during the English civil war of 1135–54 and appears to have been rewarded by being made Earl of Kent by King Stephen.[74] The anarchy of King Stephen's reign was exacerbated by the brigandage of the mercenaries, and Henry II (r. 1154–1189) gained considerable popularity by putting an end to the employment of Flemish mercenaries shortly after assuming the throne of England.

Despite this populist act, Henry II in fact often made use of mercenaries during his reign. Henry was very much a transnational person. Having been born in France, he was educated in both France and England. His first employment of mercenaries was at the age of 14 when in 1147 he hired a group of mercenaries in France and sailed to England in an ill-fated adventure that ended with him having to seek refuge with his mother and ask his cousin King Stephen to pay what he owed to the mercenaries.[75] As king of England, duke of Normandy, count of Anjou, and duke of Aquitaine, Henry ruled over a large multi-national territory and soon found that he could not do without mercenaries. As Trevelyan remarks,

> A great foreign ruler like Henry II wanted troops whom he could take to Aquitaine or beyond, and keep on foot or horse for more than the feudal forty days. He therefore extended a system begun by Henry I, by which payments called 'scutage' or 'shield-money' were, if the King wished it, received by the Exchequer from Prelates and Barons, in lieu of the military service of their knights enfeoffed upon their lands. The cash could then be used by the King to hire mercenaries either foreign or English.[76]

Thus, mercenaries once again became the mainstay of the army of the king of England, but under Henry II it was a more orderly country in which the mercenaries were more disciplined. The knights meanwhile were "in process of becoming that preeminently English figure — the country gentleman."[77]

Foreign mercenaries appeared in England again towards the end of King John's (r. 1199–1216) reign in relation to his struggle with the barons.[78] Having alienated the barons and much of the rest of the population of England leading up to his signing of the *Magna Carta* in 1215, King John had to rely on support from the Marcher Lords of the English-Welsh border region and on mercenaries that he had hired from Poitou in France.

The Hundred Years' War (1337–1453) provided a setting within which mercenaries were employed but also produced a large number of soldiers who sought employment as mercenaries outside of the war zone. As in England, mercenaries were widely used in France from the 1000s onward. Mercenaries called Brabaçons were especially prominent. Many of these Brabaçons, such as Lobar the Wolf, who was particularly active in southern France in the 1100s, actually were from the Brabant region (the southern Netherlands and northern Belgium), but the bands of Brabaçons commonly included mercenaries from a variety of nations. So-called free companies were the most prominent groups of mercenaries to emerge during the Hundred Years' War.[79] These free companies, called *routiers* (road-men) by the French, were groups of mercenaries who fought in France and generally spread terror throughout the French countryside. As Seward notes, although the French commonly referred to them as English, the majority of them were Gascons and their ranks also included Spaniards, Germans, and other Frenchmen, as well as a few English.[80] Henry II had assumed control of Gascony following his marriage to Eleanor of Aquitaine in 1152, and during the Hundred Years' War the territory passed back and forth between English and French control a number of times. Members of the free companies usually were professional soldiers who had been discharged from regular forces and who joined these bands rather than return to civilian life. Gascon officers commanded most of these companies.

The period of peace between France and England in the 1360s following the signing of the Treaty of Brétigny produced organized bands of mercenaries in France known as Great Companies.[81] *La Compagna Bianca* (the White Company) was one of the earliest of these. It was comprised mainly of Anglo-Navarrese and Gascons who had formerly been supporters of Jean V, the Count of Harcourt, and operated mostly in Provence.[82] The total number of soldiers who joined these companies was around 12,000, "of whom 3,000 to 4,000 were 'really fine soldiers,'" and their officers included Gascons, Bretons, Anglo-Navarrese, English, and Germans.[83] In addition to France, some of these companies also fought in Spain. After war between France and England resumed in 1369 many of these soldiers sought service with the two protagonists.

A number of soldiers from the campaigns of the Hundred Years' War sought employment as mercenaries in Italy where there was considerable demand for their services. As Urban and Jones note, "By the year 1000 secular rulers in Italy were hiring mercenaries to fight against Arabs, Greeks and local enemies" as "were the many bishops and abbots."[84] The first document use of mercenaries in the medieval period was in 1159, "when Pope Alexander [Alexander III] raised a mercenary army to fight Frederik Barbarosa, the Holy Roman emperor."[85] Urban and Jones refer to Barbarosa's grandson Friedrich II von Hohenstraufen (1. 1194–1250) as "the greatest employer of mercenary forces of his era," adding, "Friedrich II's most significant innovation was to hire Arabs and Berbers."[86] Friedrich II was a truly cosmopolitan monarch who ruled over a multi-national empire often with the assistance of armies composed largely of mercenaries, especially to deal with conflicts in Italy.[87] Friedrich grew up in Palermo speaking Sicilian, Greek, and Arabic and learned to speak Latin, German, and French as well. He became king of Sicily in 1198 at the age of 4 and was later to become king of Italy, Germany, and Jerusalem as well as Holy Roman Emperor in 1220. While he spent most of his life in Sicily, the Crusades took him to the Holy Lands and at times he traveled to other parts of Italy as well as to Germany.

Returning crusaders in the 1100s and 1200s helped to fill the ranks of mercenaries in Italy. Some of these crusaders formed themselves into bands of roving soldiers known as *masnada* that like the *routiers* in France often were more bandits than mercenaries. Many of the mercenaries at this time were from the Brabant region as well as from Catalonia and Aragon. Many of those from Aragon were not returning crusaders but had served with King Peter III of Aragon when he invaded Sicily in 1282. The invasion was a success and he became king of Sicily. Many of the soldiers then decided to remain in Italy rather than returning to Aragon.

The 1300s saw the emergence of a new brand of free companies of mercenaries in Italy known as *condottieri* (*condottiero* means contractor and was used to refer to the mercenary leader). They resembled the so-called Great Companies of France.[88] Some of these fought for the papacy, but most were employed by Italian city-states such as Venice, Florence, and Genoa that had amassed considerable wealth from long-distance trade. The first of these was the *Compagnia della Colomba* (Dove Company) that fought for Perugia against Arezzo in 1333. The *Compagnia di San Giorgio* (Company of St. George) was especially prominent in the mid–1300s. Lodrisio Visconti (1. *c.* 1280–1364) of Milan established the company in 1339.[89] It had around 6,500 soldiers, including prominent German mercenaries like Werner von Urslingen and Konrad von Landau as well as Swiss mercenaries from Graubünden, and was financed by Mastino II della Scalla of Verona. Werner von Urslingen (1. *c.* 1308–1354) was from Swabia and initially had fought for Venice against Verona, but later he joined the *Compagnia di San Giorgio.*

The English mercenary John Hawkwood (aka Jean Haccoudem Giovanni Acuto) is by far the most famous of the *condottieri,* being the subject of several biographies[90] and a serial by Arthur Conan Doyle,[91] as well as a series of contemporary novels.[92] Hawkwood served in the English army of Edward III in France during the Hundred Years' War. After the Treaty of Brétigny was signed in 1360 he joined a mercenary company in Burgundy and then became commander of the White Company in Avignon. In 1362 the Marquis of Montferrat (in northern Italy) hired Hawkwood and the White Company to fight in Italy at Lanzo Torinese, Turin, and then against Milan at other locales in the Piedmont. Over the next couple of years Hawkwood and the White Company fought for Pisa against Florence, for Perugia against the Pope, and then for Bernabò Visconti, the Duke of Milan, against Pisa, Milan, and other cities, and against his former employer the Marquis of Montferrat. He left the White Company in the early 1370s and fought for the Pope for a time until he changed sides to fight for anti-papal forces. The 1380s saw Hawkwood fighting for Florence and he eventually became commander of its army in its on-going war with Milan. His success in this regard resulted in his being given citizenship by the city-state and he eventually retired to his estate nearby. Hawkwood had maintained relations with England. King Richard II knighted him and appointed him ambassador to the court of Rome in 1381. When he died in 1394 he was buried in Florence, but King Richard asked that his body be returned to England. He had married an illegitimate daughter of Bernabò Visconti and his son by that marriage also moved to England, even though he had been born in Italy.

The *condottieri* continued to function until the late 1400s, when the emergence of small states in Italy with their own armies and the presence of larger armies of other European states made their service of less value.

Chinese Imperial Armies

The pre-imperial Spring and Autumn and Warring States periods (722–221 B.C.) were characterized by frequent warfare between a number of kingdoms within what is now China, including the seven main protagonists of the Warring States Period (Chu, Han, Qi, Qin, Wei, Yan, and Zhao). Throughout most of this time warfare was conducted on a seasonal basis by feudal armies of skilled soldiers and conscripts largely recruited from within the kingdoms involved, although sometimes rulers would recruit armies of soldiers from outside of their kingdoms. Lewis estimates that the armies of the major states during the Spring and Autumn Period (i.e., before 475 B.C.) numbered around 30,000, whereas during the Warring States Period they grew to between 50,000 and 100,000.[93] The larger armies of the Warring States Period were comprised mostly of conscripted peasants.

Important changes in the nature of the armies took place in the 300s B.C., including the introduction of universal military service and the rise of a class of professional military officers. Shang Yang of Qin introduced a series of reforms in the 350s B.C. that included universal military service linked to registration of population and rewards and punishments to encourage service in the military. "Military success measured by the number of heads of slain enemies was rewarded by promotion in rank" accompanied by the granting of property and slaves with such merits being transferable to one's descendants.[94] Military service was also related to nation building and assimilation in that newly conquered territories were the principal areas for recruitment and discharged soldiers were often given land in frontier areas that were lightly populated.[95]

The most significant transnational figures in relation to military activities during the latter part of the Warring States Period (roughly from the late 300s B.C. until the 260s B.C.) were not generals or soldiers, but courtiers that Lewis refers to as "persuader/diplomats ...

who moved from state to state promising a ruler to secure his interests through alliances that they could obtain through their persuasive skills."[96] There were instances of such individuals serving several states at the same time and it was often difficult to tell where their loyalty lay. Su Qin is the best-known example of these persuader/diplomats. He served the king of Yan at the outset and appears to have remained loyal to him while serving other masters. He managed to dismantle an alliance formed by Qin and create an oppositional alliance for Qi, and then he led Qi into war with Qin, Qi being "the ultimate target of Yan's ambitions."[97]

The army of the Han Empire continued to be comprised mainly of conscripts from within the empire. In general all able-bodied males between the ages of 23 and 56 were required to serve for two years in the army. Loewe estimates that "the total number of men available for call-up may be estimated variously at between 300,000 and 1,000,000," adding, "but it is certain that no Han government was ever able to draft, train, and supply the full potential."[98] It is of interest in relation to transnationalism and the process of Hanization that in addition to conscripts from the commanderies (*chün*) and kingdoms (*kuo*) of the empire — both of these are often referred to as provinces — soldiers were also recruited from the dependent or vassal states associated with the empire and, during the Later Han period in particular, from among the nomadic peoples of the Taklamakan Desert (in modern Xinjiang) who lived to the west of the empire. The latter, however, were generally only recruited for particular campaigns to serve as mounted archers. As for the conscripts from within the integral parts of the empire, they usually spent their first year in their home region being trained as infantry, cavalry, or sailors and then either continued to serve within their home region as garrison conscripts or were sent off to the frontier.[99]

Remaining away from home for such a short time, the scope for developing transnational ties was virtually non-existent for most soldiers. After completion of their service they remained in the local militia and could be called to serve in times of emergency. Nevertheless, there were some officers and other soldiers whose lives were more transnational in character. We have already mentioned Zhang Qian (aka Chang Chien) whom Emperor Wu Di sent as an emissary to the Yuezhi in 138 B.C. because of his knowledge of the nomadic tribes. The establishment of garrisons along the Silk Road in Xinjiang such as at Quici (modern Kucha) provided a context for the development of transnationalism on the part of the soldiers stationed there and the locals who catered to the soldiers' needs as translators, procurers of supplies, and providers of other services. Similar developments no doubt took place in and around frontier outposts to the south in Nam Yue and beyond. While many imperial soldiers remained in these outposts for only a short time, some remained for longer periods. As was already mentioned, when Ban Chao was appointed to the position of Protector of the Western Regions in A.D. 91 he lived in Quici almost until his death in A.D. 102.

The Tang Dynasty relied more heavily than previous imperial regimes on the use of soldiers who were recruited from outside of its borders both as members of its regular army and in times of emergency. We have already discussed the Four Garrisons of Anxi of the Protectorate General to Pacify the West that was established in Xinjiang in A.D. 648, and we have referred to the fact that the troops stationed there often were non–Han from the surrounding area (including Uyghurs and Tibetans). The presence of foreigners in the Tang army was also highlighted in the case of general Gao Xianzhi, of Goguryeo nationality (from modern northern Korea), who led the Tang army in campaigns across Central Asia in the mid–700s, and the Sogdian-Turkic general An Lushan, who had been commander of three northern garrisons and then became leader of the An Shi or An Lushan Rebellion in 755.

The Tang rulers' growing reliance on foreign troops was related to the presence of on-going threats from nomads such as the Eastern Turks and Khitans as well as the Tibetans living beyond the Tang's western and northern borders. Also of concern was the need to maintain garrisons along western trade routes. Among the important developments during the early 700s was the growth in the overall size of the Tang army, the increasing use of for-eigners, and the incorporation of large numbers of these foreigners into the army itself rather than temporary allied units. Peterson estimates that the Tang army on the frontier numbered around 500,000 in the 740s, a figure that was "five times greater than a century earlier."[100] Such numbers affected the nature of the army: "The earlier reliance on a system of small garrisons manned by troops of mixed provenance (militiamen, professional soldiers and convicts) was no longer possible. The militia (*fu-ping*) system, the effectiveness of which was already limited by the turn of the seventh century, could never conceivably have sustained large-scale permanent garrisons on the frontier."[101] A new kind of large permanent army was needed. Longer terms of military service were proclaimed in 737 in order to create a more professional army. Also more permanent regional commands were created along the frontier overseen by military governors. Many of these governors and the soldiers that they com-manded were non–Han, like An Lushan, or from nomadic tribes. The growth of such a strong frontier army coincided with a decline in militias within the empire and the army stationed at the capital.

An Lushan's rebellion saw the mobilization of about 750,000 men by the opposing forces, and even after the rebels were defeated the military remained "a major force in the life of the empire" for the next 50 years.[102] However, in the decentralized post-rebellion Tang Empire the central government no longer exercised much control over the military, and by 763 the provinces had assumed control of the military.[103] However, the military tended to control the provinces rather than the other way around: "The army remained the nucleus of the province. Essential for the security of the province, it usually absorbed the major share of local revenue."[104] Many of the provinces came to be dominated by military governors who paid little heed to central authority. An inner army (*ya-nei-chüm*) that was based in the headquarters garrison and composed of professional soldiers dominated these provincial armies. Under this decentralized system local army units also tended to be manned by local people rather than being drawn from various parts of the empire or beyond. Not always trusting the loyalty of local troops, some governors formed units that served as per-sonal bodyguards. These units were independent of the provincial army and loyal to the governor himself. The governors paid for such troops out of their personal funds and they moved with their employer.[105] Emperor Xian Zong of Tang (aka Hsien-tsung, r. 805–820) sought to curb the power of the more independent minded military governors. He waged wars against several of them and by 817 had re-unified the empire once again. This central-ization was short-lived and after his death the Tang Empire once again started to crumble.

The Aztec Military

The Aztecs provide an example of the militaries of the New World empires. The military forces that the Aztecs employed reflect the nature of their empire, which was cobbled together with allies and vassals that included a variety of city-states and tribal groups. The

Aztecs lacked a standing army. There were military orders, but even these people assumed their military duties only when called upon. This does not imply that the Aztecs were militarily weak — far from it, but there were important logistical constraints on their army. As Valliant remarks, "Due to the governmental system, wherein each town was independent, the armies did not dare live off the country for fear of inciting revolt and also because most communities lacked the food to sustain a large body of men."[106] Supplies thus had to be arranged for in advance of a campaign with the imperial granaries playing an important role. Sieges and long campaigns were not possible: "Usually a single battle decided the issue, since the attacking force could not maintain itself in the field for more than a very few days."[107] In cases of a distant war, say in Oaxaca, complex logistical calculations were required and "much of the Aztec force on such a campaign must have been composed of local tribesmen, stiffened with a *garde d'élite* of Tenochcas and Texcocans."[108] Hassig notes, "In the field the Aztec army required, and received, considerable auxiliary support in the form of Aztec colonists relocated in potentially troublesome areas, supplies provided as tribute en route, allied troops from various places in the empire, and local troops manning the frontier in lieu of tribute."[109]

Thus, the Aztec military was multi-ethnic and transnational both in terms of manpower and provisioning. The core of the army consisted of troops from the city-states of the Triple Alliance (Tenochtitlan, Texcoco, and Tlacopan) as well as from other city-states in the Valley of Mexico such as Mexicalzongo, Chimalhuacan, Acolman, Xochimilco, Chalco, Culhuacan, Ixtapalapa, and Huitzilopochco.[110] Beyond this the remainder of the army in any particular campaign varied since the army collected additional troops on the way as well as once it arrived in the general area of combat. In regard to mobilizing an army, "Although technically a standing army may have been absent, the existence of military ranks, grades, and offices clearly indicates a military infrastructure running through Aztec society, providing the organizational basis for mobilization."[111] Vaillant points out that "each quarter of the town had its tlacochcalco, or house of darts, an arsenal where the military supplies were stored.... At a call to arms the clan leaders could rapidly assemble their men and equip them."[112] All of the vassal states of the empire were subject to such mobilization. Peoples and towns in frontier areas were sometimes exempted from paying tribute in return for military service. Hassig mentions the Yopes of Guerrero, the Tlaxcalans, and the Tarascans of Michoacan, the towns of Acapetlaguaya and Teloloapa in Guerrero, and the Mixtec town of Tamazola in Oaxaca in this regard.[113] It should be noted that most Tlaxcalans and Tarascans — like the Germanic tribes along the Roman Empire's border and many of the nomadic groups of Mongolia and Xinjiang — lived outside of the empire and both groups were able to successfully thwart Aztec efforts to conquer them.

The Aztecs built fortified garrisons throughout their empire. However, those in relatively secure areas were occupied by Aztec troops only when conflicts required a military presence. In times of peace the local population was responsible for looking after the garrison. Permanent garrisons of Aztec troops were created only "adjacent to hostile polities and areas of imperial expansion" such as the Tarascan and Chichimec areas to the north and the Gulf Coast to the southeast. Such frontier garrisons were often augmented by the presence of Aztec colonists who were settled in potentially troublesome areas. Hassig mentions that unmarried men from Tenochtitlan, Texcoco, and Tlacopan in the Valley of Mexico, as well as from some more distant towns, were recruited to settle in these distant frontier regions.[115]

10

Monks and Scholars

This book began with an ancient example of transnationalism in relation to religion in Western Europe. While early religions tended to be fairly localized, pilgrimages appear to have a very long history and became even more common as the religions that achieved prominence in the ancient and medieval worlds spread beyond their points of origin, often along trade routes or as a result of conquest. This movement of religions across borders tended to lead to the creation of transnational links both during their outward spread and once they were established in diverse parts of the world.

The spread of religions beyond the point of origin influences transnationalism in a number of ways. For one thing it creates a pool of people across borders who share certain beliefs and have a sense of being connected to one another. There is also an important linguistic component since the primary language used by followers of a religion tends to be spread with its beliefs. Prominent examples include Greek and Latin in the case of Christianity, Sanskrit in the case of Buddhism and Hinduism, and Arabic in the case of Islam. This does not mean that all followers of a religion are fluent in the language, but that at least there is a group of religious specialists in a variety of nations who share the use of the language and are able to communicate with one another using it.

In addition to ideas and languages, the spread of religions also leads to the movement of people across borders. Those involved in spreading a religion are commonly referred to as missionaries. While in the past many missionaries went on a one-way trip, they nevertheless commonly maintained transnational relations with other members of their religion through correspondence or interaction with visitors. Once established, transnational relations among followers of a religion were maintained in a variety of ways, including through formal transnational organizations and by the promotion of visits to holy sites in the form of pilgrimages.

Scholarship has been closely related to religion throughout human history and during the ancient and medieval periods this was particularly so. However, there is also a long tradition of secular scholarship in some parts of the world, especially around the Mediterranean. In the past, just as today, most religious and secular scholars work and live in the countries where they were born. However, even in ancient times there were also a significant number of scholars employed outside of the countries of their birth. Moreover, transnational scholars are not a new phenomenon and there are records of scholars roaming across borders in antiquity. As in modern times, students and scholars in the past were often attracted to centers of learning away from their homes. Often when crossing borders they would move to places sharing a common language or cultural heritage with their own. The creation of empires assisted scholarly mobility by making it possible for scholars to move about to different regions within imperial borders. As we will see the spread of religions is especially noteworthy for encouraging the movement of religious scholars across borders to study with co-religionists, often well beyond their homelands and even outside of the empires where they lived.

Transnational Buddhists

Understanding the early transnational spread of Buddhism is sometimes difficult since the references to it are often of a quasi-mythical nature, but in general its initial spread is closely associated with Emperor Asoka, his conversion, and subsequent support of the religion. Asoka converted to Buddhism in reaction to the brutality of the Kalinga War (265–263 B.C.). Asoka's wife, Queen Devi, was already a Buddhist and had brought up their children, Prince Mahamahinda (aka Mahinda) and Princess Sanghamitra (aka Sanghamittaa), as Buddhists. After his conversion Asoka became a great patron of Buddhism, resulting in large numbers of people joining the Buddhist Sangha (monastic order). Asoka and Devi's two children asked their father permission to join the Sangha as well, which he granted. As Perera comments, "Vast numbers joined the Order in the reign of Asoka solely to share the benefits showered on it by the king, and such people were not only lax in their conduct, but also held doctrines counter to the teachings of the Buddha."[1] It was in an effort to reform the practice of Buddhism that Asoka convened the 3rd Buddhist Council (which came to be associated with the Vibhajjavada or Theravada school of Buddhism) in Pataliputra (modern Patna) around 250 B.C.

The 3rd Buddhist Council led to Asoka sponsoring the sending of numerous Buddhist missionaries (*dharma bhanaks*) beyond his empire. Chapter 12 of the *Mahavamsa* (aka *Great Chronicle*) of Sri Lanka, "The Converting of Different Countries," mentions Asoka sending missionaries to the following countries: Gandhara, Mahisamandala (Mysore), Banavasi (Karnataka), Aparantaka (northwestern India and Pakistan), Maharattha (Maharashtra), Himavanta (Nepal), Lankapida (Sri Lanka), Suvannabhumi (a Mon kingdom in southern Burma and central Thailand), and the Country of the Yona (the Seleucid Empire, Bactria).[2]

Chapter 13 of the *Mahavamsa*, "The Coming of Mahinda," describes how Asoka's son Mahinda brought Buddhism to Sri Lanka. It says that the prince, considering it more opportune, waited until the old king of Lankapida, Mutasiva, had died and his son Devaanampiya Tissa (aka Devanampiyatissa) had assumed the throne to travel to Sri Lanka. Prior to assuming the throne Devaanampiya Tissa was known to have been well disposed towards Asoka. As soon as he became king he sent envoys to Asoka "bearing costly presents." The envoys returned with a message from Asoka attesting to his conversion to Buddhism. Prince Mahinda, accompanied by a number of other monks — including one who was the son of his sister Princess Sanghamitra — and lay followers arrived in Sri Lanka a month later. According to the *Mahavamsa*, Mahinda and his companions "rose up in the air" at Vedisagiri and then "alighted" on Mihintale mountain near the kingdom's capital city of Anuradhapura, where he met the king who was there hunting: "There he [the king] saw the theras [monks] with shaven heads dressed in yellow robes, of dignified mien and distinguished appearance, who faced him and addressed him not as ordinary men addressing a king but as those to whom a king was their inferior. The conversation impressed the king and his immediate surrender to the wisdom and piety displayed by the thera was complete." For his part, "Mahinda then had a conversation with the king, and realizing that the king was intelligent enough to comprehend the Dhamma, preached the Cuulahatthipadopama Sutta. At the end of the discourse the king and his retinue of forty thousand people embraced the new faith. Having invited the missionaries to the city the king left for his palace." While it is obvious that the events did not happen precisely as recorded in the *Mahavamsa,* especially in regard to Mahinda flying to Sri Lanka, the account does provide insights into the dynamics of the spread of Buddhism to Sri Lanka and to the important role played by the respective rulers.

Chapter 17 of the *Mahavamsa* says that one of the things the Buddha resolved on his deathbed was that a branch of the Bodhi tree under which he had attained enlightenment at Bodh Gaya should be taken to Sri Lanka. Beyond the symbolic interpretation of spreading the religion to Sri Lanka, one year after her brother had gone to Sri Lanka Princess Sanghamitra is believed to have taken an actual branch of the tree to Anuradhapura, where the king planted it in a ceremony attended by numerous nobles from around Sri Lanka. She appears to have first taken the branch to Pataliputra and from there to the port of Tamralipti (modern Tamluk) on the Bay of Bengal. From Tamralipti she sailed to the Sri Lankan port of Jambukola (north of Jaffna) and then on to Anuradhapura. The tree is now known as Sri Maha Bodhiya and it is one of the Eight Great Places of Veneration (Atamasthana) in Anuradhapura.

Following the mass conversions in Sri Lanka the island emerged as a secondary center of Buddhism after northern India. This role was also manifest in the distribution of Buddha relics. After the Buddha was cremated a number of body parts that remained (e.g., teeth and bones) were distributed as relics. The number of relics and their whereabouts is uncertain, but the best provenanced one is a canine tooth (which one is subject to dispute). The tooth initially was in the possession of King Bramadatta of Kasi and was kept in the city of Dantapuri (modern Puri, Orissa). The Sacred Tooth Relic, as it was known, came to be linked to the right to rule over the region and, not surprisingly, generated considerable conflict between those seeking to possess it. According to legend, in the A.D. 300s the relic had come into the possession of King Guhasiva of Kalinga. King Kshiradara sought to destroy the relic and led an army against Kalinga. King Kshiradara died in battle, but his sons raised a new army to renew the attack. Faced with the threat of the relic's destruction King Guhasiva's daughter Hemamala and her husband prince Dantha from Udeni disguised themselves as Brahmins and smuggled the relic out of the city to the port of Tamralipti. From there they sailed to the port of Lankapattana in Sri Lanka and then brought the relic to King Kirthi Sri Meghavarma (r. A.D. 301–328), who placed it in the Meghagiri Vihara in Anuradhapura. The relic then became associated with the right of the king of Sri Lanka to rule, and it was subsequently moved to various shrines close to the royal palaces (it is presently in the Sri Dalada Maligawa shrine in Kandy).

The Yona (Greeks, i.e., Ionians) appear not only to have been conspicuous among those converted to Buddhism at this time (one of the Buddha relic canine teeth is also said to have been sent to Gandhara), but also subsequently to have been prominent among Buddhist missionaries who traveled elsewhere to spread the religion. Chapter 12 of the *Mahavamsa* mentions a Yona monk named Dharmaraksita (aka Dhammarakkhita) as being responsible for spreading Buddhism to Aparataka—i.e., western countries.[3] The *Milinda Panha,* which was written around 100 B.C., mentions a student of Dharmaraksita's named Nagasena converted the Hellenic Bactrian king Menander I Soter (aka Milinda, r. 155–130 B.C.) to Buddhism.[4] After his conversion Menander I in turn was influential in spreading

Buddhism throughout the western part of South Asia (Pakistan, Kashmir, and Afghanistan) and into Central Asia (Uzbekistan, Turkmenistan, and Tajikistan) and eastern parts of Iran. Chapter 29 of the *Mahavamsa* mentions a Yona monk named Mahadhammarakkhita (aka Mahadharmaksita) as traveling from the city of Alasanda (near modern Kabul) to Sri Lanka at the head of 30,000 monks to take part in the foundation ceremony of the Maha Thupa (Great Stupa) at Anuradhapura during the reign of Menander I.

Edict 13 of the 14 *Rock Edicts of King Asoka* adds to the list of places visited by Buddhist monks:

> There is no country, except among the Greeks, where these two groups, Brahmans and ascetics, are not found, and there is no country where people are not devoted to one or another religion.... Now it is conquest by Dhamma that Beloved-of-the-Gods considers to be the best conquest. And it [conquest by Dhamma] has been won here, on the borders, even six hundred yojanas away, where the Greek king Antiochos rules, beyond there where the four kings named Ptolemy, Antigonos, Magas and Alexander rule, likewise in the south among the Cholas, the Pandyas, and as far as Tamraparni. Here in the king's domain among the Greeks, the Kambojas, the Nabhakas, the Nabhapamkits, the Bhojas, the Pitinikas, the Andhras and the Palidas, everywhere people are following Beloved-of-the-Gods' instructions in Dhamma.[5]

Who are the people and places referred to in the above passage? Antiochos refers to Antiochus II Theos of the Seleucid Empire. Ptolemy refers to Ptolemy II Philadelphus of Egypt. Antignos refers to Antigonus II Gonatas of Macedon. Magas refers to Magas of Cyrene (modern Libya). Alexander refers to Alexander II of Epirus (located in parts of modern Greece and Albania). The Cholas and Pandyas lived in southern India beyond Asoka's empire. The remaining names refer to peoples living within his empire.

There is evidence, albeit very limited, that Buddhism also spread beyond the Hellenic world of the eastern Mediterranean into Europe. The evidence comes from a brief passage by Saint Origen (l. *c.* 185–254), an Egyptian who lived mainly in Alexandria and also spent time in Rome, Petra, and Caesarea.[6] Origen wrote in his *Commentary on Ezekiel,* "The island [Britain] has long been predisposed to it [Christianity] through the doctrines of the Druids and Buddhists, who already inculcated the doctrine of the Godhead." It is interesting to note that Origen favored the doctrine of rebirth and reincarnation and sought unsuccessfully to have them become part of Christian doctrine.

We have already mentioned how Buddhism survived in the tolerant environment of the Parthian Empire and how the Parthian prince An Shigao (aka An Shih-kao) renounced his title to become a monk and then traveled along the Silk Road to the Han capital of Luoyang where he introduced Buddhism to China in A.D. 148. In addition to An Shigao and some fellow Parthians, Sogdians and various monks from Central Asia also went to China to teach and translate Buddhist texts under the Han Dynasty and later. The Silk Road served as a conduit for the spread of Buddhism not only to China, but also to parts of Central Asia along its route. The spread of Buddhism along the Silk Road was a two-way affair. As Buddhism became entrenched in China, Chinese Mahayana Buddhism spread back along the Silk Road, especially among those engaged in trade with China. Thus, "on the whole, the Sogdian Buddhists were converted to Mahayana Buddhism by the Chinese, whose language they had learned for the sake of trade."[7]

Once Buddhism was established in these areas people travelled in both directions along the Silk Road to visit centers of Buddhist learning. This not only entailed going to centers in China and South Asia, but also to centers that developed along the Silk Road itself. Khotan (aka Hotan, modern Hetian), Turfan (modern Turpan), and Kucha (aka Quichi) were the three most important of these. Kucha was associated primarily with the Sarvastivada (aka Sarvastivadin) sect of Kasmira (modern Kashmir).[8] It attracted monks from neighboring regions, and its own monks traveled abroad. For example, one named Po-Yen went to Luoyang between A.D. 256 and 260 to translate Buddhist texts into Chinese. The Saka peoples of Turfan converted to Buddhism as early as A.D. 84 and employed a variant of Brahmi script to translate Buddhist texts into their own language. The city was a center of Mahayana Buddhism, attracting Chinese pilgrims, and continued to flourish as a Buddhist center into the 900s and to function as one even for a time after Muslims conquered it in the 1000s.[9]

The city of Khotan had been a Kushan center for the jade trade with the Chinese since early times and became a multi-cultural and multi-lingual entrepôt along the Silk Road and capital of the Kingdom of Khotan. People spoke various Central Asian, Indian, and Sinitic languages. The kingdom was a vassal of the Han and Tang at various times and under Tibetan rule for a short period in the 700s, before becoming a Tang vassal again. One of the kings of Khotan, Yuchi Gui (r. c. 737–746), persecuted the resident Buddhist monks, forcing them to flee to Tibet and later from there to Gandhara, but the town later re-emerged as a Buddhist center until its conquest by the Muslim Yusuf Qadr Khan in 1006.[10] A number of monks from Khotan (e.g., Devaprajna, Siksananda, and Siladharma) traveled to Luoyang and Chang'an to teach and translate Buddhist texts, and Chinese Buddhists also visited Khotan.[11]

There is some controversy about when Buddhism was introduced to northern Vietnam. Some Vietnamese, such as Tam Ha Le Cong Da, believe that missionaries sent by Asoka introduced it: "Now, in Haiphong ... there is a memorial tower to commemorate King Asoka that was built by local Vietnamese Buddhists at that time to express their gratitude to King Asoka."[12] Most scholars, however, associate it with Mau Bac (aka Mecu Fo and Mou Po in Chinese; b. c. A.D. 165–70).[13] During his time what is now northern Vietnam was part of the Han Empire. He was from Wu Chau (within modern Hong Kong) and had converted from Taoism to Buddhism around 190. Conflicts between Confucians and Buddhists at the time led him to go to northern Vietnam around A.D. 194–5, where he proselytized and gained followers. He was also the author of an influential book on Buddhism named *Reason and Doubt*. Northern Vietnam's location along the maritime trade route between India and China served to bolster its role as a center for Buddhist scholarship and propagation of Buddhism with monks coming there from both India and China. Tran mentions that Buddhism in northern Vietnam was spread not only by monks and religious refugees, but also by diplomatic envoys and merchants.[14] An Indian trader named Kang Seng Huei (aka Khang Tang Hoi, d. A.D. 280) came to northern Vietnam on a commercial trip with his father and converted to Buddhism while there. He was ordained as a monk, became a famous translator of Buddhist writings, and actively engaged in proselytizing. Among those that he converted was Suen Kuian, the ruler of the kingdom of Wu.

The outward spread of Buddhism from its place of origin in northeastern India created transnational links that led back to the Buddhist homeland on the part of Buddhist scholars and pilgrims. There are eight particularly important places of pilgrimage for Buddhists located in the Gangetic plains of northern India and southern Nepal. They are known as the *Atthamahathanani* or the Eight Great Places. Four of these were mentioned by Gautama Buddha as being suitable for pilgrimage: Lumbini (located in modern Nepal), where he was born (Kapilavastu, Kapilavatthu); Bodh Gaya, the place of his enlightenment, located in the Mahabodhi temple; Sarnath (formerly called Isipathana), where he delivered his first teaching (where he turned the wheel of Dharma); and Kusinara, where he died, located in

Kushinagar, India. These four places are mentioned in Part 5 "At Kusinara" (passages 16–20) of the *Maha-Parinibbana Sutta,* which then goes on to state (passages 21–22):

> "'These, Ananda, are the four places that a pious person should visit and look upon with feelings of reverence. And truly there will come to these places, Ananda, pious bhikkhus and bhikkhunis, laymen and laywomen, reflecting: 'Here the Tathagata was born! Here the Tathagata became fully enlightened in unsurpassed, supreme Enlightenment! Here the Tathagata set rolling the unexcelled Wheel of the Dhamma! Here the Tathagata passed away into the state of Nibbana in which no element of clinging remains! And whoever, Ananda, should die on such a pilgrimage with his heart established in faith, at the breaking up of the body, after death, will be reborn in a realm of heavenly happiness.'"

Four other places were added to the list later as pilgrimage sites because Buddha had performed an important miracle there. These are: Sravasti, "Place of the Twin Miracle," where Buddha spent the most time; Rajgir, "Place of the subduing of Nalagiri" (an angry elephant); Sankasia, "Place of descending to earth from Tusita heaven"; and Vaishali (aka Vesali), "Place of receiving an offering of honey from a monkey" and capital of the ancient Vajjian republic.

Emperor Asoka championed pilgrimages (referred to as *dhammayatra,* dhamma expedition) to the Eight Great Places and conducted such a pilgrimage himself in 249 B.C. At each locale he had stupas built and pillars made of polished sandstone erected. With the decline of Buddhism in India these structures fell into decay, but his pillars can still be seen at Lumbini and Vaishali. In addition to these sacred sites Buddhists from around Asia were also attracted to India and Sri Lanka to seek out Buddhist texts.

There are a number of famous Chinese monks who made arduous journeys to visit Buddhist sites and centers of learning in South Asia after the time of the Han Empire. Fa Xian (aka Fa Hsien, Fa Hien) appears to have been the first of these monks. He left a written account of his travels to India and Sri Lanka from A.D. 399 to 413.[15] Fa Xian was born in Wuyang, Shanxi, and then studied as a monk in Chang'an. Fa Xian organized an expedition to go to India to collect copies of Buddhist scripts and images with other Buddhist scholars. He and his companions traveled overland to Dunhuang, and then, walking through the Taklamakan desert (modern Xinjiang) beyond the western borders of China, they entered the Buddhist kingdom of Khotan on the southern edge of the desert and remained in its capital for three months. Next they walked over the Pamirs and Hindu Kush, entering India via Gandhara and Punjab. The monks that they met in India said that Fa Xian and his colleagues were the first Chinese monks to visit them since Buddhism had been introduced to China. By the time that he reached Pataliputra Fa Xian was accompanied by only one other companion who at this point decided to remain in India, leaving Fa Xian to travel on his own.

Fa Xian visited the sacred places of Buddhism (e.g., Nalanda and Bodh Gaya) and then returned to Pataliputra. He then traveled down the Ganges by boat to the port of Tamralipti. From there he sailed to Sri Lanka on a large merchant vessel. The voyage took him two weeks. Fa Xian remained in Sri Lanka for two years and then "took passage on board a large merchant-vessel on which there were over 200 souls, and astern of which there was a smaller vessel in tow, in case of accident at sea and destruction of the big vessel."[16] This precaution proved fortunate, for two days out from Sri Lanka they encountered a storm that lasted for 13 days. The merchant vessel finally sank near an island. Fa Xian and the survivors sailed on for another 90 days until reaching Java, where he stayed for about five months. He then took passage on another large merchant vessel that he says carried over 200 persons. This ship was struck by another storm that caused the captain to lose his reckoning. Lost and with provisions for only 50 days, they sailed in one direction for 70 days before the captain changed direction, and they sailed for another 12 days before reaching land. Fa Xian returned to China, landing on the coast.

Fa Xian visited about 30 countries during his 14 years away from China. He spent six of these years travelling and another six in India studying. He remained in one place for three years to learn Sanskrit so that he would be able to copy any manuscripts that he found, although in fact he found few documents to copy since most learning in India, as in China, was passed on orally. His trip points to the difficulty of travel in Asia during this period, but also to the existence of significant and fairly regular maritime commerce.

The period of the Tang Dynasty (618–907) witnessed an increase in the number of Buddhist monks and pilgrims travelling from East Asia to South Asia. Xuanzang (aka Hsüan Tsang, 1. c. 602–664) is the most famous of these Chinese Buddhist travelers to visit India at this time.[17] His account of his travels between 629 and 645, *Record of the Western World*,[18] provided the basis for the popular fictional *Journey to the West* that was written in the 1590s.[19] Xuanzang left Chang'an in 629, but had to avoid Dunhuang since he did not have the emperor's permission to leave China. Next he traveled to the oasis city of Turfan. With the assistance of the local ruler Xuanzang was able to continue on his journey along the Silk Road to Tashkent, Samarkand, Bamiyan (aka Bamyan, capital of the Buddhist Kushan-Hephthalite kingdom, where the Taliban destroyed its famous Buddhist images in 2001), Peshawar, and then to Taxila. Xuanzang remained in Taxila for two years studying at a Buddhist monastery and then went to study at the Buddhist university at Nalanda for an additional two years. Xuanzang visited the region's major Buddhist sacred sites before leaving India. In 645 he returned to China over the Silk Road.

Xuanzang's writings, which include descriptions of important Buddhist sites in India, served as inspiration for subsequent Buddhist travelers from China, including Yijing (aka I-Ching, 1. 635–713). Yijing wrote a biography that includes an account of earlier monks who had traveled to India and neighboring counties. He also traveled there himself over a 25-year period between 673 and 687.[20] Yijing left China by sea, setting sail on a Persian ship from Guangzhou. His first stop was Srivijaya (Palembang), which was an important center of Buddhist scholarship at the time. He then traveled along the coast of the Malay Peninsula to the east coast of India. He headed overland to the Indian center of Buddhist learning at Nalanda with a group of merchants and was robbed along the way after being left behind by the merchants when he fell sick. Yijing remained in Nalanda studying at its Buddhist university for 11 years and then went back to Srivijaya for a time to work on his translation into Chinese of the 400 manuscripts that he had collected and copied before returning to China by sea.

Buddhist relations between India and China developed into more of a two-way affair under the Tang Dynasty. Nalanda's university had emerged as an important center for the teaching of Vajrayana or Tantric Buddhism by the A.D. 600s and it was to remain one into the 1000s. The Buddhist monk Subhakarasimha (1. A.D 637–735) arrived in Chang'an from Nalanda in 716. A member of a royal family, he had given up a throne to become a monk and study under the Vajrayana master Dharmagupta at Nalanda. It was Dharmagupta who told Subhakarasimha to go to China.[21] Almost 80 years old when he arrived in Chang'an, Subhakarasimha quickly built a reputation for his supernatural abilities, and the Emperor Xuanzong sought his services.

Another Buddhist monk named Vajrabodhi (1. 671–741) arrived in Chang'an a few years later. Vajrabodhi was the son of a south Indian Brahmin who converted to Buddhism and came to Nalanda to study under Nagabodhi. After leaving Nalanda he did not go directly to China, but first went to Sri Lanka and then sailed on to Srivijaya, where he taught a version of Vajrayana Buddhism. In 720 he took passage on a large fleet of 35 Persian merchant vessels that had stopped at Srivijaya on its way to China. He took up residence at Jianfu Temple in Chang'an where he too soon gained a substantial reputation and attracted the patronage of Tang nobles as well as students from within China and abroad.

Amoghavajra (1. 705–774) was one of these students—one who became even more renowned than his master. Amoghavajra was born in Samarkand of an Indian father and Sogdian mother. He came to Chang'an to study Buddhism and was ordained by Vajrabodhi in 719 and became his disciple. When foreign monks were expelled from China in 741, Amoghavajra used this as an opportunity to go on a pilgrimage with several others and traveled to Southeast Asia, Sri Lanka, and India. He spent some of this time studying under Nagabodhi. When foreign monks were allowed in China once again, Amoghavajra returned to China in 746, bringing with him around 500 Buddhist texts. Back in China he became famous for performing rites to avert disasters and performed such rites for Emperor Daizong (r. 727–779).

Hye-ch'o (aka Hyecho, Hui Chao, 1. *c.* 704–787) from the Korean kingdom of Silla also came to Chang'an to study with Vajrabodhi. At Vajrabodhi's urging Hye-ch'o made a pilgrimage to India, arriving in Tamralipti in 723. In addition to visiting the major Buddhist sacred sites he traveled extensively around India. Hye-ch'o returned to China overland by the Silk Road through Central Asia in 729. Back in China he settled at Chang'an to work with Vajrabodhi and Amoghavajra translating texts. He also produced a diary and commentary on his travels.[22]

Ximing Temple in Chang'an, which was established under the patronage of Emperor Gao Zong in 656, became one of the most important centers of Buddhist scholarship in Chang'an during the Tang Dynasty. Both Xuanzang and Yijing resided at the temple after their travels to work on translating the manuscripts that they had brought back from India, and Ximing came to have the most important Buddhist library in China at the time. The famous Korean monk Woncheuk (aka Yuance, Ximing Fashi, 1. 613–696) also lived at the temple for a time. One of Amoghavajra's disciples named Hui-kuo (aka Hui-Gu0, 1. 746–805) became a master at Ximing along with the Gandharan monk Prajna (1. *c.* 734–810). Prajna was from Gandhara (modern Afghanistan) and had studied at Nalanda university before coming to China. In addition to numerous Chinese students, these two masters attracted students from Korea, Japan, Central Asia, and Java.

The movement of monks back and forth between China and Japan starting in the A.D. 700s played an important role in the development of Buddhism in Japan.[23] A Chinese monk named Daoxuan (aka Tao-hsüan, Dosen, 1. 702–760) introduced the Flower Garden school of Buddhism to Japan in 736. Next, in 740, a Korean monk named Sim-sang (aka Shinjo) from the kingdom of Silla who had studied the Flower Garden Sutra in China came to Japan to lecture on the sutra. He is considered the founder of this school in Japan and was among the monks who presided at the ceremony to consecrate the great image of Vairochana Buddha at the Todai-ji temple in Nara in 752.

In 742 a Japanese ambassador to China invited a monk from the Daming Temple in Yangzhou, Jiangsu, named Jiangzhen (aka Ganjin) to visit Japan. His story highlights the difficulties of travel between China and Japan in those days. Jiangzhen had studied in Chang'an and was a senior monk at the Daming Temple at the time. Although his fellow monks urged him not to go, the following year he made his first attempt to sail to Japan.

This effort ended in failure, as did the next four because of bad weather or government opposition. The last of these unsuccessful efforts in 748 was the most harrowing. The ship that he was on met a storm that carried it far to the south to Hainan Island. Jiangzhen crossed over to the mainland, traveled along the Gan and Yangtze rivers, and finally reached home again after three years. An infection that he developed on this trip had left him blind, but he persisted in his hope of taking Buddhist teachings to Japan. Finally, in 753 he and a group of his followers were able to join the party of another Japanese ambassador to China on his return voyage to Japan. Although the voyage also met with difficulties, after several months the ship finally landed at Kogoshima on the southern Japanese island of Kyushu. From there he traveled north to meet the Japanese emperor at Nara. He ordained the former emperor Shomu and empress Komyo in 758 and remained in Nara until his death in 763.

As Buddhism developed in Japan during the latter part of the 700s there was a growing sense of the need to send Japanese monks directly to China to study and to copy and collect Buddhist manuscripts in an effort to strengthen and purify the religion — a sentiment akin to the earlier motives of Chinese monks for making the trip to India. A program to do so was supported by the emperor who now resided in Kyoto, which had become the capital in 795. Mount Hiei was northeast of the capital and because of its direction the court's priests considered it dangerous. A monk named Saicho (1. 767–822) had taken up residence on the mountain in 785 and his presence was considered to protect the new capital. This brought him to the attention of the court, which in 803 asked Saicho to accompany the ships of the official mission to China on their voyage.[24] Saicho had studied texts of the Chinese Tien-t'ai sect (aka Tiantai) that had been brought to Japan in 754 and hoped specifically to study and collect texts related the sect. The ships were damaged during a storm and forced to return to Kyushu. The fleet set out again about a year later, carrying Saicho along with several other monks including Kukai (aka Kobo Daishi, 1. 774–835).

The fleet that set sail in 804 also encountered rough weather and two ships were lost. The ship carrying Saicho survived the storm and made it to the port of Mingzhou (modern Ningbo, Zhejiang), while the ship carrying Kukai made land further south at the port of Fuzhou (Fujian province). After a period of recuperation, Saicho went to the monastery at Mount Tiantong near Mingzhou to study Tien-t'ai Buddhism, while Kukai went to Chang'an, where he studied esoteric Tantric Buddhism under Hui-kuo and Sanskrit under Prajna at Ximing Temple.[25] Saicho returned to Japan in 805 and went on to become the founder of the Tiantai sect (aka the White Lotus School) of Buddhism in Japan in 809. Kukai returned in 806 and established a monastery near Osaka in 819, which became the headquarters for the Shingon sect of Buddhism. Saicho is of particular interest in regard to transnationalism: "Saicho looked upon himself as the first in a series of Japanese monks who were to go to China to study. He hoped to send other Japanese monks later and to be able to maintain one long-term and one short-term student in China at all times. He even had a hall built at the Ch'an-lin-ssu monastery which was to serve as living quarters for Japanese students."[26] The hall was destroyed in 845, but was later rebuilt and such a center for Japanese monks remained in operation well into the Northern Song Dynasty.

Among Saicho's disciples was one named Ennin (1. c. 794–864), who went to China in 838 to study Tien-t'ai as well as Esoteric Buddhism. Ennin remained in China until 847 and brought back a large number of sutras and religious items with him to Japan. He became the chief abbot of the Tendai sect in 854 and was influential in the sect's coming to be dominated by Esoteric Buddhism. He wrote numerous books, including a diary of his travels in China.[27]

While their journeys are not as well documented as those of the monks who traveled to China during the Tang period, it appears as if at least a few Japanese also made the effort to travel to India. For example, Kasetsiri mentions a religiously minded Japanese prince who visited the Mon city-state of Lopburi in the 700s on his way between China and India in search of Buddhist texts.[28] In this instance the prince died in Lopburi before reaching India.

Japanese Buddhists continued to travel to China during the time of the Southern Song Dynasty (1127–1279), although for political and ideological reasons their trips now focused on pilgrimages to the Tiantong Monastery in Zhejiang. The Tendai sect monk Eisai (1. 1141–1215) made a pilgrimage to Tiantai monasteries in Zhejiang in 1168 to gather texts and study over a five-month period. He made a second trip to China in 1187 "intending to go to India, but the Chinese Song authorities refused him the necessary travel documents."[29] Unable to go to India, Eisai stayed in China for four years studying with Xu'an Huaichang (1. *c.* 1125–1195), who was a master of the Chan sect of Linzi (aka Zen sect of Rinzai). As a result of these studies, Eisai came to promote the combination of meditation with Esoteric Buddhism upon his return to Japan. Eisai is also closely associated with the popularity of green tea in Japan. Tea had become a popular fixture in Chinese monasteries during the Tang Dynasty, the monks considering it helpful for meditation and for quelling hunger in the afternoon.[30] Accordingly, both Saicho and Kukai brought tea seeds back with them in the early 800s. Eisai also brought back tea seeds that were given to another monk named Myoe Shonin and became the basis for the green tea of Uji (now a suburb of Kyoto). Eisai also wrote Japan's first book devoted to tea, *Kissa Yojoki* (How to Stay Healthy by Drinking Tea), in 1211. Dôgen Kigen (1. 1200–1253) was another prominent monk from Kyoto to visit China during the Southern Song period. He sailed to Mingzhou in 1223, studied at Tiantong Monastery, and visited monasteries in Zhejiang.

The decline of Buddhism in India by the 1200s and the shift of its center to Sri Lanka as well as political instability in China resulted in a virtual end to Buddhist pilgrimages to India and China during the remainder of the medieval period. During the later part of the medieval period Buddhism lost ground to Confucians, Hindus, Christians, and Muslims in many parts of Asia and Europe. It held its ground and continued to gain adherents mainly in the highlands of the Himalayas (e.g., Tibet, Nepal, Bhutan, and some highland areas of northern India) and on Mainland Southeast Asia (e.g., Burma, Thailand, Laos, Cambodia, and Vietnam). Its expansion in these regions continued to be the result of a mixture of the efforts of traveling monks and the conversion of local rulers and the subsequent consolidation and expansion of their power. The main difference with earlier times was that the monks were not traveling so far. Rather than moving along the Silk Road and the maritime trade route between India and China, these monks mainly traveled along the inland rivers and jungle and mountain trails. In the case of Southeast Asia, for example, while more distant connections with fellow Buddhists in Sri Lanka continued to a limited extent, Buddhism within Southeast Asia became more localized and evolved into a syncretic religion that combined aspects of Buddhism, Hinduism, and local animistic and other beliefs.

Hellenic Scholars

Ancient Hellenic scholars provide an example of scholars who moved across borders not in relation to religion but as part of a general migratory trend among Hellenes in the ancient world and often particularly in search of employment rather than enlightenment. The spread of Hellenic civilization around the Mediterranean and Middle East through conquest and colonization resulted in the appearance of ethnic Greek scholars throughout this region and their movement within it. In regard to language, there were dialects of ancient Greek — Achaean, Aeolic, Arcado-Cypriot, Attic, Doric, Ionic — but they were mutually intelligible and by the 4th and 5th centuries B.C. a common dialect had emerged, "which emanated principally from Athens, and was spoken by nearly al the educated classes of the Hellenic world."[31]

As the leading city of ancient Greece, Athens not only produced many scholars of its own; such institutions as Plato's Academy, founded around 387 B.C., and Aristotle's Lyceum, founded in 334 or 335 B.C., attracted many from other parts of the Hellenic world. In fact, Aristotle himself was born in Stageira, Chalcidice (near modern Thessalonika in northern Greece), and his father was King Anyntas of Macedon's personal physician. Among those who came from elsewhere in the Hellenic world to study in Athens were Archytas and Eudoxus. The famous philosopher, mathematician, and astronomer Archytas (428–347 B.C.) was born in Tarentum, an Achaean colony in the Magna Graeca region of southern Italy, and lived in Athens for a time as a student before returning to Tarentum. The astronomer and mathematician Eudoxus was born in Cnidus (in modern Turkey). He went first to southern Italy to study under Archytas and then to Sicily to study medicine under Philistion of Locri before going to Athens around 387 B.C., where he became a student of Plato's. Next he travelled for a few years, first to Heliopolis in Egypt to study medicine, then to Mysia (modern Cyzicius) in the Propontis (modern Sea of Marmara), and finally to the court of Mausolus, the ruler of Karia in southwestern Anatolia, before returning to Athens with a group of his own students. During this stay in Athens he temporarily took over as head of Plato's Academy while Plato was away in Syracuse. He eventually left Athens and returned to Cnidus.

Herodotus was another famous non–Athenian Greek scholar who lived in Athens.[32] Herodotus is commonly referred to as the Father of History, but as Marozzi points out, he is also its "first foreign correspondent, investigative journalist, anthropologist and travel writer."[33] Herodotus was born in Halicarnassus, Karia (modern Bodrun, Turkey), around 484 B.C. Dorians had originally settled Halicarnassus, but by the time of Herodotus the Ionic dialect was widely used and this was the dialect that Herodotus wrote in. Halicarnassus was a pioneer in Greek trade with Egypt and had important commercial and cultural links with the Egyptians. The island was part of the Persian Empire when Herodotus was born and therefore also had ties with other territories within the empire. As a boy Herodotus moved with his family to the wealthy wine-producing island of Samos, which was also the birthplace of the philosopher and mathematician Pythagoras (1. c. 570–495 B.C.) — who had moved to the Greek colony of Croton (modern Crotone) in southern Italy for a time. While the details of much of his life are sketchy, it is known that Herodotus travelled extensively around the eastern Mediterranean and eastward within Persian territory at least as far as Babylon.

Some time around 447 B.C. Herodotus attended the Olympics to write his *Histories*. Unlike modern Olympics, the ancient Greek ones included artistic and literary competitions. They attracted participants from throughout the Hellenic world who were able to travel to the games safely under the Olympic Truce.[34] Herodotus settled in Athens for a few years and then migrated to Thurii (aka Thurium) in the Calabria region of southern Italy, probably in 443 B.C. He was part of a group of colonists sent to establish the colony by Pericles. Before he died in 425 B.C. Herodotus may have returned to Athens.

The Greek settlements in Asia Minor and the nearby islands produced a particularly large number of Hellenic scholars in addition to Herodotus with a distinctive secular rationalistic approach. Porter argues that the emergence of this secular scholarship at this time in the Greek colonies was possible because "the societies of the Aegean fringes absorbed a multiplicity of intellectual influences from the Mediterranean, Asian and Oriental cultures, and avoided the limiting rigidity of religious dogmatism."[35] While some of these scholars migrated to Greece itself, at least for a time as in the case of Herodotus, many remained in Asia Minor or moved to other parts of the Hellenic world. Moreover, there were important centers of learning in Asia Minor and elsewhere in the Hellenic world that attracted transnational scholars.

Medical schools provide a good example of transnational centers of learning in the Greek colonies. The first Greek medical school seems to have been established at Cnidus (aka Knidos) on the Datca peninsula in southwestern Turkey around 700 B.C. Hippocractes (1. *c.* 460–370 B.C.) established a rival school on his home island of Cos (aka Kos, Meropis, and Nymphaea). Cos was famous for its wine and was also an important trading center. It was among the earliest places in the west to have access to silk from the east (silk weaving became an industry there by the 300s B.C.). Cos had close relations with Egypt, and Egyptian ships often visited. Its ties with Egypt were evident as Cos emerged as a center of learning. It not only had links to the Ptolemaic center of learning at Alexandria, but some Ptolemy family members were sent to Cos for education. Another important medical school was established at Croton in the Calabria region of southern Italy. Croton is closely associated with the philosopher and mathematician Pythagoras (1. *c.* 570–495 B.C.). Pythagoras was born on the island of Samos and is known to have traveled extensively, including to Egypt, before setting at Croton around 530 B.C. and establishing what is commonly known as the Pythagorean school. His pupils included Almaeon of Croton.[36] He was an advocate of the notion that health was related to a balance between bodily humors that were related to external environmental as well as dietary factors. He is also considered to be a pioneer in anatomical dissection. The medical practitioner Demonedes was also born in Croton and appears to have practiced medicine in such places as Aegina, Athens, Samos, and Susa before returning to live in Croton.[37]

Ptolemy I Soter (r. 323–283 B.C.), the founder of the Ptolemaic Dynasty, established the Mouseion — a gathering place under the protection of the Muses — in Alexandria.[38] It served as a home for scholars and their students and also contained the largest library in the world at the time. Thus, it functioned somewhat like a university. The Mouseion was well financed by the Ptolemies, allowing it to attract renowned scholars and to collect an unprecedented quantity of scrolls. The subjects covered by the resident scholars and the library included philosophy, history, mathematics, astronomy, physics, and the natural sciences.

Scholars were appointed to their posts for life and in addition to generous tax-free salaries, they were provided with free lodging and board. The mathematician and "Father of Geometry" Euclid (aka Euclid of Alexandria), who lived in Alexandria at the time of Ptolemy I Soter, was among the scholars working at the Mouseion. The famous mathematician, engineer, and astronomer Archimedes, who was from the Greek colony of Syracuse in Sicily, was a student there. The astronomer Canon, who was from Samos in Ionia, was a fellow student. Whereas Archimedes returned to Syracuse, where he died during the city's siege by the Romans, Canon remained in Alexandria and became court astronomer to Ptolemy III Euergetes.

The goal of the library of Alexandria was to collect writings covering the totality of human knowledge. In addition to purchasing scrolls locally and from passing ships, it sent buyers to Rhodes, Athens, and elsewhere in search of additional works. When items could not be purchased, copies were made. Alexandria was a major producer of papyrus and in large part because of the library's activities it soon became a leading producer of scrolls as well. Demetrius of Phaleron was given the task of organizing the library. He was an Athenian (Phaleron is a suburb of Athens), who had served as governor of Athens until he was exiled in 307 B.C. After a stay in Thebes he went to Ptolemy I Soter's court in Alexandria around 297 B.C. In addition to his political activities he was also a well-respected scholar. Having been a student of Aristotle, he wrote literary criticism, history, and law.

A grammarian named Zenodotus, from the Ionian city of Ephesus in Asia Minor, was the first person to be given the position of head librarian. He was a student of Philitas of Cos. Cos had been captured by Ptolemy I Soter in 310 B.C, and Ptolemy made Philitas tutor to his son Philapelphus, who was to become Ptolemy II. A poet named Callimachus (aka Kallimachos) from Cyrene (modern Shahhat) — an important Greek town and commercial center on the coast of Libya — became the next head librarian in 245 B.C. He is known primarily for creating the *Pinakes,* the first library catalog.[39] Callimachus was from a family that claimed descent from the first ruler of Cyrene. As a young man he was sent to Athens to study. He returned to Cyrene and then moved to Alexandria. A Hellenic Egyptian named Apollonius, who was a student of Callimachus, was the next head librarian. Although born in Egypt, he spent part of his life in Rhodes and adopted Rhodian as his surname and is therefore commonly referred to as Apollonius of Rhodes. Another person from Cyrene, Eratosthenes (aka Eratosthenes of Cyrene), became the next head librarian in 235 B.C. He studied in Athens and Alexandria (along with Archimedes and Canon) and is known primarily as a geographer. He stepped down from his post in 195 B.C. when he became blind and was succeeded by Aristophanes of Byzantium, who had been born in Byzantium and then moved to Alexandria, where he studied under Callimachus. He in turn was succeeded by one of his students, a grammarian named Aristarchus, who had been born on the island of Samothrace in the Aegean Sea.

Alexandria also became an important center of medical scholarship as a result of the Ptolemies support for the Mouseion and its library. The establishment of medical study at Alexandria is associated with Herophilus (1. 335–280 B.C.) and what is commonly known as the Herophilean school, which existed from roughly 300 B.C. to A.D. 50.[40] He was born in Chalcedon (a coastal town in Bithynia, Asia Minor, the modern Kadikoy district of Istanbul). Herophilus moved to Alexandria to study at a fairly young age and remained there as a teacher and resident scholar. He was a pioneer in the field of anatomy and was the first scientist to systematically perform dissections of human cadavers — sometimes in public. Alexandria was one of the few places in the Mediterranean world that allowed the dissection of human cadavers. As a result of his dissections of humans and animals Herophilus established how blood flowed through the veins and arteries and determines that intelligence was located in the brain. Herophilus worked alongside Erasistratus (1. 304–250 B.C.). Erasistratus was probably born at Ioulis on the island of Keos (aka Ceos, modern Kea) in the Cyclades archipelago. He served as the court physician to Seleucus I Nicator — where he is best remembered for discovering that the illness from which the king's eldest son was suffering was love-sickness related to his pining for his mother-in-law. He then moved to Alexandria, where he conducted anatomical research in collaboration with Herophilus. He is credited with establishing that the heart is a pump rather than a center of sensations. While

Herophilus was the star of the school, it was the collaborative work of Herophilus and Erasistratus that resulted in its attaining fame and attracting students from throughout the Hellenic world.

Alexandria continued as an important center of learning under Roman rule, even though Julius Caesar accidentally burned the library in 48 B.C. Scholarly work then shifted to the Serapeum. It was a temple built by Ptolemy III Euergetes (r. 246–222 B.C.) that was dedicated to the Hellenic-Egyptian god Serapis and that also housed a library. It was destroyed in A.D. 391.

Whereas transnational scholarship in the Mediterranean region prior to the establishment of the Roman Empire was largely among ethnic Greeks who shared a common language and cultural heritage, under the Romans it became more multi-lingual and multi-ethnic in the sense that it now involved ethnic Greeks, ethnic Italians, and sometimes others who were bicultural and could function within their own and the Latin cultural milieu. There were a number of Hellenic scholars who moved about the Roman Empire. Many of them lived in or at least spent time in Rome. We have already encountered Lucius Cassius Dio Cocceianus in this regard. The geographer and historian Strabo (1. *c.* 63/64 B.C.–A.D. 24) provides another example. He was born in the Hellenic city of Amasya (in Pontus in modern Turkey), which was at the time part of the Roman Empire, in 63 or 64 B.C.[41] He was from an affluent family, which allowed him to travel extensively throughout the Mediterranean, Near East and even as far as Ethiopia. He studied at Nysa (modern Sultanhisar, Turkey) and then went to Rome around 44 B.C., where he studied under and befriended a number of prominent Hellenic scholars including the philosopher Xenarchus of Seleucia (who had previously taught in Athens and Alexandria before moving to Rome), Tyranion of Amisus (who was originally brought to Rome as an enslaved war captive), and the philosopher Athenodoros Cananites (who was born at Canana in modern Turkey and taught the young Octavian in Apollonia and Greece and then followed him to Rome). He remained in Rome until about 31 B.C. and then went to Greece for several years. He travelled up the Nile in 25 B.C. There are few records of how he spent his time between then and his return to Rome in A.D. 17. He began work on his 17-volume *Geographica,* an important source of information on peoples and places in the ancient world, prior to his return to Rome around A.D. 7 and did not complete it until some time shortly before he died in A.D. 24.

Transnational Christians

Christian missionary activity is based on what Christians refer to as the Great Commission. One version of the Great Commission appears in Matthew 28:16–20, which has the resurrected Jesus telling the 11 disciples, "Go therefore and make disciples of all nations, baptizing them in the name of the Father and the Son and the of the Holy Spirit, teaching them to observe all that I have commanded you." There are, however, some scholars of early Christianity who doubt that Jesus ever uttered these words and believe that the Great Commission was a later product of the Christian community.[42] Whether or not these were the words of Jesus, Christian missionaries soon set about to spread their religion within the Roman Empire.

St. Paul and St. Barnabas were among the most important early Christian missionaries. Barnabus was born a Levite Jew and became one of the earliest converts to Christianity and one of the first disciples. Paul was born in Tarsus (in what is now Turkey) and converted to Christianity while traveling on the road to Damascus in A.D. 33. After wandering around the Middle East for several years he began work as a traveling missionary in earnest in the company of Barnabas. Some time around A.D. 43 and 44 they were especially active in making converts in and near Antioch. They left Antioch around A.D. 45 and traveled to Anatolia and Cyprus where they made further converts. They then attended the Council of Jerusalem around A.D. 50. Paul and Barnabas quarreled shortly after this and parted company.

Paul resumed his missionary work and traveled to Anatolia, where he teamed up with a young convert named Timothy. After traveling around Anatolia the two of them along with another convert named Silas sailed to Macedonia, where they preached Christianity for the first time in Europe. Paul and Silas were arrested at Philippi for disturbing the peace but were released when it was discovered that they were Roman citizens. Paul then went to Thessalonika to preach among its Jewish population. He gained some converts, but the Jewish community then forced him to leave. He moved on to Athens, where there were few Jews and fewer still interested in listening to him. Next he went to the important commercial center of Corinth, where there was a large Jewish community. Here he preached in the Jewish synagogue and earned a living as a tentmaker. He was more successful in gaining converts in Corinth and after 18 months sailed to Jerusalem. After spending a short time in Jerusalem he set off again to re-visit many of the Christian communities where he had worked previously.

Paul returned to Jerusalem around A.D. 57. This time his preaching received a hostile response from some members of the local Jewish community, who had him arrested as "a pest and a disturber of the peace among Jews all over the world."[43] Rather than face trial in hostile Jerusalem, Paul asked to be tried in Rome before the emperor since he was a Roman citizen. The local Roman-appointed ruler, Agrippa II, was prepared to release him, but Paul had already made his appeal to be tried in Rome and so was put on a merchant vessel bound for Rome around A.D. 61. The ship sank on the way but Paul eventually made it to Rome where he was placed under a relatively lenient house arrest. He resumed his preaching in Rome and made some converts, but most of those in the local Christian community did not care much for his version of Christianity, which broke more thoroughly with Jewish traditions than they liked. Most of the local Christians were former Jews who preferred a more syncretic version of the religion. Eventually, around A.D. 64–65, Paul was tried and executed. Paul's former fellow missionary Barnabas also became a martyr. Christians in Cyprus believe that he was killed and buried in Salamis, and he is the patron saint of the Christian church in Cyprus.

Although they got off to a rough start, eventually Christian missionaries succeeded in establishing Christianity as the Roman Empire's dominant religion following the conversion of the Emperor Constantine I (r. 306–37). Constantine paved the way for this through such acts as the Edict of Milan in 313, which removed penalties for professing Christianity. Christian missionaries were now free to roam around the empire in order to seek converts. Constantine also sponsored the Council of Nicaea in Bithynia (modern Iznik, Turkey) in 325, which led to the creation of a uniform Christian doctrine overseen by councils of bishops.

Although today Christianity is often portrayed as a European religion, its origins in the Middle East and association with the Roman Empire provided the early Christian church with a base in the Middle East as well. We have already discussed the spread of Christianity eastward from the Mediterranean as far as China during the medieval period in earlier chapters. As was noted previously, Christian missionaries operating in the East tended to follow the main trade routes along the Silk Road and the maritime route to South Asia and on to China and often to mix commerce with religion. The Christian communities that were established further to the east were relatively small and were often centered on groups of people engaged in long-distance trade. Moreover, the rise of Islam curtailed the growth of Christianity in the East until the age of European colonialism, and the number of missionaries working in the region remained fairly small until modern times.

The situation was quite different in Europe beyond the Roman Empire and in areas where Roman power first collapsed in the western parts of Europe. Pope Gregory I (1. *c.* 540–604) revitalized Christian missionary activities in northern and far western Europe and laid the basis for all of this part of Europe becoming fundamentally Christian.[44] From the perspective of transnationalism, what is most significant about such medieval missionary activities is that they served to link Christian communities in the kingdoms of northern and northwestern Europe with the Christian church based in Rome and that some of the religious figures engaged in this early mission work maintained significant ties to both Rome and the country where they were engaged in their missionary endeavors. Pope Gregory I was born in Rome to a wealthy family shortly before the Byzantine Emperor Justinian I retook the city from the Goths in 552. He became a monk after his father died and in 579 he was sent as a papal ambassador to the Byzantine court in Constantinople. He returned to Rome in 585 and became pope in 590. Among the missions sent by Pope Gregory I was one to England in 597.[45] It was Gregory's most famous mission and is commonly referred to as the Gregorian mission.

Pope Gregory's decision to send a mission to England appears in part to have been prompted by the marriage of the pagan Anglo-Saxon king Aethelbert, who ruled over Kent (r. *c.* 590–616), to a Christian princess, Bertha, who was the daughter of Charibert I, the king of Paris. Bertha had brought her chaplain with her to England and restored a Roman-era church in Canterbury. In 595 Gregory chose an Italian Benedictine monk named Augustine (who became known as Augustine of Canterbury) to lead a group of 40 Italian missionaries to Kent. The group arrived in Kent in 597 and was allowed by Aethelbert to set about proselytizing. The king himself converted to Christianity some time prior to 601. Augustine remained in England for the rest of his life (he died in 604), but corresponded with Pope Gregory. Augustine sent a missionary named Laurence back to Rome in 601 with a report on the group's progress. The pope responded by sending an additional group of missionaries to England along with a letter asking Augustine to establish a dozen new dioceses. The pattern of transnational links between the Christian church in Kent and the pope in Rome was typical of medieval missions in that the missionary established roots in his new country of residence and remained there while maintaining contact with Rome through correspondence and through church officials who occasionally traveled back and forth.

TRANSNATIONAL CHRISTIAN ORGANIZATIONS

From the A.D. 300s on throughout the medieval period the Christian church was organized in a relatively centralized and hierarchical fashion. The pope in Rome was at the top and in the center. The centralized nature of the European Christian church developed over time. Thus, while Rome was an important center of Christianity in the early days of the religion it was only one of several and its bishop's power was limited. Saint Clement I, who served as bishop of Rome from A.D. 92 to 99, was asked his opinion in a dispute among members of the church in Corinth and wrote a letter to them on the matter in A.D. 96, but he had no power to enforce his will.

After Emperor Constantine I converted to Christianity, Constantinople and its emperors exerted considerable influence over the church. As mentioned above, Constantine convened the First Council of Nicaea in A.D. 325 in a move aimed at creating a degree of unity within the church.[46] Although Constantine invited all of the approximately 1,800 bishops of the church only about 200–300 attended. The subsequent First Council of Constantinople in A.D. 381, like all of the early councils, was held in the east, but it did affirm the important role of the bishop of Rome, even though the bishop did not attend the council.

By A.D. 400 the Christian church was well entrenched around the Mediterranean, but there were often sharp divisions that manifested themselves in its organization. Although the bishops in Rome and Constantinople were highly regarded throughout the Church, localized loyalty often was more important. The 90 Christian bishops in Egypt, for instance, recognized the leadership of the patriarch in Alexandria as Pope Dioscorus I of Alexandria. Divisions came to a head in 451 at the Council of Chalcedon (in Turkey). Patriarch Anatolius of Constantinople convened the council at the urging of the Roman Pope Leo I (r. 440–461). The council "affirmed the equal authority of the bishop of Constantinople with that of Rome" and deposed Dioscorus I as pope and sent him into exile.[47] The council's actions led to a sharp division within the eastern Christian church between those that adhered to the Melchite Church or what came to be known as Chalcedonian Christianity (the churches of Rome, Constantinople, and the Greek Orthodox patriarchates of Alexandria, Antioch, and Jerusalem) and the Coptic Church and those that came to be known as Oriental Orthodox churches (in Armenia, Syria, Egypt, and Ethiopia). In regard to transnationalism, what is of relevance here is not so much the schisms within the Christian church as the extent to which members of the church in general and those of certain factions in particular interacted with one another and viewed relations beyond national borders as important.

Over the next few centuries the power of the Christian church's leadership in Rome gradually grew in Western Europe in part as a result of successful missionary activities that led to the conversion of peoples throughout the area. Pope Gregory I, whose role in promoting such missionary activity was discussed above, was especially important in this regard. He is widely seen as an important transitional figure as European Christian beliefs changed from those of the early Christian church to those of the medieval Christian church in Western Europe.[48]

The Roman church found itself under threat after the Byzantine army had withdrawn after it overthrew the Ostrogoth kingdom in Italy. A Germanic tribe known as the Lombards entered the power vacuum and invaded Italy from the north in 569. The Lombard King Aistulf (r. 749–56) invaded papal territories. Pope Stephen II (r. 715–57) found Emperor Constantine V (r. 741–775) unwilling to provide assistance and he turned instead to the Franks for help. He had allied himself with Pepin the Short (r. 752–768), king of the Franks, having travelled to Paris to anoint him and grant him the title Patrician of the Romans in 754 — the first time that a pope crowned a civil ruler. After Pepin became king he attacked the Lombards and after defeating them returned properties to the papacy that had been seized by the Lombards. This act, known as the Donation of Pepin, led to the founding of the Papal States. Pope Leo III crowned Pepin's son Charlemagne in 800 and established a precedence of the pope's crowning the Holy Roman emperors.

The power of the popes declined considerably from the mid–800s until a revival took shape in the mid–1000s. In addition to a weakness of the popes in Western Europe at this time, especially in regard to their control over local church leaders, relations with the Christian churches to the east also soured. In response to such problems, Pope Nicholas II and Cardinal Hildebrand convened the First Lateran Council in 1059 that sought to reform the Roman Church and to strengthen to power of the pope. Prior to the council local bishops had come to exercise considerable autonomy. At the council it was decreed that all bishops had to swear obedience to the pope. In addition, territories around Europe ranging from the island of Sardinia to the kingdoms of England and Spain had to recognize the pope as their feudal lord and to send him tribute. Also at this time the power to appoint a new pope was given to seven cardinal bishops who resided near Rome. Over the years the number of cardinal bishops was increased to form a Sacred College with 70 members from various countries.

After 1059 the power of the papacy and its control over church and secular affairs throughout Europe began to grow once again. Following the sacking of Constantinople by the crusaders in 1204, the Roman church under Pope Innocent III temporarily regained control over the east as far as Armenia. The strengthened position of the pope was manifest in the Fourth Lateran Council of 1215, which was attended by 1,500 clerics from all of the important Christian countries. One of the outcomes of this council was that bishops came to be elected in co-operation with the Pope. The Inquisition also served as a representation of the power of the Pope across borders. The Inquisition had its origins with the decision of Pope Gregory IX to appoint a board of inquisitors in Florence to judge accused heretics in 1227. In 1231 Pope Gregory IX went further by adopting a law making impenitent heresy treason and punishable by death. Following this an increasing number of inquisitors under the pope's authority were sent out across Western Europe in search of Christian heretics.

The issue of control over abbots and monasteries was yet another indication of the growing power of the popes. Prior to the 1200s bishops had exercised considerable power over monasteries located within their domains. However, the power of bishops over these diminished in the 1200s "as the popes, fearing the power of the bishops, brought the monastic orders under direct papal control."[49] The monastic movement within the western Christian church can trace its origins back to the early church, but initially such monasteries were not joined together to form transnational organizations. One early founder of a monastery was St. Augustine of Hippo (l. 354–430) who was born in Numidia, North Africa, and left North Africa as a young man and went to Rome. He returned to North Africa in 387 and founded a monastery the following year, but an order bearing his name was not established until the 1200s. Benedict of Nursia established a monastery at Monte Cassino in 529 and the Order of Saint Benedict (aka Benedictines) grew from this. One of the significant characteristics of the Benedictine order was the autonomy of each individual community — a pattern that has been maintained to the present and that sets it apart from other monastic orders.

The First Lateran Council of 1059 gave monasticism a boost when it urged the clergy to live in a community like the apostles. Many responded by forming monastic communities, such as one named Citeaux, near Lyon. It was established in 1098 and the Cistercian monastic order grew from it. Focusing on manual labor and shunning learning, the Cistercians "set up new centers of their order in unsettled regions, subdued marshes, jungles and forests to cultivation, and played a leading part in colonizing eastern Germany, and in repairing the damage that William I the Conqueror had done in England."[50]

St. Francis of Assisi founded the Franciscan Order in 1209 based on a principle of living a life of apostolic poverty.[51] Pope Innocent III recognized the order. Francis himself left Italy with the Fifth Crusade in 1219 to announce the gospel to the Saracens. He returned after a short time with an eye infection. While Francis continued his work in Italy members of his order spread its presence to other countries. Caesarius of Speyer established a branch of the order in Augsburg, Germany, in 1221. Agnellus of Pisa led a group of Franciscans to England in 1224. Known as greyfriars, they soon established branches throughout England. At the time of St. Francis's death in 1226 there were some 5,000 members of his order in Italy, France, Spain, Germany, England, and Hungary. The order also had a presence in the Holy Land, where it established Custodia Terrae Sanctae in 1217. After the last Crusader stronghold fell to the Muslims in 1291, the order sent two friars to the Holy Land to serve as custodians of Christian holy places, and Pope Clement VI granted Custodia Terrae Sanctae official status in 1342. After St. Francis's death the order relaxed its rules of poverty, illiteracy, and extreme asceticism, and the Order of the Friars Minor, as the order was known, grew rapidly until there were 200,000 monks by 1280.[52]

Other important monastic orders established in the 1200s include the Dominicans and Augustinians. St. Dominic founded the Dominican Order in 1216. He was born in Castile and became an Augustinian canon in 1201, while working in France. The pope recognized Dominic and his followers as the Friars Preachers. The order's headquarters was in Rome and from there its members were sent out across Europe as far to the east as Kiev. The Augustinians, known as the Brothers of the Hermits of Saint Augustine, were established by a group of hermits living in Tuscany who wished to bring the ideals of a monastic life into urban settings. They petitioned Pope Innocent IV to recognize them as a religious order in 1243. Innocent's successor, Pope Alexander IV, called on the diverse groups of monastic hermits in Italy, Switzerland, Germany, France, England, and elsewhere in Europe to send representatives to Rome and in 1256 they came together to form the Augustinian Order.

The Christian Crusades to the Holy Land (1095–1291) were also one outcome of the reform and revitalization of the Western Christian Church in the mid-1000s. The majority of the crusaders in the First Crusade (1095–99) were French, with a significant contingent of Germans, plus an assortment of other nationalities. After conquering Jerusalem (and killing its Muslim and Jewish inhabitants) the crusaders established the Latin Kingdom of Jerusalem, which lasted until Saladin took the city in 1187. The Second Crusade (1146–48) was largely a German and French affair. It ended in defeat with most of the crusaders also returning home. After the fall of Jerusalem, Christians still held Tyre, Antioch, and Tripoli.

The Third Crusade (1189–92) was a multi-national affair that included armies led by Richard I the Lionheart of England, Philip II Augustus of France, and the Holy Roman Emperor Frederick I Barbarossa. Each of the three armies embarked separately from Europe. Frederick I Barbarossa's large German army was joined by a small group of Hungarians led by Prince Geza on the way. The German and Hungarian crusaders reached Anatolia, where they defeated a Turkish force, but then Frederick Barbarossa drowned while bathing in a river in 1190. Only a small portion of the German-Hungarian force under the command of Frederick Barbarossa's son Frederick VI of Swabia managed to make it to the Holy Land. The French and English armies fought together, but relations between the two kings were strained. Philip II returned home early, leaving Richard in command of what remained of the crusader army. The Third Crusade ended with the signing of the Treaty of Ramla by Richard and Saladin, which saw the Latin Kingdom reduced to a small coastal area from Tyre to Jaffna. Jerusalem remained under Muslim rule, but the terms of the treaty permitted

Christian pilgrims to visit. Weather and politics conspired to make Richard's trip home a difficult one. His voyage home was plagued by stormy weather and ended with his ship being wrecked in the northern Adriatic. Forced to travel overland, he was captured by the Duke of Austria, Leopold V, in late December 1192, who turned him over to the Holy Roman Emperor Henry VI, who in turn held him for ransom until early 1194.

Most crusaders who survived returned to Europe. Among those who remained in the Holy Land were men who formed new orders of military monks in part to provide protection for Christians within the Latin Kingdom of Jerusalem and in nearby lands. These included the Knights of the Hospital of St. John (aka Hospitallers), founded in 1080, who numbered around 600 members at the time and the Knights Templar that was founded in 1096 and numbered around 300. They were rivals who gained considerable reputations for their armed capabilities and grew wealthy, building large fortresses.

The Knights Templar were also know as the Poor Fellow-Soldiers of Christ and of the Temple of Solomon. The Roman church endorsed the Order in 1129. It served as a charity to receive money and land and to run commercial enterprises to help fight in the Holy Land. Nobles going to the Holy Land to fight also sometimes would place their estates under Templar management. Pope Innocent II exempted the order from local laws in 1139. This meant that its knights were able to pass through all borders and were exempt from local taxes. They answered only to the authority of the pope. In addition to its combatants, there were non-combatant members who managed its large economic and fiscal infrastructure and who developed innovative forms of banking. For example, in 1150 the order began issuing letters of credit to pilgrims who had made deposits in Europe with the order before going to the Holy Land. The Templars established a financial network throughout the Christian world and it can be argued that they were the world's first transnational corporation — although usually this honor goes to the Dutch East India Company, which was established in 1602.[53] Support for them receded with the loss of Christian power in the Holy Land and the order was disbanded in 1312.

The Templars had an important presence in France, England, Aragon, Portugal, Poitou, Apulia, Jerusalem, Tripoli (Lebanon), Antioch, Anjou, and Hungary. At the head of the order was a French Grand Master. Below him were Masters in each region. At its peak there were an estimated 15,000 to 20,000 Templars, with knights making up about 10 percent. Templars were divided into aristocratic knights, sergeants, and clergy. The knights also had squires, who were not members of the order. The sergeants might be soldiers with horses who served as cavalry; they might be administrators; or they might have performed menial tasks and worked as traders. The red cross on the mantle worn by the knights was considered a symbol of martyrdom and it was considered an honor to die in combat — something that assured the person a place in heaven.

The Hospitallers or Sovereign Military Hospitaller Order of St. John of Jerusalem of Rhodes and of Malta began with the founding of the Amalfitan hospital in Jerusalem in 1080 to provide care for the poor and sick pilgrims. After the reconquest of Jerusalem in 1099 it became a military order. The Hospitallers divided its personnel into those engaged in military activities and those who cared for the sick. The pope exempted them from all local authorities. The order grew wealthy and owned numerous buildings in the Holy Land. After the fall of Jerusalem it operated out of Rhodes, which they captured in 1309. The Hospitallers were driven out of Rhodes in 1522 and in 1530 they settled on Malta (as a vassal state under the Spanish viceroy of Sicily). Charles V of Spain gave them Malta, Gozo, and Tripoli in return for a Maltese falcon a year. The Hospitallers were given much of the property of the Knights Templar when that order was dissolved in 1312. They were organized into eight "tongues" (Aragon, Auvergne, Castile, England, France, Germany, Italy, and Provence). A prior governed each of these. The head in Rhodes and Malta was called a *bailli*. The order ceased to be associated solely with Malta after Napoleon conquered the island in 1789. The Russian ruler Paul I gave many of them refuge in St. Petersburg. By the early 1800s it had little presence in the rest of Europe outside of Russia. The order underwent a restoration in 1879 and devoted its efforts mainly to humanitarian works.

CHRISTIAN PILGRIMAGES

As the opening paragraph of this book concerning the presence of foreigners buried at Stonehenge indicates, visiting distant sacred places has an ancient history. Prior to the spread of so-called world religions this usually entailed visiting sacred locales that were relatively close to home and often within an area occupied by people sharing a similar culture. As in the case of Stonehenge, however, even in ancient times it is apparent that certain places gained widespread notoriety for their sacredness that inspired peoples from distant lands to visit them.

The spread of today's major religions from their points of origin served to increase the motivation for people from a variety of nations to visit sacred sites associated with these religions. In regard to transnationalism two things are of particular relevance: the extent to which such sacred sites and the desire to visit them gives followers of a religion a link to another land, and the actual infrastructure that is built up to make such visits possible. In regard to this last point, early pilgrims often simply followed established trade routes and took advantage of the existing infrastructure catering to commercial travelers.

Pilgrimages by European Christians to the Holy Land began in the A.D. 300s following Constantine I's conversion to Christianity. Saint Jerome (1. *c.* 347–420) was one of the most prominent of the early pilgrims.[54] Living in Antioch at the time, in 385 Jerome (serving as spiritual adviser to the group) and a small group of fellow Christians, including Bishop Paulinus of Antioch, set off as pilgrims to the Holy Land. Unlike most modern pilgrims, this group intended to take up residence for the remainder of their lives in the Holy Land. They visited Jerusalem, Bethlehem, and various sites around Galilee, and then went on to Egypt. Jerome returned to Palestine from Egypt in 388 and took up residence in Bethlehem, where he spent the rest of his life.

Christian pilgrimages on more of a mass scale did not develop until the medieval period. European Christians in the medieval period went on pilgrimages for a variety of reasons: "to fulfill a penance or a vow, or to seek a miraculous cure, or to earn an indulgence, and doubtless, like modern tourists, to see strange lands and sights, and find adventure on the way as a relief from the routine of a narrow life."[55] The bravest pilgrims set out for Palestine. Durant describes a pilgrimage from Germany and the Netherlands in 1064 in which clerics led 10,000 pilgrims, 3,000 of them dying on the way, and only 2,000 returning safely to their homes. Rome was a major destination of pilgrims within Europe: "In 1299 Pope Boniface VIII declared a jubilee for 1300, and offered a plenary indulgence to those who should come to worship in St. Peter's in that year. It was estimated that on no day in those twelve months had Rome less than 200,000 strangers within her gates; and a total of 2,000,000 visitors, each with a modest offering, deposited such treasure before St. Peter's tomb that two priests, with rakes in their hands, were kept busy night and day collecting coins."[56]

Transnational Muslims

Muslim conquest, commerce, and conversions created various forms of transnational linkages. We have already discussed Muslim long-distance traders. Here we will focus on those who were more specifically religiously motivated or whose work was more specifically related to Islam. Both within and beyond the Muslim-ruled empires missionaries actively sought to gain converts, often along long-distance trade routes. Sufism played an important role in Islamic conversion in Africa, Asia, and the Balkans from the 1200s to the 1600s.[57] Cook writes, "Sufis, more than any other single group in Islam, have been responsible for large-scale conversions to Islam."[58]

Muslim Pilgrims

We have already touched on the topic of camel caravans carrying Muslim pilgrims in the first chapter. It is important to note that pilgrims also traveled by sea. Although, as the fifth pillar of Islam, the pilgrimage to Mecca was important to all Muslims, in the past the logistics and expense meant that relatively few actually made the trip. Such a pilgrimage to a central place of worship served an important unifying role among followers. As Durant remarks in the case of Islam,

> This famous pilgrimage served many purposes. Like that of the Jews to Jerusalem, of the Christians to Jerusalem or Rome, it intensified the worshiper's faith, and bound him by a collective emotional experience to his creed and to his fellow believers. In the pilgrimage a fusing piety brought together poor Bedouins from the desert, rich merchants from the towns, Berbers, African Negroes, Syrians, Persians, Turks, Tartars, Moslem Indians, Chinese — all wearing the same simple garb, reciting the same prayers in the same Arabic tongue.[59]

The caravans carrying pilgrims usually were fairly large for security reaosons.[60] The Muslim scholar Ibn Battuta (to be discussed below) joined a caravan of pilgrims financed by the Ilkhanate Sultan Abu Said in 1326. Thanks to the "generosity" of the sultan, the caravan had camels and provisions for a number of poorer pilgrims.[61] Like other large caravans, the caravan was run by a professional caravan leader who was responsible for security, internal order, and particularly making sure that there was enough water for such a large group of people (over 1,000 in this instance) and animals. Merchants also joined such caravans because of the security that they offered and, for some, the market provided by the pilgrims.

Muslim Scholars

The spread of Islam in the medieval period provided a context for scholars and other learned people to move around the Islamic world. As Gordon has noted, "By the twelfth century there existed — for the first time — a world largely without borders for educated men. These were men who felt at home everywhere within the vast region stretching from Spain to the port cities of China. Their skills in law and religious texts were equally applicable and equally desired across the whole Muslim world."[62] In addition to centers of learning that attracted the most talented scholars, those with even a modicum of knowledge of Muslim law and religious texts and an ability to speak and read Arabic could find employment throughout this large area. Gordon estimates, "Overall, the number of people who traveled to find [such] employment was large, probably in the hundreds of thousands. At the time, there were more than a dozen Islamic capital cities and hundreds of smaller cities, any of which might offer employment."[63]

Writing of scholarship during the Umayyad Caliphate, Durant remarks, "The caliphs realized the backwardness of the Arabs in science and philosophy, and the wealth of Greek culture surviving in Syria. The Umayyads wisely left unhindered the Christian, Sabean, or Persian colleges at Alexandria, Beirut, Antioch, Harran, Nisibis, and Jund-i-Shapur."[64] The written works found at these colleges were initially studied in Greek and Syriac, but before long Nestorian Christian and Jewish scholars began to translate them into Arabic.

The Abbasid Dynasty was particularly active in promoting scholarship and Baghdad became one of world's leading intellectual centers. The Abbasid caliph Al-Ma'mun (r. 813–33) established a House of Wisdom (*Bait al-Hikma*) in Baghdad in 830. It functioned as a scientific academy, public library, and center for translation and attracted Muslim and non–Muslim scholars. Translation of important ancient written works into Arabic and Persian was an especially important activity. The Muslims had learned to make paper from the Chinese when they captured Samarkand in 712 and began manufacturing paper in Baghdad in 794. One of the House of Wisdom's head translators, Hunain ibn Ishaq (John son of Isaac, 1. 809–73), who was a Nestorian physician, was responsible for translating hundreds of works, including ones by Aristotle, Plato, and Ptolemy, and the Old Testament from Greek (perhaps being motivated by the fact that Al-Ma'mun paid him in gold equivalent to the weight of the books that he translated).

Many of the most famous scholars of the Abbasid period moved about considerably during their lifetimes. Abu Jafar al-Tabari (1. 838–923), a Persian born in Tabaristan, wandered as a poor scholar through Arabia, Syria, and Egypt before settling in Baghdad, where he composed his massive *Annals of the Apostles and Kings*. Abu al-Hasan Ali ibn al-Husayn ibn Ali (aka Al-Mas'udi) was an Arab born in Baghdad who traveled to Syria, Palestine, Arabia, Zanzibar, Persia, Central Asia, India, Sri Lanka, and possibly even parts of Southeast Asia. Among his works is an encyclopedia called *Meadows of Gold and Mines of Precious Stones* and another book called *Book of Information*. Some of his ideas appear to have upset more conservative thinkers in Baghdad and he was forced to move to Cairo, where he died in 956.[65] The famous scholar Abu al-Rayhan Muhammad ibn Ahmad al-Biruni (1. 973–1048) — known as a philosopher, historian, geographer, linguist, mathematician, astronomer, poet, and physicist — was born near Khiva in Uzbekistan. His talents resulted in his being given positions at the courts of the rulers of Khwarezm (in modern Uzbekistan) and Tabaristan (in northern Iran along the southern coast of the Caspian Sea). Mahmud of Ghazni (r. 997–1030) — the first ruler to carry the title sultan and founder of the Ghazni Sultanate — asked the ruler of Khwarezm to send al-Biruni to his capital at Ghazni in Afghanistan in 1018. Mahmud conquered parts of India and al-Biruni went to live in India for several years before returning to Mahmud's court. Al-Biruni's works included *Vestiges of the Past* and *History of India* (published in 1030, and focused on Hindu astronomy and religion more than on political history).

Hajji Abu Adbullah Muhammad Ibn Battuta (1. 1304–1368/69) is probably the most famous of medieval Islam's itinerant scholars.[66] He was a Berber who was born in Tangiers, Morocco, into a family of legal scholars. After studying Muslim law himself, at the age of 21 he left home and set off overland on a pilgrimage (*hajj*) to Mecca. He joined a caravan in Tunis where he managed to gain employment as a judge and legal adviser for fellow pilgrims. He also arranged to marry the daughter of a magistrate from Tunis. He divorced her after a dispute with her father and promptly married the daughter of a scholar from Fez who was also with the caravan. In Egypt he found his way to Arabia blocked by a local rebellion in the Aidhab region and so he headed north to Damascus, which was then also under Mamluk rule. As for how he traveled, as Gordon notes, after Ibn Battuta left the caravan in Alexandria, he "entered the network of donation-supported hostels and colleges (madrassas) found in all Muslim cities of the time."[67] Gordon also remarks that such a system resembles and may have been modeled on a similar system of supporting traveling Buddhist monks that had already been in place in Central Asia for 1,000 years, and that at the same time, "there was a parallel tradition of Jewish scholars wandering in search of knowledge."[68]

During his three weeks in Damascus, Ibn Battuta married again and left his wife pregnant before setting off alone for Mecca. Rather than returning home from Mecca like most pilgrims, Ibn Battuta remained there for about a year. From Mecca, as discussed above, Ibn Battuta traveled with a caravan of returning pilgrims to Baghdad, where he became affiliated with the court of Sultan Abu Said (r. 1316–1335), the last ruler of the Ilkhanate. The sultan provided Ibn Battuta with horses and provisions, as well as letters of introduction, in order to resume his travels. From Baghdad, Ibn Battuta traveled north around through the Caucasus and across the Black Sea to Constantinople. He also sailed south to the east coast of Africa, visiting the Muslim ports of Mogadishu, Mombasa, and Kilwa (an important trading port in what is now Tanzania from which gold, iron, ivory, and slaves were exported). In 1332 Ibn Battuta traveled to Delhi, where the sultan hired him as a judge. In 1341 he sailed from Delhi down the west coast of India, visiting important trading centers such as Calicut and Cochin along the way, and then to the Maldives, where the population had recently converted to Islam and he again found employment as a judge and married four different women. After becoming embroiled in local politics in the Maldives he spent time in Sri Lanka and then, on a voyage along the Malabar Coast, lost his wealth to pirates. He then headed towards home and arrived in Fez in 1349, after an absence from Morocco of 24 years, during which time his parents had died.

He did not remain home for long, however, and soon set off on a trip to al-Andalus (the Muslim controlled portion of the Iberian Peninsula). About a year later he left again, this time journeying over the caravan routes of the western Sahara, and spent eight months in the capital of the Mali Empire. Ibn Battuta returned to Fez in 1354 and under the patronage of the local sultan settled down to dictate his memoir during the remaining years of his life. He called his memoir *A Gift to Those Who Contemplate the Wonders of Cities and the Marvels of Travelling.* This work is commonly known as the *Rihla*— the journey.

Notes

Introduction

1. Paul Rincon, "Stonehenge Boy 'was from Med,'" *BBC News,* 28 September (2010), online at www.bbc.co.uk/news.

2. "Bronze Age Mediterraneans May Have Visited Stonehenge," British Geological Survey, online at www.bgs.ac.uk, no date.

3. Kate Ravilious, "Bejeweled Stonehenge Boy Came from Mediterranean?" *National Geographic News* (13 October 2010).

4. Ravilious, "Bejeweled Stonehenge Boy."

5. Michael C. Howard, *Transnationalism and Society: An Introduction* (Jefferson, NC: McFarland, 2011), 3.

6. Jerry H. Bentley, "Beyond Modernocentrism: Towards Fresh Vision of the Global Past," *Contact and Exchange in the Ancient World,* ed. V.H. Mair (Honolulu: University of Hawai'i Press, 2006), 17–29.

7. Bentley, "Beyond Modernocentrism," 17.

8. Bentley, "Beyond Modernocentrism," 20.

9. Samuel P. Huntington, *The Clash of Civilizations and the Remaking of the World Order* (New York: Simon and Schuster, 1996), 21.

10. Huntington, *Clash of Civilizations,* 48.

Chapter 1

1. Victor H. Mair, "Introduction: Kinesis versus Stasis, Interaction versus Independent Invention," *Contact and Exchange in the Ancient World,* ed. V.H. Mair (Honolulu: University of Hawai'i Press, 2006), 7.

2. Janet L. Abu-Lughod, *Before European Hegemony: The World System A.D. 1250–1350* (New York: Oxford University Press, 1989), 33.

3. See Richard W. Bulliet, *The Camel and the Wheel* (Cambridge, MA: Harvard University Press, 1975); Hilde Gauthier-Pilters, *The Camel, Its Evolution, Ecology, Behavior, and Relationship to Man* (Chicago: University of Chicago Press, 1981); and R.T. Wilson, *The Camel* (New York: Longman, 1984).

4. William J. Bernstein, *A Splendid Exchange: How Trade Shaped the World* (New York: Atlantic Monthly Press, 2008), 12.

5. Carleton Coon, *Caravan: The Story of the Middle East* (New York: Holt, Rinehart and Winston, 1958), 332.

6. Coon, *Caravan,* 332.

7. Richard Burton, *Personal Narrative of a Pilgrimage to El-Madinah and Meccah* (New York: Putnam, 1893), 272–4.

8. Coon, *Caravan,* 336–7.

9. James Riley, *An Authentic Narrative of the Loss of the American Brig Commerce* (Hartford: S. Andrus, 1831), 204; cited in Coon, *Caravan,* 338–9.

10. See Mike Morwood, *Stone Tools and Fossil Elephants: The Archaeology of Eastern Indonesia and Its Implications for Australia* (Armidale, NSW: University of New England, 1998); and Mike Morwood, P.B. O'Sullivan, F. Aziz, and A. Raza. "Fission-track Ages of Stone Tools and Fossils on the East Indonesian Island of Flores," *Nature* 392 (12 March, 1998), 173–6; and Mike Morwood, F. Aziz, P.B. O'Sullivan, Nasruddin, D.R. Hobbs, and A. Raza, "Archaeological and Paleontological Research in Central Flores, East Indonesia: Results of Fieldwork 1997–98," *Antiquity* 73 (1999), 273–86.

11. Lionel Casson, *Illustrated History of Ships & Boats* (New York: Doubleday, 1964), 1.

12. Casson, *Illustrated History of Ships & Boats,* 1.

13. Shelly Wachsmann, *Seagoing Ships & Seamanship in the Bronze Age Levant* (College Station: Texas A&M Press; London: Chatham, 1998), 61.

14. Lionel Casson, *Travel in the Ancient World* (London: George Allen & Unwin, 1974), 65.

15. Wachsmann, *Seagoing Ships,* ix.

16. Lionel Casson, *The Ancient Mariners: Seafarer and Sea Fighters of the Mediterranean in Ancient Times* (New York: Macmillan, 1959), 4.

17. Edwin Doran, Jr., "The Sailing Raft as a Great Tradition," in *Man Across the Sea: Problems of Pre-Columbian Contacts,* ed. C.L. Riley, J.C. Kelley, C.W. Pennington, and R.L. Rands (Austin: University of Texas Press, 1971), 123.

18. Wachsmann, *Seagoing Ships,* 39–60.

19. Paul Johnstone, *The Sea-craft of Prehistory* (London: Routledge & Kegan Paul, 1980), 56.

20. Johnstone, *The Sea-craft of Prehistory,* 58.

21. Johnstone, *The Sea-craft of Prehistory,* 67.

22. Casson, *Illustrated History of Ships & Boats,* 216.

23. George F. Bass, "Cape Gelidonya: A Bronze Age Shipwreck," *Transactions of the American Philosophical Society* 57, 8 (1967).

24. Casson, *The Ancient Mariners,* 58.

25. Casson, *The Ancient Mariners,* 61–2.

26. Casson, *The Ancient Mariners,* 61.

27. Leslie Adkins and Roy A. Adkins, *Handbook to Life in Ancient Greece* (New York: Facts on File, 1997), 199.

28. Adkins and Adkins, *Handbook to Life in Ancient Greece*, 198.

29. Casson, *Travel in the Ancient World*, 95.

30. Casson, *Travel in the Ancient World*, 104.

31. Casson, *Illustrated History of Ships & Boats*, 215.

32. Casson, *Illustrated History of Ships & Boats*, 211.

33. Johnstone, *The Sea-craft of Prehistory*, 187.

34. G.R.C. Worchester, *Sail and Sweep in China* (London: Science Museum, 1966), 3.

35. Johnstone, *The Sea-craft of Prehistory*, 189.

36. John N. Miksic, "Introduction: The Beginning of Trade in Ancient Southeast Asia: The Role of Oc Eo and the Lower Mekong River," *Art & Archaeology of Fu Nan: Pre-Khmer Kingdom of the Lower Mekong Valley*, ed. J.C.M. Khoo (Bangkok: Orchid, 2003), 22.

37. Miksic, "Introduction," 22.

38. Miksic, "Introduction," 22.

39. Kenneth R. Hall, "Economic History of Early Southeast Asia," *The Cambridge History of Southeast Asia, Volume I: From Early Times to c.1800*, ed. N. Tarling (New York: Cambridge University Press, 1992), 186.

40. Doran, "The Sailing Raft as a Great Tradition," 122, Fig. 7.7, provides a map of the distribution of the outrigger canoe.

41. S.P. Smith, *Hawaiki, The Original Home of the Maori* (Wellington: Whitcombe and Tombe, 1910), 125.

42. James Hornell, *The Canoes of Polynesia, Fiji, and Micronesia*, Volume I of A.C. Haddon and J. Hornell, *Canoes of Oceania* (Honolulu: Bernice P. Bishop Museum, 1936), 126.

43. Hornell, *The Canoes of Polynesia, Fiji, and Micronesia*, 319.

44. Hornell, *The Canoes of Polynesia, Fiji, and Micronesia*, 319.

45. Thomas Williams, *Fiji and the Fijians, Volume I: The Islands and their Inhabitants* (London: Alexander Heylin, 1858; reprint, Suva, Fiji Museum, 1972), 75.

46. Thomas West, *Ten Years in South-central Polynesia* (London: J. Nisbet, 1865), 69–70.

47. Charles Wilkes, *Narrative of the U.S. Exploring Expedition: during the years 1838, 1839, 1840, 1841, 1842* (New York: George Putnam, 1851), Volume 3, 366.

48. Felix Speiser, *Ethnology of Vanuatu: An Early Twentieth Century Study* (Honolulu: University of Hawai'i Press, 1996). Originally published as *Ethnographische Materialien aus den Neuen Hebriden und den Banks-Inseln* (Berlin: Springer-Verlag, 1923), 250.

49. Hornell, *The Canoes of Polynesia, Fiji, and Micronesia*, 334.

50. Hornell, *The Canoes of Polynesia, Fiji, and Micronesia*, 334.

51. See Thor Heyerdahl, *Kon-Tiki* (New York: Rand McNally, 1950).

52. Doran, "The Sailing Raft as a Great Tradition;" also see Johnstone, *The Sea-craft of Prehistory*, 222–4.

53. Richard Scaglion, "*Kumara* in the Ecuadorian Gulf of Guayaquil?" *The Sweet Potato in Oceania: A Reappraisal*, ed. C. Ballard, P. Brown, R.M. Bourke, and T. Harwood (Sydney: Oceania Monograph 56, 2005), 38; also see R.C. Green, "Sweet Potato Transfers in Polynesian Prehistory," *The Sweet Potato in Oceania: A Reappraisal*, ed. C. Ballard, P. Brown, R.M. Bourke, and T. Harwood (Sydney: Oceania Monograph 56, 2005), 43–62.

54. See John L. Sorenson and Carl L. Johannessen, "Biological Evidence for Pre-Columbian Transoceanic Voyages," *Contact and Exchange in the Ancient World*, ed. V.H. Mair (Honolulu: University of Hawai'i Press, 2006).

55. William Dampier, *A New Voyage Round the World* (London: James Knapton, 1697), Volume 1, 141–3.

56. Clinton R. Edwards, *Aboriginal Watercraft on the Pacific Coast of South America* (Berkeley: University of California Press, 1965), 105, 113.

57. Scaglion, "*Kumara* in the Ecuadorian Gulf of Guayaquil?" 36–7.

58. See George F. Hourani and John Carswell, *Arab Seafaring: In the Indian Ocean in Ancient and Early Medieval Times (Expanded Edition)* (New Jersey: Princeton University Press, 1995); Himanshu P. Ray, *The Archaeology of Seafaring in Ancient South Asia* (New York: Cambridge University Press, 2003); and David Parkin and Ruth Barnes, eds., *Ships and the Development of Maritime Technology in the Indian Ocean* (New York: Routledge, 2002).

59. Burzug ibn Shahriyar (L. Marcel Devic, trans.), *The Book of the Marvels of India* (New York: Dial, 1929).

60. Bernstein, *A Splendid Exchange*, 99.

61. Bernstein, *A Splendid Exchange*, 99.

62. David Andrew Graff and Robin D.S. Higham, *A Military History of China* (Boulder, CO: Westview, 2002), 86–7.

63. Joseph W. Needham, *Clerks and Craftsmen in China and the West* (Cambridge: Cambridge University Press, 1970), 240.

64. Louise Levathes, *When China Ruled the Waves: The Treasure Fleet of the Dragon Throne, 1405–33* (New York: Simon & Schuster, 1994), 41.

65. Levathes, *When China Ruled the Waves*, 43.

66. See Ma Huan (J.V.G. Mills, trans.), *Ying-Yai Sheng-Lan: The Overall Survey of the Ocean's Shores* (Cambridge, UK: Cambridge University Press, 1970).

67. Levathes, *When China Ruled the Waves*, 81.

68. Ma Huan, *Ying-Yai Sheng-Lan*, 9.

69. Ma Huan, *Ying-Yai Sheng-Lan*, 113.

70. Levathes, *When China Ruled the Waves*, 172.

71. Ma Huan, *Ying-Yai Sheng-Lan*, 3.

72. Levathes, *When China Ruled the Waves*, 175.

73. See Klaus Beyer, *The Aramaic Language: Its Distribution and Subdivisions* (Göttingen: Vandenhoeck und Ruprecht, 1986); and Wolfhart Heinrichs, ed., *Studies in Neo-Aramaic* (Atlanta, GA: Scholars, 1990).

74. See Jean-Jacques Glassner, *The Invention of Cuneiform* (Baltimore: Johns Hopkins University Press, 2002).

75. Will Durant, *Our Oriental Heritage* (New York: Simon and Schuster, 1935), 131.

76. See James P. Allen, *Middle Egyptian: An Introduction to the Language and Culture of Hieroglyphic Writing* (New York: Cambridge University Press, 1999); and Janice Kamrin, *Ancient Egyptian Hieroglyphics* (New York: Harry N. Abrams, 2004).

77. Adolf Erman, *Literature of the Ancient Egyptians* (New York: Arno, 1976, originally published in 1927), 30–1.

78. Emmanuel Guillon, *Cham Art: Treasures from the Da Nang Museum, Vietnam* (London: Thames & Hudson, 2001), 68.

79. Guillon, *Cham Art*, 68.

80. Michael Vickery, *Society, Economics, and Politics in Pre-Angkor Cambodia: The 7th-8th Centuries* (Tokyo: The Centre for East Asian Cultural Studies for UNESCO, the Toyo Bunko, 1998), 91–2.

81. See Michael D. Coe and Justin Kerr, *The Art of the Maya Scribe* (London: Thames & Hudson, 1997).

82. See Ronald Reed, *Ancient Skins, Parchments, and Leathers* (New York: Seminar, 1972).

83. Michael C. Howard, ed., *Bark-cloth in Southeast Asia* (Bangkok: White Lotus, 2006), 1.

84. Joseph W. Needham and Tsien Tsuen-Hsuin, *Science and Civilization in China, Volume 5: Chemistry and Chemical Technology, Part 1, Paper and Printing* (New York: Cambridge University Press, 1985), 1.

85. Needham and Tsien, *Science and Civilization in China, Volume 5,* 123.

86. See Dard Hunter, *A Papermaking Pilgrimage to Japan, Korea and China* (New York: Pynson Printers, 1936); and Dard Hunter, *Papermaking: The History and Technique of an Ancient Craft* (New York: Alfred A. Knopf, 1943).

87. Timothy Barrett, *Japanese Papermaking: Traditions, Tools, and Techniques* (New York: Weatherhill, 1983).

88. See Alfred Bühler, "The Geographical Extent of the Use of Bark Fabrics," *Ciba Review* 33 (1940), 1170–5; and Shun-Sheng Ling, "Stone Bark-cloth Beaters of South China, Southeast Asia and Central America," *Bulletin of the Institute of Ethnology, Academia Sinica* 13 (1962), 195–212.

Chapter 2

1. William Little, H.W. Fowler, and J. Coulson (C.T. Onions, rev. and ed.), *The Oxford Universal Dictionary, Third Edition* (Oxford: Clarendon, 1955), 2337.

2. Michael C. Howard and Wattana Wattanapun, *The Palaung in Northern Thailand* (Chiang Mai: Silkworm, 2001), 41, 74.

3. Andrew Kitchen, Christopher Ehret, Shiferaw Assefa, and Connie J. Mulligan, "Bayesian Phylogenetic Analysis of Semitic Languages Identifies an Early Bronze Age Origin of Semitic in the Near East," *Proceedings of the Royal Society, Biological Sciences* 276, 1668 (2009), 2703–10.

4. See J.P. Mallory, *In Search of the Indo-Europeans: Language, Archaeology, and Myth* (London: Thames & Hudson, 1989); and Elena Kuz'mina (J. Mallory, ed.), *The Origins of the Indo-Iranians* (Leiden: Brill, 2007).

5. See Mallory, *In Search of the Indo-Europeans,* 48–55.

6. See Mallory, *In Search of the Indo-Europeans.*

7. See Trevor R. Bryce, *The Kingdom of the Hittites* (New York: Oxford University Press, 1999).

8. See Samuel Noah Kramer, *The Sumerians: Their History, Culture and Character* (Chicago: University of Chicago Press, 1963), 51–2.

9. See Arthur Ungnad, *Subartu, Beiträge zur Kulturgeschichte und Völkerkunde Vorderasiens* (Berlin: W. de Gruyter, 1936).

10. See Alfred Haldar, *Who Were the Amorites* (Leiden: E. J. Brill, 1971).

11. See W. F. Leeman, "The Importance of Trade: Some Introductory Remarks," *Iraq* 39, 1 (1977), 1–10; and Guillermo Algaze, *Ancient Mesopotamia at the Dawn of Civilization: The Evolution of an Urban Landscape* (Chicago: University of Chicago Press, 2009), 93.

12. Algaze, *Ancient Mesopotamia at the Dawn of Civilization,* 95.

13. Leeman, "The Importance of Trade," 5.

14. Algaze, *Ancient Mesopotamia at the Dawn of Civilization,* 94–5.

15. Leeman, "The Importance of Trade," 5.

16. See Asko Parpola and Simo Parpola, "On the Relationship of the Sumerian Toponym Meluhha and Sanskrit Mleccha," *Studia Orientalia* 46 (1975), 205–38.

17. See Leeman, "The Importance of Trade," 9. On Harappa as a source of chickens see A. Al-Nasser, et al.,

"Overview of Chicken Taxonomy and Domestication," *World's Poultry Science Journal* 63, June (2007), 285–300.

18. See S.R. Rao, *Lothal and the Indus Civilisation* (New Delhi: Asia, 1974).

19. See Peter M. M. G. Akkermans and Glenn M. Schwartz, *The Archaeology of Syria: From Complex Hunter-Gatherers to Early Urban Societies (c.16,000–300 BC)* (New York: Cambridge University Press, 2004); Lucio Milano, "Ebla: A Third-Millennium City-State in Ancient Syria," *Civilizations of the Ancient Near East,* ed. Jack M. Sasson (New York: Simon & Schuster, 1996), 1221; and Daniel E. Fleming, *Democracy's Ancient Ancestors: Mari and Early Collective Governance* (New York: Cambridge University Press, 2004), 6–8, 219–21.

20. Fleming, *Democracy's Ancient Ancestors,* 4.

21. Piotr Michalowski, "Third Millennium Contacts: Observations on the Relationships between Mari and Ebla," *Journal of the American Oriental Society* 105, 2 (1985), 301.

22. Leeman, "The Importance of Trade," 8–9.

23. Leeman, "The Importance of Trade," 8.

24. Juris Zarins, "Pastoral Nomadism and the Settlement of Lower Mesopotamia," *Bulletin of the American Schools of Oriental Research* 280, November (1990), 31–65.

25. See Giorgio Buccellati, "Akkadian," *The Semitic Languages,* ed. Robert Hetzron (New York: Routledge, 1997), 69–99.

26. See Kramer, *The Sumerians,* 59–61.

27. See Kramer, *The Sumerians,* 59–66.

28. Leeman, "The Importance of Trade," 5.

29. Milano, "Ebla," 1228.

30. Michalowski, "Third Millennium Contacts," 301.

31. Giorgio Buccellati and Marilyn Kelly-Buccellati, "Tar'am-Agade, Daughter of Naram-Sin, at Urkesh," *Of Pots and Plans: Papers on the Archaeology and History of Mesopotamia and Syria Presented to David Oates in Honour of His 75th Birthday,* ed. L. al Gailani Werr, J. Curtis, H. Martin, A. McMahon, J. Oates, and J. Reade (London: Nabu, 2002).

32. Richard A. Kerr, "Sea-Floor Dust Shows Drought Felled Akkadian Empire," *Science,* 279, 5340 (1998), 325–6.

33. 2047–2030 B.C. using the short chronology.

34. Leeman, "The Importance of Trade," 5.

35. 1940 B.C. using the alternative short chronology.

36. 1830 B.C. by the short chronology.

37. Leeman, "The Importance of Trade," 6.

38. Leeman, "The Importance of Trade," 5.

39. Klaas R. Veenhof and Jesper Eidem, *Mesopotamia: The Old Assyrian Period* (Fribourg: Academic Press; Göttingen: Vandenhoeck & Ruprecht, 2008), 131.

40. Klaas R. Veenhof, "Some Social Effects of Old Assyrian Trade," *Iraq* 39, 1 (1977), 109–18.

41. See Harvey Weiss, et al., "1985 Excavations at Tell Leilan, Syria," *American Journal of Archaeology* 94, 4 (1990), 529–81; and Jesper Eidem, Lauren Ristvet, and Harvey Weiss, *The Royal Archives from Tell Leilan: Old Babylonian Letters and Treaties from the Eastern Lower Town Palace* (New Haven, CT: Yale University Press, 2010).

42. See J.M. Sasson, "The King and I: A Mari King in Changing Perceptions," *Journal of the American Oriental Society* 118, 4 (1998), 453–70.

43. See Luc-Normand Tellier, *Urban World History: An Economic and Geographical Perspective* (Québec: Presses de l'Université du Québec, 2009), 61.

44. Stephen Bartman, *Handbook of Life in Ancient Mesopotamia* (New York: Oxford University Press, 2005), 74.

45. Tellier, *Urban World History*, 64.

46. For primary accounts relating to his reign see Hayim Tadmor, *The Inscriptions of Tiglath-Pileser III, King of Assyria* (Jerusalem: Israel Academy of Sciences and Humanities, 1994).

47. Durant, *Our Oriental Heritage*, 270.

48. Leeman, "The Importance of Trade," 6.

49. Durant, *Our Oriental Heritage*, 270.

50. Tellier, *Urban World History*, 65.

51. Durant, *Our Oriental Heritage*, 270.

52. Durant, *Our Oriental Heritage*, 266.

53. See Anne Katrine Gade Kristensen (Jorgen Laessoe, trans.), *Who Were the Cimmerians, and Where Did They Come From? Sargon II, and the Cimmerians, and Rusa I* (Copenhagen, Denmark: The Royal Danish Academy of Science and Letters, 1988).

54. See Stefan Zawadzki, *The Fall of Assyria and Median-Babylonian Relation in Light of the Nabopolassar Chronicle* (Delft: Eburon, 1988).

55. Durant, *Our Oriental Heritage*, 325.

56. Durant, *Our Oriental Heritage*, 263.

57. I.M. Diakonoff, "Media I: The Medes and Their Neighbours," *The Cambridge History of Iran*, ed. Ilya Gershevitch (New York: Cambridge University Press, 1985), Volume 2, 104, n. 1.

58. See Diakonoff, "Media I: The Medes and Their Neighbours"; and T. Cuyler Young, "The Early History of the Medes and the Persians and the Achaemenid Empires to the Death of Cambyses," *The Cambridge Ancient History, IV: Persia, Greece and the Western Mediterranean, c. 525 to 479 B.C*, ed. M. Boardman, N.G.L. Hammond, D.M. Lewis, and M. Ostwald (New York: Cambridge University Press, 1988), 1–52.

59. Ernst Herzfeld, *The Persian Empire: Studies in Geography and Ethnography of the Ancient Near East* (Weisbaden: Franz Steiner, 1968), 344.

60. Alden A. Mosshammer, "Thales' Eclipse," *Transactions of the American Philological Association*, 111 (1981), 145–55.

61. Pierre Briant (Peter Daniels, trans.), *From Cyrus to Alexander: A History of the Persian Empire* (Winona Lake, IN: Eisenbrauns, 2002), 31.

62. George Rawlinson, *The Five Great Monarchies of the Ancient World* (New York: Dodd, Mead, 1870), Volume 3, 417.

63. Durant, *Our Oriental Heritage*, 363.

64. Rawlinson, *The Five Great Monarchies*, Volume 3, 425.

65. Durant, *Our Oriental Heritage*, 357–8.

66. Durant, *Our Oriental Heritage*, 358.

67. Rawlinson, *The Five Great Monarchies*, Volume 3, 427.

68. Herodotus, *The Histories* (New York: Everyman's Library, 1997); cited in Rawlinson, *The Five Great Monarchies*, Volume 3, 242.

69. Rawlinson, *The Five Great Monarchies*, Volume 3, 427.

70. Durant, *Our Oriental Heritage*, 358.

71. Rawlinson, *The Five Great Monarchies*, Volume 3, 426.

72. Durant, *Our Oriental Heritage*, 358.

73. Herodotus, *The Histories*, i 153, ii 167; cited in Rawlinson, *The Five Great Monarchies*, Volume 3, 242.

74. Rawlinson, *The Five Great Monarchies*, Volume 3, 243.

75. Robin Lane Fox, *Alexander the Great* (New York: E.P. Dutton, 1974), 301.

76. See J. Duchesne-Guillemin, "Zoroastrian Religion," *Cambridge History of Iran*, ed. Ehsan Yarshater (London: Cambridge University Press, 2008), Volume 3.2, 866–908.

77. See Glanville Downey, *Ancient Antioch* (Princeton, NJ: Princeton University Press, 1963).

78. G. Georges Aperghis, *The Seleukid Royal Economy: The Finances and Financial Administration of the Seleukid Empire* (New York: Cambridge University Press, 2004), 93–4.

79. Aperghis, *The Seleukid Royal Economy*, 76–7.

80. A.D.H. Bivar, "The Political History of Iran under the Arsacids," *Cambridge History of Iran*, ed. Ehsan Yarshater (New York: Cambridge University Press, 2000), Volume 3.1, 28–9.

81. See Pierre Lecoq, "Aparna," *Encyclopaedia Iranica* (New York: Routledge, 1987), Volume 2, 151, online at <www.iranica.com/articles/aparna-c3k>.

82. See Bivar, "The Political History of Iran under the Arsacids," 28–9.

83. Bivar, "The Political History of Iran under the Arsacids," 33.

84. Bivar, "The Political History of Iran under the Arsacids," 39.

85. See the map showing the Royal Road in Bivar, "The Political History of Iran under the Arsacids," 25; and Tellier, *Urban World History*, 141.

86. Tellier, *Urban World History*, 87.

87. Strabo, *The Geography* (Cambridge, MA: Harvard University Press, Loeb Classical Library, 1932), Book 16, Chapter 1, 219, online at <penelope.uchicago.edu/Thayer/E/Roman/Texts/Strabo/16A*.html>. Another print edition is: *The Geography of Strabo* (London: George Bell & Sons, 1903).

88. Tellier, *Urban World History*, 189.

89. Strabo, *The Geography*, Book 16, Chapter 1, 219; and see Bivar, "The Political History of Iran under the Arsacids," 39–40.

90. Strabo, *The Geography*, Book 16, Chapter 1, 219.

91. Strabo, *The Geography*, Book 16, Chapter 1, 219.

92. Gary K. Young, *Rome's Eastern Trade: International Commerce and Imperial Policy, 31 BC–AD 305* (New York: Routledge, 2001), 147.

93. Young, *Rome's Eastern Trade*, 148.

94. R.E. Emmerick, "Buddhism among Iranian Peoples," *Cambridge History of Iran*, ed. Ehsan Yarshater (New York: Cambridge University Press, 2008), Volume 3.2, 952. Also see E. Zürcher, *The Buddhist Conquest of China: The Spread and Adaptation of Buddhism in Early Medieval China*, 3rd ed. (Leiden: E.J. Brill, 1959), and Richard C. Folz, *Spirituality in the Land of the Noble: How Iran Shaped the World's Religions* (Oxford: Oneworld, 2004).

95. Emmerick, "Buddhism among Iranian Peoples," 956–7.

96. Bivar, "The Political History of Iran under the Arsacids," 81, 93–6.

97. See Nilakantha Shastri, *Age of the Nandas and Mauryas* (New Delhi: Motilal Banarsidass, 1967).

98. See Kristi L. Wiley, *Historical Dictionary of Jainism* (Lanham, MD: Scarecrow, 2004).

99. See B.C. Law, *Tribes in Ancient India* (Poona: Bhandarkar Oriental Research Institute, 1973), 245–56.

100. Durant, *Our Oriental Heritage*, 441. Also see Radha Kumud Mookerji, *Chandragupta Maurya and His Times* (New Delhi: Motilal Banarsidass, 1988).

101. Durant, *Our Oriental Heritage*, 441.

102. Durant, *Our Oriental Heritage*, 443.

103. Durant, *Our Oriental Heritage*, 444.

104. D. D. Kosambi, *The Culture and Civilisation of Ancient India in Historical Outline*, 8th ed. (New Delhi: Vikas, 1982), 160–1.

105. Kosambi, *The Culture and Civilisation of Ancient India,* 161.

106. Durant, *Our Oriental Heritage,* 444.

107. See Manoranjan Bhaumick, *History, Culture and Antiquities of Tamralipta* (Kolkata: Punthi Pustak, 2001); also see the entry on Tamluk by Amita Ray and Kaushik Gangopadhyay, online at <www.banglapedia.org/http docs/HT/T_0040.HTM>.

108. For an account of the Council see <lakdiva.org/mahavamsa/chap005.html>.

109. Ven. S. Dhammika, *Edicts of King Ashoka* (Kandy: Buddhist Publications Society, 1993), online at <www.cs.colostate.edu/~malaiya/ashoka.html>.

110. See Romila Thapar, *Asoka and the Decline of the Mauryas* (New Delhi: Oxford University Press, 2001), 185–7.

111. See H.C. Raychaudhuri, *Political History of Ancient India* (Calcutta: University of Calcutta, 1972), 312–3.

112. Strabo, *The Geography.*

113. J.W. McCrindle, *Ancient India as Described by Megasthenes and Arrian: A Translation of the Fragments of the Indika of Megasthenes Collected by Dr. Schwanbeck, and of the First Part of the Indika of Arrian* (London: Trüber & Co.; Bombay: Thacker & Co., and Calcutta: Thacker, Spink & Co., 1877), online at <www.archive.org/stream/ancientindiaasd02mccrgoog#page/n6/mode/2up> and also at <www.sdstate.edu/projectsouthasia/upload/Megasthene-Indika.pdf>.

114. Durant, *Our Oriental Heritage,* 446.

115. Pliny the Elder (John Bostock and H.T. Riley, eds.), *The Natural History: Book VI, An Account of Countries, Nations, Seas, Towns, Haven, Mountains, Rivers, Distances, and Peoples Who Now Exist, or Formerly Existed* (London: Taylor and Francis, 1855), Chapter 21, online at <perseus.mpiwg-berlin.mpg.de/cgi-bin/ptext?lookup=Plin.+Nat.+6.21>.

116. See Thapar, *Asoka and the Decline of the Mauryas.*

117. See John Marshall, *A Guide to Sanchi* (Calcutta: Manager of Publications, Government of India, 1955).

118. See Elizabeth Errington and Joe Cribb, eds., *The Crossroads of Asia: Transformation in Image and Symbol in the Art of Ancient Afghanistan and Pakistan* (Cambridge: Ancient India and Iran Trust, 1992).

119. Radhakumud Mookerji, *The Gupta Empire* (New Delhi: Motilal Banarsidass, 1995), 11; also see Vincent A. Smith, *The Oxford History of India* (New York: Oxford University Press, 1981, originally published 1924).

120. Mookerji, *The Gupta Empire,* 49.

121. Mookerji, *The Gupta Empire,* 50.

122. Mookerji, *The Gupta Empire,* 119; and N.K. Ojha, *The Aulikaras of Central India: History and Inscriptions* (Chandigarh: Arun, 2001), 52. Also see Ashvivi Agarwal, *Rise and Fall of the Imperial Guptas* (New Delhi: Motilal Banarsidass, 1989).

123. See Agarwal, *Rise and Fall of the Imperial Guptas,* 238–9.

124. Will Durant, *Caesar and Christ: A History of Roman Civilization and of Christianity from their Beginnings to A.D. 325* (New York: Simon and Schuster, 1944), 414.

125. Michael Grant, *History of Rome* (New York: Charles Scribner, 1978), 264.

126. See Richard Talbert, "The Senate and Senatorial and Equestrian Posts," *Cambridge Ancient History, X: The Augustan Empire, 43 B.C.–A.D. 69,* ed. Alan K. Brown, Edward Champlin, and Andrew Lintott (New York: Cambridge University Press, 1996), 324–43.

127. See George Long, "Foederatae Civitaes," *A Dictionary of Greek and Roman Antiquities,* ed. William Smith (London: John Murray, 1875), 542–543, online at <penelope.uchicago.edu/Thayer/E/Roman/Texts/secondary/SMIGRA*/Foederatae_Civitates.html>.

128. Durant, *Caesar and Christ,* 121.

129. Durant, *Caesar and Christ,* 121.

130. See Durant, *Caesar and Christ,* 122; Long, "Foederatae Civitaes," 543; and E. T. Salmon, "Notes on the Social War," *Transactions and Proceedings of the American Philological Association,* 89 (1958), 159–84.

131. See Durant, *Caesar and Christ,* 193–4, 216; and Mark Hassall, "Romans and non–Romans," *The Roman World,* ed. John S. Wacher (New York: Routledge, 1987), Volume 1, 685–700.

132. Durant, *Caesar and Christ,* 194.

133. Durant, *Caesar and Christ,* 622–3.

134. David Noy, *Foreigners at Rome: Citizens and Strangers* (London: Duckworth & Classical Press of Wales, 2000), 32.

135. Noy, *Foreigners at Rome,* 24.

136. Alan K. Bowman, "Provincial Administration and Taxation," *Cambridge Ancient History, Volume X: The Augustan Empire, 43 B.C.–A.D. 69,* ed. Alan K. Brown, Edward Champlin, and Andrew Lintott (New York: Cambridge University Press, 1996), 344, 346.

137. Christopher Kelly, "Bureaucracy and Government," *The Cambridge Companion to the Age of Constantine,* ed. Noel Lenski (New York: Cambridge University Press, 2006), 185–7.

138. Talbert, "The Senate and Senatorial and Equestrian Posts," 324–5.

139. Talbert, "The Senate and Senatorial and Equestrian Posts," 337.

140. Talbert, "The Senate and Senatorial and Equestrian Posts," 351.

141. Talbert, "The Senate and Senatorial and Equestrian Posts," 351.

142. His full name was Quintus Flavius Maesius Egnatius Lollianus signo Mavortius; see François Chausson, "Les Egnatii et l'aristocatie italienne des IIe–IVe siècles," *Journal des Savants* 2 (1997), 211–331, which provides a genealogical diagram relating to Lollianus Mavortius on p. 216.

143. On provincial administration in general see Talbert, "The Senate and Senatorial and Equestrian Posts"; Ramsay MacMullen, "Imperial Bureaucrats in the Roman Provinces," *Harvard Studies in Classical Philosophy,* 68 (1964), 305–316; and Graham Burton, "Government and the Provinces," *The Roman World,* ed. John S. Wacher (New York: Routledge, 1987), Volume 1, 423–39.

144. Talbert, "The Senate and Senatorial and Equestrian Posts," 347.

145. Talbert, "The Senate and Senatorial and Equestrian Posts," 353.

146. Talbert, "The Senate and Senatorial and Equestrian Posts," 357.

147. See P. Faure, "Les Centurions Frumentaires et le Commandment des Castra Peregrina," *Mélanges de l'Ecole française de Rome Antiquité* 115 (2003), 377–427.

148. See William J. Sinnegen, "Two Branches of the Roman Secret Service," *The American Journal of Philology* 80, 3 (1959), 238–54.

149. Sinnegen, "Two Branches of the Roman Secret Service," 249.

150. Christopher Kelly, *Ruling the Later Roman Empire* (Cambridge, MA: Harvard University Press, 2004), 207.

151. Jeremy Paterson, "Trade and Traders in the Roman World: Scale, Structure, and Organisation," *Trade, Traders and the Ancient City,* ed. H. Parkins and C. Smith

(New York: Routledge, 1998), 150. Also see A.J. Parker, "Trade within the Empire and Beyond the Frontiers," *The Roman World,* ed. John S. Wacher (New York: Routledge, 1987), Volume 1, 635–57.

152. Paterson, "Trade and Traders in the Roman World," 150.

153. Durant, *Caesar and Christ,* 328–9.

154. Durant, *Caesar and Christ,* 330.

155. Paterson, "Trade and Traders in the Roman World," 161–2; and Gary K. Young, *Rome's Eastern Trade: International Commerce and Imperial Policy, 31 BC—AD 305* (New York: Routledge, 2001), 59–60.

156. Young, *Rome's Eastern Trade,* 59–60.

157. Young, *Rome's Eastern Trade,* 49–50. The duties were figured in terms of drachmas and oboli. These were Greek measurements and monetary terms. A drachma was divided into six oboli. A drachma weighed about 3.4 to 4.3 grams of silver and was worth about the daily wage of a skilled worker.

158. Young, *Rome's Eastern Trade,* 55–7.

159. Young, *Rome's Eastern Trade,* 57.

160. Young, *Rome's Eastern Trade,* 54.

161. Talbert, "The Senate and Senatorial and Equestrian Posts," 349.

162. Talbert, "The Senate and Senatorial and Equestrian Posts," 349.

163. Walter C. Perry, *The Franks, from Their First Appearance in History to the Death of King Pepin* (London: Longman, Brown, Green, Longmans, and Roberts, 1857), 43; and Cornelius Tacitus (Robert G. Latham, trans.), *The Germania of Tacitus: With Ethnological Dissertations and Notes* (London: Taylor, Walton, and Maberly, 1851), lvii, lx. Also see Lucien Musset, *The Germanic Invasions: The Making of Europe, AD 400–600* (University Park: Pennsylvania State University Press, 1975).

164. Perry, *The Franks,* 47.

165. Perry, *The Franks,* 47; and see John Casey, *Carausius and Allectus: British Usurpers* (New York: Routledge, 1994). His full name was Marcus Aurelius Mausaeus Valerius Carausius. The Menapian lived in an area roughly corresponding to modern Belgium.

166. Pat Southern, *The Roman Empire from Severus to Constantine* (New York: Routledge, 2001), 152.

167. Anthony R. Birley, *The Roman Government in Britain* (New York: Oxford University Press, 2005), 373.

168. Perry, *The Franks,* 53–4.

169. John F. Drinkwater, "The Revolt and Ethnic Origin of the Usurper Magnentius (350–53), and the Rebellion of Vetranio (350)," *Chiron: Mitteilungen der Kommission für Alte Geschichte und Epigraphikdes Deutschen Archäologischen Instituts* 30 (2000), 131–59.

170. David S. Potter, *The Roman Empire at Bay, AD 180–395* (New York: Routledge, 2004), 471–2.

171. According to Zonaras, in his history (v. 13, 8.17), cited in Thomas Banchich and Eugene Lane, *The History of Zonaras from Alexander Severus to the Death of Theodosius the Great* (New York: Routledge, 2009).

172. Potter, *The Roman Empire at Bay,* 474.

173. Potter, *The Roman Empire at Bay,* 481.

174. Potter, *The Roman Empire at Bay,* 481.

175. See Potter, *The Roman Empire at Bay,* 481–2.

176. Perry, *The Franks,* 54–5.

177. Perry, *The Franks,* 55–6.

178. Perry, *The Franks,* 57.

179. See Kwang-Chih Chang, "China on the Eve of the Historical Period," *The Cambridge History of Ancient China, From the Origins of Civilization to 221 B.C.,* ed. Michael Loewe and Edward L. Shaughnessy (New York: Cambridge University Press, 1999), 57–8.

180. On their common heritage see Chang, "China on the Eve of the Historical Period," 52.

181. On the origins of rice see, "Rice's Origins Point to China, Genome Researchers Conclude," *Science Newsline Biology* 3 May 2011, online at <www.sciencenewsline.com/biology/2011050313000047.html>.

182. See *Bark-cloth in Southeast Asia,* ed. Michael C. Howard (Bangkok: White Lotus, 2006).

183. See Herald J. Wiens, *Han Chinese Expansion in South China* (Hamden, CT: Shoe String, 1967), 42, 55, 60.

184. Friedrich Hirth, *The Ancient History of China to the End of the Chóu Dynasty* (Freeport, NY: Books for Libraries, 1969, originally published 1908), 195.

185. Jay Xu, "Sichuan before the Warring States Period," *Ancient Sichuan: Treasures from a Lost Civilization,* ed. Robert Bagley (Seattle: Seattle Art Museum, 2001), 32.

186. Chang, "China on the Eve of the Historical Period," 71.

187. Chang, "China on the Eve of the Historical Period," 72.

188. Robert Bagley, "Shang Archaeology," *The Cambridge History of Ancient China, From the Origins of Civilization to 221 B.C.,* ed. Michael Loewe and Edward L. Shaughnessy (New York: Cambridge University Press, 1999), 181.

189. Bagley, "Shang Archaeology," 201.

190. David K. Keightley, "The Shang: China's First Historical Dynasty," *The Cambridge History of Ancient China, From the Origins of Civilization to 221 B.C.,* ed. Michael Loewe and Edward L. Shaughnessy (New York: Cambridge University Press, 1999), 281.

191. Bagley, "Shang Archaeology," 197, 230.

192. Keightley, "The Shang," 276–7.

193. Keightley, "The Shang," 288.

194. Edward L. Shaughnessy, "Western Zhou History," *The Cambridge History of Ancient China, From the Origins of Civilization to 221 B.C.,* ed. Michael Loewe and Edward L. Shaughnessy (New York: Cambridge University Press, 1999), 311.

195. Shaughnessy, "Western Zhou History," 312–3.

196. Jessica Rawson, "Western Zhou Archaeology," *The Cambridge History of Ancient China, From the Origins of Civilization to 221 B.C.,* ed. Michael Loewe and Edward L. Shaughnessy (New York: Cambridge University Press, 1999), 404.

197. Shaughnessy, "Western Zhou History," 322.

198. Constance A. Cook and Barry B. Blakeley, "Introduction," *Defining Chu: Image and Reality in Ancient China,* ed. Constance A. Cook and Barry B. Blakeley (Honolulu: University of Hawai'i Press, 1999), 4.

199. Cook and Blakeley, "Introduction," 9.

200. James R. Chamberlain, "The Origins of the Sek: Implications for Tai and Vietnamese History," *Journal of the Siam Society* 86, 1–2 (1998), 38–9.

201. Leonard Aurousseau, "Le première conquête chinois des pays Annamites," *Bulletin de l'Ecole Française d'Extrême Orient* 23 (1923), 255.

202. C. Madrolle, "Le Tonkin ancien," *Bulletin de l'Ecole Française d'Extrême Orient* 37, 2 (1937), 313–4, 319.

203. See Rawson, "Western Zhou Archaeology," 427–30.

204. Xu, "Sichuan before the Warring States Period," 34.

205. Cook and Blakeley, "Introduction," 1.

206. Michael C. Howard, *Textiles of the Highland Peoples of Burma, Volume II* (Bangkok: White Lotus, 2005), 173.

207. Michael C. Howard, "Religious and Status-Marking Functions of Textiles among the Tai Peoples of Vietnam," *The Secrets of Southeast Asian Textiles,* ed. Jane Puranananda (Bangkok: River, 2007), 194.

208. The history of Nam Yue is recorded in "Chapter 113: Ordered Annals of Nanyue" (aka "Treatise on the Nanyua") in Sima Qian (Burton Watson, trans.), *Records of the Grand Historian: Han Dynasty* (Hong Kong: Chinese University of Hong Kong; New York: Columbia University Press, 1993).

209. John N. Miksic, "The Beginning of Trade in Ancient Southeast Asia: the Role of Oc Eo and the Lower Mekong River," *Art & Archaeology of Funan,* ed. James C.M. Khoo (Bangkok: Orchid, 2003), 7; and see Wang Gungwu, "The Nanhai Trade: Early Chinese Trade in the South China Sea," *Journal of the Malaysian Branch of the Royal Asiatic Society* 32, 2 (1958), 7.

210. The Cuong temple near the battle site commemorates the defeat and contains shrines dedicated to Thuc Phan and his general Cao Lo. See Michael C. Howard, "Searching for the Identity of the Bird on Dongson Drums," *Arts of Asia* 34, 2 (2004), 140–1; and Howard, "Religious and Status-Marking Functions of Textiles among the Tai Peoples of Vietnam," 194–5.

211. Burton Watson, *Records of the Grand Historian of China, Volume II: The Age of Emperor Wu 140 to Circa 100 BC.* (New York: Columbia University Press, 1961). Also see Homer H. Dubs (trans.), *The History of the Former Han Dynasty,* 3 volumes (Baltimore: Waverly, 1938–55), available online in digitalized form.

212. Watson, *Records of the Grand Historian of China, Volume II,* 123.

213. See Wang, "The Nanhai Trade," 17.

214. See Taishan Yu, *A History of the Relationships between the Western and Eastern Han, Wei, Jin, Northern and Southern Dynasties and the Western Regions,* Sino-Platonic Papers 131 (Philadelphia: Department of East Asian Languages and Civilizations, University of Pennsylvania, 2004).

215. John E. Hill, *Through the Jade Gate to Rome: A Study of the Silk Routes during the Later Han Dynasty, First to Second Centuries CE* (Charleston, SC: BookSurge, 2009), 5. Accounts of Ban Chao also appear in Watson, *Records of the Grand Historian of China,* and in Sima Qian (Homer H. Dubs, trans.), *The History of the Former Han Dynasty,* 3 volumes (Baltimore: Waverly, 1938–55), as well as Sima Qian, *Records of the Grand Historian: Han Dynasty.*

216. In addition to versions of this such as Watson, *Records of the Grand Historian of China,* and Dubs, *The History of the Former Han Dynasty,* an online version of the portion on trade is available: John E. Hill, *The Western Regions according to Hou Hanshu: The Xiyu Juan, Chapter on the Western Regions from Hou Hanshu 88,* 2nd ed. (Seattle: University of Washington, 2003), online at <depts.washington.edu/silkroad/texts/hhshu/hou_han_shu.html>.

217. See Irene Good, "On the Question of Silk in Pre-Han Eurasia," *Antiquity* 69, 266 (1995), 959–68.

218. Felicitas Maeder, "The Project Sea-silk — Rediscovering an Ancient Textile Material," *Archaeological Textiles Newsletter* 35 (2002), 8–11; and Daniel L. McLinley, "Pinna and Her Silken Beard: A Foray into Historical Misappropriations," *Ars Textrina* 29 (1998), 9–22.

219. Wang, "The Nanhai Trade: Early Chinese Trade in the South China Sea," 20.

220. Wang, "The Nanhai Trade: Early Chinese Trade in the South China Sea," 26.

221. Georges Maspero, *The Champa Kingdom: The History of an Extinct Vietnamese Culture* (Bangkok: White Lotus, 2002, originally published 1928), 24.

222. Maspero, *The Champa Kingdom,* 24.

223. Maspero, *The Champa Kingdom,* 26.

224. See Michael Rogers, *The Rise of the Former Ch'in State and Its Spread under Fu Chien, through 370 A.D.* (Berkeley: University of California Press, 1953); and Michael Rogers, *The Chronicle of Fu Chien: A Case of Exemplar History,* Chinese Dynastic Histories Translations No. 10 (Berkeley: University of California Press, 1968).

225. Wang, "The Nanhai Trade: Early Chinese Trade in the South China Sea," 35.

226. See J.O. Maenchen-Helfen, *The World of the Huns: Studies in Their History and Culture* (Berkeley: University of California Press, 1973).

227. See Peter Heather, *The Fall of the Roman Empire: A New History of Rome and the Barbarians* (New York: Oxford University Press, 2005).

228. Nicola Di Cosmo, "The Northern Frontier in Pre-imperial China," *The Cambridge History of Ancient China: From the Origins of Civilization to 221 B.C.,* ed. Michael Loewe and Edward L. Shaughnessy (New York: Cambridge University Press, 1999), 965.

229. René Grousset (Naomi Walford, trans.), *The Empire of the Steppes: A History of Central Asia* (Piscataway, NJ: Rutgers University Press, 2002), 27.

230. The Han historian Sima Qian (l. 145–86 B.C.) relates the story of the initial practice; see Sima Qian, *Records of the Grand Historian: Han Dynasty.* Also see Tamara T. Chin, "Defamiliarizing the Foreigners: Sima Qian's Ethnography and Han-Xiongu Marriage Diplomacy," *Harvard Journal of Asiatic Studies* 70, 2 (2010), 311–354; and Cui Mingde, *The History of Chinese Heqin: Brief Charts of Heqin Events* (Beijing: Renmin Chubanshe, 2005).

231. See Uradyn E. Bulag, *The Mongols at China's Edge* (Lanham, MD: Rowman & Littlefield, 2002), Ch. 3.

Chapter 3

1. Will Durant, *The Age of Faith: A History of Medieval Civilization — Christian, Islamic, and Judaic — from Constantine to Dante: A.D. 325–1300* (New York: Simon and Schuster, 1950), 119.

2. Durant, *The Age of Faith,* 118.

3. Durant, *The Age of Faith,* 436.

4. Sukumar Dutt, *Buddhist Monks and Monasteries of India: Their History and Contribution to Indian Culture* (London: George Allen & Unwin, 1962), 352–3.

5. Dutt, *Buddhist Monks and Monasteries of India,* 373.

6. See R.C. Majumdar, *Ancient India* (New Delhi: Motilal Banarsidass Publications, 1987), 407.

7. C.W. Previté-Orton, *The Shorter Cambridge Medieval History* (New York: Cambridge University Press, 1971), Volume 1, 239.

8. Durant, *The Age of Faith,* 208.

9. Durant, *The Age of Faith,* 208.

10. Bernstein, *A Splendid Exchange,* 81–2.

11. Bernstein, *A Splendid Exchange,* 82.

12. George F. Hourani and John Carswell, *Arab Seafaring: In the Indian Ocean in Ancient and Early Medieval Times,* Expanded ed. (Princeton, NJ: Princeton University Press, 1995), 77.

13. See Charles Benn, *China's Golden Age: Everyday Life in the Tang Dynasty* (New York: Oxford University Press, 2002).

14. See Marc S. Abramson, *Ethnic Identity in Tang China* (Philadelphia: University of Pennsylvania Press, 2008).

15. Benn, *China's Golden Age*, 11.

16. Edward H. Schafer, *The Golden Peaches of Samarkand: A Study of T'ang Exotics* (Berkeley: University of California Press, 1963), 15.

17. Raphael Israeli, *Islam in China* (Lexington, MA: Lexington, 2002), 291.

18. Schafer, *The Golden Peaches of Samarkand*, 11.

19. Schafer, *The Golden Peaches of Samarkand*, 11; and Edwin O. Reischauer, "Notes on T'ang Dynasty Sea Routes," *Harvard Journal of Asiatic Studies* 5, 2 (1940), 155–7.

20. Reischauer, "Notes on T'ang Dynasty Sea Routes," 155–6.

21. See John S. Bowman, *Columbia Chronologies of Asian History and Culture* (New York: Columbia University Press, 2000), 104–5.

22. Benn, *China's Golden Age*, 11.

23. Schafer, *The Golden Peaches of Samarkand*, 15.

24. Durant, *The Age of Faith*, 242.

25. Shen Fuwei, *Cultural Flow between China and the Outside World* (Beijing: Foreign Languages Press, 1996), 163.

26. Shen, *Cultural Flow between China and the Outside World*, 155.

27. Louise Levathes, *When China Ruled the Waves: The Treasure Fleet of the Dragon Throne, 1405–33* (New York: Simon & Schuster, 1994), 38.

28. Shen, *Cultural Flow between China and the Outside World*, 158; and S.A.M. Adshead, *T'ang China: The Rise of the East in World History* (New York: Palgrave Macmillan, 2004), 80.

29. Shen, *Cultural Flow between China and the Outside World*, 159–61.

30. See Christopher P. Atwood, *Encyclopedia of Mongolia and the Mongol Empire* (New York: Facts on File, 2004); and John J. Saunders, *The History of the Mongol Conquests* (London: Routledge & Kegan Paul, 1971).

31. See Morris Rossabi, *Khubilai Khan: His Life and Times* (Berkeley: University of California Press, 1988).

32. See Reuven Amitai and Michael Biran, eds., *Mongols, Turks, and Others: Eurasan Nomads and the Sedentary World* (Leiden: E.J. Brill, 2005); Charles J. Halperin, *Russia and the Golden Horde: The Mongol Impact on Medieval Russian History* (Bloomington: Indiana University Press, 1985); and George Vernadsky, *The Mongols and Russia* (New Haven, CT: Yale University Press, 1953).

33. Henry Yule (trans.), *The Travels of Friar Odoric* (Grand Rapids, MI: William B. Eerdmans, 2002).

34. Jonathan D. Spence, *The Search for Modern China* (New York: W.W. Norton, 1991).

35. Timothy Brook, *The Confusions of Pleasure: Commerce and Culture in Ming China* (Berkeley: University of California Press, 1998), 19.

36. William H. Prescott, *History of the Conquest of Mexico* (Philadelphia: David McKay, 1891), Volume 1, 51.

37. Prescott, *History of the Conquest of Mexico*, Volume 1, 52.

38. Prescott, *History of the Conquest of Mexico*, Volume 1, 52.

39. Prescott, *History of the Conquest of Mexico*, Volume 1, 52.

40. Prescott, *History of the Conquest of Mexico*, Volume 1, 52, 65.

41. Prescott, *History of the Conquest of Mexico*, Volume 1, 54–5.

42. Prescott, *History of the Conquest of Mexico*, Volume 1, 65.

43. Prescott, *History of the Conquest of Mexico*, Volume 1, 65.

44. Juan de Torquemada, *Monarquía Indiana* (Mexico: Editorial Cultura, 1975–9), Volume 4, 320–1; and Prescott, *History of the Conquest of Mexico*, Volume 1, 66.

Chapter 4

1. See Christopher Beckwith, *Empires of the Silk Road: A History of Central Eurasia from the Bronze Age to the Present* (Princeton, NJ: Princeton University Press, 2009); John E. Hill, *Through the Jade Gate to Rome: A Study of the Silk Routes during the Later Han Dynasty, 1st to 2nd Centuries CE* (Charleston, SC: BookSurge, 2009); René Grousset (Naomi Walford, trans.), *The Empire of the Steppes: A History of Central Asia* (Piscataway, NJ: Rutgers University Press, 2002); and Nicola Di Cosmo, *Ancient China and Its Enemies: The Rise of Nomadic Power in East Asian History* (New York: Cambridge University Press, 2002).

2. Xinru Liu, "Migration and Settlement of the Yuezhi-Kushan: Interaction and Interdependence of Nomadic and Sedentary Societies," *Journal of World History* 12, 2 (2001), 265.

3. Liu, "Migration and Settlement of the Yuezhi-Kushan," 272.

4. Liu, "Migration and Settlement of the Yuezhi-Kushan," 273.

5. K. Enoki, G.A. Koshelenko, and Z. Haidary, "The Yüeh-chih and their Migrations," *History and Civilizations of Central Asia, Volume II*, ed. János Harmatta, B.N. Puri, and G.F. Etemadi (New Delhi: Motilal Banarsidass, 1999), 175, 179.

6. Enoki, Koshelenko, and Haidary, "The Yüeh-chih and their Migrations," 175–6; and Craig G.R. Benjamin, *The Yuezhi: Origins, Migration and the Conquest of Northern Bactria* (Louvain: Brepols, 2006), 71–4.

7. See Enoki, Koshelenko, and Haidary, "The Yüeh-chih and their Migrations"; Benjamin, *The Yuezhi;* and Sima Qian, *Records of the Grand Historian: Han Dynasty, Part II*, 234.

8. Enoki, Koshelenko, and Haidary, "The Yüeh-chih and their Migrations," 179.

9. Enoki, Koshelenko, and Haidary, "The Yüeh-chih and their Migrations," 179.

10. P. Bernard, "The Greek Kingdoms of Central Asia," *History and Civilizations of Central Asia, Volume II*, ed. János Harmatta, B.N. Puri, and G.F. Etemadi (New Delhi: Motilal Banarsidass, 1999), 103. Greek and Roman sources such as *The Geography of Strabo* (Book 11, Ch. 1, Sec. 1) refer to them as Tocharoi; see Liu, "Migration and Settlement of the Yuezhi-Kushan," 266–8.

11. Enoki, Koshelenko, and Haidary, "The Yüeh-chih and their Migrations," 180.

12. Sima Qian, *Records of the Grand Historian: Han Dynasty*, 123.

13. See Enoki, Koshelenko, and Haidary, "The Yüeh-chih and their Migrations."

14. Enoki, Koshelenko, and Haidary, "The Yüeh-chih and their Migrations," 185.

15. Liu, "Migration and Settlement of the Yuezhi-Kushan," 264.

16. Joseph Hackin, *Recherches archéologiques à Begram* (Paris: Les Editions d'art et histoire, 1939); and Joseph Hackin, *Nouvelle recherches archéologiques à Begram (an-*

cienne Kâpicî), 1939–1940 (Paris: Imprimère Nationale, Presses Universitaires, 1954). Also see John M. Rosenfield, *The Dynastic Art of the Kushans* (New Delhi: Munshiram Manoharlal, 1993).

17. Liu, "Migration and Settlement of the Yuezhi-Kushan," 281.

18. See Shinu A. Abraham, "Chera, Chola, Pandya: Using Archaeological Evidence to Identify the Tamil Kingdoms of Early Historic South India," *Asian Perspectives: The Journal of Archaeology for Asia and the Pacific* 42, 2 (2003), 207–23.

19. E.H. Warmington, *The Commerce between the Roman Empire and India,* 2nd ed. (London: Curzon Press, 1974), 50; and Lionel Casson, "Ancient Naval Technology and the Route to India," *Rome and India: The Ancient Sea Trade,* ed. V. Bagley and R.D. De Puma (Madison: University of Wisconsin Press, 1992), 9–10.

20. Roberta Tomber, *Indo-Roman Trade: From Pots to Pepper* (London: Duckworth, 2008), 150.

21. Warmington, *The Commerce between the Roman Empire and India,* 68.

22. See V. Bagley and R.D. De Puma, eds., *Rome and India: The Ancient Sea Trade* (Madison: University of Wisconsin Press, 1992); R. Jeyasurya, "The Trading Community in Early Tamil Society Up to 900 AD," *Language in India* 8, 11 (2008); and Tomber, *Indo-Roman Trade.*

23. Strabo, *The Geography,* Book 11, Chapter 5, Sec. 12.

24. Warmington, *The Commerce between the Roman Empire and India,* 265–72.

25. Young, *Rome's Eastern Trade,* 30.

26. Young, *Rome's Eastern Trade,* 31.

27. Tomber, *Indo-Roman Trade,* 148.

28. Tomber, *Indo-Roman Trade,* 153.

29. See Vimala Begley, *The Ancient Port of Arikamedu: New Investigations and Researches 1989–1992* (Pondicherry: Ecole Française d'Extrême Orient, 1996); and Mortimer Wheeler, *Rome beyond the Imperial Frontiers* (London: Philosophical Library, 1955).

30. See Tomber, *Indo-Roman Trade,* 149.

31. Jeyasurya, "The Trading Community in Early Tamil Society Up to 900 AD," 375.

32. R. Nagaswamy, *Roman Karur* (Chennai, India: Brahadish, 1995), online at <www.tamilartsacademy.com/books/roman%20karur/>.

33. Nagaswamy, *Roman Karur.*

34. Warmington, *The Commerce between the Roman Empire and India,* 65.

35. Warmington, *The Commerce between the Roman Empire and India,* 77.

36. Warmington, *The Commerce between the Roman Empire and India,* 75.

37. Tomber, *Indo-Roman Trade,* 73.

38. Tomber, *Indo-Roman Trade,* 74, 76.

39. Tomber, *Indo-Roman Trade,* 75.

40. See Kenneth R. Hall, *Trade and Statecraft in the Age of the Colas* (New Delhi: Abhinav, 1980); Tansen Sen, *Buddhism, Diplomacy, and Trade: The Realignment of Sino-Indian Relations, 600–1400* (Honolulu: University of Hawai'i Press, 2003); Kanakalatha Mukund, *The Trading World of the Tamil Merchant: Evolution of Merchant Capitalism in the Coromandel* (Chennai: Orient Longman, 1999); K.A. Nilakanta Sastri, *A History of South India from Prehistoric Times to the Fall of Vijayanagar* (New Delhi: Oxford University Press, 1976), 304–6; and Hermann Kulke and Diethard Rothermund, *A History of India* (London: Routledge, 2004), 117–8.

41. See Celie W.M. Arokiaswamy, *Tamil Influences in Malaysia, Indonesia, and the Philippines* (Manila: s.n., 2000), 146.

42. Kenneth R. Hall, "Economic History of Early Southeast Asia," *The Cambridge History of Southeast Asia, Volume I: From Early Times to c.1800,* ed. N. Tarling (New York: Cambridge University Press, 1992), 247; and Wilhelm Geiger (C. Mabel Rickmers, trans.), *The Culavamsa: Being the More Recent Part of the Mahavamsa* (London: Pali Text Society, 1929–30), 8–9, 58.

43. Hall, "Economic History of Early Southeast Asia," 248; also see Hall, *Trade and Statecraft in the Age of the Colas.*

44. Hall, "Economic History of Early Southeast Asia," 207.

45. J.G. de Casparis and I. W. Mabbett, "Religion and Popular Beliefs of Southeast Asia before c. 1500," *The Cambridge History of Southeast Asia, Volume I: From Early Times to c.1800,* ed. N. Tarling (New York: Cambridge University Press, 1992), 295.

46. I-Ching (J. Takakusu, trans.), *Record of the Buddhist Religion: As Practised in India and the Malay Archipelago (A.D. 671–695)* (New Delhi: AES, 2005); and I-Ching, *Chinese Monks in India: Biography of Eminent Monks Who Went to the Western World in Search of the Law During the Great T'ang Dynasty* (New Delhi: Motilal Banarsidass, 1995).

47. Keith W. Taylor, "The Early Kingdoms," *The Cambridge History of Southeast Asia, Volume I: From Early Times to c.1800,* ed. N. Tarling (New York: Cambridge University Press, 1992), 173.

48. See O.W. Wolters, *Early Indonesian Commerce: A Study of the Origins of Srivijaya* (Ithaca, NY: Cornell University Press, 1967), 150–8.

49. Wang, "The Nanhai Trade," 75–6.

50. Casparis and Mabbett, "Religion and Popular Beliefs of Southeast Asia," 320.

51. Wolters, *Early Indonesian Commerce,* 156.

52. Hall, "Economic History of Early Southeast Asia," 174–5.

53. Hall, "Economic History of Early Southeast Asia," 174–5.

54. Ma Huan (J.V.G. Mills, trans.), *Ying-Yai Sheng-Lan: The Overall Survey of the Ocean's Shores* (Cambridge, UK: Cambridge University Press, 1970), 98, n. 2.

55. Ma Huan, *Ying-Yai Sheng-Lan,* 98–9.

56. Ma Huan, *Ying-Yai Sheng-Lan,* 99.

57. Ma Huan, *Ying-Yai Sheng-Lan,* 99, n. 1.

58. Ma Huan, *Ying-Yai Sheng-Lan,* 99.

59. Ma Huan, *Ying-Yai Sheng-Lan,* 99.

60. Gordon, *When Asia Was the World,* 126.

61. Taylor, "The Early Kingdoms," 175.

62. Maspero, *The Champa Kingdom,* 26; and Emmanuel Guillon, *Cham Art: Treasures from the Da Nang Museum, Vietnam* (London: Thames & Hudson, 2001), 14.

63. Maspero, *The Champa Kingdom,* 41.

64. Maspero, *The Champa Kingdom,* 43.

65. Maspero, *The Champa Kingdom,* 27.

66. Maspero, *The Champa Kingdom,* 27.

67. Maspero, *The Champa Kingdom,* 27.

68. Hall, "Economic History of Early Southeast Asia," 259.

69. See Paul Wheatley, "Geographical Notes on Some Commodities Involved in Sung Maritime Trade," *Journal of Malaysian Branch of the Royal Asiatic Society* 32, 2 (1959), 1–139.

70. Maspero, *The Champa Kingdom,* 113.

71. Nicolo de Conti (J.W. Jones, trans.), *The Travels of Nicolo Conti in the East in the Early Part of the Fifteenth Century* (London: Hakluyt Society, 1857) p. 8–9.

72. Maspero, *The Champa Kingdom,* 87.

73. Maspero, *The Champa Kingdom,* 87.

74. Maspero, *The Champa Kingdom*, 55.
75. Maspero, *The Champa Kingdom*, 30.
76. Maspero, *The Champa Kingdom*, 57.

Chapter 5

1. Colin Renfrew, J.E. Dixon, and J.R. Cann, "Obsidian and Early Cultural Contact in the Near East," *Proceedings of the Prehistorical Society* 32 (1966), 1–29; also see Steven Shackley, ed., *Archaeological Obsidian Studies* (New York: Kluwer Academic/Plenum, 1998).

2. Joseph Yellin, Thomas E. Levy, and Yorke M. Rowan, "New Evidence on Prehistoric Trade Routes: The Obsidian Evidence from Gilat, Israel," *Journal of Field Archaeology* 23, 3 (1996), 361–68.

3. See Patrick V. Kirch, *The Lapita Peoples: Ancestors of the Oceanic World* (Oxford: Blackwell, 1997); and Peter Bellwood, *Man's Conquest of the Pacific: The Prehistory of Southeast Asia and Oceania* (Auckland: Collins, 1978), 244–55.

4. Bellwood, *Man's Conquest of the Pacific*, 244.

5. C.A. Key, "The Identification of New Guinea Obsidians," *Archaeology and Physical Anthropology in Oceania* 4 (1969), 47–55; W.R. Ambrose and R.C. Green, "First Millennium BC Transport of Obsidian from New Britain to the Solomon Islands," *Nature* 237, 31 (1972), 31; and W.R. Ambrose, "3000 years of Trade in New Guinea Obsidian," *Australian Natural History*, September (1973), 370–3.

6. Bellwood, *Man's Conquest of the Pacific*, 248.

7. R.C. Green, "Lapita Pottery and the Origins of Polynesian Culture," *Australian Natural History*, June (1973), 332–337; and R.C. Green, "Sites with Lapita Pottery: Importing and Voyaging," *Mankind* 9 (1974), 253–9.

8. Michael C. Howard and Naffi Sanggenafa, "The People of Northern Papua," *Indigenous Peoples and Migrants of Northern Papua, Indonesia*, ed. Michael C. Howard and Naffi Sanggenafa (Bangkok: White Lotus, 2005), 4.

9. Norman Hammond, "Obsidian Trade Routes in the Maya Area," *Science* 178, 4065 (1972), 1092–3.

10. William L. Rathje, "The Origin and Development of Lowland Classic Maya Civilization," *American Antiquity* 36, 3 (1971), 275–85; and see Lee A. Parsons and Barbara J. Price, "Mesoamerican Trade and Its Role in the Emergence of Civilization," *University of California Archaeological Research Facility*, Contribution 11 (1971), 169–95.

11. Jane W. Pires-Ferreira, "Obsidian Exchange in Formative Mesoamerica," *The Early Mesoamerican Village*, ed. K.V. Flannery (New York: Academic Press, 1976), 292–305.

12. Michael C. Howard, *Political Change in a Mayan Village in Southern Belize*, Katunob Occasional Publications in Mesoamerican Anthropology 10 (Greeley, CO: University of Northern Colorado, 1977), 33–4.

13. Lois Sherr Dubin, *The History of Beads from 30,000 B.C. to the Present* (New York: Harry N. Abrams, 1987), 9.

14. Dubin, *The History of Beads*, 21.

15. Dubin, *The History of Beads*, 30.

16. Maurizo Tosi and Marcello Piperno, "Lithic Technology Behind the Ancient Lapis Lazuli Trade," *Expedition* 16, 1 (1973), 15–23.

17. James Mellaart, "Egyptian and Near Eastern Chronology: A Dilemma?" *Antiquity* 53, 207 (1979), 18.

18. M.A. Besborodov and J.A. Zadneyprovsky, "Early Stages of Glassmaking in the USSR," *Slavia Antiqua* 12 (1965), 127.

19. Gladys Davidson Weinberg, "Glass Manufacture in Hellenistic Rhodes," *Archaiologikon Deltion* 24 (1971), 143–151, plus plates 76–88.

20. Peter Francis, Jr., *Asia's Maritime Bead Trade: 300 B.C. to the Present* (Honolulu: University of Hawaii Press, 2002), 90.

21. Mieczyslaw Rodziewicz, *Alexandrie III: Les Habitations Romains Tardives d' Alexandrie à la luminière des fouilles polonaises à Kom el-Dikka* (Varsovie: Editions Scientifiques de Pologne, 1984), 241–3.

22. Peter Francis, Jr., "Beads of the Early Islamic Period," *Beads* 1 (1989), 21–39; and Peter Francis, Jr., "The Beads from Fustat in the Awad Collection," *Margaretologist* 8, 2 (1995), 7–11.

23. Dubin, *The History of Beads*, 54.

24. Dubin, *The History of Beads*, 55.

25. Francis, *Asia's Maritime Bead Trade*, 88–9.

26. Francis, *Asia's Maritime Bead Trade*, 88.

27. Jean-Francis Jarrige and Richard H. Meadow, "The Antecedents of Civilization in the Indus Valley," *Scientific American* 244, 8 (1980), 130–1.

28. Francis, *Asia's Maritime Bead Trade*, 104.

29. Francis, *Asia's Maritime Bead Trade*, 105.

30. Tertius Chandler, *Four Thousand Years of Urban Growth: An Historical Census* (Lewiston/Queenstown: St. David's University Press, 1987), 462–9.

31. Francis, *Asia's Maritime Bead Trade*, 115.

32. Ian C. Glover, "The Southern Silk Road: Archaeological Evidence for Early Trade between India and Southeast Asia," *Ancient Trade and Cultural Contacts in Southeast Asia* (Bangkok: The Office of the National Culture Commission, 1996), 65; and B. Bronson, "Glass Beads at Khuan Lukpad, Southern Thailand," *Southeast Asian Archaeology 1986*, ed. I. Glover and E. Glover (Oxford: BAR International Series, 1990), 213–30.

33. Louis Malleret, *L'Archaeologie du Delta du Mekong: Tome Troisième: Le Culture du Fou-Nan* (Paris: l'Ecole Française d'Extrême-Orient, 1962), 152–65.

34. Peter Francis, Jr., "Bead, the Bead Trade and State Development in Southeast Asia," *Ancient Trade and Cultural Contacts in Southeast Asia* (Bangkok: The Office of the National Culture Commission, 1996), 141.

35. Dubin, *The History of Beads*, 95.

36. Francis, "Bead, the Bead Trade and State Development in Southeast Asia," 141.

37. E.J.W. Barber, *Prehistoric Textiles: The Development of Cloth in the Neolithic and Bronze Ages with Special Reference to the Aegean* (Princeton, NJ: Princeton University Press, 1991), 12.

38. Barber, *Prehistoric Textiles*, 25.

39. Bernstein, *A Splendid Exchange*, 7.

40. W.F. Leeman, *Foreign Trade in the old Babylonian Period, as Revealed by Texts from Southern Mesopotamia* (Leiden: E.J. Brill, 1960); and Irene Good, "Textiles as a Medium of Exchange in Third Millennium B.C.E. Western Asia," *Contact and Exchange in the Ancient World*, ed. V.H. Mair (Honolulu: University of Hawai'i Press, 2006), 200.

41. Gregory L Possehl, *Kulli: An Exploration of Ancient Civilization in Asia* (Durham, NC: Carolina Academic, 1986), 73.

42. Possehl, *Kulli*.

43. Philip L. Kohl, "A Note on Chloraite Artifacts from Shahr-I Sokhta," *East and West* 27 (1977), 111–27; and Philip L. Kohl, "The Balance of Trade in Southwest Asia," *Current Anthropology* 19 (1978), 463–92.

44. See Michael C. Howard, *Textiles of the Highland Peoples of Burma, Volume II* (Bangkok: White Lotus, 2005), 173; and Wolfram Eberhard, *The Local Cultures of South and East China* (Leiden: E.J. Brill, 1968), 42.

45. Philip L. Kohl, ed. *The Bronze Age Civilisation of Central Asia: Recent Soviet Discoveries* (Armonk, NY: M.E. Sharpe, 1981), xxi.

46. Barber, *Prehistoric Textiles,* 31.

47. Barber, *Prehistoric Textiles,* 32.

48. Barber, *Prehistoric Textiles,* 32; and J. Marshall, *Mohenjo-Daro and the Indus Civilization* (New Delhi: Asian Educational Service, 1973, originally published, London: Arthur Probsthain, 1931), 194.

49. F.R. Allchin, "Early Cultivated Plants in India and Pakistan," *The Domestication and Exploitation of Plants and Animals,* ed. P.J. Ucko and G.W. Dimbleby (London: Duckworth, 1969), 326.

50. Karen R. Nemet-Nejat, *Daily Life in Ancient Mesopotamia* (Santa Barbara, CA: Greenwood, 1998), 153.

51. Young, *Rome's Eastern Trade,* 28.

52. Andrew Sherratt, "The Trans-Eurasian Exchange: The Prehistory of Chinese Relations with the West," *Contact and Exchange in the Ancient World,* ed. V.H. Mair (Honolulu: University of Hawai'i Press, 2006), 44.

53. Gregory L. Possehl, "Mehrgarh," *Oxford Companion to Archaeology,* ed. B. Fagan (New York: Oxford University Press, 1996), online at <www.oxfordreference.com>.

54. J. R. Caldwell, ed. *Investigations at Tal-I Iblis* (Springfield, IL: Illinois State Museum, 1967).

55. See N. Nezafati, M. Momenzadeh, and E. Pernicka, "New Insights into the Ancient Mining and Metallurgical Researches in Iran," *Ancient Mining in Turkey and the Eastern Mediterranean,* ed. Ü. Yalcin, H. Özbal, and A.G. Pa amehmeto lu (Ankara, Turkey: Atilim University, 2008), 307–28.

56. See Ü. Yalchin, H. Özbal, and A. G. Pa amehmeto lu, eds., *Ancient Mining in Turkey and the Eastern Mediterranean* (Ankara, Turkey: Atilim University, 2008).

57. Philip L. Kohl, *The Making of Bronze Age Eurasia* (New York: Cambridge University Press, 2007), 28–38.

58. Colin Renfrew, "Sitagroi, Radiocarbon Dating and the Pre-history of South-east Europe," *Antiquity* 45, 180 (1971), 275–82.

59. Kathryn Bard, ed., *Encyclopedia of the Archaeology of Ancient Egypt* (New York: Routledge, 1988), 522.

60. Carol Meyer, "Bir Umm Fawakhir: Insights into Ancient Egyptian Mining," *JOM* (Journal of the Minerals, Metals and Materials Society) 49, 3 (1997), 64–8.

61. Andreas Hauptmann, "The Earliest Periods of Copper Metallurgy in Feinan," *Old World Archaeometallurgy,* ed. A. Hauptmann, E. Pernicke, and G.A. Wagner (Heidelberg: Der Anschnitt, Beiheft 7, 1989), 88–112; and Bard, *Encyclopedia of the Archaeology of Ancient Egypt,* 522.

62. Noel H. Gale, "Metals and Metallurgy in the Chalcolithic Period," *Bulletin of the American School of Oriental Research* 282/283 (1991), 37–61.

63. Sherratt, "The Trans-Eurasian Exchange," 46.

64. K. Aslihan Yener, "An Early Bronze Age Tin Production Site at Göltpepe, Turkey," *The Oriental Institute News and Notes* 140 (1991).

65. Paul Yule, *Metal Work of the Bronze Age in India* (Munich: Beck'sche, 1985).

66. Kohl, *The Making of Bronze Age Eurasia,* 146–56.

67. See Kohl, *The Making of Bronze Age Eurasia,* 166–79; Sherratt, "The Trans-Eurasian Exchange," 47–8; and L.G. Fitzgerald-Huber, "Qiji and Erlitou: The Question of Contacts with Distant Cultures," *Early China* 20 (1995), 17–67.

68. Robert Bagley, "Shang Archaeology," *The Cam-bridge History of Ancient China: From the Origins of Civilization to 221 B.C.,* ed. Michael Loewe and Edward L. Shaughnessy (New York: Cambridge University Press, 1999), 139–40.

69. Bagley, "Shang Archaeology," 170.

70. Bagley, "Shang Archaeology," 174.

71. Bagley, "Shang Archaeology," 174.

72. Lothar von Falkenhausen, "The Waning of the Bronze Age: Material Culture and Social Development, 770–481 B.C," *The Cambridge History of Ancient China: From the Origins of Civilization to 221 B.C.,* ed. Michael Loewe and Edward L. Shaughnessy (New York: Cambridge University Press, 1999), 531.

73. Von Falkenhausen, "The Waning of the Bronze Age," 530.

74. Von Falkenhausen, "The Waning of the Bronze Age," 538.

75. Von Falkenhausen, "The Waning of the Bronze Age," 542.

76. Charles Higham, *The Bronze Age of Southeast Asia* (New York: Cambridge University Press, 1996), 17–38.

77. Higham, *The Bronze Age of Southeast Asia,* 94.

78. Higham, *The Bronze Age of Southeast Asia,* 95–6.

79. Richard M. Cooler, *The Karen Bronze Drums of Burma* (Leiden: E.J. Brill, 1995), 51–5.

80. Cooler, *The Karen Bronze Drums of Burma,* 51.

81. Cooler, *The Karen Bronze Drums of Burma,* 51.

82. Cooler, *The Karen Bronze Drums of Burma,* 55.

83. Cooler, *The Karen Bronze Drums of Burma,* 56.

84. On the shoulder-bags see Howard, *Textiles of the Highland Peoples of Burma, Volume II,* 199.

85. Cooler, *The Karen Bronze Drums of Burma,* 55.

86. Pamela Swadling, *Plumes from Paradise: Trade Cycles in Outer Southeast Asia and Their Impact on New Guinea and Nearby Islands until 1920* (Boroko: Papua New Guinea National Museum, 1996).

87. F.C. Kamma, "De Verhouding tussen Tidore e de Papoese eilaanden in Legende en Historie," *Indonesië* 1 (1947–48), 361–70, 536–59; and 2 (1948–49), 17–188, 256–75; John-Erik Elmberg, *Balance and Circulation: Aspects of Tradition and Change among the Mejprat of Irian Barat* (Stockholm: Etnografiska Museet, 1968); and Michael C. Howard, "Beaded Skirts from Ambai Island," *Indigenous Peoples and Migrants of Northern Papua, Indonesia,* ed. M.C. Howard and N. Sanggenafa (Bangkok: White Lotus, 1995), 96–9.

88. P.R.S. Moorey, *Ancient Mesopotamian Materials and Industries: The Archaeological Evidence* (Winona Lake, IN: Eisenbrauns, 1999), 78.

89. Walter Schumann, *Gemstones of the World* (New York: Sterling, 1977), 51.

90. Exodus 28: 17–22 (RSV).

91. See Fred Ward, *Rubies & Sapphires,* 4th ed. (Bethesda, MD: Gem, 2003), 4.

92. Fred Ward, *Emeralds,* Rev. ed. (Bethesda, MD: Gem, 2001), 46.

93. Ward, *Emeralds,* 4.

94. Ward, *Emeralds,* 6.

95. Ward, *Rubies & Sapphires,* 5.

96. Gary W. Bowersox and Bonita E. Chamberlain, *Gemstones of Afghanistan* (Tucson, AZ: Geoscience, 1995).

97. Fred Ward, *Diamonds,* Rev. ed. (Bethesda, MD: Gem, 1998), 3.

98. Barbara Ashton, James Harrelm and Ian Shaw, "Stone," *Ancient Egyptian Materials and Technology,* ed. P.T. Nicolson and E. Shaw (New York: Cambridge University Press, 2000), 51; and Barry J. Kemp, "Old Kingdom, Middle Kingdom and Second Intermediate Period in Egypt," *The Cambridge History of Africa, Volume I:*

From the Earliest Times to C. 500 B.C., ed. J.D. Clark, J.D. Fage, and R.A. Oliver (New York: Cambridge University Press, 1982), 709.

99. Moorey, *Ancient Mesopotamian Materials and Industries,* 76–8, 94.

100. Moorey, *Ancient Mesopotamian Materials and Industries,* 77, 81.

101. Schumann, *Gemstones of the World,* 146.

102. Ward, *Rubies & Sapphires,* 5.

103. Diane Morgan, *From Satan's Crown to the Holy Grail: Emeralds in Myth, Magic, and History* (Santa Barbara, CA: Praeger, 2007), 131.

104. Peter Francis, Jr., "South Indian Stone Beadmaking," *Margaretologist* 6, 2 (1993), 3–6; and Peter Francis, Jr., "More on South Indian Stone Beadmaking," *Margaretologist* 7, 1 (1994), 7.

105. Warwick Ball, *Rome in the East: The Transformation of an Empire* (New York: Routledge, 2001), 127.

106. Doris Dohrenwend, *Chinese Jades in the Royal Ontario Museum* (Toronto: Royal Ontario Museum, 1971), 11.

107. Marc Aurel Stein, *Ancient Khotan: Detailed Report of Archaeological Exploration in Chinese Turkestan* (Oxford: Clarendon, 1907), Volume 1, 182; and Dohrenwend, *Chinese Jades in the Royal Ontario Museum,* 10.

108. Gillett G. Griffin, "Formative Guerrero and Its Jade," *Precolumbian Jade: New Geological and Cultural Interpretations,* ed. F.W. Lange (Salt Lake City: University of Utah Press, 1993), 206.

109. Doris Z. Stone, "Jade and Jade Objects in Precolumbian Costa Rica," *Precoluumbian Jade: New Geological and Cultural Interpretations,* ed. F.W. Lange (Salt Lake City: University of Utah Press, 1993), 143.

110. James F. Garber, David C. Grove, Kenneth G. Hirth, and John W. Hooper, "Jade Use in Portions of Mexico and Central America: Olmec, Maya, Costa Rica, and Honduras — A Summary," *Precolumbian Jade: New Geological and Cultural Interpretations,* ed. F.W. Lange (Salt Lake City: University of Utah Press, 1993), 211–31.

111. Michael D. Coe, *America's First Civilization: Discovering the Olmec* (New York: American Heritage, 1968), 94, 103.

112. Patricia Crone, *Meccan Trade and the Rise of Islam* (Piscataway, NJ: Gorgias, 2004), 19; also see Jean-Francois Breton (A. LaFarge, trans.), *Arabia Felix: From the Time of the Queen of Sheba, Eighth Century B.C. to First Century A.D* (Notre Dame, IN: University of Notre Dame Press, 2000).

113. Young, *Rome's Eastern Trade,* 104.

114. Young, *Rome's Eastern Trade,* 91.

115. Young, *Rome's Eastern Trade,* 105.

116. Young, *Rome's Eastern Trade,* 114.

117. Young, *Rome's Eastern Trade,* 114.

118. Hall, "Economic History of Early Southeast Asia," 194–5.

119. Hall, "Economic History of Early Southeast Asia," 195.

120. Hall, "Economic History of Early Southeast Asia," 195.

121. Hall, "Economic History of Early Southeast Asia," 195.

122. Maspero, *The Champa Kingdom,* 56.

123. De Conti, *The Travels of Nicolo Conti,* 8–9.

124. Ma Huan, *Ying-Yai Sheng-Lan.*

125. Ma Huan, *Ying-Yai Sheng-Lan,* 81.

126. Little, *The Oxford Universal Dictionary,* 1968.

127. Bernstein, *A Splendid Exchange,* 40; also see J. Innes Miller, *The Spice Trade of the Roman Empire* (Oxford: Clarendon, 1969).

128. Bernstein, *A Splendid Exchange,* 40.

129. Hall, "Economic History of Early Southeast Asia," 217.

130. P.N. Ravindran, *Black Pepper: Piper Nigrum* (Amsterdam: Harwood Academic, 2000).

131. Hall, "Economic History of Early Southeast Asia," 198.

132. See Ma Huan, *Ying-Yai Sheng-Lan,* 115–21.

133. Hall, "Economic History of Early Southeast Asia," 211.

134. Hall, "Economic History of Early Southeast Asia," 212.

135. Hall, "Economic History of Early Southeast Asia," 219; based on Rakawi of Majapahit Prapanca (Th. Pigeaud, trans.), *Java in the Fourteenth Century: A Study of Cultural History — the Nagara-Kertagama by Rakawi Prapanca of Majapahit, 1365 A.D.,* 5 volumes (The Hague: Martinus Nijhoff, 1960–3).

136. Crone, *Meccan Trade and the Rise of Islam,* 261.

137. Crone, *Meccan Trade and the Rise of Islam,* 258.

138. Crone, *Meccan Trade and the Rise of Islam,* 256.

139. W.R. Schoff, trans. and ed., *The Periplus of the Erythraean Sea: Travel and Trade in the Indian Ocean by a Merchant of the First Century* (London: Longman, Green, 1912).

140. Lynda N. Shaffer, *Maritime Southeast Asia to 1500* (Armonk, NY: M.E. Sharpe, 1996), 15.

141. Shaffer, *Maritime Southeast Asia to 1500,* 16.

142. See <www.lemrinc.com/cinamon.html>.

143. See Joanna Hall Brierly, *Spices* (Kuala Lumpur: Oxford University Press, 1994); R.A. Donkin, *Between East and West: The Moluccas and the Traffic in Spices Up to the Arrival of Europeans,* Memoir 248 (Philadelphia, PA: American Philosophical Society, 2003); Giles Milton, *Nathaniel's Nutmeg: How One Man's Courage Changed the Course of History* (London: Hodder & Stoughton, 1999); and Jack Turner, *Spice: The History of a Temptation* (New York: Vintage, 2004).

144. Turner, *Spice,* xv.

145. Marco Polo (Henry Yule, ed.), *The Travels of Marco Polo* (London: 1870; reprint, New York: Dover, 1983).

146. Bernstein, *A Splendid Exchange,* 110.

147. Bernstein, *A Splendid Exchange,* 110.

148. Frederic C. Lane, *Venice: Maritime Republic* (Baltimore: Johns Hopkins University Press, 1973), 228.

149. See Bret Hinsch, *The Ultimate Guide to Chinese Tea* (Bangkok: White Lotus, 2008), 8.

150. William H. Ukers, *All About Tea* (New York: Tea and Coffee Trade Journal Company, 1935); also see Hinsch, *The Ultimate Guide to Chinese Tea,* 19–33.

151. Cited in and translated by Ukers, *All About Tea.*

152. Cited in and translated by Ukers, *All About Tea.*

153. Cited in and translated by Ukers, *All About Tea.*

154. Cited in and translated by Ukers, *All About Tea.*

155. See Yang Fuquan, "The 'Ancient Tea and Horse Caravan Road,' the 'Silk Road' of Southwest China," *The Silkroad Foundation Newsletter* 2, 1 (2004), online at <www. silkroadfoundation.org/newsletter/>.

156. Jia Daquan, "The Historic Function of the Sichuan Tea Sold to Tibet," *The Collection of Papers of Tibetology of Sichuan* (Tibetology Publishing House, 1993, in Chinese), 4; cited by Yang Fuquan, "The 'Ancient Tea and Horse Caravan Road,' the 'Silk Road' of Southwest China."

Chapter 6

1. Bernstein, *A Splendid Exchange,* 7.

2. Bernstein, *A Splendid Exchange,* 7.

3. Pierre A. Zalloua et al., "Identifying Genetic

Traces of Historical Expansions: Phoenician Footprints in the Mediterranean," *The American Journal of Human Genetics* 83, 5 (2008), 633–42.

4. Herodotus, *The Histories,* iv, 42.

5. William Culican, *The First Merchant Venturers: The Ancient Levant in History and Commerce* (New York: Mc-Graw-Hill, 1966), 43, 46.

6. Culican, *The First Merchant Venturers,* 46.

7. See Cardon, *Natural Dyes,* 553–82.

8. Cardon, *Natural Dyes,* 563, fig. 12.

9. Barber, *Prehistoric Textiles,* 229.

10. Durant, *The Life of Greece,* 575.

11. Quoted in Durant, *The Life of Greece,* 175.

12. Durant, *The Life of Greece,* 276.

13. Durant, *The Life of Greece,* 172.

14. Casson, *Travel in the Ancient World,* 65–6.

15. See Michael Whitby, "The Grain Trade of Athens in the Fourth Century BC," *Trade, Traders and the Ancient City,* ed. H. Parkins and C. Smith (New York: Routledge, 1998), 102–28.

16. Durant, *The Life of Greece,* 275–6.

17. Gocha R. Tsetskhladze, "Trade on the Black Sea in the Archaic and Classical Periods: Some Observations," *Trade, Traders and the Ancient City,* ed. H. Parkins and C. Smith (New York: Routledge, 1998), 58.

18. Tsetskhladze, "Trade on the Black Sea," 61.

19. Cited in D. Braud, "Fish from the Black Sea: Classical Byzantium and the Greekness of Trade," *Food in Antiquity,* ed. M.J. Dobson, D. Harvey, and J. Wilkins (Exeter: University of Exeter Press, 1995), 168.

20. Adkins and Adkins, *Handbook to Life in Ancient Greece,* 189.

21. Casson, *Travel in the Ancient World,* 76.

22. Casson, *Travel in the Ancient World,* 98.

23. Casson, *Travel in the Ancient World,* 87.

24. Arnold W. Gomme, *The Population of Athens in the Fifth and Fourth Centuries BC* (Oxford: Oxford University Press, 1933).

25. Culican, *The First Merchant Venturers,* 109.

26. Richard N. Frye, *The Heritage of Central Asia: From Antiquity to Turkish Expansion* (Princeton: Markus Wiener, 1996), 194–5.

27. Luce Boulnois (Helen Loveday, trans.), *Silk Road: Monks, Warriors & Merchants on the Silk Road* (Geneva: Editions Olizane, 2004), 238; also Étienne de la Vaissière, *Histoire des marchands sogdiens* (Paris: Collège de France, Institut des Heutes Etudes Chinoises, 2002).

28. G. Azarpay, *Sogdian Painting* (Berkeley: University of California Press, 1981), 216.

29. Azarpay, *Sogdian Painting,* 213.

30. The Sogdians also traded with India; see Nicholas Sims-Williams, "The Sogdian Merchants in China and India," *Cina e Iran da Alessandro Magno alla dinastia Tang,* ed. A. Cadonna and L. Lanciotti (Florence: Leo S. Olschki editore, 1996), 45–67.

31. Boulnois, *Silk Road,* 241.

32. Menander Protector (Roger C. Blockley, trans.), *The History of Menander the Guardsman* (Liverpool: Francis Cairns, 1985).

33. Boulnois, *Silk Road,* 244.

34. Frye, *The Heritage of Central Asia,* 197.

35. Frye, *The Heritage of Central Asia,* 197.

36. See De la Vaissière, *Histoire des marchands sogdiens.*

37. Etienne de la Vaissière, "Sogdians in China: A Short History and Some New Discoveries," *The Silk Road Foundation Newsletter* 1, 2 (2003), online at <www.silkroadfoundation.org/newsletter/>.

38. Cited by Sims-Williams, "The Sogdian Merchants in China and India," 49.

39. De la Vaissière, "Sogdians in China."

40. De la Vaissière, "Sogdians in China."

41. See Rong Xinjang, *Middle-period China and Outside Cultures* (Beijing: Shenhuo dusho xinzhi Sanlian shudian, 2001, in Chinese); Rong Xinjang, "Sogdians around Ancient Tarim Basin," *The Silk Road Foundation Newsletter* 1, 2, (2003), online at <www.silkroadfoundation.org/newsletter/>; and Valerie Hansen, "New Work on the Sogdians, the Most Important Traders on the Silk Road, A.D. 500–1000," *T'oung Pao* 89, 1–3 (2003), 149–61.

42. Chapter 83 of the *Sui shi,* cited by Boulnois, *Silk Road.*

43. Boulnois, *Silk Road,* 241.

44. Hansen, "New Work on the Sogdians," 154.

45. Hansen, "New Work on the Sogdians," 154.

46. Hansen, "New Work on the Sogdians," 155.

47. Rong Xinjang, *Middle-period China and Outside Cultures.*

48. Cited by Rong Xinjang, *Middle-period China and Outside Cultures,* 138–9; and Hansen, "New Work on the Sogdians," 156.

49. Rong Xinjang, *Middle-period China and Outside Cultures.*

50. De la Vaissière, "Sogdians in China."

51. De la Vaissière, "Sogdians in China."

52. De la Vaissière, "Sogdians in China."

53. De la Vaissière, "Sogdians in China."

54. See Dierk Lange, *Ancient Kingdoms of West Africa: Africa-Centered and Canaanite-Israelite Perspectives* (Dettelbach, Germany: J.H. Roll, 2004).

55. Horace Miner, *The Primitive City of Timbuctoo,* Rev. ed. (New York: Anchor, 1965), 71–4; Henry Barth, *Travels and Discoveries in North and Central Africa. Including Accounts of Timbuktu, Sokoto, and the Basins of the Niger and Benuwe* (London: Ward, Lock, 1890), Volume 2, 352–3.

56. Miner, *The Primitive City of Timbuctoo,* 72.

57. Miner, *The Primitive City of Timbuctoo,* 2–3.

58. H.A.R. Gibb and C.F. Beckingham, eds. and trans., *The Travels of Ibn Battuta, A.D. 1325–1354* (Cambridge: Hakluyt Society, 1993), Volume 4, 969–70; and C. Defrémery and B.R. Sanguinetti, eds. and trans., *Voyages d'ibn Batoutah* (Paris: Société Asiatic, 1853–1858, online at <books.google.co.uk/books?id=mdQOAAAAQ AAJ>, Volume 4, 376–404, on his trip to West Africa.

59. John O. Hunwick, *Timbuktu and the Songhay Empire: Al-Sadhi's Tarikh al-Sudan down to 1613 and Other Contemporary Documents* (Leiden: Brill, 1999), 275.

60. Jacqueline Simpson, *Everyday Life in the Viking Age* (New York: G.P. Putnam's Sons; London: B.T. Batsford, 1967), 114.

61. H.R. Ellis Davidson, *The Viking Road to Byzantium* (London: George Allen & Unwin, 1976), 62.

62. Simpson, *Everyday Life in the Viking Age,* 26.

63. Simpson, *Everyday Life in the Viking Age,* 22.

64. Davidson, *The Viking Road to Byzantium,* 11.

65. Davidson, *The Viking Road to Byzantium,* 74.

66. Fuat Sezgin, ed. *Collection of Geographical Works by Ibn al-Faqih, Ibn Fadlan, Abu Dulaf Al-Khazraji* (Frankfurt am Main: Institute for the History of Arabic-Islamic Science at the Johann Wolfgang Goethe University, 1987).

67. Davidson, *The Viking Road to Byzantium,* 17.

68. Davidson, *The Viking Road to Byzantium,* 52–4.

69. Simpson, *Everyday Life in the Viking Age,* 113.

70. Davidson, *The Viking Road to Byzantium,* 54.

71. Simpson, *Everyday Life in the Viking Age,* 98.

72. Davidson, *The Viking Road to Byzantium,* 93–4.

73. Simpson, *Everyday Life in the Viking Age,* 97.

74. W.C. Green, trans., *The Story of Egil Skallagrimsson* (online at www.sacred-texts.com/neu/egil/index.htm), Chapter 17, "Hildirida's sons in Finmark and at Harold's court"; also available in Snori Sturuson and Hermann Pálsson, *Egil's Saga* (Harmondsworth, UK: Penguin, 1976).

75. Simpson, *Everyday Life in the Viking Age,* 101.

76. Simpson, *Everyday Life in the Viking Age,* 107.

77. Constantine Porphyrogenitus (Gyula Moravcik, ed.; Romilly J.H. Jenkins, trans.). *Constantine Porphyrogenitus: De Administrando Imperio (Corpus Fontium Historiae Byzantinae).* Washington, DC: Dumbarton Oaks Research Library and Collection, 1967.

78. Irene Sorlin, "Les traits de Byzance avec la Russie au Xe. siècle," *Cahiers du Monde Russe et Soviétique* (1961), 313–60, 447–75.

79. Translation in Davidson, *The Viking Road to Byzantium,* 90.

80. Simpson, *Everyday Life in the Viking Age,* 108.

81. Davidson, *The Viking Road to Byzantium,* 79.

82. Ahmad ibn Rustah (G. Wiet, trans.), *Les Atours Precieux* (Cairo, 1955).

83. Eric Otto Winstedt, ed. and trans., *The Christian Topography of Cosmos Indicopleustes* (Malden, MA: Forbes, 2008).

84. Winstedt, *The Christian Topography of Cosmos Indicopleustes.*

85. John P. Newman, *The Thrones and Palaces of Babylon and Nineveh from Sea to Sea: A Thousand Miles on Horseback* (New York: Harper & Brothers, 1876), 363.

86. Newman, *The Thrones and Palaces of Babylon and Nineveh,* 363.

87. See Samuel Hugh Moffett, *A History of Christianity in Asia: Volume 1, Beginnings to 1500* (Maryknoll, NY: Orbis, 1998); and <www.nestorian.org>.

88. Shiu Keung Lee, *The Cross and the Lotus* (Hong Kong: Christian Study Center on Chinese Religion and Culture, 1971).

89. Nicolas Trigault (L.J. Gallagher, trans.), *China in the Sixteenth Century: The Journals of Mathew Ricci: 1583–1610* (New York: Random House, 1953).

90. See Elkan Adler, *Jewish Travellers in the Middle Ages* (New York: Dover, 1987); Elinoar Bareket, "R d- h nites," *Jewish Civilization: An Encyclopedia,* ed. Norman Roth (New York: Routledge, 2002), 558–561; Shlomo Goitein, *Letters of Medieval Jewish Traders* (Princeton, NJ: Princeton University Press, 1973); and Sidney Shapiro, ed. *Jews in Old China: Studies by Chinese Scholars* (New York: Hippocrene, 2000).

91. See Goitein, *Letters of Medieval Jewish Traders;* and Gordon, *When Asia was the World,* 75–95.

92. Gordon, *When Asia was the World,* 75–6.

93. Gordon, *When Asia was the World,* 88–9.

94. Gordon, *When Asia was the World,* 95.

95. Philip D. Curtain, *Cross-cultural Trade in World History* (New York: Cambridge University Press, 1984), 116.

96. Will Durant, *The Age of Faith: A History of Medieval Civilization—Christian, Islamic, and Judaic—from Constantine to Dante: A.D. 325–1300* (New York: Simon and Schuster, 1950), 628.

97. See D.S. Chambers, *The Imperial Age of Venice, 1380–1580* (London: Thames & Hudson, 1970); Frederic C. Lane, *Venice: Maritime Republic* (Baltimore: Johns Hopkins University Press, 1973); and John J. Norwich, *A History of Venice* (New York: Alfred A. Knopf, 1982).

98. Curtain, *Cross-cultural Trade in World History,* 117.

99. See Maria Georgopoulou, *Venice's Mediterranean Colonies* (New York: Cambridge University Press, 2001);

and Sally McKee, *Uncommon Dominion: Venetian Crete and the Myth of Ethnic Purity* (Philadelphia: University of Pennsylvania Press, 2000).

100. McKee, *Uncommon Dominion.*

101. See A.J. Schoenfeld, "Immigration and Assimilation in the Jewish Community of Late Venetian Crete (15th–17th Centuries)," *Journal of Modern Greek Studies* 25, 1 (2007), 1–15; and J. Starr, "Jewish Life in Crete Under the Rule of Venice," *Proceedings of the American Academy for Jewish Research* 12 (1942), 59–114.

102. See John E. Dotson, ed. and trans., *Merchant Culture in Fourteenth Century Venice: The Zibaldone Da Canal* (Tempe, AZ: Medieval & Renaissance Texts & Studies, Arizona Center for Medieval and Renaissance Studies, 1994), 116, 119.

103. Marco Polo (Henry Yule, ed.), *The Travels of Marco Polo* (London: 1870; reprint, New York: Dover, 1983).

104. See Krishanlal Mohanlal Jhaveri, ed., *The Gujaratis: The People, Their History, and Culture* (New Delhi: Cosmo, 2003).

105. Tomé Pires (A. Cortesao, trans. and ed.), *The Suma Oriental of Tomé Pires: An Account of the East, from the Red Sea to Japan, Written in Malacca and India in 1512–1515* (London: Hakluyt Society, 1944), 40.

106. Pires, *The Suma Oriental,* 40.

107. Pires, *The Suma Oriental,* 41.

108. Pires, *The Suma Oriental,* 42.

109. Pires, *The Suma Oriental,* 42.

110. Pires, *The Suma Oriental,* 42.

111. Pires, *The Suma Oriental,* 42.

112. Pires, *The Suma Oriental,* 45.

113. Pires, *The Suma Oriental,* 45–6.

114. Pires, *The Suma Oriental,* 45.

115. Pires, *The Suma Oriental,* 45.

116. Pires, *The Suma Oriental,* 46.

117. Pires, *The Suma Oriental,* 47.

118. See Shunz Sakamaki, "Ryukyu and Southeast Asia," *Journal of Asian Studies* 23, 3 (1964), 382–404; R.K. Sakai, "The Satsuma Ryukyu Trade and the Tokugawa Seclusion Policy," *Journal of Asian Studies* 23, 3 (1964), 405–416; and Shosuke Murai et al., *Studies of Medieval Ryukyu within Asia's Maritime Network,* Special Issue of *Acta Asiatica* 95 (2008), especially the chapter by Okamoto.

119. Charles E. Nowell, "The Discovery of the Pacific: A Suggested Change of Approach," *The Pacific Historical Review* 16, 1 (1947), 8.

120. Pires, *The Suma Oriental,* 5.

121. Pires, *The Suma Oriental,* 129.

122. Pires, *The Suma Oriental,* 130.

123. Pires, *The Suma Oriental,* 93.

124. Pires, *The Suma Oriental,* 265.

125. Pires, *The Suma Oriental,* 192–3.

126. Pires, *The Suma Oriental,* 130.

127. Pires, *The Suma Oriental,* 131.

128. Prescott, *History of the Conquest of Mexico,* Volume 2, 125.

129. Prescott, *History of the Conquest of Mexico,* Volume 1, 155.

130. Prescott, *History of the Conquest of Mexico,* Volume 1, 156–7.

131. See Miguel Acosta Signes, "Los pochteca," *Acta Anthropologica* 1 (1945), 9–54; Bente Bittmann Simons and Thelma D. Sullivan, "The Pochteca," *Atti del XL Congresso Internazionale degli Americanisti* 4 (1972), 203–12; Lee A. Parsons and Barbara J. Price, "Mesoamerican Trade and Its Role in the Emergence of Civilization," *University of California Archaeological Research Facility* 11

(1971), 169–95; and Anne E. Chapman, "Port of Trade Enclaves in Aztec and Maya Civilizations," *Trade and Market in the Early Empires,* ed. K. Polanyi, C.M. Arensberg, and H.W. Pearson (Chicago: Henry Regnery, 1971), 114–53.

132. Prescott, *History of the Conquest of Mexico,* Volume 1, 155.

133. Prescott, *History of the Conquest of Mexico,* Volume 1, 156.

134. Bernardo de Sahagun (J.O. Anderson and C.E. Dibble, trans.), *General History of the Things of New Spain* (Salt Lake City: University of Utah Press, 1959), Book 9, Chapter 2, "The Merchants."

135. Prescott, *History of the Conquest of Mexico,* Volume 1, 156.

136. Prescott, *History of the Conquest of Mexico,* Volume 1, 156, n. 32; also see Frances Frei Berdan, "Tres formas de intercambio en la economia azteca," *Economia política e ideologia en el México prehispánico,* ed. P. Carrasco and J. Broda (Mexico: Editorial Nueva Imagen, 1978).

137. Ross Hassig, *Trade, Tribute, and Transportation: The Sixteenth-century Political Economy of the Valley of Mexico* (Norman: University of Oklahoma Press, 1985), 300, n. 89.

138. Acosta Signes, "Los pochteca."

139. Hassig, *Trade, Tribute, and Transportation,* 114.

140. Hassig, *Trade, Tribute, and Transportation,* 114.

141. Hassig, *Trade, Tribute, and Transportation,* 114.

142. Hassig, *Trade, Tribute, and Transportation,* 120.

143. See Chapman, "Port of Trade Enclaves in Aztec and Maya Civilizations," 115–8; Simons and Sullivan, "The Pochteca," 204; Berdan, "Tres formas de intercambio en la economia azteca," 93; and Parsons and Price, "Mesoamerican Trade and Its Role in the Emergence of Civilization," 173.

144. France V. Scholes and Ralph L. Roys, *The Maya Chontal Indians of Acalan-Tixchel: A Contribution to the History and Ethnography of the Yucatan Peninsula* (Norman: University of Oklahoma Press, 1968), 31.

145. Scholes and Roys, *The Maya Chontal Indians,* 31.

146. Scholes and Roys, *The Maya Chontal Indians,* 32.

147. Ralph L. Roys, *The Indian Background of Colonial Yucatan* (Norman: University of Oklahoma Press, 1972), 101.

148. Scholes and Roys, *The Maya Chontal Indians,* 33.

149. Scholes and Roys, *The Maya Chontal Indians,* 36.

150. Francis Augustus MacNutt, trans. and ed., *Hernando Cortés: His Five Letters of Relation to the Emperor Charles V 1519–1526* (Whitefish, MT: Kessinger, 2006, originally published 1908), Volume 1, 152.

151. J. Eric S. Thompson, *Maya History and Religion* (Norman: University of Oklahoma Press, 1970), 134.

152. Thompson, *Maya History and Religion,* 134.

153. Thompson, *Maya History and Religion,* 127.

154. MacNutt, *Hernando Cortés,* Volume 2, 231.

155. Thompson, *Maya History and Religion,* 128.

156. Thompson, *Maya History and Religion,* 74.

157. Thompson, *Maya History and Religion,* 75.

158. See Roys, *The Indian Background of Colonial Yucatan,* 56; and Scholes and Roys, *The Maya Chontal Indians,* 33–4.

159. Thompson, *Maya History and Religion,* 74.

160. MacNutt, *Hernando Cortés,* Volume 2, 306.

161. Roys, *The Indian Background of Colonial Yucatan,* 114, 320.

162. Thompson, *Maya History and Religion,* 78.

163. Thompson, *Maya History and Religion,* 78.

164. Thompson, *Maya History and Religion,* 78.

Chapter 7

1. Anne E. Chapman, "Port of Trade Enclaves in Aztec and Maya Civilizations," *Trade and Market in the Early Empires,* ed. K. Polanyi, C.M. Arensberg, and H.W. Pearson (Chicago: Henry Regnery, 1971), 115.

2. Chapman, "Port of Trade Enclaves in Aztec and Maya Civilizations," 116.

3. Robert B. Revere, "'No Man's Coast': Ports of Trade in the Eastern Mediterranean," *Trade & Market in the Early Empires,* ed. Karl Polanyi, Conrad M. Arensberg, and Harry W. Pearson (Chicago: Henry Regnery, 1971), 52.

4. Gil J. Stein, *Rethinking World Systems Diasporas, Colonies, and Interaction in Uruk Mesopotamia* (Tucson: University of Arizona Press, 1999), 117–69.

5. See Louis L. Orlin, *Assyrian Colonies in Cappadocia* (Berlin: Walter de Gruyter, 1970); and P. Garelli, "Le commerce assyiren de la Cappadoce au XIXe siècle av. n.e.," *Akkadica* 88 (1994), 1–17.

6. Zoltán Pálfi. *Territorial Cooperation in the Old Assyrian Trade (Analysis of Four Regions),* PhD dissertation (PhD School of History and PhD Program of Assyriology, Budapest, 2008), 9.

7. M. Gawlikowski, "Palmyra as a Trading Centre," *Iraq* 56 (1994), 27; and see Michael I. Rostovtzeff (D. and T. Talbot Rice, trans.), *Caravan Cities* (Oxford: Clarendon, 1932).

8. Gawlikowski, "Palmyra as a Trading Centre"; and Young, *Rome's Eastern Trade,* 136.

9. Young, *Rome's Eastern Trade,* 137.

10. Young, *Rome's Eastern Trade,* 38.

11. Young, *Rome's Eastern Trade,* 168.

12. Ernest Will, "Marchands et chefs de caravanes à Palmyre," *Syria* 34, 3/4 (1957), 262–77; and see Gawlikowski, "Palmyra as a Trading Centre," 31; Richard Stoneman, *Palmyra and Its Empire: Zenobia's Revolt against Rome* (Ann Arbor: University of Michigan Press, 1991), 63; and Young, *Rome's Eastern Trade,* 150.

13. Young, *Rome's Eastern Trade,* 154–5, 157.

14. Young, *Rome's Eastern Trade,* 159–66.

15. Ma Huan, *Ying-Yai Sheng-Lan,* 154.

16. Pires, *The Suma Oriental,* 15.

17. Pires, *The Suma Oriental,* 15.

18. Pires, *The Suma Oriental,* 16.

19. Pires, *The Suma Oriental,* 17.

20. Pires, *The Suma Oriental,* 13.

21. Duarte Barbosa (M. Longworth Dames, trans.), *The Book of Duarte Barbosa: An Account of the Countries Bordering on the Indian Ocean and Their Inhabitants* (London: Hakluyt Society, 1921).

22. Pires, *The Suma Oriental,* 19, 20.

23. Pires, *The Suma Oriental,* 20.

24. Pires, *The Suma Oriental,* 35.

25. Pires, *The Suma Oriental,* 41–2.

26. See Walter J. Fischel, ed. *Unknown Jews in Unknown Lands, the Travels of Rabbi David D'Beth Hillel (1824–1832)* (New York: Ktar, 1973); Nathan Katz, *Who Are the Jews of India?* (Berkeley: University of California Press, 2000); Nathan Katz and Ellen S. Goldberg, *The Last Jews of Cochin: Jewish Identity in Hindu India* (Columbia, SC: University of South Carolina Press, 1993); Nathan Katz and Ellen S. Goldberg, "Leaving Mother India: Reasons for the Cochin Jews' Migration to Israel," *Population Review* 39, 1–2 (1995), 35–53; S.S. Koder, "History of the Jews of Kerala," *Thomapedia: Christian Encyclopaedia of India,* ed. George Menachery (Ollur, India: B.N.K., 2000), 183–185; and James Henry Lord, *The Jews in India and the Far East* (Kolhapur, India: Mission, 1907; reprint, Westport, CT: Greenwood, 1977).

27. See A.E. Medlycott, *India and the Apostle Thomas: An Inquiry with a Critical Analysis of the Acta Thomae* (Piscataway, NJ: Gorgias, 2005, originally published 1905); and George Smith, *The Conversion of India: From Pantaenus to the Present Time (AD 193–1893)* (Piscataway, NJ: Gorgias, 2004).

28. Pires, *The Suma Oriental,* 73.

29. Ma Huan, *Ying-Yai Sheng-Lan,* 143.

30. Pires, *The Suma Oriental,* 78.

31. Ma Huan, *Ying-Yai Sheng-Lan,* 132–5.

32. Pires, *The Suma Oriental,* 79.

33. Pires, *The Suma Oriental,* 80.

34. Pires, *The Suma Oriental,* 233.

35. See Vivian Wee, *Melayu, Indigenism and the 'Civilising Process': Claims and Entitlements in Contested Territories,* Working Paper Series 78 (Hong Kong: City University of Hong Kong, 2005), 4.

36. Pires, *The Suma Oriental,* 238.

37. Pires, *The Suma Oriental,* 238.

38. Pires, *The Suma Oriental,* 238.

39. Pires, *The Suma Oriental,* 238.

40. Pires, *The Suma Oriental,* 240.

41. Pires, *The Suma Oriental,* 242.

42. Pires, *The Suma Oriental,* 243.

43. Pires, *The Suma Oriental,* 245.

44. Pires, *The Suma Oriental,* 251.

45. Pires, *The Suma Oriental,* 254–5.

46. Pires, *The Suma Oriental,* 93.

47. Pires, *The Suma Oriental,* 269.

48. Pires, *The Suma Oriental,* 268.

49. Pires, *The Suma Oriental,* 269–71.

50. From their introduction to Chau Ja-kua (F. Hirth and W.W. Rockhill, eds. and trans.), *Chau Ju-kua: His Work on the Chinese and Arab Trade in the Twelfth and Thirteenth Centuries, Entitled Chu-fan-chï* (Amsterdam: Oriental, 1966), 17–8.

51. Chau Ja-kua, *Chau Ju-kua,* 14, n. 4.

52. Chau Ja-kua, *Chau Ju-kua,* 15.

53. Chau Ja-kua, *Chau Ju-kua,* 16, n. 2.

54. Cited in Chau Ja-kua, *Chau Ju-kua.*

55. Abu Zayd Hassan ibn Yazid Sirafi (Eusebius Renaudot, trans.), *Ancient Accounts of India and China, by Two Mohammedan Travellers. Who Went to Those Parts in the 9th Century* (London, 1733; reprint, New Delhi: Asian Educational Service, 1995).

56. Chau Ja-kua, *Chau Ju-kua,* 17.

57. Chau Ja-kua, *Chau Ju-kua,* 23.

58. Pires, *The Suma Oriental,* 120–1.

59. Pires, *The Suma Oriental,* 121–2.

60. Frederic Mauro, "Merchant Communities, 1350–1750," *The Rise of Merchant Empires,* ed. James D. Tracy (New York: Cambridge University Press, 1990), 256.

61. Mauro, "Merchant Communities," 257–8.

62. Mauro, "Merchant Communities," 262.

63. Mauro, "Merchant Communities," 262.

64. Mauro, "Merchant Communities," 262.

Chapter 8

1. Tellier, *Urban World History,* 30.

2. See Nicholas Wade, "Europe's Plagues came from China, Study Finds," *New York Times* 31 October (2010), online at <www.nytimes.com/2010/11/01/health/01plague.html?_r=1>.

3. Ping-ti Ho, "An Estimate of the Total Population of Sung-Chin China," *Etudes Song* 1, 1 (1970), 33–53.

4. J.F.C. Hecker (B.G. Babington, trans.), *Epidemics of the Middle Ages* (London: Trüber, 1859), 21.

5. Ibn Battuta, *The Travels of Ibn Battuta,* Volume 3, 920.

6. Norman F. Cantor, *In the Wake of the Plague: The Black Death and the World It Made* (New York: The Free Press, 2001), 7.

7. Tellier, *Urban World History,* 39.

8. P.R.S. Moorey, *Ur of the Chaldees: A Revised and Updated Edition of Sir Leonard Woolley's Excavations at Ur* (Ithaca, NY: Cornell University Press, 1982).

9. See Tellier, *Urban World History,* 47; and Charles Gates, *Ancient Cities: The Archaeology of Urban Life in the Ancient Near East and Egypt, Greece and Rome* (New York: Routledge, 2003), 56.

10. See R.L. Zettler and L. Horne, eds., *Treasures from the Royal Tombs of Ur* (Philadelphia: University of Pennsylvania Museum of Archaeology and Anthropology, 1998).

11. See Joan Oates, *Babylon* (London: Thames & Hudson, 1986); and I.L. Finkel and M.J. Seymour, *Babylon* (New York: Oxford University Press, 2009).

12. Tellier, *Urban World History,* 60.

13. Tellier, *Urban World History,* 60.

14. Durant, *Our Oriental Heritage,* 227.

15. Durant, *Our Oriental Heritage,* 229.

16. See V. Minorsky and S.S. Blair, "Tabriz," *Encyclopedia of Islam,* ed. P.J. Bearman et al. (Leiden: Brill, 2009), Volume 10.

17. See William B. Fisher, ed., *The Cambridge History of Iran: The Land of Iran* (New York: Cambridge University Press, 1968), 14.

18. Rodney Castleden, *The Mycenaeans* (New York: Routledge, 2005), 188.

19. See John Chadwick, *The Mycenean World* (New York: Cambridge University Press, 1976); Elizabeth B. French, *Mycenae: Agamemnon's Capital: The Site and Setting* (Stroud, Gloucestershire: Tempus, 2002); and Castleden, *The Mycenaeans.*

20. Castleden, *The Mycenaeans,* 194.

21. Castleden, *The Mycenaeans,* 188.

22. Castleden, *The Mycenaeans,* 194.

23. Castleden, *The Mycenaeans,* 195.

24. Durant, *The Life of Greece,* 122.

25. Durant, *The Life of Greece,* 275.

26. Durant, *The Life of Greece,* 276.

27. Durant, *The Life of Greece,* 273.

28. Durant, *The Life of Greece,* 273.

29. See Maria Eugenia Aubet, *The Phoenicians and the West: Politics, Colonies and Trade* (New York: Cambridge University Press, 1987); Gilbert Charles-Picard and Colette Charles-Picard, *Daily Life in Carthage* (New York: Macmillan, 1961); David Soren, Aicha ben Abed ben Kader, and Heidi Slim, *Carthage: Uncovering the Mysteries and Splendors of Ancient Tunisia* (New York: Simon and Schuster, 1990); and B.H. Wormington, *Carthage* (New York: Frederick A. Praeger, 1960).

30. Andrew Erskine, "Culture and Power in Ptolemaic Egypt: The Museum and Library of Alexandria," *Greece & Rome* 42 (2nd Ser.), 1 (1995), 42.

31. See Peter M. Fraser, *Ptolemaic Alexandria* (Oxford: Clarendon, 1972); and Edward M. Forster, *Alexandria* (London: M. Haag, 1982).

32. Richard Alston, "Trade and the City in Roman Egypt," *Trade, Traders and the Ancient City,* ed. H. Parkins and C. Smith (New York: Routledge, 1998), 195.

33. Durant, *Caesar and Christ,* 499.

34. Durant, *Caesar and Christ,* 500.

35. Tellier, *Urban World History,* 138–9.

36. Glenn R. Storey, "The Population of Ancient Rome," *Antiquity* 71, 274 (1997), 966; N. Morely, *Metrop-*

olis and Hinterland: The City of Rome and the Italian Economy, 200 BC–AD 200 (New York: Cambridge University Press, 1996), 38; and David Noy, *Foreigners at Rome: Citizens and Strangers* (London: Duckworth & Classical Press of Wales, 2000), 15–16.

37. The original version was *Mille viae ducunt homines per saecula Romam* (A thousand roads lead men forever to Rome); see Samuel Singer, *Thesaurus Proverbiorum Medii Aevi: Lexikon der Sprichwörter des romanisch-germanischen Mittelters* (Berlin: Walter de Gruyter, 1995).

38. Michael Grant, *History of Rome* (New York: Charles Scribner, 1978), 264.

39. David Matz, *Daily Life of the Ancient Romans* (Westport, CT: Greenwood, 2002), 49.

40. Durant, *Caesar and Christ*, 325.

41. Gustav Hermansen, *Ostia: Aspects of Roman City Life* (Edmonton: University of Alberta Press, 1982), 8.

42. See L. Michael White, "Synagogue and Society in Imperial Ostia: Archaeological and Epigraphic Evidence," *The Harvard Theological Review* 90, 1 (1997), 23–58.

43. Plutarch, *Moralia* (Cambridge, MA: Harvard University Press, 2004), 604.

44. Durant, *Caesar and Christ*, 325.

45. Durant, *Caesar and Christ*, 324.

46. Pausanias (W.H.S. Jones, trans.), *Description of Greece* (Cambridge, MA: Harvard University Press; London, William Heinemann, 1918); and see S.E. Alcock, J.F. Cherry, and J. Elsner, *Pausanias: Travel and Memory in Roman Greece* (New York: Oxford University Press, 2001); Christian Habicht, "An Ancient Baedeker and His Critics: Pausanias' 'Guide to Greece,'" *Proceedings of the American Philosophical Society* 129, 2 (1985), 220–24; and Aubrey Diller, "The Manuscripts of Pausanias," *Transactions and Proceedings of the American Philological Association* 88 (1957), 169–88.

47. Noy, *Foreigners at Rome*, 17, 22.

48. Noy, *Foreigners at Rome*, 23.

49. Noy, *Foreigners at Rome*, 59–60.

50. Noy, *Foreigners at Rome*, 257.

51. Fergus Millar, *The Roman Empire and Its Neighbours* (London: Weidenfeld & Nicolson, 1967), 178.

52. Durant, *Caesar and Christ*, 113–5.

53. Cassius Dio's *Historia Romana* (Roman History) covers the period up to A.D. 229 and provides biographical information on the Roman emperors. The *Historia Augusta* is another Roman source on the lives of the emperors, although it is commonly believed to contain numerous inaccuracies. See these online at <http://penelope.u chicago.edu/Thayer/E/Roman/Texts/Cassius_Dio/home. html>.

54. See Anthony R. Birley, *Septimus Severus: The African Emperor* (New York: Routledge, 1999).

55. The cult of the sun god Elagabalus may be linked to the Roman cult of the *Sol Invictus* that was made an official Roman cult by the Emperor Aurelian in 274, although this view is disputed by some scholars; see Gaston Halsberhe, *The Cult of Sol Invictus* (Leiden: Brill, 1972); and Steven E. Hijmans, "The Sun That Did Not Rise in the East," *Babesch* 71 (1996), 115–50.

56. Noy, *Foreigners at Rome*, 88.

57. See Fergus Millar, *A Study of Cassius Dio* (Oxford: Clarendon, 1964).

58. Noy, *Foreigners at Rome*, 115.

59. Noy, *Foreigners at Rome*, 115.

60. Noy, *Foreigners at Rome*, 160.

61. Noy, *Foreigners at Rome*, 163.

62. Noy, *Foreigners at Rome*, 225.

63. Durant, *Caesar and Christ*, 339.

64. Noy, *Foreigners at Rome*, 47.

65. Matz, *Daily Life of the Ancient Romans*, 97.

66. Noy, *Foreigners at Rome*, 119.

67. Peter Struck, "Greatest of All Time," *Lapham's Quarterly* (19 May, 2011), online at <www.laphamsquar terly.org>.

68. Durant, *Caesar and Christ*, 378.

69. Noy, *Foreigners at Rome*, 20.

70. Noy, *Foreigners at Rome*, 20–1.

71. Yves Le Bohec, *The Imperial Roman Army* (London: B.T. Batsford, 1994), 99; cited by Noy, *Foreigners at Rome*, 21.

72. Noy, *Foreigners at Rome*, 21.

73. Noy, *Foreigners at Rome*, 22.

74. Noy, *Foreigners at Rome*, 101.

75. Noy, *Foreigners at Rome*, 106.

76. See Frank Kolb, *Rom: Die Geschichte der Stadt in der Antike* (Munich: C.H.Beck, 1995), 461; and Noy, *Foreigners at Rome*, 78.

77. Noy, *Foreigners at Rome*, 11, 78.

78. Noy, *Foreigners at Rome*, 250.

79. Noy, *Foreigners at Rome*, 245.

80. Noy, *Foreigners at Rome*, 243.

81. Noy, *Foreigners at Rome*, 265.

82. Leonard V. Rutgers, *The Jews of Late Rome* (Leiden: E.J. Brill, 1995), 48–9.

83. Noy, *Foreigners at Rome*, 264.

84. Noy, *Foreigners at Rome*, 267.

85. Noy, *Foreigners at Rome*, 23.

86. Brian Crooke, "Justinian's Constantinople," *The Cambridge Companion to the Age of Justinian*, ed. Michael Mass (New York: Cambridge University Press, 2005), 67; also see Glanville Downey, *Constantinople in the Age of Justinian* (Norman: University of Oklahoma Press, 1960).

87. Crooke, "Justinian's Constantinople," 73–4.

88. Durant, *The Age of Faith*, 119.

89. Crooke, "Justinian's Constantinople," 69.

90. Durant, *The Age of Faith*, 436.

91. Crooke, "Justinian's Constantinople," 73.

92. See Cyril A. Mango, *Byzantium: The Empire of New Rome* (London: Weidenfeld and Nicolson, 1980).

93. Halil Inalcik, "The Policy of Mehmed II toward the Greek Population of Istanbul and the Byzantine Buildings of the City," *Dumbarton Oaks Papers* 23 (1969), 236.

94. See Janet L. Abu-Lughod, *Cairo: 1001 Years of the City Victorious* (Princeton, NJ: Princeton University Press, 1971).

95. Tellier, *Urban World History*, 197.

96. Monica Smith, "The Archaeology of South Asian Cities," *Journal of Archaeological Research* 14 (2006), 100.

97. Smith, "The Archaeology of South Asian Cities," 120.

98. E. A. Schwanbeck (J.W. McCrindle, trans.), *Ancient India as Described by Megasthenes and Arrian* (London: Thacker, Spink, 1877; reprint, New York: Oxford University Press, 2007).

99. Smith, "The Archaeology of South Asian Cities," 120.

100. Durant, *Our Oriental Heritage*, 457; also see John M. Fritz and George Mitchell, eds., *New Light on Hampi: Recent Research at Vijayanagar* (Mumbai: MARG, 2001).

101. See Smith, *The Oxford History of India* (New York: Oxford University Press, 1981), 304–13.

102. W.H. Moreland and Atul Chandra Chatterjee, *A Short History of India* (New York : David McKay, 1962), 177; K.A. Nilakanta Sastri, *A History of South India from Prehistoric Times to the Fall of Vijayanagar* (New Delhi: Oxford University Press, 2002), 304–6; and Robert Sewell, *A Forgotten Empire (Vijayanagara)* (New Delhi: Asian Education Services, 1982), 246–7.

103. Moreland and Chatterjee, *A Short History of India*, 177; Sastri, *A History of South India*, 304–6; and Sewell, *A Forgotten Empire*, 246–7.

104. Moreland and Chatterjee, *A Short History of India*, 177; Sastri, *A History of South India*, 304–6; and Sewell, *A Forgotten Empire*, 246–7.

105. See Suryanath U. Kamath, *A Concise History of Karnataka: From Pre-historic Times to the Present* (Bangalore: Jupiter, 2001), 181.

106. Vijayanagara Research Project, "Foreign Visitors," online at <www.vijayanagara.org>.

107. Von Falkenhausen, "The Waning of the Bronze Age," 455.

108. Von Falkenhausen, "The Waning of the Bronze Age," 455.

109. Nancy S. Steinhardt, *Chinese Imperial City Planning* (Honolulu: University of Hawai'i Press, 1990), 68.

110. Patricia Buckley Ebrey, Anne Walthall, and James B. Palais, *East Asia: A Cultural, Social, and Political History* (Boston: Houghton Mifflin, 2006), 112; and Studwell, 2003, 4.

111. Edward H. Schafer, *The Golden Peaches of Samarkand: A Study of T'ang Exotics* (Berkeley: University of California Press, 1963), 21.

112. Schafer, *The Golden Peaches of Samarkand*, 25.

113. See Xu Xin, *The Jews of Kaifeng: History, Culture, and Religion* (Jersey City: KTAV, 2003); William Charles White, *Chinese Jews: A Compilation of Matters Relating to the Jews of K'aifêng fu* (New York: Paragon Book Reprint, 1966, originally published 1942); and Michael Pollack, *Mandarins, Jews, and Missionaries: The Jewish Experience in the Chinese Empire* (New York: Weatherhill, 1998).

114. Anthony Reid, "Economic and Social Change, c. 1400–1800," *The Cambridge History of Southeast Asia, Volume 1: From Early Times to c.1800*, ed. Nicholas Tarling (New York: Cambridge University Press, 1992), 460.

115. Nguyen Van Huyen, *The Ancient Civilization of Vietnam* (Hanoi: Gioi, 1995), 122–3.

116. Hall, "Economic History of Early Southeast Asia," 267–8.

117. Hall, "Economic History of Early Southeast Asia," 269.

118. Charnvit Kasetsiri, *The Rise of Ayudhya: A History of Siam in the Fourteenth and Fifteenth Centuries* (Kuala Lumpur: Oxford University Press, 1976), 16.

119. See L.P Briggs, "Dvaravati, the Mon Ancient Kingdom in Siam," *Journal of the American Oriental Society* 65, 2 (1945), 98, 101.

120. O.C. Blagden, "The Mon or Talaing and Pyu Faces of the Myazedi Inscription at Pagan," *Epigraphia Birmanica*, eds. Charles Duroiselle and Taw Sein Ko (Rangoon: Superintendent of Government Printing, 1919), Volume 1, Part 1; and see Gordon H. Luce, *Old Burma-Early Pagan* (Locust Valley, PA: J.J. Augustine, 1969–70), plate 338.

121. G.E Harvey, *History of Burma from the Earliest Times to 10 March 1824 the Beginning of the English Conquest* (London: Longmans Green, 1925), 348. See Michael Aung-Thwin, *The Mists of Ramanna: The Legend That was Lower Burma* (Honolulu: University of Hawai'i Press, 2005), for an examination of Mon influence on Bagan.

122. Keith W. Taylor, "The Early Kingdoms," 165.

123. Sylvia Fraser-Lu, *Burmese Crafts Past and Present* (Kuala Lumpur: Oxford University Press 1994), 59. Fraser-Lu, 79, n. 61, cites Susan Huntington and John Huntington, *Leaves from the Bodhi Tree: The Art of Pala India (8th–12th Centuries) and Its International Legacy* (Seattle: University of Washington Press and Dayton Art Institute, 1990), 201, who say that Pagan art is a "conflation of Bihar styles and the artistic traditions of Assam."

124. John Strong, *The Legend and Cult of Upagupta* (New Delhi: Motilal Banarsidass, 1994), 12.

125. Hall, "Economic History of Early Southeast Asia," 244.

126. D.G.E. Hall, *Burma* (London: Hutchinson's University Library, 1956), 140.

127. Hall, "Economic History of Early Southeast Asia," 237.

128. Tellier, *Urban World History*, 220.

129. Zhou Daguan (Peter Harris, trans.), *A Record of Cambodia: The Land and Its People* (Chiang Mai: Silkworm, 2007), 12.

130. Zhou, *A Record of Cambodia*, 12.

131. Zhou, *A Record of Cambodia*, 58–9.

132. Zhou, *A Record of Cambodia*, 69.

133. Zhou, *A Record of Cambodia*, 70.

134. Zhou, *A Record of Cambodia*, 61.

135. Zhou, *A Record of Cambodia*, 75–6.

136. Zhou, *A Record of Cambodia*, 76.

137. Zhou, *A Record of Cambodia*, 50.

138. Zhou, *A Record of Cambodia*, 71.

139. Zhou, *A Record of Cambodia*, 70.

140. Zhou, *A Record of Cambodia*, 81.

141. Kasetsiri, *The Rise of Ayudhya*, 20.

142. Kasetsiri, *The Rise of Ayudhya*, 21.

143. See Kasetsiri, *The Rise of Ayudhya*, 76–89.

144. Jeremias van Vliet (Leonard Y. Andaya, translator, Miriam J. Verkuijl-van den Berghe, transcription, David K. Wyatt, ed.), *The Short History of the Kings of Siam* (Bangkok: Siam Society, 1975); and see Christopher J. Baker, *Van Vliet's Siam* (Chiang Mai: Silkworm, 2005). Also see David K. Wyatt, *Thailand: A Short History* (New Haven, CT: Yale University Press, 1982), 65; and Kasetsiri, *The Rise of Ayudhya*, 52.

145. Kasetsiri, *The Rise of Ayudhya*, 66.

146. H.G. Wales, *Dvaravati: The Earliest Kingdom of Siam* (London: Quaritch, 1969), 4, 10; and Kasetsiri, *The Rise of Ayudhya*, 23.

147. See Kasetsiri, *The Rise of Ayudhya*, 80.

148. G. William Skinner, *Chinese Society in Thailand* (Ithaca, NY: Cornell University Press, 1957), 1–2.

149. Levathes, *When China Ruled the Seas*, 105–6.

150. Kasetsiri, *The Rise of Ayudhya*, 81.

151. Kasetsiri, *The Rise of Ayudhya*, 66.

152. Wyatt, *Thailand*, 66.

153. Wyatt, *Thailand*, 89.

154. Wyatt, *Thailand*, 71.

155. Kasetsiri, *The Rise of Ayudhya*, 100.

156. Kasetsiri, *The Rise of Ayudhya*, 85–86.

157. Kasetsiri, *The Rise of Ayudhya*, 139.

158. E. Thaddius Flood, "Sukhothai-Mongol Relations," *Journal of the Siam Society* 57, 2 (1969), 203–34.

159. Suebsaeng Promboon, *Sino-Siamese Tributary Relations: 1282–1853* (PhD, dissertation, University of Wisconsin, 1971).

160. Kasetsiri, *The Rise of Ayudhya*, 80.

161. Kasetsiri, *The Rise of Ayudhya*, 112.

162. Kasetsiri, *The Rise of Ayudhya*, 109, 111–2; and Suebsaeng Promboon, *Sino-Siamese Tributary Relations*, 158.

163. Kasetsiri, *The Rise of Ayudhya*, 112; and Suebsaeng Promboon, *Sino-Siamese Tributary Relations*, 162–5.

164. Kasetsiri, *The Rise of Ayudhya*, 112.

165. Levathes, *When China Ruled the Seas*, 105; Kasetsiri, *The Rise of Ayudhya*, 113; and Suebsaeng Promboon, *Sino-Siamese Tributary Relations*, 75.

166. Levathes, *When China Ruled the Seas*, 105.

167. Kasetsiri, *The Rise of Ayudhya,* 112; and Levathes, *When China Ruled the Seas,* 105.

168. Kasetsiri, *The Rise of Ayudhya,* 113.

169. Levathes, *When China Ruled the Seas,* 184.

170. Wyatt, *Thailand,* 67.

171. Ma Huan, *Ying-Yai Sheng-Lan,* 107.

172. Ma Huan, *Ying-Yai Sheng-Lan,* 107.

173. Ma Huan, *Ying-Yai Sheng-Lan,* 105–6.

174. See John Guy, *Woven Cargoes: Indian Textiles in the East* (London: Thames & Hudson, 1998), 123.

175. Wyatt, *Thailand,* 73–74; and Kasetsiri, *The Rise of Ayudhya,* 78.

176. See John Guy, *Oriental Trade Ceramics in Southeast Asia: Ninth to Sixteenth Centuries* (Singapore: Oxford University Press, 1986); and John Guy, *Woven Cargoes,* 121.

177. Guy, *Woven Cargoes,* 107–8.

178. Anthony Reid, *Southeast Asia in the Age of Commerce 1450–1680, Volume One: The Lands Below the Winds* (New Haven, CT: Yale University Press, 1988), 95; "Traibhumikatha c. 1345," in Frank Reynolds and Mani Reynolds, trans., *Three Worlds According to King Ruang: A Thai Buddhist Cosmology* (Berkeley: University of California Press, 1982), 176.

179. Wyatt, *Thailand,* 86.

180. Atsushi Kobata and Mitsugu Matsuda, trans., *Ryukyuan Relations with Korea and South Sea Countries: An Annotated Translation of Documents in the Rekidai Hoan* (Kyoto: Kobata Atsushi, 1969), 64.

181. Pires, *The Suma Oriental,* 103.

182. Pires, *The Suma Oriental,* 104.

183. Kasetsiri, *The Rise of Ayudhya,* 79.

184. I discuss Ayutthaya in the 1500s and 1600s in Howard, *Transnationalism and Society,* 81–84. During those centuries in addition to Chinese, Ayutthaya had significant numbers of Persians, Japanese, Malays, Cham, Bugis-Makassarese, as well as various Europeans living in and around the city.

185. Kasetsiri, *The Rise of Ayudhya,* 81.

186. Kasetsiri, *The Rise of Ayudhya,* 81–2.

187. See Kathleen Berrin and Esther Pasztory, eds., *Teotihuacan: Art from the City of the Gods* (New York: Thames & Hudson, 1994); George L. Cowgill, "State and Society at Teotihuacan, Mexico," *Annual Review of Anthropology* 26 (1997), 129–61; and Karl E. Meyer, *Teotihuacán: First City in the Americas* (New York: Newsweek Book Division, 1980).

188. René Millon, "Teotihuacan: Completion of Map of Giant Ancient City in the Valley of Mexico," *Science* 170 (1970), 1080.

189. René Millon, *The Teotihuacan Map, Volume 1, Part 2 (maps)* (Austin: University of Texas Press, 1973).

190. Richard E.W. Adams, *Prehistoric Mesoamerica* (Boston: Little, Brown, 1977), 200.

191. Millon, *The Teotihuacan Map.*

192. Sigvald Linné, *Archaeological Researches at Teotihuacan, Mexico* (Stockholm: The Ethnographical Museum of Sweden, 1934), 97.

193. Arthur G. Miller, *The Mural Painting of Teotihuacan* (Washington, DC: Dunbarton Oaks Research Library and Collection, 1978), 68.

194. Richard E.W. Adams, *Ancient Civilizations of the New World* (Boulder, CO: Westview, 1997), 47.

Chapter 9

1. See Mark Healy, *Qadesh 1300 BC: Clash of the Warrior Kings* (Oxford: Osprey, 1993), 28–30.

2. The identity of the Sea Peoples is subject to considerable debate. See Eliezer D. Oren, ed., *The Sea Peoples and Their World: A Reassessment* (Philadelphia: The University of Pennsylvania Museum of Archaeology and Anthropology, 2000).

3. See Kitchen, 1982, p. 40–4.

4. See Hans Goedicke, "Considerations on the Battle of Kadesh," *The Journal of Egyptian Archaeology* 52 (1966), 71–80.

5. Herodotus, *The Histories,* 1.28.

6. Herodotus, *The Histories,* 1.94; and Xenophanes (James H. Lesher, trans. and ed.), *Xenophanes of Colophon: Fragments: A Text and Translation with a Commentary* (Toronto: University of Toronto Press, 1992), fragment 4, see pages 17, 65, 129, 133, 135, 151–2, 160.

7. Later, coins were made of gold or silver rather than electrum.

8. Xenophon (H.G. Dakyns, trans), *Cyropaedia: The Education of Cyrus* (London: Macmillan, 1897), Book 2, online at <ebooks.adelaide.edu.au/x/xenophon/x5cy/>.

9. Charles Anthon, *A Classical Dictionary: Containing an Account of the Principal Proper Names Mentioned in Ancient Authors* (New York: Harper & Brothers, 1848), 388.

10. M. Cogan and H. Tadmor, "Gyges and Ashurbanipal: A Study in Literary Transmission," *Orientalia* 46 (1977), 68.

11. Jona Lendering, "Gyges of Lydia," *Livius, Articles on Ancient History,* online at <www.livius.org/men-mh/mermnads/gyges.html>.

12. Diodorus (C.H. Oldfather, trans.), *The Library of History* (1933), 1.66, online at: <penelope.uchicago.edu/Thayer/E/Roman/Texts/Diodorus_Siculus/home.html>; also see Herodotus, *Histories,* 2.152.3–154.5, 178.1–182.2; R. Ball, "The Karians's Place in Diodoros' Thalassocracy List," *The Classical Quarterly* 27 (n.s.), 2 (1977), 317–22; and M.M. Austin, "Greece and Egypt in the Archaic Age," *Proceedings of the Cambridge Philological Society Supplement* 2 (1970), 15–6.

13. Diodorus, *The Library of History,* 1.67.

14. Herodotus, *Histories,* 2.154.

15. Diodorus, *The Library of History,* 1.67.

16. Diodorus, *The Library of History,* 1.67.

17. Diodorus, *The Library of History,* 1.67.

18. Matthew Dillon and Lynda Garland, *Ancient Greece: Social and Historical Documents from Archaic Times to the Death of Alexander the Great,* 3rd ed. (New York: Routledge, 2010), 69–70.

19. Peter A. Clayton, *Chronicle of the Pharaohs: The Reign-by-Reign Record of the Rulers and Dynasties of Ancient Egypt* (London: Thames & Hudson, 2006), 197.

20. See Herodotus, *Histories,* 1.3.

21. See Guy T. Griffith, *Mercenaries of the Hellenistic World* (Cambridge: Cambridge University Press, 1935).

22. Durant, *The Life of Greece,* 468.

23. Charles D. Hamilton, "The Hellenistic World," *War and Society in the Ancient Worlds,* ed. K. Raaflaub and N. Rosenstein (Cambridge, MA: Harvard University Press, 1999), 180.

24. Rawlinson, *The Five Great Monarchies,* Volume 3, 242.

25. Rawlinson, *The Five Great Monarchies,* Volume 3, 419.

26. Rawlinson, *The Five Great Monarchies,* Volume 3, 242.

27. Rawlinson, *The Five Great Monarchies,* Volume 3, 434.

28. Pierre Briant, "The Achaemenid Empire," *War and Society in the Ancient Worlds,* ed. K. Raaflaub and N.

Rosenstein (Cambridge, MA: Harvard University Press, 1999), 118–20.

29. Glenn E. Markoe, *The Phoenicians* (Berkeley: University of California Press, 2000), 60.

30. Rawlinson, *The Five Great Monarchies,* Volume 3, 511.

31. Rawlinson, *The Five Great Monarchies,* Volume 3, 531. For information on some of the lesser known groups mentioned here see George Rawlinson, "Essay I: On the Obscurer Tribes Contained within the Empire of Xerxes," *History of Herodotus* (London: John Murray, 1875), Volume 4, 198–235.

32. G. Georges Aperghis, *The Seleukid Royal Economy: The Finances and Financial Administration of the Seleukid Empire* (New York: Cambridge University Press, 2004), 194.

33. Polybius, *The Histories of Polybius,* 5.79; and cited in Aperghis, *The Seleukid Royal Economy,* 192. Daniel T. Potts, *The Archaeology of Elam: Formation and Transformation of an Ancient Iranian State* (New York: Cambridge University Press, 1999), 339–40, discusses the Kissians and argues that they are Elamites whose territory was included in the same satrapy as Susiana. The Agrianians (aka Agrianes) are a Thracian tribe from Macedonia who later served as javelin throwers in the army of Alexander the Great.

34. Aperghis, *The Seleukid Royal Economy,* 199–200.

35. See Polybius, *The Histories of Polybius.*

36. Lawrence Keppie, "The Army and the Navy," *Cambridge Ancient History, Volume X: The Augustan Empire, 43 B.C.–A.D. 69,* ed. Alan K. Brown, Edward Champlin, and Andrew Lintott (New York: Cambridge University Press, 1996), 371.

37. Polybius, *The Histories of Polybius,* vi.39.12.

38. Keppie, "The Army and the Navy," 371–2.

39. Keppie, "The Army and the Navy," 381.

40. Keppie, "The Army and the Navy," 373.

41. Keppie, "The Army and the Navy," 375.

42. See Peter Richardson, *Herod: King of the Jews and Friend of the Romans,* (New York: Continuum, 1999); and Joseph Jacobs and Isaac Broydé, "Herod," online at JewishEncyclopedia.com (originally published 1901–1906), 356–60.

43. Keppie, "The Army and the Navy," 377.

44. See Keppie, "The Army and the Navy," 388, Table 3. On the imperial army in general also see Alistair Scott Anderson, "The Imperial Army," *The Roman World,* ed. John S. Wacher (London: Routledge, 1987), Volume 1, 89–106.

45. Keppie, "The Army and the Navy," 387.

46. Brian Campbell, "The Roman Empire," *War and Society in the Ancient Worlds,* ed. K. Raaflaub and N. Rosenstein (Cambridge, MA: Harvard University Press, 1999), 218.

48. Keppie, "The Army and the Navy," 387.

49. Keppie, "The Army and the Navy," 391.

50. Keppie, "The Army and the Navy," 389.

51. Keppie, "The Army and the Navy," 389.

52. Campbell, "The Roman Empire," 222.

53. Campbell, "The Roman Empire," 222.

54. Keppie, "The Army and the Navy," 395.

55. Keppie, "The Army and the Navy," 396.

56. See Birley, *Septimus Severus.*

57. Durant, *Caesar and Christ,* 670. Also see R.S.O. Tomlin, "The Army of the Late Empire," *The Roman World,* ed. John S. Wacher (New York: Routledge, 1987), Volume 1, 107–33.

58. Durant, *Caesar and Christ,* 670.

59. Durant, *The Age of Faith,* 108.

60. H.R. Ellis Davidson, *The Viking Road to Byzantium* (London: George Allen & Unwin, 1976), 178.

61. Davidson, *The Viking Road to Byzantium,* 178.

62. Davidson, *The Viking Road to Byzantium,* 179.

63. Robert Crowley and Geoffrey Parker, eds., *The Reader's Companion to Military History* (New York: Houghton Mifflin, 1996), 300.

64. Richard Huscroft, *Ruling England, 1042–1217* (Harlow, UK: Pearson, 2005), 169–70.

65. Durant, *The Age of Faith,* 294.

66. Durant, *The Age of Faith,* 295.

67. See Rafael Altamira, "Il Califfato Occidentale," *Storia del Mondo Medievale* 2 (1999), 477–515.

68. David Bates, *William the Conqueror* (Stroud, UK: Tempus, 2001), 79–81.

69. See Eljas Oksanen, "The Anglo-Flemish Treaties and Flemish Soldiers in England, 1101–1163," *Mercenaries and Paid Men: The Mercenary Identity in the Middle Ages,* ed. John France (Leiden: E.J. Brill, 2008), 261–73.

70. Cited by Christopher Daniell, *From Norman Conquest to Magna Carta: England, 1066–1215* (New York: Routledge, 2003), 13–4; and see William of Tyre (E.A. Babcock and A.C. Krey, trans.), *A History of Deeds Done Beyond the Sea* (New York: Columbia University Press, 1943); and Peter W. Edbury and John G. Rowe, *William of Tyre: Historian of the Latin East* (New York: Cambridge University Press, 1988).

71. Krijna Nelly Ciggaar, *Western Travellers to Constantinople: The West and Byzantium, 962–1204* (Leien: E.J. Brill, 1996), 140–1.

72. Ian Heath, *Byzantine Armies, AD 1118–1461* (Oxford: Osprey, 1995), 23.

73. Ciggaar, *Western Travellers to Constantinople,* 140–1.

74. Richard Eales, "William of Ypres, Styled Count of Flanders (*d.* 1164/5)," *Oxford Dictionary of National Biography* (2004), online at <www.oxforddnb.com/index/101029465/William-of-Ypres>.

75. Richard Barber, *Henry Plantagenet* (Melton, Suffolk, UK: Boydell & Brewster, 2003), 278.

76. George Macaulay Trevelyan, *A Shortened History of England* (Harmondsworth, UK: Penguin, 1959), 128–9.

77. Trevelyan, *A Shortened History of England,* 129.

78. Warren W. Lewis, *King John* (London: Methuen, 1991), 55.

79. See Desmond Seward, *The Hundred Years War: The English in France 1337–1453* (Harmondsworth, UK: Penguin, 1999), 9, 88–90, 104, 105–06, 127, 147.

80. Seward, *The Hundred Years War,* 90.

81. Kenneth A. Fowler, *Medieval Mercenaries, Volume 1: The Great Companies* (Oxford: Blackwell, 2001).

82. Fowler, *Medieval Mercenaries,* 4.

83. Fowler, *Medieval Mercenaries,* 6.

84. William L. Urban and Terry Jones, *Medieval Mercenaries: The Business of War* (London: Greenhill Books; St. Paul, MN: MBI, 2006), 43.

85. Urban and Jones, *Medieval Mercenaries,* 43.

86. Urban and Jones, *Medieval Mercenaries,* 44.

87. See Ernst Kantorowicz, *Frederick the Second, 1194–1250* (London: Constable, 1931, and New York: Frederick Ungar, 1957); and David Abulafia, *Frederick II: A Medieval Emperor* (Harmondsworth, UK: Allen Lane, 1988).

88. See Michael Mallett, *Mercenaries and Their Masters: Warfare in Renaissance Italy* (Lanham, MD: Rowman and Littlefield, 1974).

89. Claudio Rendina, *I capitani di ventura* (Rome: Newton & Compton, 1999).

90. William Caferro, *John Hawkwood: An English Mercenary in Fourteenth-century Italy* (Baltimore: Johns Hopkins University Press, 2006); Stephen Cooper, *Sir John Hawkwood: Chivalry and the Art of War* (Barnsley: Pen and Sword, 2008); and Frances Stonor Saunders, *Hawkwood: The Diabolical Englishman* (London: Faber & Faber, 2004).

91. Arthur Conan Doyle, *The White Company* (New York: HarperCollins, 1988), originally published in 1891; set in France and loosely based on the exploits of John Hawkwood.

92. Hubert Cole, *Hawkwood* (London: Eyre & Spottiswoode, 1967); Hubert Cole, *Hawkwood in Paris* (Colchester, UK: The Book Service, 1969); Hubert Cole, *Hawkwood and the Towers of Pisa* (London: Methuen, 1973).

93. Mark Edward Lewis, "Warring States: Political History," *The Cambridge History of Ancient China,* ed. Michael Loewe and Edward L. Shaughnessy (New York: Cambridge University Press, 1999), 625–627.

94. Lewis, "Warring States: Political History," 612.

95. Lewis, "Warring States: Political History," 614–5.

96. Lewis, "Warring States: Political History," 633.

97. Lewis, "Warring States: Political History," 633.

98. Michael Loewe, "The Structure and Practice of Government," *The Cambridge History of China, Volume I: The Ch'in and Han Empires, 221 B.C.–A.D. 220,* ed. Denis Twitchett and John K. Fairbank (New York: Cambridge University Press, 1987), 479.

99. Loewe, "The Structure and Practice of Government," 479; and Hans Bernstein, "The Institutions of Later Han," *The Cambridge History of China, Volume I: The Ch'in and Han Empires, 221 B.C.–A.D. 220,* ed. Denis Twitchett and John K. Fairbank (New York: Cambridge University Press, 1987), 512.

100. C.A. Peterson, "Court and Province in Mid- and Late T'ang," *The Cambridge History of China, Volume 3: Sui and T'ang China, 589–906, Part I,* ed. Denis Twitchett (New York: University Press, 1979), 466.

101. Peterson, "Court and Province in Mid- and Late T'ang," 465.

102. Peterson, "Court and Province in Mid- and Late T'ang," 485.

103. Peterson, "Court and Province in Mid- and Late T'ang," 485.

104. Peterson, "Court and Province in Mid- and Late T'ang," 515–6.

105. Peterson, "Court and Province in Mid- and Late T'ang," 516.

106. George C. Vaillant, *Aztecs of Mexico* (Harmondsworth, UK: Penguin, 1965), 220.

107. Vaillant, *Aztecs of Mexico,* 220.

108. Vaillant, *Aztecs of Mexico,* 221.

109. Hassig, *Trade, Tribute, and Transportation,* 97.

110. Hassig, *Trade, Tribute, and Transportation,* 98.

111. Hassig, *Trade, Tribute, and Transportation,* 95.

112. Vaillant, *Aztecs of Mexico,* 220.

113. Hassig, *Trade, Tribute, and Transportation,* 98.

114. Hassig, *Trade, Tribute, and Transportation,* 96.

115. Hassig, *Trade, Tribute, and Transportation,* 98.

Chapter 10

1. H.R. Perera, *Buddhism in Sri Lanka: A Short History* (Kandy: Buddhist Publication Society, 1988), online at <www.accesstoinsight.org/lib/authors/perera/wheel 100.html>.

2. There are numerous versions of the *Mahavamsa* available in English both in print form and on the internet.

3. James Bird, *Historical Researches on the Origin and Principles of the Buddha and Jaina Religions* (Bombay: American Mission Press, 1847), 60.

4. There are several versions of the *Milinda Panha* in English; see T.W. Rhys Davids, trans., *Questions of King Milinda* (Oxford: Clarendon, 1890–94; reprint, New York: Dover, 1963).

5. S. Dhammika, *The Edicts of King Ashoka* (Kandy, Sri Lanka: Buddhist Publication Society, 1993), online from DharmaNet and at <www.cs.colostate.edu/~malai ya/ashoka.html>.

6. See Joseph Wilson Trig, *Origen* (New York: Routledge, 1998).

7. Emmerick, "Buddhism among Iranian Peoples," 961.

8. Charles S. Prebish, *Buddhism: A Modern Perspective* (University Park, PA: Pennsylvania State University Press, 1971), 42–3.

9. Emmerick, "Buddhism among Iranian Peoples," 962.

10. Stein, *Ancient Khotan,* Volume 1, 180.

11. Emmerick, "Buddhism among Iranian Peoples," 963.

12. Tam Ha Le Cong Da, "Introduction to Buddhism in Viet Nam & Vietnamese Zen," online at <www.bud dhismtoday.com/english/vietnam>.

13. See Tran Van Giap, "Le Bouddhisme en Annam, des Origines au XIII Siècle." *Bulletin de l'Ecole Française d'Extrême Orient* 32 (1932), 191–268.

14. Tran, "Le Bouddhisme en Annam," 227.

15. James Legge, *A Record of Buddhistic Kingdoms: Being an Account by the Chinese Monk Fa-Hien of His Travels in India and Ceylon (AD 399–414) in Search of the Buddhist Books of Discipline* (Oxford: Clarendon, 1886), online at <etext.library.adelaide.edu.au>, and reprinted by Paragon in 1965; and see Mookerji, *The Gupta Empire,* 56–63.

16. Mookerji, *The Gupta Empire,* 61–2.

17. See Arthur Waley, *The Real Tripitaka* (New York: Macmillan, 1952); and Sally Hovey Wriggins, *Xuanzang: A Buddhist Pilgrim on the Silk Road* (Boulder, CO: Westview, 1996).

18. Samuel Beal, *Si-Yu-Ki: Buddhist Records of the Western World* (New York: Paragon Book Reprint, 1968).

19. Arthur Waley, *Monkey: Folk Novel of China* (New York: Evergreen, 1958); and Anthony Yu, *The Journey to the West,* 4 volumes (Chicago: University of Chicago Press, 1977–83).

20. I-Ching, *Chinese Monks in India: Biography of Eminent Monks Who Went to the Western World in Search of the Law During the Great T'ang Dynasty* (New Delhi: Motilal Banarsidass, 1995); and I-Ching (J. Takakusu, trans.), *Record of the Buddhist Religion: As Practised in India and the Malay Archipelago (A.D. 671–695)* (New Delhi: AES, 2005, originally published 1896).

21. Bibbhuti Baruah, *Buddhist Sects and Sectarianism* (New Delhi: Sarup & Son, 2008), 170.

22. Hye-ch'o (Jan Yun-Hua, Iida Shotaro, and Yang Han-Sung, eds.; Laurence Preston, trans.), *The Hye Ch'o Diary: Memoir of the Pilgrimage to the Five Regions of India* (Freemont, CA: Asian Humanities, 1984).

23. Soka Gakkai International (SGI) has a useful website for its *The Soka Gakkai Dictionary of Buddhism* that includes entries on prominent monks during this period: <www.sgilibrary.org/search_dict.php>.

24. See Paul Groner, *Saicho: The Establishment of the*

Japanese Tendai School (Honolulu: University of Hawai'i Press, 1984), 39–65.

25. Ryuichi Abe, *The Weaving of Mantra: Kukai and the Construction of Esoteric Buddhist Discourse* (New York: Columbia University Press, 1999), 118–27.

26. Groner, *Saicho,* 64.

27. Ennin (Edwin O Reischauer, trans.), *Ennin's Diary: The Record of a Pilgrimage to China in Search of the Law* (New York: Ronald Press, 1955).

28. Kasetsiri, *The Rise of Ayudhaya,* 18.

29. Louis Frédéric (Käthe Roth, trans.), *Japan Encyclopedia* (Cambridge, MA: Harvard University Press, 2002), 172.

30. Hinsch, *The Ultimate Guide to Chinese Tea,* 25.

31. Durant, *The Life of Greece,* 204; and see Roger D. Woodard, "Greek Dialects," *The Ancient Languages of Europe,* ed. R.D. Woodward (New York: Cambridge University Press, 2008).

32. See Justin Marozzi, *The Way of Herodotus: Travels with the Man Who Invented History* (London: John Murray/Cambridge, MA: Da Capo, 2008); and James S. Romm, *Herodotus* (New Haven, CT: Yale University Press, 1998). Biographies of many of the ancient Greeks discussed here are available in William Smith, ed. *A Dictionary of Greek and Roman Biography and Mythology,* 3 volumes (Boston: Little, Brown, 1867, originally published 1849), online at <http://quod.lib.umich.edu/cgi/t/text/text-idx?c=moa;idno=ACL3129.0001.001>.

33. Marozzi, *The Way of Herodotus,* 7.

34. See Nigel Spivey, *The Ancient Olympics* (Oxford: Oxford University Press, 2005); and Judith Swaddling, *The Ancient Olympic Games* (Austin: University of Texas Press, 1999).

35. Dorothy Porter, *Health, Civilization, and the State: A History of Public Health from Ancient to Modern Times* (New York: Routledge, 1999), 10.

36. See James Longrigg, *Greek Rational Medicine: Philosophy and Medicine from Alcmaeon to the Alexandrians* (New York: Routledge, 1993).

37. Durant, *The Life of Greece,* 342; Herodotus, Volume 3, 125–38.

38. See Lionel Casson, *Libraries of the Ancient World* (New Haven, CT: Yale University Press, 2001); Roy Macleod, ed., *The Library of Alexandria: Centre of Learning in the Ancient World* (New York: I.B. Tauris, 2000); and Justin Pollard and Howard Reid, *The Rise and Fall of Alexandria: Birthplace of the Modern World* (New York: Viking, 2006).

39. See Rudolf Blum (Hans H. Wellsch, ed. and trans.), *Kallimachos: The Alexandrian Library and the Origins of Bibliography* (Madison, WI: University of Wisconsin Press, 1991); and Alan Cameron, *Callimachus and His Critics* (Princeton, NJ: Princeton University Press, 1995).

40. Heinrich Von Staden (ed. and trans.), *Herophilus: The Art of Medicine in Early Alexandria* (Cambridge: Cambridge University Press, 1989).

41. See Daniela Dueck, *Strabo of Amasia: Greek Man of Letters in Augustan Rome* (New York: Routledge, 2000); and Daniela Dueck, H. Lindsay, and S. Pothecary, eds., *Strabo's Cultural Geography: The Making of a Kolossourgia* (New York: Cambridge University Press, 2005).

42. See Robert W. Funk, Ron W. Hoover, and The Jesus Seminar, *The Five Gospels: The Search for the Authentic Words of Jesus* (Sonoma, CA: Polebridge, and New York: Macmillan, 1993; reprint, New York: HarperOne, 1996).

43. Durant, *Caesar and Christ,* 586.

44. See R.A. Markus, "Gregory the Great and a Papal Missionary Strategy," *The Mission of the Church and the Propagation of the Faith,* ed. G.J. Cumming (New York: Cambridge University Press, 1970), 29–38; and R.A. Markus, *Gregory the Great and His World* (New York: Cambridge University Press, 1997).

45. See Nicholas Brooks, *The Early History of the Church of Canterbury: Christ Church from 597 to 1066* (London: Leicester University Press, 1984); Richard A. Fletcher, *The Barbarian Conversion: From Paganism to Christianity* (New York: H. Holt, 1998); Henry Mayr-Harting, *The Coming of Christianity to Anglo-Saxon England* (University Park: Pennsylvania State University Press, 1991); and Barbara Yorke, *The Conversion of Britain: Religion, Politics, and Society in Britain c. 600–800* (London: Pearson/Longman, 2006).

46. See Lewis Ayres, *Nicaea and Its Legacy: An Approach to Fourth-century Trinitarian Theology* (New York: Oxford University Press, 2004); and Leo D. Davis, *The First Seven Ecumenical Councils (325–787): Their History and Theology* (Collegeville, MN: The Order of St. Benedict, 1983).

47. Durant, *The Age of Faith,* 49.

48. See Markus, *Gregory the Great and His World.*

49. Durant, *The Age of Faith,* 758.

50. Durant, *The Age of Faith,* 788.

51. See John R.H. Moorman, *A History of the Franciscan Order: From Its Origins to the Year 1517* (Oxford: Oxford University Press, 1968).

52. Durant, *The Age of Faith,* 802.

53. Howard, *Transnationalism and Society,* 121.

54. See Stefan Rebenich, *Jerome* (New York: Routledge, 2002).

55. Durant, *The Age of Faith,* 752.

56. Durant, *The Age of Faith,* 753.

57. See Dine Le Gall, *Culture of Sufism: Naqshbandis in the Ottoman World, 1450–1700* (New York: State University of New York Press, 2005); and Knut S. Vikyr, *Sufi and Scholar on the Desert Edge: Muhammad B. Oali Al-Sanusi and His Brotherhood* (Evanston, IL: Northwestern University Press, 1995).

58. David Cook, *Martyrdom in Islam* (New York: Cambridge University Press, 2007), 74.

59. Durant, *The Age of Faith,* 216.

60. Coon, *Caravan,* 333.

61. Defémery and Sanguinetti, *Voyages d'ibn Batoutah,* Volume 1, 404.

62. Gordon, *When Asia was the World,* 106.

63. Gordon, *When Asia was the World,* 106.

64. Durant, *The Age of Faith,* 239. Jund-i-Shapur (aka Gundedhapur) was a famous teaching hospital in the city of Jondi Shapour founded by the Sassanid ruler Shapur I in A.D. 271. Under the Sassanids it attracted scientists from throughout the Mediterraean and Middle East. It remained an important center of learning for a time under Muslim rule and served as a link between Hellenic and Muslim scholarship.

65. See Abu al-Hasan Ali ibn al-Husayn ibn Ali al-Mas'udi (Barbier de Meynard and Pavet de Courteille, trans.), *Prairies d'or* (Paris: L'Imprimerie Impériale 1861–77), 9 volumes, online at <openlibrary.org/books/OL23311746M/Les_prairies_d'or>; and see Ahmad A. M. Shboul, *Al-Mas'udi and His World* (London: Ithaca, 1979).

66. See Defémery and Sanguinetti, *Voyages d'ibn Batoutah;* and Gibb and Beckingham, *The Travels of Ibn Battuta.*

67. Gordon, *When Asia was the World,* 102.

68. Gordon, *When Asia was the World,* 103.

Bibliography

Abe, Ryuichi. *The Weaving of Mantra: Kukai and the Construction of Esoteric Buddhist Discourse*. New York: Columbia University Press, 1999.

Abraham, Shinu A. "Chera, Chola, Pandya: Using Archaeological Evidence to Identify the Tamil Kingdoms of Early Historic South India." *Asian Perspectives: The Journal of Archaeology for Asia and the Pacific* 42, 2 (2003), 207–223.

Abramson, Marc S. *Ethnic Identity in Tang China*. Philadelphia: University of Pennsylvania Press, 2008.

Abulafia, David. *Frederick II: A Medieval Emperor*. Harmondsworth, UK: Allen Lane/Penguin, 1988.

Abu-Lughod, Janet L. *Cairo: 1001 Years of the City Victorious*. Princeton, NJ: Princeton University Press, 1971.

_____. *Before European Hegemony: The World System A.D. 1250–1350*. New York: Oxford University Press, 1989.

Acosta Signes, Miguel. "Los pochteca." *Acta Anthropoloica* 1 (1945), 9–54.

Adams, Richard E.W. *Prehistoric Mesoamerica*. Boston: Little, Brown, 1977.

_____. *Ancient Civilizations of the New World*. Boulder, CO: Westview, 1997.

Adkins, Lesley, and Roy A. Adkins. *Handbook to Life in Ancient Greece*. New York: Facts on File, 1997.

Adler, Elkan. *Jewish Travellers in the Middle Ages*. New York: Dover, 1987.

Adshead, S.A.M. *T'ang China: The Rise of the East in World History*. New York: Palgrave Macmillan, 2004.

Agarwal, Ashvivi. *Rise and Fall of the Imperial Guptas*. New Delhi: Motilal Banarsidass, 1989.

Akkermans, Peter M.M.G., and Glenn M. Schwartz. *The Archaeology of Syria: From Complex Hunter-Gatherers to Early Urban Societies (c.16,000–300 BC)*. New York: Cambridge University Press, 2004.

Alcock, S.E., J.F. Cherry, and J. Elsner. *Pausanias: Travel and Memory in Roman Greece*. New York: Oxford University Press, 2001.

Algaze, Guillermo. *Ancient Mesopotamia at the Dawn of Civilization: The Evolution of an Urban Landscape*. Chicago: University of Chicago Press, 2009.

Allchin, Bridget, and Raymond Allchin. *Birth of Indian Civilization: India and Pakistan before 500 BC*. Harmondsworth, UK: Penguin, 1968.

Allchin, F.R. "Early Cultivated Plants in India and Pakistan." In P.J. Ucko and G.W. Dimbleby, eds., *The Domestication and Exploitation of Plants and Animals: 323–329*. London: Duckworth, 1969.

Allen, James P. *Middle Egyptian: An Introduction to the Language and Culture of Hieroglyphic Writing*. New York: Cambridge University Press, 1999.

Al-Mas'udi, Abu al-Hasan Ali ibn al-Husayn ibn Ali. (Barbier de Meynard and Pavet de Courteille, trans.) *Prairies d'or*. 9 volumes. Paris: L'Imprimerie Impériale 1861–77. Online at <openlibrary.org/books/OL233117 46M/Les_prairies_d'or>.

Al-Nasser, A., et al. "Overview of Chicken Taxonomy and Domestication." *World's Poultry Science Journal* 63, June (2007), 285–300.

Alston, Richard. "Trade and the City in Roman Egypt." In H. Parkins and C. Smith, eds., *Trade, Traders and the Ancient City:* 168–202. New York: Routledge, 1998.

Altamira, Rafael. "Il Califfato Occidentale." *Storia del Mondo Medievale* 2 (1999), 477–515.

Ambrose, W.R. "3000 Years of Trade in New Guinea Obsidian." *Australian Natural History,* September 1973: 370–373.

_____, and R.C. Green. "First Millennium BC Transport of Obsidian from New Britain to the Solomon Islands." *Nature* 237, 31 (1972), 31.

Amitai, Reuven, and Michael Biran, eds. *Mongols, Turks, and Others: Eurasian Nomads and the Sedentary World*. Leiden: E.J. Brill, 2005.

Anderson, Alistair Scott. "The Imperial Army." In John S. Wacher, ed., *The Roman World,* Volume 1: 89–106. London: Routledge, 1987.

Anthon, Charles. *A Classical Dictionary: Containing an Account of the Principal Proper Names Mentioned in Ancient Authors*. New York: Harper & Brothers, 1848.

Aperghis, G. Georges. *The Seleukid Royal Economy: The Finances and Financial Administration of the Seleukid Empire*. New York: Cambridge University Press, 2004.

Arokiaswamy, Celine W.M. *Tamil Influences in Malaysia, Indonesia, and the Philippines*. Manila: s.n., 2000.

Ashton, Barbara, James Harrelm and Ian Shaw. "Stone." In P.T. Nicolson and E. Shaw, eds., *Ancient Egyptian Materials and Technology:* 5–77. New York: Cambridge University Press, 2000.

Atwood, Christopher P. *Encyclopedia of Mongolia and the Mongol Empire*. New York: Facts on File, 2004.

Aubet, Maria Eugenia. *The Phoenicians and the West: Politics, Colonies and Trade*. New York: Cambridge University Press, 1987.

Aung-Thwin, Michael. *The Mists of Ramanna: The Legend That Was Lower Burma*. Honolulu: University of Hawai'i Press, 2005.

Aurousseau, Leonard. "Le première conquête chinois des

pays Annamites." *Bulletin de l'Ecole Française d'Extrême Orient* 23 (1923), 137–264.

Austin, M.M. "Greece and Egypt in the Archaic Age." *Proceedings of the Cambridge Philological Society Supplement* 2 (1970).

Ayres, Lewis. *Nicaea and Its Legacy: An Approach to Fourth-century Trinitarian Theology.* New York: Oxford University Press, 2006.

Azarpay, G. *Sogdian Painting.* Berkeley: University of California Press, 1981.

Bagley, Robert. "Shang Archaeology." In Michael Loewe and Edward L. Shaughnessy, eds., *The Cambridge History of Ancient China: From the Origins of Civilization to 221 B.C.:* 124–231. New York: Cambridge University Press, 1999.

Baker, Christopher J. *Van Vliet's Siam.* Chiang Mai: Silkworm Books, 2005.

Ball, R. "The Karians's Place in Diodoros' Thalassocracy List." *The Classical Quarterly* 27 (n.s.), 2 (1977), 317–322.

Ball, Warwick. *Rome in the East: The Transformation of an Empire.* New York: Routledge, 2001.

Banchich, Thomas, and Eugene Lane. *The History of Zonaras from Alexander Severus to the Death of Theodosius the Great.* New York: Routledge, 2009.

Barber, E.J.W. *Prehistoric Textiles: The Development of Cloth in the Neolithic and Bronze Ages with Special Reference to the Aegean.* Princeton, NJ: Princeton University Press, 1991.

Barber, Richard. *Henry Plantagenet.* Melton, Suffolk, UK: Boydell & Brewer, 2003.

Barbosa, Duarte. (M. Longworth Dames, trans.) *The Book of Duarte Barbosa: An Account of the Countries Bordering on the Indian Ocean and Their Inhabitants.* London: Hakluyt Society, 1921.

Bard, Kathryn, ed. *Encyclopedia of the Archaeology of Ancient Egypt.* New York: Routledge, 1988.

Bareket, Elinoar. "Rādhānites." In Norman Roth, ed., *Jewish Civilization: An Encyclopedia:* 558–561. New York: Routledge, 2002.

Barrett, Timothy. *Japanese Papermaking: Traditions, Tools, and Techniques.* New York: Weatherhill, 1983.

Barth, Henry. *Travels and Discoveries in North and Central Africa: Including Accounts of Timbuktu, Sokoto, and the Basins of the Niger and Benuwe.* 2 volumes. London: Ward, Lock, 1890.

Bartman, Stephen. *Handbook of Life in Ancient Mesopotamia.* New York: Oxford University Press, 2005.

Baruah, Bibbhuti. *Buddhist Sects and Sectarianism.* New Delhi: Sarup & Son, 2008.

Bass, George F. "Cape Gelidonya: A Bronze Age Shipwreck." *Transactions of the American Philosophical Society* 57, 8 (1967).

Bates, David. *William the Conqueror.* Stroud, UK: Tempus, 2001.

Beal, Samuel. *Si-Yu-Ki: Buddhist Records of the Western World.* New York: Paragon Book Reprint, 1968.

Beckwith, Christopher. *Empires of the Silk Road: A History of Central Eurasia from the Bronze Age to the Present.* Princeton, NJ: Princeton University Press, 2009.

Begley, Vimala. *The Ancient Port of Arikamedu: New Investigations and Researches 1989–1992.* Pondicherry: Ecole Française d'Extrême Orient, 1996.

_____, and Richard D. De Puma, eds. *Rome and India: The Ancient Sea Trade.* Madison: University of Wisconsin Press, 1992.

Bellwood, Peter. *Man's Conquest of the Pacific: The Prehistory of Southeast Asia and Oceania.* Auckland, NZ: Collins, 1978.

Benjamin, Craig G.R. *The Yuezhi: Origins, Migration and the Conquest of Northern Bactria.* Louvain: Brepols, 2006.

Benn, Charles. *China's Golden Age: Everyday Life in the Tang Dynasty.* New York: Oxford University Press, 2002.

Bentley, Jerry H. "Beyond Modernocentrism: Towards Fresh Vision of the Global Past." In V.H. Mair, ed., *Contact and Exchange in the Ancient World:* 17–29. Honolulu: University of Hawai'i Press, 2006.

Berdan, Frances Frei. "Tres formas de intercambio en la economia azteca." In P. Carrasco and J. Broda, eds., *Economia política e ideologia en el México prehispánico.* Mexico: Editorial Nueva Imagen, 1978.

Bernard, P. "The Greek Kingdoms of Central Asia." In János Harmatta, B.N. Puri, and G.F. Etemadi, eds., *History and Civilizations of Central Asia,* Volume 2: 99–129. New Delhi: Motilal Banarsidass, 1999.

Bernstein, Hans. "The Institutions of Later Han." In Denis Twitchett and John K. Fairbank, eds., *The Cambridge History of China, Volume 1: The Ch'in and Han Empires, 221 B.C.–A.D. 220:* 491–519. New York: Cambridge University Press, 1987.

Bernstein, William J. *A Splendid Exchange: How Trade Shaped the World.* New York: Atlantic Monthly Press, 2008.

Berrin, Kathleen, and Esther Pasztory, eds. *Teotihuacan: Art from the City of the Gods.* New York: Thames & Hudson, 1994.

Besborodov, M.A., and J.A. Zadneyprovsky. "Early Stages of Glassmaking in the USSR." *Slavia Antiqua* 12 (1965).

Beyer, Klaus. *The Aramaic Language: Its Distribution and Subdivisions.* Göttingen: Vandenhoeck und Ruprecht, 1986.

Bhaumick, Manoranjan. *History, Culture and Antiquities of Tamralipta.* Kolkata: Punthi Pustak, 2001.

Bird, James. *Historical Researches on the Origin and Principles of the Buddha and Jaina Religions.* Bombay: The American Mission Press, 1847.

Birley, Anthony R. *Septimus Severus: The African Emperor.* New York: Routledge, 1999.

_____. *The Roman Government in Britain.* New York: Oxford University Press, 2005.

Bivar, A.D.H. "The Political History of Iran under the Arsacids." In Ehsan Yarshater, ed., *The Cambridge History of Iran,* Volume 3.1: 21–99. London: Cambridge University Press, 2000.

Blagden, O.C. "The Mon or Talaing and Pyu Faces of the Myazedi Inscription at Pagan." In Charles Duroiselle and Taw Sein Ko, eds., *Epigraphia Birmanica,* Volume 1, Part 1. Rangoon: Superintendent of Government Printing, 1919.

Blum, Rudolf. (Hans H. Wellisch, trans.) *Kallimachos: The Alexandrian Library and the Origins of Bibliography.* Madison, WI: University of Wisconsin Press, 1991.

Boulnois, Luce. (Helen Loveday, trans.) *Silk Road: Monks, Warriors & Merchants on the Silk Road.* Geneva: Editions Olizane, 2004.

Bowersox, Gary W., and Bonita E. Chamberlain. *Gemstones of Afghanistan.* Tucson, AZ: Geoscience, 1995.

Bowman, Alan K. "Provincial Administration and Taxation." In Alan K. Bowman, Edward Chaplin, and Andrew Lintott, eds., *Cambridge Ancient History, X: The Augustan Empire, 43 B.C.–A.D. 69:* 344–370. New York: Cambridge University Press, 1996.

Bowman, John S. *Columbia Chronologies of Asian History and Culture.* New York: Columbia University Press, 2000.

Braund, D. "Fish from the Black Sea: Classical Byzantium and the Greekness of Trade." In M.J. Dobson, D. Harvey, and J. Wilkins, eds., *Food in Antiquity:* 162–170. Exeter: University of Exeter Press, 1995.

Breton, Jean-François. (A. LaFarge, trans.) *Arabia Felix: From the Time of the Queen of Sheba, Eighth Century B.C. to First Century A.D.* Notre Dame: University of Notre Dame Press, 2000.

Briant, Pierre. "The Achaemenid Empire." In K. Raaflaub and N. Rosenstein, eds., *War and Society in the Ancient Worlds:* 105–128. Cambridge, MA: Harvard University Press, 1999.

_____. (Peter Daniels, trans.) *From Cyrus to Alexander: A History of the Persian Empire.* Winona Lake, IN: Eisenbrauns, 2002.

Brierly, Joanna Hall. *Spices.* Kuala Lumpur: Oxford University Press, 1994.

Briggs, L.P. "Dvaravati, the Mon Ancient Kingdom in Siam." *Journal of the American Oriental Society* 65, 2 (1945), 98–106.

British Geographical Survey. "Bronze Age Mediterraneans May Have Visited Stonehenge." *British Geographical Survey,* no date. Online at <www.bgs.ac.uk>.

Bronson, B. "Glass Beads at Khuan Lukpad, Southern Thailand." In I. Glover and E. Glover, eds., *Southeast Asian Archaeology 1986:* 213–230. Oxford: BAR International Series, 1990.

Brook, Timothy. *The Confusions of Pleasure: Commerce and Culture in Ming China.* Berkeley: University of California Press, 1998.

Brooks, Nicholas. *The Early History of the Church of Canterbury: Christ Church from 597 to 1066.* London: Leicester University Press, 1984.

Bryce, Trevor R. *The Kingdom of the Hittites.* New York: Oxford University Press, 1999.

Buccellati, Giorgio. "Akkadian." In Robert Hetzron, ed., *The Semitic Languages:* 69–99. New York: Routledge, 1997.

_____, and Marilyn Kelly-Buccellati. "Tar'am-Agade, Daughter of Naram-Sin, at Urkesh." In L. al Gailani Werr, J. Curtis, H. Martin, A. McMahon, J. Oates, and J Reade, eds., *Of Pots and Plans: Papers on the Archaeology and History of Mesopotamia and Syria Presented to David Oates in Honour of His 75th Birthday.* London: Nabu, 2002.

Bühler, Alfred. "The Geographical Extent of the Use of Bark Fabrics." *Ciba Review* 33 (1940), 1170–1175.

Bulag, Uradyn E. *The Mongols at China's Edge.* Lanham, MD: Rowman & Littlefield, 2002.

Bulliet, Richard W. *The Camel and the Wheel.* Cambridge, MA: Harvard University Press, 1975.

Burton, Graham. "Government and the Provinces." In John S. Wacher, ed., *The Roman World,* Volume 1: 423–439. New York: Routledge, 1987.

Burton, Richard. *Personal Narrative of a Pilgrimage to El-Madinah and Meccah.* 2 volumes. New York: Putnam, 1856.

Caferro, William. *John Hawkwood: An English Mercenary in Fourteenth-century Italy.* Baltimore: Johns Hopkins University Press, 2006.

Caldwell, J.R., ed. *Investigations at Tal-I Iblis.* Springfield: Illinois State Museum, 1967.

Cameron, Alan. *Callimachus and His Critics.* Princeton, NJ: Princeton University Press, 1995.

Campbell, Brian. "The Roman Empire." In K. Raaflaub and N. Rosenstein, eds., *War and Society in the Ancient and Medieval Worlds:* 217–240. Cambridge, MA: Harvard University Press, 1999.

Cantor, Norman F. *In the Wake of the Plague: The Black Death and the World It Made.* New York: The Free Press, 2001.

Cardon, Dominique. *Natural Dyes: Sources, Tradition, Technology and Science.* London: Archetype, 2007.

Casey, John. *Carausius and Allectus: British Usurpers.* New York: Routledge, 1994.

Casson, Lionel. *The Ancient Mariners: Seafarer and Sea Fighters of the Mediterranean in Ancient Times.* New York: Macmillan, 1959.

_____. *Illustrated History of Ships & Boats.* New York: Doubleday, 1964.

_____. *Travel in the Ancient World.* London: George Allen & Unwin, 1974.

_____. "Ancient Naval Technology and the Route to India." In V. Bagley and R.D. De Puma, eds., *Rome and India: The Ancient Sea Trade:* 8–11. Madison: University of Wisconsin Press, 1992.

_____. *Libraries of the Ancient World.* New Haven, CT: Yale University Press, 2001.

Castleden, Rodney. *The Mycenaeans.* New York: Routledge, 2005.

Chadwick, John. *The Mycenaean World.* New York: Cambridge University Press, 1976.

Chamberlain, James R. "The Origins of the Sek: Implications for Tai and Vietnamese History." *Journal of the Siam Society* 86, 1–2 (1998), 27–48.

Chambers, D.S. *The Imperial Age of Venice, 1380–1580.* London: Thames & Hudson, 1970.

Chandler, Tertius. *Four Thousand Years of Urban Growth: An Historical Census.* Lewiston/Queenstown: St. David's University Press, 1987.

Chang, Kwang-Chih. "China on the Eve of the Historical Period." In Michael Loewe and Edward L. Shaughnessy, eds., *The Cambridge History of Ancient China: From the Origins of Civilization to 221 B.C.:* 37–73. New York: Cambridge University Press, 1999.

Chapman, Anne E. "Port of Trade Enclaves in Aztec and Maya Civilizations." In K. Polanyi, C.M. Arensberg, and H.W. Pearson, eds., *Trade and Market in the Early Empires:* 114–153. Chicago: Henry Regnery, 1971.

Charles-Picard, Gilbert, and Colette Charles-Picard. *Daily Life in Carthage.* New York: Macmillan, 1961.

Chau Ju-kua. (F. Hirth and W.W. Rockhill, eds. and trans.) *Chau Ju-kua: His Work on the Chinese and Arab Trade in the Twelfth and Thirteenth Centuries, Entitled Chu-fan-chï.* Amsterdam: Oriental, 1966.

Chausson, François. "Les Egnatii et l'aristocatie italienne des IIe-IVe siècles." *Journal des Savants* 2 (1997), 211–331.

Chin, Tamara T. "Defamiliarizing the Foreigners: Sima Qian's Ethnography and Han-Xiongu Marriage Diplomacy." *Harvard Journal of Asiatic Studies* 70, 2 (2010), 311–354.

Ciggaar, Krijna Nelly. *Western Travellers to Constantinople: The West and Byzantium, 962–1204.* Leiden: E.J. Brill, 1996.

Clayton, Peter A. *Chronicle of the Pharaohs: The Reign-by-Reign Record of the Rulers and Dynasties of Ancient Egypt.* London: Thames & Hudson, 2006.

Coe, Michael D. *America's First Civilization: Discovering the Olmec.* New York: American Heritage, 1968.

_____, and Justin Kerr. *The Art of the Maya Scribe.* London: Thames & Hudson, 1997.

Cogan, M., and H. Tadmor. "Gyges and Ashurbanipal: A Study in Literary Transmission." *Orientalia* 46 (1977), 66–85.

Cole, Hubert. *Hawkwood.* London: Eyre & Spottiswoode, 1967.

_____. *Hawkwood in Paris.* Colchester, UK: The Book Service, 1969.

_____. *Hawkwood and the Towers of Pisa.* London: Methuen, 1973.

Conan Doyle, Arthur. *The White Company.* New York: HarperCollins, 1988. (Originally published 1891.)

Constantine Porphyrogenitus. (Gyula Moravcik, ed., and Romilly J.H. Jenkins, trans.) *Constantine Porphyrogenitus: De Administrando Imperio (Corpus Fontium Historiae Byzantinae).* Washington, DC: Dumbarton Oaks Research Library and Collection, 1967.

Cook, Constance A., and Barry B. Blakeley. "Introduction." In Constance A. Cook and Barry B. Blakeley, eds., *Defining Chu: Image and Reality in Ancient China:* 1–5. Honolulu: University of Hawai'i Press, 1999.

Cook, David. *Martyrdom in Islam.* New York: Cambridge University Press, 2007.

Cooler, Richard M. *The Karen Bronze Drums of Burma.* Leiden: E.J. Brill, 1995.

Coon, Carleton. *Caravan: The Story of the Middle East.* New York: Holt, Rinehart and Winston, 1958.

Cooper, Stephen. *Sir John Hawkwood: Chivalry and the Art of War.* Barnsley: Pen and Sword, 2008.

Cowgill, George L. "State and Society at Teotihuacan, Mexico." *Annual Review of Anthropology* 26 (1997), 129–161.

Crone, Patricia. *Meccan Trade and the Rise of Islam.* Piscataway, NJ: Gorgias, 2004.

Crooke, Brian, "Justinian's Constantinople." In Mass, Michael, ed., *The Cambridge Companion to the Age of Justinian:* 60–84. New York: Cambridge University Press, 2005.

Crowley, Robert, and Geoffrey Parker, eds. *The Reader's Companion to Military History.* New York: Houghton Mifflin, 1996.

Cui Mingde. *The History of Chinese Heqin: Brief Charts of Heqin Events.* Beijing: Renmin Chubanshe, 2005.

Culican, William. *The First Merchant Venturers: The Ancient Levant in History and Commerce.* New York: McGraw-Hill, 1966.

Curtain, Philip D. *Cross-cultural Trade in World History.* New York: Cambridge University Press, 1984.

Da, Tam Ha Le Cong. "Introduction to Buddhism in Viet Nam & Vietnamese Zen." Online at <www.buddhismtoday.com/english/vietnam>.

Daniell, Christopher. *From Norman Conquest to Magna Carta: England, 1066–1215.* New York: Routledge, 2003.

Davids, T.W. Rhys, trans. *Questions of King Milinda.* Oxford: Clarendon, 1890–94; reprint, New York: Dover, 1963.

Davidson, H.R. Ellis. *The Viking Road to Byzantium.* London: George Allen & Unwin, 1976.

Davis, Leo D. *The First Seven Ecumenical Councils (325–787): Their History and Theology.* Collegeville, MN: Order of St. Benedict, 1990.

De Casparis, J.G., and I.W. Mabbett. "Religion and Popular Beliefs of Southeast Asia before c. 1500." In N. Tarling, ed., *The Cambridge History of Southeast Asia, Volume I: From Early Times to c.1800:* 276–340. New York: Cambridge University Press, 1992.

De Conti, Nicolo. (J.W. Jones, trans.) *The Travels of Nicolo Conti in the East in the Early Part of the Fifteenth Century.* London: Hakluyt Society, 1857.

Defrémery, C., and B.R. Sanguinetti, trans. and eds. *Voyages d'ibn Batoutah.* 4 volumes. Paris: Société Asiatic, 1853–1858. Online at <books.google.co.uk/books?id=mdQOAAAAQAAJ>.

De la Vaissière, Étienne. *Histoire des marchands sogdiens.* Paris: Collège de France, Institut des Heutes Études Chinoises, 2002.

_____. "Sogdians in China: A Short History and Some New Discoveries." *The Silk Road Foundation Newsletter* 1, 2, December (2003).

_____. *Sogdian Traders: A History.* Leiden: E.J. Brill, 2005.

De Sahagun, Bernardo. (J.O. Anderson and C.E. Dibble, trans.) *General History of the Things of New Spain: Florentine Codex: The Merchants, Book 9.* Salt Lake City: University of Utah Press, 1959.

Dhammika, Ven. S. *Edicts of King Ashoka.* Kandy: Buddhist Publications Society, 1993. Online at DharmaNet and at <www.cs.colostate.edu/~malaiya/ashoka.html>.

Diakonoff, I.M. "Media I: The Medes and Their Neighbours." In Ilya Gershevitch, ed., *The Cambridge History of Iran,* Volume 2: 36–148. New York: Cambridge University Press, 1985.

Di Cosmo, Nicola. "The Northern Frontier in Pre-imperial China." In Michael Loewe and Edward L. Shaughnessy, eds., *The Cambridge History of Ancient China: From the Origins of Civilization to 221 B.C.:* 885–966. New York: Cambridge University Press, 1999.

_____. *Ancient China and Its Enemies: The Rise of Nomadic Power in East Asian History.* New York: Cambridge University Press, 2002.

Diller, Aubrey. "The Manuscripts of Pausanias." *Transactions and Proceedings of the American Philological Association* 88 (1957), 169–188.

Dillon, Matthew, and Lynda Garland. *Ancient Greece: Social and Historical Documents from Archaic Times to the Death of Alexander the Great.* 3rd ed. New York: Routledge, 2010.

Dio Cassius. *Roman History.* Originally published by the Loeb Classical Library (Cambridge, MA: Harvard University Press, 1914–1927). Online at <http://penelope.uchicago.edu/Thayer/E/Roman/Texts/Cassius_Dio/home.html>.

Diodorus. (C.H. Oldfather, trans.) *The Library of History.* (Originally published 1933.) Online at <penelope.uchicago.edu/Thayer/E/Roman/Texts/Diodorus_Siculus/home.html>.

Dohrenwend, Doris. *Chinese Jades in the Royal Ontario Museum.* Toronto: Royal Ontario Museum, 1971.

Donkin, R.A. *Between East and West: The Moluccas and the Traffic in Spices Up to the Arrival of Europeans.* Philadelphia, PA: American Philosophical Society, Memoir 248, 2003.

Doran, Edwin, Jr. "The Sailing Raft as a Great Tradition." In C.L. Riley, J.C. Kelley, C.W. Pennington, and R.L. Rands, eds., *Man Across the Sea: Problems of Pre-Columbian Contacts:* 115–137. Austin: University of Texas Press, 1971.

Dotson, John E., ed. and trans. *Merchant Culture in Fourteenth Century Venice: The Zibaldone Da Canal.* Tempe: Medieval & Renaissance Texts & Studies, Arizona Center for Medieval and Renaissance Studies, 1994.

Downey, Glanville. *Constantinople in the Age of Justinian.* Norman: University of Oklahoma Press, 1960.

_____. *Ancient Antioch.* Princeton, NJ: Princeton University Press, 1963.

Drinkwater, John F. "The Revolt and Ethnic Origin of the Usurper Magnentius (350–53), and the Rebellion of Vetranio (350)." *Chiron: Mitteilungen der Kommission für Alte Geschichte und Epigraphikdes Deutschen Archäologischen Instituts* 30 (2000), 131–59.

Dubin, Lois Sherr. *The History of Beads from 30,000 B.C. to the Present.* New York: Harry N. Abrams, 1987.

Duchesne-Guillemin, J. "Zoroastrian Religion." In Ehsan

Yarshater, ed., *The Cambridge History of Iran*, Volume 3.2: 866–908. London: Cambridge University Press, 2008.

Dueck, Daniela. *Strabo of Amasia Greek Man of Letters in Augustan Rome*. New York: Routledge, 2000.

_____, H. Lindsay, and S. Pothecary, eds. *Strabo's Cultural Geography: The Making of a Kolossourgia*. New York: Cambridge University Press, 2005.

Durant, Will. *Our Oriental Heritage*. New York: Simon & Schuster, 1935.

_____. *The Life of Greece*. New York: Simon & Schuster, 1939.

_____. *Caesar and Christ: A History of Roman Civilization and of Christianity from Their Beginnings to A.D. 325*. New York: Simon & Schuster, 1944.

_____. *The Age of Faith: A History of Medieval Civilization — Christian, Islamic, and Judaic — from Constantine to Dante: A.D. 325–1300*. New York: Simon & Schuster, 1950.

Dutt, Sukumar. *Buddhist Monks and Monasteries of India: Their History and Contribution to Indian Culture*. London: George Allen and Unwin, 1962.

Eales, Richard. "William of Ypres, Styled Count of Flanders (*d.* 1164/5)." *Oxford Dictionary of National Biography* (2004). Online at <www.oxforddnb.com/index/101029465/William-of-Ypres>.

Eberhard, Wolfram. *The Local Cultures of South and East China*. Leiden: E.J. Brill, 1968.

Ebrey, Patricia Buckley, Anne Walthall, and James B. Palais. *East Asia: A Cultural, Social, and Political History*. Boston: Houghton Mifflin Company, 2006.

Edbury, Peter W., and John G. Rowe. *William of Tyre: Historian of the Latin East*. New York: Cambridge University Press, 1988.

Edwards, Clinton R. *Aboriginal Watercraft on the Pacific Coast of South America*. Berkeley: University of California Press, 1965.

Eidem, Jesper, Lauren Ristvet, and Harvey Weiss. *The Royal Archives from Tell Leilan: Old Babylonian Letters and Treaties from the Eastern Lower Town Palace*. New Haven, CT: Yale University Press, 2010.

Elmberg, John-Erik. *Balance and Circulation: Aspects of Tradition and Change among the Mejprat of Irian Barat*. Stockholm: Etnografiska Museet, 1968.

Emmerick, R.E. "Buddhism among Iranian Peoples." In Ehsan Yarshater, ed., *The Cambridge History of Iran*, Volume 3.2: 949–964. London: Cambridge University Press, 2008.

Ennin. (Edwin O Reischauer, trans.) *Ennin's Diary: The Record of a Pilgrimage to China in Search of the Law*. New York: Ronald Press Company, 1955.

Enoki, K., G.A. Koshelenko, and Z. Haidary. "The Yüeh-chih and Their Migrations." In János Harmatta, B.N. Puri, and G.F. Etemadi, eds., *History and Civilizations of Central Asia, Volume II:* 171–189. New Delhi: Motilal Banarsidass, 1999.

Erman, Adolf. *Literature of the Ancient Egyptians*. New York: Arno, 1976. (Originally published 1927.)

Errington, Elizabeth, and Joe Cribb, eds. *The Crossroads of Asia: Transformation in Image and Symbol in the Art of Ancient Afghanistan and Pakistan*. Cambridge: Ancient India and Iran Trust, 1992.

Erskine, Andrew. "Culture and Power in Ptolemaic Egypt: The Museum and Library of Alexandria." *Greece & Rome* 42 (2nd Ser.), 1 (1995), 38–48.

Fan Chuo. (G.H. Luce, trans.) *The Man Shu, Book of Southern Barbarians*. Ithaca, NY: Southeast Asia Program, Department of Far Eastern Studies, Cornell University, 1961.

Faure, P. "Les Centurions Frumentaires et le Commandment des Castra Peregrina." *Mélanges de l'Ecole française de Rome Antiquité* 115 (2003), 377–427.

Finkel, I.L., and M.J. Seymour. *Babylon*. New York: Oxford University Press, 2009.

Fischel, Walter J., ed.. *Unknown Jews in Unknown Lands, the Travels of Rabbi David D'Beth Hillel (1824–1832)*. New York: Ktar, 1973.

Fisher, William B., ed.. *The Cambridge History of Iran: The Land of Iran*. New York: Cambridge University Press, 1968.

Fitzgerald-Huber, L.G. "Qiji and Erlitou: The Question of Contacts with Distant Cultures." *Early China* 20 (1995), 17–67.

Fleming, Daniel E. *Democracy's Ancient Ancestors: Mari and Early Collective Governance*. New York: Cambridge University Press, 2004.

Fletcher, Richard A. *The Barbarian Conversion: From Paganism to Christianity*. New York: H. Holt, 1998.

Flood, E. Thaddius. "Sukhothai-Mongol Relations." *Journal of the Siam Society* 57, 2 (1969), 203–234.

Folz, Richard C. *Spirituality in the Land of the Noble: How Iran Shaped the World's Religions*. Oxford: Oneworld, 2004.

Forster, Edward M. *Alexandria*. London: M. Haag, 1982.

Fowler, Kenneth A. *Medieval Mercenaries, Volume 1: The Great Companies*. Oxford: Blackwell, 2001.

Fox, Robin Lane. *Alexander the Great*. New York: E.P. Dutton, 1974.

Francis, Peter, Jr. "Beads of the Early Islamic Period." *Beads* 1 (1989), 21–39.

_____. "South Indian Stone Beadmaking." *Margaretologist* 6, 2 (1993), 3–6

_____. "More on South Indian Stone Beadmaking." *Margaretologist* 7, 1 (1994), 7.

_____. "The Beads from Fustat in the Awad Collection." *Margaretologist* 8, 2 (1995), 7–11.

_____. "Bead, the Bead Trade and State Development in Southeast Asia." In *Ancient Trade and Cultural Contacts in Southeast Asia:* 139–152. Bangkok: Office of the National Culture Commission, 1996.

_____. *Asia's Maritime Bead Trade: 300 B.C. to the Present*. Honolulu: University of Hawai'i Press, 2002.

Fraser, Peter M. *Ptolemaic Alexandria*. 3 volumes. Oxford: Clarendon, 1972.

Fraser-Lu, Sylvia. *Burmese Crafts Past and Present*. Kuala Lumpur: Oxford University Press, 1994.

Frédéric, Louis. (Käthe Roth, trans.) *Japan Encyclopedia*. Cambridge, MA: Harvard University Press, 2002.

French, Elizabeth B. *Mycenae: Agamemnon's Capital: The Site and Setting*. Stroud, Gloucestershire, UK: Tempus, 2002.

Fritz, John M., and George Mitchell, eds. *New Light on Hampi: Recent Research at Vijayanagar*. Mumbai: MARG, 2001.

Frye, Richard N. *The Heritage of Central Asia: From Antiquity to Turkish Expansion*. Princeton, NJ: Markus Wiener, 1996.

Funk, Robert W., Ron W. Hoover, and the Jesus Seminar. *The Five Gospels: The Search for the Authentic Words of Jesus*. Sonoma, CA: Polebridge; New York: Macmillan, 1993; reprint, New York: HarperOne, 1996.

Gale, Noel H. "Metals and Metallurgy in the Chalcolithic Period." *Bulletin of the American School of Oriental Research* 282/283 (1991), 37–61.

Garber, James F., David C. Grove, Kenneth G. Hirth, and John W. Hooper. "Jade Use in Portions of Mexico and Central America: Olmec, Maya, Costa Rica, and Honduras — A Summary." In F.W. Lange, ed., *Pre-*

columbian Jade: New Geological and Cultural Interpretations: 211–231. Salt Lake City: University of Utah Press, 1993.

Garelli, P. "Le commerce assyiren de la Cappadoce au XIXe siècle av. n.e." Akkadica 88 (1994), 1–17.

Gates, Charles. Ancient Cities: The Archaeology of Urban Life in the Ancient Near East and Egypt, Greece and Rome. New York: Routledge, 2003.

Gauthier-Pilters, Hilde. The Camel, Its Evolution, Ecology, Behavior, and Relationship to Man. Chicago: University of Chicago Press, 1981.

Gawlikowski, M. "Palmyra as a Trading Centre." Iraq 56 (1994), 27–33.

Geiger, Wilhelm. (Mabel Rickmers, trans.) The Culavamsa: Being the More Recent Part of the Mahavamsa. London: Pali Text Society, 1929–30.

Georgopoulou, Maria. Venice's Mediterranean Colonies. New York: Cambridge University Press, 2001.

Gibb, H.A.R., and C.F. Beckingham, eds. and trans. The Travels of Ibn Battuta, A.D. 1325–1354. 4 volumes. Cambridge: Hakluyt Society, 1993.

Glassner, Jean-Jacques. The Invention of Cuneiform. Baltimore: Johns Hopkins University Press, 2002.

Glover, Ian C. "The Southern Silk Road: Archaeological Evidence for Early Trade Between India and Southeast Asia." In Ancient Trade and Cultural Contacts in Southeast Asia: 57–94. Bangkok: The Office of the National Culture Commission, 1996.

Goedicke, Hans. "Considerations on the Battle of Kadesh." The Journal of Egyptian Archaeology 52 (1966), 71–80.

Goitein, Shlomo. Letters of Medieval Jewish Traders. Princeton, NJ: Princeton University Press, 1973.

Gomme, Arnold W. The Population of Athens in the Fifth and Fourth Centuries BC. Oxford: Oxford University Press, 1933.

Good, Irene. "On the Question of Silk in Pre-Han Eurasia." Antiquity 69, 266 (1995), 959–968.

_____."Textiles as a Medium of Exchange in Third Millennium B.C.E. Western Asia." In V.H. Mair, ed., Contact and Exchange in the Ancient World: 191–214. Honolulu: University of Hawai'i Press, 2006.

Gordon, Stewart. When Asia Was the World: Traveling Merchants, Scholars, Warriors, and Monks Who Created the "Riches of the East." Philadelphia: Da Capo, 2008.

Graff, David Andrew, and Robin D.S. Higham. A Military History of China. Boulder, CO: Westview, 2002.

Grant, Michael. History of Rome. New York: Charles Scribner, 1978.

Green, R.C. "Lapita Pottery and the Origins of Polynesian Culture." Australian Natural History, June 1973: 332–337.

_____. "Sites with Lapita Pottery: Importing and Voyaging." Mankind 9 (1974), 253–259.

_____. "Sweet Potato Transfers in Polynesian Prehistory." In C. Ballard, P. Brown, R.M. Bourke, and T. Harwood, eds., The Sweet Potato in Oceania: A Reappraisal: 43–62. Sydney: Oceania Monograph 56, 2005.

Green, W.C., trans. The Story of Egil Skallagrimsson. Online at <www.sacred-texts.com/neu/egil/index.htm>.

Griffin, Gillett G. "Formative Guerrero and Its Jade." In F.W. Lange, ed., Precolumbian Jade: New Geological and Cultural Interpretations: 203–210. Salt Lake City: University of Utah Press, 1993.

Griffith, Guy T. Mercenaries of the Hellenistic World. Cambridge: Cambridge University Press, 1935.

Groner, Paul. Saicho: The Establishment of the Japanese Tendai School. Honolulu: University of Hawai'i Press, 1984.

Grousset, René. (Naomi Walford, trans.) The Empire of the Steppes: A History of Central Asia. Piscataway, NJ: Rutgers University Press, 2002.

Guillon, Emmanuel. Cham Art: Treasures from the Da Nang Museum, Vietnam. London: Thames & Hudson, 2001.

Guy, John. Oriental Trade Ceramics in South-east Asia: Ninth to Sixteenth Centuries. Singapore: Oxford University Press, 1986.

_____. Woven Cargoes: Indian Textiles in the East. London: Thames & Hudson, 1998.

Habicht, Christian. "An Ancient Baedeker and His Critics: Pausanias' 'Guide to Greece.'" Proceedings of the American Philosophical Society 129, 2 (1985), 220–224.

Hackin, Joseph. Recherches archéologiques à Begram. Paris: Les Editions d'art et histoire, 1939.

_____. Nouvelle recherches archéologiques à Begram (ancienne Kâpici), 1939–1940. Paris: Imprimérie Nationale, Presses Universitaires, 1954.

Haldar, Alfred. Who Were the Amorites. Leiden: E. J. Brill, 1971.

Hall, D.G.E. Burma. London: Hutchinson's University Library, 1956.

Hall, Kenneth R. Trade and Statecraft in the Age of the Colas. New Delhi: Abhinav, 1980.

_____. "Economic History of Early Southeast Asia." In N. Tarling, ed., The Cambridge History of Southeast Asia, Volume I: From Early Times to c.1800: 183–275. New York: Cambridge University Press, 1992.

Halperin, Charles J. Russia and the Golden Horde: The Mongol Impact on Medieval Russian History. Bloomington: Indiana University Press, 1985.

Hamilton, Charles D. "The Hellenistic World." In K. Raaflaub and N. Rosenstein, eds., War and Society in the Ancient Worlds: 163–191. Cambridge, MA: Harvard University Press, 1999.

Hammond, Norman. "Obsidian Trade Routes in the Maya Area." Science 178, 4065 (1972), 1092–1093.

Hansen, Valerie. "New Work on the Sogdians, the Most Important Traders on the Silk Road, A.D. 500–1000." T'oung Pao 89, 1–3 (2003), 149–161.

Harvey, G.E. History of Burma from the Earliest Times to 10 March 1824 the Beginning of the English Conquest. London: Longmans Green, 1925.

Hassall, Mark. "Romans and non–Romans." In John S. Wacher, ed., The Roman World, Volume 1: 685–700. New York: Routledge, 1987.

Hassig, Ross. Trade, Tribute, and Transportation: The Sixteenth-century Political Economy of the Valley of Mexico. Norman: University of Oklahoma Press, 1985.

Hauptmann, Andreas. "The Earliest Periods of Copper Meallurgy in Feinan." In A. Hauptmann, E. Pernicke, and G.A. Wagner, eds., Old World Archaeometallurgy: 88–112. Heidelberg: Der Anschnitt, Supplement 7, 1989.

Healy, Mark. Qadesh 1300 BC: Clash of the Warrior Kings. Oxford: Osprey, 1993.

Heath, Ian. Byzantine Armies, AD 1118–1461. Oxford: Osprey, 1995.

Heather, Peter. The Fall of the Roman Empire: A New History of Rome and the Barbarians. New York: Oxford University Press, 2005.

Hecker, J.F.C. (B.G. Babington, trans.) Epidemics of the Middle Ages. London: Trüber, 1859.

Heinrichs, Wolfhart, ed. Studies in Neo-Aramaic. Atlanta: Scholars, 1990.

Hermansen, Gustav. Ostia: Aspects of Roman City Life. Edmonton: University of Alberta Press, 1982.

Herodotus. The Histories. New York: Everyman's Library, 1997.

Herzfeld, Ernst. *The Persian Empire: Studies in Geography and Ethnography of the Ancient Near East.* Weisbaden: Franz Steiner, 1968.

Heyerdahl, Thor. *Kon-Tiki.* New York: Rand McNally, 1950.

Higham, Charles. *The Bronze Age of Southeast Asia.* New York: Cambridge University Press, 1996.

Hill, John E. "The Western Regions According to *Hou Hanshu:* The *Xiyu Juan,* 'Chapter on the Western Regions' from *Hou Hanshu* 88, Second Edition." Seattle: University of Washington, 2003. Online at <depts.washington.edu/silkroad/texts/hhshu/hou_han_shu.html>.

_____. *Through the Jade Gate to Rome: A Study of the Silk Routes during the Later Han Dynasty, First to Second Centuries CE.* Charleston, SC: Book Surge, 2009.

Hinsch, Bret. *The Ultimate Guide to Chinese Tea.* Bangkok: White Lotus, 2008.

Hirth, Friedrich. *The Ancient History of China to the End of the Chóu Dynasty.* Freeport, NY: Books for Libraries, 1969. (Originally published 1908.)

Hornell, James. *The Canoes of Polynesia, Fiji, and Micronesia.* Volume I of A.C. Haddon and J. Hornell, *Canoes of Oceania.* Honolulu: Bernice P. Bishop Museum, 1936.

Hourani, George F., and John Carswell. *Arab Seafaring: In the Indian Ocean in Ancient and Early Medieval Times.* Expanded ed. Princeton, NJ: Princeton University Press, 1995.

Howard, Michael C. *Political Change in a Mayan Village in Southern Belize.* Greeley, CO: University of Northern Colorado, Katunob Occasional Publications in Mesoamerican Anthropology 10, 1977.

_____. "Searching for the Identity of the Bird on Dongson Drums." *Arts of Asia* 34, 2 (2004), 136–142.

_____. "Beaded Skirts from Ambai Island." In M.C. Howard and N. Sanggenafa, eds., *Indigenous Peoples and Migrants of Northern Papua, Indonesia:* 92–103, 223–209. Bangkok: White Lotus, 2005.

_____. *Textiles of the Highland Peoples of Burma, Volume II.* Bangkok: White Lotus, 2005.

_____. "Religious and Status-Marking Functions of Textiles among the Tai Peoples of Vietnam." In Jane Puranananda, ed., *The Secrets of Southeast Asian Textiles:* 194–215. Bangkok: River, 2007.

_____. *Transnationalism and Society: An Introduction.* Jefferson, NC: McFarland, 2011.

_____, ed. *Bark-cloth in Southeast Asia.* Bangkok: White Lotus, 2006.

_____, and Naffi Sanggenafa. "The People of Northern Papua." In M.C. Howard and N. Sanggenafa, eds., *Indigenous Peoples and Migrants of Northern Papua, Indonesia:* 1–22, 217–222. Bangkok: White Lotus, 2005.

_____, and Wattana Wattanapun. *The Palaung in Northern Thailand.* Chiang Mai: Silkworm, 2001.

Hunter, Dard. *A Papermaking Pilgrimage to Japan, Korea and China.* New York: Pynson Printers, 1936.

_____ *Papermaking: The History and Technique of an Ancient Craft.* New York: Alfred A. Knopf, 1943.

Huntington, Samuel P. *The Clash of Civilizations and the Remaking of World Order.* New York: Simon & Schuster, 1996.

Huntington, Susan, and John Huntington. *Leaves from the Bodhi Tree: The Art of Pala India (8th–12th Centuries) and Its International Legacy.* Seattle: University of Washington Press and Dayton Art Institute, 1990.

Hunwick, John O. *Timbuktu and the Songhay Empire: Al-Sadhi's Tarikh al-Sudan Down to 1613 and Other Contemporary Documents.* Leiden: E.J. Brill, 1999.

Huscroft, Richard. *Ruling England, 1042–1217.* Harlow, UK: Pearson, 2005.

Hye-ch'o. (Jan Yun-Hua, Iida Shotaro, and Yang Han-Sung, eds., Laurence Preston, trans.) *The Hye Ch'o Diary: Memoir of the Pilgrimage to the Five Regions of India.* Freemont, CA: Asian Humanities, 1984.

Ibn Rustah, Ahmad. (G. Wiet, trans.) *Les Atours Precieux.* Cairo: 1955.

Ibn Shahriyar, Buzurg. (L. Marcel Devic, trans.) *The Book of the Marvels of India.* New York: Dial, 1929.

I-Ching. *Chinese Monks in India: Biography of Eminent Monks Who Went to the Western World in Search of the Law During the Great T'ang Dynasty.* New Delhi: Motilal Banarsidass, 1995.

_____. (J. Takakusu, trans.) *Record of the Buddhist Religion: As Practised in India and the Malay Archipelago (A.D. 671–695).* New Delhi: AES, 2005. (Originally published 1896.)

Inalcik, Halil. "The Policy of Mehmed II toward the Greek Population of Istanbul and the Byzantine Buildings of the City." *Dumbarton Oaks Papers* 23 (1969), 229–249.

Israeli, Raphael . *Islam in China.* Lexington, MA: Lexington, 2002.

Jacobs, Joseph, and Isaac Broydé. "Herod." *The Jewish Encyclopedia:* 356–360. (Originally published 1901–1906.) Online at <JewishEncyclopedia.com>.

Jarrige, Jean-Francis, and Richard H. Meadow. "The Antecedents of Civilization in the Indus Valley." *Scientific American* 244, 8 (1980), 12–133.

Jeyasurya, R. "The Trading Community in Early Tamil Society Up to 900 AD." *Language in India* 8, 11 (2008). Online at <www.languageinindia.com/>.

Jhaveri, Krishanlal Mohanlal, ed. *The Gujaratis: The People, Their History, and Culture.* New Delhi: Cosmo, 2003.

Johnstone, Paul. *The Sea-craft of Prehistory.* London: Routledge & Kegan Paul, 1980.

Kamath, Suryanath U. *A Concise History of Karnataka: From Pre-historic Times to the Present.* Bangalore: Jupiter, 2001.

Kamma, F.C. "De Verhouding tussen Tidore e de Papoese eilaanden in Legende en Historie." *Indonesië* 1 (1947–48), 361–370, 536–559; 2 (1948–49), 17–188, 256–275.

Kamrin, Janice. *Ancient Egyptian Hieroglyphics.* New York: Harry N. Abrams, 2004.

Kantorowicz, Ernst. *Frederick the Second, 1194–1250.* London: Constable, 1931, and New York: Frederick Ungar, 1957.

Kasetsiri, Charnvit. *The Rise of Ayudhya: A History of Siam in the Fourteenth and Fifteenth Centuries.* Kuala Lumpur: Oxford University Press, 1976.

Katz, Nathan. *Who Are the Jews of India?* Berkeley: University of California Press, 2000.

_____, and Ellen S. Goldberg. *The Last Jews of Cochin: Jewish Identity in Hindu India.* Columbia: University of South Carolina Press, 1993.

_____, and _____. "Leaving Mother India: Reasons for the Cochin Jews' Migration to Israel." *Population Review* 39, 1–2 (1995), 35–53.

Keightley, David K. "The Shang: China's First Historical Dynasty." In Michael Loewe and Edward L. Shaughnessy, eds., *The Cambridge History of Ancient China: From the Origins of Civilization to 221 B.C.:* 232–291. New York: Cambridge University Press, 1999.

Kelly, Christopher. *Ruling the Later Roman Empire.* Cambridge, MA: Harvard University Press, 2004.

_____. "Bureaucracy and Government." In Noel Lenski,

ed., *The Cambridge Companion to the Age of Constantine:* 183–204. New York: Cambridge University Press, 2006.

Kemp, Barry J. "Old Kingdom, Middle Kingdom and Second Intermediate Period in Egypt." In J.D. Clark, J.D. Fage, and R.A. Oliver, eds., *The Cambridge History of Africa, Volume 1: From the Earliest Times to C. 500 B.C.:* 658–773. New York: Cambridge University Press, 1982.

Keppie, Lawrence. "The Army and the Navy." In Alan K. Brown, Edward Champlin, and Andrew Lintott (eds), *Cambridge Ancient History, X: The Augustan Empire, 43 B.C.–A.D. 69:* 371–396. New York: Cambridge University Press, 1996.

Kerr, Richard A. "Sea-Floor Dust Shows Drought Felled Akkadian Empire." *Science* 279, 5340 (1998), 325–326.

Key, C.A. "The Identification of New Guinea Obsidians." *Archaeology and Physical Anthropology in Oceania* 4 (1969), 47–55.

Kirch, Patrock V. *The Lapita Peoples: Ancestors of the Oceanic World.* Oxford: Blackwell, 1997.

Kitchen, Andrew, Christopher Ehret, Shiferaw Assefa, and Connie J. Mulligan. "Bayesian Phylogenetic Analysis of Semitic Languages Identifies an Early Bronze Age Origin of Semitic in the Near East." *Proceedings of the Royal Society, Biological Sciences* 276, 1668 (2009), 2703–2710.

Kitchen, Kenneth. *Pharaoh Triumphant: The Life and Times of Ramesses II, King of Egypt.* London: Aris & Phillips, 1982.

Kobata, Atsushi, and Mitsugu Matsuda, trans. *Ryukyuan Relations with Korea and South Sea Countries: An Annotated Translation of Documents in the Rekidai Hoan.* Kyoto: Kobata Atsushi, 1969.

Koder, S.S. "History of the Jews of Kerala." In George Menachery, ed., *Thomapedia: Christian Encyclopaedia of India:* 183–185. Ollur, India: B.N.K., 2000.

Kohl, Philip L. "A Note on Chlorate Artifacts from Shahr-I Sokhta." *East and West* 27 (1977), 111–127.

_____. "The Balance of Trade in Southwest Asia." *Current Anthropology* 19 (1978), 463–492.

_____. *The Making of Bronze Age Eurasia.* New York: Cambridge University Press, 2007.

_____, ed. *The Bronze Age Civilization of Central Asia: Recent Soviet Discoveries.* Armonk, NY: M.E. Sharpe, 1981.

Kolb, Frank. *Rom: Die Geschichte der Stadt in der Antike.* Munich: C.H.Beck, 1995.

Kosambi, D.D. *The Culture and Civilization of Ancient India in Historical Outline.* 8th ed. New Delhi: Vikas, 1982.

Kramer, Samuel. *The Sumerians: Their History, Culture and Character.* Chicago: University of Chicago Press, 1963.

Kristensen, Anne Katrine Gade. (Jorgen Laessoe, trans.) *Who Were the Cimmerians, and Where Did They Come From?: Sargon II, and the Cimmerians, and Rusa I.* Copenhagen: The Royal Danish Academy of Science and Letters, 1988.

Kulke, Hermann, and Dietmar Rothermund. *A History of India.* London: Routledge, 2004.

Kuz'mina, Elena. (J. Mallory, ed.) *The Origins of the Indo-Iranians.* Leiden: E.J. Brill, 2007.

Lane, Frederic C. *Venice: Maritime Republic.* Baltimore: Johns Hopkins University Press, 1973.

Lange, Dierk. *Ancient Kingdoms of West Africa: Africa-Centered and Canaanite-Israelite Perspectives.* Dettelbach, Germany: J.H. Roll, 2004.

Law, B.C. *Tribes in Ancient India.* Poona: Bhandarkar Oriental Research Institute, 1973.

Le Bohec, Yves. *The Imperial Roman Army.* London: B.T. Batsford, 1994.

Lecoq, Pierre, "Aparna." *Encyclopedia Iranica,* Volume 2: 151. New York: Routledge, 1987. Online at <www.iranica.com/articles/aparna-c3k>.

Lee, Shiu Keung. *The Cross and the Lotus.* Hong Kong: Christian Study Center on Chinese Religion and Culture, 1971.

Leeman, W.F. *Foreign Trade in the Old Babylonian Period, as Revealed by Texts from Southern Mesopotamia.* Leiden: E.J. Brill, 1960.

_____. "The Importance of Trade: Some Introductory Remarks." *Iraq* 39, 1 (1977), 1–10.

Le Gall, Dina. *A Culture of Sufism: Naqshbandis in the Ottoman World, 1450–1700.* New York: State University of New York Press, 2005.

Legge, James. *A Record of Buddhistic Kingdoms: Being an Account by the Chinese Monk Fa-Hien of His Travels in India and Ceylon (AD 399–414) in Search of the Buddhist Books of Discipline.* Oxford: Clarendon, 1886; reprint, New York: Paragon, 1965. Online at <etext.library.adelaide.edu.au>.

Lendering, Jopna. "Gyges of Lydia." *Livius, Articles on Ancient History.* Online at <www.livius.org/men-mh/mermnads/gyges.html>.

Levathes, Louise. *When China Ruled the Waves: The Treasure Fleet of the Dragon Throne, 1405–33.* New York: Simon & Schuster, 1994.

Lewis, Mark Edward. "Warring States: Political History." In Michael Loewe and Edward L. Shaughnessy, eds., *The Cambridge History of Ancient China: From the Origins of Civilization to 221 B.C.:* 587. New York: Cambridge University Press, 1999.

Lewis, Warren W. *King John.* London: Methuen, 1991.

Ling, Shun-Sheng. "Stone Bark-cloth Beaters of South China, Southeast Asia and Central America." *Bulletin of the Institute of Ethnology, Academia Sinica* 13 (1962), 195–212.

Linné, Sigvald. *Archaeological Researches at Teotihuacan, Mexico.* Stockholm: The Ethnographical Museum of Sweden, 1934.

Little, William, H.W. Fowler, and J. Coulson. (Rev. and ed. by C.T. Onions). *The Oxford Universal Dictionary on Historical Principles.* 3rd ed. Oxford: Clarendon, 1955.

Liu, Xinru. "Migration and Settlement of the Yuezhi-Kushan: Interaction and Interdependence of Nomadic and Sedentary Societies." *Journal of World History* 12, 2 (2001), 261–292.

Loewe, Michael. "The Structure and Practice of Government." In Denis Twitchett and John K. Fairbank, eds., *The Cambridge History of China, Volume 1: The Ch'in and Han Empires, 221 B.C.–A.D. 220:* 463–490. New York: Cambridge University Press, 1987.

Long, George. "Foederatae Civitaes." In William Smith, ed., *A Dictionary of Greek and Roman Antiquities:* 542–543. London: John Murray, 1875. Online at <penelope.uchicago.edu/Thayer/E/Roman/Texts/secondary/SMIGRA*/Foederatae_Civitates.html>.

Longrigg, James. *Greek Rational Medicine: Philosophy and Medicine from Alcmaeon to the Alexandrians.* New York: Routledge, 1993.

Lord, James Henry. *The Jews in India and the Far East.* Kolhapur, India: Mission, 1907; reprint, Westport, CT: Greenwood, 1977.

Luce, Gordon H. *Old Burma–Early Pagan.* Locust Valley, PA: J.J. Augustine, 1969–70.

Ma Huan. (J.V.G. Mills, trans.) *Ying-Yai Sheng-Lan: The Overall Survey of the Ocean's Shores.* Cambridge, UK: Cambridge University Press, 1970.

Macleod, Roy, ed. *The Library of Alexandria: Centre of Learning in the Ancient World.* New York: I.B. Tauris, 2000.

MacMullen, Ramsay. "Imperial Bureaucrats in the Roman Provinces." *Harvard Studies in Classical Philosophy,* 68 (1964), 305–316.

MacNutt, Francis Augustus, trans. and ed. *Hernando Cortés: His Five Letters of Relation to the Emperor Charles V 1519–1526.* 2 volumes. Whitefish, MT: Kessinger, 2006. (Originally published 1908.)

Madrolle, C. "Le Tonkin ancien." *Bulletin de l'Ecole Française d'Extrême Orient* 37, 2, (1937), 263–332.

Maeder, Felicitas. "The Project Sea-silk — Rediscovering an Ancient Textile Material." *Archaeological Textiles Newsletter* 35 (2002), 8–11.

Maenchen-Helfen, J.O. *The World of the Huns: Studies in Their History and Culture.* Berkeley: University of California Press, 1973.

Mair, Victor H. "Introduction: Kinesis versus Stasis, Interaction versus Independent Invention." In V.H. Mair, ed., *Contact and Exchange in the Ancient World:* 1–16. Honolulu: University of Hawai'i Press, 2006.

Majumdar, R.C. *Ancient India.* New Delhi: Motilal Banarsidass, 1987.

Malleret, Louis. *L'Archaeologie du Delta du Mekong: Tome Troisième: Le Culture du Fou-Nan.* Paris: L'Ecole Française d'Extrême-Orient, 1962.

Mallett, Michael. *Mercenaries and Their Masters: Warfare in Renaissance Italy.* Lanham, MD: Rowman and Littlefield, 1974.

Mallory, J.P. *In Search of the Indo-Europeans: Language, Archaeology, and Myth.* London: Thames & Hudson, 1989.

Mango, Cyril A. *Byzantium: The Empire of New Rome.* London: Weidenfeld and Nicolson, 1980.

Markoe, Glenn E. *The Phoenicians.* Berkeley: University of California Press, 2000.

Markus, R.A. "Gregory the Great and a Papal Missionary Strategy." In G.J. Cuming, ed., *The Mission of the Church and the Propagation of the Faith:* 29–38. New York: Cambridge University Press, 1970.

_____. *Gregory the Great and His World.* New York: Cambridge University Press, 1997.

Marozzi, Justin. *The Way of Herodotus: Travels with the Man Who Invented History.* London: John Murray; Cambridge, MA: Da Capo, 2008.

Marshall, John. *A Guide to Sanchi.* Calcutta: Manager of Publications, Government of India, 1955.

_____. *Mohenjo-Daro and the Indus Civilization.* New Delhi: Asian Educational Service, 1973. (Originally published, London: Arthur Probsthain, 1931.)

Maspero, Georges. *The Champa Kingdom: The History of an Extinct Vietnamese Culture.* Bangkok: White Lotus, 2002. (Originally published 1928.)

Matz, David. *Daily Life of the Ancient Romans.* Westport, CT: Greenwood, 2002.

Mauro, Frederic. "Merchant Communities, 1350–1750." In James D. Tracy, ed., *The Rise of Merchant Empires:* 255–286. New York: Cambridge University Press, 1990.

Mayr-Harting, Henry. *The Coming of Christianity to Anglo-Saxon England.* University Park: Pennsylvania State University Press, 1991.

McCrindle, J.W. *Ancient India as Described by Megasthenes and Arrian: A Translation of the Fragments of the Indika of Megasthenes Collected by Dr. Schwanbeck, and of the First Part of the Indika of Arrian.* London: Trüber & Co.; Bombay: Thacker & Co.; Calcutta: Thacker, Spink & Co., 1877. Online at <www.archive.org/stream/ancientindiaasd02mccrgoog#page/n6/mode/2 up> and at <www.sdstate.edu/projectsouthasia/upload/Megasthene-Indika.pdf>.

McKee, Sally. *Uncommon Dominion: Venetian Crete and the Myth of Ethnic Purity.* Philadelphia: University of Pennsylvania Press, 2000.

McLinley, Daniel L. "Pinna and Her Silken Beard: A Foray into Historical Misappropriations." *Ars Textrina* 29 (1998), 9–22.

Medlycott, A. E. *India and the Apostle Thomas: An Inquiry with a Critical Analysis of the Acta Thomae.* Piscataway, NJ: Gorgias, 2005. (Originally published 1905.)

Mellaart, James. "Egyptian and Near Eastern Chronology: A Dilemma?" *Antiquity* 53, 207 (1979), 6–18.

Menander Protector. (Roger C. Blockley, trans.) *The History of Menander the Guardsman.* Liverpool: Francis Cairns, 1985.

Meyer, Carol. "Bir Umm Fawakhir: Insights into Ancient Egyptian Mining." *JOM* (Journal of the Minerals, Metals and Materials Society) 49, 3 (1997), 64–68.

Meyer, Karl E. *Teotihuacán: First City in the Americas.* New York: Newsweek Book Division, 1980.

Michalowski, Piotr. "Third Millennium Contacts: Observations on the Relationships between Mari and Ebla." *Journal of the American Oriental Society* 105, 2 (1985), 293–302.

Miksic, John N. "Introduction: The Beginning of Trade in Ancient Southeast Asia: The Role of Oc Eo and the Lower Mekong River." In J.C.M. Khoo, ed., *Art & Archaeology of Fu Nan: Pre-Khmer Kingdom of the Lower Mekong Valley:* 1–34. Bangkok: Orchid, 2003.

Milano, Lucio. "Ebla: A Third-Millennium City-State in Ancient Syria." In Jack M. Sasson, ed., *Civilizations of the Ancient Near East:* 1219–1230. New York: Simon & Schuster, 1996.

Millar, Fergus. *A Study of Cassius Dio.* Oxford: Clarendon, 1964.

_____. *The Roman Empire and Its Neighbours.* London: Weidenfeld & Nicolson, 1967.

Miller, Arthur G. *The Mural Painting of Teotihuacan.* Washington, DC: Dunbarton Oaks Research Library and Collection, 1978.

Miller, J. Innes. *The Spice Trade of the Roman Empire.* Oxford: Clarendon, 1969.

Millon, René. "Teotihuacan: Completion of Map of Giant Ancient City in the Valley of Mexico." *Science* 170 (1970), 1077–1082.

_____. *The Teotihuacan Map, Volume 1, Part 2 (maps).* Austin: University of Texas Press, 1973.

Milton, Giles, *Nathaniel's Nutmeg: How One Man's Courage Changed the Course of History.* London: Hodder & Stoughton, 1999.

Miner, Horace. *The Primitive City of Timbuctoo.* Rev. ed. New York: Anchor, 1965. (Originally published 1953.)

Minorsky, V., and S.S. Blair. "Tabriz." In P.J. Bearman, et al., eds., *Encyclopedia of Islam,* Volume 10. Leiden: E.J. Brill, 2009.

Moffett, Samuel Hugh. *A History of Christianity in Asia, Volume 1: Beginnings to 1500.* Maryknoll, NY: Orbis, 1998.

Mookerji, Radhakumud. *Chandragupta Maurya and His Times.* New Delhi: Motilal Banarsidass, 1988.

_____. *The Gupta Empire.* New Delhi: Motilal Banarsidass, 1995.

Moorey, P.R.S. *Ur of the Chaldees: A Revised and Updated Edition of Sir Leonard Woolley's Excavations at Ur.* Ithaca, NY: Cornell University Press, 1982.

_____. *Ancient Mesopotamian Materials and Industries: The Archaeological Evidence*. Winona Lake, IN: Eisenbrauns, 1999.

Moorman, John R.H. *A History of the Franciscan Order: From Its Origins to the Year 1517*. Oxford: Oxford University Press, 1968.

Moorwood, Mike. *Stone Tools and Fossil Elephants: The Archaeology of Eastern Indonesia and Its Implications for Australia*. Armidale, NSW: University of New England, 1998.

_____, F. Aziz, P.B. O'Sullivan, Nasruddin, D.R. Hobbs, and A. Raza. "Archaeological and Paleontological Research in Central Flores, East Indonesia: Results of Fieldwork 1997–98." *Antiquity* 73 (1999), 273–286.

_____, P.B. O'Sullivan, F. Aziz, and A. Raza. "Fission-track Ages of Stone Tools and Fossils on the East Indonesian Island of Flores." *Nature* 392, 12 March (1998), 173–176.

Moreland, W.H., and Atul Chandra Chatterjee. *A Short History of India*. New York: David McKay, 1962.

Morely, N. *Metropolis and Hinterland: The City of Rome and the Italian Economy, 200 BC—AD 200*. New York: Cambridge University Press, 1996.

Morgan, Diane. *From Satan's Crown to the Holy Grail: Emeralds in Myth, Magic, and History*. Santa Barbara, CA: Praeger, 2007.

Mosshammer, Alden A. "Thales' Eclipse." *Transactions of the American Philological Association* 111 (1981), 145–155.

Mukund, Kanakalatha. *The Trading World of the Tamil Merchant: Evolution of Merchant Capitalism in the Coromandel*. Chennai: Orient Longman, 1999.

Murai, Shosuke, et al. *Studies of Medieval Ryukyu within Asia's Maritime Network*. Special Issue of *Acta Asiatica* 95 (2008).

Musset, Lucien. *The Germanic Invasions: The Making of Europe, AD 400–600*. University Park: Pennsylvania State University Press, 1975.

Nagaswamy, R. *Roman Karur*. Brahadish Publications, 1995. Online at <www.tamilartsacademy.com/books/roman%20karur/>.

Needham, Joseph W. *Clerks and Craftsmen in China and the West*. New York: Cambridge University Press, 1970.

_____, and Tsien Tsuen-Hsuin. *Science and Civilization in China, Volume 5: Chemistry and Chemical Technology, Part 1, Paper and Printing*. New York: Cambridge University Press, 1985.

Nemet-Nejat, Karen R. *Daily Life in Ancient Mesopotamia*. Santa Barbara, CA: Greenwood, 1998.

Newman, John P. *The Thrones and Palaces of Babylon and Nineveh from Sea to Sea: A Thousand Miles on Horseback*. New York: Harper & Brothers, 1876.

Nezafati, N., M. Momenzadeh, and E. Pernicka. "New Insights into the Ancient Mining and Metallurgical Researches in Iran." In Ü. Yalcin, H. Özbal, and A.G. Paşamehmetoğlu, eds., *Ancient Mining in Turkey and the Eastern Mediterranean*: 307–328. Ankara: Atilim University, 2008.

Nguyen Van Huyen. *The Ancient Civilization of Vietnam*. Hanoi: Gioi, 1995.

Nilakanta Sastri, K.A. *A History of South India from Prehistoric Times to the Fall of Vijayanagar*. 4th rev. ed. New Delhi: Oxford University Press India, 1976.

Norwich, John J. *A History of Venice*. New York: Alfred A. Knopf, 1982.

Nowell, Charles E. "The Discovery of the Pacific: A Suggested Change of Approach." *The Pacific Historical Review* 16, 1 (1947), 1–10.

Noy, David. *Foreigners at Rome: Citizens and Strangers*. London: Duckworth & Classical Press of Wales, 2000.

Oates, Joan. *Babylon*. London: Thames & Hudson, 1986.

Ojha, N.K. *The Aulikaras of Central India: History and Inscriptions*. Chandigarh: Arun, 2001.

Oksanen, Eljas. "The Anglo-Flemish Treaties and Flemish Soldiers in England, 1101–1163." In John France, ed., *Mercenaries and Paid Men: The Mercenary Identity in the Middle Ages*: 261–273. Leiden: E.J. Brill, 2008.

Oren, Eliezer D., ed. *The Sea Peoples and Their World: A Reassessment*. Philadelphia: The University of Pennsylvania Museum of Archaeology and Anthropology, 2000.

Orlin, Louis L. *Assyrian Colonies in Cappadocia*. Berlin: Walter De Gruyter, 1970.

Pálfi, Zoltán. *Territorial Cooperation in the Old Assyrian Trade (Analysis of Four Regions)*. PhD diss., PhD School of History and PhD Program of Assyriology, Budapest, 2008.

Parker, A.J. "Trade Within the Empire and Beyond the Frontiers." In John S. Wacher, ed., *The Roman World*, Volume 1: 635–657. New York: Routledge, 1987.

Parkin, David, and Ruth Barnes, eds. *Ships and the Development of Maritime Technology in the Indian Ocean*. New York: Routledge, 2002.

Parpola, Asko, and Simo Parpola. "On the Relationship of the Sumerian Toponym Meluhha and Sanskrit Mleccha." *Studia Orientalia* 46 (1975), 205–238.

Parsons, Lee A., and Barbara J. Price. "Mesoamerican Trade and Its Role in the Emergence of Civilization." *University of California Archaeological Research Facility*, Contribution 11 (1971), 169–195.

Paterson, Jeremy. "Trade and Traders in the Roman World: Scale, Structure, and Organization." In H. Parkins and C. Smith, eds., *Trade, Traders and the Ancient City*: 149–167. New York: Routledge, 1998.

Pausanias. (W.H.S. Jones, trans.) *Description of Greece*. 4 volumes. Cambridge, MA: Harvard University Press; London, William Heinemann, 1918.

Perera, H.R. *Buddhism in Sri Lanka: A Short History*. Kandy: Buddhist Publication Society, 1988. Online at <www.accesstoinsight.org/lib/authors/perera/wheel100.html>.

Perry, Walter C. *The Franks, from Their First Appearance in History to the Death of King Pepin*. London: Longman, Brown, Green, Longmans, and Roberts, 1857.

Peterson, C.A. "Court and Province in Mid- and Late T'ang." In Denis Twitchett, ed., *The Cambridge History of China, Volume 3: Sui and T'ang China, 589–906, Part 1*: 464–560. New York: Cambridge University Press, 1979.

Ping-ti Ho. "An Estimate of the Total Population of Sung-Chin China." *Études Song* 1, 1 (1970), 33–53.

Pires, Tomé. (A. Cortesao, ed. and trans.) *The Suma Oriental of Tomé Pires: An Account of the East, from the Red Sea to Japan, Written in Malacca and India in 1512–1515*. London: Hakluyt Society, 1944.

Pires-Ferreira, Jane W. "Obsidian Exchange in Formative Mesoamerica." In K.V. Flannery, ed., *The Early Mesoamerican Village*: 292–305. New York: Academic Press, 1976.

Pliny the Elder. (John Bostock and H.T. Riley, eds.) *The Natural History: Book VI, An Account of Countries, Nations, Seas, Towns, Havens, Mountains, Rivers, Distances, and Peoples Who Now Exist, or Formerly Existed*. London: Taylor and Francis, 1855. Online at <perseus.mp iwg-berlin.mpg.de/cgi-bin/ptext?lookup=Plin.+Nat.+6.21>.

Plutarch. *Moralia*. Cambridge, MA: Harvard University Press, 2004.

Pollack, Michael. *Mandarins, Jews, and Missionaries: The*

Jewish Experience in the Chinese Empire. New York: Weatherhill, 1998.

Pollard, Justin, and Howard Reid. *The Rise and Fall of Alexandria: Birthplace of the Modern World.* New York: Viking, 2006.

Pollock, Sheldon I. *The Language of the Gods in the World of Men: Sanskrit, Culture and Power in Premodern India.* Berkeley: University of California Press, 2006.

Polo, Marco. (Henry Yule, ed.) *The Travels of Marco Polo.* New York: Dover, 1983. (Originally published, London: 1870).

Polybius. *The Histories.* Online at <penelope.uchicago. edu/Thayer/E/Roman/Texts/Polybius/home.html>.

_____. *The Histories of Polybius.* 2 volumes. Bloomington: Indiana University Press, 1962.

_____. (I. Scott-Kilvert, trans.) *The Rise of the Roman Empire.* Harmondsworth, UK: Penguin, 1980.

Porter, Dorothy. *Health, Civilization, and the State: A History of Public Health from Ancient to Modern Times.* New York: Routledge, 1999.

Possehl, Gregory L. *Kulli: An Exploration of Ancient Civilization in Asia.* Durham, NC: Carolina Academic Press, 1986.

_____. "Mehrgarh." In Brian M. Fagan, ed., *Oxford Companion to Archaeology.* New York: Oxford University Press, 1996. Online at <www.oxfordreference.com>.

Potter, David S. *The Roman Empire at Bay, AD 180–395.* New York: Routledge, 2004.

Potts, Daniel T. *The Archaeology of Elam: Formation and Transformation of an Ancient Iranian State.* New York: Cambridge University Press, 1999.

Prapanca, Rakawi of Majapahit. (Th. Pigeaud, trans.) *Java in the Fourteenth Century: A Study of Cultural History—the Nagara-Kertagama by Rakawi Prapanca of Majapaht, 1365 A.D.* 5 volumes. The Hague: Martinus Nijhoff, 1960–1963.

Prebish, Charles S. *Buddhism: A Modern Perspective.* University Park: Pennsylvania State University Press, 1971.

Prescott, William H. *History of the Conquest of Mexico, with a Preliminary View of the Ancient Mexican Civilization and the Life of the Conqueror, Hernando Cortés.* 3 volumes. Philadelphia: David McKay, 1891.

Previté-Orton, C.W. *The Shorter Cambridge Medieval History.* New York: Cambridge University Press, 1971.

Promboon, Suebsaeng. *Sino-Siamese Tributary Relations: 1282–1853.* PhD diss., University of Wisconsin, 1971.

Rao, S.R. *Lothal and the Indus Civilization.* New Delhi: Asia, 1974.

Rathje, William L. "The Origin and Development of Lowland Classic Maya Civilization." *American Antiquity* 36, 3 (1971), 275–285.

Ravilious, Kate. "Bejeweled Stonehenge Boy Came from Mediterranean?" *National Geographic News,* 13 October (2010).

Ravindran, P.N. *Black Pepper: Piper Nigrum.* Amsterdam: Harwood Academic, 2000.

Rawlinson, George. *The Five Great Monarchies of the Ancient World.* 3 volumes. 2nd ed. New York: Dodd, Mead, 1870.

_____. "Essay I: On the Obscurer Tribes Contained within the Empire of Xerxes." *History of Herodotus,* Volume 4: 198–235. London: John Murray, 1875.

Rawson, Jessica. "Western Zhou Archaeology." In Michael Loewe and Edward L. Shaughnessy, eds., *The Cambridge History of Ancient China: From the Origins of Civilization to 221 B.C.:* 352–449. New York: Cambridge University Press, 1999.

Ray, Himanshu P. *The Archaeology of Seafaring in Ancient*

South Asia. New York: Cambridge University Press, 2003.

Raychaudhuri, H.C. *Political History of Ancient India.* Calcutta: University of Calcutta, 1972.

Rebenich, Stefan. *Jerome.* New York: Routledge, 2002.

Reed, Ronald. *Ancient Skins, Parchments, and Leathers.* New York: Seminar, 1972.

Reid, Anthony. *Southeast Asia in the Age of Commerce 1450–1680, Volume One: The Lands Below the Winds.* New Haven, CT: Yale University Press, 1988.

_____. "Economic and Social Change, c. 1400–1800." In Nicholas Tarling, ed., *The Cambridge History of Southeast Asia, Volume 1: From Early Times to c.1800:* 460–507. New York: Cambridge University Press, 1992.

Reischauer, Edwin O. "Notes on T'ang Dynasty Sea Routes." *Harvard Journal of Asiatic Studies* 5, 2 (1940), 142–164.

Rendina, Claudio. *I capitani di ventura.* Rome: Newton, 1999.

Renfrew, Colin. "Sitagroi, Radiocarbon Dating and the Pre-history of South-east Europe." *Antiquity* 45, 180 (1971), 275–282.

_____, J.E. Dixon, and J.R. Cann. "Obsidian and Early Cultural Contact in the Near East." *Proceedings of the Prehistorical Society* 32 (1966), 1–29.

Revere, Robert B. "'No Man's Coast': Ports of Trade in the Eastern Mediterranean." In Karl Polanyi, Conrad M. Arensberg, and Harry W. Pearson, eds., *Trade & Market in the Early Empires:* 38–63. Chicago: Henry Regnery, 1971.

Reynolds, Frank, and Mani Reynolds, trans. *Three Worlds According to King Ruang: A Thai Buddhist Cosmology.* Berkeley: University of California Press, 1982.

Richardson, Peter. *Herod: King of the Jews and Friend of the Romans.* New York: Continuum, 1999.

Riley, James. *An Authentic Narrative of the Loss of the American Brig Commerce.* Hartford: S. Andrus, 1831.

Rincon, Paul. "Stonehenge Boy 'was from Med.'" *BBC News,* 28 September (2010). Online at www.bbc.co.uk/news/.

Rodziewicz, Mieczyslaw. *Alexandrie III: Les Habitations Romains Tardives d'Alexandrie à la luminière des fouilles polonaises à Kom el-Dikka.* Varsovie: Editions Scientifiques de Pologne, 1984.

Rogers, Michael. *The Rise of the Former Ch'in State and Its Spread under Fu Chien, through 370 A.D.* Berkeley: University of California Press, 1953.

_____. *The Chronicle of Fu Chien: A Case of Exemplar History.* Berkeley: University of California Press, Chinese Dynastic Histories Translations 10, 1968.

Romm, James S. *Herodotus.* New Haven, CT: Yale University Press, 1998.

Rong Xinjiang. *Middle-period China and Outside Cultures.* Beijing: Shenhuo dusho xinzhi Sanlian shudian, 2001 (in Chinese).

_____. "Sogdians around Ancient Tarim Basin." *The Silk Road Foundation Newsletter* 1, 2, December (2003).

Rosenfield, John M. *The Dynastic Art of the Kushans.* New Delhi: Munshiram Manoharlal, 1993.

Rossabi, Morris. *Khubilai Khan: His Life and Times.* Berkeley: University of California Press, 1988.

Rostovtzeff, Michael I. (D. and T. Talbot Rice, trans.) *Caravan Cities.* Oxford: Clarendon, 1932.

Roys, Ralph L. *The Indian Background of Colonial Yucatan.* Norman: University of Oklahoma Press, 1972.

Rutgers, Leonard V. *The Jews of Late Rome.* Leiden: E.J. Brill, 1995.

Sakai, R.K. "The Satsuma Ryukyu Trade and the Tokugawa Seclusion Policy." *Journal of Asian Studies* 23, 3 (1964), 405–416.

Sakamaki, Shunzō. "Ryukyu and Southeast Asia." *Journal of Asian Studies* 23, 3 (1964), 382–404.

Salmon, E.T. "Notes on the Social War." *Transactions and Proceedings of the American Philological Association,* 89 (1958), 159–184.

Sasson, J.M. "The King and I: A Mari King in Changing Perceptions." *Journal of the American Oriental Society* 118, 4 (1998), 453–470.

Sastri, K.A. Nilakanta. *A History of South India from Prehistoric Times to the Fall of Vijayanagar.* New Delhi: Oxford University Press, 2002.

Saunders, Frances Stonor. *Hawkwood: The Diabolical Englishman.* London: Faber & Faber, 2004.

Saunders, John J. *The History of the Mongol Conquests.* London: Routledge & Kegan Paul, 1971.

Scaglion, Richard. "*Kumara* in the Ecuadorian Gulf of Guayaquil?" In C. Ballard, P. Brown, R.M. Bourke, and T. Harwood, eds., *The Sweet Potato in Oceania: A Reappraisal:* 35–41. Sydney: Oceania Monograph 56, 2005.

Schafer, Edward H. *The Golden Peaches of Samarkand: A Study of T'ang Exotics.* Berkeley: University of California Press, 1963.

Schoenfeld, A.J. "Immigration and Assimilation in the Jewish Community of Late Venetian Crete (15th–17th Centuries)." *Journal of Modern Greek Studies* 25, 1 (2007), 1–15.

Schoff, Wilfred H., trans. and ed. *The Periplus of the Erythraean Sea: Travel and Trade in the Indian Ocean by a Merchant of the First Century.* London: Longman, Green, 1912.

Scholes, France V., and Ralph L. Roys. *The Maya Chontal Indians of Acalan-Tixchel: A Contribution to the History and Ethnography of the Yucatan Peninsula.* Norman: University of Oklahoma Press, 1968.

Schumann, Walter. *Gemstones of the World.* New York: Sterling, 1977.

Sen, Tansen. *Buddhism, Diplomacy, and Trade: The Realignment of Sino-Indian Relations, 600–1400.* Honolulu: University of Hawai'i Press, 2003.

Seward, Desmond. *The Hundred Years War: The English in France 1337–1453.* Harmondsworth, UK: Penguin, 1999.

Sewell, Robert. *A Forgotten Empire (Vijayanagara).* New Delhi: Asian Education Services, 1982.

Sezgin, Fuat, ed. *Collection of Geographical Works by Ibn al-Faqih, Ibn Fadlan, Abu Dulaf Al-Khazraji.* Frankfurt am Main: Institute for the History of Arabic-Islamic Science at the Johann Wolfgang Goethe University, 1987.

Shackley, Steven, ed. *Archaeological Obsidian Studies.* New York: Kluwer Academic/Plenum, 1998.

Shaffer, Lynda N. *Maritime Southeast Asia to 1500.* Armonk, NY: M.E. Sharpe, 1996.

Shapiro, Sidney, ed. *Jews in Old China: Studies by Chinese Scholars.* New York: Hippocrene, 2000.

Sharma, Arvind. "Ancient Hinduism as a Missionary Religion." *Numen* 39, 2 (1992), 175–192.

Shastri, Nilakantha. *Age of the Nandas and Mauryas.* New Delhi: Motilal Banarsidass, 1967.

Shaughnessy, Edward L. "Western Zhou History." In Michael Lowe and Edward L. Shaughnessy, eds., *The Cambridge History of Ancient China: From the Origins of Civilization to 221 B.C.:* 292–351. New York: Cambridge University Press, 1999.

Shboul, Ahmad A.M. *Al-Mas'udi and His World.* London: Ithaca, 1979.

Shen, Fuwei. *Cultural Flow between China and the Outside World.* Beijing: Foreign Languages, 1996.

Sherratt, Andrew. "The Trans-Eurasian Exchange: The Prehistory of Chinese Relations with the West." In V.H. Mair, ed., *Contact and Exchange in the Ancient World:* 30–61. Honolulu: University of Hawai'i Press, 2006.

Sima Qian. (Homer H. Dubs, trans.) *The History of the Former Han Dynasty.* 3 volumes. Baltimore: Waverly, 1938–55.

_____. (Burton Watson, trans.) *Records of the Grand Historian: Han Dynasty.* Hong Kong: Chinese University of Hong Kong and New York City: Columbia University Press, 1993.

Simons, Bente Bittmann, and Thelma D. Sullivan. "The Pochteca." *Atti del XL Congresso Internazionale degli Americanisti* 4 (1972), 203–212.

Simpson, Jacqueline. *Everyday Life in the Viking Age.* New York: G.P. Putnam's Sons, and London: B.T. Batsford, 1967.

Sims-Williams, Nicholas. "The Sogdian Merchants in China and India." In A. Cadonna and L. Lanciotti, eds., *Cina e Iran da Alessandro Magno alla dinastia Tang:* 45–67. Florence: Leo S. Olschki, 1996.

Singer, Samuel. *Thesaurus Proverbiorum Medii Aevi: Lexikon der Sprichwörter des romanisch-germanischen Mittelters.* Berlin: Walter de Gruyter, 1995.

Sinnegen, William J. "Two Branches of the Roman Secret Service." *The American Journal of Philology* 80, 3 (1959), 238–254.

Sirafi, Abu Zayd Hassan ibn Yazid. (Eusebius Renaudot, trans.) *Ancient Accounts of India and China, by Two Mohammedan Travellers. Who Went to Those Parts in the 9th Century.* London, 1733; reprint, New Delhi: Asian Educational Service, 1995.

Skinner, G. William. *Chinese Society in Thailand.* Ithaca, NY: Cornell University Press, 1957.

Smith, George. *The Conversion of India: From Pantaenus to the Present Time (AD 193–1893).* Piscataway, NJ: Gorgias, 2004.

Smith, Monica. "The Archaeology of South Asian Cities." *Journal of Archaeological Research* 14 (2006), 97–142.

Smith, S.P. *Hawaiki, The Original Home of the Maori.* Wellington: Whitcombe and Tombe, 1910.

Smith, Vincent A. *The Oxford History of India.* New York: Oxford University Press, 1981. (Originally published 1924).

Smith, William, ed. *A Dictionary of Greek and Roman Biography and Mythology.* 3 volumes. Boston: Little, Brown, 1867.

Soka Gakkai International. *The Soka Gakkai Dictionary of Buddhism.* Online at <www.sgilibrary.org/search_dict.php>.

Soren, David, Aicha ben Abed ben Kader, and Heidi Slim. *Carthage: Uncovering the Mysteries and Splendors of Ancient Tunisia.* New York: Simon & Schuster, 1990.

Sorenson, John L., and Carl L. Johannessen. "Biological Evidence for Pre-Columbian Transoceanic Voyages." In V.H. Mair, ed., *Contact and Exchange in the Ancient World:* 238–297. Honolulu: University of Hawai'i Press, 2006.

Sorlin, Irene. "Les traits de Byzance avec la Russie au Xe. siècle." *Cahiers du Monde Russe et Soviétique* (1961), 313–360, 447–475.

Southern, Pat. *The Roman Empire from Severus to Constantine.* New York: Routledge, 2001.

Speiser, Felix. *Ethnology of Vanuatu: An Early Twentieth Century Study.* Honolulu: University of Hawai'i Press, 1996. (Originally published as *Ethnographische Materi-*

alien aus den Neuen Hebriden und den Banks-Inseln, Berlin: Springer-Verlag, 1923.)

Spence, Jonathan D. *The Search for Modern China.* New York: W.W. Norton, 1991.

Spivey, Nigel. *The Ancient Olympics.* New York: Oxford University Press, 2005.

Starr, J. "Jewish Life in Crete Under the Rule of Venice." *Proceedings of the American Academy for Jewish Research* 12 (1942), 59–114.

Stein, Gil J. *Rethinking World Systems: Diasporas, Colonies, and Interaction in Uruk Mesopotamia.* Tucson: University of Arizona Press, 1999.

Stein, Marc Aurel. *Ancient Khotan: Detailed Report of Archaeological Exploration in Chinese Turkestan.* 2 volumes. Oxford: Clarendon, 1907.

Steinhardt, Nancy S. *Chinese Imperial City Planning.* Honolulu: University of Hawai'i Press, 1990.

Stone, Doris Z. "Jade and Jade Objects in Precolumbian Costa Rica." In F.W. Lange, ed., *Precolumbian Jade: New Geological and Cultural Interpretations:* 141–148. Salt Lake City: University of Utah Press, 1993.

Stoneman, Richard. *Palmyra and Its Empire: Zenobia's Revolt against Rome.* Ann Arbor: University of Michigan Press, 1991.

Storey, Glenn R. "The Population of Ancient Rome." *Antiquity* 71, 274 (1997), 966–979.

Strabo. *The Geography.* Cambridge, MA: Harvard University Press, Loeb Classical Library, 1932. Online at <penelope.uchicago.edu/Thayer/E/Roman/Texts/Strabo/16A*.html>.

_____. *The Geography of Strabo.* London: George Bell & Sons, 1903.

Strong, John. *The Legend and Cult of Upagupta.* New Delhi: Motilal Banarsidass, 1994.

Swaddling, Judith. *The Ancient Olympic Games.* Austin: University of Texas Press, 1999.

Swadling, Pamela. *Plumes from Paradise: Trade Cycles in Outer Southeast Asia and Their Impact on New Guinea and Nearby Islands until 1920.* Boroko: Papua New Guinea National Museum, 1996.

Tacitus, Cornelius. (Robert G. Latham, trans.) *The Germania of Tacitus: With Ethnological Dissertations and Notes.* London: Taylor, Walton, and Maberly, 1851.

Tadmor, Hayim. *The Inscriptions of Tiglath-Pileser III, King of Assyria.* Jerusalem: Israel Academy of Sciences and Humanities, 1994.

Talbert, Richard. "The Senate and Senatorial and Equestrian Posts." In Alan K. Brown, Edward Champlin, and Andrew Lintott, eds., *The Cambridge Ancient History, X: The Augustan Empire, 43 B.C.–A.D. 69:* 324–343. New York: Cambridge University Press, 1996.

Taylor, Keith W. "The Early Kingdoms." In N. Tarling, ed., *The Cambridge History of Southeast Asia, Volume I: From Early Times to c.1800:* 137–182. New York: Cambridge University Press, 1992.

Tellier, Luc-Normand. *Urban World History: An Economic and Geographical Perspective.* Québec: Presses de l'Université du Québec, 2009.

Thapar, Romila. *Asoka and the Decline of the Mauryas.* New Delhi: Oxford University Press, 2001.

Thompson, J. Eric S. *Maya History and Religion.* Norman: University of Oklahoma Press, 1970.

Tomber, Roberta. *Indo-Roman Trade: From Pots to Pepper.* London: Duckworth, 2008.

Tomlin, R.S.O. "The Army of the Late Empire." In John S. Wacher, ed., *The Roman World,* Volume 1: 107–133. New York: Routledge, 1987.

Torquemada, Juan de. *Monarquía Indiana.* 6 volumes. Mexico: Editorial Cultura, 1975–1979.

Tosi, Maurizio, and Marcello Piperno. "Lithic Technology behind the Ancient Lapis Lazuli Trade." *Expedition* 16, 1 (1973), 15–23.

Tran Van Giap. "Le Bouddhisme en Annam, des Origines au XIII Siecle." *Bulletin de l'Ecole Francaise d'Extrême Orient* 32, 1932 (1933), 191–268.

Trevelyan, George Macaulay. *A Shortened History of England.* Harmondsworth, UK: Penguin, 1959.

Trigault, Nicolas. (L.J. Gallagher, trans.) *China in the Sixteenth Century: The Journals of Mathew Ricci: 1583–1610.* New York: Random House, 1953.

Trigg, Joseph Wilson. *Origen.* New York: Routledge, 1998.

Tsetskhladze, Gocha R. "Trade on the Black Sea in the Archaic and Classical Periods: Some Observations." In H. Parkins and C. Smith, eds., *Trade, Traders and the Ancient City:* 52–74. New York: Routledge, 1998.

Turner, Jack. *Spice: The History of a Temptation.* New York: Vintage, 2004.

Ukers, William H. *All About Tea.* New York: Tea and Coffee Trade Journal Company, 1935.

Ungnad, Arthur. *Subartu, Beiträge zur Kulturgeschichte und Völkerkunde Vorderasiens.* Berlin: W. de Gruyter, 1936.

Urban, William L., and Terry Jones. *Medieval Mercenaries: The Business of War.* London: Greenhill; St. Paul, MN: MBI, 2006.

Vaillant, George C. *Aztecs of Mexico.* Harmondsworth, UK: Penguin, 1965.

Van Vliet, Jeremias. (Leonard Y. Andaya, translator, Miriam J. Verkuijl-van den Berghe, transcription, David K. Wyatt, ed.) *The Short History of the Kings of Siam.* Bangkok: Siam Society, 1975.

Veenhof, Klaas R. "Some Social Effects of Old Assyrian Trade." *Iraq* 39, 1 (1977), 109–118.

_____, and Jesper Eidem. *Mesopotamia: The Old Assyrian Period.* Fribourg: Academic Press; Göttingen: Vandenhoeck & Ruprecht, 2008.

Vernadsky, George. *The Mongols and Russia.* New Haven: Yale University Press, 1953.

Vickery, Michael. *Society, Economics, and Politics in Pre-Angkor Cambodia: The 7th–8th Centuries.* Tokyo: The Centre for East Asian Cultural Studies for UNESCO, the Toyo Bunko, 1998.

Vikyr, Knut S. *Sufi and Scholar on the Desert Edge: Muhammad B. Oali Al-Sanusi and His Brotherhood.* Evanston, IL: Northwestern University Press, 1995.

Von Falkenhausen, Lothar. "The Waning of the Bronze Age: Material Culture and Social Development, 770–481 B.C." In Michael Loewe and Edward L. Shaughnessy, eds., *The Cambridge History of Ancient China: From the Origins of Civilization to 221 B.C.:* 450–544. New York: Cambridge University Press, 1999.

Von Staden, Heinrich, ed. and trans. *Herophilus: The Art of Medicine in Early Alexandria.* New York: Cambridge University Press, 1989.

Wachsmann, Shelley. *Seagoing Ships & Seamanship in the Bronze Age Levant.* College Station: Texas A&M Press; London: Chatham, 1998.

Wade, Nicholas. "Europe's Plagues Came from China, Study Finds." *New York Times,* 31 October (2010), online at <www.nytimes.com/2010/11/01/health/01plague.html?_r=1>.

Wales, H.G. *Dvaravati: The Earliest Kingdom of Siam.* London: Quaritch, 1969.

Waley, Arthur. *The Real Tripitaka.* New York: Macmillan, 1952.

_____. *Monkey: Folk Novel of China.* New York: Evergreen, 1958.

Wang Gungwu. "The Nanhai Trade: A Study of the Early History of Chinese Trade in the South China Sea." *Journal of Malaysian Branch of the Royal Asiatic Society* 31, 2 (1958), 1–135.

Ward, Fred. *Diamonds.* Rev. ed. Bethesda, MD: Gem Books, 1998.

_____. *Emeralds.* Rev. ed. Bethesda, MD: Gem Books, 2001.

_____. *Rubies & Sapphires.* 4th ed. Bethesda, MD: Gem Books, 2003.

Warmington, E.H. *The Commerce between the Roman Empire and India.* 2nd ed. London: Curzon, 1974.

Watson, Burton. *Records of the Grand Historian of China, Volume II: The Age of Emperor Wu 140 to Circa 100 BC.* New York: Columbia University Press, 1961.

Wee, Vivian. *Melayu, Indigenism and the 'Civilising Process': Claims and Entitlements in Contested Territories.* Hong Kong: City University of Hong Kong, Working Paper Series 78, 2005.

Weinberg, Gladys Davidson. "Glass Manufacture in Hellenistic Rhodes." *Archaiologikon Deltion* 24 (1971), 143–151, plus plates 76–88.

Weins, Herald J. *Han Chinese Expansion in South China.* Hamden, CT: Shoe String, 1967.

Weiss, Harvey, et al. "1985 Excavations at Tell Leilan, Syria." *American Journal of Archaeology* 94, 4 (1990), 529–581.

West, Thomas. *Ten Years in South-central Polynesia.* London: J. Nisbet, 1865.

Wheatley, Paul. "Geographical Notes on Some Commodities Involved in Sung Maritime Trade." *Journal of Malaysian Branch of the Royal Asiatic Society* 32, 2 (1959), 1–139.

Wheeler, Mortimer. *Rome beyond the Imperial Frontiers.* London: Philosophical Library, 1955.

Whitby, Michael. "The Grain Trade of Athens in the Fourth Century BC." In H. Parkins and C. Smith, eds., *Trade, Traders and the Ancient City:* 102–128. New York: Routledge, 1998.

White, L. Michael. "Synagogue and Society in Imperial Ostia: Archaeological and Epigraphic Evidence." *The Harvard Theological Review* 90, 1 (1997), 23–58.

White, William Charles. *Chinese Jews: A Compilation of Matters Relating to the Jews of K'aifêng fu.* New York: Paragon Book Reprint, 1966. (Originally published 1942.)

Wiley, Kristi L. *Historical Dictionary of Jainism.* Lanham, MD: Scarecrow, 2004.

Wilkes, Charles. *Narrative of the U.S. Exploring Expedition: during the years 1838, 1839, 1840, 1841, 1842.* 5 volumes. New York: George Putnam, 1851.

Will, Ernest. "Marchands et chefs de caravanes à Palmyre." *Syria* 34, 3/4 (1957), 262–277.

William of Tyre. (E.A. Babcock and A.C. Krey, trans.) *A History of Deeds Done Beyond the Sea.* New York: Columbia University Press, 1943.

Williams, Thomas. *Fiji and the Fijians, Volume I: The Islands and their Inhabitants.* London: Alexander Heylin, 1858; reprint, Suva: Fiji Museum, 1972.

Wilson, R. T. *The Camel.* New York: Longman, 1984.

Winstedt, Eric Otto, ed. and trans. *The Christian Topography of Cosmos Indicopleustes.* Malden, MA: Forbes, 2008.

Wolters, O.W. *Early Indonesian Commerce: A Study of the Origins of Srivijaya.* Ithaca, NY: Cornell University Press, 1967.

Woodard, Roger D. "Greek Dialects." In R.D. Woodward, ed., *The Ancient Languages of Europe:* 50–72. New York: Cambridge University Press, 2008.

Worchester, G.R.G. *Sail and Sweep in China.* London: Science Museum, 1966.

Wormington, B.H. *Carthage.* New York: Frederick A. Praeger, 1960.

Wriggins, Sally Hovey. *Xuanzang: A Buddhist Pilgrim on the Silk Road.* Boulder, CO: Westview, 1996.

Wyatt, David K. *Thailand: A Short History.* New Haven, CT: Yale University Press, 1982.

Xenophanes. (James H. Lesher, trans. and ed.) *Xenophanes of Colophon: Fragments: A Text and Translation with a Commentary.* Toronto: University of Toronto Press, 1992.

Xenophon. (H.G. Dakyns, trans.) *Cyropaedia: The Education of Cyrus.* London: Macmillan, 1897. Online at <ebooks.adelaide.edu.au/x/xenophon/x5cy/>.

Xu, Jay. "Sichuan before the Warring States Period." In Robert Bagley, ed., *Ancient Sichuan: Treasures from a Lost Civilization:* 21–38. Seattle: Seattle Art Museum, 2001.

Xu Xin. *The Jews of Kaifeng: History, Culture, and Religion.* Jersey City: KTAV, 2003.

Yalcin, Ü., H. Özbal, and A. G. Paşamehmetoğlu, eds. *Ancient Mining in Turkey and the Eastern Mediterranean.* Ankara: Atilim University, 2008.

Yang Fuquan. "The 'Ancient Tea and Horse Caravan Road,' the 'Silk Road' of Southwest China." *The Silkroad Foundation Newsletter* 2, 1 (2004). Online at <www.silkroadfoundation.org/newsletter/>.

Yellin, Joseph, Thomas E. Levy, and Yorke M. Rowan. "New Evidence on Prehistoric Trade Routes: The Obsidian Evidence from Gilat, Israel." *Journal of Field Archaeology* 23, 3 (1996), 361–368.

Yener, K. Aslihan. "An Early Bronze Age Tin Production Site at Göltepe, Turkey." *The Oriental Institute News and Notes* 140 (1991).

Yorke, Barbara. *The Conversion of Britain: Religion, Politics, and Society in Britain c. 600–800.* London: Pearson/Longman, 2006.

Young, Gary K. *Rome's Eastern Trade: International Commerce and Imperial Policy, 31 BC–AD 305.* New York: Routledge, 2001.

Young, T. Cuyler. "The Early History of the Medes and the Persians and the Achaemenid Empires to the Death of Cambyses." In M. Boardman, N.G.L. Hammond, D.M. Lewis, and M. Ostwald, eds., *The Cambridge Ancient History, IV: Persia, Greece and the Western Mediterranean, c. 525 to 479 B.C.:* 1–52. New York: Cambridge University Press, 1988.

Yu, Anthony. *The Journey to the West.* 4 volumes. Chicago: University of Chicago Press, 1977–83.

Yu, Taishan. *A History of the Relationships between the Western and Eastern Han, Wei, Jin, Northern and Southern Dynasties and the Western Regions.* Philadelphia: Department of East Asian Languages and Civilizations, University of Pennsylvania, Sino-Platonic Papers 131, 2004.

Yule, Henry, trans. *The Travels of Friar Odoric.* Grand Rapids, MI: William B. Eerdmans, 2002.

Yule, Paul. *Metal Work of the Bronze Age in India.* Munich: Beck'sche, 1985.

Zalloua, Pierre A., et al. "Identifying Genetic Traces of Historical Expansions: Phoenician Footprints in the Mediterranean." *The American Journal of Human Genetics* 83, 5 (2008), 633–642.

Zarins, Juris. "Pastoral Nomadism and the Settlement of Lower Mesopotamia." *Bulletin of the American Schools of Oriental Research* 280, November (1990), 31–65.

Zawadzki, Stefan. *The Fall of Assyria and Median-Baby-*

lonian Relation in Light of the Nabopolassar Chronicle. Delft: Eburon, 1988.

Zettler, R.L., and L. Horne, eds. *Treasures from the Royal Tombs of Ur.* Philadelphia: University of Pennsylvania Museum of Archaeology and Anthropology, 1998.

Zhou Daguan. (Peter Harris, trans.) *A Record of Cambodia: The Land and Its People.* Chiang Mai: Silkworm, 2007.

Zürcher, E. *The Buddhist Conquest of China: The Spread and Adaptation of Buddhism in Early Medieval China.* 3rd ed. Leiden: E.J. Brill, 1959.

Index